THE IVP NEW TESTAMENT COMMENTARY SERIES

John

Rodney A. Whitacre

Grant R. Osborne
series editor

D. Stuart Briscoe
Haddon Robinson
consulting editors

INTERVARSITY PRESS
DOWNERS GROVE, ILLINOIS, USA
LEICESTER, ENGLAND

InterVarsity Press, USA
P.O. Box 1400, Downers Grove, IL 60515. USA
World Wide Web: www.ivpress.com
E-mail: mail@ivpress.com

Inter-Varsity Press, England
38 De Montfort Street, Leicester LE1 7GP, England

InterVarsity Press®, USA, is the book-publishing division of InterVarsity Christian Fellowship/USA®, a student movement active on campus at hundreds of universities, colleges and schools of nursing in the United States of America, and a member movement of the International Fellowship of Evangelical Students. For information about local and regional activities, write Public Relations Dept., InterVarsity Christian Fellowship/USA, 6400 Schroeder Rd., P.O. Box 7895, Madison, WI 53707-7895.

Inter-Varsity Press, England, is the book-publishing division of the Universities and Colleges Christian Fellowship (formerly the Inter-Varsity Fellowship), a student movement linking Christian Unions in universities and colleges throughout the United Kingdom and the Republic of Ireland, and a member movement of the International Fellowship of Evangelical Students. For information about local and national activities write to UCCF, 38 De Montfort Street, Leicester LE1 7GP.

USA ISBN 0-8308-1804-9
UK ISBN 0-85111-685-X

Printed in the United States of America ♾

Library of Congress Cataloging-in-Publication Data

Whitacre, Rodney A.
   John/Rodney A. Whitacre.
      p.   cm.—(the IVP New Testament commentary series: 4)
   Includes bibliographical references.
   ISBN 0-8308-1804-9 (alk. paper)
      1. Bible.   N.T. John Commentaries.   I. Title.   II. Series.
   BS2615.3.W55   1999
   226.5'07—DC21
                                                                          99-36484

                                                                                CIP

British Library Cataloguing in Publication Data

A catalogue record for this book is available from the British Library

19	18	17	16	15	14	13	12	11	10	9	8	7	6	5	4	3	2	1
14	13	12	11	10	09	08	07	06	05	04	03	02	01	00	99			

For the glorification of God,
the Father, the Son and the Holy Spirit:
Holy Trinity, One God,
and in memory of my parents,
Charles and Leah Whitacre
and my father-in-law, William Nigel Kerr

General Preface

In an age of proliferating commentary series, one might easily ask why add yet another to the seeming glut. The simplest answer is that no other series has yet achieved what we had in mind—a series to and from the church, that seeks to move from the text to its contemporary relevance and application.

No other series offers the unique combination of solid, biblical exposition and helpful explanatory notes in the same user-friendly format. No other series has tapped the unique blend of scholars and pastors who share both a passion for faithful exegesis and a deep concern for the church. Based on the New International Version of the Bible, one of the most widely used modern translations, the IVP New Testament Commentary Series builds on the NIV's reputation for clarity and accuracy. Individual commentators indicate clearly whenever they depart from the standard translation as required by their understanding of the original Greek text.

The series contributors represent a wide range of theological traditions, united by a common commitment to the authority of Scripture for Christian faith and practice. Their efforts here are directed toward applying the unchanging message of the New Testament to the ever-changing world in which we live.

Readers will find in each volume not only traditional discussions of authorship and backgrounds, but useful summaries of principal themes and approaches to contemporary application. To bridge the gap between commentaries that stress the flow of an author's argument but skip over exegetical nettles and those that simply jump from one difficulty to another, we have developed our unique format that expounds the text in uninterrupted form on the upper portion of each page while dealing with other issues underneath in verse-keyed notes. To avoid clutter we have also adopted a social studies note system that keys references to the bibliography.

We offer the series in hope that pastors, students, Bible teachers and small group leaders of all sorts will find it a valuable aid—one that stretches the mind and moves the heart to ever-growing faithfulness and obedience to our Lord Jesus Christ.

Author's Preface

For the first fifteen years of my Christian life the Gospel of John was more confusing than edifying to me. It was not that I did not honor it as God's Word and have favorite verses in it. But its distinct style did not communicate much to me. In fact, it was disturbing because I did not know what to make of it in the light of the first three Gospels. I learned much about the Synoptics, but could not see how the Fourth Gospel fit with them.

Only after I had a course in seminary on John from J. Ramsey Michaels did I begin to appreciate this marvelous document. When I went on to doctoral studies, my supervisor, Morna D. Hooker, suggested that for the topic I had chosen I should focus on 1 John. My studies in the letter then led me back into the Gospel and so, through no design of my own, I spent a couple of years intensively studying John and 1 John.

My respect for this material deepened from appreciation to awe and wonder. St. Gregory the Great said the Scriptures are "a kind of river . . . which is both shallow and deep, in which both the lamb may find a footing and the elephant float at large" (*Moralia* Epistle 4.177-78; cf. C. Koester 1995:232 n.27), and this is certainly true of St. John's Gospel, as many have noted.

My early lack of enthusiasm for this Gospel is not the typical reaction. For many Christians it is a favorite text for their own spiritual lives and for use in evangelism and the instruction of new Christians. I pray this commentary will be of help to them as well as to those confused by this marvelous oracle.

Our great need is to see Jesus better. In him dwells the fullness of deity and through him that fullness is given to those who believe in him (Col 2:9-10). John's Gospel was written that we might indeed know Jesus and share in the very life of God. I pray that God may use this commentary, despite its deficiencies, to help make himself known.

I am grateful for the love and encouragement which I have received during this project from family and friends, especially my wife Margaret and our sons Seth and Chad. I am very thankful for the help in understanding this Gospel which I have received, by the grace of God, from my teachers (including the many whom I have met only through their writings), from my students at Gordon-Conwell Theological Seminary, Trinity Episcopal School for Ministry and in the church, and from my colleagues over the years. Editors Jim Hoover and Grant Osborne have been of much help, not least through their patience and encouragement. Jennifer Conrad Seidel's copy editing has made this a more accurate and readable book. Finally, I want to thank Ron Marr for the indexes he prepared for the publication of my doctoral dissertation (Whitacre 1982). The requirements of the series in which the dissertation was published prevented me from thanking him at the time, so I am happy to have the chance now to publicly express my gratitude for his work.

Shed upon your Church, O Lord, the brightness of your light, that we, being illumined by the teaching of your apostle and evangelist John, may so walk in the light of your truth, that at lengh we may attain to the fullness of eternal life; through Jesus Christ our Lord, who lives and reigns with you and the Holy Spirit, one God, for ever and ever. Amen.

(Book of Common Prayer)

Introduction

John's Gospel is a profound witness to Jesus, the Son of God. Yet John makes it clear that the more we know Jesus, the more we realize we have yet more to learn—the lion is never tamed! What is true of the central character is also true of the document itself. When we try to discover who wrote it, how it was written and in what circumstances, we find the clues confusing. As Edwyn Hoskyns says, the commentator on this document "will not be true to the book he is studying if, at the end, the gospel does not still remain strange, restless and unfamiliar" (1940a:7). A great many detectives have been on the case and have produced an abundance of theories to account for the Fourth Gospel. Robert Kysar (1975; 1983) and Gerard Sloyan (1991) offer helpful guides to the research that has been done in recent decades.

☐ How Was This Gospel Written, and Who Was Responsible?

We will dive in at the deep end with some of the most difficult questions. The answers to these questions will not affect our respect for this material as inspired Scripture, but they will give us an appreciation for the wondrous complexity of its production, very much analogous to God's organic working in the realm of nature. Our answers to these questions will also affect how we interpret John's Gospel.

First View: A Single Author   An ancient icon of John pictures him sitting in a cave with his disciple Prochorus. He is looking back over his shoulder, and a shaft of light is coming down to his head from the upper corner of the icon. Prochorus is writing, *en archē,* "In the beginning . . ." This icon expresses wonderfully the truth of John's inspiration by God. Many people would see it as also illustrating how the Gospel came to be written, the apostle sitting down one day and beginning to write as God gave him the words. While a number of scholars would agree that this Gospel was written by the son of Zebedee, virtually all scholars would say the process by which it was written was more complex.

B. F. Westcott provided the classic statement of John's authorship when he worked point by point to show that there is evidence in the Gospel that it was written by a Jew, someone from Palestine, an eyewitness and an apostle and, finally, that the author was John, the son of Zebedee (Westcott 1908:1:ix-lii; cf. Lightfoot 1893:1-198; Morris 1969:215-280). The first points are not questioned by most scholars, not even the notion that there is eyewitness tradition behind the text. The last two points, however, are more controversial. The evidence that he was an apostle is derived from the author's knowledge of the apostles' activities, feelings, movements and thoughts. Moreover, "he speaks as one to whom the mind of the Lord was laid open" (Westcott 1908:1:xlv). The clue that he was John, the son of Zebedee, is found in the figure of the Beloved Disciple. In the Synoptics the disciples closest to Jesus were Peter, James and John. James was martyred early (Acts 12:2), and Peter is mentioned several times in the Fourth Gospel in special association with the Beloved Disciple (13:24; 20:2-10; 21:7, 20). No one but the son of Zebedee seems to fit the description of the Beloved Disciple, and, according to 21:24, this Beloved Disciple was the author of the Gospel. He is therefore understood to be the author in a simple, direct manner. The evidence from the early church, beginning with Irenaeus near the end of the second century (*Against Heresies* 3.1.1), supports this position (Westcott 1908:1:lix-lxvii).

Other scholars, however, have identified many other individuals as the Beloved Disciple, including John Mark, Lazarus and Thomas (Charlesworth 1995:127-287). Papias (c. 60-130) refers to an elder named John, apparently in distinction to the apostle John (Eusebius *Ecclesiastical History* 3.39.3-4, 7), and some take this elder to be the Beloved Disciple (for example, Hengel 1989). Papias's statement, however, is obscure, so he may actually be referring to only one person, the son of Zebedee (Smalley 1998:80-81). In any case, none of these suggestions have gained widespread support. Other scholars think the Beloved Disciple is an ideal figure. There is no doubt he plays such a role, but John makes it clear that he is also an actual person (for example, 21:24). If there is a single person behind this Gospel, the best evidence points to the apostle John.

Second View: More Than One Hand at Work When we look at the Gospel itself for clues to how it was written, its overall coherence and general uniformity of style support the view that it was written by one person. But there is also evidence of a more complicated process. It seems clear that the document we now have contains material from more than one person and includes material added at various points in time. The question of authorship used to be like a true-false question: The apostle John, the son of Zebedee, wrote the Fourth Gospel—true or false? Now it is more like an essay question.

Editorial Insertions. That more than one person was involved is clear at the end of the Gospel (21:24-25), where later disciples bear witness to the truthfulness of the one known as the Beloved Disciple (cf. v. 20). Similar testimony by these disciples, concerning the one who witnessed the flow of blood and water from Jesus' side on the cross, may occur at 19:35.

Seams. Many find evidence of instances where material has been patched together. For example, chapter 21 seems to many to have been added later since 20:30-31 reads like the conclusion of the Gospel. At the end of chapter 14 Jesus concludes his teaching by saying "Come now; let us leave." What follows is not their departure but chapter 15, beginning, "I am the true vine. . . ." However, when we turn to 18:1 we find exactly what we would have expected to find following 14:31, "When Jesus had spoken these words, he went forth with his disciples

. . ." (RSV; obscured by the NIV, which paraphrases *eipōn* as "praying" in 18:1). It appears that chapters 15—17 may have been inserted.

Other Evidence. Various scholars claim to have detected much more evidence of extensive editing, and they have produced a variety of theories to account for such data. The evidence includes signs of editorial roughness, such as the identification of Mary as "the same one who poured perfume on the Lord and wiped his feet with her hair" (11:2) when the account of the anointing does not occur until chapter 12, Jesus' statement that no one asks where he is going (16:5) when Peter had done so (13:36) and awkward repetitions (cf. 5:19-25 with 5:26-30; 14:1-31 with 16:4-33). Some would say there are also differences in grammar, style, vocabulary and theology between various texts in the Gospel that suggest there are different hands at work.

Three Explanations for the Complexity What are we to make of these clues? That more than one person worked on this Gospel is recognized by virtually everyone. There are three basic approaches to a solution.

A Single Author's Material Has Been Edited by Others. The first solution is that we have the work of a single author, with material from later disciples only at obvious points like 21:24-25. The roughness of the material could mean that the author did not care to edit his material and left it in this condition (cf. Robinson 1985:17-18). Or it could mean that the author's material was in the form of individual stories, perhaps from sermons or teachings, which were then put together by his later disciples. The work of these disciples would have been very conservative, perhaps out of reverence for their teacher. They merely patched the material together, thereby creating the roughness (cf. Hengel 1989:104-7). From 21:24 it would seem this material, at least in part, was actually written by the Beloved Disciple. This verse could, however, mean that the Beloved Disciple *caused* these things to be written down, the emphasis falling on the witness of this disciple (cf. Beasley-Murray 1987:lxxii). In either case the document would be the product of a master teacher. The author's material could have come from different periods in his life and that of his community. Thus it could reflect developments in his thinking and the changing needs of his community. So the differences in language and thought could reflect a single teacher's complexity.

Multiple Sources Have Been Used. The second solution says that more than one hand was at work in the formation of this material so that what we have is the product of editors at work on several sources from outside the Johannine community.

One of the more influential of the theories that non-Johannine source material is included is that of Rudolf Bultmann (1971). He distinguished between the work of an editor known as the Evangelist and a later editor, the identity of both being unknown. The Evangelist wove together material from three main sources along with other miscellaneous materials. The sources included a collection of miracle stories written in Greek with Semitic influence (the Signs Source), a collection of Gnostic discourses (the Revelatory Discourse Source) and an account of the Passion and Easter. The Evangelist, formerly a member of a Gnostic group of John the Baptist's disciples, christianized his source material where necessary. His product was still too Gnostic, so a later editor (often referred to as the Ecclesiastical Redactor) finished the job, harmonizing the material with the Synoptic Gospels and adding material on the sacraments and the second coming to bring the Gospel more in line with church teaching.

Bultmann's hypothesis in its full form has not found general acceptance, but parts of it have been further developed. For example, the idea of a Gnostic Revelatory Discourse Source, rejected by most scholars, is being advanced in the light of the Gnostic materials discovered in the 1940s at Nag Hammadi, Egypt (cf. H. Koester 1990:173-271). Most scholars, however, think this Gnostic material is dependent on the canonical Gospels (cf. Meier 1991:112-166) and continue to doubt the existence of this source. But more work has also been done on detecting a Signs Source (for example, Fortna 1970; 1988; von Wahlde 1989), and this work is finding some acceptance. This Signs Source, however, is often viewed as a product from within the community itself, essentially an earlier edition of the Gospel. Those who take such a view, such as Urban C. von Wahlde, are therefore representatives of the third major approach, discussed below.

Source studies are admittedly speculative. Indeed, Robert T. Fortna only claims 70 percent confidence in his proposals and would be happy if readers can accept more than half of what he offers (1988:xii). Many would accept that sources were used, but a number of scholars doubt whether it is possible to retrieve them (cf. Morris 1971:58; Kysar 1975:33-37; Robinson 1985:14-35; Carson 1991:41-45). They doubt whether the tools at our disposal are sharp enough for this task, with perhaps the most significant problem being the uniformity of style (Carson 1991:45-49). Commenting on one such theory, B. H. Streeter says, "If the sources have undergone anything like the amount of amplification, excision, rearrangement and adaptation which the theory postulates, then the critic's pretense that he can unravel the process is grotesque. As well hope to start with a string of sausages and reconstruct the pig" (Streeter 1926:377).

Composition Took Place Within the Community. A third solution suggests that this Gospel developed mostly within the community itself. One particularly influential version of this theory proposes the Gospel developed in five stages (Brown 1966:xxxiv-xxxix). The first stage consisted of traditional material like that behind the Synoptics but not dependent on the Synoptic tradition. The second stage was the development of this material into distinctively Johannine patterns through oral preaching and teaching, with written forms taking shape near the end of this period. Some of the miracle stories were developed into dramas and some of the sayings into discourses. More than one person was involved at this stage in the Johannine school, but there was one principal preacher, whom Raymond Brown refers to as the evangelist. The third stage brought the first edition of a consecutive Gospel, probably organized by the evangelist of stage two. Brown sees this as more comprehensive than a mere collection of signs. Not all of the Johannine material would have been included at this point, and alternative forms of the material that was included would continue to circulate. Some of this additional or repetitious material will be added at stage five.

Stage four was a reediting of the Gospel (at least once) by the evangelist. He added material to meet new problems faced by the community. For example, he probably added 9:22-23 at this point in the light of the expulsion of Christians from the synagogue for confessing

Christ. It is not always possible to say what comes from this stage (the second edition) as opposed to the fifth and last stage (the final edition, our Gospel). Stage five is the final editing by someone other than the person behind stages two through four, probably a close friend or disciple, whom Brown refers to as the redactor. Much of the material added at this stage actually comes from the evangelist but was not included by him earlier. The redactor does not feel free to rewrite the Gospel, so he simply inserts this additional material, thus causing the repetitions and rough transitions. For example, chapters 15—17 were added at this time without smoothing the transition from 14:31 to 15:1. Brown argues that the account of the public ministry in the earlier edition ended at 10:40-42 and the redactor added chapters 11—12, though this process could have occurred between stages three and four—that is, between the first and second editions by the evangelist—instead of at the last by the redactor. Inserting these chapters probably caused the shift of the account of the temple cleansing to chapter 2. There is a stronger stress on sacramental material, though sacramentalism is found at all stages of the Gospel. Finally, there is some material added by the redactor, notably the prologue (1:1-18) and chapter 21, which did not come from the evangelist. Brown proposes the difference in style between the last chapter and the rest of the Gospel suggests this distinction and also argues that the prologue was originally a Johannine community hymn independent of the Gospel itself.

Such a hypothesis is incapable of being proven, as Brown himself recognizes (1966:cii), but many scholars find some such solution to best account for the very puzzling data. Within the general framework of a series of stages there is much room for differences concerning the details. For example, many scholars think three stages are all that are needed to account for the data and that a Signs Source was used (cf. Brown's later view, 1988:12) or rather that the first edition of the Gospel focused on the signs.

While such theories are popular among scholars, they are not without their difficulties. In particular, they rely on detecting tensions within the text. Many of the tensions that scholars take to be evidence of different hands are actually aspects of the profundity of John's thought. Furthermore, many scholars play off the earlier and later stages of the Gospel, failing to do justice to the fact that the earlier material is retained in the later editions. The alleged later additions help prevent possible misunderstanding and supplement the earlier thought in profound ways. While there were stages in the composition, it is arguable that the Beloved Disciple himself was involved throughout (with exceptions such as 21:24-25), as the first view of composition above allows. It is far more likely that one individual stands behind this document than that a community does (Hengel 1989:80-83). In any case, for Christians it is the final edition of the Gospel that is authoritative and that is the focus of this commentary.

John, the Son of Zebedee The role of the son of Zebedee is debated, of course. In his commentary Brown sees the son of Zebedee as the key witness in stage one and another master teacher behind stages two through four (1966:xcviii, c-ci). More recently he has come to the conclusion that the Beloved Disciple is not the son of Zebedee (1988:9-11). Furthermore, since the differences between John and the Synoptics are "the product of editorial and theological development," they "make it most implausible (nay impossible) that the Fourth Gospel was written by an eyewitness of the ministry of Jesus" (1979:178). Brown has concluded that the tradition about Jesus behind the Fourth Gospel comes from an unknown disciple. The tradition was reflected on for many years, and then the evangelist, presumably a disciple of the Beloved Disciple, "wove the theologically reflected tradition into a work of unique literary skill" (1988:11; so also, for example, Beasley-Murray 1987:lxxiv).

Difficulties with John's Involvement. Those who argue that John, the son of Zebedee, was the primary author must respond to the doubts raised by the literary, social and theological styles of this Gospel. This does not sound like the writing of a peasant Galilean fisherman nor like what we would expect from the description of him in the Synoptics or from his place as a pillar of the Jerusalem church (Gal 2:9). But, in fact, it is not unreasonable to think that a Galilean fisherman could be literate, articulate, relatively prosperous and perhaps even acquainted with someone at the high priest's household (Robinson 1985:116-17). That he could also develop his style and thought along very idiosyncratic lines is also striking but not impossible. Most of us probably know living examples of such change. Thus, the son of Zebedee should not be ruled out as the author, but if he were involved beyond the earliest stage of the Gospel's development, then he probably went through enormous changes in thought and expression.

John's Role. I think the silence regarding the sons of Zebedee in this story, when we know they were known to the community (21:2), indicates that John was somehow involved in the production of this Gospel. As Brown says in another connection, there are silences that are significant for they concern a matter that the author "could scarcely have passed over accidentally" (1979:21; cf. p. 34 n. 47). I will refer to John as the author not in the sense that he necessarily wrote it all as it stands, but in recognition that it is his witness that is presented here and that he at least caused it to be written (21:24).

John and the Synoptics There is clearly some connection between John and the Synoptics. A number of the stories are similar, ten of them even following in the same order (Barrett 1978:43). So it is possible to argue that John made use of one or more of the Synoptic Gospels (cf. Barrett 1978:15-18, 42-54; Carson 1991:49-58). Others would say that the differences between John and the Synoptics, even when they are telling the same story, suggest John did not use them as sources for his Gospel. Instead of using the Synoptics themselves he may have had access to some of the same traditions that went into the making of the first three Gospels (cf. Kysar 1975:54-66). While the majority of scholars still hold the latter view, there is much ferment in this field of study at present. After examining the various approaches to the question taken by scholars in this century, D. Moody Smith concludes, "We have now reached a point at which neither assumption is safe, that is, neither can be taken for granted" (1992:189). If the son of Zebedee is behind the testimony of this Gospel, then the Gospel has grounding in the actual history being recounted, which complicates matters further.

General Differences. Instead of a one-year ministry that moves from Galilee to Jerusalem, John describes at least a three-year ministry that moves back and forth between these settings. Instead of parables about the kingdom of God, the dominant topic is Jesus' relationship with the

Father, which he discusses through debates and extended monologues in highly symbolic language. Perhaps most striking of all is the style—everyone sounds the same in this Gospel; that is, they all speak in Johannine style, the same style as in John's letters. The christology of John is not higher than that of the Synoptics, but how it is expressed is strikingly diferent (see comments on 7:53—8:11).

Chronological Differences. All four Gospels contain historically accurate details of place and local color, John's no less than the others. He is also at least as accurate as the Synoptics concerning chronology. For example, it is historically reasonable that Jesus had a ministry longer than one year and that he made more than one trip to Jerusalem. The Synoptics have simplified the story and even included details that imply the Johannine description (Robinson 1985:123-57). Differences in chronology occur over and over between all four Gospels, which makes it clear that none of the Gospels share our standards of chronological accuracy. On this level of chronology and details of location and local color, John and the Synoptics are fairly similar in their approach.

Differences in Jesus' Teaching and Style. The way Jesus responds to questions is one of the striking features of his speech in John's Gospel. Over and over in this Gospel, Jesus does not appear to respond directly to a question or comment, but instead offers profound revelation from a transcendent perspective. A. D. Nuttall says this form of discontinuous answer, which he claims is "virtually unique" in literature (1980:139), implies Jesus saw himself as divine. "Jesus did not claim to have heard the divine voice. He claimed to be the divine voice" (1980:137). Nuttall's own assessment is that Jesus was mad, which leaves him with an irony since this particular madman's "real claim upon our reverence is immense" (1980:142). Nuttall's dilemma is somewhat similar to that of the Jewish opponents in this Gospel as they are confronted with one whose great deeds and strange words cannot be understood in traditional categories and so accuse him of being demon possessed and mad (7:20; 8:48-52; 10:20-21).

Turning to what Jesus actually says in this Gospel we see that frequently John has taken particular sayings of Jesus, which we often can identify from the Synoptic material, and developed them into extended symbolic discussions, often centering on Jesus' identity (for example, Dodd 1963; Lindars 1980-1981; 1981). Even more striking, in Jesus' speech there is a mixture of past and present, time and eternity, heaven and earth. The words of the earthly Jesus are indeed here, as we have just noted, but they are developed under the guidance of the Spirit (cf. 14:12-13, 26; 16:12-15). The result is that we also have the risen Jesus speaking in this story to the situation in which the Johannine Christians find themselves (cf. Beasley-Murray 1987:xlvii-liii). This feature of John's witness is achieved by what Franz Mussner calls an "act of vision" (1967:17-47). Mussner's study suggests there is an important sense in which John is a visionary. But instead of ascending to heaven, as some whom he opposes are claiming (see below), he has seen heaven opened: the one from heaven has come amongst us and remains with us by his Spirit. Now, as he writes his Gospel, it is as if he is looking down on the historical story from above with a Skycam and pointing out the eternal realities at work in the various encounters and teachings. Now the acts and speech of Jesus make sense in the light of Scripture (see comment on 2:22). But John is not just a player looking at the tapes after the game and analyzing the plays. Here *the* player, Jesus, continues to speak, but he speaks now by his Spirit leading the disciples into all truth (cf. 16:13).

All of the characters in the Gospel speak in the same style. From the Johannine letters we know that this is the style of John and perhaps his community. One intriguing hypothesis is that this style came from Jesus himself. At times his teaching in each of the Gospels is expressed in a way that is oracular, as if he were partly detached from the setting and speaking of divine reality from within that reality. Furthermore, in the Synoptics we find at times this oracular style in a form very similar to what we find in John, most notably in Matthew 11:25-30. There is every reason to think that Jesus used more than one style and no reason to doubt he used this one. So perhaps John took the oracular style Jesus used at times and told the whole story in that form of expression. With this hypothesis not only is Jesus' teaching in John's Gospel grounded in the historical Jesus, but so is the inspiration for the style.

Indeed, perhaps there is a connection between this style and the content of the Gospel. The examples of this style in the Synoptics usually occur in Jesus' statements about the kingdom of God and about himself.

Jesus' self-description as the Son in Matthew 11:27 is especially striking. Jesus' references to the Son of Man often have this oracular quality (for example, Mk 2:28; 8:38; 9:31; 14:21, 62). In the Fourth Gospel this oracular expression of Jesus' identity is especially evident in the I AM sayings, which point to Jesus' deity and the divine life he offers. The oracular style thus corresponds with Jesus' identity as the divine Son who has come down from heaven and become flesh to give life to the world. Since Jesus' identity as the Son of God is the great fact of existence that dominates John's vision, the adoption of this style, if it had such associations, would be understandable. Indeed, judging from the letters, this style came to characterize John's own expression; it is as if he sees all of life from this oracular center and speaks from this center.

The Significance of This Perspective. John's Gospel is thus a very exciting form of witness in which Jesus, both earthly and risen, speaks to later disciples. This does not mean this Gospel is the product of a proto-Gnostic New Ager with little concern for history, for this Gospel is grounded in history (cf. Morris 1969:65-138; Thompson 1996; D. Wenham 1997:30-47). But the Gospel does not give us the equivalent of a transcript of a videotape. John is thoroughly committed to the importance of history, but he wants to tell the story of Jesus as interpreted by the abiding Spirit. One of the themes throughout the Gospel is how cryptic Jesus' words and deeds are within the story. What was cryptic then is now clear in the light of the glorification. John wants us to understand Jesus' identity and significance in a way no one at the time possibly could, in order that we may respond in faith, continue to respond in faith and thereby share in the very life of God.

□ Date

The main question regarding date is whether this Gospel was written before or after the destruction of the temple in A.D. 70. A further question arises from the complex history of the text, namely, the date of the various stages.

No Later than A.D. 110 A papyrus fragment dating from early in the second century that contains John 18:31-33, 37-38 has been found in Egypt. Assuming this is a fragment of a copy of the Gospel and not of one of its sources, the date of the Gospel could not be much later than 110. Irenaeus says John lived on into the reign of Trajan (A.D. 98-117), but it is not clear that this is when he was writing.

One Option: Pre-A.D. 70 Some scholars think the Gospel was written before the destruction of the temple in A.D. 70 (Morris 1971:30-35; Robinson 1976:254-84; 1985:67-93). Since most scholars agree that John did not use the Synoptic Gospels themselves as source material, it is possible to argue that John goes back to source as directly as the Synoptics (Robinson 1985). If that is the case, then there is no reason to expect a long period of writing while sources were gathered. On this theory he did not use the Synoptics because they were being written at the same time he was writing. Furthermore, the presence of many features of pre-70 conditions in Israel, not least the presence of the temple, suggest an early date. There is no clear indication in this Gospel that the temple has been destroyed. A statement like that made by Caiaphas (11:48) is quite in keeping with a pre-70 context.

Another Option: A.D. 80-100 Most scholars would accept a date between 80 and 100. While the thought in this Gospel has contacts with the sort of tradition found in the Synoptics, it has been reworked extensively. The presumption is that it takes time to develop a coherent tradition. This point is probably correct, but there is no way of saying how much time such development would take. A theological genius such as the one that appears to be behind this Gospel could, presumably, see things fall together rapidly. There is also the matter of the inspiration of the Holy Spirit, claimed by this author. So there is no way to say such development must take seventy years rather than thirty-five, but some gestation time is reasonable.

The historical settings within Judaism and Johannine Christianity provide further reasons for this date. First, the highly developed polemic against the Jewish opponents probably reflects the extreme tensions between Jewish leaders and Johannine Christians in John's own day. John seems to reflect a separation between church and synagogue. Three times reference is made to being put out of the synagogue (9:22; 12:42; 16:2). According to many, one of the decisive moments of separation was the introduction into the liturgy of the synagogue a prayer, known as the Twelfth Benediction, that cursed the heretics. It is thought that Christians, among others, were targeted by this prayer. Thus, Christians could no longer attend synagogue without hearing prayer for their own cursing! This benediction was introduced probably in the 80s, though perhaps slightly later. This change in the liturgy reflects the sort of situation in which John writes, though whether the Twelfth Benediction was the specific catalyst behind the expulsion is debated (see comment on 9:22). Some would say the hostility reflected in John may be of a more local nature such as existed from the beginning, as Acts describes, as well as in Paul's experience (for example, 1 Thess 2:14-16). Nevertheless, the hostility is intense enough to suggest a period of time has passed and tensions have increased. Thus a date later in the century is more probable, though not required.

The same must be said regarding the developments within the Johannine community itself. We know from the letters something of the tensions within this community, and these tensions may be reflected in some passages in the Gospel itself (for example, 15:1-17). Thus, it is possible that the major part of the Gospel was written before the letters but that a final redaction came after they were written. Robinson attempts to date the letters and the tensions they represent to A.D. 60-65 (1976:284-311), but most scholars put them in the 90s. Thus a date for the Gospel in the early 90s, with a final redaction perhaps a few years later, may best account for the evidence.

☐ **Location**

Nothing is said in the Gospel about where it was written. There is evidence of familiarity with Palestine, but there is very little data that helps locate this document. If the complexity of the composition is acknowledged, then it is possible the material was formed in more than one location over a period of time.

Ephesus Church tradition says it was written in Ephesus (Irenaeus *Against Heresies* 3.1.1), and there is no reason to reject this. Ephesus was a cosmopolitan center where most of the religious and philosophical winds of the day were blowing. Since this Gospel contains echoes of many of these currents, a location where they are present would make sense. The apocalyptic mysticism that was a particular concern of John had a strong presence in this area (cf. Goulder 1991), so again this would support this proposal. But these currents were present elsewhere, even in Israel, so a center such as Ephesus is not required. A further significant point in favor of Ephesus is the location of the book of Revelation in this area. Many scholars deny these two books were written by the same person but admit they seem to come from the same Christian community (cf. Beasley-Murray 1987:lxix-lxxx).

Other Suggestions   Scholars have, of course, suggested other locations. The similarities between John's thought and that of Philo of Alexandria has commended that Egyptian location to a few (Brownlee 1990:189-91). But these similarities are part of larger currents of thought not restricted to Alexandria. A more attractive setting has been Syria, perhaps Antioch, for some the contacts with Ignatius of Antioch (c. 110) and the Odes of Solomon are significant (Kümmel 1975:247). Theophilus of Antioch (c. 170-180) gives the first clear citation of John, whom he says was inspired by the Spirit (*Ad Autolycum* 2.22, citing Jn 1:1). Others look to Syria because they find within John evidence that it comes from the sphere of Palestinian Judaism yet outside the jurisdiction of the Jerusalem Sanhedrin (H. Koester 1982:2:178-81). Others would see the location simply in Israel, since the Gospel shows intimate knowledge of the geography and politics of Israel and the story focuses often on the conflicts with Jewish authorities in Israel.

A Chronological and Geographical Combination   Since something could be said for Israel, Syria and Ephesus, a number of scholars would combine these options (cf. Kümmel 1975:247 n. 222; Robinson 1985:48). George Beasley-Murray summarizes one such proposal by T. W. Manson: "He suggested that the Fourth Gospel originated in a tradition which had its home in Jerusalem, and was taken to Antioch; there it influenced literature connected with that city, the liturgical usage of the Syrian church, the teaching of missionaries who went out from it (for example, Paul) and its later leaders (for example, Ignatius); from Antioch it was taken to Ephesus, where 'the final literary formulation was achieved in the Gospel and Epistles attributed to John' " (Beasley-Murray 1987:lxxxi, referring to Manson 1946-1947:320). Such a view may do most justice to the data we have, such as it is.

☐ Purposes

The purpose of the Gospel is clearly stated: "Jesus did many other miraculous signs in the presence of his disciples, which are not recorded in this book. But these are written that you may believe that Jesus is the Christ, the Son of God, and that by believing you may have life in his name" (20:30-31). His primary purpose is to tell the story of Jesus for faith. There is debate, however, whether this means he is writing for the purpose of evangelism, that his readers might learn of Jesus and come to faith, or for the encouragement of Christians, that they may continue in the faith. Indeed, the manuscripts offer two different forms of the word for "believe" that illustrate these two interpretations (see the NIV margin and the commentary). There is evidence for both concerns in the Gospel. I think his specific purpose was assurance for Christians but his great passion was to bear witness to Jesus, and he does so in a way that is very effective for evangelism.

Evidence Against Evangelism as the Primary Purpose John clearly expects his readers to have at least a general knowledge of many of the people, places, institutions and events mentioned in the story (Culpepper 1983:211-23). For example, he expects them to already know near the beginning of the story that Jesus was raised from the dead (2:22). Knowledge of such a central Christian fact might be expected of a potential convert, but there are other details that one would not expect a non-Christian to know. Mary of Bethany is described by referring to an event that does not occur until later in the story (11:2; cf. 12:1-8). As we have seen, such features in the text could well indicate that the Gospel consists largely of stories originally told separately. But even when they were separate, the stories that contained these allusions were told for a Christian audience.

Two Challenges Calling for Reassurance If the specific focus is not evangelism but the encouragement of Christians to continue in the faith, why would they need such encouragement? Their faith appears to be challenged primarily from two directions.

Conflict with the Synagogue. Conflict with the synagogue is reflected throughout the Gospel. Indeed, Jesus' conflict with Jewish leaders is one of the major plot lines of the Gospel. It is expressed in the prologue in the abstract symbolism of light versus darkness (1:5) and the rejection of the light by "his own" (1:11). The drama of first part is the growing conflict with the Jewish opponents (chaps. 1—12), and then future conflict is promised to the disciples (chaps. 13—17). The climax of Jesus' conflict comes in the crucifixion (chaps. 18—19), but there are still echoes in the resurrection account (20:19). Presumably John emphasizes this conflict because of its relevance to his readers. They are experiencing the same sort of conflict as described in the story, as was promised to them (for example, 15:18—16:4).

The specific problem the disciples face is expulsion from the synagogue (16:2; cf. 9:22; 12:42). Up to this point Christians have been able to remain in the synagogue, but now they are being forced to withdraw. Some are even suffering death (16:2). In John's situation the conflict has reached the point of separation between church and synagogue with extreme hostility on both sides. The pain, frustration and hostility evident in naming Jesus' opponents simply "the Jews" is indicative of the polarization (see comments on 1:19; 8:44). They have rejected Jesus on the grounds of their Judaism, so now John, a Jew himself, takes that which is most precious in their eyes and uses it as a negative term full of irony. It is similar to Paul's reference to the "super-apostles" (2 Cor 11:5; 12:11). This language has, of course, provided an excuse for ungodly attitudes and actions toward Jews throughout history. But the term represents a break with the leadership of Judaism not because they are Jewish (see comment on 19:11), but because they have rejected God's Son. It is their form of Judaism that is found wanting, but their form was in the process of becoming official Judaism.

Up to this point the Christians have viewed themselves as, in some sense, Jewish. Perhaps they still do when John is writing. But now the mother community has rejected them and thereby severely challenged their identity as Jewish followers of the Jewish Messiah. The significance of this crisis lies in the fact that it has forced the Christians to change their understanding of both themselves and the synagogue. I think the primary purpose of John in telling the story of Jesus for faith is to interpret this division that has taken place. He is concerned first and foremost with comforting and assuring his Christian readers in their new situation, separated from the synagogue.

He seeks to accomplish this task in two interrelated ways. First, there is the positive side: he assures his readers by establishing their identity as children of God. It is they who worship the Jewish God in spirit and truth, for they have the Spirit, and they live in Jesus, the Son who perfectly reveals the Father. But if Christians are the ones worshiping the Jewish God, what does that say about their opponents? On the negative side John says their Jewish opponents are children of the devil (8:44). In rejecting Jesus the Jewish opponents are rejecting the God of Israel. As far as John is concerned, if church and synagogue must divide, there is no doubt as to who is of the truth—who really knows, worships and serves the true God.

At the heart of the conflict with the synagogue are claims for Jesus' deity. The problem was not the claim that Jesus is the Messiah but the additional claim that he is the unique Son of God. Judaism knew of leaders set apart by God as his agents in a special sense, but now the Johannine Christians were claiming for Jesus not only that he was God's agent, like a prophet, but that he is God. Jesus existed with God before creation, he shares in the divine prerogatives of judgment and life giving, and he is, in a word, the self-revelation of God. The figure of Wisdom in the wisdom literature was described in similar terms (for example, Prov 8—9; Sirach 24; Wisdom of Solomon 7—9), and, as we will see, John's Gospel is saturated with allusions to such material (cf. Brown 1966:cxxii-cxxv; Witherington 1995:18-27; Willett 1992). John is claiming, among other things, that Jesus is the fulfillment of this figure of Wisdom, one who is divine and yet distinguishable from God.

Not surprisingly, such a claim was seen by the Jewish leaders as a challenge to monotheism, the very heart of the Jewish faith. This was no time to tolerate such thoughts. Late in the first century, after the destruction of Jerusalem, Judaism itself was having a major identity crisis. When they had gone into exile in Babylon in 587 B.C., losing the land and the temple, all they had left was the Torah, and that became their focus. Now, when the temple was again taken from them, they intensified their attention to the Torah. It is at this time that rabbinical Judaism was coming into existence, and it is this protorabbinism that is reflected in the opponents in this Gospel. For them Wisdom, the focus of God's revelation, is found in the Torah, the law (cf. Hengel 1974:1:169-75). In this Gospel a major theme is the struggle over where God's revelation is located, either in the law or in Jesus.

This conflict raises the question of where God is truly known, where his life is available. John's assurance to his readers is based on faith in Jesus as God's Son revealing God's glory. This revelation of the Father by the Son is the other primary plot line of the Gospel, along with the conflict. Knowledge of the Father and the Son is eternal life (17:3). The purpose statement (20:31) can be read as a call to remain in this life, which is available in Jesus' name, in the face of pressure to deny Christ.

Claims by Mystics. There were strands within Judaism that both the rabbis and the Christians found required a response. Apocalypticism and mysticism were two interrelated movements within Judaism with connections to both the prophetic and wisdom traditions (cf. Gruenwald 1980:3-28; Rowland 1982:193-213; J. Collins 1987:1-32; Dunn 1991; Kanagaraj 1998). Such influences are evident to one degree or another in various types of Judaism at this time, including that at Qumran and even among the rabbis themselves. An important feature of apocalypticism and mysticism was the notion of having direct knowledge of the mysteries of God through visions or ascensions to heaven. We have a number of writings from these movements, which ascribe visions and trips to heaven to such people as Enoch, Abraham, Moses and Isaiah, among many others. Some of the mystics had visions of the chariot-throne of God, described in Ezekiel 1, granted to them through mediation on that passage of Scripture.

One particular theme among some of the mystics was especially disturbing to the rabbis. These mystics claimed to have ascended to heaven and seen a second power in heaven along with God (cf. Segal 1977; 1987). They could ground this notion in Scripture by appeal to Daniel 7:9, where more than one throne is mentioned in Daniel's vision of heaven. The rabbis found this teaching a threat to monotheism. Thus, for them both the "two powers" heretics and the Johannine Christians were threatening the heart of the Jewish faith.

These mystics and apocalyptic seers were a challenge not only to the rabbis but also to the Christians. The conflict was not specifically about the claim by a few that there was a second power in heaven. Rather, it was the more general theme of heavenly ascents and visions. There is a very strong emphasis in John that "no one has ever seen God" (1:18) and "no one has ever gone into heaven" (3:13), suggesting a denial of the claims of these Jewish mystics. John's witness is that heaven has been opened (cf. 1:51) and Jesus is the locus of God's presence.

Although there was conflict with the mystics and apocalyptic seers, there were similarities also, especially regarding dualism and eschatology. Indeed, such conflict and similarities are reflected in much of the New Testament. There was also a similarity between all of these groups and the rabbis, for they all claimed the Scriptures.

In Sum: A Three-Way Conflict Late in the First Century. So the stage was set for major conflict. The apocalyptic and mystical strands had been around at least a couple of centuries, and the Jewish concern for the law, even longer. But now, late in the first century, with the Messiah having come and the temple destroyed, the situation became intense. And out of the spiritual, intellectual, social and political pressures of this time and the conflicts between these groups, the definitive shape was being given to three major movements. The focus on the law and the consolidation of the Jewish identity was giving shape to rabbinical Judaism. The "two powers" heresy developed later into radical Gnosticism with a much more extreme dualism (Segal 1987:24-29). And in John the flower of Christianity was continuing to unfold to a very significant degree. The recognition of Jesus' deity was expressed early on in the church's devotional life, and it increased in clarity as time went on (cf. Hurtado 1988). Now in this Gospel we have a clear vision of Jesus' humanity (cf. Thompson 1988) but also the clearest expression of his deity.

So John is defending his understanding of Jesus over against both establishment and nonestablishment forms within Judaism. In doing so the formation of a distinctive Christian identity is further developed. The conflict here with protorabbinical Judaism speaks to the church's past within the Jewish fold. The conflict with proto-Gnosticism prepares the church for the near future when radical Gnosticism emerged in the second century. These later Gnostics were happy to make use of John's Gospel since so much of its language was congenial. But John's gnosticism includes a rejection of radical Gnosticism, and the church found it a powerful weapon. He claimed gnosticism for Christianity just as the book of Revelation claimed apocalyptic for Christianity. In both cases changes are rung through a focus on Jesus, for in both books the center is the cross. In the Gospel, John argues against both protorabbinism and proto-Gnosticism yet claims the heart of both. In Jesus the Christians have the law and heaven—that is, God's revelation and his presence. John claims that Christians are the true interpreters of the law and that Christians are the true gnostics.

The Evangelistic Significance of John Thus, the primary focus is assurance for Christians. Such a focus, however, not only would bolster the faith of Christians, but would also work as an evangelistic tool. The latter has often been seen as the primary purpose, but the signs that supposedly suggest this purpose are actually ambiguous. For example, the emphasis throughout the Gospel on Jesus as the Messiah and the Son of God, the use of the widely recognized term *logos* ("word") and the provision of a number of footnotes translating Jewish terms (for example, 1:38, 41, 42) are taken as indicating evangelistic concern. But the focus on Jesus as Messiah and Son of God would also serve to assure Christians, and the explanations for non-Jewish readers would be helpful for converts as well as prospective converts.

Nevertheless, the witness to Jesus as Messiah and the Son of God, the presence of the God of Israel and the fulfillment of the Jewish scriptures and festivals would be a powerful witness to Jews, both rabbinical and mystical, who were open to the message and put off neither by language like "the Jews" nor by the pressures from the synagogue and the conflict in general. There may also be a specific interest in evangelizing the Samaritans (cf. 4:34-42), an intriguing suggestion in light of the role John had in the evangelization of Samaria (Acts 8:14-17). Indeed, the Samaritans may have played an important role in the life of the Johannine community as a catalyst for both new insight into Christ and increased conflict with the synagogue (cf. Brown

1979:36-40).

Finally, and most significantly, the use of language that speaks to virtually every major religious and philosophical system in the world of John's time (cf. MacRae 1970; Beasley-Murray 1987:liii-lxvi; Dodd 1953:3-285) not only is a powerful way of interpreting Jesus for Christians, but would also help make the Gospel accessible to non-Christians. John proclaims Jesus as the fulfillment of the Old Testament in its legal, prophetic and wisdom traditions and also of all religious and philosophical insight. In part this is accomplished by using such archetypical symbols as light, darkness, wine, water and bread, and also by revealing Jesus as the focal point for such universal religious concerns as truth and love.

But this does not mean that Jesus is presented as a composite of parts taken from various systems. He, not these systems, is the starting point. In fact, the longings of the religions and philosophies are fulfilled in Jesus even though he is not what anyone was looking for. This is true even of Judaism; the Jews were not looking for a crucified messiah! Jesus does not fit any of the specific systems or expectations, but John claims that once we see Jesus, we will find in him what we were really seeking. C. H. Dodd demonstrates this aspect of John's thought for theme after theme in the Fourth Gospel (1953:133-285). The Gospel, however, is unique at two key points. First, the incarnation claims that history and eternity have met in a person who embodies God's own grace and glory, his light and life and love. Second, the cross reveals the heart of God to be self-sacrificing love.

Some Possible Secondary Purposes Such is the primary purpose with its specific focus on assurance and its more general focus on evangelism. There may be several secondary purposes as well. The evidence for these, as for the primary purposes, comes from distinctive emphases within John that can be understood as corrections of errors he finds in other groups.

Correction of Other Christians. A number of scholars think that John is in disagreement with fellow Christians outside his own community on issues like Christology, eschatology, church order and the sacraments. Indeed, many would see John as representing an isolationist, sectarian mentality (for example, Meeks 1972). Many see conflict reflected in the contrast between the Beloved Disciple and Peter (13:22-24; 20:1-9; 21), with these two serving as representative figures for different Christian groups late in the first century. However, it is not at all clear that figures in the story carry such significance. Even if they do, there is no conflict between Peter and the Beloved Disciple. The insight of the Beloved Disciple is greater than Peter's, but Peter's place of prominence is recognized and not disputed. Indeed, it is Thomas, and not the Beloved Disciple, who has the Gospel's punch line (20:28). Thus, while John's thought and expression is certainly distinctive, he is in agreement with other Christians rather than in debate.

Correction of Followers of John the Baptist. The extreme emphasis in this Gospel on denying that the Baptist is the Messiah has suggested to many that John has in view claims made in his own day by disciples of the Baptist. That groups of the Baptist's disciples continued on after his death may be suggested in Acts (19:1-7), and there is evidence for their existence at least into the third century (cf. Brown 1966:lxviii). Within the Gospel, disciples of the Baptist certainly express antagonism toward Jesus and his followers (3:26), but we do not know any details about the Baptist's followers late in the first century. This suggestion is, however, quite plausible even if its significance remains unclear.

□ Themes

The Gospel contains a very complex pattern of thought, many individual themes woven tightly together; there is no one central theme. Rather, Jesus is the point of reference for each theme, and the web they form together is a vision of reality, that is, of life itself. Accordingly, one of the key themes for John is life (cf. 1 Jn 1:1). Our survey of this grand vision will begin with some general characteristics of John's thought and then move to clusters of themes.

Characteristics of Johannine Thought We must begin with a brief description of some of the most important features of John's thought, otherwise we will miss his profundity and probably even misunderstand what he is trying to say.

Dualism. John often works with contrasts like above and below, heaven and earth, love and hate, light and darkness, truth and lie. One is either of God or of the devil, though he does not see the devil as equal to God, as in more radical dualism. This view of reality and John's form of expression can give the impression that he has no appreciation for the ambiguities of life, but in fact he does recognize that we live with gray areas. For example, the purest group has Judas the betrayer within it, and the core of the Jewish opponents, the Pharisees, has Nicodemus within it. John sees life in terms of stark contrasts that seem almost static. Yet his picture is one of dynamic activity as God sends his Son to redeem the world and as people are in motion either toward the light or away from it.

Antinomies. John paints with bold, bright colors, but he expresses subtle complexity by setting side by side things that seem to clash. For example, he has some of the strongest statements in the Bible on the topic of divine election and also some of the clearest statements about human responsibility. And he often puts them right next to each other (cf. 1:12-13; 6:39-40). John is our theological master. He is saying both of these are true even though we cannot see how they can both be true. The thought John is expressing is greater than what our language can convey or our minds entirely grasp, and so these juxtapositions are used to circle around the truth when he is not able to simply state it. Such pairs of seemingly contradictory statements, called *antinomies,* are a favorite of both classical rhetoricians and Jewish writers, and this Gospel has a number of them as well. Such antinomies are to be expected in a revelation that actually comes from beyond the human sphere.

Symbolism. Another means for expressing such thought is symbolism, which is found throughout this Gospel. Its symbolism comes from within Judaism, especially from the Old Testament, but most of it also reflects non-Jewish traditions: for example, the use of *logos* or "word" (see comment on 1:1). John's use of symbols suggests he is not trying merely to label or describe Jesus. They are textured so that layer upon layer of meaning is found as one reflects on the associations conveyed by the symbol. What does it mean that Jesus is the bread of life (see Jn 6)? The historical allusions involved in this symbol will help us understand it, but they will hardly exhaust its meaning. This use of symbols also means that the conversation in the Gospel is often working on more than one level: the woman at the well (chap. 4) thinks Jesus is speaking of physical water, but he is speaking of spiritual water. We will find the truth of the symbol on both literal and spiritual levels of reference.

Irony. The use of multiple levels results in a great deal of irony. Sometimes it is stated explicitly (1:15; 9:39), while at other times it is evident in the events. For example, Caiaphas says Jesus must be eliminated or else "the Romans will come and take away both our place and our nation" (11:48). The readers in John's day realize the irony here, for these leaders did get Jesus killed and the Romans came anyway. At the very heart of the gospel are the twin ironies that we are to look at this human being, Jesus, in order to see God and that life comes through Jesus' death (cf. O'Day 1986).

Signs. This Gospel makes much of what it calls *signs* (cf. 20:30). Signs are symbols in action, that is, actions full of significance. They are windows into the ultimate realities at work in Jesus' revelation of God's glory in deed as well as word. "These stories do not merely illustrate or symbolize divine actions. They are the record of divine action itself" (Newbigin 1982:25). At several points the signs and the symbols are used in conjunction with each other, as in chapter 6, where the sign of the feeding of the five thousand is the occasion for Jesus' teaching on the bread of life.

☐ Three General Clusters of Themes

What then is being revealed through this cryptic, symbolic speech and action? In order to provide a framework for understanding John's thought, I will focus on three general areas. This Gospel is about God, so our first focus with be on the Father, the Son and the Holy Spirit. All of John's thought flows from his vision of God, therefore I will then survey his thought under the headings of light, life and love, since John particularly associates these images with God (cf. 1 Jn 1:1, 5; 4:8). Thirdly, I will take up aspects of discipleship not covered under these other headings.

Father, Son and Holy Spirit While John obviously does not express Trinitarian theology in all of its later sophistication, he does bear witness to the fundamental reality that later trinitarian thought tries to express. John was rightly named "the Theologian" by the ancient church, for in its ancient meaning this term refers to one who knows God and makes him known.

Son. John wants us to believe that Jesus is the Messiah, the Son of God. There are over two dozen titles and descriptions of Jesus used in this Gospel. Many of these terms show Jesus to be the fulfillment of Jewish hopes—he is the Messiah, the King, the Prophet. Others have connections with the Old Testament but also distinctively develop Jesus' teaching in the Synoptics. For example, in Luke 15 Jesus tells a parable about a shepherd who searches for his lost sheep, and in John, Jesus *is* the Good Shepherd. Similarly, images of the kingdom now have their referent directly in Jesus. But these categories only supplement the central thought—namely, that Jesus is the Son of God the Father. The "I Am" sayings affirm Jesus' deity and point to the divine life he offers. While he is one with God and equal to God, he is also utterly dependent on God. Like a model Jewish son he only does what he sees the Father doing and only speaks what he hears from the Father. In this he also fulfills the role of a faithful agent, whose obedience to the one who sent him is the authentication of his message. He is the very presence of God, but he points not to himself, but rather to the Father. His whole mission is to reveal God and enable people to become one with God. He accomplishes this task by glorifying God, particularly on the cross where the love of God is revealed at its brightest. As Son of God he is the fullness from which all of these other images have flowed in the past and now point back to him.

Spirit. After Jesus has revealed the glory and ascends to the Father he sends the Spirit to continue the divine presence on earth. As Jesus always pointed to the Father, so the Spirit will point to Jesus, bringing to remembrance and interpreting his life and teaching. He is referred to as the *paraklētos,* one who is present (see comment on 14:16). This word can have several nuances depending on the context. In situations where there is accusation, a *paraklētos* defends; where there is perplexity, he offers counsel; where there is adversity, he offers comfort. The Johannine Christians found themselves in need of all these forms of help, and they are all provided by the *paraklētos:* defense (16:7-11), counsel (16:12-15) and comfort (14:26-27).

Father. Since the Spirit points to Jesus and Jesus points to the Father, it is clear that this Gospel is ultimately about God the Father. "There is no intention of instituting a separate cult of Jesus" (Lee 1962:33), and yet if we are to know God, we must find him in Jesus. This Gospel utterly rejects unmediated God-mysticism: "No one has ever seen God" apart from Christ (1:18). Jesus reveals God as he exercises the divine functions of life giver and judge and as he reveals God's heart of love. But there is one distinctive aspect of the Father that the Son does not share. The Father is the source of all, including the Son and the Spirit, though in their cases, as later theology makes clear, their origin is an eternal relationship rather than a temporal beginning.

Light, Life, Love The three general categories of light, life and love reveal the character of this God in his relationship with humanity. I will put in italics the key terms for each cluster.

Light. This first cluster of images teaches us about God's *revelation*. The image of *light* itself is only used in the first twelve chapters, as Jesus proclaims himself to be the light of the world and demonstrates what that means by revealing the divine *glory* through his life and teaching. In this revelation he depends on what he *hears* and *sees* from the Father (cf. 8:38). Thus, in a sense he is the true mystic, in contrast with the others who claim to have had visions of God. However, he is not just a mystic; rather he is himself the locus of the divine presence (cf. 1:51). Thus, he enables people to have a vision of God, for to see him is to see God (see comment on 1:18). The revelation of God sought by the mystics is available in Jesus. He also speaks to the rabbis' concern for revelation, for he shows, through debate with the Jewish leaders, that his teaching is true to Scripture. He claims the Scriptures actually speak of him (5:39). Similarly, he is the *fullness* from which the Jewish revelation, comes and thus completes and therefore replaces the temple, the festivals, the land and the law. Accordingly, he is *truth* itself, for truth is the eternal reality and its revelation, and Jesus is both. But when the really real is revealed, not all receive it. The conflict that arises from Jesus' claim is the presence of *judgment*. Jesus does not come to condemn, but condemnation occurs as people reject him—they stand self-condemned. As the light shines, one either hates the light or approaches it (cf. 3:19-21). The stories in this Gospel illustrate both reactions.

Life. Jesus as the divine revealer is not simply trying to convey information or a mystical experience; he is offering life, *eternal life,* the life of God. It is his life that is our light (1:4), and he gives his life not just for our instruction, but so we also may share in his life. These ideas of revelation and life come together in 17:3: "Now this is eternal life: that they may know you, the only true God, and Jesus Christ, whom you have sent." In seeing the relation between the Father and the Son and by experiencing the love that is the essence of their relationship, one *knows* God. John never uses the word *knowledge (gnōsis)* but always the verb "to know." Perhaps this is part of his attempt to distinguish his thought from the knowledge claimed by the proto-Gnostics. The knowledge Jesus offers is not insight into the cosmos, though insight into God's plan in history and understanding of his will are included. But fundamentally Jesus desires that we share in his own relation with the Father, *becoming one* with him and one another (cf. 17:20-23)! As we *abide* in him we bear the fruit of a life that reflects Jesus' own life.

Love. The chief characteristic of this divine life is love. The Johannine understanding of love is expressed clearly in 1 John 3:16: "This is how we know what love is: Jesus Christ laid down his life for us." Thus, God is love, and love is the laying down of one's life—hence the centrality of the *cross* for John. Throughout the story God's gracious love is expressed by Jesus in word and deed in the context of his "hour," that is, his crucifixion. The cross is already in view before Jesus says or does anything (1:29), and it provides the frame of reference for his first sign (2:11). The crucifixion is referred to as his glorification because here we see the *glory* of God shining at its brightest. In the cross we have the revelation of the heart of God, namely, his love.

Discipleship

John wants his readers not just to see this vision of God, but to enter into the divine life that God is offering. He seems to have in mind the needs of second-generation Christians (cf. Minear 1977). Some in his churches seem to have wished they could have seen and heard and touched Jesus themselves. John makes it clear that no matter how great a privilege contact with Jesus was (cf. 1 Jn 1:1), those who live after the giving of the Spirit have it far better. Most of Jesus' words and deeds were puzzling, but now they are clear by the ministry of the Spirit in the church. In fact, we now have his very life within us; we are united to him and his Father by the Spirit. So although it was an unspeakable honor to have seen Jesus, "blessed are those who have not seen and yet have believed" (20:29). But how is one to enter into this union with God? In this third major area, discipleship, the twin foci for John are the well known fundamentals: trust and obey. He develops these in his own distinctive way.

Faith. John reflects throughout the story on why some people *believe* and some disbelieve. He does not unravel this mystery entirely, but he does have an answer. His answer is twofold; it is one of our antinomies. The first answer is God's call. Those whom the Father gives to the Son will come to him and remain with him (6:37-40). The second answer is the human heart. One's interior disposition determines whether one will accept Jesus as the Son of God or not. It is a matter of what one loves and hates (3:19-21). Divine sovereignty and human responsibility are interwoven in the text. For example, there are at least a half dozen references to each scattered throughout 6:27-65. John is quite clear that it is God who takes the initiative; all is of grace. But he is clear that human response also plays an essential role, and it is this part of the antinomy that he develops most in his concept of faith.

Faith, for John, is a very dynamic response to God, as is suggested, perhaps, from the fact that he never uses the noun "faith," but always the verb "to believe." It is not simply an intellectual grasp of truths about God nor a once-and-for-all decision to follow Christ. Rather, it is an openness to God that trusts Jesus is who he claims to be and God is like what Jesus reveals him to be. It is the desire of the heart, a will to do God's will (7:17). As God continues to reveal more of himself this response is required over and over. After the very first sign it is said that his disciples put their faith in him (2:11), but this faith is tested as Jesus does and says things that are increasingly puzzling or even scandalous (cf. 6:60-69). The disciples are holding on for dear life as Jesus takes them for a wild ride. They are usually in the dark about what is going on and what Jesus is talking about. A great deal of what Jesus says in this Gospel is cryptic and therefore misunderstood. This is quite intentional on Jesus' part, for he admits at the end of his teaching ministry that he has been speaking in unclear dark sayings (16:25; the NIV "figuratively" is not adequate). What he is revealing is the glory of God, and until that revelation is complete in the cross, the resurrection and the ascension and until the Spirit is given, it is not possible to grasp what he is saying, for one must be born from above to even see the kingdom (3:3).

Humility. One must have a great deal of humility in order to continue trusting in such circumstances. We see such humility again and again in those who receive Jesus. In contrast, those who reject him are characterized by an attitude of self-assurance based on their own concepts of God and his ways. This does not mean that John thinks openness, of itself, is always good. One can be open to evil and fail to hold fast to God, as happens later in his community (cf. 1 Jn 2:19; 2 Jn 9). Nor does it mean that the only ones who received Jesus were those who had no opinions about God and his ways. Right at the outset we find Nathanael, who doubts Jesus could be "the one Moses wrote about in the Law, and about whom the prophets also wrote" (1:45). And some of his reasons for doubting are the same ones the opponents will have later in the story. The difference between Nathanael and the opponents is that his *interior disposition* is different, for he is "a true Israelite, in whom there is nothing false" (1:47). He is willing to come and see, while the opponents do not come and see. Rather, they are of their father the devil in whom there is no truth (8:44).

Such humility may explain why neither the Beloved Disciple nor the mother of Jesus is ever named in this Gospel even though they are both important models of discipleship. Perhaps, like John the Baptist, another such model, they have "decreased that Jesus might increase" to such an extent that their identities have become one with their relation to Jesus. Indeed, even the title Beloved Disciple could come from his humble wonder at being loved by the Son of God (cf. Carson 1991:76). The Beloved Disciple has special insight precisely at those points that reveal the glory most brightly—the cross (13:21-26; 19:35) and the resurrection

(20:2-10; 21:7). Such references attest to his insight and thus the value of his testimony. By painting himself into the picture like this we see his humility, but we see also that it is not a false humility. He recognizes the authority that comes from what he has been given to see and understand, but he exalts in what he has heard, seen and touched, not in himself. In his humility he keeps pointing to Jesus, in the same way the Spirit points to Jesus and Jesus himself keeps pointing to the Father.

Obedience. Such humility is closely associated not only with belief but also with obedience. It takes humility to put oneself under someone's direction, and it takes humble trust to remain there. Obedience is not to a set of rules as such, but to Jesus' example of servitude (13:14-17) and his command to love one another (13:34-35; 15:9-17). These are closely related both to one another and to humility, since love is the laying down of one's life. The command of Jesus is that we lay down our lives for one another in humble service. Such service characterizes Jesus' friends (15:13-14) as it flows from his own relationship with the Father. It is in the context of such love that evangelism can take place (13:35; cf. 17:21-23), because as Christians embody this love the divine life continues to be manifested on earth, the light continues to shine in the darkness.

Community. At the heart of the universe is the one God—monotheism is true. But this one God turns out to be a community of Persons. The Jewish (and Muslim) understanding of monotheism is woefully inadequate, and the mystic's flight of the alone to the Alone is misguided. God is much more marvelous than any of these visions. This vision of the Holy Trinity, present here in John's Gospel in seed form, affects how we understand all of life. For instance, the great goal of God revealed in the Bible, and in this Gospel in particular, is the formation of community (for example, see comments at the beginning of Jn 9 and on 19:25-27). The revelation of the Trinity shows this goal to be grounded in God's very being. We are in God's image as individuals and as community, hence John's Gospel focuses on these.

This is a startling vision, but the real shock is the revelation that the divine life is life laid down. Here is a revelation unlike any other view of God anywhere. Indeed, it is a vision of God to which Christians themselves have had a difficult time remaining true. Jesus said he only does what he sees the Father doing, and the washing of his disciples' feet is not said to be an exception. The God of the universe washes feet! Jesus is deity as much as the Father is, yet the Father is greater than he, he only does what he sees the Father doing, and he only speaks what he hears from the Father. This means that to obey is as divine as to command. At every point in the Gospel this divine life is revealed in order that we might live the divine, heavenly life, being born from above and filled with his presence, reflecting his glory in our own lives as individuals and in community. This is what it means to have life in his name (20:31).

Outline of John

Some scholars believe the entire Gospel is composed of an intricate series of chiasms (Ellis 1984; Barnhart 1993). While these proposals probably go too far, there is no doubt that John does at times make use of chiasms to pattern his material, some of which will be noted in the commentary. This outline, however, follows more obvious plot lines in the Gospel.

13:21-30 _____ Jesus Predicts His Betrayal

13:31-35 _____ Jesus Introduces Major Themes of His Farewell Discourse

13:36—14:4 _ Jesus Predicts Peter's Denial and Speaks of His Own Departure

14:5-7 _____ Jesus Declares Himself to Be the Way to the Father

14:8-21 _____ Jesus Speaks of Both His Relation to the Father and His Disciples' Relation to the Father

14:22-31 _____ Jesus Contrasts His Disciples' Relation to God with the World's Relation to God

15:1-17 _____ Jesus Calls the Disciples to Remain in Him, the True Vine

15:18—16:15 Jesus Speaks of the Conflict with the World and of the Paraclete

16:16-33 _____ Jesus Predicts Joy and Suffering

17:1-26 _____ Jesus Concludes His Time Alone with His Disciples by Praying to His Father

18:1—19:42 __ The Climax of the Glorification Begins: Jesus' Passion and Death

18:1-11 _____ Jesus Is Arrested

18:12-27 _____ Jesus Is Confronted by Annas; Peter Is Confronted by People in the Courtyard

18:28—19:16_ Pilate Interrogates Jesus

19:16-30 _____ Jesus Is Crucified

19:31-42 _____ Enemies and Friends Attend to Jesus' Body

20:1—21:23 __ The Climax of the Glorification Continues: Jesus Is Raised and Meets with His Disciples

20:1-29 _____ Jesus Appears to His Disciples

20:30-31 _____ John Declares His Purpose in Writing This Gospel

21:1-23 _____ Jesus Appears Again to His Disciples

21:24-25 _____ Later Disciples Bear Witness to the Beloved Disciple's Witness

COMMENTARY

□ **John Introduces the Story of the Revelation of the Glory of God (1:1-18)**

We are at the outset of a story that will reveal to us the most profound mysteries of life. This story is simply about God, the glory of his character, the nature of his life and his desire to share that life with his creatures. It is about God come amongst us and the mixed response he received to his offer of divine life.

John does not ease us into such awesome topics; he plunges us immediately into the heart of the revelation by giving in the prologue an overview of the themes that will be worked out in narrative form in the story. The prologue helps us understand the significance of what takes place in the story and gives us clues as to what to watch for.

John Presents the Revelation in a Nutshell (1:1-5) These first five verses provide the frame of reference and the main components for the story to follow—sort of a prologue to the prologue. We get the story in the right perspective by beginning in eternity (vv. 1-2) and then moving to creation (v. 3). The key ingredients follow, namely, incarnation (v. 4) and conflict (v. 5).

John's opening echoes Genesis (Gen 1:1), but whereas Genesis refers to the God's activity at the beginning of creation, here we learn of a being who existed before creation took place. In the beginning the Word already *was*. So we actually start before the beginning, outside of time and space in eternity. If we want to understand who Jesus is, John says, we must begin with the relationship shared between the Father and the Son "before the world began" (Jn 17:5, 24). This relationship is the central revelation of this Gospel and the key to understanding all that Jesus says and does.

The first verse is very carefully constructed to refer to the personal distinctness yet the essential oneness of the Word with God. To be *with* God means the Word is distinct from him. The word *with (pros)* in a context like this is used to indicate personal relationship, not mere proximity (cf. Mk 6:3). But he also *was* God; that is, there is an identity of being between them. These two truths seem impossible to reconcile logically, and yet both must be held with equal firmness. At this point John simply affirms this antinomy, but later he will reveal more of the relations of the Father and the Son, as well as of the Holy Spirit. John does not reflect philosophically on the Holy Trinity but bears witness to it as the eternal reality, leaving it to later teachers to try to expound its bright mystery.

To speak of the *Word (logos)* in relation to the beginning of creation would make sense to both Jews and Greeks. In some schools of Greek thought, the universe is *kosmos,* an ordered place, and what lies behind the universe and orders it is reason *(logos)*. For the Jews, creation took place through God's speech (Gen 1; Ps 33:6). Furthermore, in John's day "word" was often associated with "wisdom" (for example, Wisdom of Solomon 9:1; cf. Breck 1991:79-98), and John will often use wisdom motifs to speak of Jesus (cf. Willett 1992). For example, like the *Word* who was *with God,* Wisdom is said to have been "at his side" at the creation (Prov 8:30). As this passage suggests, God's word and wisdom were often spoken of as if they were persons (for example, Wisdom of

---

1:1-18 The style, structure and content of these verses suggest to many scholars they form a hymn that has been adapted for use as the prologue (cf. Beasley-Murray 1987:3-5). If so, it was probably composed by John or a close disciple since its style and content are so thoroughly in keeping with the rest of the Gospel. There is, however, no agreement among scholars on the structure or content of the original hymn nor even that this material was a hymn.

1:1 There is no definite article in front of *God* in *the Word was God,* leading some to

Solomon 18:14-16; Prov 8:1—9:18; Job 28; cf. Hengel 1974:1:153-56). The Jews did not view these personifications as divine personal beings distinct from God, thereby challenging monotheism (Hurtado 1988:41-50). However, a redefinition of monotheism *is* called for with the coming of Jesus (for example, Jn 1:14, 18; 5:16-18). Thus the use of "word" and "wisdom" within Judaism was of enormous help to the Christians as they tried to understand and express the reality they found in Jesus. Jesus is what the "word" and "wisdom" were, and much more.

The description of Wisdom as the master worker at God's side at creation (Prov 8:22-31) is now echoed in John's declaration that the *Word* was the agent of all creation (1:3). As agent he is distinct from the Creator. God the Father is viewed throughout the Gospel as the ultimate source of all, including the Son and the Spirit. But life did not simply come *through* the Word but was *in* the Word (1:4). Only God is the source of life, and it is a mark of Jesus' distinctness and deity that the Father "has granted the Son to have life in himself" (5:26).

By stating both positively and negatively that the Word is the agent of all creation (1:3), John emphasizes that there were no exceptions: the existence of absolutely all things came by this Word. Although with verse 3 we move from eternity to creation, we are still dealing with facts hard to comprehend. Until discoveries made in the 1920s, the Milky Way was thought to be the entire universe, but now we realize there are many billions of galaxies. Science is helping us spiritually, for it silences us before God in wonder and awe. But this verse also helps us put science in its proper place. The universe is incredibly wonderful, so how much more wonderful must be the one upon whose purpose and power it depends. "The builder of a house has greater honor than the house itself" (Heb 3:3).

Because the earliest manuscripts had no verse numbers, nor even spaces between words and sentences, it is sometimes hard to know

---

translate it "a god" or "divine." But John's grammar is "the most concise way he could have stated that the Word was God and yet was distinct from the Father" (Wallace 1996:269). If John had included a definite article before *God,* this would be too emphatic, obliterating the distinctness between the Word and God. A later heresy, Sabellianism, went this route by failing to distinguish sufficiently between the persons of the Godhead, seeing them as different modes or operations of one person.

where one sentence ends and another begins. Such is the case with verses 3 and 4. Many commentators, ancient and modern, divide the text as in the NIV, but many others think the final words of verse 3 belong with verse 4: "What has come into being in him was life, and the life was the light of all people" (NRSV). Either option would fit John's style and thought, but the NRSV option reflects how all the earliest commentators took the text, suggesting this was the more natural reading for native speakers. At a later date the orthodox began taking it as in the NIV because of misuses by false teachers who took *ho gegonen* ("what was made in him") to include the Holy Spirit, thus making the Spirit a creature (cf. Chrysostom *In John* 5.1).

If the text reads "what has come into being in him was life," this could refer to those who came to have union with God in the Son, a major theme of this Gospel. If so, John has moved from creation in verse 3 to re-creation, as it were, in verse 4. The quality of life in the sphere of creation is not yet the deepest life, the divine life in the Word. This idea is true to John's thought, but he does not use *light of men* to refer to the new order of life now offered in Jesus. So most likely the reference is to the incarnation, declaring that what took place in the Word at his incarnation was the manifestation of life itself (cf. 1 Jn 1:1-2). This allusion to the incarnation would only be evident to those who understand Jesus' identity as revealed in the rest of the Gospel.

His life, manifest in the incarnation, is our light (Jn 1:4). In this Gospel light always refers to the revelation and salvation that Jesus is and offers (cf. 8:12; 11:9 is the one exception). In order to have life we need to know God, and Jesus is our source of such knowledge. As our light, his life is our guide. He is our wisdom, that which reveals all else to us and enables us to see. In Jewish thought it is the law that plays this role (for example, Wisdom of Solomon 18:4; cf. Hengel 1974:1:171; 2:112; Kittel 1967:134-36), but for John it is the incarnation of the Word that makes sense of all of life.

1:4 That the Word is *the light of men* may pick up a theme among the Jewish mystics (Kanagaraj 1998:295-300). This phrase could also mean that the light of Jesus' life illumines human beings (*tōn anthrōpon* as an objective genitive), a thought that will be developed later in the Gospel (for example, 3:19-21). In Christ we see God, but we also have our own hearts revealed.
1:5 Here also we have an echo of Wisdom: "Compared with the light [of the sun] she [Wisdom] is found to be superior, for it is succeeded by the night, but against wisdom evil

Thus, here at the outset we have the two most fundamental affirmations about Jesus in this Gospel, namely that he himself is the presence of God's own life and light and that he makes this life and light available to human beings. In one profound sentence we have the central assertion of this Gospel concerning the revelation of the Son and the salvation he offers.

The story will reveal the glory described in these opening verses, but it will be a tragic story of conflict, because humanity is in the darkness of rebellion. The shining of the light is an ongoing, continuous activity (*phainei,* present tense, v. 5), for it is the very nature of light to shine. But when that light and life came amongst us as a human being, the darkness did not grasp, or master, the light; it neither comprehended it nor overcame it (*katelaben;* cf. the NIV text and note). The story will show both senses of this word to be true.

The Light Came into the World (1:6-13) Using the image of light John now describes the incarnation in more detail, but he still does not refer to it explicitly. Nothing in this section, as in the last, need refer to a distinct person at all. Throughout there are analogies to what is said of Wisdom in the wisdom literature. Wisdom was God's agent at creation (Prov 3:19-20; 8:22-31), has come down to earth seeking those who will give heed (Prov 1:20-21; 8:1-11), is rejected by some (Prov 1:22-33; 8:36) and is received by others whom she enables to receive life and favor from the Lord (Prov 3:13-18; 8:35). Thus, John is working with what would be familiar from Judaism to establish the context for appreciating the radically new thing that has occurred in Jesus.

This section begins with the ministry of John the Baptist (Jn 1:6-8), as in the Synoptics. The Baptist is presented in very exalted terms, for the language of being sent *from God* is also used of Jesus (16:27) and the Holy Spirit (15:26). But John's own identity is not dwelt on, other

does not prevail" (Wisdom of Solomon 7:29-30 RSV).
1:6-13 The major sources in wisdom literature for primary analogies with John's thought include the following: Job 28; Prov 1—9; Baruch 3:9—4:4; Sirach 1; 4:11-19; 6:18-31; 14:20—15:10; 24; Wisdom of Solomon 6:12—10:21. See Brown 1966:cxxii-cxxv for a summary survey of the analogies based on these texts, and, for much more extensive treatment, see Willett 1992.

than to insist that he himself was not the light (1:8). He is described solely in terms of his mission *to testify concerning that light* (v. 7), a point that will be developed later (vv. 19-28). This mission is universal; it is that *all* might believe. What is in view, therefore, is not just John's preaching to the Jews who went out to hear him, but the witness he continues to have through his place in the proclamation of the story of Jesus (cf. vv. 15, 31).

This universality is also reflected in the cry in verse 9 concerning the coming of the light *that gives light to every man.* The phrase *coming into the world* could refer to the people rather than the light (see NIV margin), but since the focus of the passage is on the coming of the light the NIV text is probably correct. If so, it could be translated "This was the true light that enlightens everyone by coming into the world" (cf. v. 4). In any case, here we have the universal significance of the light for every individual, an important theme in this Gospel and a controversial one. The light of Jesus is as universal as the light of creation. He did not come merely to some Gnostic elite, nor did he come to a single nation or culture. This light is the Word that became flesh in a given time and place. At the heart of Christianity is the so-called scandal of particularity. People of all cultures and times are to receive the light that shines in this first-century Jew—he who has been given authority over all people (17:2). This does not mean the light of God is not manifested to some degree throughout the world's religions and philosophies. But even such light is derived from the one who became incarnate in Israel. Indeed, it is only by his light that we can recognize what is genuine light elsewhere. This is something of what it means that the *true light* has come. The word *true* means for John, in part, that which is really real, that which is genuine. John's own example in this Gospel encourages us to recognize that which is of the truth from whatever quarter. But among all the claims to wisdom, revelation and truth, John is claiming that in Jesus we have received the real thing, the truth from which all truth

1:11 The phrase *ta idia (that which was his own)* is probably an idiom for a generality like "his own home" or "place" (cf. 19:27). The following phrase *(hoi idioi, his own)* shifts to masculine since it refers to the response of his people at his place.
1:12 In receiving the Son *(hyios)* believers receive the power to become children *(tekna).*

flows and the criterion for recognizing truth wherever it may be found.

God is working out his salvation through one nation, and specifically one person within that nation, but his is a universal salvation. This light shines on everyone (v. 9). The tragedy is the mixed response he gets, for some "wilfully close the eyes of their mind" (Chrysostom *In John* 8.1). This light *was in the world* (v. 10), probably referring to the incarnation, since that is the focus of the context. *The world* in this Gospel usually refers to those who oppose God, but here it is used first of the created order before shifting to a negative sense: *the world did not recognize him*. When the author appeared in his own story he was not recognized, not even by *his own* (v. 11), that is, those who knew him not just through the general revelation of creation but through the special revelation of covenant. The Old Testament, especially throughout the Prophets, witnesses to such rejection of God as the common human response. Thus an old familiar pattern is repeated, though the identity of this messenger makes this rejection especially shocking.

Why do some believe and others do not? John has two answers, and they are both found in verses 12-13. If we had only verse 12 the answer would be human response, for it says that after they receive and believe they are given *the right to become children of God*. The word *right (exousia)* may be misleading since it suggests a legal claim. *Exousia* can also mean "power" or "authority." The imagery of coming alive as God's children suggests the focus here is on the power that produces divine life. But it is a power that must be exercised by the person—John does not say "he made them children of God" but "he gave them power to become children of God" (cf. Chrysostom *In John* 10.2).

On the other hand, if we had only verse 13 the answer would be divine initiative. The general meaning of this verse is clear enough, though the imagery taken from physical childbirth is obscure. *Natural descent* is literally "of bloods" *(ex haimatōn)*. The NIV seems to suggest the reference is to lineage (cf. Carson 1991:126), but this usage is extremely rare in Jewish material. More likely, the reference is to the

---

John does not mix these terms, a sign that although believers share in some sense in the relation Jesus has with the Father (see comment on 17:21), he remains the only, unique Son (*monogenēs,* 1:14, 18).

physical contribution of the woman, or of both parents, which is matched with the third expression that refers to the will or desire of the husband. In other words, the begetting of children of God depends on neither human material nor planning. It is Christ's blood and the Father's will that produce children of God (Jn 6:37-40, 53-57). These two elements—human material and planning—are the bookends for the middle expression, which is literally "nor of the will of the flesh." " 'Flesh' here is not a wicked principle opposed to God. Rather, it is the sphere of the natural, the powerless, the superficial, opposed to 'spirit,' which is the sphere of the heavenly and the real (iii 6, vi 63, viii 15)" (Brown 1966:12). This middle term thus conveys the key point of the verse: This birth owes nothing to the natural sphere of life. The other two images express this thought through reference to childbirth in particular.

So the question of why some believe and others do not is answered by another of John's antinomies. There is no doubt that God's gracious sovereign initiative comes first, for he is the source of all life and it is only by his grace that any life occurs and abides at all. The *right* (or power) *to become children of God* must be given by God. The images of verse 13 rule out any role for human power or authority in the process of becoming a child of God. But unlike in natural birth the one being born of God does play a part; this life is not forced on the believer but must be received. Those who are receptive to the Son are offered the gift of becoming children of God themselves.

Throughout this Gospel John will show examples of this receptivity and its opposite. He does not, however, address the further question of why some have receptive hearts and some do not. But by holding fast to these two foci of divine sovereignty and human responsibility John avoids two views common in his day and ours, namely, a fatalistic determinism in which one is an automaton and a merit theology in which one earns or deserves eternal life (cf. further Carson 1981).

On the human side everything depends on one's response to the light who has come. Receiving him is described as believing in his name (1:12), a very striking expression that occurs only in John and 1 John (2:23; 3:18; 1 Jn 3:23; 5:13). For most ancient peoples, "the name is inextricably bound up with the person" (Bietenhard 1976:648). The name is a point of contact between the person and those around, as when we refer to one's name, colloquially, as a "handle." For the ancients this contact goes below the surface, for the name reveals something of who the person actually is. Therefore changing a name means changing one's identity (cf. Jn 1:42). In the Old Testament this tight connection between the name and the person is especially important for God's revelation of himself (Bietenhard 1976:649-50). Indeed, a major element in Israel's claim to know God is the fact that they have received the revelation of his name (Ex 3:13-15). This idea is picked up in John's Gospel (cf. Bietenhard 1976:653) when it is said Jesus has come in order to reveal the Father's name (17:26; completely obscured in the NIV). In Jesus we see the revelation of God himself, for the Father has given his own name to Jesus (17:11-12). God's giving of his name to Jesus continues the theme that the Father has given the Son the divine prerogatives of life-giving and judgment (5:19-30). In this way the "name" is a summary of the gospel itself, and so the missionaries from the later Johannine community go forth "for the sake of the Name" (3 Jn 7).

In our text, therefore, to believe in Jesus' name "implies the acceptance of Jesus to the full extent of his self-revelation" (Schnackenburg 1980a:263), including, especially, his deity. This belief developed slowly among the disciples as Jesus' self-revelation and his revelation of the Father unfolded during his ministry. They apply many exalted titles to Jesus during the first days of their discipleship (Jn 1:41-49), but their belief remains immature until the revelation has been given in its fullness in the cross, resurrection and ascension and until the Spirit comes to guide them into all truth.

Becoming children of God means we begin to share his divine life, without ceasing to be creatures. Believing in Jesus as the Messiah, the Son of God, enables us to have "life in his name" (20:31). Given the significance of the "name," it is clear that "life in his name" is another way of referring to being a child of God because it means sharing in the divine life (cf. 6:40) and reflecting God's character. Thus the revelation of God in Jesus includes a revelation of the type of life we are offered as members of his family.

The story will make clear that believing is not just an intellectual assent to some ideas but a relationship of discipleship to Jesus in which we trust and obey his revelation and receive his ongoing presence through the Spirit.

The Word Became Flesh (1:14-18) We now come to the climax of the prologue. There have been references to the incarnation in the previous verses, but they were expressed in a veiled way. In fact, everything up to this point could be interpreted in a way that would have been compatible, even attractive, to various ancient thinkers. But now comes the break with all non-Christian thought. This Word, the agent of creation, has become a creature. He who brought the universe into existence now is born within the universe as a human being. This thought is so familiar in Christianity we may no longer be staggered by it. A prayer of the Eastern churches conveys well the breathtaking wonder: "We see most eloquent orators voiceless as fish when they must speak of Thee, O Jesus our Savior. For it is beyond their power to tell how Thou art both perfect man and immutable God at the same time."

When we look at this Word become flesh John says we see glory (v. 14). Often in John the "flesh" is that which is natural, powerless and superficial (cf. v. 13). But now the flesh becomes the sphere of the supernatural, the all-powerful, the really real. Matter becomes spirit bearing, and we see the divine glory not through the flesh but precisely in the flesh (Bultmann 1971:63).

The word *glory* means "brightness" or "splendor." When it is used of a person, *glory* has to do with how a person appears to others, suggesting a character that is attractive and honorable. In Jewish thinking a son was to replicate the character of his father, thereby honoring the father and showing the son himself to be honorable. The lack of definite articles in the Greek suggests John is referring to such a relation in general, not to the specific relation between Jesus and the Father (contrast the NIV). An elder son held a position of special responsibility, and an only son, as here, was very special indeed. The term *One and Only (monogenēs)* means "one of a kind" (*genos;* cf. Brown 1966:13-14). It refers to a child who is distinctive in some sense, perhaps "only begotten" as in the case

---

1:14 When John says that this Word *made his dwelling among us,* he uses the verb *skēnoō,* which in its narrow usage refers to living in a tent *(skēnē).* The allusion seems to be to

of Jephthah's daughter (Judg 11:34), but not necessarily so, as its use in describing Isaac illustrates (Heb 11:17). While the word does not in itself mean "only begotten," this sense is true of Jesus (cf. NIV note) since his relation to the Father is distinct from that of all other people. So here is a picture of honor such as is seen when an only son obeys his father and thus reflects his father's character. This general human relation is fulfilled par excellence in the relation of Jesus to the Father.

But *glory* is more than an image of honor, for it is used to refer to God's revealed character. In the Old Testament, "it does not mean God in his essential nature, but the luminous manifestation of his person, his glorious revelation of himself" (Aalen 1976:45; cf. Dodd 1953:206-7). Frequently this glory is seen in God's power, both in nature (Ps 19:1) and in salvation history (Num 14:22). But it is also associated with his gracious mercy, as when Moses asks to see God's glory and the Lord replies, "I will cause all my goodness to pass in front of you, and I will proclaim my name, the LORD, in your presence. I will have mercy on whom I will have mercy, and I will have compassion on whom I will have compassion" (Ex 33:19). This description of God's glory in terms of his sovereign goodness and mercy, or graciousness, is echoed by John's witness to the *glory* of the Son who is *full of grace and truth.*

This *grace* answers to the *ḥeseḏ* of the Old Testament—God's covenant-keeping, gracious love. *Truth* answers to *'emet,* God's covenant-keeping, faithful reliability in which there is nothing false or deceitful. The two terms occur together in the very next story in Exodus when God graciously gives two new stone tablets. "Then the LORD came down in the cloud and stood there with him and proclaimed his name, the LORD. And he passed in front of Moses, proclaiming, The LORD, the LORD, the compassionate and gracious God, slow to anger, abounding in love and faithfulness" (34:5-6). The God of the Old Testament, who was "abounding in love and faithfulness," is now revealed in the Son who is *full of grace and truth.*

John also uses the term *truth (alētheia)* in a more Hellenistic way to refer to divine reality and its revelation. Thus, Jesus is the truth (Jn

the tabernacle (Ex 25:8), since John goes on to say *we have seen his glory,* an allusion to the tabernacle that was filled with the glory of the Lord (Ex 40:34-35).

14:6) and speaks the truth (8:40, 45-46). To say the Son is full of *truth* is to claim he is the perfect revelation of the divine reality (cf. 15:15; 17:10), and saying he is full of *grace* expresses the character of that reality, the truth about God. "The glory of God is shown by his acting in faithfulness to his own character, and by his character's revealing itself in mercy" (Barrett 1978:167).

The primary focus is on this *grace,* as is evident in what follows after the parenthetical reference in verse 15 to the Baptist's witness. The Son is not simply full of grace; he has a fullness from which he shares with others (v. 16). The verse reads literally, "For from his fullness we all (have) received even grace upon grace." In part the image may be of an unending supply of grace similar to the water he will offer the Samaritan woman (4:14; cf. 7:38). But John has something more specific in mind for the next verse says this "grace upon grace" is somehow explained by the relation Moses has to the law and that which Jesus Christ has to grace and truth.

Verse 17 is sometimes read as a rejection of Moses and the law. But the relation here between Jesus Christ (now named for the first time in the prologue) and Moses and the law is one of fulfillment—the graciousness of God revealed in Scripture has now been perfectly manifested in Jesus. The careful construction of verse 17 even allows us to say more precisely how this is the case. The significant contrast in John is not of the law over against grace and truth, since it is the same graciousness of the same God that is revealed in both. Rather, it is the contrast between the verbs *was given (edothē)* and *came (egeneto).* The verb "to give" itself speaks of the divine graciousness, because it obviously talks of God's gifts. Indeed, we just saw that "grace and truth" were manifest at the giving of the law (Ex 34:6). So these verbs are not contrasting a negative with a positive. Rather, the divine graciousness evident in the divine *was given* is tremendously intensified in the divine *came.* The same graciousness has now been manifested in an entirely new mode: the Word *became (egeneto)* flesh.

So there is a contrast here, but it is one of degree. The grace received

---

1:18 The reading the NIV adopts has the best manuscript support. The readings in the NIV

in Jesus is added upon the grace that came through Moses and the law. The association between the two is basically one of continuity, of the partial contrasted with the full. While there is continuity it is, nevertheless, a quantum leap that has occurred in Jesus, as verse 18 makes clear. The references we noted to Wisdom's coming from God and offering knowledge of God's ways were taken by many Jews as a reference to the law (for example, Sirach 24). John does not deny the truth of this but says there is a greater fulfillment of this picture, for the law itself points to Jesus (5:39). The law points to *the* revelation of the Father, the one who was *at the Father's side,* or, better, "close to the Father's heart" (NRSV; *eis ton kolpon tou patros,* literally, "in the bosom of the Father," NASB), who *has made him known (exēgēsato).* Here we have the answer to the question in Sirach, "Who has seen him [God] and can describe [*ekdiēgēsetai*] him?" (Sirach 43:31). When God reveals God, it is the ultimate revelation. "The absolute claim of the Christian revelation could not be put more definitely" (Schnackenburg 1980a:278).

Many would say, therefore, that John presents Jesus as replacing Judaism. In a sense this is true. If the glory of the divine presence that filled the tabernacle (and later the temple) has now come to us in Jesus, then he is the place where we now seek God's presence. Accordingly, we will see John presenting Jesus as the fulfillment of Judaism, since he is the archetype behind Jacob, the temple and its feasts and many other persons and institutions. But this replacement comes through fulfillment, not rejection. Replacement does not mean there is no longer any role for the Old Testament, but it does mean any attempt to know God that is not centered in Jesus is defective, since in him is the fullness. No one has seen God, but now the one who was with the Father reveals the glory of God that he shared with him "before the world began" (Jn 17:5, 24; cf. 6:46; 14:8-9). The revelation of God in Jesus is not contradictory to Judaism, but rather the very thing for which Judaism had been preparing. So when the Jewish opponents reject Jesus later in the story they do so despite their Judaism, not because of it.

This last section of the prologue speaks powerfully of the identity of

---

note perhaps came about through the influence of verse 14 and Johannine usage elsewhere (3:16, 18; 1 Jn 4:9).

Jesus and the character of God revealed in him. Understanding Jesus' deity is crucial to understanding all that he says and does in the story, especially that which is most cryptic. The connection between glory and grace is also extremely important, for we are told that in this story we will see the glory that is grace and truth. This is the only place the word *grace* occurs in this Gospel (vv. 14, 16-17), but the rest of the story presents this grace in narrative form, coming to a climax at the cross (Hoskyns 1940a:148).

John also critiques claims to have seen God apart from Christ. The topic of the vision of God is somewhat complex in Scripture. No one may see God and live (Ex 33:20), but there are a number of visions of God mentioned in the Old Testament (Gen 16:13; Ex 24:9-10; Num 12:6-8; Job 42:5; Is 6:1, 5; perhaps Ezek 1:1; 8:3; 40:2). Similarly, in the Johannine material, there is an emphasis on the fact that no one has seen God (Jn 1:18; 5:37; cf. 1 Jn 4:12), but believers are promised that they will see God at the end of salvation history (1 Jn 3:2), and the Seer of Revelation has a vision of God (Rev 4:2-3, though note the Father is described symbolically in terms of stones, not anthropomorphically).

It is helpful to distinguish three basic types of sight (cf. Kirk 1932:106 n. 4; Bultmann 1971:608 n. 4), which include (1) physical sight; (2) rational sight, that is, perception through rational thought and inference; and (3) spiritual sight with the "eyes of the heart" (Eph 1:18), that is, perception of the soul that comes through intuition, communion, faith and love, as mediated by the Spirit to those who are willing to do the will of God (Jn 7:17). The second and third types do not necessarily involve visual perceptions, and thus the themes of vision and knowledge overlap considerably (cf. Dodd 1953:166-68). When Scripture says it is not possible to see God, it is referring to vision in the physical sense, since God is not a physical object. It is possible to see him with the second form of sight (that is, sight in the sense of intellectual perception) for Scripture says truth about God can indeed be inferred from the natural order (for example, Ps 19:1-4; Acts 14:17; Rom 1:19-20). The third form of sight occurs in the context of covenant relationship and love. It includes mystical experiences, such as those experienced by Isaiah (Is 6:1) and John (Rev 4:2-3), but also less visual perceptions.

John's emphasis is on the incarnation's effect on the human quest for the vision of God. He says that in this life we have not been able to see God with our normal human sight—until now. Jesus claims, "Anyone who has seen me has seen the Father" (Jn 14:9). The incarnation has brought a new way to apprehend God. Yet even now it is not God in his essence that is seen (cf. 1 Tim 6:16), for creatures do not have the capacity to apprehend God in himself; we can only see him as he makes himself accessible to our limited organs of perception (cf. Chrysostom *In John* 15.1). Furthermore, the opponents saw Jesus but did not recognize his deity, so the other two forms of sight are also required (see comment on 14:9-10). Thus the incarnation adds to the complexity of Scripture on this subject, but it also provides the criterion for assessing claims to have seen God. Throughout this Gospel John will deny such claims made by Jewish mystics (cf. 1:51; 3:13; 6:46; 14:8-9).

☐ He Came to His Own (1:19—4:54)

The prologue has prepared us to see nothing less than the coming of the divine light, the Son of God, revealing the glory of God, full of grace and truth. The Son comes on the scene in the context of the ministry of John the Baptist. Jesus' first followers come from among the Baptist's disciples, and then several others are gathered together. All of this is preparation for the revelation of the glory beginning in chapter 2. With a core of disciples in place from the beginning who will be able to witness to everything (15:27), Jesus is ready to reveal God to them. In 2:1—4:54 the glory is revealed with increasing intensity with each story, for God's grace is evident in each of these opening stories. Finally, after one more climactic revelation of the glory (5:1-15), the light is shining so brightly that the darkness responds and the conflict begins (5:16-18). At this point Jesus gives his first major public teaching, a keynote address (5:19-30), which is followed by a series of confirming witnesses (5:31-40) and concludes with Jesus' condemning accusation against his opponents (5:41-47). In this way chapter 5 is a transitional text, rounding off this opening section and beginning the next. The conflict that starts at that point will continue throughout the story as the light continues to shine in the darkness and the darkness fails to grasp it.

Preparation Is Made for the Revelation of the Glory (1:19-51) The preparation takes place in two stages. As in the other Gospels, Jesus' ministry begins in the context of the Baptist's ministry (Mt 3:1-17 par. Mk 1:2-13 par. Lk 3:1-22). In John, the Baptist acknowledges that the Spirit's descent upon Jesus at his baptism is what enables him to recognize Jesus (1:32-33), but the event itself is not recounted. The emphasis is on the Baptist's testimony arising from this event (1:34). It is when the Baptist identifies Jesus as the Lamb of God in the hearing of some of his disciples that they become his first followers (1:35-37). The Baptist had an extensive ministry quite apart from his testimony to Jesus (Mt 3; Lk 3; Josephus *Antiquities of the Jews* 18.116-19), but in John all of this is eclipsed. For John, the Baptist is a witness to Jesus and a model of true discipleship.

The second stage is the gathering of disciples around Jesus, beginning with two of the Baptist's own disciples. This section offers many insights into the nature of discipleship. It is also striking for the number of titles given to Jesus right from the outset, including Son of God (1:34, 49). These titles are part of the preparation for the glory, though the characters in the story do not yet understand their true significance. The section closes with Jesus' promise that they will "see heaven open, and the angels of God ascending and descending on the Son of Man" (1:51), which prepares us for the revelation of God's glory that follows.

John the Baptist Witnesses About Himself and Jesus (1:19-34)
The leaders in Jerusalem send an investigating team, referred to as *the Jews* (*Ioudaios,* v. 19). This term can mean either Jew in an ethnic sense (for example, 4:9) or Judean. When used of Jesus' opponents it seems to refer, in general, to a sect of Jews who were particularly associated with Judea, whether living there or not. More specifically, "the term frequently designates adherents of a particularly strict, Torah- and Temple-centred religion found especially (but not exclusively) in Judea and Jerusalem" (Motyer 1997:56). The Pharisees and a number of the leaders of Israel were important members, and at times the term is used of them in particular, as it is here. The term itself, however, refers to a wider group (cf. Motyer 1997:46-57) but still only one faction of Judaism (cf. Ashton 1991:132-59). In John's day they had become the representatives of official Judaism.

Those sent to interview John had a task that was far from simple.

The Baptist was a religious leader outside the mainstream. He appeared in the wilderness with an eschatological message, that is, a message about the expected time of God's judgment and restoration. But although his message was not mainstream, it was not unique. Within Judaism there were many popular movements (cf. Horsley 1992) and much speculation concerning the Coming One prophesied in Scripture. It was as confusing a time as our own. Even the hope for a coming messiah was not a single, simple idea, but rather a complex variety of expectations that had been developing for several centuries (cf. Schürer 1973-1987:2:488-554).

The interrogation falls into two sections, the first concerning the Baptist's identity (1:19-23) and the second concerning his activity (1:24-28). As the interrogation begins, John emphatically denies that he is the Christ (v. 20). They then ask him, almost as if they were working through a check list of expected eschatological figures, if he is Elijah or the Prophet (v. 21). Elijah was expected to return just before the day of God's wrath to turn people hearts and thereby avert God's curse (Mal 4:5-6; Sirach 48:1-11) and *the Prophet* probably refers to the prophet like Moses (Deut 18:15-18; cf. Jn 4:19-25). When John rejects both of these suggestions they change their approach and allow him to identify himself in his own way (1:22). He does so by referring to an entirely obscure figure—not really a "figure" at all but only a voice (v. 23).

In this brief interchange we see that the Jewish authorities believe they are capable of passing judgment on religious claims, presumably on the basis of their understanding of Scripture. They come to the Baptist as those who know God's ways, even possessing a list by which to evaluate him. But when the Baptist quotes from Scripture to identify himself (v. 23) they ignore it entirely (v. 25). Despite their desire to be loyal to God, they lack an openness to God and his Scripture.

This lack of genuine openness is matched by a lack of personal desire. The Jews of Jerusalem are not interested enough to come themselves (v. 19), and those who come are not themselves interested—they only want to have an answer for those who sent them (v. 22; contrast Mt 3:7). So even when they ask what seems to be an open question (v. 22), they do so with a closed attitude of indifference. Such an attitude can never receive spiritual instruction, and therefore true teachers will not accommodate such spiritual voyeurism. Neither John the Baptist nor Jesus will cast pearls before swine. But while such people are not ready for pearls, it does not mean they are not ready for instruction altogether. It is said you can lead a horse to water, but you can't make him drink. True enough, but you can feed him salt. Much of Jesus' teaching is a matter of giving salt, seeking to arouse a thirst deep enough to enable a person to come and drink (cf. Jn 7:37).

In the Synoptic Gospels this "salty" teaching is given in parables (cf. Mk 4:10-12), but in this Gospel it is given through cryptic sayings. Almost none of Jesus' teaching could be understood at the time, yet it gives the hearer a hint at an answer and, in fact, actually contains a profound answer for those who can understand. The Baptist's reference to the "voice" of Isaiah 40:3 is also such a saying. It is a highly significant expression of who he is, what he is doing and why he is doing it. His identity is his task, and this task is directed entirely toward the Lord's coming and not his own. His reply does answer them and should arouse their curiosity. Unfortunately, it goes right over their heads; they do not even acknowledge it (Jn 1:25). It is outside their expectations, and they do not have the inner openness to be able to hear it.

What we have seen of the Baptist and his questioners is repeated in the second section of his testimony concerning his activity (1:24-28). They ask him why he is baptizing, but he does not respond to their question. He simply says that he is baptizing (v. 26) and then goes on to identify himself solely in terms of *the one who comes after me* (v. 27). His statement *among you stands one you do not know* sums up the picture of the opponents in this Gospel (cf. 1:10-11). This one of whom they are ignorant is far greater than the Baptist himself (v. 27). By such a response John the Baptist is true to his task, for he is testifying to the light (cf. 1:7). Even when he is asked to testify concerning himself he points to Jesus. Thus he is a model of humility, a key characteristic of discipleship in this Gospel. So the Baptist himself is a lamp (5:35), both shining on Christ and exposing the ignorance of the opponents. We find in him a powerful example of humility, single-mindedness and witness.

1:27 The Baptist's humility is dramatically illustrated by the contrast with "a Rabbinical maxim . . . to the effect that a disciple might offer any service to his teacher which a slave did for his master, except that of unfastening his shoes, which was counted as a menial's

This brief encounter between the officials and the Baptist raises searching questions for us. First, do we have the inner openness and deep desire necessary to receive God's revelation? Second, since our identity, like that of the Baptist, is most truly seen in relation to Christ, how does our life—our relationships and responsibilities—flow from our relation to God? What would we say if asked "Who are you?" (v. 22) and "Why are you doing what you are doing?" (v. 25)?

The Baptist may be cagey about his own identity, but he is not so about Jesus' identity (vv. 29-34). Here also there are two parts, the first identifying Jesus as the Lamb of God who comes after the Baptist (vv. 29-31) and the second identifying Jesus as the one upon whom the Spirit rests, the Son of God (vv. 32-34). Taken together these verses read like a summary of his testimony, though there is no indication of where he gives it nor of who hears it.

He first testifies that Jesus is *the Lamb of God, who takes away the sin of the world!* (v. 29). It is difficult to know what precise background the Baptist has in mind here, since the Old Testament does not mention a lamb who is said to take away sins. Since Jesus is identified with the Passover lamb (cf. Jn 19:31-37; cf. Beasley-Murray 1987:25), this may be the primary allusion. While the Passover lamb was not specifically associated with taking away sins, it did represent the general theme of redemption. There may also be allusion here to such motifs as the lamb provided for Abraham (Gen 22:8), the ewe of the sin offering (Lev 4:32-35), the suffering servant of Isaiah 53 and the goat that bore away the sins of the people on the Day of Atonement (Lev 16:21-22). Echoes of the apocalyptic figure of the conquering lamb (for example, Rev 6:16; 17:14; *1 Enoch* 89:41-50; 90:8-12; *Testament of Joseph* 19:8) may also be present (cf. Dodd 1953:230-38). The primary focus, however, is obviously the bearing away of sins. The fact that it is the sin of *the world* that is taken away continues the theme of the universal scope of Jesus' ministry and the Baptist's witness (1:7).

In this passage we have the only clear expression in John of the idea of taking away sin (vv. 29, 36), though there are numerous instances of

duty" (Bernard 1928:1:44). This maxim is attributed to Rabbi Joshua ben Levi, who lived c. A.D. 239 (*b. Ketubot* 96a), but the fact that the Baptist uses this image suggests that at least the general idea was earlier.

sacrificial language (6:51; 10:15; 11:50; 17:19). The only reference to forgiveness of sins occurs when the disciples are told "If you forgive anyone his sins, they are forgiven" (20:23). John thus affirms the atoning significance of the cross but does not develop this theme extensively. Later when some in the community begin to affirm they are without sin John stresses the need for atonement (for example, 1 Jn 2:2; cf. Whitacre 1982:156-57). But in the Gospel the focus is on the cross as the revelation of God's love. This is a good example of the lush variety of language and imagery used in the New Testament to describe Jesus and his salvation. We are given not a single note, but a marvelous chord in which each note has a role to play. It is vital that we allow each writing to sound its distinct notes, thereby contributing to the harmony of the chord of Scripture.

The Baptist next says that Jesus is the one who *has surpassed me because he was before me* (v. 30). Some have suggested that the Baptist thought he was preparing for the coming of Elijah and therefore the statement *he was before me* would be a simple matter of history since Elijah lived 900 years before John (Brown 1966:64). But as it now stands this clause clearly refers to the preexistence of Jesus (Brown 1966:56, 63; Schnackenburg 1980a:302-3, 494-506). Thus the Baptist is speaking a more profound truth than he realizes, a common occurrence in this Gospel.

In the second section of his testimony the Baptist is able to recognize Jesus by the sign of the Spirit (v. 32). Here in a nutshell we have the Johannine teaching about the Spirit as the one who comes from God and points to Jesus. This "remaining" (*menon*, present tense) implies that all of Jesus' ministry, "must be understood as accomplished in communion with the Spirit of God" (Barrett 1978:178).

The Baptist concludes his testimony to Jesus with the central title for

---

1:28 The location of Bethany is not certain. Many scholars think it was on the east side of the Jordan several miles north of the Dead Sea, while others place it in the region of Batanea in the north (Riesner 1992; cf. Carson 1991:147).

1:31 In contrast to the word *Jew* that occurs some seventy times in John, the word *Israel* occurs only four times (1:49; 3:10; 12:13; cf. Israelite, 1:47), each instance being highly significant. In this Gospel, "*Israēl* is the people of God. To be related to it is to be related to God's people, and consequently to God" (Gutbrod 1965:385). John is baptizing so that the coming one might be revealed to the true people of God.

1:33 It is not explained what the Baptist meant by *baptize with the Holy Spirit*. In the

Jesus in this Gospel: *I have seen and I testify that this is the Son of God* (v. 34). His testimony is a model of Christian witness to Jesus! He is also a model of Christian discipleship in his humility. His admission, *I myself did not know him* (v. 31) is startling since what he had just asserted concerning his examiners (v. 26) he now confesses of himself. It is important to see that such ignorance of Jesus is not bad in itself—everyone begins ignorant of Jesus. Even the fact that the Baptist's cryptic saying went over their heads (vv. 23-25) is not necessarily an indictment of them, as we will see later (for example, 4:1-26). But their ignorance and the Baptist's ignorance are two very different things. They thought they already knew all about the Messiah and other eschatological figures. The Baptist, however, knows his ignorance and is looking for the one to be revealed. In fact, it is for this very reason that he came baptizing (v. 31). So we see his humility in his recognition of his ignorance and in his waiting and watching for God's promised one.

Such humility is part of being receptive and obedient to God. One with such a heart is able, like the Baptist (v. 33), to hear God. Later in the story we will be told of God's speaking directly to people who are not able to understand (12:28-30). It seems clear that the Baptist must have had an inner receptivity that enabled him to receive God's message.

This section thus introduces us to four important truths about Jesus, one of which has already been introduced (preexistence; cf. Jn 1:1-18), another that is not developed further (Lamb of God), a third that is developed later (Spirit) and a fourth that is central in John (Son of God). We also see the Baptist as a significant model of humility, openness and obedience.

Jesus Appears and His First Disciples Are Gathered (1:35-51)
The prologue prepared us for the coming of the very Son of God himself.

---

original context it would presumably have been a reference to the renewal of life and righteousness by the Spirit of God expected in the future (for example, Is 32:15-18; 44:3-5; Ezek 36:25-27; *Jubilees* 1:23; *4 Ezra* 6:26; *Testament of Judah* 24:3; cf. Schnackenburg 1980a:305).

1:34 Instead of having *the Son of God,* some ancient sources have "the Chosen One of God," which many scholars accept as original (for example, Barrett, Brown, Schnackenburg). " 'Son' possibly represents the Gospel writer's interpretation of John the Baptist's own term 'Chosen One' " (Michaels 1989:36).

We caught a glimpse of him as he approached the Baptist (v. 29), but then, instead of being shown the Son, we heard the Baptist's testimony. Now such preparatory testimony is over, and the time has come for the Son himself to take center stage. Our present passage gives us both a distinctive picture of Jesus and a description of the first disciples' initial experiences of Jesus, providing further reflections on the nature of discipleship. This material is divided in two parts. In the first (vv. 35-42) the disciples take the initiative to follow Jesus, and in the second (vv. 43-51) Jesus takes the initiative. The events conclude with a climactic promise by Jesus (v. 51).

John does not tell us of Jesus' initial call to his disciples (cf. Mt 4:18-20 par. Mk 1:16-20; cf. Lk 5:1-11). There is nothing but a declaration by the Baptist: *Look, the Lamb of God!* (1:36). There is not even any indication that the Baptist said this for the benefit of the two disciples with him. He could have been talking to himself, even under his breath! The initiative to follow Jesus was solely theirs; they heard and followed (v. 37). Indeed, far from calling them to follow him, Jesus turns around and looks at them after they are already following him (v. 38). He is going on ahead and they must catch up.

His question to them, *What do you want?* could be spoken in an off-putting tone. It is a question that can reveal their hearts by indicating their attitude toward Jesus and their reason for following him. It also allows them to set the agenda. They could ask him, for instance, why the Baptist called him the Lamb of God. Instead they accept the role of receivers and express a desire to be with Jesus: *"Rabbi" (which means Teacher), "where are you staying?"* (v. 38). They address him with a term of respect, which indicates they regard him as a teacher, as the disciple John the Evangelist, or perhaps a later discile in a non-Jewish setting, indicates by providing a translation. The disciples' question, *where are you staying?* passes the initiative back over to Jesus. His response, *Come . . . and see* (v. 39), gives no information, such as the address where he

---

1:38 Jesus' role as rabbi is an important theme in this Gospel (Köstenberger 1998a). The term *rabbi* is used of Jesus nine times, far more frequently than in the other Gospels.

The theme of seeking plays a key role in this Gospel—both God's searching for those who will believe and various people's seeking Jesus, either to follow him or to harm him (cf. R. Collins 1990:94-127; Painter 1993). That Jesus' first utterance is a question is also

is staying. It shifts the initiative back to the disciples again for his answer reveals nothing and promises nothing, except that they will see where he is staying. It gives no information, but it invites relationship. The disciples, in their docility, are acting like true disciples, and Jesus encourages them. They respond and spend the day with him (v. 39).

John puts a great emphasis on Jesus' almost mysterious silence, as becomes evident when we compare his account with the Synoptics. Leading up to the coming of the first disciples in John there is no heavenly voice identifying Jesus (Mt 3:17 par. Lk 3:22), no reference to the temptation of Jesus (Mt 4:1-11 par. Mk 1:12-13 par. Lk 4:1-13), no preaching of the kingdom of God (Mt 4:17 par. Mk 1:14-15), no teaching in synagogues and healing (Lk 4:14-41) and no call for disciples (Mt 4:18-22 par. Mk 1:16-20; cf. Lk 5:1-11). In John, Jesus comes on the scene as one silently walking past (1:29, 36). Instead of a voice from heaven there is only the human voice of John the Baptist applying to Jesus a term that may have been confusing (vv. 29, 36). In the other Gospels Jesus teaches, preaches and calls people to follow him, yet here Jesus has said almost nothing (vv. 38-39). So, compared with the Synoptics' picture, Jesus in John appears as one hidden and aloof. These first disciples, therefore, are characterized by initiative and willingness to examine claims they have heard concerning this silent one. Most importantly, they are not put off by his silence, nor do they seek to break it. Rather they are humbly receptive, seeking only to be where Jesus is staying.

The two disciples, Andrew and the unnamed disciple, stay with Jesus. We are not told how Jesus began teaching such open-hearted people. The implication is that something impressive occurred, for we find Andrew going to his brother Simon Peter and telling him, *We have found the Messiah* (v. 41). If Peter had been expecting something impressive, he was not disappointed. Jesus immediately claims sovereign authority

---

suggestive. There are 161 questions in this Gospel, many of them on the lips of Jesus as he teaches and confronts his hearers (cf. Wijngaards 1986:37-45).

1:40 This unnamed disciple is often taken to be John, the son of Zebedee, who is among the first disciples to be called in the Synoptics (Mt 4:18-22; Mk 1:16-20; Lk 5:1-11).

over him by renaming him (v. 42). Since one's identity is connected with one's name (see comment on 1:12) this means that meeting Jesus was a life-changing event for Peter.

The picture of Jesus that emerges from this opening scene is quite different from the picture we usually have of him. The great activity surrounding Jesus that we usually think of will in fact be described by John. But here at the outset John gives us a glimpse of the enormous depths of silence that lay behind all that Jesus does. Jesus is fully engaged in his historical circumstances, but he is not centered in them nor controlled by them. We hear later that Jesus acts in accordance with God's time and God's will, and the depiction here at the beginning of the story hints at the same. Even his silence speaks powerfully of a life centered in God (cf. Ignatius of Antioch *Letter to the Ephesians* 15.1-2). Similarly, these disciples, who will shortly be so full of words, opinions and activity, are characterized at the outset by a desire for the presence of Jesus more than for answers to questions. Their immaturity will become evident immediately, but the crucial issue in discipleship is not whether we are mature but whether we desire to come and see and then abide in the divine presence, the only source of eternal life and growth in grace and truth.

The second section (vv. 43-51), which deals with the gathering of the disciples, is important in two ways. First, in Nathanael we have a major example of a model disciple. If we pay careful attention to him, we will gain valuable insights into understanding the reactions to Jesus, both positive and negative, that will follow in the story. Second, the series of titles given to Jesus in this opening chapter culminates with *Son of God* and *King of Israel* (v. 49). Jesus concludes by pointing to the deeper significance of these titles in his promise that they will *see heaven open, and the angels of God ascending and descending on the Son of Man* (v. 51). This Gospel's use of these titles right from the outset is different than the Synoptics', where Peter does not confess Jesus as Messiah until halfway into the story (Mt 16:16 par. Mk 8:29 par. Lk 9:20). It is unlikely that the disciples would have taken long to begin

---

1:43 In the rabbinic model the rabbi does not call disciples but rather the disciples take the initiative to attach themselves to the teacher (Hengel 1981:50-52). Jesus is acting more like God, who calls, than like a rabbi.

wondering whether Jesus were the Messiah, but John, agreeing with the Synoptics, allows that they had to grow in their understanding of who Jesus really is.

The section begins with the calling of Philip. The main point to notice is precisely that now Jesus does call someone to follow him, unlike the first disciples' having taken initiative themselves. Andrew found Simon (v. 41), and now Jesus finds Philip (v. 43). Philip also goes to find another person to tell about Jesus (v. 45), which suggests that such sharing is a characteristic of the disciples. Many sermons on missions and evangelism have rightly been based on these passages: to find and share the divine presence found in Jesus is to take part in the Son's own mission to the world (see comment on 20:21-23).

Philip tells Nathanael about Jesus. Nathanael is a model disciple because he stands in striking contrast with the picture of the opponents that will emerge. He reacts to Jesus initially in exactly the same way they will later in the story. He says, *Nazareth! Can anything good come from there?* (v. 46). That is, for Nathanael, Jesus' origin raises doubts whether he could be *the one Moses wrote about in the Law, and about whom the prophets also wrote* (v. 45), just as it will later for the Jewish opponents (7:41-42, 52).

The reason Nathanael has trouble with Jesus' coming from Nazareth is probably because the Messiah was not expected to be associated with Nazareth. Nathanael's question is usually understood as a negative one, though some of the church fathers took the tone as positive—that something good could come from Nazareth (Westcott 1908:1:55). It is probably neither entirely negative nor positive but simply a genuine question, expressing his doubts. He has reason to question whether Jesus is the one promised, but he is open to the possibility that Jesus is, as his subsequent action and confession show.

Both Nathanael and Jesus' opponents begin by questioning Jesus' identity on the basis of his origin, but unlike the opponents Nathanael ends by confessing Jesus and being promised greater revelation. The reason for the difference must lie in the fact that Nathanael is *a true Israelite, in whom is nothing false* (1:47). This designation, *true Israelite,*

1:49 The title *king* may also contain an allusion to the Jewish mystics' view of the divine glory on the throne (cf. Kanagaraj 1998:233-47), a connection Jesus may draw out in his response to Nathanael (v. 51).

marks Nathanael as a genuine member of the people of God, unlike "the Jews," who consider themselves such but are not. Nathanael accepts Jesus despite his skepticism and thereby shows that he is a member of the people of God. In contrast with the opponents—whose rejection is traced to their relationship to the devil, in whom there is no truth (8:44)—Nathanael is described as *one in whom there is nothing false* (1:47). This does not mean that he has no wrong beliefs, as the word *false* in the NIV might suggest. Rather, the word *dolos* suggests a more fundamental internal disposition in which there is no deceit. He is honest and clear-sighted, his eye is single (cf. Lk 11:34 RSV), he has a clear conscience (cf. 2 Tim 1:3). He is the sort who seeks God before all else. No one is without falseness within, but there are those who nevertheless desire truth before anything. Most of us must be pruned for years before we approach such single-hearted desire for God. Mercifully God accepts us before we even begin to desire him, and by his grace he undertakes the purging of all our duplicity and deceitfulness.

So that which distinguishes Nathanael from the opponents is a clear heart in which there is no deceit and a humble docility that is open to God, willing to *come and see* (1:46). The "seeing" involved here is not just physical sight—the opponents also had that. A favorite term of the Gospel writer's, "seeing" means being insightful, grasping the revelation that is present. Indeed, Jesus' own identity is revealed here by his ability to see. Nathanael accepts that Jesus has seen into his heart (vv. 47-48) and has seen him from afar (v. 48b), and this confirms the accuracy of Philip's claim to have found *the one Moses wrote about in the Law, and about whom the prophets also wrote* (v. 45).

The reference to Moses and the prophets (v. 45) suggests the titles Nathanael uses for Jesus are messianic. One popularly held expectation of the Messiah was that he would be a king in the line of David (for example, 2 Sam 7:12-16; *Psalms of Solomon* 17:21; cf. Rengstorf 1976:335-37; Michel 1978:648-51). The title *Son of God* could be understood in this way, as when in the Old Testament the king is called God's

---

1:51 The formula *I tell you the truth (amēn, amēn)* occurs twenty-five times in John. The word *amēn* is added to prayers to signal confirmation of what has been said. By putting

son (for example, Ps 2:6-7; cf. Michel 1978:636-37). Thus, in calling Jesus *the Son of God* and *the King of Israel* (Jn 1:49) Nathanael is the true Israelite acknowledging his King. This view of Jesus is right, as Jesus acknowledges when he affirms that Nathanael believes (1:50), but it is far short of the deep truth expressed by these titles. Jesus is truly King, but his kingdom is not of this world (Jn 18:36). He is indeed the Son of God, but in a sense far beyond anything expected by Moses and the prophets. Each of Jesus' titles affirmed in this chapter is true, so the disciples have glimpsed something of Jesus' identity. But much purging of error and further illumination will be necessary before they truly grasp what they are saying.

So Nathanael has a correct though limited understanding of who Jesus is, just as we will see that the opponents have a correct though limited view in their acknowledgment that Jesus is a teacher come from God (Jn 3:2). The opponents will continue to question (3:4, 9) whereas Nathanael, instead, wholeheartedly accepts and confesses. Nathanael is promised further enlightenment and is represented as receiving it, for he is one of the disciples who meets Jesus after the resurrection (21:2). We will see the opponents, on the other hand, go from questioning to antagonism to violent hostility.

At the end of this section Jesus—introduced as one who comes on the scene, moving silently past, and then shown as one who has extraordinary knowledge and authority—makes an amazing claim: *I tell you the truth, you shall see heaven open, and the angels of God ascending and descending on the Son of Man* (v. 51). Jesus is speaking to Nathanael (*autō,* omitted in the NIV), but the verbs he uses are in the plural, so this is intended for the rest of the disciples also. The allusion is clearly to Jacob's vision (Gen 28:12). The picture could be of Jesus as the ladder upon which the angels are moving, but no ladder is mentioned. It is more likely that he is on earth as a new Jacob. Thus the *King of Israel,* acknowledged by the true Israelite, turns out to be the fulfillment of Israel (Jacob) himself.

Here, as elsewhere in this first chapter, we have a vague reference

---

a double *amēn* at the beginning of his statements Jesus is signaling that what he is about to say is utterly true—one can confirm it before even hearing it.

to that which will become clear in what follows: in this case, the fact that Jesus fulfills and thus replaces the revelation to Israel (cf. 1:17-18). He is in truth greater than Jacob (Jn 4:12), for he is the real Jacob-Israel, the locus and source of the real people of God (cf. Dodd 1953:244-46; Kim 1985:82-86). It also means that "Jesus as Son of Man has become the locus of divine glory, the point of contact between heaven and earth. The disciples are promised figuratively that they will come to see this; and indeed, at Cana they do see his glory" (Brown 1966:91). Jacob's exclamation that "This in none other than the house of God; this is the gate of heaven" (Gen 28:17) is fulfilled in Jesus, who is himself the temple (Jn 2:19-21) and the gate (Jn 10:7). But there is no literal vision of angels later in the story such as is mentioned in this verse. Rather, this verse is the clue to the significance of everything that follows in the Gospel (Dodd 1953:294). Specifically, the promise here is that they will recognize who Jesus really is and thereby see God, for John uses the term *Son of Man* to speak of Jesus' deity manifested in humanity (cf. comments on 3:13-14; 5:27). This promise is fulfilled when Thomas sees the crucified one now living and confesses, "My Lord and my God!" (Jn 20:28). "Jesus Christ *even in his humanity* is united to heaven and enjoys perfect communion with God his Father" (Michaels 1989:43).

Heaven has been opened, but there is no need for us to ascend because the Son of Man has come down to us. The one Isaiah saw (Is 6:1-5; Jn 12:38-41) has come into our midst! Jesus, not heaven, is the focal point of revelation. The desire of the mystics has been fulfilled. Therefore from now on it is those who do *not* see and yet believe who are blessed (Jn 20:29), for if we are to see God, we must look back to Jesus under the continuing guidance of the Spirit (16:13-15). It is not that heavenly visions are impossible (cf. comment on 1:18) but that an intimacy with God is possible quite apart from such visions (cf. chaps. 13—17).

The Glory Begins to Be Revealed (2:1—4:54) As John begins to recount Jesus' ministry, he emphasizes Jesus' deeds. There is mention of Jesus' teaching (4:41), but apart from private discourses (3:10-15; 4:7-26) John does not relate the public teaching until 5:19. The significance of this early activity is made clear by Jesus' statement that "My Father is always at his work to this very day, and I, too, am working" (5:17).

These stories form a coherent section, as the link between 2:11 and 4:54 indicates. A common theme in 2:1—4:42 (cf. Dodd 1953:297) is the replacement of the old with the new: wine in place of water (2:1-11), a new temple (2:14-19), a new birth (3:1-21), a new well of water (4:7-15) and new worship (4:16-26). Thus, these stories reveal the fulfillment that has come in Jesus, providing grace upon grace (cf. 1:16).

As we progress through these stories we see the glory of God, which is his grace (cf. 1:14), shining ever more brightly. It shines first in kosher Jewish settings, both in the Galilean countryside (2:1-11) and in Jerusalem (2:12—3:21). At the end of this kosher section, John the Baptist returns to the stage to bear witness, setting his seal to what has been revealed (3:22-36). Then the glory shines among various despised people who are less than kosher, including a Samaritan adulteress and a Herodian official (4:1-54).

In the transitional section that follows, grace is given to one who betrays Jesus (5:1-15), bringing to a climax this opening series of stories and initiating the conflict that follows. As God's scandalous grace is offered not just to the kosher but to the unkosher, the glory is revealed with increasing intensity until it provokes a reaction (5:16-18). At this point Jesus delivers his keynote address (5:19-30), provides a list of witnesses to the truth of what he is saying (5:31-40) and adds his own accusation against his opponents (5:41-47). Thus chapter 5 brings to a head the opening revelation of the glory and introduces the conflict that will then dominate the story.

The Glory Is Revealed in a Kosher, Domestic Setting (2:1-11)
This story begins the revelation of the glory and continues the presentation of examples of discipleship. Jesus' mother, who is never named in this Gospel, has the same essential characteristics as found in the other disciples. Indeed, the very fact that she, like the Beloved Disciple, is not named may be in keeping with her humility, a key aspect of discipleship in this Gospel.

A wedding is said to take place in Cana *on the third day* (2:1), a note that connects this story with those in 1:19-51. Many see this initial period as a seven-day cycle symbolizing the dawn of the new creation, though this idea is not made clear in the text itself (Schnackenburg 1980a:297,

325). In fact, even the pattern of a week is not clear (Robinson 1985:163). Be that as it may, it seems John loosely connects these events together primarily because they prepare for the revelation of the glory and then begin that revelation.

John says the mother of Jesus was there at the wedding and that Jesus and his disciples were also invited *(eklēthē de kai),* perhaps implying that they got into town at the last minute and were invited to come along. Their unexpected presence at the wedding may account for the wine shortage. Since guests were to provide some of the wine (cf. Derrett 1970:232-34), it is also possible that the supply ran out because Jesus did not contribute, either because of his last minute arrival or because of his poverty.

When the wine runs out Jesus' mother says, *They have no more wine* (2:3). There are significant similarities between her statement and the way the first disciples relate to Jesus. The first two disciples took the initiative in following Jesus (1:37), and now his mother takes the initiative in speaking to him. The response of the first two disciples allowed Jesus to set the agenda (1:38), and so also his mother's statement does not dictate what he is to do about the problem that has arisen. The request that Jesus do something about the wine shortage is clear, but implicit. The implication is that she believes he is able to do something about it, but whether he will do something, and what it will be, her statement leaves open for him to decide.

Jesus' response to his mother is also similar to his way of relating to the first disciples. He responds to her with a cryptic saying that tests her: *"Dear woman, why do you involve me?" Jesus replied. "My time has not yet come"* (2:4). The phrase *why do you involve me?* is literally "what [is there] to me and to you?" It occurs a number of times in the Septuagint (Judg 11:12; 2 Sam 16:10; 1 Kings 17:18; 2 Kings 3:13; 2 Chron 35:21) as well as in the New Testament (Mt 8:29; Mk 1:24; 5:7; Lk 8:28). An enormous amount of ink has been spilt trying to guard against the implication that Jesus is saying something uncomplimentary to his mother. Even the NIV's *dear woman* instead of simply *woman (gynai)* indicates such a concern. The word *woman* does not necessarily connote coldness, but the idiom "what [is there] to me and to you?" does express either a harsh rejection or a mild form of detachment, depending on the context. Here it expresses distance but not disdain. It is part of the larger theme that Jesus is guided by his heavenly Father and not by the agenda of any human beings, even his family (cf. Jn 7:1-10; Mk 3:33-35; Lk 2:49).

Here in Cana this aloofness is followed by an enigmatic statement concerning his *time,* literally, "hour" *(hōra).* This hour is a reference to his death and the events that follow (Jn 13:1; 17:1). It will be mentioned a number of times in the story, but no one is able to comprehend what he is talking about. Not surprisingly, then, this first mention of Jesus' "hour" is quite unintelligible to his mother. It is an entirely cryptic saying and, as with the other cryptic sayings in John, it reveals everything and nothing. Those who know the whole story realize Jesus is saying all of his ministry, even his signs in Galilee, are to be understood as done under the shadow of the cross, resurrection and ascension.

But his mother grasps none of this. She responds by turning to the servants and saying, *Do whatever he tells you* (2:5; cf. Gen 41:55). That is, in the face of Jesus' thoroughly enigmatic statement she leaves the initiative entirely with him. His saying has gone over her head. It sounds like it is slightly, or even completely, negative, but since she does not know what this "hour" is she cannot really be sure of what he means. So she continues her request for him to do something about the problem, but she does so in a way that leaves him entirely free to respond as he will. So a key element in Jesus' mother's character, as in that of the first disciples, is her leaving of the initiative with Jesus. In this openness to Jesus' will, we see her humility.

This picture of the mother of Jesus is very similar to that which shines through in the Synoptic accounts, especially in the Lukan infancy narratives (Lk 1—2). Mary's response to the annunciation, "May it be to me as you have said" (Lk 1:38), and the spirituality of the Magnificat (Lk 1:46-55) express this same docility before God. She is entirely Godward. She is poor in spirit and thus has entered the door of the kingdom of God described in the beatitudes (Mt 5:3). It is as true now spiritually as it was true for her physically that a person with such a disposition is the one to whom God comes and implants his seed and begets divine life (cf. 1 Jn 3:9). All generations are to call her blessed (Lk 1:48) because of the ineffable honor God has bestowed upon her: she was chosen from among all women to carry in her womb the Word that became flesh. She bore in her body for nine months the one who bears the universe in his hands. It is not without reason that Mary has held such an important place in Christian thought and life, both as the one who bore God the Son and as a model of someone who lived a truly Christian life. It is a great tragedy that she has become a figure of controversy within Christendom.

While this story provides a powerful picture of true discipleship, the main point is that it reveals Jesus' glory (2:11). It does this in part by revealing something of Jesus' identity through associations with the Old Testament. Such a miracle might suggest, for example, the deeds of Elijah (1 Kings 17:7-16) or Elisha (2 Kings 4:1-7). More specifically, the promised time of restoration is expressed in the imagery of marriage (Is 54:4-8; 62:4-5) and of an abundance of wine (Is 25:6; Jer 31:12; Amos 9:13-14; *1 Enoch* 10:19; *2 Apocalypse of Baruch* 29:5). Indeed, in Hosea these images appear together (Hos 2:14-23). Thus, through both the supernatural power of the miracle and the imagery associated with it the disciples' confessions of Jesus in the first chapter are confirmed. Here indeed is the one they have been waiting for. He himself is the good wine that has been kept back until now.

The glory is also evident in the graciousness of this event, as the prologue has prepared us to notice (1:14). In response to a humble request Jesus provides wine in abundance, over 100 gallons. Here is a free, full, extravagant outpouring, and it is precisely the Son of God's gratuitous, gracious generosity that is the glory revealed in this sign. Throughout the Gospel the signs will provide windows into the ultimate realities at work in Jesus' revelation of God's glory, in deed as well as word (cf. Morris 1989:1-42).

In response to this sign it is said that his disciples *put their faith in him* (2:11). For John this means that they see what Jesus is doing and understand it, however dimly, in the context of God's revelation of himself in the Old Testament. They see in Jesus the very acts of power and graciousness that are like his Father's. Their understanding is very limited, but they see something of the Father in the Son and accept him as one come from God and align themselves with him.

This effect of this sign on the disciples is in contrast to the experience of those who most directly reap the benefits—the master of the banquet and the bridegroom. Jesus keeps a very low profile throughout the story with the result that only the servants realize what has happened. How often something similar happens in our lives! God's grace constantly surrounds us; his love is constantly active in our lives. Yet often we fail to discern his love, seeing only the hands of those who give us the wine and not realizing where it comes from and the grace it represents.

The Glory Is Revealed in Jerusalem: A Confrontation at the Temple (2:12-22) The first disciples found following Jesus to be something of a wild roller-coaster ride. The miracle at Cana took place in a pleasant domestic setting. The demonstration of their master's powers was striking, but this experience was more exciting than it was challenging. But as they move from the countryside to the temple in Jerusalem, Jesus switches from low profile to high profile and does something not only exciting but very strange.

After the wedding Jesus, along with his family and his disciples, goes to Capernaum (2:12), a distance of about 18 miles as the crow flies. During his ministry Capernaum is his home town, the family perhaps having moved there after the death of Joseph (Robinson 1985:121). After being at home a short while Jesus goes up to Jerusalem for the feast of Passover. John mentions three or four Passovers during Jesus' ministry (2:13; 6:4; 11:55; perhaps 5:1), which provides the main basis for the assumption that Jesus' ministry lasted roughly three years (see comment on 8:57). At this Passover Jesus performs a sign that points to his death and reveals his replacement of the temple, thereby implying the fulfillment of the redemption of God that Passover itself represents. In the context of Passover in chapter 6 Jesus teaches about the significance of his death at great length. And then at the third Passover (chapter 11) he accomplishes his work and dies as the true Passover lamb. Thus the whole of Jesus' ministry occurs in the framework of Passover and has the effect of replacing the Passover and all associated with it (cf. 1:16-17). Accordingly, this is a *Jewish* feast (2:13); that is, it is now "abandoned by the Evangelist and his readers" (Ridderbos 1997:114) because Jesus himself, rather than the temple and its feasts, has become the new focal point.

The confrontation in the temple (2:13-16) culminates in Jesus' words:

Get these out of here! How dare you turn my Father's house into a market! (v. 16). Jesus' authority and his identity are revealed in this statement. As the Synoptics tell the story, Jesus quotes Scripture at this point, combining Isaiah 56:7 and Jeremiah 7:11: "It is written," he said to them, " 'My house will be called a house of prayer,' but you are making it a 'den of robbers' " (Mt 21:13, with slight differences in Mk 11:17; Lk 19:46). Jesus is obviously exercising some sort of authority in the Synoptics, but perhaps this sense of authority is heightened in John since Jesus speaks in his own words.

This authority is based on his identity. Instead of contrasting God's house of prayer with a den of robbers, as in the Synoptics, he contrasts *my Father's house* with *a market*. Here is the first use outside the prologue of the term *Father,* the single most important designation for God in Johannine literature. Equally significant is the implication that Jesus is God's Son: he refers to *my Father's house*. Jesus' provocative act is based on his relation to God as his Son.

While John helps us see Jesus' identity revealed in this event he also indicates that the original participants did not have such insight. Indeed, the emphasis in John is as much on the response to this action as it is on Jesus' own statement (v. 16). John begins with the response of the disciples. It seems that right in the midst of the event the disciples recall a verse of Scripture (v. 17). This verse has the potential for putting this rather enigmatic action of Jesus in its proper interpretive frame. Psalm 69:9 is spoken by the Righteous One who is persecuted by those who hate God. This text connects Jesus' activity to a certain strand of Old Testament thought that plays a very important role in this Gospel, especially in relation to Jesus' death (cf. comments on 19:24, 36). As we will see, this particular text has the potential for revealing a great deal more about Jesus, but the disciples do not grasp this at the time.

2:14 The Synoptics all place the confrontation in the temple at the end of Jesus' ministry. It is possible that there were two such confrontations, but given the Gospels' freedom with matters of chronology it is also possible that John has shifted the timing of this story. Though John is not concerned with our standards of historical accuracy, this does not mean he sits loose to history (see comments on 20:27-29). He claims that the details of this story were recalled (with interpretation) by the disciples in the postresurrection church (v. 22). For a comparison of the accounts of this story in John and the Synoptics see Brown 1966:116-20.

In the case of the opponents, Jesus' action is met with a question (v. 18) instead of with an Old Testament text that places Jesus' action in the light of Scripture, however vaguely. Their request for a sign is not hostile; indeed they appear genuinely open to the possibility that Jesus might be able to defend his audacious activity (cf. 3:2). Presumably if a text of Scripture that placed Jesus in relation to some feature of the scriptural tradition had occurred to them, as it had to the disciples, they would not have needed to ask such a question. Furthermore, Jesus has already given them the answer to their question; it is his identity as Son that authorizes his action. But it will become increasingly clear that the opponents do not understand Scripture because they cannot see Jesus' relation to it (5:39), which is due, in turn, to their inability to grasp his identity as Son of the Father (for example, 8:19, 27, 42, 54-55).

To their request for a sign Jesus responds with another of his cryptic sayings that reveal everything and nothing (v. 19). This enigma about destroying the temple tests their hearts. There is no way anyone could have understood this saying at the outset of Jesus' ministry. They respond with an incredulous question (v. 20). Nathanael also had heard something he considered unlikely, if not impossible, but he reserved final judgment, he came and saw, and he ended by confessing Jesus (1:45-49). These Jewish leaders, on the other hand, seem able only to question. In contrast to the disciples they jump to conclusions; they cannot be silent and wait. So the opponents are left with their questions, while the disciples have a vague but substantial hint at the fact that Jesus' action can be seen in the light of Scripture.

This is the last we hear of the Jewish leaders in this scene. John returns to the disciples, and something of the significance of their remembering the text of Scripture now becomes apparent. John first interprets Jesus'

2:20 Since work on the temple began in 20/19 B.C. (Wise 1992:812), this incident occurred in A.D. 26.

In Judaism, disciples were expected to raise questions as the teachers and students debated the interpretation of the law (cf. Köstenberger 1998a:120-21). Jesus, however, is not merely one teacher among others. Rather, his words and deeds are the equivalent of the law itself. The disciples' questions are in accord with faith; the opponents' questions are based in unbelief.

cryptic saying about the temple (v. 21). By associating his own body with the temple, which is his Father's house, Jesus again points to his own special relationship with God and his replacement of the revelation in Judaism (cf. comments on 1:16-17). The vision Jacob had of the house of God (Gen 28:17) is here fulfilled in Jesus (cf. 1:51; 10:7). Thus, in both his first statement (2:16) and his cryptic reply (2:19) he does give the leaders an answer to their question. Here the Son is offering revelation to these questioners, and in this offering itself we see the glory of God's gracious love. But there is really no way the opponents could have understood what he meant by *destroy this temple*. Even the disciples did not understand it until after the event (2:22).

The later recollection (v. 22) refers to more than what we usually mean by "remembering." In John, to remember something means to recall it and to understand it (cf. Mussner 1967). The NIV brings out this nuance in a related passage, when after the climactic entrance into Jerusalem it is said, "At first his disciples did not understand all this. Only after Jesus was glorified did they realize [*emnēsthēsan,* literally, "remember"] that these things had been written about him and that they had done these things to him (12:16). Here John is showing us how the Scripture was used after the "glorification" (John's language for Jesus' death, resurrection and ascension) to make sense out of events in Jesus' life. Later he will refer to the agent of this interpretive process, the Spirit (14:26), who is given after the glorification (7:39). What emerges, then, is that after Jesus' glorification the disciples are able, by the presence of the Spirit, to recall Jesus' actions and words and to interpret them in the light of Scripture. This insight arising from a connection between the Scripture and Jesus' words and actions seems to be what is meant by *they believed the Scripture and the words that Jesus had spoken* (2:22). The old and the new revelation function together, under the influence of the Spirit, to interpret Jesus, the fulfillment of the old.

The use of Scripture here is not a simple rational process of lining up texts to get an answer to Jesus' puzzling action. Something more subtle is involved, something requiring the aid of the Spirit. It is also more complex, for John implies a process of several stages. First there is the recall of Scripture during the event (v. 17), which indicates in some vague way the significance of this activity. Then comes the postglorification faith in the Scripture (v. 22). Psalm 69 seems related to the event in two different ways through the double meaning of *consume (kataphagetai)*. In the midst of Jesus' action the disciples could have understood this text as referring to the extent of his zeal. But after Jesus' death they would have understood this same verse in a different way—as referring to his death itself.

Such an application of the Old Testament is typical of the way it is used in the New Testament generally as well as in the church throughout its history: Christ is the key to understanding the Old Testament. Verses that were never taken as messianic stand out now that Jesus has come on the scene. The events, institutions and characters of the Old Testament reveal patterns that are found repeated in Jesus and in the experience of believers. Such interpretation remains valid and valuable today.

Jesus' death is the central topic in this passage for it is the deeper meaning of both the Scripture (v. 17) and the saying concerning the destruction of the temple of Jesus' body (v. 19). In this one image of the temple Jesus' sonship and his death are set side by side. The center of John's thought is his theology, that is, the revelation of God, and the center of his theology is God's love. God is love, and love is the laying down of one's life (3:16; 1 Jn 3:16; 4:8). Thus, it is precisely in the incarnate Son's death that God himself is revealed. The death of the Son of God in Jerusalem at the instigation of these Jewish opponents during a later Passover is already referred to here in the opponent's first provocation at this earlier Passover in Jerusalem. By including this event at the outset of the story and bringing out the themes we have noted, John shows the glory of the cross shining through Jesus' life from the start. The divine gracious love is crucial to Jesus' life, and it is at the heart of this story, both in the reference to his death and in his gracious teaching of those who will become his opponents.

Jesus' identity as the Father's Son and the centrality of his death are revealed in this story, and we begin to see how upsetting these truths are. At this point the confrontation is all on Jesus' part. What are we to make of a Jesus who responds to honest, open questions with cryptic words and deeds? Jesus is indeed compassionate, but there is always a wildness, an otherness, about him. Perhaps most Christians have experienced the upheaval that results when he confronts elements of shallow religion in their lives. Out of love he will use extraordinary means to break through our hardness of heart so that we might realize our need and come to him for life. The disciples did not understand what Jesus was doing, but they stuck with him and were open despite their questions; the Jewish leaders had only their questions. Spiritual growth demands questions. It is evident from this story that God wants us to have questions—we see his Son here, and throughout the story, raising one question after another through his words and deeds. The answer to all of these questions is found in the heart of God himself as Jesus reveals him. All of our language is but a pointer to the reality of God himself. John is writing not so we might understand all mysteries but so we might have life in his name (20:31).

The Glory Is Revealed in Jerusalem: Signs and a Teaching (2:23—3:21) John has focused our attention on the enigmatic confrontation at the temple, but he mentions that Jesus also performed a number of miraculous signs at this time. In response many people *believed in his name* (v. 23), but Jesus did not *entrust himself to them* (v. 24). The problem is not that their faith is based on Jesus' deeds, for these do provide grounds for belief (Jn 10:38; 12:37; 14:11; 20:30-31; cf. Brown 1966:525-29). Rather, it seems to be due in part to the nature of faith. All faith is immature until after the glorification (that is, the climactic revelation in the cross, resurrection and ascension) and the coming of the Spirit. The signs of sovereign love and power throughout Jesus' ministry cannot be adequately understood and responded to until after Easter Sunday. Jesus does not trust even the disciples' profession of faith late in his ministry (16:29-32); how much less would he trust this faith at the outset.

Jesus' reason for not entrusting himself to these people goes deeper still. The events in Cana made it clear that Jesus only takes his cues from his Father. In this sense Jesus does not entrust himself to anyone. He is present to all with God's love, but he is also detached from all in his attachment to God. Jesus' inner disposition is not shared by these believers. What he sees in them stands in contrast to what he found in

---

2:25 What is said about these people is the exact opposite of the description of Jesus throughout the rest of the Gospel. Jesus knows everyone and needs no one to bear witness (v. 25), whereas no one knows him and therefore everyone has need of witness. In a later

Nathanael, for in him he saw nothing false (1:47). Nathanael heard something that seemed questionable, but he came and began to see more deeply. These people see something attractive and remain on that level, thereby missing the whole point. That which is in them is not trustworthy because it is not open to God, as is made clear in the story of Nicodemus that follows.

Nicodemus is one of these who have an untrustworthy faith. John signals this connection by his repetition of the word *man* (2:25; 3:1) and by the fact that Nicodemus's assessment of Jesus is based on the signs he had seen (3:2; cf. 2:23). Later in the story we find him defending Jesus among his fellow Pharisees (7:50-52) and assisting Joseph of Arimathea in burying Jesus (19:38-42). He will end the story as a disciple, but here at the beginning he is something less.

He comes to Jesus under cover of night and makes a grand statement of faith (3:2). He is identified with the Pharisees, so we understand that when he says *we know,* his assessment of Jesus is more than his own private opinion. This makes it clear that there is not yet a settled opposition to Jesus, though his coming by night suggests, as we would expect, that not all share his positive view of Jesus after what took place in the temple. Within the group at the heart of the opposition to Jesus in this Gospel, there is at least one who is attracted to him. This shows that John, despite his strongly dualistic language, recognizes the grayness of life. Only Jesus and the devil are absolutes; all other characters are in motion either toward the light or away from it.

In response to Nicodemus' profession of faith Jesus once again expresses a cryptic saying that tests the heart (3:3; cf. 1:49-51). How uncomfortable it must have been to be around Jesus! He has been approached as a spiritual master, and he responds as one. He has been recognized as *a teacher who has come from God* (v. 2), and he responds by speaking of *the kingdom of God* (v. 3). Nicodemus may think he is talking to a rabbi, but in fact Jesus is the King of Israel (1:49). The kingdom of God is his own kingdom, but it is not of this world (18:36). One must be born from above even to see it (v. 3), let alone enter it (v. 5).

Jewish text it is said, "No man knows what is in the heart of his fellow man" (*Mekilta* on Ex 16:32). From this point of view Jesus' knowledge of the heart witnesses to his divinity.

Thus, in his response to Nicodemus, Jesus is giving Nicodemus the opportunity to recognize who it is that stands before him. But Nicodemus gets confused. When Jesus says one must be born from above *(anō then)*, Nicodemus takes it as being born again (cf. NIV text and note). Jesus is speaking of the spiritual realm, but Nicodemus thinks he is referring to the physical. Such a mistake need not be an absolute barrier to understanding Jesus. The Samaritan woman will have the same problem, and yet Jesus will use her misunderstandings to reveal himself to her (4:1-26). But Nicodemus is unable to pick up on the additional clues Jesus gives.

Jesus explains being born from above in terms of being born *of water and the Spirit* (3:5). The water of baptism and the coming of the Spirit have already been associated in this Gospel (1:31-33), and cleansing by water and new life from the Spirit were already associated with one another in the Old Testament, especially in Ezekiel 36:25-28:

> I will sprinkle clean water on you, and you will be clean; I will cleanse you from all your impurities and from all your idols. I will give you a new heart and put a new spirit in you; I will remove from you your heart of stone and give you a heart of flesh. And I will put my Spirit in you and move you to follow my decrees and be careful to keep my laws. You will live in the land I gave your forefathers; you will be my people, and I will be your God.

What follows in Ezekiel is the vision of the valley of dry bones in which the Spirit's restoration of the people is described as bringing the dead to life (chap. 37). What is needed is a new heart and a new life; that is, the Spirit must give birth to spirit (Jn 3:7). Only those alive in the realm of the spirit by the Spirit will be able to recognize and enter that realm.

The fundamental point is God's initiative in bringing spiritual life, which is reinforced by an illustration from nature (3:8). One can see the effects of the presence of the wind, but one cannot see the wind itself nor map out where it comes from nor where it goes (at least before modern technology). So also in the spiritual realm people can see the effects (cf. 3:2), but they cannot map out nor control the activity of the

---

3:8 This statement about the Spirit and the believer corresponds with what is said elsewhere about Jesus: people do not know where he is from nor where he is going (for example,

Spirit. It is God alone who initiates and produces this birth from above (cf. 1:13). Thus, once again we are back to the theme of God's grace, for this begetting is an act of sovereign gracious love initiated by God, not by us.

The image of begetting is not very common in the Old Testament (cf. Brown 1966:138-39), though there are texts that link the metaphor of childbirth with God's new life for his people (for example, Is 26:17-19; 66:7-14; Hos 13:13-14). But this fundamental point of the divine initiative of God's grace is central to Old Testament religion. No wonder Jesus reproves Nicodemus' obtuseness (3:10). A teacher of Israel should have recognized such a vital theme, especially as it is conveyed so clearly in imagery from Ezekiel. Instead, we leave Nicodemus stammering his question, How? His problem, as Jesus points out, is precisely one of receptivity (3:11). Although it was acceptable for a student to question his rabbi (cf. note on 2:20), if Nicodemus really believes that God is with Jesus, then he should receive what Jesus says. But he does not, and thereby his heart is revealed. The signs have shown him that Jesus has come from God, yet he does not receive Jesus' teaching as teaching come from God.

As Nicodemus fades from view we have Jesus' first monologue. He begins by referring to his testimony: *I tell you the truth, we speak of what we know, and we testify to what we have seen, but still you people do not accept our testimony* (3:11). These words echo what the Johannine Christians say to their Jewish opponents in John's own day. The striking use of *I* and *we* seems to be an example of the voice of the risen Christ speaking as the head of the community of those who have received the Spirit and bear witness (cf. 14:26; 15:26-27; 16:7-11). The *we know* of a ruler of the Jews (3:2) is countered by the *we know* of the Lord of the Christians.

Jesus distinguishes teaching about *earthly things* from teaching about *heavenly things* (3:12). It seems strange to call the topics of divine begetting and entrance into the kingdom of God *earthly!* But they are earthly in the sense that they refer to the effects of divine activity here

---

8:14). The whence and the whither for Jesus is the same as for the Spirit and for the one born of the Spirit, namely, the Father.

on earth. He immediately goes on to speak of the heavenly things, that is, the heavenly source behind this divine activity on earth. These *heavenly things* have to do with Jesus himself as the Son of Man who *came from heaven* (3:13). In the Synoptics *Son of Man* is used of Jesus as a human being on earth, as the future judge and as the one coming in glory. In John, Jesus is indeed on earth and is certainly human (1:14); but the future has entered the present, and already on earth judgment takes place through the presence and revelation of the Son of Man. Already he is glorified, though it is on the cross. Therefore the Son of Man sayings in John refer to the Messiah from heaven who brings God's life and judgment, especially through the cross (cf. Schnackenburg 1980a:529-42; Moloney 1978; Lindars 1983:145-57). The term itself obviously speaks of a human, perhaps even of a representative human (cf. Pamment 1985), yet because the Son of Man comes from heaven and exercises divine prerogatives (cf. comment on 5:27) he also shares in divinity. Thus the term is a complex one, speaking to Jesus' deity and his humanity (cf. Marshall 1992:780-81).

Jesus' strong denial that anyone else has ascended into heaven (3:13) has in mind the claims of the Jewish mystics (cf. Odeberg 1968:72-98), in particular the traditions concerning Moses' ascension (cf. Borgen 1968; Meeks 1967). Moses did not ascend into heaven; he only lifted up the serpent, which was a figure of Christ (3:14). Moses is indeed a source of revelation, but he is so through his witness to Jesus (cf. 5:39, 45-47). Thus, John does not simply reject the claims of the Jewish mystics; he also shows that what they were after is available in Jesus. Among those who pursued heavenly journeys some "sought to find an answer to the question of what would follow death" and "others desired the vision of God which could bring with it eternal life" (Grese 1988:688). In our passage, as well as throughout the Gospel, John is speaking to these desires (see comments on 1:18; 6:46; 14:8-10).

When Jesus says *the Son of Man must be lifted up* (3:14) he means it

---

3:14 This saying is similar to the Son of Man sayings in the Synoptics in which Jesus predicts his Passion (for example, Mk 8:31). The double meaning of *lifted up*, referring to both crucifixion and exaltation, "may be confidently traced to the suffering servant prophecy, where the servant of the Lord 'will be lifted up and glorified' (Isa. 52.13, LXX: *hypsōthēsetai kai doxasthēsetai*)" (Lindars 1983:146). This comparison with Numbers 21:8-9 occurs only here in the New Testament, though it is reflected on in other early Christian

is God who lifts him up, since *must (dei)* often refers to God's plan (cf. Grundmann 1964:22-24), and *be lifted (hypsōthēnai)* is an example of a passive verb used to refer to God's action, a common form of expression in the New Testament. In this way Moses has a role analogous to that which God plays, but the older revelation is now fulfilled in Jesus (cf. 6:32).

The lifting up of the Son of Man points us to the center of his revelation, the cross. The cross itself is a heavenly thing for it reveals the life of heaven that Jesus has come to offer us (3:15). Since God is love (1 Jn 4:8) and love is the laying down of one's life (1 Jn 3:16), it is precisely in the cross that we see God most clearly. Jesus humbles himself to the point of crucifixion *because* he is God, not despite it (cf. Phil 2:6, reading *hyparchōn* as causal). That God is love *is* the good news—this revelation *is* the gospel.

The heart of John's message is summed up in the justly famous sixteenth verse, which declares that the Son of Man's coming down from heaven and being lifted on the cross is the activity of God himself, of his gracious love, the love that gives. As Jesus will declare clearly at the end of his teaching, summing up his revelation, "the Father himself loves you" (16:27).

Thus in these verses we hear of the agent from heaven and the act whereby he reveals the reality of heaven, the heart of the Father. To believe that Jesus is the Son of Man from heaven and that his revelation of God is true gives one *eternal life,* that is, a share in God's own life (3:15). This message is clear enough to John's readers, including us, but within the story verses 13-15 contain a very cryptic message that, Jesus says, Nicodemus and those like him (the *you* in vv. 11-12 is plural) cannot receive.

With verse 16 we have not only the core of the revelation but also the beginning of a commentary on the different responses to this revelation. Since Greek does not use quotation marks it is sometimes

---

texts (for example, *Barnabas* 12:5-7; Justin Martyr *1 Apology* 1.60) as well as in Philo and among the rabbis, Jewish mystics and Gnostics (cf. Odeberg 1968:99-110). In Wisdom of Solomon 16:5-14 the story of the snake is used to speak of God's salvation (cf. Wisdom of Solomon 16:7), which is accomplished by his "word" (Wisdom of Solomon 16:12; cf. "oracles" in 16:11). So perhaps this figure also speaks to Jesus' fulfillment of the law: he, not the law, is the Savior; the law saves only as it witnesses to him.

unclear, as it is here, where a quotation ends (see NIV note to v. 21). This section reads like a commentary on what precedes it, but as there is no indication of a change of speaker, it could be either Jesus or the Evangelist. Since the voice of the earthly Jesus and the voice of the risen Jesus through John are so interwoven in this book, there is no great difference between putting the quotation mark at verse 15 or verse 21. However, a similar commentary occurs in 3:31-36, and there it is likely that we have the Evangelist (see comment on 3:31). Accordingly, it may be likely that here also John is stepping back to summarize and reflect on what has just been narrated.

God's purpose is clearly stated: not condemnation but salvation for the whole world (vv. 16-17). Jesus has come not just for the Jews or the elect, but for the world. He has come not to save some and to condemn others, but solely for salvation. Nevertheless, condemnation does take place—not through God's rejection of some, but by their rejection of him (v. 18). Judgment is a matter of what people do with the light, as Jesus emphasizes at the end of the first half of the Gospel (12:46-48). One's response to Jesus is one's judgment because Jesus is the revelation of God himself (12:49-50).

Why is it that some come to the light and some do not? John does not unravel this mystery entirely, but verses 19-21 shed some light. At first glance this passage seems to say that one's response to the light is determined by one's moral behavior prior to encountering the light. This cannot be correct, however, since John describes people living immoral lifestyles, such as the Samaritan woman, who come to the light. The key is in the terms *be exposed* (*elenchō,* v. 20) and *be seen plainly* (*phaneroō,* v. 21). It is sometimes assumed that the image in verse 20 is of someone working under cover of darkness so no one will know what is taking place. That person does not come into the light lest his or her activity, which is obviously wrong, be seen. But a preferable image is of a person involved in some activity that is morally neutral or even virtuous. This person does not come to the light because it would expose that what was considered virtuous is actually evil. This latter interpretation best fits this context, and we know it was held very early because some manuscripts, including $\mathbf{p}^{66}$ (from about A.D. 200), read, "He does not come to the light lest his deeds be exposed, that they are evil" (*hina mē elenchthē ta erga autou hoti ponēra estin*).

But whoever lives by the truth (*ho de poiōn tēn alētheian*, literally, "but whoever does the truth") seems to refer to specific deeds, thus suggesting moral activity and raising again the interpretation ruled out by the context. The only other use of this phrase (1 Jn 1:6) is instructive. The letter is speaking of Christians, so the Gospel's concern with coming to the light is here changed to walking in the light. But the basic meaning of the phrase is the same. In the letter, not to do the truth is equivalent to lying, in particular, to saying one has fellowship with God and yet walking in darkness. This is exactly the problem of the Jewish opponents in the Gospel. They claim to be children of God, yet they reject the Son of God; they are self-deceived and, according to Jesus, liars (8:42-47, 55). Thus "doing the truth" is not just a matter of morality—it involves not being deceived, having a right evaluation of oneself in relation to God. Truth, for John, has to do with reality, and here the issue is the reality of one's claim to have fellowship with God.

But what does it mean that a deed is evil? In 1 John an evil deed is one that is of the evil one (3:12). John seems to be working with the same idea here, for in the parallel clause (3:21) that which is *seen plainly* about the deeds of those who come to the light is not that they do the truth, but that their actions are done *through God*. Both verses indicate there is something about the deeds that is not obvious on the surface. As the true deeds are seen to have been done through God, the evil deeds are revealed as *evil;* that is, they are of the evil one, which is to say they have not been done through God.

This interpretation finds confirmation as the story unfolds, for what is said to this representative of the Jews is worked out further throughout the story. The problem with the Jewish opponents is their self-deception (9:39-41). They are self-satisfied, thinking they know God's ways, and they are, in fact, his children. But they only receive glory from one another, and this keeps them from believing in Jesus (5:44). When Jesus, the Son of God, comes he shows up the opponents' alienation from God. It is this alienation that the opponents cannot stand to have exposed, and so they hate this light that shows them up. Jesus reveals that their virtue is not of God but of their father the devil (8:44). The problem is at the level of their wills—what they love and hate, as our passage puts it. They claim to love God, but they have set their wills against Jesus (5:40), thereby revealing that God's love is not in their hearts (5:42) and that it is not their will to do God's will (7:17).

So the judgment that comes as the light shines reveals the terrible possibility, already recognized in Jewish thought, that even though one may be virtuous and have the Scriptures of God it is still possible to be alienated from God and closed to him. In this passage the issue is not that their deeds were morally wrong, but that these Jewish opponents hate the light, which is to say they share the character of the evil one. No matter how good their deeds may have appeared to be, these deeds separated them from God, and therefore the deeds were evil. This evil, which is the source of hatred of the light, is the pride and self-satisfaction of religious people who think they know God and yet are far from him.

This does not mean that John is a libertine who thinks morality is unimportant. In fact, in 1 John the question of believers' behavior is explicitly addressed, and there one's behavior indicates something about one's relation to God. But the emphasis in the Gospel is on the initial response to Jesus in Israel. One's response to Jesus is connected to one's openness to God, no matter how morally pure or impure one may be.

Thus we again find the antinomies of divine sovereignty and human responsibility woven together. This passage undermines the point of view held by many that everyone is a child of God and that all we have to do is get to work and then we will achieve eternal life. Instead, we learn that we lack life and do not have it within ourselves to cause our spiritual birth. We are utterly dependent on God, whose Spirit blows where he will. A second view is also clearly condemned, namely the self-satisfaction of religious folk who have made idols even out of the teachings in the Bible. This is a difficult area because we *are* to hold fast to what God has revealed. The point is that we must hold fast to the living God himself and realize that our understanding of him will continue to develop. In Christ we have the full and perfect revelation

---

3:22 Here and at verse 26 it is clearly said that Jesus was baptizing, but 4:2 clarifies the point by saying it was not Jesus but only his disciples. Many would see the correction at 4:2 as evidence of later editorial work (for example, Brown 1966:164). But why was not the clarifying note added at 3:22 or the misleading language of 3:22, 26 and 4:1 simply corrected? We seem to have stories told at separate times combined with a minimum of editorial work.

of God, as John insists, but that does not mean our grasp of him is perfect. We, like Paul, "see but a poor reflection as in a mirror" (1 Cor 13:12) and have need of the Spirit to lead us into all truth (1 Cor 2:6-16). When Paul met the risen Christ he had to rethink things. He did so in the light of the Scriptures, for God's further revelation unfolds his earlier revelation rather than destroys it (cf. 1:16-17; Mt 5:17). Thus, we should test everything by Scripture, in keeping with the guidance the Spirit has given the church (14:26; 15:26), and expect our personal understanding of Christ to be deepened.

A third lesson is at the heart of this passage—indeed, of the whole Gospel. For here is proclaimed the incredibly good news that what we need is a birth from above by the Spirit and that it is God's desire for us to have precisely this. If we are to be saved God must take the initiative, and he *has* taken the initiative, for he has sent his Son. In the Son we see heaven opened and the heart of God, which is love, revealed.

John the Baptist Endorses Jesus (3:22-36) Jesus' ministry was launched from the ministry of John the Baptist (1:19-37). Now that Jesus has begun his ministry the Baptist returns to the stage to bear witness, setting his seal to what has been revealed. But he does so after it is made clear that there are in fact differences between the Baptist and Jesus himself. That which is new in Jesus, going beyond the Baptist's own message, is accepted and affirmed by John the Baptist on the basis of his recognition of who Jesus is, the one who comes from heaven.

Just as Jesus' first disciples came from among the ranks of the Baptist's disciples, so the first real offense taken with Jesus is on the part of the Baptist's own disciples (3:25-26). They argue with *a certain Jew* over *ceremonial washing,* literally, "purification" (*katharismos,* v. 25). This *certain Jew* seems to be simply a figure representing those who came out to the wilderness seeking purification in baptism. Since this argument causes them to go to the Baptist and complain about Jesus (v. 26), it is evident that these disciples perceive differences between their

---

This is the only passage in the New Testament that clearly states Jesus authorized baptism during his ministry, that is, prior to the commission after the resurrection (Mt 28:19). This baptism was not Christian baptism since the Spirit was not yet given (Jn 7:39), but neither was it exactly like John's since it "gained special significance as obedient response to him who was in the process of bringing the saving sovereignty" (Beasley-Murray 1987:52).

master and Jesus. They are also upset because Jesus is becoming more popular that the Baptist. This *certain Jew* would be one of those more attracted to Jesus, and the differences between Jesus and the Baptist must have to do with purification. One of the most obvious things about Jesus that a Jew would notice is his rejection of the various purificatory practices of the Pharisees and his nonascetical ways compared with those of the Baptist (cf. Mt 11:18-19; Lk 7:33-35). So we see the Baptist's disciples rejecting Jesus' teaching, but it is made clear that they are also rejecting their own master's instruction as well. They themselves state that he has borne witness to Jesus, but they do not accept his testimony. Like Nicodemus (3:2), the Baptist's disciples use the term "rabbi" without really meaning it. They call the Baptist their teacher but do not receive his teaching.

But we should not be too harsh with them. Perhaps they were not only envious but also confused about the differences between Jesus and their master, wondering whether Jesus was the one after all. If so, the Baptist's further witness that he now gives should set them straight. It seems strange to us that all the disciples who heard John testify to Jesus did not flock to him. But the Baptist's testimony must not have been as clear as we imagine from the Evangelist's account. A more complicated picture is also suggested by John's doubts while in prison (Mt 11:2; Lk 7:19). The Baptist continued to have a following and, indeed, it is probably part of John the Evangelist's purpose to set straight followers of the Baptist in his own day.

Jesus' success, which the Baptist's disciples complain about, is accepted by John the Baptist as evidence for his earlier testimony to Jesus (3:27-28). His statement *a man can receive only what is given him from heaven* (v. 27) could be a misleading criterion of truth for it seems to say all success is from God. This is true if one is taking the long view, since any success evil may appear to have is temporary. However, given the fact that evil can appear to succeed, this saying does not provide a general criterion of truth. Furthermore, the fact that evil can prevail for an extended period of time (according to our standards), the similar

_____

3:24 The Evangelist does not recount John the Baptist's imprisonment, nor does he refer to it again. This verse suggests this Gospel was written for those already familiar with the

principle stated by Gamaliel (Acts 5:38-39) is of limited help in discerning truth from error. Gamaliel's principle does, however, include useful advice: In the face of confusion one should sit tight and see how God shakes things down. This thought might be implied also in the Baptist's statement of divine sovereignty, in which case his disciples erred in that they leapt to conclusions, despite what their master had said.

John's disciples had, in addition to Jesus' success, the Baptist's own testimony (3:28), a combined witness that points to God's presence with Jesus. This success is linked to heaven, as was his testimony (1:32-34). The earlier testimony expressed clearly the sovereign initiative. Now the Baptist's statement about the gift from heaven (3:27) is also a powerful expression of divine sovereignty, a theme of great importance in this Gospel and in this chapter in particular (3:3-8, 16-18). All of life is gift, all is of grace. This key Johannine theme is here echoed by the Baptist as he testifies to Jesus once again, now in the light of Jesus' ministry.

Unlike his disciples the Baptist is filled with joy, the joy of a best man at a wedding. The friend of the bridegroom was to wait outside the bridal chamber for the groom's indication that the marriage had been consummated in sexual intercourse. "The Talmud evidences an indelicate, but probably ancient, custom whereby the bridegroom would signify a successful attempt at intercourse by pronouncing the *Shema* ('Hear, O Israel . . . !')" (Derrett 1970:230; cf. Jeremias 1967b:1101). This image fits the present context, for as the shout of the bridegroom signifies the new family is off and running, so Jesus' activity indicates his ministry has begun successfully.

At a wedding attention is obviously focused on the bride and the groom. Thus, we again see John as a model of humility. As we saw earlier (1:19-34) he is completely self-emptied, being defined solely in terms of Jesus. His example of humility is expressed most memorably here: *He must become greater; I must become less* (3:30). This word *must (dei)* signifies the outworking of God's plan (cf. comment on 3:14). John's joy is in fulfilling God's will for his life—a model of Christian discipleship. He raises the question for all who would be disciples of

Baptist's life, which would include Jews and Christians but not Hellenistic folk outside of Israel.

Jesus, Where do we find our joy? It is easy to get distracted by the pleasurable blessings of this life. We should be thankful and receive gratefully God's blessings, but our joy's deepest foundation is God in himself. That he is as Jesus revealed him to be is our joy, as is the fulfilling of his purposes for our own lives (cf. 15:10-11), and we see this joy here in the Baptist.

With verse 31 there is a shift from narrative to a general comment by either the Baptist (as in the NIV), or, more likely, the Evangelist, since this section (vv. 31-36) summarizes the whole of chapter 3 by weaving together many of its major themes. In particular, the failure of the people to receive Jesus' testimony is again noted (vv. 32-33; cf. v. 11). One who receives Jesus' testimony is described as having certified that God is true, a thought that may recall verse 21. The next two verses (vv. 34-35) are particularly rich in allusions to previous themes: *For the one whom God has sent* (cf. 3:2, 16-17) *speaks the words of God* (cf. 3:11-12), *for God gives the Spirit without limit* (cf. 3:5-8). *The Father loves the Son and has placed everything in his hands* (cf. 3:27). The final verse summarizes the theme of judgment (v. 36; cf. 3:16-21). Indeed, this last verse combines the central motifs of the two meditational passages (3:16-21, 31-35). In 3:16-21 the issue is faith in Jesus himself (vv. 16, 18), which is represented in verse 36a: *Whoever believes in the Son has eternal life*. In 3:31-35 the issue is receiving Jesus' testimony (cf. 3:11-12), and this is reflected in the notion of obedience in verse 36. Thus, we are told who Jesus is and what it means to accept or reject him.

John's contrast between *the one who comes from above* and *the one who is from the earth* (v. 31) in the context refers to Jesus and John the Baptist. But by putting the contrast in these terms we are brought back to the story of Nicodemus. That is, this passage begins at the same point verse 13 does, but now Jesus' identity as the one from heaven is contrasted with the Baptist, who is of the earth. He bears witness to the things of God that have been revealed to him, but they are the things God is doing on earth. In contrast, Jesus speaks of heavenly things, that

---

3:33 John states categorically that no one received Jesus' testimony, but then he goes on to speak of those who do receive it (cf. 1:11-12). This is another example of John's dualistic language.

3:34 The one giving the Spirit could be Jesus (cf. 15:26), but the primary reference is

is, of the God of heaven who is behind this activity on earth (cf. v. 12).

Accordingly, to accept Jesus' testimony is to say something about God, namely, *that God is truthful* (v. 33). In other words, because Jesus has been sent by God, speaks God's words and has received the Spirit *without limit* (v. 34), to hear him is to hear God. Jesus thus fulfills the role of an agent: "He speaks the words of God and no more, but he does so with full authority. Behind this is the old Jewish axiom, that a man's envoy is like himself" (Schnackenburg 1980a:386; cf. *m. Berakot* 5:5; see note on 5:21). But Jesus is not just an envoy; he is the Son, and as such he is able to do more than simply proclaim a message from a distant God. As Son he receives not just a message but God's Spirit and, as we hear in the next verse, God's love: *The Father loves the Son and has placed everything in his hands* (v. 35). The chief characteristic of this true God, who is behind what Jesus is doing, is love. Behind God's love for the world and his giving of his Son (v. 16) is this love of the Father for the Son and the fact that he *has placed* (literally, "has given," *dedōken*) everything into his hands. In these two verses we have one of John's glimpses of the Holy Trinity—we see heaven opened, and heavenly things are revealed to us. The Son and the Spirit both come from heaven. The Father is the source, for both this Spirit and the Son's possession of all things are given by the Father. The Son has received the Spirit without limit, unlike any other envoy, and all things have been given into his hand; that is, he has supreme authority over all.

Thus, in Jesus we see the presence of God, by which he reveals the love of God and speaks with the authority of God. Given such a vision it naturally follows that believing in him brings eternal life and that rejecting him (*ho apeithōn,* literally, "the one disobeying") means one remains under the wrath of God (v. 36; cf. 1 Jn 5:19). The divine prerogatives of life-giving and judgment are exercisd by Jesus (see comment on 5:19-30), which means he plays roles of the utmost significance in the life of each person.

We have, then, a brief but profound glimpse into Jesus' identity and

---

probably to the Father's giving the Spirit to the Son. That this giving is *without limit* (*ou . . . ek metrou,* literally, "without measure") distinguishes Jesus from believers (Eph 4:7; 1 Cor 12:8-30; cf. Augustine *In John* 14.10).

the heavenly reality of the relationship between the Father and the Son. We also are confronted with the high stakes in this game. In Jesus the presence of God has come into our midst: the visitation of God expected in the last days has come bringing eschatological blessing and danger. The wrath of God is here seen as the opposite of sharing in his life. Alienation from his life is the condition of all who have not been born from above. The enormous difference between what we take to be normal life and the life God offers us in his Son could not be more graphically expressed. There will be a future judgment (5:28-30), but it is already active now (5:22-23), so the believer is beyond the judgment (5:24-27). At this point John is concerned that we understand who Jesus is as well as the eschatological realities present in his ministry. Those who have experienced the reality of what this section describes—the gift of the Father, the supremacy of the Son and the eschatological reality of passing from death to life (cf. 5:24)—have received the good news. Later John will make the point that those who enter this reality are commissioned themselves to share it (20:21-22).

The Glory Is Revealed Among the Despised: A Samaritan Woman (4:1-42) In chapters 2 and 3 the glory of God is revealed within kosher Jewish settings, first in the countryside and then in Jerusalem. We now move on to see Jesus offer God's grace to folk despised by most Jews, namely a Samaritan and a Herodian (who may even be a Gentile). These accounts are followed in chapter 5 with a pivotal scene in which we see Jesus' graciousness to one whom even Christians would be tempted to despise, a man who betrays Jesus to the authorities, a Judas figure. In each of these stories we continue to see Jesus, who is God's presence on earth, revealing God's gracious love.

After illustrating the faulty faith described in 2:23—3:36, John offers examples of true faith, beginning with the Samaritan adulteress. The story depicts a series of barriers that must be overcome in order for her to have faith in Jesus. Thus, in this story we learn more about who Jesus is and the grace he offers, as well as more about discipleship.

Jesus moves back into Galilee from Judea because the Pharisees have learned of his popularity (4:1). There has been no opposition from them

---

4:1-2 On Jesus as a baptizer see note on 3:22.

up to this point, though the commotion in the temple has raised questions. Jesus is not "on the lam" yet (contrast 7:1), but he nevertheless clearly wants to avoid contact with the Pharisees. If Nicodemus had shared with his fellow Pharisees something of his conversation with Jesus, then they would have even more questions. They had sent agents to the Baptist to ask whether he was the Christ and to find out why he was baptizing (1:19-28). By moving on, Jesus avoids such questions and the confrontation that would inevitably follow. But he moves not merely for the sake of expediency; he moves because it is God's will. He only does God's will, and it is God's will not only that he avoid the Pharisees but also that he meet this Samaritan woman. Jesus *had to go through Samaria* (4:4). There is no geographical necessity for going through Samaria. The necessity is due to God's plan, as *had (edei)* indicates (cf. comment on 3:14). The Father was sending him there to look for those who would worship him in spirit and truth (4:23).

At noon Jesus stops to rest outside of Sychar and sends his disciples into town for food. It was the hottest time of day, not the best time to be traveling and a very unusual time for a woman to fetch water. The fact that it was noon may highlight both Jesus' desire to avoid the Pharisees and the woman's desire to avoid her neighbors, who would come to draw water at cooler periods of the day. Since she had had six of the men of the village, the other women would have little love for her. Her immorality is well known to the villagers (4:29), as one would expect.

As she comes to draw water Jesus initiates the conversation, in contrast to his encounter with his first disciples (1:37). The woman is shocked that he, a Jew, would speak to her, a Samaritan woman (4:9). The Samaritans were held in contempt as religious apostates who had mixed the purity of Israel's worship with idolatry and the worship of pagan gods (cf. 2 Kings 17:24-41; Ezra 4:1-3; Sirach 50:25-26). While these texts reflect a Jewish explanation of the Samaritans, they probably do not refer to Samaritans (cf. Williamson 1992:726). Certainly the Samaritans were at least as zealous in their monotheism as the Jews. The animosity toward the Samaritans was greatly intensified about twenty years before Jesus' ministry when some Samaritans defiled the temple in Jerusalem by scattering human bones in the courtyard during Passover (Josephus *Antiquities of the Jews* 18.30). This conflict at the temple highlights one of the fundamental differences between the Samaritans and the Jews, namely, the question of where God has centered his worship. Apart from this issue most of their beliefs are represented within segments of Judaism, that is, until the Pharisees came to dominate the scene (cf. Gowan 1982:163-77; Haacker 1978; Williamson 1992).

For Jesus to have dealings with this woman was to risk ritual defilement (4:9). The expression *do not associate with (ou . . . synchrōntai)* can mean "use together with" (cf. NIV note; Daube 1956:373-82). The ritual impurity of the person was thought to pass to whatever he or she had contact with, like spiritual germs. There is thus an enormous religious barrier between this woman and Jesus, the first of several barriers. Jesus takes the initiative and will keep at it until all of the barriers are dealt with. This gentle persistence should be a great comfort to us who are not without barriers ourselves.

While the differences between the Jews and Samaritans were not as great as most Jews believed, there was indeed a difference between Jew and Samaritan, and the truth of Judaism over against Samaritanism is ratified by Jesus (4:22). But the hatred and the alienation are not accepted by the Son. The Samaritans do in fact offer worship, though they are in ignorance of the one they worship (v. 22). But the one they are desiring to worship wants their worship and comes to them, revealing himself and bringing salvation. Like the world (3:16-18), the Samaritans are worthy of condemnation and yet are loved. The distinction between Judaism and Samaritanism is maintained, but individuals within both of these communities either receive or reject God's salvation. John's characteristic appreciation of the importance of both the group and the individual is evident here.

The woman has asked Jesus a question, and he replies with another of his cryptic sayings: *If you knew the gift of God and who it is that asks you for a drink, you would have asked him and he would have given you living water* (4:10). She could not have understood in depth what Jesus was saying, as is the case with his other cryptic sayings, but she could have picked up on something in it that would point her in the right direction. The phrase *gift of God* was a very common expression, "a comprehensive term for everything that God bestows on man for his salvation" (Schnackenburg 1980a:426). So this term should have at least indicated to the woman that Jesus was talking about God's revelation. The image of *water* is also used in both Jewish and Samaritan sources as an image of God's revelation, the Torah, as well as of the Spirit.

On the basis of such general associations she could have understood Jesus to be saying, in effect, "If you knew the Scriptures and the salvation they reveal and if you were aware of my identity as Messiah, then you would ask me as the bearer of revelation and salvation and I would give you revelation and salvation." The woman does in fact have some knowledge of the gift of God in that she expects the Messiah (4:25). She obviously would not understand the role of the Holy Spirit and the death and resurrection of the Son of God, but she could have understood that Jesus was speaking of the revelation of God. She could also see he was implying not just that his request for water that was strange, but that his own identity was unusual. The purpose of the conversation is to reveal something of this identity.

The woman's reply shows that she misunderstands Jesus entirely (4:12). She does not make any of the connections that Jesus' cryptic saying might have triggered. Rather, she thinks he is talking about physical water. This superficial level of reference is the second barrier to her belief. Jesus uses this barrier itself as a stepping stone. She says, *Are you greater than our father Jacob, who gave us the well and drank from it himself, as did also his sons and his flocks and herds?* (v. 12). Even though she thinks they are speaking only of physical water, she recognizes that Jesus' cryptic statement implies he is greater than the patriarch Jacob.

What would it mean to a Samaritan that someone is greater than Jacob? Jacob was central to the covenant identity of the people. Among the patriarchs, "Jacob Israel, the son of Isaac, became the actual progenitor of the elect, the Hebrew tribes" (MacDonald 1964:16). And by the same fact, "Jacob Israel represents the last of a line, the line of the Patriarchs, and the beginning of a new line, the line of the elect" (MacDonald 1964:448). These covenants were of primary importance for the Samaritans' identity as the elect of God. Furthermore, God chose Jacob because of the way Jacob lived (MacDonald 1964:227). These features of Samaritan thought are paralleled in the Jewish evaluation of Jacob (cf. Odeberg 1965). Crucial for both Samaritan and Jew is that "it is the name of Jacob which defines the people of the covenant" (Odeberg 1965:191-92). Thus, to make a claim to be greater than Jacob would set oneself up as more virtuous than a major model of piety, and, most importantly, it would suggest a superiority to the covenant, which was central to the identity of both Jew and Samaritan.

Jesus makes it evident in his statement concerning the coming change in the religion of both Jew and Samaritan that he intends to suggest some such notion of superiority (4:21). What is necessary is spirit and truth (4:23-24), which have come in Jesus (1:17; 3:6; 20:22). Jesus' superiority to Jacob means that both Judaism and Samaritanism have been superseded in Jesus. Jacob gave a well that provides water, but Jesus is the giver of a greater gift, *living water* (4:10). The provision of *living water* speaks of the superiority of Jesus' revelation to that of the old covenant, for Jesus not only brings revelation of God but gives the Spirit by which this revelation is internalized in believers, giving birth to spirit (3:6). Such is the basic thrust of this story in its revelation of Jesus and what he is doing.

Jesus' offer of water leads the woman to focus on his identity (4:12). Jesus blows on this ember of understanding by continuing to use the idea of water to lead her to an understanding of himself. He makes another of his testing comments, contrasting the water Jacob gave with the water he gives. What he says about this water—that in a person it will become *a spring of water welling up to eternal life*—is very cryptic indeed (vv. 13-14). The man-made well is contrasted with a God-given spring (cf. Loyd 1936:63). The woman's response seems disappointing, for she remains on the superficial level (v. 15). She wants this *spring of water welling up to eternal life* so she will not have to come to the well anymore. The phrase *living water (hydōr zōn)* can mean "running water." So Jesus is offering her eternal life, but she thinks he is talking about indoor plumbing.

Although she remains on this superficial level, she also makes a profound movement toward faith. For even on this superficial level, by asking for this marvelous private supply of running water she is actually putting faith in Jesus as one greater than Jacob. While as yet her level of faith is very shallow and her misunderstanding is great, nevertheless she has begun to believe in Jesus. It is a source of great comfort to us to realize how patiently God works with each of us to lead us out of our misunderstanding and shallowness to come to ever deeper levels of faith, knowledge and union with God.

Next Jesus seems to change the subject entirely, but in fact he is responding to her request for living water by revealing more about himself. She has shown an openness toward him, and now he responds to her. He indicates his own special identity by revealing something of her identity, or at least of her marital status (4:16-18). He tells her something about her personal life, as he had done with Nathanael (1:48), and his preternatural knowledge indicates to the woman that he is a prophet (4:19). With this realization she has come to the place of understanding that she would have reached earlier had she understood Jesus' first statements about the gift of God and the living water. Those previous cryptic statements had contained hints that Jesus is special in a religious way, and she now realizes this.

Her recognition of Jesus as a prophet could be a very significant statement of faith, much more so than it would be if she were a Jew. For the Samaritans, unlike the Jews, did not recognize a succession of prophets. Rather, their expected one, their "Messiah," called *Taheb* *(tā 'ē ḇ)*, was the prophet like Moses (Deut 18:15). But since she is not calling Jesus the Messiah (cf. 4:25), she probably does not use the word *prophet* in this Samaritan sense. She is engaging in ecumenical dialogue, using the word *prophet* more like a Jew would, to signify a holy man rather than the expected one. She is moving in the right direction, but there are still difficulties to be overcome.

It is very significant that she does not react defensively to Jesus' knowledge of her domestic relationships. Many interpreters see here an attempt on her part to avoid the subject. But her interest in pursuing religious questions is actually in keeping with what we have already learned about her, namely, her consciousness of differences between Samaritans and Jews and her pride in the patriarch Jacob. By implicitly affirming that Jesus is greater than Jacob, she focuses on his person, not her own. So her attention remains on Jesus' person even though her own life is being used to reveal something more of his identity. This focus on Jesus is a key characteristic of true faith.

She now returns to the original barrier between herself and Jesus: the religious differences. She has met a genuine religious figure, but he is a Jew. She thinks, What about the religious separation? She does not ask about the relations between Jews and Samaritans; she simply states the differences in terms of places of worship (4:20). In this simple statement of the problem we are reminded of the way Jesus' mother presented the problem at Cana (2:3). Jesus' response is, not surprisingly, quite mystifying (4:21-24). Here is God's assessment of the division between Jews and Samaritans: in essence Jesus says that salvation is indeed of the Jews, but now with the coming of that salvation in himself as the Messiah people will be able to worship God in a qualitatively different way that supersedes the worship of the past and the controversies associated with it. The blessings expected in the last days have come (cf. comment on 4:35-38).

This new worship is characterized by spirit and truth (*pneuma kai alētheia*, 4:23). Like most of the key terms in this conversation, these words function on more than one level. On one level to worship *in spirit* could mean to worship not just with words or thoughts or mere emotion but with one's innermost self, at one's center, one's heart. Such worship engages the mind, emotions and body, but it is centered deeper, in the spirit. And to worship *in truth* could mean to worship as who one really is, with no hypocrisy, falseness, deception. Such a reference to the human spirit and integrity develops thoughts already introduced in the Gospel (for example, 1:47; 3:6).

But even on this earthly level the reference is not merely to human qualities, for one must be born from above (3:3-8). To worship *in spirit and truth* means to worship as one who is spiritually alive, living in the new reality Jesus offers, referred to here as *the gift of God,* which is *living water.* For behind the earthly things are the heavenly things, that is, God himself (cf. 3:12). Worshiping in spirit is connected to the fact that *God is spirit* (4:24). And worshiping in truth is connected with Jesus, the Messiah who explains everything (4:25-26). This picture of Jesus will be developed more when it is said that his words are spirit and truth (6:63) and he is himself the truth (14:6). So worshiping *in spirit and truth* is related to the very character of God and the identity of Christ. It is to worship in union with the Father, who is spirit, and according to the revelation of the Son, who is the truth. Indeed, it is to be taken into union with God through the Spirit (chaps. 14—17).

This profound response to the woman's statement goes completely over her head. Jesus has spoken directly to the issue she raised, but she is not able to hear it at all: *The woman said, "I know that Messiah" (called Christ) "is coming. When he comes, he will explain everything to us"* (4:25). In effect she is saying, "I do not know what you are talking about, but I believe that the Messiah will come and teach us about all of these things." This view of the Messiah is true to the Samaritan understanding. They were expecting not a Davidic king, but rather the *Taheb* who would be primarily a lawgiver, teacher, restorer, revealer (MacDonald 1964:362-65; Dexinger 1989:272-76). She is expecting someone who will clear up all the confusion.

Her reply reveals her basic openness and receptivity, which are crucial elements of true faith in this Gospel. This is the sort of person the Father is looking for (cf. 2 Chron 16:9). She recognizes that things are not right, and she is waiting for God to act. She is expecting one who will teach, which is to say she is open to revelation. This response epitomizes an appropriate response to Jesus and his cryptic sayings. Faced with such openness Jesus reveals himself to her immediately: *I who speak to you am he (egō eimi, ho lalōn soi,* v. 26). His use of *egō eimi* here is primarily self-designation, but it conceals yet deeper revelation since it is God's own self designation as I AM (cf. comment on 8:58). Thus, Jesus identifies himself as the awaited Messiah of the Samaritans, but he does so in language that hints he is God's own presence, the Jewish God who brings the living water of salvation, who indeed *is* "the spring of living water" (Jer 2:13).

The woman's response to his declaration is not given. The starkness and clarity of Jesus' statement is exceptional in light of what has been seen up to this point in the Gospel. But now the disciples arrive on the scene, and the woman heads to town (4:27-28). In the background her response is hinted at: *Come, see a man who told me everything I ever did. Could this be the Christ?* (4:29). She is entertaining the possibility that Jesus is the Messiah, but with some question still.

This question is the last we hear of her. We are not told whether it is a question that results in solid faith, as in Nathanael's case, or in rejection, as it does for the Jewish opponents later in the Gospel. The impression left is favorable, because of what is revealed of her heart (4:25) and the parallel between her and the first disciples. Like Andrew and Philip she is characterized by her testimony to others who come and see and believe (4:28-29, 39-42). Also, the Samaritans want Jesus to stay with them (4:40), just as the first disciples wanted to stay with Jesus (1:38). The story concludes with a confession reminiscent of Nathanael's (4:42; cf. 1:49).

The woman's receptivity stands in obvious contrast to the opponents' unwillingness to receive. Nathanael began by asking one of the very same questions later raised by the Jewish opponents concerning Jesus' origin (cf. 1:49). In the same way, the woman's question of whether Jesus is greater than *our father Jacob* (4:12) is identical with the opponents' later question of whether Jesus is greater than "our father Abraham" (8:53). But John makes it clear that "the Samaritan woman, who is ready, seemingly, to desert her traditional religion (verse 15), is in reality faithful toward the element of truth received from the fathers, whereas the Jews, who were apparently unswervingly loyal to the inheritance from their father Abraham and to the Tora *[sic]* of Moses, in opposition to the demands of Jesus, had already severed themselves spiritually and intrinsically from the way of Abraham and the Tora of Moses" (Odeberg 1968:178-79). Thus, the woman stands alongside the disciples as an example of one who is receptive of Jesus. The docility before God and his law that figures so prominently in the opponents' self-understanding is actually present in the followers of Jesus, including this Samaritan adulteress.

The Samaritan woman was surprised that Jesus would talk to a Samaritan (4:9). When the disciples return they are surprised he is talking to a woman (4:27), reflecting the sensitivities of their time. "Sir [Sirach] ix 1-9 describes the care to be taken lest one be ensnared by a woman;

4:29 The woman's question, *Could this be the Christ?* uses *mēti,* a word that usually expects

and rabbinic documents (*Pirqe Aboth* i 5; TalBab *'Erubin* 53b) warn against speaking to women in public" (Brown 1966:173). In particular, the woman's presence at the well at this unusual hour might have raised the disciples' suspicions, in which case their question could reflect warnings regarding the adulteress (Prov 5; 6:20—7:27).

But they neither snap at her *What do you want?* nor ask Jesus *Why are you talking with her?* In these unasked questions we again see their confusion and also their docility. These private questions point up the fact that Jesus has just revealed his identity to a Samaritan adulteress, which is to say, he has acted about as shockingly as he possibly could. While it is true that God hates divorce (Mal 2:16), here we see God's incredible love toward one with multiple marriages or perhaps just affairs. The glory of God continues to be revealed as we see the scandalous graciousness of God. Jesus is talking with this woman because God loves her. He is looking for true worshipers (4:23), those who will enter into life (4:36).

The woman leaves the scene, and we hear her preaching her evangelistic sermon (4:29). She connects her understanding of the Scriptures concerning the Christ with her own experience and encourages folk to come out to the well. At the heart of any true evangelism is an invitation to come to Jesus himself, not just a call to accept the evangelist's own ideas or experiences.

Her witness is effective, for in the background we see a crowd coming to see Jesus (v. 30). The significance of what is taking place in the background is explained by the dialogue in the foreground (vv. 31-38). These verses reveal Jesus to be God's agent who fulfills God's promises for the last days, the eschatological reality now present in our midst in Jesus.

The section begins with the disciples' encouraging Jesus to eat something (v. 31). This expression of loving concern is met by an obscure response from Jesus: *I have food to eat that you know nothing about* (v. 32). His disciples are still very ignorant of who he really is and what he is really about. They have yet to see him as the revelation of

---

a negative answer but that here suggests indecision; her faith is real but still tenuous. Cf. Blass and Debrunner 1961:221 par. 427.2.

the Father. Accordingly, the disciples do not get Jesus' point and so have more unasked questions, such as wondering if someone has brought him food (v. 33). They repeat exactly the woman's incomprehension concerning living water; she did not know how he could get a drink, and they do not know how he could get food. But there is an important difference, for whereas Jesus did not tell the woman what he meant by living water, he does give an explanation to the disciples: *My food . . . is to do the will of him who sent me and to finish his work* (v. 34). This saying calls attention to what is significant about his encounter with the Samaritan woman and indeed about all of his activity: he does God's will and finishes God's work. Jesus is the true Son of God, living out the obedience that was expected of the people of Israel, who were not to "live on bread alone but on every word that comes from the mouth of the LORD" (Deut 8:3). Jesus is thus not only God's presence on earth but also the model of discipleship. Doing the will of God is Jesus' food and is such for his followers also.

Again questions are raised for modern disciples. Are we walking as he walked (1 Jn 2:6)? How is our diet? Are we malnourished? Are we starving ourselves by failing to nourish God's life within us through obedience? As we pray for our daily bread we should have in mind not only physical nourishment, but this spiritual nourishment as well. Indeed, the word for "daily" *(epiousion)* in the Lord's Prayer (Mt 6:11; Lk 11:3) is not the common word for "daily," suggesting that something more than just ordinary food is in mind (cf. Dunn 1992:622). In John's Gospel this deeper sort of nourishment is to share in God's very life (6:53-58). The point of reference behind these strands of thought is the cross, which is the greatest expression of Jesus' obedience to the will of God and also the deepest revelation of God's love and the means by which we receive the life of God.

Of special significance is his claim to *finish his* [God's] *work* (4:34). The Father has begun a project, and now Jesus is bringing it to its perfect completion *(teleiōsō autou to ergon)*. Israel was to be a source of God's salvation for the whole world, and this is now coming to fulfillment, beginning with the Samaritans. Its extension to the rest of the world is represented later by the Greeks who come to Jesus, thereby indicating that the hour had come for him to be lifted up and draw all people to himself (12:20-23, 32).

But if God began the work and if Jesus now completes this divine work, he must be divine himself. Once again, then, we see Jesus' identity as central to the story. Before long this same theme of Jesus' working with God as his equal will get through to the Jewish opponents, causing them to reject Jesus (5:17-18) and launch the conflict that will dominate the rest of the story.

The remaining verses in this section dwell on the notion of Jesus' completion of the Father's work. The eschatological theme that the awaited time has now come (4:23) is developed with the image of a harvest. In the Old Testament this image usually represented God's coming judgment (for example, Joel 3:13), though it was also used of God's gathering in the Israelites who had been scattered among the nations (Is 27:12; cf. Demarest 1978:526). In our text this image implies eschatological blessings. The *crop for eternal life* (4:36) is starting to be gathered, as is evidenced by the fields that are *ripe for harvest,* literally, "white for harvest" (4:35). Jesus may well be referring to the approaching Samaritans, who probably would be wearing white clothing.

In this completion of the Father's work our standard expectations must be set aside. Normally in Israel it takes at least four months between the latest sowing and the earliest reaping. But in Jesus' work the sowing and harvesting are taking place simultaneously (4:35-36). This is another eschatological image of the abundance of God's blessings in the last days taken from the Prophets (Amos 9:13).

The imagery of sower and reaper is used in several ways in these few verses. Since Jesus is completing his Father's work, presumably the Father would be the sower and Jesus the reaper (cf. Schnackenburg 1980a:447). In another sense, however, here the same person is both sower and reaper, for Jesus has just spoken with the woman and already many are coming to him. But even though Jesus has functioned in these two capacities, in a deeper sense the Father is still the sower, for "it is the Father who 'gives' believers to Jesus and 'draws' them to him (cf. 6:37ff., 44, 65; 10:29; 17:6)" (Schnackenburg 1980a:451).

Jesus goes on to speak of the work his disciples will do in the future (4:37-38). He uses a well-known proverb to speak of a division of labor between sower and reaper. The idea of one sowing and another reaping is found in the Old Testament as a description of catastrophe and judgment (Lev 26:16; Deut 28:30, 33, 51; Job 31:8; Mic 6:15). The opposite picture—of reaping what one has sown—is a description of eschatological blessing (Is 65:21-22). Jesus, however, is describing a division of labor among those who are part of a common enterprise. The proverb in verse 37 is given as an explanation of verse 36, which literally says, "Already the one who harvests receives wages and gathers fruit unto life eternal, so that the one who sows and the one who harvests may rejoice together." At first it seems the sower and the harvester are the same person, but then they are clearly distinguished. This ambiguity, both reflects the mystery of the relation between the Father and the Son and, along with the implication of immediate harvest, suggests the abnormality of this time of eschatological fulfillment (cf. Bultmann 1971:197-200).

Jesus' disciples are to reap the harvest of what others have sowed and labored over. This prediction will be fulfilled specifically by John and the Samaritans: John and Peter will follow up on Philip the Evangelist's work in Samaria. The Samaritans have been "baptized into the name of the Lord Jesus," but when the apostles lay their hands on them, the Holy Spirit falls (Acts 8:14-17). Here indeed is a harvest *for eternal life* (4:36). But this is just one instance of what 4:38 is referring to. The general language used in verse 38 suggests that the whole ministry of the disciples is in view. They are being taught that their ministry is dependent on that of earlier laborers. *Others* probably refers to all those through whom the Father has been accomplishing his work, the work that is now coming to a perfect completion in Jesus.

This verse is thus part of the theme of Jesus as the fulfillment of Judaism and, indeed, of all God's work in the world. It is also the first glimpse of Jesus' teaching the disciples about their own ministry, a major theme in chapters 13—17. Already the fundamental point is clear: the work of the disciple is an extension of Jesus' own work (20:21)—doing

---

4:38 Jesus' statement is strange because he uses the past tense, *I sent* (*apesteila,* aorist, v. 38) when he has not yet sent them anywhere. At this point we probably again have the voice of the risen Jesus expanding on the historical Jesus' statement. Others would explain this text as the earthly Jesus' looking into the future (Schnackenburg 1980a:452) or as a text coming from a later period in Jesus' ministry, a time after, according to the Synoptics,

the Father's will by the presence of the Spirit and embodying and proclaiming the eternal life available in Jesus, the one who completed the Father's work. Jesus' work is to reveal the Father and make available eternal life (17:3-4, 6). He has done so in the present context of his revelation to the Samaritan woman by telling her of the worship that the Father desires and by demonstrating, in his relationship with her, God's acceptance of Samaritans. So both in his action and in his teaching he has revealed God's love for Samaritans, his willingness to reveal himself to them and receive their worship.

The story concludes with the response of the Samaritans who went out to see Jesus (4:39-42). Their faith goes from being based on the woman's testimony (v. 39) to being based on their own experience (v. 42). There is no indication that their initial faith was false, but it obviously needed to be deepened. They had heard about Jesus, and now they needed to hear him for themselves (cf. 1:45-49). The lesson for our own lives is perhaps obvious: our faith also must be based on hearing Jesus for ourselves, not just on hearing about him. The folk in Jerusalem saw Jesus' deeds and thought they had faith, but it was faulty (2:23-25). These Samaritans have seen no deeds of power, no signs, but have come to have faith in Jesus. The signs and the teaching were meant to reveal Jesus' identity and the character of the Father. We who live after the coming of the Spirit, who illumines Jesus' words and deeds, are better off than the first disciples were while they were with him. We now understand him and actually share, through the Spirit, in his life with the Father. We hear about Jesus as we read the Gospels in the light of the insight the Spirit has provided to the church, but we must come to the well ourselves to meet him through the means of grace he provides.

These Samaritans want Jesus to stay with them for two days. The initial religious barrier that had kept the woman from Jesus has obviously broken down. These Samaritans—unlike Nathaniel, the Jews and this woman—are not put off by Jesus' origin (cf. Schnackenburg 1980a:455).

---

he had sent out the disciples (Beasley-Murray 1987:64).

4:42 The title *Savior of the world* does not occur in Samaritan texts (cf. Haacker 1978:462) nor in the Old Testament nor elsewhere in the New Testament except 1 John 4:14. It occurs in connection with emperor worship and with the Asclepius cult (Schnackenburg 1980a:458), but nothing in John's text suggests either of these are in view.

This is an eschatological sign, an indication that the awaited time has arrived (4:23). The Father is seeking worshipers from among the Jews but also from the whole world, for he loves the whole world (3:16-17). This universal love must have been something of what Jesus taught these Samaritans as he stayed with them, for they come to believe that he is *the Savior of the world* (4:42). This powerful title summarizes the cosmic dimensions of Jesus' work revealed in the prologue (1:1-18), which was touched on in the Baptist's preaching (1:29) and in the story of Nicodemus (3:15-17) and which will recur again (6:33, 51; 12:32, 47).

The Glory Is Revealed Among the Despised: A Herodian (4:43-54) As Jesus moves back into Galilee the faith of the Samaritans, which has just been described, is contrasted with the lack of faith among the Galileans. Yet we meet a royal official who is an amazing example of one who has the characteristics of true discipleship. In this story we will have another reflection on the nature of faith as well as a continuation of the revelation of God's grace.

The transitional section (4:43-45) addresses the people's reaction to Jesus, but it does so in a somewhat ambiguous fashion. Jesus says, *a prophet has no honor in his own country,* but he is then immediately welcomed by the Galileans. He comes from Nazareth in Galilee (1:45), but, given this welcome by the Galileans, our text seems to suggest that Galilee was not his own country. This text, however, is commenting on the reception given him by these Galileans, not on whether Galilee is his country. The Galileans are identified as those who had seen what Jesus had done in Jerusalem at Passover, which means these Galileans are associated with the many in Jerusalem who had a faith that was faulty (2:23-25). Thus, there is something wrong with this welcome, as will be confirmed in the story (4:48). Accordingly, both Judea and Galilee are viewed as Jesus' own country because in neither does he receive real honor.

Then we are back in Cana (v. 46), where we see Jesus healing the son of a certain *royal official (basilikos),* a servant of Herod's court. This

---

4:44 John does not say where or when Jesus gave this saying. Most other sources also fail to locate it exactly (Mt 13:57; Mk 6:4; *Gospel of Thomas* 31; *Oxyrhynchus Papyrus* 1), but Luke locates it at Nazareth, with an allusion to a healing in Capernaum (Lk 4:16, 23-24).
4:46-53 There are many similarities between this story and the healing of the centurion's

official could be either a Jew or a Gentile, and if he was a Gentile, then the divine grace revealed in this story is even more remarkable. But John does not indicate that the official is a Gentile, so we cannot be certain. In any case, for many Jews a servant at Herod's court would be little better than a Gentile, so the scandalous nature of God's grace is evident here even if the official is a Jew.

In response to this man's request that Jesus come and heal his son Jesus says to him, *Unless you people see miraculous signs and wonders . . . you will never believe* (v. 48). At first glance Jesus' saying seems clear enough, though rather harsh. But when we look closer it becomes evident that it is completely inappropriate as addressed to this man, for the request that Jesus heal his son implies that this official already believes in Jesus, or at least he believes that Jesus is able and willing to heal even his son, the son of a Herodian official. Faith is belief that God is who and what Jesus reveals him to be, the loving Father, and it is trust in this God. This official seems to have something of this faith.

So while this rebuke is spoken to the official (*Jesus told him,* v. 48), it is addressed also to those standing around *(you people),* which suggests that this one saying has two purposes. It is directed in part to the Jews of Galilee, who would not think too highly of a servant of Herod. They need to see signs and wonders performed for such a despised person before they will understand that God loves him also and is willing to freely grant life to his son. In Galilee, with its "freedom-loving inhabitants" (Schürer 1973-1987:1:341), Jesus' acceptance of a member of Herod's court would perhaps be the best possible example of God's scandalous, gracious love, whether or not this official is a Gentile.

This official does have such faith, and so, addressed to him, we understand that Jesus' second purpose is to test the one to whom he speaks. From what the official says, we see that he passes the test. To Jesus' provocative statement the official simply says, *Sir, come down before my child dies* (v. 49). With this response the official demonstrates

---

slave (or son, *pais* can mean either) in the Synoptics (Mt 8:5-13 par. Lk 7:1-10). These may be independent accounts of the same event (cf. Brown 1966:192-93; Schnackenburg 1980a:471-75), though the notion that verses 48-49 are a later addition is not likely (Beasley-Murray 1987:71).

perseverance, which is like the humble patience of Jesus' true disciples. To this request Jesus answers, *You may go. Your son will live* (v. 50). The NIV catches the meaning but not the ambiguity of this statement. Literally it says, simply, "Go, your son lives" *(poreuou, ho hyios sou zē)*. This need not convey the rather positive message implied in the NIV. The official could have heard this as a simple command to go away, especially since "lives" need not imply healing. Despite this possible misunderstanding, however, it says that the man *took Jesus at his word and departed* (v. 50). Here it becomes yet clearer that Jesus' statement about needing to see signs and wonders does not apply to this official. He believed Jesus' word alone, even a potentially ambiguous word. Even though he had requested that Jesus come with him to heal his son (v. 47), he believes Jesus can do it without coming with him. Here is faith indeed!

This faith is confirmed and deepened when he learns of his son's recovery (v. 53). His faith in Jesus as one who is willing and able to heal the son of a Herodian official progressed to faith in Jesus' bare word. Now at the end of the story it is simply said that he *believed,* with no other qualifiers. This form of expression is used often in this Gospel, usually in reference to a person who has insight into Jesus' special identity and accepts of him (for example, 1:50; 20:8). As the Samaritans had their faith confirmed and deepened, recognizing Jesus as Savior of the world, so this man has his faith confirmed by this healing. It is not said what deeper insight the man gains, but the description of the healing in terms of life and death might suggest he catches a glimpse of Jesus as the giver of life. If so, then this healing illustrates a theme developed earlier (3:15-16, 36), which is about to come to the fore (5:19-30).

Whether or not the official grasped any of this significance, it is there for the reader. The grace here is obvious, for God is revealed as willing to grant life to the son of a Herodian official. The universal love of God, already noted (1:4, 7, 9; 3:16), is seen active in these two stories in chapter 4.

This story ends with a reference that *This was the second miraculous sign that Jesus performed, having come from Judea to Galilee* (4:54). It is common to take this verse as evidence that John is using a source that consisted only of signs. Originally, then, this story was the second sign in the Signs Source (see introduction, under "Three Explanations for the Complexity"). While it is possible that an earlier draft of the Gospel focused on the signs, this verse fits its present context very well. John does not say this is Jesus' second sign, but his second sign *having come from Judea to Galilee;* that is, he lays as much stress on the geographical motif as on the signs. These two signs are done when Jesus goes "out of Judea" *(ek tēs Ioudaias).* Immediately we hear of a feast of "the Jews" *(tōn Ioudaiōn,* 5:1). If Jesus' opponents are called "the Jews" at least in part because of their attachment to Judea (cf. 1:19), perhaps John is linking these two stories through a common word, as he has done earlier (cf. 2:25 and 3:1). The fact that Jesus does signs outside Judea as well as within indicates that Judea is not the favored place the opponents think it is (cf. 4:21).

Twice now Jesus has moved into Galilee, and both times he has performed very significant signs. Both signs have pointed to God's gratuitous generosity: the first one, at the wedding, was in a presumably kosher Jewish setting, and the other seems to have involved the healing of one whom many Jews would not consider kosher. These two signs in Galilee stand in contrast to the many signs he did in Jerusalem, for each of the two signs performed in Galilee are received in faith by someone, whereas the signs in Jerusalem were not received in true faith.

The account of these two signs is not only a summary of what has happened, but an anticipation of what immediately follows. Twice now Jesus has moved into Galilee, and twice he has revealed God's glory, and some have been able to receive it. Now he will go to Jerusalem again, and this time he performs a revelatory act that *is* grasped by the Jewish opponents. But this is a provocative act, as are all of Jesus' actions and teachings. Unlike during his disturbance at the temple, the opponents' hostility is aroused (5:16). Jesus' provocation has finally resulted in confrontation. Up to this point in the Gospel there has been no controversy as such. But we have been prepared for controversy by the dualistic language (1:5), the contrast between those who believe in him and those who do not (10-13; 3:18-20, 32-36), the scandals Jesus has caused (2:18-20; 3:4-10; 4:27) and the difficulties that those who do receive him have had to overcome (1:46; 2:4, 17, 22; 4:9-27, 33, 48). Thus the note in verse 54 not only concludes the previous sections, but sets off the one that follows and hints that the story has reached a transition.

□ Jesus' Revelation Reaches a Climax and the Conflict Begins, Leading to Jesus' Keynote Address (5:1-47)

Many scholars think the order of chapters 5 and 6 should be reversed since 6:1 assumes Jesus is in Galilee, but chapter 5 is set in Jerusalem. There is, however, no reason to doubt that Jesus moved around in this fashion. The vague expression "after these things" (*meta tauta,* 5:1; 6:1) suggests that although John is giving us a sequence of events, he is not concerned with giving us a detailed itinerary (cf. Carson 1991: 267). Furthermore, shifting the chapters would destroy the thematic development, for chapter 5 is linked to the initial stories, which have revealed God's glory and the conflict that is now evoked. The healing of the man by the pool (5:1-15) reveals the glory at its brightest and triggers the conflict (5:16-18) that will dominate the rest of the story. The challenge of the Jewish opponents leads to Jesus' keynote address (5:19-30), a statement by Jesus that is fundamental to understanding him and all of his activity. Then follows a series of confirming witnesses (5:31-40) and Jesus' condemning accusation of his opponents (5:41-47).

The Opening Revelation of the Glory Reaches a Climax (5:1-15)

Jesus has revealed God's love both for Jews and for those despised by many Jews. Now we come to the man at the pool, one whom Christians would be tempted to despise, since he betrays Jesus. In God's love for this Judas figure we see the full picture of God's love, a love that excludes no one (3:16, see comments on 13:23-26).

Jesus is back in Jerusalem at an unspecified feast. He visits a pool at the northeast corner of the city where people with various illnesses gathered to seek healing. This pool was actually two large trapezoid-

---

5:1 The term *Jews* may provide a link with the previous story (cf. 4:54). John will show Jesus as fulfilling the meaning of the feasts of Israel, but the fact that this feast is not named suggests no specific association is here intended.

5:2 The manuscripts contain alternatives to the name *Bethesda* (see NIV note), but a scroll from Qumran (3Q15, dated A.D. 35-65) has established that *Bethesda* is the preferred reading, meaning "house of two springs" (Barrett 1978:252-53; Jeremias 1966b:34-36).

5:3-4 The explanation found in these verses (cf. NIV note) was not originally in the story,

shaped pools with a twenty-one-foot-wide space between them. The whole structure was enclosed by porches on each side, with a fifth porch over the area dividing the two pools. The water was occasionally disturbed, perhaps from an underground source such as a spring with irregular flow or drainage from another pool. People believed one could be healed by getting into the pool when this disturbance occurred. It is implied that at least some of those who got into the pool when it was stirred actually were healed (5:7).

Jesus takes the initiative, as he did with the woman of Samaria, and approaches a man lying by this pool who had been ill for thirty-eight years. We are not told exactly what was wrong with him. The NIV translates the general term *astheneia* ("weakness," "disease") as *invalid,* due to the present context, but a later reference to healing "the whole man" may suggest a more general illness (7:23). We are also not told how long the man had been coming to this pool, but he had been there long enough to miss the stirring of the water a number of times.

The man is there with no one to help him. So here is an unpredictable source of healing that can affect only a few people, and this man has no hope of getting healed anyway because he cannot get to the pool. In other words, this is a situation of utter hopelessness and futility. But while the man cannot get to the pool, Jesus can get to him. The man is met by the one who is the stable, constant source not just of healing but of life itself, indeed, of eternal life.

Although Jesus knows the man has been ill for a long time and also knows what is in his heart (2:24-25), he nevertheless initiates the contact by asking if he wants to get well (5:6). This Gospel stresses both divine sovereignty and human responsibility, and here we see both Jesus' sovereign approach to this man and the importance of the man's own will. This is another of Jesus' questions that are intended to reveal one's heart. What would we say to Jesus if he asked us whether we wanted

---

but it may reflect accurately the beliefs held at that time.

5:6 The NIV says Jesus *learned* that this man had been ill a long time. This takes *gnous* as an ingressive use of the aorist, which is possible. But given the theme of Jesus' special knowledge of people (1:47; 2:23-25) and his abrupt way of addressing folk, we probably have such special knowledge here, with no conversation occurring prior to his testing question.

to be healed of our own illnesses, physical or otherwise? Do we want to be rid of our addictions and other sins? Ten minutes hard thought on this question could lead us to new depths of repentance. It seems like a silly question—of course he would want to be healed. But perhaps the man has grown accustomed to his disability and would prefer the known pain to the terror of the unknown, with its new responsibilities. While such speculation is true to human nature, John does not develop this line of thought (Carson 1991: 243). He is, however, quite clear on the basic point that what one wants or wills or desires (all of these can be conveyed by the verb *thelō*) plays a vital role in determining whether one can recognize Christ and receive him (7:17). God finds each of us as helpless as this man. The good news is that he desires to grant each of us life, not necessarily mere healing in this life, but eternal life beginning now.

The man's answer implies that he wants to be healed, for he explains to Jesus how it can take place. All he needs is someone to help him into the pool at the right time. By explaining the situation to Jesus he seems to interpret Jesus' question as an offer to help (Schnackenburg 1980b:95). He is right in assuming that Jesus wants to help him, but it is not in the way he expects. Jesus helps indeed! How little is needed on our part for God to work! This man has no idea who Jesus is. He indirectly asks for Jesus' help the same way the Samaritan woman wanted the indoor plumbing she thought Jesus was offering (4:15). In both cases they get far more than they expected. Instead of giving him a hand into the pool Jesus gives him immediate and complete healing. To be able to walk and carry his mat after thirty-eight years meant he received not just healing from his illness, but also strength and muscle tone. "Just as the thirty-eight years prove the gravity of the disease, so the carrying of the bed and the walking prove the completeness of the cure" (Barrett 1978:254). How gracious God is! In the power and the grace revealed in this healing we see the glory of God shining brightly.

After describing this healing John introduces the dramatic note that this occurred on a sabbath (v. 9), thereby setting the stage for the second scene of this story. *The Jews* reproach the man for carrying his mat on the sabbath (v. 10). The Old Testament does not prohibit this activity, but rabbinic interpretation of the command not to work on the sabbath did prohibit it (*m. Šabbat* 7:2; cf. Carson 1991:244). Since Jesus explicitly commanded the man to carry his mat we have a conflict between interpretations of God's will. The Jewish opponents believe the man is sinning as he obeys Jesus' command. A more striking illustration of the conflict between Jesus and these opponents could not be imagined. Indeed, this story becomes a point of reference as the conflict deepens (7:19-24).

The opponents ask, *Who is this fellow who told you to pick it up and walk?* (5:12). On one level they are simply asking for his name. But on another level this question epitomizes their basic problem: nothing that Jesus does makes godly sense to them because they do not know who he is. The major question of this Gospel is *Who is this fellow?* One's answer to that question makes the difference between eternal life and death.

It turns out that the man at the pool does not himself know who Jesus is (5:13). As in the first story in this series (2:1-11) Jesus keeps a very low profile, and the beneficiary does not know who Jesus is. The reason given for this is not the man's ingratitude or dullness, but the fact that Jesus had slipped away in the crowd. The description of the healing gives the impression that it happened quite suddenly and surprisingly, right after Jesus had approached the man. But in his complete ignorance of Jesus, not even knowing his name, this man is like those who earlier had seen Jesus' signs in Jerusalem but had no true faith (2:23-25). This man does not just see signs but is himself the one who receives the benefit of Jesus' action. Yet like those others he fails to receive that which the sign points to, the revelation of God in Jesus.

Jesus does not leave him in this ignorance but, in the final scene (5:14-15), he finds him in the temple. Again Jesus is taking the initiative. It is almost as if this is a two-stage miracle with an interval separating the healing and Jesus' manifestation of himself to the man. In any event, he now speaks to him in his usual abrupt manner: *See, you are well again. Stop sinning or something worse may happen to you* (v. 14). The man had earlier obeyed Jesus' command, but it had gotten him into trouble with the Jews, who accused him of sinning. Now he disobeys (at least from a Johannine point of view) Jesus' order to stop sinning, for he immediately betrays Jesus to the Jewish opponents. Jesus' command to this man could have functioned like his order to the Samaritan woman to go and call her husband (4:16). That command and the woman's response were part of Jesus' imparting of eternal life. The woman passes the test, but not so this man. He is caught between Jesus and the Jewish opponents, and he does not choose wisely. He now knows Jesus' name, but he continues to be ignorant of Jesus' identity.

Jesus' command focuses on the man as a sinner. This is in striking contrast to the later healing of the man born blind, in which Jesus declines to connect the illness with sin (9:3). These two passages taken together provide important insight into the relation between sin and catastrophes such as illness (cf. Carson 1991:245-46, 361-62). Here a connection is clearly drawn between this man's sin and his illness (5:14), whereas the later passage (9:3) seems to suggest that not every illness is directly linked with particular sins (as opposed to the general effects of the Fall). We should thus avoid the view that illness is always connected to some particular sin, almost as if one could work out a precise formula for the connection. We should also reject the idea that there is never such a connection. In practical terms it seems wise to take any illness or calamity as an occasion for an examination of conscience, which one should be doing daily anyway. But we should not necessarily expect to find a specific sin that has caused the distress. Any sin found must, of course, be repented of and put to death by the power of the Spirit (cf. Rom 8:13). Also, just because there are no catastrophes in a person's life does not mean he or she does not have sin to turn from (cf. Lk 13:1-5)!

Asking this man to sin no more seems like an impossible request, an intolerable burden, but it is actually part of the good news. In the first place it implies that he has been forgiven (cf. Jn 8:11; Mt 9:1-8 par. Mk 2:1-12 par. Lk 5:17-26). Here we see the Lamb of God at work, taking away the sins of the world, forgiving even those who will go on to betray him. But furthermore there is a theme in John and 1 John that Christians have been freed from the power of sin. Jesus is challenging this man to a new life, the life from above (Jn 3:3, 5). The barest glimmer of faith

---

5:14 In this Gospel, freedom from sin comes from knowing the truth, that is, from knowing and receiving Jesus (8:34-36). 1 John develops this freedom in terms of continual confession of sin and maintaining fellowship with God within the community where his light, life and

on this man's part brought Jesus' healing to his life, and now he is to move far beyond his weakness, both physically and spiritually. As George MacDonald has put it, God is easy to please but hard to satisfy.

Failing to turn to this new life will result in *something worse* happening—something worse than being an invalid for thirty-eight years! Jesus is offering the man life and threatening him with judgment. These are two sides of a single coin, and together they are the hallmark of all of Jesus' ministry, as will be stated shortly in his keynote address (5:24-29). The light of God's love brings division (3:16-21); one is heading toward either life or death. This image of Jesus threatening a man with hell is not very popular in some circles, but it is a fundamental element in the portrait of all four Gospels. No one in Scripture talks about hell more than Jesus. And he never talks about it, as George MacDonald does, as a purifying fire that will burn you until you are good. God's love is indeed a purifying fire, and that very fire is a part of the good news. If we love God we will want him to purge all sin from us, and the good news is that he is willing and able to do so. The Great Physician will not allow any of the disease to remain within us. Thanks be to God! Jesus, however, never speaks of hell in these terms; it is always spoken of as something to avoid at all cost (for example, Mt 5:29-30; 18:8-9; Mk 9:43-48).

John portrays this man, therefore, in a very negative light. He is a sinner, unlike the blind man in chapter 9, and he betrays the one who healed him. He knows that these leaders were upset with Jesus (5:10). So when he informs the opponents he is prefiguring informers later (11:46) as well as Judas' betrayal at a later feast in Jerusalem (18:2-3). This man's betrayal of Jesus is in marked contrast to the blind man's devotion (chap. 9), for the blind man confesses Jesus by standing up to the very opponents this man sides with against Jesus. The man's ingratitude is apparent.

Thus Jesus is healing one who is totally unworthy, and in doing so he reveals God's graciousness. Here we have revealed God's love, which embraces even one who betrays him. The light of God's glory is shining

---

love dwell (1 Jn 1:8—2:2; 3:1-12; 5:16-17; cf. Whitacre 1982:136-40). Perfection is not possible in this life, but growth in holiness is.

at its brightest in this manifestation of his love for his enemies.

The Conflict Begins (5:16-18) In this short transitional section we hear for the first time of the Jews' persecuting Jesus (v. 16). Jesus' response captures in a nutshell the heart of all that he is and does, for he reveals himself to be doing God's work as one equal to God. Accordingly, the Jews wish to kill him for such a claim. The monologue that follows will focus on this central claim (5:19-30), after which witnesses will be brought in for support (5:31-40). All that follows in the Gospel will be an unfolding of what is expressed here.

Jesus' deeds, beginning with the miracle at the wedding in Cana, have revealed the glory of God, his gracious love. Thus they provide the evidence for Jesus' assertion that his Father is working and he is working (5:17). The gratuity of God's love becomes more evident each time he expresses favor to increasingly less-worthy recipients until it is seen clearly in Jesus' healing of a man who, having been healed, betrays him. The rejection of Jesus by the invalid echoes the rejection by the opponents in that they themselves have been graciously offered divine revelation in Jesus. Instead of accepting that which is graciously offered them by Jesus, the opponents seek to kill him (5:18). Thus 5:1-18 is pivotal because it brings to a climax the revelation of grace that began in these initial stories and because it also triggers the opponents' hostility, which in turn leads to Jesus' death, the supreme revelation of this same gracious love.

Jesus has healed one who is totally unworthy, thereby revealing God's love. But by doing it on the sabbath he provokes the Jewish opponents. Jesus' defense is that his Father is working and he is working. This is a statement extraordinary in its clarity, not at all cryptic. And

---

5:16 The word translated *persecuted (diōkō)* could also be translated "began to prosecute" (Liddell, Scott and Jones 1940:440, Harvey 1976:50-51). Jesus is indeed on trial at this point (see notes on vv. 17, 31), but this informal prosecution is a part of the larger pattern of persecution.

The expression *was doing these things* (*tauta epoiei,* an imperfect) suggests John is keying in on one event among others that were similar. So also the imperfect *was breaking* (*elyei*) in verse 18. Cf. 20:30.

5:17 *Jesus said* is literally "Jesus answered" *(apekrinato).* The form used here, aorist middle, occurs in John only here and in verse 19 whereas the aorist passive *(apekrithē)* occurs

indeed, the opponents understand that he is claiming to be uniquely related to God. This claim is implied in two ways. First, he does not say "My Father is working and *therefore* I am working." Rather, he simply coordinates the two sayings, setting them on equal footing. Second, according to Jewish thought God alone is allowed to work on the sabbath, so to claim such a right would make one equal to God, as they say (5:18). According to *Exodus Rabbah* 30:9 the idea that God worked on the sabbath was held by rabbis at the time John is writing in the 90s. These rabbis argued that God is exempt from the prohibition to work on the sabbath (Ex 20:11; Deut 5:14) because "a man is permitted to carry on the sabbath in his own courtyard" and Isaiah 6:3 indicates that the whole world is God's courtyard when it says "the whole earth is full of his glory." Similarly, a person is permitted to carry "a distance of his own height," and since God fills heaven and earth (Jer 23:24) there is no limit to his carrying. These arguments may focus on "carrying" because God must continue to carry the universe even on the sabbath or it would collapse. The use of carrying as a reference point in rabbinic arguments in John's day may account for why John chose this type of story about sabbath breaking—in which a man carries his mat—to stand for all the instances in which Jesus challenged his opponents' ideas about the sabbath.

Yet another rabbinic argument is also strikingly related to the themes here in John. "He rested from the work of [creating] His world, but not from the work of the wicked and the work of the righteous, for He works with the former and with the latter. He shows the former their essential character, and the latter their essential character" (*Genesis Rabbah* 11:10). That is, the work of judgment takes place on the sabbath, presumably because people die on the sabbath and go before God.

---

more than fifty times. This middle form suggests a legal setting in which one is answering a charge or offering a defense (Abbott 1906:391-92). The witnesses brought in later (vv. 31-47) also contribute to this theme.
5:18 This Gospel does reveal Jesus to be equal *(isos)* with God, "very God of very God" as the creed puts it. The material that follows, however, shows that this equality does not mean interchangeability, as most commentators point out (for example, Carson 1991:250-51). While John is not teaching trinitarian doctrine with the philosophical framework of later centuries, he is certainly revealing something of the relations of the three persons of the holy Trinity, a revelation reflected on in the later formulations.

Raymond Brown also suggests that because births occur on the sabbath, God's work of giving life must occur on the sabbath (Brown 1966:217). It is precisely these divine prerogatives of life-giving and judgment that Jesus is exercising according to the monologue that follows (Jn 5:21-22).

The work Jesus sees the Father doing and the work he himself does is characterized by gratuitous love. But the opponents fail to recognize this divine love in Jesus and thereby show the depth of their alienation from God. Their rejection of Jesus, who reveals the Father, shows that they have never heard nor seen God (5:37), or else they would have recognized him in his Son. They are utterly unlike their gracious God who is revealed in Jesus. As Jesus himself says in what follows, "I know you. I know that you do not have the love of God in your hearts" (5:42). They have grasped something of Jesus' claim, but they reject it.

Jesus Delivers His Keynote Address: The Revelation of the Father's Son (5:19-30) The prologue began with the relation of the Father and the Son, and now Jesus' first major public teaching in this Gospel begins with the same topic. It is this relationship that makes sense out of everything Jesus says or does, and so this rich passage requires special attention.

Jesus begins his defense by saying *the Son can do nothing by himself; he can do only what he sees his Father doing* (v. 19). He is completely dependent upon the Father. In this expression of humility, obedience and dependence we see the Semitic version of the ideal son, since a son is to reproduce his father's thought and action. He does nothing *by himself,* or more literally, "from himself" *(aph heautou);* his source of being and activity is not himself but his Father. He cannot act from himself, for to do so would be to exist autonomously from God. There is one who is autonomous, namely, the devil (cf. comment on 8:44).

5:19 It has been suggested that behind verse 19-20 there is a parable about a son learning his father's trade. While this image may be in mind, there is little to suggest a parable has here been used (cf. Beasley-Murray 1987:75).

5:20 Here we find the only use in John of the verb *phileō* for the love between the Father and the Son. The more common verb is *agapaō*. Many scholars deny that John intends a

The Son is distinct from the Father (or he would not be the Son), but he is not autonomous.

More is involved, however, for Jesus is not simply the ideal son, but the unique Son, "the One and Only" (1:14, 18). Therefore, when Jesus says the Son *sees* what his Father is doing he is not saying that he makes rational deductions regarding God's activity from what he can observe in Scripture or history or nature. Rather, since Jesus is in the bosom of the Father (1:18), totally at one with the Father (10:30), he sees God differently than anyone else ever has (1:18; 6:46). While he is referring to his human experience, as the next verse makes clear, he has a sensitivity beyond human experience to God's voice, because his intimacy with God is unclouded by sin. This sight, then, refers to his constant communion with his Father, and thus the actions he refers to are not some special signs done now and then to illustrate what the Father is like. Rather, Jesus' whole life, everything he does, is reflective of what he sees the Father doing. According to this verse, such is all he, the Son, can do.

Jesus himself, who is the unique Son and who alone has seen God, is nevertheless the model of true humanity in that he is thoroughly open to God, humble, doing nothing of his own. The birth from above makes us God's children, and we share in something of the same sort of relationship with God through the Spirit as we see in the Son (cf. chaps. 13—17).

Jesus explains his relationship with the Father through a series of four explanatory clauses (5:19-23), each headed by the conjunction *gar* (variously translated in the NIV). He begins by saying he can only do what he sees the Father doing *because [gar] whatever the Father does the Son also does* (v. 19). Here the same unity of action is stated, yet it is not in terms of limitation (the Son can *only* do what he sees the Father doing), but through a mind-boggling claim of completeness. He does everything *(ha gar an,* translated *whatever)* the Father does. That is, not

---

special nuance to each of the words (for example, Barrett 1978:259; Carson 1991:251), but others disagree. Rudolf Schnackenburg, for example, says *phileō* is used when "the evangelist wanted a more strongly affective love to be indicated" (1980b:462; cf. 1980b: 104; Westcott 1908:1:190). See comments on 21:15-17.

5:21 In Judaism there was a principle that "a man's agent *[šalîaḥ]* is like to himself" *(m.*

only is everything in Jesus' life reflective of God the Father, but also everything the Father does is reflected in Jesus' life. Jesus is claiming to be the full revelation of the Father (cf. 15:15; 16:13, 15; 17:10).

Next, the Son's complete revelation of the Father is grounded in the Father's own love for the Son and the fact that the Father has not held anything back from the Son. *For [gar] the Father loves the Son and shows him all he does* (5:20). The Father's love is the heart of everything. It is this love between the Father and the Son "that moves the sun and the other stars" (Dante, *The Divine Comedy: Paradise* 33.145). God's love for the world (3:16) leads him to send the Son so we may be able to share through the Spirit in the Father's love for the Son (16:27; 17:23). This eternal relationship is the source of Jesus' activity for it leads the Father to show the Son all he does. We see again in verse 20 that the Father takes the initiative; he is in control, and he is the source of all. This passage also emphasizes that the Father has held back nothing of his activity from the Son. All that God does is revealed to Jesus, and Jesus passes everything on to us (15:15).

Jesus' healing on the sabbath and his other deeds have amazed people, but he promises the Father will show the Son *even greater things* ("works," *erga*) *than these* (5:20). Jesus' desire for his opponents to be amazed is not due to any interest he might have in their acclaim—he does not care for human praise (5:30, 41). Rather, Jesus works miracles that, like the miracles of Moses (Ex 3), will make people sit up and take notice and recognize that God has sent him. But on a deeper level God seeks an amazement that comes from recognizing the Father in the Son, for the miracles actually reveal the identity of Jesus and the character of the Father. This amazement is a part of faith, as seen, for example, in the case of Nathanael (1:49-50): he was amazed, and Jesus promised him he would see even greater things. As we learn more of God we continue to be amazed. If we are not amazed by Jesus, then we, like these opponents, have not yet really seen him.

Berakot 5:5; *m. Terumot* 4:4; *m. Me'ilah* 6:4; cf. Mt 10:40-42; 25:40; Lk 10:16; Jn 5:23; 12:44-45; Acts 9:4-5; 22:7-8; 26:14-15; Talbert 1992:195). Such an agent could be used, for example, both for betrothing and divorcing (Rengstorf 1964a:415). God uses agents to execute judgment, but three areas were viewed as normally the prerogatives of God: provision of water, birth and resurrection. The fact that Moses, Elijah, Elisha and Ezekiel were used by

Jesus then explains that these greater works have to do with giving life and judging. *For [gar] just as the Father raises the dead and gives them life, even so the Son gives life to whom he is pleased to give it. Moreover, the Father judges no one, but has entrusted all judgment to the Son* (5:21-22). The Father has put everything into the Son's hands (3:35), including the most fundamental realities of human existence, the giving of life and judgment. These two activities are at the heart of everything Jesus does in this Gospel, and these verses spell out his right to such responsibility and power.

He has been commissioned by God as his agent, but he transcends that role. He does not simply commit to the Father's plan and faithfully execute it, as a good agent would do according to Jewish ideals (cf. Rengstorf 1964a:415; see note on 5:21). He is to give life *to whom he is pleased [thelei] to give it* (5:21). Jesus' own will is involved. While Jesus can do nothing by himself (5:19), he does have a will of his own, and the Father authorizes Jesus to act according to that will. His human will, however, is completely in harmony with the Father's will. So again we see the distinctness and the oneness of the Father and the Son. An agent might bring life in the name of God, but no agent could say "*I am* the resurrection and the life" (11:25). This statement, spoken by Jesus at the raising of Lazarus, helps us perceive the significance of his staggering claims made here in chapter 5. Indeed, the raising of Lazarus is one of the greater works that does cause onlookers to marvel.

The last explanatory clause (5:22) states emphatically that *the Father judges no one [oude . . . ouden], but has entrusted all judgment to the Son.* Jesus is given this authority because of who he is; it is part of his identity (5:27). Jesus is the light of the world (8:12) and the truth itself (14:6), and his very presence is a judgment on all that is evil and false.

In these verses Jesus' equality with God is revealed with the result (v. 23, *hina*) *that all may honor the Son just as they honor the Father.* Here their complete equality is expressed in terms of people's proper

God in connection with these matters shows their greatness (Rengstorf 1964a:419). They are the exceptions that prove the rule, and thereby they also provided types for Jesus to fulfill and transcend, as he transcends the category of agent itself (see comments on 3:34; 7:37; 8:58; 10:36, 38; 14:9).

attitude toward Jesus: the very same honor given to the Father is to be given to the Son. Again the Jewish idea of agent is used and transcended (see note on 5:21). An agent was to be received as the one who sent him would be received. But here God is the one sending, and no one sent by God in the Old Testament ever claimed equal honor with God! Unless Jesus is wholly and completely God this verse promotes blasphemy. Indeed, the last part of the verse makes the point even more strongly: failure to honor the Son is failure to honor the Father. Honoring God, which was at the heart of the Jewish religion, is said to be dependent on honoring Jesus as the Son of God.

This keynote section states clearly the scandal of particularity that some Christians find discomforting today. The complex language of these verses shows the struggle to guard the truth of monotheism while claiming that Jesus is God. The concerns of monotheists such as Jews and Muslims are legitimate, and this Gospel reveals that God is indeed One, though not in the way these other religions understand. This Gospel encourages monotheists to understand their truth in light of what has now been revealed by the Son of God about himself and the Holy Spirit. This Gospel, however, offers no encouragement to Christians who wish to say that Jesus is not the unique Son of God with exclusive and ultimate authority over every person on earth. *All* judgment has been given to him, and *all* are to honor the Son just as they honor the Father. John allows for no syncretism, for that would deny the uniqueness and exclusivity of Jesus.

The next section of the keynote address (5:24-29) deals with how the Son exercises these two divine prerogatives. The first two verses (vv. 24-25) mention a present experience of life and judgment; the second two verses (vv. 26-27) return to the relationship between the Father and Son, which lies behind this activity of the Son; and finally, the Son's divine activity in the future is referred to (vv. 28-29).

To give life and to judge are interrelated, for to have life is to escape condemnation (v. 24). The great events of the last day are already taking place (v. 25). The judge they were expecting has come surprisingly,

---

5:25 Such a "call" does not seem to be a feature in Jewish eschatology (Schnackenburg 1980b:111). There appears to be a parallel in 1 Thessalonians 4:16 (*pace* Schnackenburg 1980b:112).

before the final end of this age; the life of the age to come is already available. All of this is accomplished, Jesus says, in the one who *hears my word and believes him who sent me*. This phrasing again points to the unity of the Father and the Son. Those who recognize Jesus as the unique Son receive his words as having come from God and, accordingly, believe the Father who sent him. To know God is to have eternal life (17:3). Until we receive life from the Son we are dead (5:24), under God's wrath (3:36).

The hearing *(akouō)* Jesus refers to (5:24) obviously requires more than having been present when he spoke or simply reading his words in Scripture now. The opponents hear, but do not receive and obey. The Old Testament emphasizes God's giving of his word and the necessity of our attending to it; and these are the themes again when the Word himself speaks: The cry of Wisdom in the streets is heard by the wise and ignored by the fools (Prov 8). One greater than Ezekiel is here speaking to the dry bones (Ezek 37).

Jesus' grounds for such audacious claims is the Father's authorization of the Son (5:26-27). The earlier thought (5:19-23) is repeated with two new developments. First, the deity of Christ is clear from the fact that the Father *has granted the Son to have life in himself* (v. 26). That is, the Son himself is the source of life and not just an agent of God's power of life. Yet this possession of life was given by the Father *(edōken)*. So again we have glimpses into the mystery of the relations within the Godhead and an emphasis on the gracious giving of the Father, who is the source of all.

Second, the Son's authority to judge, which also comes from the Father, is bound up with his identity as the Son of Man (5:27). Something of the meaning of this term has been mentioned previously (cf. comments on 1:51; and 3:13-14), but we encounter in this instance more of its complexities. Jesus' use of the term picks up Daniel 7:13-14 (C. F. D. Moule 1977:11-22; 1995:278; cf. J. Collins 1995:173-94), where the Son of Man is an eschatological figure who is given "authority, glory and sovereign power" and whom "all peoples, nations and men of every language worshiped." There is no explicit mention of judgment in

---

5:27 The lack of definite articles with *Son of Man* (occurring only here in the New Testament) does not suggest this phrase means at this point simply "man." Definite predicate nouns preceding the verb regularly lack articles (Blass and Debrunner 1961:143 par. 273).

Daniel, but there is in *1 Enoch* (for example, 48; 62:7-16; 63; 69:27-29, material from the first century A.D.), where the Son of Man is also associated with giving life. The Son of Man as judge is common in Christian literature (for example, Mt 13:41; 25:31-46; cf. Schnackenburg 1980b:466 n. 82). So Jesus is saying that if they recognized him as the eschatological Son of Man and if they understood this identity aright, they would know they were facing their judge. In passing judgment on Jesus they were condemning their ultimate judge and thus passing judgment on themselves. The irony of this situation comes up over and over in the story.

Jesus' claim to be the Son of Man, whom we understand to already be life-giver and judge, includes the expectation that the Son of Man will fill such a role in the future. If the opponents recognized Jesus for who he is, they would not be amazed that he is giving life and judging. The Son of Man's present activity does not preclude his acting again at the end of the ages. John, like the rest of the New Testament authors, believes that the Jews' eschatological timetable has become more complex with the coming of Jesus. Instead of the Jewish notion of two ages, this age and the age to come, Christians saw an overlap in these ages. The age to come has already begun while the old age continues on for a while. John emphasizes this inaugurated eschatology—the presence right now of the age to come—more heavily than any other author in the New Testament. But he does not reject the belief in a future expectation as well.

In the future there will be a universal judgment by the Son of Man (*all who are in their graves*, v. 28), since all judgment has been given to him (v. 22). This judgment is connected with life-giving (as in v. 24), which is described here as two resurrections. Verse 29 reads literally, "and they will come forth, those who did good things unto a resurrection of life and those who committed evil things unto a resurrection of

5:28-29 These verses contain the clearest reference to future eschatology in John. The view held by many that these verses are a foreign intrusion is rightly rejected by C. K. Barrett: "We are not justified in omitting vv. 28f. in order to make John a heretic. It is his intention to assert both present and future aspects of eschatology" (1978:261; cf. 1978:263; so also Carson 1991:258-59; Dahl 1990:326-30).

5:29 This verse echoes Daniel 12:2 and is similar to Revelation 20:11-15 with its two different books. There is indeed a judgment of works, both for non-Christians (Mt 25:31-46; Rom

judgment." This seems to suggest that judgment will be made on the basis of works. But the context has already made it clear that the issue is whether one hears the Son and believes the Father (v. 24, to be emphasized in the next chapter; 6:29, 40, 54). Thus we see again (cf. 3:19-21) that evil deeds are those which prevent us from coming to the light or, as here, from hearing the Son and believing the one who sent him. If we wish to share in the resurrection of life we should make sure we do those deeds that enable us to have faith in Jesus. We see in chapters 3 and 4 that an immoral lifestyle might not prevent a person from being open to Jesus and neither might a moral lifestyle make a person receptive. Nevertheless, once one is walking in the light it is clear that actions in keeping with God's commands keep us open toward God. That is why God commands them. That is, they are in keeping with his very nature, so to live according to their pattern is to open oneself to God. We are to walk as Jesus walked (1 Jn 2:6), obeying his commands (Jn 15:9-17). The first step of spiritual life is recognizing our need, which some immoral people may do and some moral people may not. The lifestyle we are called to in the Son is one of moral purity, in constant consciousness of absolute and utter dependence on God. "Apart from me you can do nothing" (15:5).

Having contemplated this future judgment we look again at the judgment Jesus exercises in the present (5:30). This verse repeats the themes of verse 19, thus tying this section together. All Jesus does—speaking, giving life and judging—comes from the Father and therefore reveals the Father. His life is entirely at the disposal of the Father, which is to say, he models true discipleship. The opponents are not able to "make a right judgment" *(hē dikaia krisis)* because, unlike Jesus, they do not will to do God's will (7:17).

This verse rounds out the section and prepares for the next. Jesus judges by his very presence—the light comes and exposes. Since people

---

2:6-8) and Christians (Mt 7:21-27; 1 Cor 3:10-15). While a Christian's works are judged, it is faith in Christ that saves. But salvation is a matter of having eternal life, and what is life without the actual living? The act of living ("works") does not generate life; that must come from God (Jn 3:3, 5). But life ("salvation") without living ("works") is literally unthinkable. The composite picture of Scripture might be summarized by saying we are not saved by works, nor are we saved apart from them.

judge themselves by their response to the light, Jesus can say that he himself does not judge or condemn. But in a sense Jesus does judge in that he draws peoples' attention to how they respond to him. By exposing their response he makes them all the more culpable. Thus, in what follows he will say that their rejection of him means they do not know God (vv. 37-38). He says this not to condemn them and harden them in their sin, but so they may be saved (v. 34). But there is something wrong with their hearts—they do not will to come to him (v. 40). It is not their will to do God's will, no matter how much they claim the contrary. Jesus will keep pointing this out in various ways from here through chapter 12.

Jesus Concludes His Keynote Address (5:31-47) In his keynote address (5:19-30) Jesus claims to be equal with God. But why should anyone believe him? What evidence could back up such a claim? In one sense it is tragic that these folk need evidence when truth incarnate is standing before them. But such is our blindness after the Fall. Such also is God's overwhelming grace that he provides what we need.

In 5:31-47 Jesus begins by calling attention to several witnesses who should confirm his identity to these Jewish opponents (vv. 31-40). He is aware, however, that his opponents do not receive these witnesses. So he goes on to explain why they are not attending to the evidence. He accuses them of seeking human praise (*doxa,* "glory") rather than God's praise (vv. 41-47). This section reveals more about the nature of belief and unbelief and provides insight into the witness that God gives to himself.

Jesus speaks as if he were on trial. The calling of witnesses is crucial because "Jewish legal procedure was not based on the interrogation of the accused but on the examination of witnesses" (Schnackenburg 1980b:120). According to the law there had to be at least two or three witnesses (Deut 19:15), and it was later specified that "no one can bear

---

5:31 The theme of witness (or testimony) is important in John. The noun *witness (martyria)* is found thirty-seven times in the New Testament, fourteen of which are in John. Of seventy-six uses of the verb *martyreō* in the New Testament, thirty-three are in John. The trial motif also recurs throughout John's Gospel (for example, chaps. 5, 7, 8, 10; cf. Harvey 1976).

The theme of God's bearing witness to himself is present in the Old Testament, especially

witness for himself" (*m. Ketubot* 2:9), though in some circumstances this was unavoidable. More specifically, these opponents wish to kill Jesus, but according to Deuteronomy 17:6, "no one shall be put to death on the testimony of only one witness." In situations where there was only one witness, "the court would simply have to make up its mind whether to take his word for it" (Harvey 1976:48). They might require an oath on the ground that God would then punish the person if he were guilty (cf. Gen 31:50). Because Jesus appeals to his Father's testimony, he is in essence providing such an oath (Harvey 1976:58). In doing so he goes on the offensive, since "it was as dangerous to disbelieve a statement made on oath as to make a statement on oath that was not true" (cf. Harvey 1976:58, cf. 49). The informal nature of Jewish legal procedure in such settings and the focus on witnesses meant it was not always clear who was judging whom. So it was not unusual for the accused to turn the tables, as Jesus does here with increasing clarity (5:41-47; also 8:15; cf. Harvey 1976:57).

The main focus was on the reliability of the witnesses. According to Josephus it is the previous life of the witnesses that will accredit *(alē thē poiē sei,* "make true") their testimony (*Antiquities of the Jews* 4.219). "The question was not so much, How can he prove it? as, Whose word can we trust? . . . The all-important question was the character of the witnesses" (Harvey 1976:20).

Such were the expectations, but whom could Jesus call as a witness to his deity? Only the Father, the Spirit and he himself really knew who he was. The Spirit is the Spirit of truth (16:13) and does indeed bear witness (see 16:8-11; 1 Jn 5:6), but he had not yet been given (Jn 7:39). The Son is truth (14:6), and his testimony about himself is true (8:14), but testimony about himself would not be valid (*alē thēs,* "true").

It would not be valid in the eyes of Jewish legal procedure, but on a deeper level it would not be valid if Jesus were acting on his own. The Son only speaks what he hears from the Father, and thus his

---

Isaiah 42—44 (cf. Schnackenburg 1980b:121; Beasley-Murray 1987 28-29). God's deeds on Israel's behalf bear witness to him (Is 43:8-13), just as Jesus' works bear witness to Jesus in our passage. Within this material in Isaiah is one of the main instances when God uses "I am" *(egō eimi)* of himself (Is 43:10); it comes in a passage in which he calls upon Israel to bear witness to his revelation and salvation. The analogous role of the disciples as witnesses to Jesus will be developed later (cf. Jn 15:27).

testimony of himself is only true as it is in conjunction with the Father's bearing witness (8:14, 18). If his testimony were "self-prompted" (West-cott 1908:1:197) it would not be valid. Jesus is equal with God, but again we see that the Father is distinct from the Son, for the Father is *another* (5:32; cf. comment on 1:1). So really there is only one witness who is qualified, namely the Father. And it is only the testimony of this witness that Jesus cares about (5:32, 34, 37). He points his opponents to several witnesses but, as we will see, these are all really expressions of the one valid witness, the Father (cf. Brown 1966:227). Only God, and those whom he uses, can testify to God.

If the witness of the Father is fundamental (5:32; cf. 1 Jn 5:9-12), what access do the Jewish opponents have to this testimony? There are four expressions of the Father's witness: the Baptist, Jesus' works, Jesus' words and the Scripture. Each of these has been acknowledged earlier (1:35—2:22) as the basis of the disciples' faith (cf. von Wahlde 1981), and most of them will be developed further in later material: Jesus' works in 8:12-59, Jesus' words in 10:22-39 and the Scriptures in 6:30-59. The witness of John the Baptist is not developed further, but it is drawn upon again (10:40-41).

John the Baptist (5:33-35), like Jesus, spoke what he heard from the Father (1:31-34). What he heard concerned Jesus, and so he bore witness to the truth; the truth is Christ (14:6). Not that Jesus had need of John's testimony (5:34). Jesus is one with the Father, so he has no need of human testimony for confirmation or help in knowing who he is. But the rest of us do have need of witnesses if we are to recognize him, so for our benefit he points out authentic witnesses.

Specifically, he does so for the sake of these Jewish opponents' salvation (5:34), for divine grace motivates and characterizes all that he does. God desires that these opponents be saved, and so Jesus affirms the testimony of one whom the Jews themselves highly honored. John the Baptist was not the light (1:8), but he was at least a lamp (5:35). They rejoiced in his light but did not heed his teaching concerning Jesus.

5:35 There is perhaps an allusion here to Psalm 132, which speaks of God's blessing of Zion and of her saints singing for joy (Ps 132:16). God says, "Here I will make a horn grow for David and set up a lamp for my anointed one. I will clothe his enemies with shame, but the crown on his head will be resplendent" (132:17-18). Here are the themes of God's

They failed to benefit from John.

The witness of the Baptist is valid, but it is the least significant of the four. The testimony of *the very work* (*ta erga,* "works") the Father has given Jesus *to finish* is *weightier* (5:36), for here we have not merely a voice (1:23) directing our attention to Jesus as the Christ, but the divine activity itself. As Jesus says in Matthew, a false prophet, like a tree, is known by his or her fruit (Mt 7:15-20). The important point is that Jesus' works are given to him by God and are in keeping with God's own character (cf. Jn 5:16-18). One who knows God through his previous revelation will recognize the family resemblance in Jesus.

Jesus then speaks of the Father's own testimony (5:37). It is not clear what he is referring to, but most likely he is continuing to develop the Father's testimony evident in his own activity. Now his words, as well as his works, are in view (8:37-38; cf. von Wahlde 1981:386-94). Jesus does the works of God and speaks only what he hears from God, so those who have seen him have seen the Father (14:8-11). If one can see and hear Jesus and not recognize him as God's Son, then it is evident that this person has never seen nor heard the true God (5:38).

Jesus' condemnation of the opponents cuts to the heart of their own identity (5:37). Both rabbinic and mystical strands of Judaism are judged at this point. Whatever they have heard or seen, whether in Scripture or in visions, it has not been revelation of the true God, or at least has not really benefited them, for they do not recognize the truth himself when he stands before them. By saying that they do not have God's word dwelling in them Jesus is denying they have a relationship with God. They need to come to him to have life, yet they are refusing to do so (5:40). Their problem is a matter of their own will. They are being given a chance to enter into life, but by rejecting it they condemn themselves. Here is an affirmation of Jesus' earlier claim to be the giver of life (5:21) as well as an example of his judgment (5:22). In their rejection of Jesus they stand self-condemned; they are not on the side of truth (cf. 18:37).

---

providing a lamp for his Christ ("anointed one") and also of the shame he will bring on his enemies, a point of contrast with the praise Jesus' opponents receive from one another (Jn 5:44).

Both rabbinic and mystical strands of Judaism focused on the Scripture. But they missed its testimony to the Christ and thus missed its main point. In Jesus' reference to this fourth witness we have the clearest expression of the Christian view of the Old Testament (5:39). This Christ-centered understanding of the Scriptures is affirmed throughout the New Testament and throughout the history of the church. Jesus is the Word, the point of reference for all the words of Scripture. The importance of the Scripture is here affirmed, but Scripture is presented as a means to an end, as a witness to Jesus the Christ. For the New Testament authors, Jesus is the key to the interpretation of the Old Testament, and our passage affirms they got this view from Jesus himself (cf. Lk 24:25-27, 44-45; Dodd 1952:109-10).

Assuming that verse 37 alludes to Jesus' words, we have here four witnesses. The opponents had respected Jesus' words and works earlier, but they reject him after he heals on the sabbath and makes a disturbing interpretation of his activity. They fail to hear the witness of those they still respect—the Baptist and the Scriptures.

What is their problem? The Great Physician goes on to diagnose their disease. It has to do with their hearts (5:41-44). Jesus accuses them of caring about one another's praise instead of seeking to obtain praise from God. In a word, they lack love for God in their hearts. In this portrait we see them as opposites to Jesus himself. He is completely centered in God, caring only for God's glory. He even states at this point that he does not *accept praise from men* (v. 41). This does not mean that he does not accept praise and honor from his followers, as if Christian worship were against Christ's will! He is to be honored as the Father is honored (5:23; cf. 16:14). But he is not looking for our praise as a petty king or politician would do. Our praise of Jesus does not add to the glory he already has from the Father. The witnesses he has mentioned are "the means by which men are enabled to recognize His glory; they in no wise add to it" (Hoskyns 1940a:305). The point here

---

5:39 As the NIV footnote indicates, *study (eraunate,* "search"*)* may be either a statement or a command. The context suggests it is a statement of what they already are doing, reflecting the zeal the Jews have always had for studying the Scriptures. An early text of the Mishnah connects the study of Scripture with having life: "The more study of the Law the more life. . . . If a man has gained a good name he has gained [somewhat] for himself; if he has gained for himself words of the Law he has gained for himself life in the world

is his union with the Father. As he has no need of human testimony (5:34), neither does he need human praise.

The metaphor Jesus uses to describe himself is that of a faithful agent, for coming "in the name" refers to being sent with a commission (Bietenhard 1967:260-61; see note on 5:21). They not only fail to recognize the one sent from God, they actually accept folk who come with no authority outside themselves, those who come in their own name (5:43). So they not only reject the true, they embrace the false. If they took to heart what Jesus is saying about them they would have to question their own ability to discern the things of God, which would require great humility.

After diagnosing their problem Jesus concludes with a warning (5:45-47). Rejecting the words of God's ultimate messenger puts them in grave danger. Jesus is the prophet like Moses (Deut 18:18; cf. Friedrich 1968:845-48; Boismard 1993:1-68), regarding whom God said, "If anyone does not listen to my words that the prophet speaks in my name, I myself will call him to account" (Deut 18:19). Jesus accuses them of lacking the love of God and of failing to accept the agent who has come in his name, yet Jesus does so to give them a chance to come to their senses. The judgment he passes is itself an aspect of the grace of God intended for their salvation (see comment on 3:17).

But he will not be their accuser before God. They will be judged in the end by the light they have embraced, *Moses, on whom your hopes are set* (5:45). Here again is a great blow to their identity. Jesus has undercut the views they hold of themselves as zealous for God and loyal to his revelation. Now he says Moses will be their accuser, though they have believed that Moses would be their intercessor, as he had in the past (Ex 32:30-32; Num 21:7). God had used Moses as a witness against the people in the past (Deut 31:19-29), and this role will be fulfilled and expanded. In his witness to the Christ, Moses is a witness against the Jewish opponents' rejection of Jesus (5:46). Indeed, John makes a point

to come" (*m. 'Abot* 2:7).

5:42 *The love of God* could refer to their love for God or to having God's own love within them. Since the context is about their attitudes toward God, the former is more likely.

5:45 For the belief that Moses would be an intercessor, see Meeks 1967:159-61, 200-204. The first-century text *Testament of Moses* 12:6 is often cited, but it is, unfortunately, fragmentary at this point (cf. Charlesworth 1983:934 n. 12c).

of countering every Scripture-based argument made against Jesus with counterarguments from Scripture (cf. Whitacre 1982:25-39). Thus, despite their claims, they do not really believe Moses. If they are not open to Moses, whom they desire to honor, how much less will they be able to put faith in Jesus (5:47)! Here it is clearly taught that an understanding of the Old Testament which is not centered in Jesus Christ is a deficient understanding (vv. 46-47). Once again, we see people honor someone as a teacher yet reject his teaching (cf. comments on 3:2, 26).

Jesus' condemnation of the Jewish opponents plays a key role in the Gospel's message in its original setting. These opponents viewed themselves as the true children of God (8:41), an identity based on their being disciples of Moses (9:28) and children of Abraham (8:39). Some Jewish sources go so far as to say that having faith in Moses "is the same as having faith in Him who spoke and the world came into being" (*Mekilta* 7.126 on Ex 14:31). Thus, the issue of who really understands Moses and receives his teaching is part of the deeper issue of who is truly a child of God. This is the issue at stake between the Christians and their Jewish opponents late in the first century.

The implications of our text for today are both comforting and challenging. That Jesus is the final and ultimate revelation of God by which we may judge all other revelation gives Christians confidence. The witnesses to Jesus mentioned in this text are all still available to us: The witness of the Old Testament is obviously still present, but so is the witness of the Baptist and the words and works of Jesus. The latter three come to us in the New Testament, not least in the Gospel of John. In addition, Christians have the witness of the Holy Spirit, who has enabled the church to understand the revelation of God in Jesus (cf. 14:26; 15:26; 16:12-15). Faith in Jesus gives confidence, joy and peace because of who he is—the unique Son of God, equal with God.

Such a teaching also challenges us in several ways. In our ecumenical environment some would challenge the exclusiveness of Jesus' claims. They would attribute the strong language to the polemical setting of his

---

6:1 For the suggestion that chapters 5 and 6 are out of order see the introduction to 5:1-47.

The story of this feeding is one of the few events narrated in all four of the Gospels. Some scholars argue that John is drawing upon the accounts in one or more of the Synoptics, in particular Mark (for example, Barrett 1978:271; Carson 1991:267), whereas most scholars

confrontations with the Jewish opponents or to John's similar confrontations later in the first century. Certainly hatred between Jews and Christians is to be denounced. But the claims of Jesus' divinity, his unique primacy as the Son of God, continues to divide us. This is not a secondary matter; it is the heart of the Gospel.

This text is also challenging to Christians on another level. For those who accept the primacy and uniqueness of Jesus there is no place for smugness. The New Testament, especially 1 John, bears abundant witness that those who claim to believe in Jesus may themselves be alienated from God. Our great need is for God himself. We should rejoice in all that God gives us in Scripture, in the church and in natural revelation. But to benefit from these gifts of God, we must be humble before God. We should pray constantly that God would correct our personal misperceptions and enable us to see ever more correctly and directly the glory of God in the face of Jesus Christ, for the one immovable rock is Jesus Christ. He will be either one's cornerstone or one's stumbling block. He can only be accepted on his own terms or rejected.

What are the witnesses in our lives that have pointed us to Jesus as the Christ of God, the Son of the living God? Have we made the effort to hear and grasp the message of these four witnesses to Jesus, understanding the true significance of the Old Testament, John the Baptist and Jesus' own words and works? Indeed, in this Gospel itself we have one of the greatest witnesses to Jesus (cf. 15:27; 1 Jn 1:1-4). May we receive the grace to benefit from his witness.

□ Jesus, the Life-Giver and Judge, Is Revealed as the Bread of Life (6:1-59)

The heart of the revelation has now been given in Jesus' keynote address (chap. 5), in which he claims to have the divine prerogatives of life-giver and judge. These two rights will be depicted throughout the rest of the Gospel, beginning immediately with the description of Jesus as the

would say John is independent of the Synoptics, perhaps drawing instead upon common traditions (for example, Brown 1966:236-44; Schnackenburg 1980b:21-23, 28). John A. T. Robinson argues that John is independent of the Synoptics but provides material necessary for making sense of the Synoptic accounts (1985:190-211).

Bread of Life—the one who not only gives life but sustains it. We also see judgment taking place as people are unable to receive this revelation. First the Jews and then most of Jesus' disciples are offended rather than enlightened. By the end of the chapter only the Twelve are left.

Jesus Demonstrates His Authority in Two Nature Miracles (6:1-24)

John follows Jesus' speech (5:19-47) with further disclosure of Jesus as the one who can give and take life; he is the life-giver and the judge. Jesus has said that Moses "wrote about me" (5:46), and now we learn how this is the case. Under Moses' leadership Israel escaped through the Red Sea, traveled through the wilderness and miraculously received food there. These stories are now echoed in Jesus' miraculous feeding of the five thousand (6:1-15) and his rescue of his disciples as he walks to them on the sea (6:16-21). These miracles clearly reveal Jesus as sovereign over the forces of nature. But in his teaching that follows and the controversy it arouses, we discover that he is not merely one who works miracles within the realm of nature, nor merely a leader of God's people like Moses, but the source of eternal life itself (6:22-59). He fulfills the role of Moses and utterly transcends it.

The revelation at this point, however, is too difficult to accept even for most of Jesus' disciples (6:60-71). This gracious revealing is itself a test of hearts and thus a judgment. Jesus tests Philip (6:6), and then, as we see the reaction to his teaching and the events leading up to it, we find that the crowd and the disciples are all being put to the test. As God tested his people in the wilderness, so here the Son of God tests hearts. As with Israel, many grumble and fail, yet Jesus does find some who are receptive enough to pass the test.

Jesus Feeds the Five Thousand (6:1-15) Jesus has said that Moses wrote about him, and now, when he miraculously feeds the five thousand, the people conclude that he is the prophet Moses wrote about (6:14; cf. Deut 18:15). Jesus is indeed the prophet, but he is also something much greater. He is not only the prophet that Moses wrote about but the God that Moses wrote about, the one who gave bread in the wilderness.

Once again we find Jesus in Galilee with people attracted to him because of the signs he has done (cf. 4:45). The crowd's faith is defective, as was the faith of the earlier crowd. The fact that it is described as a *great crowd* at the outset (6:2) contrasts sharply with the desertion of all but the Twelve at the conclusion of the story (6:66). As we watch the dynamics that lead from acceptance to rejection we learn something about the nature of discipleship.

The reference to the Passover (6:4) alerts us to another developing motif in this Gospel. At a previous Passover feast (2:13) Jesus made reference to his coming death (2:19-22; 3:14-15), and the opponents sought to kill him (5:18). Here, again in the context of Passover, he provides one of the most profound discussions of his coming death, which is to occur at a later Passover. The exodus of this new Moses is accomplished in his own sacrificial death as the Passover lamb, whose flesh and blood give life to the world (6:51-58). "The multitude, by coming to Jesus instead of going to Jerusalem, finds in him the true meaning of Passover" (Talbert 1992:131-32).

The account of the feeding begins with Jesus' asking Philip, *Where shall we buy bread for these people to eat?* (v. 5). Since Philip is from the area (1:44) this could come across as a simple question of where the shops are located posed to a local boy. But in fact it is a test (v. 6), and Philip fails. He is asked "where" and can think only in terms of "how." It is a very difficult test because Jesus refers to "buying" bread. A correct answer, in keeping with faithful responses earlier in the Gospel (for example, 1:38; 2:5), might be something like, "Lord, you know." Or perhaps even more could be expected: Jesus' question echoes that of Moses in the wilderness (Num 11:13), and if Philip caught this allusion and remembered that Jesus has turned water into wine, he might have said, "You, Lord, are able to provide." But Philip does not grasp the full significance of his earlier confession that Jesus is "the one Moses wrote about in the Law, and about whom the prophets also wrote" (1:45).

Thus the test is ultimately concerned with the recognition of Jesus' identity and the graciousness of God. In fact, even in this test itself Jesus' identity and God's graciousness are evident. Jesus is acting like God, for in testing Philip, Jesus is treating him like God treats his own people in the Old Testament. Indeed, in the Old Testament, God tests only his own people, not those outside the covenant relationship; and the only individuals God is said to test are the godly, not the ungodly. What God is looking for is faith, trust that God will be loyal to his covenant obligations to care for his people (Schneider and Brown 1978:799-800). This question is meant to reveal Jesus as the presence of that gracious God who is providing the ultimate blessing—eternal life.

God's children continue to be tested in this same way today. We who have the benefit of the revelation of the New Testament and the witness of the Spirit still find ourselves in situations that challenge us to think and act in keeping with our recognition of God as the ultimate reality in every situation, even situations of great fear or grief, when God seems absent or cruel (cf. comments on 6:20 and 11:27). Such testing is not comfortable, but it is part of God's graciousness, for it achieves a deepening of our faith by revealing our own weakness and God's all-sufficiency.

Philip has called attention to the enormity of the problem. Then Andrew points to the meagerness of the resources (v. 9). The availability of twelve baskets for collecting the leftovers (v. 13) suggests this child was not the only one who had brought food. But there is no suggestion that this feeding was accomplished by getting people to share their lunches. Indeed, the reference to this event as a "sign" rules out such an interpretation (6:26; cf. Mk. 6:52). Rather, Jesus takes a child's lunch and from it provides for all. Andrew does not see how the child's lunch can be of help, but just such weakness is characteristic of the way God provides. He produces sons from barren women (Gen 18:11) and even from a virgin (Mt 1:18); he chooses what is foolish, weak, lowly, despised and even nonexistent (1 Cor 1:27-28). He is the God of the impossible (Mk 10:27), as the salvation of each of us testifies.

Given the allusions to Moses and the stress on both the enormity of the need and the meagerness of the resources, the actual account of the

---

6:11 This description is very similar to the accounts of the Last Supper in Paul and the Synoptics (1 Cor 11:23-24; Mt 26:26 par. Mk 14:22 par. Lk 22:19), with the main exception being the lack of reference to breaking the bread. It is doubtful any Christian could read this without thinking of the Eucharist, a connection that will become clearer in the discourse that follows (especially Jn 6:53). This is striking because John does not give an account of the institution of the Lord's Supper.

6:13 Presumably there were twelve baskets because the Twelve were the collectors. John has not referred to the twelve apostles yet, but he does so at the end of this chapter (vv.

miracle is striking in its spare simplicity. The disciples are told to get the people to sit down. The disciples play no further role, unlike in the Synoptics where they are the ones who distribute the food (Mt 14:19 par. Mk 6:41 par. Lk 9:16). John does not suggest otherwise, but his focus is entirely on Jesus. He *took the loaves, gave thanks, and distributed* (v. 11). Jesus is clearly in charge from first to last, having taken the initiative (v. 5; contrast Mt 14:15 par. Mk 6:35-36 par. Lk 9:12) and now distributing the food himself. He is acting as the father of a family, but in giving thanks he refers it all back to his Father, as will be developed in the following discourse.

Everyone received *as much as they wanted* (v. 11), they were all full (v. 12), and twelve baskets full of food was left over (v. 13). This leftover food echoes the account of Elisha's feeding a hundred people from only twenty barley loaves (2 Kings 4:42-44). Here we see the same gracious abundance evident in the provision of more than one hundred gallons of wine at the wedding (2:6-9). It is a sign that reveals Jesus' identity and the Father's gracious gifts. All food and drink come from God, so Jesus here continues to do what he sees his Father doing (5:19). But provision of nourishment for physical life is itself a sign of nourishment for life in a deeper sense, as will become clear later in the chapter.

The people who have been following him because they saw signs now interpret this sign correctly. They identify Jesus as the prophet like Moses (Deut 18:15) and want to make him king. Among at least some Jews, Moses was viewed as both the greatest prophet and the ideal king (Meeks 1967), a connection that seems reflected in the response of this crowd. But, like the disciples in chapter 1, they are applying correct titles to Jesus with no real understanding of what they are saying. They think of kingship in earthly, political terms whereas Jesus' kingdom is not of this world (Jn 18:36). Furthermore, their attitude is as wrong as

---

67, 70). John does not focus much attention on the Twelve, but if this explanation of the twelve baskets is correct, then John at times uses the word *disciple (mathētēs)* to refer to the Twelve. According to the Synoptics, Jesus had chosen the Twelve before the feeding miracle (for example, Mk 3:13-19; cf. Mk 6:30-44).

6:15 The reference to withdrawing *again* is puzzling. Either *oros* ("hill," "mountain") here refers to the hill country and Jesus is depicted as withdrawing further up into the hills (cf. Carson 1991:268, 271) or Jesus perhaps came down the mountain for the feeding.

their understanding. The desire *to come and make him king by force* (6:15) is totally opposite to the humble and docile attitude that is characteristic of true disciples. They are working on their own agenda, not God's, and thus ironically they share a chief characteristic of Jesus' opponents. Jesus escapes from them, just as he will escape from the opponents later (8:59; 12:36).

Each of us probably knows from experience how easy it is to come up with our own ideas and confuse them with the Lord's will. Only great humility and docility before the Lord and his revelation can protect us. Part of God's grace is seen in his continual correction of our false views. In the discourse that follows in this chapter we see him trying to correct and deepen these folks' understanding, but to no avail. We should fear lest we also are as obtuse as these people. True receptivity is itself a gift from God for which we can trust him.

Jesus Rescues His Disciples on the Sea (6:16-21) The account of the feeding of the five thousand shows Jesus as a new Moses, but Jesus is more than a new prophet like Moses, as is confirmed in what follows. The imagery, language and action in the story of Jesus' walking on water all echo descriptions of God in the Old Testament. In Jesus' rescue of his disciples we see yet another example of the divine glory, God's grace.

In these six verses two miracles are recorded that each reveal Jesus as the master over the natural realm. The first is his walking on the water to reach the disciples. Many have suggested that John does not intend for us to believe Jesus walked upon water but that John is saying Jesus was walking along the shore next to the sea. The Greek allows such an interpretation (*epi tēs thalassēs* has this meaning in 21:1), and it is quite possible that they had begun their trip along the coastline, expecting to pick up Jesus. But John says that they were heading across the lake and had rowed several miles, which does not speak of a trip along the coast. Furthermore, if Jesus had merely walked along the coast, then the disciples' fear (v. 19) and the puzzlement of the crowds (vv. 22-25)

_____

6:17 The note that Jesus had *not yet* joined them is puzzling. According to Mark (6:45) Jesus sent them on ahead to Bethsaida. Since Bethsaida was on the northeast shore of Galilee, probably only a short distance from where the feeding took place, it seems the disciples were to go by boat to Bethsaida and meet Jesus there before sailing across the

would not be accounted for.

The second miracle is the way they arrived at Capernaum after taking Jesus into the boat (v. 21). Again, it is possible that this verse does not describe anything miraculous. Some suggest that once the sea had calmed down, the normal travel seemed as though it took no time at all, especially with Jesus present in the boat after his spectacular approach. Thus the immediate arrival would say something about the disciples' perception rather than about physical motion. Such an interpretation is possible, but the text focuses attention on what happened to the boat: *immediately the boat reached the shore where they were heading*. John seems to suggest that Jesus' walk on the water was not the only unnatural mode of transportation that night.

Such stories raise questions regarding the miraculous. Many believe that such things do not happen, so therefore John is making up a story to convey something of Jesus' authority and power. The story certainly does show Jesus' authority and power, but did he really have such authority and power? Was he really able to walk on water? As science is coming to accept views of the universe that are not as mechanistic as views in the past were, it is perhaps easier today to believe that such unusual events are possible.

If we accept that this passage recounts events in history, there are three ways we might view them. An older view of miracle spoke of the suspension of a natural law. Alternatively, it could be that Jesus is drawing upon forces in nature to which most of us do not have access but which are part of the created order. Widespread evidence, both ancient and modern, of "faith healing" that can be explained neither by medicine nor psychology suggests such forces exist. A third possibility is that something unique is happening. That is, there is here neither the suspension of a natural law nor the drawing upon a natural law as yet unobserved by natural science, but rather there is "a new force called into exercise" (Westcott 1908:1:217). Because we do not really know the nature and scope of these unstudied forces and laws of nature, it would

---

lake. "Probably Jesus had directed the apostles to wait for Him at some point on the eastern shore on their way to Capernaum, but not beyond a certain time. The phrase 'not yet' implies that He had led them to expect that He would be with them, and that they clung in some way to the expectation even in their disappointment" (Westcott 1908:1:218).

seem we cannot say for certain whether this is a "new force" or the operation of natural laws unknown to most people.

In any case, we have here nature miracles that reveal Jesus' identity to us: he is God present in our midst, saving his people. This identity is signaled in part by Jesus' statement, *It is I [egō eimi]; don't be afraid* (v. 20). The expression *egō eimi* plays a major role in this Gospel. Rudolf Bultmann (1971:225-26) has identified four uses of this formula: (1) a presentation formula, in which one tells who one is ("I am John"); (2) a qualifying formula, in which one tells what one is ("I am a teacher"); (3) an identification formula, in which one identifies oneself in terms of another person or thing ("I am a servant of Christ"); and (4) a recognition formula, in which one identifies oneself as the one expected, spoken to, seen, and so on ("It is I"). John's uses fall in the latter two categories. These uses in themselves can be either secular or sacred, but in John the usage is most characteristically an expression of Jesus' close relationship with God. For a fifth use, the divine name of God, I AM, overshadows the other uses.

The exact significance of this formula is, however, debated. Rudolf Schnackenburg and George Beasley-Murray believe that the *egō eimi* formula signifies that Jesus is "God's eschatological revealer in whom God utters himself" (Schnackenburg 1982:88; cf. Beasley-Murray 1987:90) but that it does not signify Jesus' identification with God. This is true in the sense that Jesus is not the Father; the first verse of the Gospel reveals that there is both identity and distinction between the Father and the Son, and the very terms *father* and *son* suggest the same. We cannot be certain the use of *egō eimi* in 6:20 is a divine formula, but nevertheless in John's Gospel this ambiguous formula is made "a leitmotiv of the Gospel as that form of the divine name which the Father has given to Jesus and by which he identifies himself. . . . The majesty of Jesus is that he can bear the *divine* name" (Brown 1966:252, 254-55, 533-38). This formula seems to be a part of the larger theme of the charge of blasphemy against Jesus (8:58-59; cf. 5:18; 10:33), suggesting the term is understood as Jesus' claim to be more than a human agent of God. So although Jesus' assurance, *It is I (egō eimi),* could be simply a call for the disciples to recognize that it is Jesus who is standing there in front of them, the Johannine reader, knowing Jesus uses it as the divine name (for example, 8:58), hears an echo of that more weighty use in all this Gospel's references to Jesus.

The story of Jesus' walking on water alludes to several Old Testament passages, which builds the case for Jesus' divine identity. It is said of God, "he alone stretches out the heavens and treads on the waves of the sea" (Job 9:8). Psalm 107 speaks of those who "went out on the sea in ships" (Ps 107:23) and were caught in a great storm. They should "give thanks to the Lord for his unfailing love" (Ps 107:31) because "he stilled the storm to a whisper; the waves of the sea were hushed. They were glad when it grew calm, and he guided them to their desired haven" (Ps 107:29-30). The poetic imagery of these passages is reenacted on a historical level in the actual event John is describing. The image of walking on the sea mentioned in Job now actually occurs; and though John does not mention the calming of the sea, the deliverance to "their desired haven" is attributed to God in the psalm and, by implication, to Jesus in the Gospel. When Jesus brings his people safely through the sea, he repeats the pattern of God's leading his people through the Red Sea by the hand of Moses and Aaron (Ex 13:17—15:21; Ps 77:16-20). Thus, Jesus' superiority to Moses, seen clearly in the feeding of the five thousand, is implied in this story as well.

So John continues to witness to Jesus' identity and his gracious activity. The feeding shows that Jesus is able to provide even when our resources are very small. The rescue on the sea shows that he can protect and guide in the midst of great adversity, when we have no control over the forces of chaos. In both cases the physical realm reveals his identity and his loving care. In this way, these stories also begin to prepare us for the startling teaching that comes next in the discourse on the bread of life, when he tells his would be followers they are to eat his flesh and drink his blood.

The miracles in this chapter have presented a challenge to a secular view of the physical realm. In the teaching that follows, secular views and even many religious views of the relationship between the material and the spiritual are challenged. We do not expect a small amount of food to feed many people nor the surface of the water to support a human being, and neither do we expect body and blood to bring us eternal life. But, just as Jesus is far superior to Moses, so too the salvation he brings is far more than the provision of physical food and the protection from physical danger. We will now learn of the eternal life he offers and the means of its provision.

The Crowds Seek Jesus (6:22-24) This brief transition section provides important information about the crowd. John also uses this transition to emphasize the two miracles that he has just depicted.

We learn at the beginning of this section that this crowd is well aware that something very strange has happened. They realize that Jesus is no longer present at the scene of the feeding but also that he did not leave in the one boat that had been present (v. 22). Thus, while the crowd did not witness Jesus walking on the water, they come to realize that the feeding miracle was not the only unusual event that had taken place.

Once they realize the situation and boats arrive from Tiberias (v. 23), they set out for Capernaum in search of Jesus (v. 24). It is not clear why they knew to search for Jesus in Capernaum. They may have heard the disciples talking as they departed (v. 17) or assumed the destination from the direction they took. But it is also possible that they realized Capernaum was Jesus' base of operations (cf. Mt 4:13; Mk 1:21; 9:33) and the residence of Andrew, Peter, James and John. In any case, in doing so they repeat the pattern of the first disciples, who took the initiative and sought out Jesus as he went on ahead of them (1:35-39). But others, like Nicodemus, also sought Jesus out yet failed to have the openness and trust to receive his teachings. This transition passage shows us that, like Nicodemus, this crowd has seen miraculous signs and has come to Jesus. In what follows we will discover whether or not they have the inner disposition to be Jesus' disciples in truth.

As verse 22 draws our attention to the fact that Jesus' departure the night before had been unusual, so verse 23 helps focus our understanding of the feeding miracle. Boats from Tiberias arrive *near the place where the people had eaten the bread after the Lord had given thanks.* The additional phrase *after the Lord had given thanks* seems unnecessary and is, indeed, omitted in some manuscripts (for example, D, 091). But

---

6:22-24 The NIV smoothes out some difficulties in the Greek in these verses. The simplest solution is either that verse 23 is parenthetical (Beasley-Murray 1987:90) or that "St. John has inserted two explanatory clauses, the first [v. 22] to explain why they still lingered on the eastern shore in the hope of finding Jesus . . . and the second [v. 23] to explain how

its presence puts Jesus at the center of attention. The people had eaten, but the Lord's gracious activity had preceded this miracle. And the specific action John focuses us on, Jesus' giving thanks, speaks of the relationship between the Son and the Father and of the Son's dependency. It also shows Jesus acting in the family role of a father at meal. So this brief clause touches on the deepest revelation about Jesus in this Gospel, the relation between the Father and the Son, and it also speaks of Jesus as the agent of God's gracious provision.

Do we miss the important point in the events of our lives? Behind all blessings and all sorrows, the Son of God is present and interceding for us with the Father. In all circumstances God the Spirit is present with us. Do we get caught up in the melodrama, whether pleasant and exciting as in this story or painful and confusing as we will see in the story of Lazarus (chap. 11)? We need to have eyes to see the gracious God active in our midst in both the joyful and the painful, in both the spectacular and the mundane.

Jesus Reveals Himself to Be the Bread of Life (6:25-59) Jesus has claimed to share God's prerogatives of life-giving and judgment and has demonstrated supernatural power. Now the claims in chapter 5 and the power demonstrated in chapter 6 are put in perspective through the series of teachings around the theme of the bread of life (vv. 25-59). The deeds of power are signs of something even more wondrous than the witnesses first thought, for Jesus speaks further of his role as the giver of eternal life and of how people are to share in this life he offers. The crowd's response to this teaching illustrates the judgment that is taking place through Jesus' ministry. In this section we also receive more revelation of the relation between the Father and the Son spoken of in the keynote address.

Jesus Teaches About the Work of God (6:25-29) The crowd that had come across the lake in search of Jesus ask him, *Rabbi, when did you get here?* Quite often in this Gospel people call Jesus "Rabbi" and

---

they were themselves able to cross over" (Westcott 1908:1:221).
6:22 The crowd referred to in this section is not the entire multitude that had been fed the previous day. "It was not an armada that crossed the Lake to find Jesus!" (Beasley-Murray 1987:90).

then do not treat him as a rabbi; that is, they do not receive his teaching. As this dialogue unfolds we see this crowd fitting this pattern. Indeed, their uncertain attachment to Jesus may be evident even in this question. We would expect them to ask *how* Jesus arrived, not *when*. By asking *when* they seem to assume he slipped away undetected and arrived by normal means. They have already observed something unusual about Jesus' travel (v. 22), yet they are slow to believe that Jesus is unusual, too.

Jesus' reply, as is often the case, is neither polite nor seemingly directed to the question asked. He responds as a holy man would, revealing their own state of heart. That they are looking for him is good (cf. 1:35-39), but Jesus says there is something wrong with their motivation. The proper motivation has to do with seeing *miraculous signs* (*sēmeia,* v. 26). A sign is a deed that is full of significance, revealing Jesus' identity and God's saving activity in his ministry. They had seen a miracle, but it did not focus their attention on Jesus. Rather, he was seen as a means to the filling of their stomachs (v. 26). Jesus did not come to fill stomachs with food, but to fill lives with the very presence of God, as he will make clear in this dialogue.

This crowd is focusing on the physical realm. In John the physical and the spiritual are interconnected, for the physical is spirit-bearing: the Word became flesh. The present dialogue will teach us this lesson very clearly. This crowd, then, is faulted not for their interest in the physical, but for lacking perception of the spiritual through and in the physical. The same problem afflicts some disciples today, since matter is still spirit-bearing. Too often we fail to have eyes to see and ears to hear the God who is present in our lives, through either the sacraments or the events of everyday life.

These folk had to work hard for their daily bread, so when they found a miraculous source of food this was good news. But Jesus tries to redirect their attention: *Do not work for food that spoils* (v. 27). Sure, they have to work for a living, but what is their deeper vocation? Their focus is on physical food, which is temporal. Like the manna in the wilderness,

---

6:27 Jesus is not saying that we should not work for our necessities, a point confirmed by Paul (2 Thess 3:6-13). The petition for "daily bread" in the Lord's Prayer (Mt 6:11; Lk 11:3) probably has an eschatological and spiritual dimension to it similar to the meaning of bread in John 6. The word for "daily" *(epiousios)* in both Matthew and Luke is not the normal

it does not last long. But more profoundly, the life it nourishes is also all too brief. Our physical lives of flesh and blood are given by God, and they are significant, but they are not the whole story; this life is transitory. There is a *food that endures to eternal life* (v. 27); it does not rot but instead nourishes real life, divine life, life that continues on forever. Jesus is repeating what he told the Samaritan woman: "Indeed, the water I give him will become in him a spring of water welling up to eternal life" (4:14). What do we really hunger and thirst for (cf. Mt 5:6)? What is "blue chip"—of highest value—in our lives (cf. Ward 1994: 23-29)? Are we like this crowd?

Jesus says the crowd is to *work . . . for food that endures,* but he also says that this is food *which the Son of Man will give you* (v. 27). So it is both work and gift, concepts that have often been thought to be in opposition to one another. The Son of Man will give this food by giving his own life and also by providing a means by which we may share in that life, as he explains later. Thus, the reference to *the Son of Man* in this passage (cf. 6:53, 62) is part of the pattern in this Gospel in which *Son of Man* refers to the Messiah from heaven who brings God's life and judgment, especially through the cross (cf. comment on 3:13).

Verse 27 in the NIV does not represent the word because *(gar),* which is important for understanding the reason Jesus, the Son of Man, can give eternal life: *the Son of Man will give you* [food that endures to eternal life] *because on him God has placed his seal of approval.* It is not clear what in particular the Father's seal of approval refers to. *Has placed his seal* is in the aorist *(esphragisen),* so it could refer to some particular event, such as the incarnation or the baptism (1:33-34). It is similar to the references to the Father's bearing witness to the Son (5:32, 37; 8:18). It means that Jesus is, as it were, the authorized dealer. Constantly Jesus is reminding us, as spelled out in his keynote address (5:19-30), that he is utterly dependent on the Father. This thought is vital for understanding everything about Jesus, not least his role in giving eternal life (cf. 6:57). It is the Father, the source of all, who has given Jesus the life that he

---

Greek word for "daily." The petition probably refers to the nourishment we need for life in this age and in the age to come, which would include both physical and spiritual nourishment. Thus, the dialogue here in John 6 provides something of an exposition on this petition in the Lord's Prayer.

offers here (cf. 5:21, 26).

The crowd next asks, *What must we do to do the works God requires?* (v. 28). This is an incredible question. How many Christians today reach the height of this question? For how many of us is this a burning question? How would we answer this question? Many would think of God's work as acting morally or doing evangelism or apologetics or even worship. As important as all of these are, Jesus goes to the heart of the matter, to the source from which all of these vital aspects of eternal life flow—belief in the one sent by God. Without this faith none of these activities benefit us. Our primary work is being receptive to God. All our actions and plans are dependent on the most important action—union with God in Christ by the Spirit. Ultimately it is not a matter of our working for God, but a matter of God's living his life and doing his work through us as we trust him and align ourselves with him by his grace (see comment on 20:27-29).

So this question by the crowd shows that they have gained some understanding since the conversation began in verse 25. They appear to be trying to get on board with Jesus' teaching, for they are talking about the work of God. But they are still missing the main point: they do not pick up on Jesus' revelation of himself and of his role in giving them the food that endures to eternal life. Instead of looking to the giver and the gift, they look to their own role. Somewhere in the midst of trying to please God it is easy to lose sight of, and lose trust in, God's own sovereign graciousness. Jesus' reply to their question sharply refocuses their attention on trust in God and his grace—*The work of God is this: to believe in the one he has sent* (v. 29). Once again Jesus describes himself by referring to the Father who sent him. Everything the crowd has said and done has failed to focus on the central figure, Jesus himself. Jesus, the Good Shepherd, has finally gotten them to face in the right direction. It is not many *works* that God requires but one *work*. And that work is *to believe,* to trust in Jesus as the one sent from God, as God's unique Son who offers God's grace. Jesus' work is to reveal the Father

---

6:28 *The works God requires* is literally "the works of God" *(ta erga tou theou)*. This genitive, "of God," is usually taken as objective, as in the NIV. The objective genitive, however, may mean not just the works required by God, but those that "correspond with God's actions . . . works 'done in God' " (Schnackenburg 1980b:39; cf. 3:21; 9:4). On the other hand, the

(cf. 4:34), and our work is to receive that revelation and align our lives with it.

Once again we see the overwhelming grace of God and his amazing patience with our dullness and stupidity. Just as he worked through the Samaritan woman's misunderstandings to bring her to faith, so here he works with an unpromising situation to get the people to see what is right before their eyes. This is great good news for all of us, for we are also quite dull at times. We too can have stiff necks. Fortunately, as John Shea has said, God has a stiffer neck! We can take great comfort in his patience and the picture we see in this account of his working in all human hearts. We can be assured that God is trying to break through to the heart of every person we come in contact with, and he may want to use us in the process.

While there is much comfort in what we see here in Jesus' dealings with the crowd, we should not take false comfort. The folk in this crowd will end up rejecting Jesus. Indeed, almost all of Jesus' disciples will reject him by the end of the chapter, at least for the present. God's patience is forever, but we can reject him and reject the gift of life he offers. Jesus' presence not only brings the offer of eschatological blessing, but also includes the threat of eschatological danger. The stakes are high for us and everyone we meet.

Many Christians, as John Wesley said, have just enough religion to be miserable. They are like this crowd, missing God's gift of life in his Son. They are not experiencing abiding life, which will be described in this chapter. We, like this crowd, need God's help to understand who Jesus is and what he offers us. We also need help to appropriate this gift of divine life.

Jesus Reveals the Source of Life (6:30-40) Jesus has finally succeeded in directing the people's attention to himself and to the necessity of faith in him. Now that their attention is fixed, he reveals himself to them as the bread of life. Jesus speaks of a bread superior to the bread that was provided for Israel in the desert, and the crowd says

---

genitive could be subjective, meaning that God himself is active in some sense. "There is a true sense in which this 'work' is 'a work of God,' as inspired and sustained by him" (Westcott 1908:1:225). The ambiguity of this genitive seems to capture something of the antinomy in John's thought between divine sovereignty and human responsibility.

it wants to receive this bread (vv. 30-34). Jesus then grants their request by revealing that he himself is that bread (vv. 35-40). He speaks of the role of the divine call and the human response in people's coming to faith, thereby challenging them to believe in him, if indeed God is their God.

Jesus focused their attention on the importance of believing in the one sent by God (6:29). As good Jews they are already aware of how important such faith is. This is quite in keeping with their loyalty to Moses as the one sent from God (5:45; 9:28-29). But they realize that Jesus is talking not about Moses, but about himself (6:27). So they ask, *What miraculous sign then will you give that we may see it and believe you? What will you do?* (v. 30). These are amazing questions, for this crowd is actually willing to entertain the possibility that Jesus is in the same league as Moses. The Samaritan woman was willing to consider the possibility that Jesus is greater than Jacob, and in this faith she was brought closer to him. This crowd seems to have a similar willingness, but the results will not be as good.

The NIV, and the interpretation of most commentators, understands these questions as a request for a sign, with the assumption that the crowd goes on to suggest something along the lines of Moses' provision of bread in the desert (v. 31). But this is strange since they have, in fact, just been given bread in the desert. It could be that they are extremely dense or that they are suggesting Jesus' feeding was inferior to Moses'. Yet they had seen in this last sign reason to make him king (6:15), so the questions in verse 30 are puzzling. Indeed, a number of scholars suspect that they are evidence of a patchwork of more than one source.

However, a more satisfactory interpretation is found when we take the verbs in the sentence, which are in the present tense, as referring to the present rather than the future: "What sign therefore are you doing, that we may see and believe you? What work are you doing?" The crowd is not asking for another sign to be given, but rather they want an interpretation of the feeding that has just occurred. Verse 31 then follows quite naturally, for the feeding reminds them of what happened through

---

6:31 According to *Midrash Rabbah Ecclesiastes* 1:9, "As the former redeemer caused manna to descend . . . so will the latter Redeemer [the Messiah] cause manna to descend." If this

Moses in the desert. The quote from Scripture cited by the crowd is not an exact quote of a particular verse. It is a summary of several passages, including Exodus 16:4, Nehemiah 9:15 and Psalm 78:24-25. Given the fact that some Jews viewed Moses as a king (see comment on 6:15), the questions in verse 31 would seem to be the crowd's way of seeking confirmation from Jesus that their interpretation of the miracle was correct. They are suggesting that Jesus should allow them to get on with the coronation.

Jesus' response (v. 32) follows a pattern familiar in rabbinic teaching styles (Borgen 1965:61-67). Jesus corrects what he understands to be their interpretation of the Scripture just cited. *He* who gave them bread was not *Moses* but *my Father,* and the giving of the *true bread* was not past *(has given)* but present *(gives).* The claims implied in these changes are astonishing. He is not claiming to be a giver of bread like Moses. Rather, he focuses their attention of the real giver, God. But he identifies God as *my Father,* thus making himself and his relationship with God the defining expression of God. Such an enormous claim is then backed up with the focus on the present: his Father is giving them bread. This bread is the *true bread from heaven* (v. 32), the real bread that is the source and standard of all else that can be called "bread from heaven." God is the one who always provides bread, but now in the person and ministry of Jesus, the Father is doing a unique work. Jesus is far more than the giver of bread like Moses was; he is the bread itself, as he is about to make clear.

This style of interpreting Scripture is very typical of the way Christians in the New Testament understand the Old Testament (see comment on 2:22). Jesus is the interpretive key. As the Word and Wisdom of God, he is the fount of all revelation to begin with. It all points to him and coheres in him. This way of interpreting Scripture differs from many modern forms of interpretation, but is not incompatible with them. Unless we interpret the Scriptures in the same way that the authors of the New Testament did, we will miss the great organic beauty of the revelation and its coherent truth.

expectation was present at the time of Jesus, the messianic views of the crowd would be all the clearer.

Jesus continues by explaining *(gar,* translated *for)* more about this bread his Father is giving them (v. 33). The language used here is subtle. It could refer to a person coming from heaven, as the NIV takes it: *he who comes down from heaven.* Or the reference could be more general: the bread of God is "that which" comes down from heaven. Jesus is, of course, referring to himself, as he makes clear in the next section. But the crowd hears it in the more general sense, and they say, *from now on give us this bread* (v. 34). The phrase *from now on* translates *pantote,* which simply means "always." The crowd wants an unending supply of this bread, perhaps like the Samaritan woman wanted a continuous supply of water so she would not have to go to the well again (4:15). Once the crowd realizes he is referring to himself, however, they become far less receptive (6:41)!

Jesus continues to correct their thinking about Moses and the bread as he explains that this bread of God *gives life to the world* (v. 33). The scope of God's concern is not just Israel, as it was in the wilderness, but the whole of the world (cf. 3:16). And the need is not just for sustenance, but for life itself. The world, apart from God, is dead. Our need is extreme and radical. We need a new birth (cf. 3:3), for apart from Christ we have no real life and are under God's wrath (cf. 3:36). By telling this Jewish crowd that the Father gives *you* this bread and then saying that it gives life *to the world,* Jesus includes this Jewish crowd in "the world." Salvation in Jesus does indeed come *from* the Jews (4:22), but it is also *for* the Jews. Recent "two-covenant theology," which asserts that God saves Jews through his covenant with them apart from Jesus the Christ, is not in accord with the truth as it is in Christ Jesus.

Jesus grants the crowd's request to receive this bread (vv. 35-40). This request for bread from heaven is met by a revelation similar to that received by the woman of Samaria: when she requested the water, Jesus responded by revealing himself to her. As always, Jesus' revelation of himself means a revelation of his relationship with the Father. Here the revelation of the relation of the Father and the Son is centered on the work of redemption, developing further what was revealed in the keynote address (5:19-30).

Jesus claims, *I am the bread of life* (v. 35). Seven times in John the phrase *I am* is used with a predicate, including the passages on bread of life (6:35, 51); the light of the world (8:12; 9:5); the gate (10:7, 9); the Good Shepherd (10:11, 14); the resurrection and the life (11:25); the way, the truth and the life (14:6); and the true vine (15:1, 5). "The predicate is not an essential definition or description of Jesus in himself; it is more a description of what he is in relation to man" (Brown 1966:534). In these sayings Jesus' own identity and the salvation he offers are brought together (cf. Witherington 1995:158). It is in union with him that believers receive his salvation.

He is claiming to be that which one needs in order to have life and continue to live. What he said earlier about the one sent from God (v. 29) and the bread coming down from heaven (v. 33) is now clearly identified with himself. Here is the revelation of the significance of the feeding of the five thousand: it was a sign of who Jesus is—the fount of life (5:26) who gives life (5:21).

Jesus as bread is a very rich image in which we can see connections with God's Word. We are not to "live on bread alone but on every word that comes from the mouth of the LORD" (Deut 8:3). The idea of the Torah as bread was common in Jewish thinking. At times it is combined with the Wisdom motif, as when Wisdom says, "Those who eat me will hunger for more, and those who drink me will thirst for more" (Sirach 24:21). This Wisdom is identified as "the book of the covenant of the Most High God, the law which Moses commanded us as an inheritance for the congregations of Jacob" (Sirach 24:23). Jesus' claim (Jn 6:35) thus makes his teaching superior to the Torah. Jesus later makes this point more explicit: "The words I have spoken to you are spirit and they are life" (6:63).

Jesus, the bread of life, promises, *He who comes to me will never go hungry, and he who believes in me will never be thirsty* (v. 35). He expands the promise he made to the Samaritan woman (4:10, 13-14), vowing to satisfy not just thirst but hunger. He makes this promise not privately to an individual, but openly to a crowd. What is required of us is that we come to him and believe. Jesus had chastised the Jewish opponents for refusing to come to him and receive life (5:40), but now he is talking to a crowd that has indeed come to him, even at the cost of some effort (6:22-25). So something more than coming to Jesus is needed, and that something more, as our verse indicates, is faith. But even this is not the whole story, since we have already seen people professing to believe in him who do not do so in truth (2:23-25).

What, then, is needed in order to come to Jesus and actually receive what he offers? In this central section of chapter 6 we have one of the major teachings on why some receive and some do not. There are two sides to this mystery—the divine and the human. On the human side, 6:35 says we need to come and believe, and later it is said we must hear and learn from the Father (v. 45). But behind the human is the divine (v. 45). Those who come and receive have been given to Jesus by his Father (v. 37); they have been drawn by the Father (v. 44). The divine will is fundamental, for "no one can come to me unless the Father has enabled him" (6:65; literally, "it is granted him by the Father").

Thus, the will of the Father is fundamental. Jesus has asserted this to be true in his own life (5:19), and he repeats this in 6:38. What is true for Jesus is also true for his disciples. It is God's gracious action in our lives that saves us from beginning to end. God's choice has been fundamental from the beginning, starting with the act of creation itself and continuing through the acts of redemption from the Fall through the call of Abraham, Jacob/Israel and so forth. The biblical teaching is not, however, mere determinism. For example, Jesus has chosen the Twelve, but one of them was "a devil" (Jn 6:70).

Along with the revelation of God's sovereignty is the revelation of his desire that all be saved (1 Tim 2:4). He is the savior of all, though only those who receive him benefit from that salvation (cf. 1 Tim 4:10). Indeed, we have one of the universal invitations in chapter 7: "If anyone is thirsty, let him come to me and drink" (Jn 7:37).

It is a mystery how salvation can be open to all yet dependent on the will of God. Several explanations have been offered over the centuries (cf. Browne 1998: 401-42), but they all seem to collapse one side of the mystery or the other. In practical terms, this dual teaching of Scripture leads us to two responses. The first is a life of praise and joy in the revelation of a gracious heavenly Father who is utterly good and completely for us. The second is a life of real effort, taking seriously our Lord's call to enter the narrow gate (Mt 7:13) and to persevere to the end (Mt 10:22; Mt 24:13 par. Mk 13:13 par. Lk 21:19). We heed the warnings in Hebrews about drifting, hardness of heart and rebellion

(Heb 2:1-4; 3:7—4:13; 5:11—6:20; 10:26-39; 12:14-29), and we obey the risen Lord's call in Revelation to be one who conquers (Rev 2—3).

These two responses are not separate from one another, because we can only do our part by relying on God's grace. We work out our salvation because he is at work within us "to will and to act according to his good purpose" (Phil 2:12-13). Without Christ abiding in us we can do nothing (Jn 15:5). All is of grace. It is not so much a matter of just living for him, but a matter of living from him as we abide in him.

After revealing the truth about himself Jesus proceeds to reveal to this crowd the truth about themselves: *But as I told you, you have seen me and still you do not believe* (v. 36). They saw his sign (v. 26), but it did not function as a sign for them. They saw him with their physical eyes, but they did not have the faith that sees the revelation of the Father in what Jesus was doing. Therefore, they do not qualify for the benefits Jesus has just spelled out (v. 35). By revealing their condition to them Jesus is exercising the judgment that is part of his job description (5:22). The light comes and reveals not only God's presence but also the state of the human heart.

Jesus goes on to explain why they do not believe. The Father is the God who wills salvation, and Jesus is the agent of that will (vv. 37-40). Jesus begins with God's grace, that is, his act of giving: *All that the Father gives me will come to me* (v. 37). We just heard of the Father as the one giving them true bread from heaven (v. 32), and now the Father gives disciples to Jesus (cf. 17:2, 6, 9, 24). We are the Father's gift to his Son (cf. Loyd 1936:89)! Again the Father is seen to be the source of all. In one sense believers come to the Father through the Son (cf. 14:6), but in another sense they were already the Father's before they became disciples of Jesus. At this point we are at the edge of a great mystery, peering into the ineffable realms of eternity. Here we have a clear affirmation of divine sovereignty. If this text were all we had in this Gospel on this topic, then we would be confronted with pure and simple determinism. We have already noted, however, that the teaching in John's Gospel is more complex than that.

This text also affirms that no one who is to come to the Son will fail to do so. Yet deeper comfort is conveyed when Jesus adds, *and whoever comes to me I will never drive away* (v. 37). The combination of *all* in the first part of the verse and *will never drive away* in the second part of the verse (very emphatic in the Greek; cf. Wallace 1996:468) has made this text the source of great comfort to many believers. Some, however, have misused it, as though a someone's one-time decision for Jesus guarantees a ticket into heaven, assuring salvation no matter how ungodly a life one then lives. We are not to sin that grace may abound (Rom 6:1)! Salvation is a matter of sharing in God's life through an intimate relationship with him. The one who has such a relationship will not live a life characterized by contempt and rebellion, even though we all have pockets of resistance as we live out the war between flesh and Spirit (Gal 5). Our assurance is not in our decision to follow Jesus, but in the graciousness and faithfulness of the Father and the Son who hold fast to those who are of God.

But how do I know whether or not I am one of those who are of God? Any number of people have been driven to despair by this question. The teaching of the Bible on assurance is many sided, but at the end of the day it comes down to trusting God for our salvation. Since we know he wills all to be saved we can be sure that we are included. The only way for that salvation to be effectual in a person's life is by God's grace. So we trust him for that grace, and we live our lives accordingly. In this way our assurance is complete because our confidence is entirely in him. Our job is to receive, trusting him for both the ability to receive and the obedience that is part of the life of salvation. The Christian life is both a resting in God and a supreme effort.

The reason Jesus will not drive away any that the Father gives him is because he has not come to do his own will but the will of him who sent him (v. 38). Jesus' complete obedience is fundamental to his relationship with the Father. In this he is the model of true discipleship.

He then expands further his message of assurance: *And this is the will of him who sent me, that I shall lose none of all that he has given me, but raise them up at the last day* (v. 39). Not only will he not drive them away, but nothing else will be able to tear them from him. The security is complete. As Paul says, nothing can separate us from the love of God (Rom 8:35-39). Neither an evil impulse from within God (as if such a thing existed) nor evil forces from within or without ourselves can thwart God's gracious gift of eternal life in the Son.

This gift is already experienced in this life, but is not for this life only. Jesus adds a reference to the believer's resurrection, another indication that Jesus is expanding on his keynote address (5:27-29). Jesus concludes this section by combining both the present and the future aspects of salvation: *For my Father's will is that everyone who looks to the Son and believes in him shall have eternal life, and I will raise him up at the last day* (v. 40). In this one statement the major themes of this section are brought together—the Father's will, human seeing and believing and the gift of eternal life.

Here is the antinomy of divine sovereignty and human responsibility. If we only had verse 40, then the teaching of this Gospel regarding salvation would be based in human decision. When we put the determinism of verse 37 alongside the decisionism of verse 40 we see the two parts of the antinomy, both of which are brought together in Jesus. Our response to him reveals the truth about ourselves in relation to God and thus whether or not we share in God's eternal life.

Jesus Challenges the Jews to Believe in Him (6:41-51) This crowd, now called *the Jews* (v. 41), fails to respond with faith in Jesus. Jesus does not reject them, but he challenges them to stop grumbling and believe in him. He repeats his claims but now clearly refers to himself as the *bread of life* (v. 48). He also continues his teaching about the divine will, clarifying the relation between the will of the Father and the human response of faith. This section of his dialogue concludes with Jesus' deepening the scandal by saying that this bread is his flesh.

The description of the people grumbling recalls the response the children of Israel in the wilderness had to the Lord's salvation (Ex 15—17; Num 14—17; 21:4-5; Deut 1:27; Ps 106:25; Sirach 46:7). Now they grumble because of Jesus' claim to be the bread of life. As with Nathaniel (1:46), their problem is with where Jesus is from. They know Joseph and Jesus' mother (6:42), and they judge Jesus' claims on the basis of what they think they already know. It seems they believe that a being who has come from heaven would not have earthly parents. This helps highlight the central claim Jesus is making, his divine origin (6:33, 38, 41, 50-51, 58), and also the fact that the divine has come amongst us within humanity. Here, in the incarnation, is the supreme example of matter as spirit-bearing.

Jesus calls upon them to stop grumbling (v. 43), to not repeat the pattern of their ancestors but instead to respond in faith. It is, in effect, a call to repent. But the only way they could stop grumbling would be to become receptive of his teaching about himself. This they are incapable of doing.

Jesus says that by their response they are judging themselves. Their rejection of him reveals their relationship with God, for *no one can come to me unless the Father who sent me draws him* (v. 43). In putting it this way Jesus indicates that he and the believer have the same origin, the Father. The Father sent the Son and the Father draws the believer. Earlier he said *all that the Father gives me will come to me* (v. 37). Now he restates that teaching from the point of view of his Father's work in the believer.

By repeating his promise to raise the believer *at the last day* (v. 44; cf. v. 39) Jesus is claiming to be the one who fulfills the promises of resurrection in the age to come. This future hope is combined in this discourse with a present fulfillment, for Jesus will shortly say that those who eat the bread of heaven will not die but will live forever (vv. 50-51).

Jesus confirms and explains his teaching about the role of the Father with a quote from Isaiah 54:13—*It is written in the Prophets: "They will all be taught by God"* (v. 45). Isaiah 54 speaks of God's future restoration of Jerusalem to intimacy with himself. By applying this text to his own ministry, Jesus is claiming that the eschatological blessings of the last day are already being experienced in his ministry; God's promise to Jerusalem is being fulfilled now. Those who know Jesus' real identity understand how this is so, for they realize that those hearing Jesus are themselves being taught by God! But the point Jesus makes is different. He is explaining the way the Father draws people. He does so by teaching, as the rest of the verse makes clear: *Everyone who listens to the Father and learns from him comes to me.* To listen and to learn require humility, a key characteristic of disciples in this Gospel. The one who listens to God and learns will be taught by God and be drawn to Jesus, for Jesus is the one who speaks God's word and manifests his presence. Here we have a very profound reflection on the mystery of the roles of the divine and the human in a person's coming to faith.

Indeed, faith itself includes receptive openness to God. Thus, the drawing by God and the reception of the person are intimately interwoven (cf. Bultmann 1971:231-32).

Jesus' claim that *everyone* who listens and learns from God will come to him is both a comfort and a challenge. It is comforting because it says no one who is really open to God will be left out. But it is also a challenge because it is another one of Jesus' claims to unique, supreme authority. God has indeed not left himself without a witness. General revelation has made something of the truth about himself known, and certainly the Scriptures have done so more clearly. But all such knowledge of God is partial and finds its fulfillment and point of reference in Jesus. All revelation before or outside of Jesus leads one to come to him. When a Jew or Muslim or Buddhist or other religious person who has really learned from God sees Jesus in truth (not as he is too often revealed by Christians' poor witness) they will recognize in him the fullness of what they have already learned. Thus, we once again find in this Gospel the scandal of the Christian claims of Jesus' exclusive supremacy.

Jesus' supreme authority is further established in the next verse when he explains that *no one has seen the Father except the one who is from God; only he has seen the Father* (v. 46). Jesus' shift from hearing God to seeing him is probably significant. The Old Testament is saturated with references to people who have heard God, but it is more ambiguous about those who have received a vision of God (see comment on 1:18). The emphasis in this Gospel is that no one has seen God (1:18; 5:37; cf. 1 Jn 4:12), yet those who have seen Jesus have seen the Father (14:8-9). Thus, John again denies the claims of the mystics (cf. comments on 1:18 and 3:13). So the exalted claims about Jesus are matched by the claims John makes for the believers. He claims they have eternal life (v. 47), which goes beyond what the rabbis or the mystics claimed for themselves. The believer not only encounters God but actually comes to share in his life, a thought that will be developed in the Jesus' farewell discourse (13:31—17:26).

Jesus now concludes this section of his teaching by returning to the story of God's provision of manna in the wilderness (vv. 48-50; cf. vv. 32-35). He repeats his claim to be the bread of life and draws out the significance of the word *life*. This bread he speaks of is a food that keeps one from dying, in contrast to the manna eaten by the wilderness generation, who nevertheless died. Obviously, any food keeps one from dying for a period of time; it sustains life. Jesus, however, is talking about food that is much more powerful than regular food, for the one who eats this bread *will live forever* (v. 51). It is God's own life that is shared through this bread.

What sort of bread could give eternal life? Jesus' teaching comes to a head as he declares, *This bread is my flesh, which I will give for the life of the world* (v. 51). The Word that became flesh (1:14) now says he will give his flesh for the life of the world, so that the world may have life. Giving of life to the world (v. 33) requires that he give his flesh. This giving is in the future, so it refers to more than his teaching. It is also on behalf of *(hyper)* the life of the world, which suggests sacrifice (see comment on 10:11). Christ's death is indeed a sacrifice on behalf of his flock (10:11, 15), the Jewish people (11:50-51), the nations (11:52) and his disciples (17:19; cf. Beasley-Murray 1987:94).

This crowd has now received the interpretation of the sign as they had requested (6:30). Earlier the Jews had asked for a sign to legitimate Jesus' action in the temple, and he had spoken of the temple of his body and of his death and resurrection (2:18-21). Now this crowd has received teaching about the manna of his flesh and about how the divine gift of eternal life will be given through the Messiah's death. Here is a cryptic saying indeed! His reference to his flesh only heightens the scandal, as we see in the next scene.

Jesus Deepens the Scandal: Eat My Flesh, Drink My Blood (6:52-59) When Jesus mentions his flesh, the tension in the crowd increases. The people are not just grumbling (v. 41); they are arguing sharply with one another (v. 52). Once again we see people who come to Jesus as a rabbi, who even wanted to make him king, but who are far from treating him as either a king or a rabbi. They are not receiving his teaching, as cryptic and offensive as it is. Like Nicodemus, they can

---

6:51 The use of *flesh* in John instead of "body" as in Paul and the Synoptics may actually go back to the Aramaic original that Jesus used at the Last Supper. It may be reflected also in the writings of Ignatius of Antioch (*Letter to the Romans* 7.3; *Letter to the Philadelphians* 4.1; *Letter to the Smyrneans* 7.1) very early in the second century (cf. Brown 1966:285).
6:55 Francis J. Moloney (1998:198, 223) notes other possible echoes of the Eucharist,

only ask how such a thing can be (v. 52; cf. 3:9). "When questioning concerning the 'how' comes in, there comes in with it unbelief" (Chrysostom *In John* 46.2). And Jesus does not make it easy for them. He now makes sure they get the point that real eating and drinking are involved. As he deepens the offense in these verses, he also explains in a very profound way the eternal life he is offering.

Jesus begins by revealing more sharply our need of the life he offers: *I tell you the truth, unless you eat the flesh of the Son of Man and drink his blood, you have no life in you* (v. 53). He claims that the life he is talking about is not merely some optional gift that we can afford to ignore. Apart from the life he offers, we are dead. Here is a claim as demanding as are his earlier claims about his own identity and what he offers to those who believe in him (vv. 30-51). Our utter neediness is seen clearly when set against the greatness of his offer: *Whoever eats my flesh and drinks my blood has eternal life, and I will raise him up at the last day* (v. 54). Jesus is promising a new quality of life now and resurrection in the future.

He says, *my flesh is real food and my blood is real drink* (v. 55). What does *real* mean here? C. K. Barrett captures part of what Jesus is saying when he explains, "My flesh and blood really are what food and drink should be, they fulfill the ideal, archetypal function of food and drink" (1978:299). This insight is confirmed by what follows: *Whoever eats my flesh and drinks my blood remains in me, and I in him* (v. 56). The eating and the drinking has to do with shared life, mutual indwelling. In the physical realm one of the most powerful examples of shared life is eating and drinking—the laying down of life by a plant or animal and the interpenetration of life as molecules are transferred, thereby nourishing life. So once again Jesus' mystifying words are referring to something that could not be understood until after his death, resurrection and ascension and the coming of the Spirit. His death will be the ultimate laying down of life; his resurrection, ascension and sending the Spirit bring onto the human scene the new possibility of actually sharing in

---

including the language for gathering the fragments (*synagō ta klasmata*, vv. 12-13; cf. *Didache* 9.3-4; Clement of Rome *1 Clement* 34.7; Ignatius of Antioch *Letter to Polycarp* 4.2), the promise of "food that endures to eternal life" (v. 27) and the reference to food that satisfies all hunger and thirst (v. 35).

the life of God (cf. 17:21-23) as he, the incarnate one, has shared in our life.

The ultimate source of our life is the Father, as Jesus next explains: *Just as the living Father sent me and I live because of the Father, so the one who feeds on me will live because of me* (v. 57). Our union with the Son enables us to share his life, just as he in turn lives because of the Father. Once again we find the full explanation of who Jesus is and of what he offers when we understand his relationship with the Father. There is an ordering in this relationship, a clear hierarchy, for the Father is the source of all. Our life is entirely dependent on Jesus, as is his on the Father (cf. chaps. 13—17).

In this section, therefore, Jesus is speaking of his death and the shared life that his death will make possible. The language of eating and drinking "appear to be a very graphic way of saying that men must take Christ into their innermost being" (Morris 1971:378). There may also be an allusion to martyrdom, to sharing in the way of the cross (Michaels 1989:116), for "there can be no participation in the life of God except by an equally concrete factual participation in the self-surrender of Jesus" (Newbigin 1982:86). More controversial is whether there is reference here also to the Eucharist.

There are several hints in the text that Jesus is referring to the sacrament here. First, the image of drinking Christ's blood (6:53) does not correspond to the starting point, namely, to the feeding of the five thousand and the manna in the wilderness. Jesus started with the simple image of bread, and now he brings in the idea of blood and drink. Drinking blood is not a natural image for receiving his revelation, though it might be suggestive of receiving his life, since "the life of every creature is its blood" (Lev 17:14; Deut 12:23). But it is a very scandalous image for a Jew since drinking any blood, let alone human blood, was forbidden by the law (Lev 3:17; 17:14; Deut 12:23). Second, although the reference to "real" food and drink (6:55) means this eating and drinking "fulfill the ideal, archetypal function of food and drink" (Barrett

---

6:57 In light of later controversies I should note that in my view this passage supports neither transubstantiation (the view that the bread and wine become in the Eucharist that body and blood of Jesus which was born of Mary and crucified on Calvary) nor memorialism

1978:299), it does not mean that this eating and drinking are something other than actual eating and drinking. This is archetypal, "real" *(alēthēs)* food and drink, just as Nathaniel was "really" *(alēthōs)*, archetypically, an Israelite (1:47). Being archetypal did not mean Nathaniel was not also an actual Israelite, nor would the flesh and blood's being archetypal food and drink necessarily mean they are not also actual food and drink. If there is a reference here to actual food and drink, then it must refer somehow to the Eucharist since there is nothing else to which it would correspond. We know from the Synoptics and Paul that Jesus commanded us to observe this rite and that Christians did indeed do so. Christians then, as now, naturally find reference here to the Eucharist unless controversies lead them to find some other explanation.

A third hint is found in the occurrence of the verb form of *Eucharist (eucharisteō)* earlier in this story (6:11, 23). This may be significant since it is rather superfluous in verse 23. Fourth, the wording of verse 53 follows the pattern given in the Synoptic account of the institution of the Eucharist; for example, Matthew 26:26-28 reads, "Take and eat; this is my body. . . . Drink. . . . This is my blood" (cf. Brown 1966:284-85). A fifth hint is the word used for *eats* in 6:54. Instead of *esthiō,* which is used elsewhere in this chapter (6:5, 23, 26, 31, 49-53, 58), John uses *trōgō* (also in 6:56-58). While *esthiō* is often used metaphorically, *trōgō* is not; it is a word tied almost entirely to the physical process of eating food.

If there is indeed reference here to the Eucharist, a number of questions are raised, and we must be careful not to read into this text all of the later controversies and refinements. The most obvious point of the text would be that there is some connection between partaking of Christ's flesh and blood in the Eucharist and having eternal life. This would be puzzling, since it appears to put this activity on the level of faith. Both faith and this eating and drinking would be necessary for eternal life (6:47, 51). Apparently, it is not for nothing that our Lord commands us to hold Eucharist (1 Cor 11:25)!

This parallel between faith and Eucharist does not, however, deny

(the view that the bread and wine are only symbols or signs). Rather, the bread and wine are efficacious signs through which we encounter the real spiritual presence of Christ and the life he offers (cf. Browne 1998:583-609, 683-731).

the primacy of faith. If both are necessary for life, faith is still the more primary in that it is necessary for obtaining the benefits of the Eucharist. God's life is available in the Eucharist because he promises to be present. We do not attract him there or make him present by our faith. He is present where people gather for Eucharist at his command. But if we do not appropriate it rightly by faith, it may do us no good or even cause harm (cf. 1 Cor 10:1-22; 11:27-30). The actual life-giving efficacy in feeding is only appropriated by faith—the Eucharist is not magically efficacious. The Eucharist is a point of contact with divine reality; it is a means of grace, a means of God's power and life in our lives. But it is not a way to manipulate God, nor does it make this spiritual contact by magic, apart from God's own gracious activity and a person's response of faith.

To say the Eucharist is necessary for eternal life is not necessarily as scandalous as it might seem at first. In the strictest sense of the word, very little is absolutely *essential,* as the thief on the cross demonstrates: all he had was faith in Jesus as the King of the Jews and a desire to be with him. Jesus here is talking about that which is generally necessary. "The sacrament is normally necessary; but it is the communion alone that is vital" (Temple 1945:95); abiding in him on the basis of his sacrificial death is what is essential. In a sense, the necessity of the Eucharist would be similar to saying one must be a member of the church. Here also we could get embroiled in controversies. But suffice it to say, the church in the New Testament is the locus of divine life, the very body of Christ. Eucharist is one of the central features of church life, and it actually effects our oneness, according to Paul (1 Cor 10:16-17). It is an occasion on the social level that feeds the spiritual life by getting in touch with the divine love of God manifest in the divine self-giving on the cross. The New Testament knows nothing of a Christianity apart from the church. The New Testament is very concrete. It points to this man Jesus and says he is the Son of God. And it points to this community and says, Here is the body of Christ, the center of divine life on earth in its fullest expression. The necessity of the Eucharist is a part of the necessity of the church. It is a part of God's dealing with us as material and relational beings.

Here, then, is some of the deepest New Testament teaching about the Eucharist. The focus of this teaching is on sacrifice and shared life. These are inseparable since there is no sharing of life without the laying down of life. The once-for-all sacrifice of Christ is the pouring out of his life for the life of the world, bringing forgiveness and a new power of life. That sacrifice also shows us the deepest reality about God—his love—and about life: all true life is sacrificial. Life is a matter of exchange: my life for yours, yours for mine. In this sacrificial web of exchange we find the communion, the community, of the Godhead. At Eucharist we receive into ourselves, into our bodies and souls, the life-giving power of God, and precisely by eating and drinking we proclaim the Lord's once-for-all death until he comes (1 Cor 11:26).

The insistence on the Eucharist, this physical activity for eternal life, is theologically and spiritually very important. It protects us from an overly cerebral or falsely spiritual form of Christianity. Salvation itself is something that encompasses all of life. It is a transformation of life and a renewal of life, including physical life. Salvation is not simply a matter of having right opinions or even right actions. Indeed, it is something larger than the human dimension, since all of creation is involved (Rom 8). John teaches us not to simply embrace spirit and oppose matter like the Gnostics did. The incarnate one in his very incarnation has shown physical matter to be "spiritual," that is, to share in divine life. Our bodies themselves are to be transformed. So the imagery involved in eating and drinking, in notions of laying down life and interpenetration, is present in this passage and in the Eucharist itself. But more than mere imagery is present—eternal life is present. The divine and human realms meet in the flesh of Jesus, and that is what a sacrament is: a material point of contact between physical and spiritual reality. Jesus' own body is the convergence of these realms, and he provides points of contact for the nourishment of his body, the church. This passage is referring to Christ's death and our life in him, as is the Eucharist. So it is fitting that the Eucharist is alluded to here, though the primary reference is to Jesus' death and the life he offers.

Obviously, this teaching is especially unclear to these people. They do not understand Jesus' identity, nor do they catch the allusion to his death, let alone the way the Lord will provide for his followers to eat his flesh and drink his blood. This cryptic, scandalous teaching took place openly in Capernaum in the synagogue (6:59), which is the place where the Torah is expounded. In the Capernaum synagogue on this particular day the eternal Word himself is giving the manna of a greater revelation.

□ Jesus Experiences Rejection by His Disciples (6:60-71)

Having recounted the controversy among the Jews over Jesus' claim to be the bread of life (6:52), John now says this controversy divided Jesus' own followers as well. Jesus responds to the people by confronting them with the implications of their reaction, and then he presses the Twelve for their response. He certainly does not change his message or try to make it more "user-friendly." In Jesus' statements and in Peter's confession we learn more about Jesus and what it takes to truly be his disciple.

This section is in two parts, verses 60-65 and verses 66-71. Each part begins with the response of *many of his disciples* (vv. 60, 66), which is then followed by a statement regarding Jesus' identity and his teaching made first by Jesus himself (vv. 61-65) and then by Peter (vv. 67-69). Each part includes a statement by Jesus about his betrayer (vv. 64-65, 70-71).

What is the relationship between being in the church and being, in fact, a Christian? This question has exercised the church from the beginning, as it did Judaism before. The issue arose in Jesus' own ministry, for these people who have difficulty with Jesus' teaching and who end up turning away from him are called *his disciples* (vv. 60, 66). They were disciples in the sense of having come to Jesus and heard his teaching. But this level of discipleship would not count for much in the end. The soil in their hearts was not such that Jesus' seed could take root and produce fruit.

The question they raise reveals their real problem: *This is a hard teaching. Who can accept it?* (v. 60). This is a profound question that points to their own hearts. By saying *Who can accept it?* they suggest they are not to blame, that this is too much for anyone to accept. But in fact it shows that they are not humbly docile, as true disciples in this

---

6:62 The reference to the Son of Man ascending speaks clearly of the "unchanged person-

Gospel are. A mark of docility is the ability and willingness to listen and receive. In this Gospel one's identity is known by whom one can and does listen to (6:45; 8:43, 47; 10:3-5, 16, 27; 12:48; 18:37). Their question—which is rendered more literally as Who can hear *(akouō)* it?—alludes to this theme. By saying they are unable to hear or to listen to Jesus' teaching they stand self-condemned.

They are grumbling like the others had done earlier in the chapter and like Israel had done in the wilderness. Instead of cutting them slack, Jesus confronts them with their response by asking, *Does this offend you?* (v. 61). Here we see the light revealing the darkness. Their offense is the opposite of faith, and Jesus makes sure they realize what they are saying. This question searches the soul of each of us. Do we find any of Jesus' teachings offensive? What causes us to falter? There is much in Jesus' teaching to scandalize each of us. But those who are born from above, those who have faith, trust in Jesus even when his teachings or his ways are puzzling.

In fact, none of Jesus' teaching makes sense unless we realize who he really is. He says as much in the verses that follow about the Son of Man (v. 62), yet he is speaking very cryptically when he refers to the ascension of the Son of Man *to where he was before*. A reference to preexistence, mingled with associations from Daniel 7, would be very hard to grasp. The one standing before them was claiming to be a person beyond their imagination. The strangeness of his reference to eating his flesh and drinking his blood is matched by the claims he is making about himself. In a sense he is saying, "You haven't seen anything yet. There will be plenty more to come that will be offensive to fallen human reason." For the ascent of the Son of Man to where he was before begins with the cross (cf. 3:14), the ultimate source of offense. If they are offended by this talk about eating his flesh and drinking his blood, how will they be able to tolerate the cross, which lies behind Jesus' talk of giving his flesh and blood?

Jesus continues his diagnosis of the problem by returning to the twin themes developed earlier in the chapter, the themes of divine sover-

---

ality of Christ" (Westcott 1908:1:248); that is, the earthly and the heavenly Christ are one and the same.

eignty and human responsibility. He interweaves these themes by speaking first of the need for the Spirit (v. 63), then of the need for faith (v. 64) and then of the Father's decisive action (v. 65). The need for the Spirit was already developed in the conversation with Nicodemus (3:3-8). By identifying the Spirit as the one who *gives life* (v. 63), he provides the foundation for what was said earlier about the necessity of being "born of the Spirit" (3:8).

The life Jesus is talking about is God's own eternal life, which can only come from God himself. He must give the Bread of Life or else the world will remain in death. Human nature in itself apart from God, here called the *flesh,* is completely incapable of generating such life. Just as God had to breathe into Adam's nostrils in order for his dead flesh to become a living being (Gen 2:7), so must we receive the Spirit of God if we are to become alive with the life God offers us. The Spirit's role in bringing life both physically and spiritually was known in the Old Testament (for example, Job 34:14-15; Ps 104:29-30; Ezek 37; see Bultmann 1971:446 n. 2), but we learn that the Son also has a role; he receives authority from the Father and "gives life to whom he is pleased to give it" (5:21). Here Jesus says, *The words I have spoken to you are spirit and they are life* (6:63). The teaching they have found offensive is actually that which could convey to them the truth regarding the Father and the Son, and to know the Father and Son is to have eternal life (17:3). Jesus' words are not just human teaching, but the teachings of the divine agent from God (3:34; see note on 5:21). They are words of power like the divine speech that created the heavens and the earth (Gen 1:1; Ps. 33:6; 2 Pet 3:5). Keeping Jesus' word enables one to "never see death" (Jn 8:51).

Thus, the word of Jesus is parallel to the flesh and blood he offers. Both are vehicles of his life for they enable one to be united with Jesus and to abide in him who is himself the life. The required response to this divine initiative is faith, and some of his disciples lack this faith (v.

6:63 *Flesh* in this verse *counts for nothing* whereas in verses 51-58 *flesh* counts for much—it conveys eternal life and mutual abiding in Christ. The referent for the word, therefore, must be different in the two passages. Raymond Brown (1966:299-303), among others, has argued that verses 51-58 are a later insertion. While these verses may be a later addition, there is no compelling reason that would require them to be so. The passage makes sense as it stands.

64). This does not surprise Jesus, for *Jesus had known from the begin-ning which of them did not believe* (v. 64), but this lack of faith had not been evident up to this point. Now Jesus' scandalous teaching has brought it out into the open, and therefore he is revealing their own condition to them. The light continues to expose the darkness. There is also the foreshadowing of further rejection, as he refers to the one who will betray him. The lack of belief among those who called themselves his disciples is here seen to be in fact a form of betrayal.

God knows the condition of our hearts and sends circumstances that will reveal our hearts to us. How do we respond to such exposure? Does it drive us to despair or to deeper dependency upon the Lord? For those whose trust is in God alone, even the exposure of their lack of faith can be an occasion of deeper faith. We are not saved by faith, but by the one in whom we have faith, whom we may trust to increase our faith through a deeper experience of himself as we, by his grace, live in obedience to what we have received from him.

Jesus concludes by returning to the role of the Father. No one comes to Jesus *unless the Father has enabled him* (v. 65; cf. 6:37, 45). A more literal translation captures better the element of grace here: "unless it has been given to him from the Father." Again we see the Father as the source of all. In this passage the role of the Father, the foreknowledge of Jesus and the life-giving role of both the Spirit and Jesus are all coordinated as an antinomy to the role of the believer's faith.

Jesus has challenged the people who are offended. In saying *there are some of you who do not believe* (v. 64) he implies that there are also some who do believe. He is not condemning the whole group. They have to decide for themselves what their reaction will be, and John tells us next that *from this time many of his disciples turned back and no longer followed him* (v. 66). So Jesus issues another challenging question, this time to the Twelve: *You do not want to leave too, do you?* (v. 67). This question tests the heart, like the earlier one did (v. 61). What do

---

6:67 This is the first reference to the Twelve in this Gospel (cf. 6:70-71; 20:24). References in the Synoptics are more frequent (eight in Matthew; ten in Mark; seven in Luke), but the main difference in John's account is that he does not recount the calling of the Twelve, nor does he have Jesus' saying that they would sit on twelve thrones judging the twelve tribes of Israel (Mt 19:28; Lk 22:30). John seems to assume his readers are familiar with the existence of the Twelve, an indication he is writing for Christian readers.

they want *(thelō)?* They must make a choice then and there. Since Jesus knows people's interior dispositions (v. 64; cf. 2:25), he would know of their faith, so his question tests their hearts and reveals their response to themselves and to one another.

Simon Peter responds on behalf of the Twelve: *Lord, to whom shall we go? You have the words of eternal life* (v. 68). The others had been offended by Jesus' words, but the Twelve accept Jesus' claim that his words are spirit and life (v. 63). They do not claim to have understood what Jesus' has been saying. They will not be able to understand until after the crucifixion has taken place and the Spirit has guided them into all truth regarding Jesus and all that he has done and taught (14:26; 15:26; 16:13). But they do recognize that Jesus is speaking from God: *We believe and know that you are the Holy One of God* (v. 68). The verbs translated *believe* and *know* are in the perfect tense, which often suggests a state that began in the past and continues to the present. This nuance fits this context, since Peter stands in contrast to those who, although attracted to Jesus by the feeding miracle, were immediately scandalized. The Twelve came to faith in Jesus some time ago and have hung in with him since then, including through this most recent challenge to their faith by his strange teaching.

The Holy One of God may have been a messianic title, but there is no evidence for such a use. It expresses Jesus' nearness to God, who is the Holy One of Israel. This Old Testament title signifies that God is set apart from all others. It is used often in Isaiah to refer to the one who makes and redeems Israel. In Jesus we see the one whom the "Holy Father" (17:11) has "set apart" (10:36). The Twelve recognize the one who is set apart and who is redeeming Israel by offering eternal life—redemption indeed!

Jesus does not address Peter's confession (contrast Mt 16:17-20). They might have expected a pat on the back or some confirmation, but instead Jesus says it is he who has chosen them, not the other way around (v. 70; cf. Jn 15:16). The divine initiative has been discussed throughout this chapter, and it is now coordinated with Jesus' choice (cf. Mt 11:25, 27).

6:69 Many note that the meanings of *believe* and *know* are very similar in John, with the significant exception being that Jesus is often said to know God but never to believe in

But disturbing questions are raised, for Jesus goes on immediately and adds, *Yet one of you is a devil!* (v. 70). Not only were *his disciples* (vv. 60, 66) a mixed lot, so were the twelve he himself had chosen! One of them would betray him to his death, thus acting in accordance with Satan, who was "a murderer from the beginning" (Jn 8:44). Indeed, he will be under Satan's supervision (Jn 13:2, 27). The presence of Judas among the Twelve shows us that no group is entirely pure, just as Nicodemus's presence among the Pharisees indicates that no group is entirely alienated from God. John's dualistic language is very stark, but he realizes the ambiguities of life.

This passage also speaks of human responsibility. In a chapter that so strongly affirms the necessity of divine initiative, here we have another note regarding the importance of faith. Even Jesus' choice for someone to be a member of his inner circle of disciples is not going to save that person unless one has faith. We are not saved by faith, but neither are we saved without it. Judas had the most intimate access to Jesus; he had one of the best seats in the house for seeing God revealed in the flesh. But he lacked humble trust and love for Jesus as Jesus actually was. This thought is very sobering in light of much false optimism among Christians today. The human heart is capable of seeing God in his great beauty and of rejecting him. Indeed, all of us are capable of such betrayal, as our sin testifies. What is our inner disposition? Have we found in Jesus the Holy One of God who has the words of eternal life? Do we actually live our lives as those who believe this truth? Have we met God in such a way that we can trust his character even when we do not understand his words and deeds?

□ The Conflict Intensifies at the Feast of Tabernacles (7:1—8:59)

Jesus has clearly revealed his identity, causing deep offense to both the opponents (5:16-18) and his own disciples (6:66). Now he increases the controversy by revealing himself yet more clearly. The central motif in chapters 7 and 8 is Jesus' role as a prophet and as something much more than a prophet. He is the dispenser of living water (7:38),

---

him (Brown 1966:298; Carson 1991:303). There may be an order to the words since faith is necessary in order to have personal knowledge of God.

he is the light of the world (8:12), and he is the I AM (8:58). As his claims become clearer the rift between himself and the Jewish leaders grows.

This revelation takes place during the Feast of Tabernacles, a week-long feast in September or early October. This feast was given in thanksgiving for God's gracious provision for Israel, both in the past and in the present. God's graciousness in the present is seen in the harvest that has just occurred at this time of year (Deut 16:13-15). His past blessing is his provision during the wilderness wanderings (Lev 23:39-43). By recalling the wilderness pilgrimage while thanking God for the blessings of the land, participants realized their profound dependence upon God for provision. The feast's emphasis on God's provision fits perfectly with the teaching Jesus has just given, in which he revealed himself as the bread of life, and with the revelation in this chapter of himself as one who gives living water. He is the one who provides nourishment for eternal life even during the present time of our pilgrimage.

Even the details of the feast correspond to Jesus' activity and teaching during the feast. The Jews lived in huts during the feast to commemorate how the Israelites lived in tents in the wilderness. In these chapters Jesus is depicted as a pilgrim, through the many references to where he is from and where he is going. Another feature of the feast was a series of water libations each morning in the temple, commemorating the provision of water in the wilderness. This provides a striking setting for Jesus' great invitation to come to him to drink (7:37-38). Similarly, Jesus' proclamation that he is the light of the world (8:12) was made in the part of the temple where the feast's lamp-lighting ceremonies took place, ceremonies that commemorated the pillar of fire during the wilderness wanderings. Thus, Jesus is revealed as the fulfillment of the major themes of this feast. The very God to whom they are giving thanks in this wonderful feast has come into their midst (8:58).

These chapters depict the sharp give and take of debate between Jesus and various people and provide a detailed picture of the confusion and controversy his revelation has aroused among the people. The people are confused, and the opponents' hostility now turns violent. There are eleven references to death threats and attempts to arrest Jesus

(7:1, 13, 19, 25, 30, 32, 44; 8:20, 37, 40, 59). Thus, the low point reached at the end of chapter 6 gets even lower. The opponents' increased hostility leads Jesus to state clearly that they are alienated from God, and Jesus' clearest statement about their identity as people alienated from God is spoken at the same time that Jesus makes one of his clearest claims regarding his own relationship with God (8:31-59). In this way, the end of chapter 8 is the theological center of the controversy in this Gospel. It also marks a break between Jesus and the temple (8:59).

Jesus Goes Up to the Feast in God's Way (7:1-13) It appears Jesus' movement is falling apart. Many disciples have left Jesus (6:66), his betrayal is in view (6:71), and he has to lay low in Galilee because of death threats in Judea (7:1). Jesus' brothers give him some family advice: he should go back to Judea and do some miracles *so that your disciples may see the miracles you do* (7:3). Apparently, when his disciples left him they went to Judea. Maybe if Jesus did another sign they would give him a second chance. If Jesus wants to be a public figure, he should show himself to the world (7:4). This might look like a great statement of faith by Jesus' brothers, but John sets us straight: *For even his own brothers did not believe in him* (7:5). Recognizing that Jesus is a miracle worker does not make one a believer. Rather, here the world is offering the Son of God some marketing strategies. They assume he wants to be in the limelight and will do what is necessary to gain a following. In this they echo Satan's temptation (Mt 4:1-11 par. Lk 4:1-13). But Jesus rejects their suggestion just as he rejected the earlier attempt by some to make him king (6:15). Jesus' aim is not to gain a following but to reveal his Father by being faithful and obedient to him. Jesus does not need suggestions from others, even those closest to him in his family.

Jesus contrasts himself with his brothers, saying they are part of the world and alienated from God (7:6-8): *The right time* [*hōra,* "hour"] *for me has not yet come; for you any time [hōra] is right* (v. 6). Jesus will indeed go to Judea to perform a great work—his death. But it is not yet time for him to die. Jesus has not come to do his own will, he has come to do the will of his Father (6:38), and thus his schedule is determined by God. However, by saying any time is right for his brothers he is saying they are not under the Father's guidance. The problem with their *time* is precisely that it is theirs and not God's. Rather than being of God they are of the world (7:7); that is, they are among those who are alienated from God.

Jesus says the world hates him *because I testify that what it does is evil* (7:7). Jesus testifies like the prophets of old did, an association important later in this chapter (7:40, 52). He reveals that many of those who appear godly are in fact alienated from God (see comment on 3:19-21). Evil is understood as that which is not of the Father. Jesus' statement to his brothers is an example of his testimony to the world's evil, for he reveals that their apparent faith is, in fact, not faith at all. The world hates him, for it does not want its evil exposed by the light (3:20; 8:12). Therefore this rejection of Jesus, emphasized by John (*even his own brothers did not believe in him,* v. 5), itself bears witness to his identity as the revealer of the Father, as the light who has come into the world.

Jesus says he is not going to the feast *because for me the right time has not yet come* (7:8). When he made the statement to them he had only their word that he should go, and he rejects them as a source of guidance. The fact that he does actually go to the feast suggests that he received instructions from the Father to go after he spoke to his brothers. Such apparent inconsistency is a common feature in the lives of believers who are sensitive to the Lord's leading. "There never was a more inconsistent Being on this earth than Our Lord, but He was never inconsistent to His Father. The one consistency of the saint is not to a principle, but to the Divine life" (Chambers 1935:319, Nov. 14; cf. 184, July 2).

There are some important similarities between this story and the wedding in Cana, where Jesus' mother had requested something but his hour had not yet come (2:1-11). In both cases Jesus goes on to do what his relatives had suggested, but he does so on his own terms. These two stories emphasize Jesus' loyalty to his heavenly Father's will. Not even those closest to Jesus in human terms—his mother and brothers—could influence him. He must be entirely open and obedient to God. Here we

_____

7:8 As the NIV notes, some very early manuscripts ($\mathbf{p}^{66,75}$) read "not yet" *(oupō)* rather

see again Jesus as the model of discipleship (cf. Mt 12:50).

The conclusion to this opening section introduces the dynamics of what is about to unfold at the feast. Jesus went to the feast *not publicly, but in secret* (7:10), and he leaves the same way (8:59). Jesus' secret arrival and departure are part of the theme in these chapters of where Jesus is from and where he is going (7:27-29, 34-36, 41-42, 52; 8:14, 21-23, 42). This motif is very significant theologically, for Jesus is from and is going to the Father.

John continues by giving a very skillful depiction of the situation. The Jews are on the lookout for "that guy" (*ekeinos,* v. 11). The people are afraid to talk about Jesus publicly because of the authorities (v. 13), but in private they debate with one another (v. 12). Some say Jesus is a good man, and others say he is a deceiver (vv. 12-13). The accusation that Jesus is a deceiver is a very serious charge, and it continued on in the polemic later between Jews and Christians (for example, Justin Martyr *Dialogue with Trypho the Jew* 69, 108; *b. Sanhedrin* 43a; 107a; *b. Sota* 47a). Labeling Jesus as a deceiver is probably like charging him with being a false prophet who should be put to death for leading Israel astray in her relationship with God (Deut 13:1-11). Hence John notes the threats against his life (7:1,19, 25; 8:37, 40), which culminate in an actual attempt to kill him by stoning (8:59).

The Jewish leaders understand the enormity of Jesus' claims and the foundational issues he raises. Their reaction is justified if Jesus' claims are indeed false. If Jesus' claims are not true, then he is not a harmless teacher who can be tolerated or ignored. In our pluralistic society we have lost the sense of significance regarding religious views. While we need not return to stoning false prophets, believers should have a sense of urgency in opposing false teaching. Jesus and his opponents cannot both be correct, and the choosing between them has eternal consequences. If Jesus is Lord, then he cannot be wedded to any other religion or philosophy. Rather, he is the standard of truth by which we assess all other claims. There are elements of truth in all religions, but we are able to recognize those elements precisely because they cohere with

---

than "not" *(ouk)*. This change was probably made to smooth out the text, given the fact that Jesus did go to the feast (v. 10).

Jesus, the truth incarnate. If Jesus is not the truth, then he cannot offer us life (1 Jn 5:20). Contrary to the view of many today, false teaching is a serious matter!

Jesus Reveals Himself as a Disciple of God, Not of the Rabbis (7:14-24) On the last day of the feast Jesus makes his startling claim to offer living water (7:37-39) and to be the light of the world (8:12). In the time between his secret entrance and dramatic conclusion he goes up to the temple and begins to teach (7:14). "What does this mean but a fulfillment of the prophecy, 'The Lord whom ye seek shall suddenly come to his temple' (Mal 3:1)?" (Dodd 1953:351).

His teaching prompts the question, *How did this man get such learning without having studied?* (7:15). He had not studied under a rabbi, nor had he been in a rabbinic school. He did not support his teaching by appealing to recognized teachers, yet his teaching made use of rabbinic-style arguments, as is evident later in this section. In the Talmud (*b. Soṭa* 22a) it is said that the person who studied the Scriptures and even the Mishnah but yet "did not attend upon Rabbinical scholars" is no better than an *'am hā 'ā reṣ*—one of the "people of the land" who are cursed because they do not keep the law with the strictness of the Pharisees. This text from the Talmud is dated later than the New Testament, but the sentiment was current in the days of Jesus, and indeed it is reflected in this very story (7:49).

Although Jesus has not studied under a rabbi, that does not mean he is on his own. Throughout the Gospel he is emphatic about his dependency on the Father. In this passage he agrees with the theory behind the rabbinic succession of teachers (v. 18) but says, *My teaching is not my own. It comes from him who sent me* (v. 16). In saying this Jesus is claiming to be not just another rabbi, but rather a prophet whose *teaching comes from God* (v. 17). Jesus is a disciple of God, not of a rabbi.

How is such a claim to be assessed? Jesus and the Jewish opponents agreed that Scripture is the word of God, but whose interpretation of

---

7:15 It is said *the Jews* ask this question. Two verses earlier this term clearly referred to Jesus' opponents among the leaders of Israel, but this meaning does not fit verse 15 since they would have already known what Jesus' teaching was like. Here *the Jews* either must

Scripture is correct? Jesus does not point to confirmation from external sources. He points rather to the internal disposition of the individual, a heart that is God-centered: *If anyone chooses to do God's will, he will find out whether my teaching comes from God or whether I speak on my own* (v. 17). One who is centered in God rather than in oneself will be able to recognize God's voice in a teacher come from God. To choose to do God's will is not just a matter of moral purity as such; it is a hungering and thirsting after righteousness, a seeking first the kingdom. Such a heart is open to God, committed to him and his ways and willing to act on what is revealed. It is a heart like Jesus' own heart—like is known by like (cf. Beasley-Murray 1987:108).

Jesus spells out the alternative: *He who speaks on his own does so to gain honor for himself* (v. 18), or, more literally, "The one who speaks from himself seeks his own glory." One either speaks from God or one speaks from self, no matter how many external authorities are appealed to. One seeking God, who is caring for God's glory rather than one's own, such as Jesus refers to, is able to believe (5:44). Jesus', "humility and obedience allow him to speak with the authority of God" (Barrett 1978:318), and these are the same qualities that enable a person to recognize God's word in Jesus' teaching.

He then addresses the Jewish ideal behind the appeal to rabbinic authority: *He who works for the honor of the one who sent him is a man of truth; there is nothing false about him* (v. 18). In this saying Jesus affirms the Jewish view of tradition. His disciples are to pass on faithfully what they have received from him (cf. Jn 15:27; 21:24; Mt 28:16-20) and to ensure that it continues to be passed on by faithful teachers (2 Tim 2:2). So the rabbinic ideal is not wrong, but it must be coupled with a heart that is open to God, in contact with God and guided by his Spirit.

This ideal is a true test of the character of the messenger, but it is not a guarantee of the truth of the message—that depends on the one who sends the messenger. If Jesus is a true messenger, passing on what he has received, then the opponents do not have a problem with him but with the one who sent him to deliver this message. Since God is the one

---

refer to Judeans or Jerusalemites or must be a very general term that includes those who had come to Jerusalem for the feast from throughout the diaspora. See comment on 1:19.

who has sent Jesus, the opponents' alienation from God is again made clear.

The rabbinic teachers trace their teaching back to Moses himself, so Jesus turns from defending himself to attacking their claim to Moses (cf. 5:45-47). The foundation on which they build is wrong. Moses indeed gave them the law (v. 19); Moses was a faithful teacher who passed on what he received from God, not caring for his own glory but for the glory of the one who sent him. The issue is not with Moses and the law, it is with the opponents who do not keep the law (v. 19).

Jesus' charge that his opponents are not keeping the law turns up the heat of the debate. They believe Jesus does not keep the law, and now he says the same of them. Jesus brings two pieces of evidence to show they fail to keep the law. The first piece of evidence is that they desire to kill him (Jn 5:18; 7:1). Jesus could be referring to a violation of the sixth commandment (Ex 20:13), but something much more profound is going on. If Jesus is a false prophet, he deserves to die according to the law (Deut 13:5). But Jesus is actually the one of whom Moses wrote in the law (Jn 1:45; 5:46). So their desire to put Jesus to death shows they violate their own law because the law itself witnesses to Jesus.

While Jesus is addressing the whole crowd, he is speaking primarily to his opponents (v. 21). Most of the people listening would be either citizens of Jerusalem or pilgrims present for the feast. The Jerusalemites are aware of the authorities' desire to kill Jesus (v. 25), so only the out-of-towners would not know anything of the controversy surrounding Jesus. Some of these pilgrims respond, saying, *You are demon-possessed. . . . Who is trying to kill you?* (v. 20). Here is another example of the people's failure to recognize who Jesus is. The very Word incarnate, who is the truth, is said to be wrong about something which is common knowledge to the Jerusalemites. Most commentators view the crowd's saying Jesus is demon-possessed as their way of saying, "You're nuts." Perhaps this is all that the crowd intended. If so, they are still completely clueless, ignorant of both Jesus and the Jewish authorities. But the larger context is the debate about the source of Jesus' teaching. The charge of being a false teacher would put one in league with the devil. So we may have another of John's double-entendres: the crowd would mean "you're nuts," but the opponents would mean something more sinister (cf. 8:48).

Jesus reminds the opponents of their response to his healing on the sabbath (v. 21). They had been *astonished,* not in the sense of giving God glory, but in the sense that they were scandalized, some to the point of seeking his death (5:16-18; Schnackenburg 1980b:134). This response is unjustified even on the basis of the law, as Jesus now demonstrates in good rabbinic fashion.

Jesus begins by bringing forth a second piece of evidence that shows they do not keep the law. Moses gave them circumcision (Lev 12:3), though in fact it was a sign of the earlier covenant, from Abraham on (Gen 17:10-14). According to the law a male child is to be circumcised on the eighth day after birth, but what happens if the eighth day is a sabbath? Circumcision takes precedence over the sabbath. "They may perform on the Sabbath all things that are needful for circumcision: excision, tearing, sucking [the wound], and putting thereon a bandage and cummin" (*m. Šabbat* 19:2). Thus, in order to keep the law regarding circumcision they must do what is not otherwise lawful on the sabbath.

They would not have viewed this as a breaking of the law since this order of precedence among the commands existed precisely in order to keep the law (cf. Carson 1991:315). Therefore Jesus says the "work" of circumcision is performed on the sabbath *so that the law of Moses may not be broken* (v. 23). Jesus questions them, saying, if this work is allowed in order to keep the law, *why are you angry with me for healing the whole man on the Sabbath?* (v. 23). In other words, he is also working with an order of precedence, and his activity on the sabbath should be viewed from this perspective rather than as a breaking of the law.

Jesus is using a "how much more" type of argument, which was popular in the ancient world, not least among the rabbis. Indeed, at the time John was writing, this very point was being argued by rabbis using the same type of argument. Rabbi Eliezer (c. A.D. 90) said, "If one supersedes the sabbath on account of one of his members [in circumcision], should he not supersede the sabbath for his whole body if in danger of death?" (*t. Šabbat* 15:16; cf. *b. Yoma* 85b). So there is an order of precedence not only between commands in the law, but for the sake of saving a life. Jesus, however, goes even further and says not only does the saving of a life take precedence, but so does doing good (Mt 12:12 par. Mk 3:4 par. Lk 6:9; cf. Acts 10:38), which includes healing. This is an application of his principle that "the Sabbath was made for man, not man for the Sabbath" (Mk 2:27). If this principle is accepted, then Jesus is not a lawbreaker.

Indeed, circumcision is a sign of the covenant, and the covenant itself is about doing good, about acting in keeping with God's own character of love and mercy. Jesus makes this connection when he says, literally, "Because of this Moses gave you circumcision" (v. 22). The "this" refers back to Jesus' deed of healing on the sabbath (v. 21). So Jesus' form of sabbath observance—healing and doing good—was the very purpose for which Moses gave them circumcision. "Jesus' attitude is not a sentimental liberalizing of a harsh and unpractical law . . . nor the masterful dealing of an opponent of the Law as such; it is rather the accomplishment of the redemptive purpose of God toward which the Law had pointed" (Barrett 1978:320-21). Thus it is not Jesus but his opponents who are going against Moses. They are breaking the law by their observance of the sabbath because their observance does not include doing good.

Jesus concludes by telling them, *Stop judging by mere appearances, and make a right judgment* (v. 24). He is using language from Moses' teaching regarding the responsibility of the judges and officers of the people (Deut 16:18). The opponents are not acting in accordance with this injunction, and thus their disobedience is exposed yet again. The right judgment of which Moses speaks includes such things as refraining from showing partiality and taking bribes. Jesus' opponents are not blinded by bribes (cf. Deut 16:19) but are blinded by receiving glory from one another (Jn 5:44). They are observing the letter of the law, but do not understand what the law is really about, neither in its witness to Jesus nor in its goal of expressing God's own love and mercy in the life of God's people. Making a *right judgment (hē dikaia krisis)* is dependent on seeking God's will and not one's own (5:30). They lack this disposition; they are too shallow. They have no depth in themselves

---

7:25 NIV takes *oun* as a transitional conjunction, *at that point,* as does Daniel B. Wallace (1996:674). However, it could be inferential, giving the conclusion the Jerusalemites drew

and thus cannot recognize God at work among them. God himself is the one who is *dikaios* ("right," "righteous"; cf. Jn 17:25; 1 Jn 2:29; 3:7; Rev 16:5), so their lack of *right judgment* is yet another indication not only of their law breaking but of their alienation from God.

This call to right judgment is a challenge to each of us, for we are all guilty at times of judging by appearances. The only way to avoid such shallowness is to be united with God and to share in his truth about Jesus and about our own lives. This requires that we will God's will (7:17), which means God's will as God knows it, not as our prejudices and sins tailor it. To will God's will is to have a purity of heart and a clarity of vision that come through death to self. Until we have found our own heart (which lies deeper than our emotions and imagination) and made contact with God there, we will be in danger of judging by appearances instead of with right judgment.

Jesus Reveals Himself as the Messiah Who Has Come from God and Who Is Returning to God (7:25-36) The people of Jerusalem now question Jesus' messiahship on the basis of where he has come from. They think that the Messiah's origin will be unknown; so since they know where Jesus is from, he is disqualified (v. 27). Later we will hear of others among the crowd who think the Messiah's origin *is* known and who disqualify Jesus because he comes from Galilee (vv. 41-42). Neither of these opinions is accurate, which reveals the confusion and ignorance of the people, who, like the opponents, are judging by appearances rather than with right judgment.

Jesus' teaching about the sabbath and his reference to the people seeking to kill him (vv. 19-23) leads some Jerusalemites to conclude that he is the man the authorities *are trying to kill* (v. 25). They realize Jesus is claiming to be the Messiah (v. 26), so the fact that he is speaking *publicly* and without interference from the authorities raises the question of whether the authorities have concluded that Jesus is the Messiah after all. If false teaching is not opposed, then people get the impression that either it is not false or it is not significant.

---

from the teaching they had just heard about sabbath keeping and from Jesus' reference to their seeking to kill him.

So the people think the authorities might be confused. We will learn later (chap. 9) that the authorities themselves are indeed divided over Jesus. But these Jerusalemites assume the authorities could not have concluded that Jesus is the Messiah because he does not fit their own messianic expectations: *But we know where this man is from; when the Christ comes, no one will know where he is from* (v. 27). They seem to have in mind the idea that the Messiah would be hidden until his public debut (cf. Beasley-Murray 1987:110-11). As a Jew in the second century reportedly put it, "Christ—if he has indeed been born, and exists anywhere—is unknown, and does not even know himself, and has no power until Elijah come to anoint him, and make him manifest to all" (Justin Martyr *Dialogue with Trypho the Jew* 8).

Among the apocalypticists the origin of the Messiah had more profound implications. In two texts that probably come from late in the first century, about the same time John is finalizing his gospel, we read of the mysterious origin of the Messiah in God and his hiddenness there (*1 Enoch* 48:7; *4 Ezra* 13:51-52). The figures depicted in these texts may not be divine, but they are more than human (J. Collins 1995:208). Such notions build on earlier reflections regarding divine Wisdom. For example, Job 28 says the place of Wisdom is hid from all creatures; only God knows where Wisdom is to be found.

In Jesus we see the fulfillment of this motif from the wisdom and apocalyptic writings. The one hidden with God has now come forth and revealed himself. In response to the Jerusalemites' musings Jesus *cried out (krazō)* in the temple (Jn 7:28), an expression John uses for significant proclamation, even revelation (1:15; 7:37; 12:44; cf. Bultmann 1971:75 n. 1). He begins by saying, *Yes, you know me, and you know where I am from* (v. 28). In keeping with good Jewish reckoning, a person is usually known by where he or she comes from (Talbert 1992:146). So to know where Jesus is from is to know him. But this is bitingly ironic since their knowledge of him as a Nazarene misses the most significant truth of his origin; they are judging by appearances. For in fact they do not really know where he is from because he is from the

---

7:29 Some take the two clauses *I am from him* and *he sent me* as referring to the historical mission (for example Schnackenburg 1980b:147). Others (for example, Westcott 1908:1:273) take the first clause *from him (par' autou)* as a reference to "continuance of being," that

Father. They do not know his ultimate origin, and therefore they do not really know him.

Jesus continues by speaking again of the Father and of his dependency on the Father. He has just said that he does not speak from himself (*ap' emautou,* 7:17-18) and that fact establishes that he is true (*alēthēs,* v. 18). Now he says that he has not come *on my own* (*ap' emautou,* v. 28) and that the one who sent him is *true* (*alēthinos,* v. 28). For John, truth is objective reality—that which corresponds to reality and reveals it (cf. Dodd 1953:177). The Father is the source and standard of all truth, so truth is based on relationship with him. Jesus has such a relationship, and his opponents do not, as Jesus says flat out: *You do not know him, but I know him because I am from him and he sent me* (vv. 28-29).

The people of Jerusalem have raised the question of Jesus' origin. This is a good issue to raise, for instead of disqualifying him, the answer is in fact one of the main witnesses to who he is and to the validity of his message and deeds. Like the Son of Man of *1 Enoch,* Jesus has come forth from the presence of the Lord. Like the prophets of old, he has been sent by God with God's own message. The issue at stake is knowledge, as the use of the word *know* seven times in verses 26-29 indicates. These Jerusalemites claim to have knowledge, but they do not. Jesus is the one who knows God, knows who he himself is and knows the truth about his opponents. The opponents are out of touch with reality.

Jesus, the truth incarnate, has just spoken to these people of Jerusalem, and they respond by rejecting him: *At this they tried to seize him* (v. 30). Presumably they were intending to take him to the authorities, who, as they knew, wanted to kill Jesus (v. 25). In any case, they are unable to carry out their will because it is not God's will: *his time* ["hour," *hōra*] *had not yet come* (v. 30; cf. 2:4). These people, like Jesus' brothers (7:5-7), are of the world and have no sense of God's sovereign plan, which is at work among them. Their action confirms that they do not will to do God's will (v. 17). Again the judgment is taking place, for the light is shining but these people are preferring darkness.

is, his eternal relation to the Father (cf. 1:14). The present context could include either idea, and both interpretations fit John's thought.

These Jerusalemites turn against Jesus, yet many in the crowd are more responsive and *put their faith in him* on the basis of the signs they have seen (v. 31). It is unclear which signs they are referring to. John has only recounted five signs up to this point (changing water into wine, healing the royal official's son, healing the paralytic at the pool on the sabbath, feeding the five thousand and walking on water), but he has indicated that there were many other signs as well (2:23; 3:2). Signs are certainly intended to lead people to faith, but it is unclear whether the faith of these people is solid. They may be like those in the next chapter who believe but whose faith is not good soil for the seed (see comment on 8:31).

Having seen his impact on the crowd the Pharisees get together with the chief priests and send servants to arrest Jesus (v. 32). We know this attempt will be no more successful than the crowd's effort to *seize* Jesus (v. 30; the word *piazō* is translated *seized* in v. 30 and *arrest* in v. 32). But John does not tell us whether they seize him until after he relates Jesus' teaching about his departure (the great invitation to come to him for living water) and describes further the division of the people (v. 45). John's storytelling conveys how inconsequential their threat is. Those who seem to have such power, whom the people greatly fear (note their *whispering* in v. 32), are not able to disrupt even slightly God's purposes for Jesus. God's purposes are just as secure for those of us who, like Jesus, will to do his will.

After commenting on his origin Jesus speaks of his departure and destination (vv. 33-36). The leaders want Jesus off the scene. They are threatening him with arrest and death. He tells them serenely and sovereignly that he will indeed be leaving soon. The crucifixion is probably about six months away, though we cannot be sure of this since we do not know how much John is leaving out of the story (cf. 21:25). They will indeed put him to death, but even in death he will go to the one who sent him (v. 33; cf. v. 29).

7:31 Miracles are not associated with the expectations regarding a royal, Davidic Messiah. But there were several messianic paradigms in the first century, including a prophetic paradigm that included signs (cf. Meeks 1967:162-64). Several messianic claimants promised signs to those who would follow them in revolt against Rome (Josephus *Antiquities of the Jews* 20.97-98, 169-72; *Jewish Wars* 6.283-87; 7.438-39; cf. J. Collins 1995:196-99). The Gospels themselves depict the peoples' expectations of signs (Mt 11:2-6 par. Lk 7:18-23; Lk

After the guards are sent, Jesus says, *You will look for me, but you will not find me; and where I am, you cannot come* (v. 34). The opponents had been looking for him at this feast (v. 11), but they were not able to find him until he appeared openly. Their seeking has not been like the disciples' seeking (cf. 1:38; 6:24); they are judges who stand self-condemned by their response to him. He will be with the Father. Since he is the way to the Father (14:6), they cut themselves off from the Father when they reject Jesus. Again, Jesus implies that they are alienated from God.

These opponents are fulfilling a pattern from the prophetic and wisdom traditions (cf. Brown 1966:318; Cory 1997). Amos says the days are coming when people will search for the word of the Lord and not find it (8:12). Hosea says the peoples' hearts are full of prostitution and arrogance, so they will seek the Lord but not find him since he has withdrawn himself from them (5:3-6). Wisdom says,

Then they will call to me but I will not answer;

 they will look for me but will not find me.

Since they hated knowledge

 and did not chose to fear the Lord,

since they would not accept my advice

 and spurned my rebuke,

they will eat the fruit of their ways

 and be filled with the fruit of their schemes. (Prov 1:28-31)

Part of God's judgment is to withdraw access to his revelation. The "judgment will consist in the very fact that he has gone, and therefore that the time of the revelation is past. . . . They will long for the revelation, but in vain; for then it will be too late; he will no longer be accessible to them" (Bultmann 1971:307). Those who seek God's word and wisdom with their unfaithful hearts cannot expect to find what they seek. Jesus, as the incarnate Word and Wisdom of God, must be sought with a heart that wills to do God's will.

4:18-19; Mt 24:24 par. Mk 13:22; Mt 16:1-4 par. Mk 8:11-12; Mt 12:38-42 par. Lk 11:29-32; Jn 6:30).

7:32 *Chief priests* may refer to the present high priest and other past high priests who have been deposed by the Romans or possibly to "the higher temple officials, including, besides the high priest himself, the captain of the temple, the temple overseer and the treasurers" (Schnackenburg 1980b:149; cf. Jeremias 1969:147-81).

We can see from the response of these opponents, now referred to as *the Jews* (7:35; see comment on 1:19), that they are alienated from God. Jesus has spoken of the Father, but they completely miss his point. They speculate on where Jesus intends to go. If he were to go *among the Greeks* (v. 35), then they would not find him since they would not want to go looking for him there. Or perhaps they think that because he has been exposed as a false prophet in Israel he will go to the Greeks to try to drum up a following there (Talbert 1992:147). They are keying in on Jesus as a teacher (v. 35), as they did earlier in the chapter (vv. 14-17, 28), but they are not receiving his teaching.

There is, of course, enormous irony in their thinking Jesus might go among the Greeks. It is the arrival of the Greeks, who ask to see Jesus (12:20), that signals the coming of his hour. Through the witness of his disciples he will indeed go and teach the Greeks (cf. 10:16; 17:20). These opponents say more than they realize, just as Caiaphas will later (11:49-50). In both cases what is said refers to Jesus' death. These opponents are seeking to kill Jesus, but through his death the world will be saved.

A number of scholars see traces of Gnostic thought here: the themes of origin and destiny, whence and whither, are two major concerns among the Gnostics. The *gnōsis* (knowledge) they sought was largely concerned with understanding the cosmos and human nature (Schmitz and Schütz 1976:393-94). "But for the Christian the answer . . . does not lie in *gnōsis* about his own origin, but in faith in the one sent by God, who truly comes from God and leads the way to him (cf. 14:2-6)" (Schnackenburg 1980b:147). Jesus is here seen as the true gnostic with the ultimate answers about whence and whither. Salvation is indeed a matter of *gnōsis* (17:3), but this knowledge is a relationship with the Father through the Son. Knowledge, for John, "has primarily the sense of the recognition and reception of love" (Bultmann 1964:711).

Jesus, the Source of Living Water, Extends an Invitation to All Who

---

7:37 The feast of Sukkoth was seven days long (Deut 16:13, 15; Ezek 45:25; *Jubilees* 16:20-31), to which was added a separate feast on the eighth day (Lev 23:34-36; Num 29:12-39; 2 Macc 10:6). Some think the last day of the feast is the eighth day, but Jewish

Thirst (7:37-39) John now takes us to Jesus' shocking, clear claim made *on the last and greatest day of the Feast* (v. 37). On each day of the feast there was a procession of priests to the pool of Siloam to draw water (*m. Sukka* 4:9). The priests returned to the temple, where the water was taken in procession once around the altar with the choir chanting Psalms 113-118, and then the water was poured out as a libation at the morning sacrifice. All-night revelry lead up to this morning libation. This was a time of joy so great that it was said, "He that never has seen the joy of the Beth he-She'ubah [water-drawing] has never in his life seen joy" (*m. Sukka* 5:1; cf. Deut 16:14-15; *Jubilees* 16:20, 25). This joy was associated with Isaiah 12:3, "With joy you will draw water from the wells of salvation." On the seventh day of the festival the priests processed around the altar with the water not once but seven times (Bloch 1980:200; cf. Beasley-Murray 1987:113 for a more detailed description).

At this high point of the festival Jesus dramatically cries out loudly (*krazō,* as in v. 28), *If anyone is thirsty, let him come to me and drink* (v. 37). If he spoke this invitation during the revelry, he would have to shout just to be heard. But we have also an allusion to the image of Wisdom, calling out, inviting all mankind to come and drink (cf. Prov 8—9; Sirach 24:19). What Jesus offers is the fulfillment of the very things they were celebrating. Here is grace upon grace (Jn 1:16). Here the Son is repeating the offer of the Father, "Come, all you who are thirsty, come to the waters" (Is 55:1). Indeed, he is fulfilling the role of God, who "will guide them and lead them beside springs of water" (Is 49:10). His offer shows he is far more than just a prophet or an agent; here we have God himself offering us life.

In Jewish writings water is a very rich symbol (cf. Goppelt 1972:318-22). God himself can be called "the spring of living water" (Jer 2:13; 17:13). Other texts that use water imagery speak of Wisdom (Baruch 3:12; Sirach 15:3; 24:21, 25-27, 30-31), the law (*Sifre on Deuteronomy* 48) and, as here in John 7:39, the Holy Spirit (*Genesis Rabbah* 70:8;

---

sources did not view this eighth day as a part of the feast of Sukkoth (Bloch 1980:205), so the last and great day of the feast would be the seventh day.

Targum of Isaiah 44:3). Jesus, in offering the Spirit (v. 39), is claiming to be able to satisfy people's thirst for God. The cries of the psalmists are answered. David prayed, "O God, you are my God, earnestly I seek you; my soul thirsts for you, my body longs for you, in a dry and weary land where there is no water" (Ps 63:1). The sons of Korah sang, "As the deer pants for streams of water, so my soul pants for you, O God. My soul thirsts for God, for the living God. When can I go and meet with God?" (Ps 42:1-2). Both of these psalms go on to speak of meeting God in the temple: David has seen God in the sanctuary (Ps 63:2), and the sons of Korah speak of "leading the procession to the house of God, with shouts of joy and thanksgiving among the festive throng" (Ps 42:4). When Jesus cries out at the end of the Feast of Tabernacles on this particular day, the worshipers meet God in his sanctuary—in the person of his Son. The longing for God is met with God's invitation to come and be satisfied. In Jesus, God's own desire for man is expressed and the desire of man for God is met. All that the temple represented is now found in Jesus.

This invitation to come and drink is the climax of a series of references to water in this Gospel: the water turned to wine (chap. 2), the water of the new birth (chap. 3), the living water (chap. 4), the cleansing water of Bethesda (chap. 5) and the calming of the waters (chap. 6). All of these have revealed Jesus as the agent of God who brings God's gracious offer of life.

In offering them the Spirit he is claiming that the age to come has already arrived. Just as water flowed out from the Garden of Eden (Gen 2:10-14), so a river flows from the eschatological temple (Ezek 47). Ezekiel's vision has begun to be fulfilled in Jesus' offer in the temple, and it will come to completion in heaven in "the river of the water of life, as clear as crystal, flowing from the throne of God and of the Lamb" (Rev 22:1). That heavenly water of life is already available through Jesus.

7:38 Since teaching in the New Testament associates baptism with a person's entrance into the life of Christ (for example, Acts 2:38; Rom 6:1-11; Tit 3:5; cf. Beasley-Murray 1962:263-305), this invitation refers to the same general reality involved in baptism. However, since baptism is not explicitly referred to and since this water is to be drunk, it appears there is no primary reference to baptism here (though cf. 1 Cor 12:13). "In these verses water is an image of the Spirit, not a means by which the Spirit is conveyed" (Barrett 1978:329).

His invitation at the Feast of Tabernacles is repeated in the invitation at the end of the book of Revelation: "Whoever is thirsty, let him come; and whoever wishes, let him take the free gift of the water of life" (Rev 22:17).

The words of Jesus' invitation echo in our ears. Jesus stands at the doors of our hearts and speaks to the heart of each person on earth, offering the water of eternal life—the life that flows from God. Evangelism is a matter of our giving voice to this spiritual call. Christians need to hold up Jesus in all his beauty, that those with a desire for God may find the God who is offering himself.

While Jesus is clearly offering the water of the Spirit, it is not entirely clear to whom *him* refers (v. 38). Both the ancient church and modern scholars are divided over whether *him* refers to Jesus or the believer (cf. NIV text and margin). A reference here to Christ is more in keeping with John's thought. Christ is clearly described as the one through whom believers receive the Spirit; he breathes on them and says, "Receive the Holy Spirit" (20:22). Although John 4:14—"Indeed, the water I give him will become in him a spring of water welling up to eternal life"—refers to the believer with language similar to that in verse 38, Jesus speaks there not of an outward flow to others, but of an inward well of eternal life. Christ indeed dwells in believers and radiates from them his light and life and love, but, despite the claims of some contemporary ministers, believers do not mediate the Spirit to others. Rather, they bear witness to Jesus (4:39), and people come to him (4:40-42) and receive the living water of the Spirit (4:10) from him. This is clear in the context of Jesus' invitation, for it is to himself that he invites the people to come (7:38) and those who believe in him are the ones who receive the Spirit (7:39).

No Old Testament verse speaks of living water that flows *from within him,* him being either a believer or the Messiah. But there are many

---

7:39 *The Spirit had not been given* is more literally "the Spirit was not yet" or "there was not yet a Spirit." John obviously does not believe the Spirit did not yet exist (cf. 1:32). It is probably rather that "the Holy Spirit was not given in the characteristically Christian manner and measure until the close of the ministry" (Barrett 1978:329). John is referring to "a giving or sending of the Holy Spirit of such a kind as there had never been before" (Augustine *On the Trinity* 4.20).

Scriptures that speak of God's provision of water as evidence of his grace and as an image of his gift of life in his presence. Indeed, many of these texts were read at this festival, such as the gift of water from the rock (Ex 17:1-6), the water from the eschatological temple (Ezek 47:1-11; cf. Joel 3:18) and the water from Jerusalem that will flow in the age to come (Zech 14:8; cf. Beasley-Murray 1987:116). In Nehemiah there is a reference to the water from the rock in the wilderness (Neh 9:15), which is followed by a description of God's gracious provision: "You gave your good Spirit to instruct them. You did not withhold your manna from their mouths, and you gave them water for their thirst" (9:20; cf. Carson 1991:326-27). In Nehemiah the focus is on the giving of the law, but the connection between the gift of the Spirit and the giving of manna and water suggests correlations in the Jewish tradition. Given John's motif of Jesus as the fulfillment of God's earlier revelation, the reference here to Scripture probably recalls a general set of images in the Old Testament rather than one particular text. Jesus provides the promised water of the age to come, which was itself a fulfillment of earlier provisions of water.

The people could not receive this Spirit until Jesus was glorified (Jn 7:39), that is, until his death (cf. 12:16, 23; 17:1). In the Son's death the glory of God shines brightest since God is love and love is the laying down of one's life (1 Jn 4:8; 3:16). One of the Spirit's roles is to bear witness to Jesus (Jn 15:26), and he could not do this until the revelation was complete. Until the Son's death, the heart of God could not be known and thus eternal life, which is knowledge of God (Jn 17:3), could not yet be experienced (cf. 1 Jn 2:20). Until the death of the Son, the life of God could not be conveyed by the Spirit.

Jesus' offer of the Spirit is both universal and addressed to individuals: *If anyone is thirsty, let him come to me and drink* (v. 37). The first requirement is thirst. Everyone has spiritual thirst, for it is part of the human condition. Our need, our thirst, is what we bring to our relationship with God. This verse is one of many revealing, diagnostic texts in John. What do we thirst for? What do we really desire? Sin is our seeking relief from this thirst in something other than God.

7:40 *People* ("crowd," *ochlos*) seems to refer to the pilgrims who have come to Jerusalem for the feast, as in verse 20. The strong geographical theme in this section may point to the local loyalties of the Jerusalemites, affirming the Davidic Bethlehem connections over

Jesus invites those who know their need, those who are poor in spirit (cf. Mt 5:3), to take the initiative and come to him and drink (v. 37). Drinking refers to believing (cf. v. 38), which means aligning oneself with him, trusting him, receiving his teaching and obeying his commands. Such faith will enable one to receive the Spirit and enter an abiding relationship with Christ after his glorification. All of this is based on who God is and what he has done for us. When we believe we open our hands to receive what his grace offers—we come and drink.

Both the Crowd and the Pharisees Are Divided over Jesus (7:40-52)
Jesus' dramatic invitation to come to him for living water provokes strong reactions. Some in the crowd believe he is from God, but for others Jesus' is disqualified because of where he is from (vv. 40-44). The Pharisees are certain he is not from God and are desperate to arrest him, despite the witness of their own guards and Nicodemus, one of their own members (vv. 45-52). Thus, the pattern of events earlier in the chapter is repeated (vv. 25-32; cf. Brown 1966:331), but this time there is the added problem concerning Jesus' origin and more detail concerning the leaders' rejection of Jesus. The light is shining, but the leaders of God's people are showing a determined preference for the darkness (cf. 3:19; 7:7).

John describes the crowd's very mixed response to Jesus. Some associate Jesus with one or another of the eschatological expectations, while others reject such claims. The words Jesus has spoken lead some in the crowd to affirm that Jesus is the prophet like Moses (v. 40; cf. Deut 18:15,18). Perhaps Jesus' offer of water is seen as a claim to be a second Moses, one who would repeat Moses' miracle of striking the rock and providing running water for the people in the wilderness (Ex 17:1-7; Num 20:1-13; cf. Jeremias 1967a:277).

Others in the crowd draw the conclusion that Jesus is the Messiah (v. 41). They seem to share the view expressed in a later rabbinic text that the Messiah was expected to provide bread and water like Moses did: "As the former redeemer caused manna to descend, as it is stated,

---

against claims from Galilee. Perhaps we are to see the out-of-town crowds as having less loyalty to Jerusalem and thus more openness to Jesus.

'Behold, I will cause to rain bread from heaven for you' (Ex 16:4), so will the latter Redeemer cause manna to descend, as it is stated. 'May he be as a rich cornfield in the land' (Ps 72:16). As the former redeemer made a well to rise, so will the latter Redeemer bring up water, as it is stated, 'And a fountain shall come forth of the house of the Lord, and shall water the valley of Shittim' (Joel 4:18)" (*Midrash Ecclesiastes Rabbah* 1:9).

These reactions reflect the variety of views within Judaism concerning the one (or ones) God would send to rescue his people. Despite this diversity, Jesus' words and deeds reveal him to be the expected one. Those in the crowd who recognize him as the Prophet or the Messiah still do not fully realize who it is they are dealing with any more than the Samaritan woman did when she accepted him as the Messiah. But such faith is the right start and true as far as it goes. The sower has sown seed, and some of it is producing fruit.

But John does not dwell on those who have seen something of the truth about Jesus. Rather, he contrasts them with those who reject the idea that Jesus is the Messiah. Earlier some people rejected Jesus because they knew where he came from and Messiah's origin was to be unknown (7:27). Now a different tradition is in view—that Messiah was to come from Bethlehem since he was the Son of David (v. 42; cf. Mic 5.2). Both conclusions are ironic. Earlier the people thought Jesus' origins were known when in fact they were unknown, for he came from the Father. Now those who reject Jesus do so because he is not from Bethlehem, when in fact he is.

John does not state elsewhere that Jesus is from Bethlehem, so a number of scholars have questioned whether he was actually aware of this fact. But Jesus' descent from David was well known in the early church (Mt 2:4-5; Lk 2:4; Rom 1:3; 2 Tim 2:8). "It seems strange that any one should have argued from this passage that the writer of the Gospel was unacquainted with Christ's birth at Bethlehem. He simply relates the words of the multitude who were unacquainted with it (comp. Luke 4:23)" (Westcott 1908:1:280). The point is to reveal how ignorant those

---

7:41 The fact that some think of Jesus as *the Prophet* and others as *the Christ* suggests these figures were distinct from each other in the people's thought (cf. 1:25). Such a distinction is clearly made by those at Qumran (cf. *Rule of the Community* 9.9-11).

who rejected Jesus were and how unjust their rejection was.

This is another example of rejecting Jesus on the basis of Scripture (cf. 5:46). As this story continues it is clear that the role of Scripture is a major focus (vv. 49-52). The problem is not with Scripture nor with their desire to be faithful to it—Jesus shares this attitude. The problem is their ignorance of Jesus. If they knew him better, these objections would be met, for his origin is not known: he is from the Father, and he is in fact from Bethlehem. There is more to it than this, of course. For if Jesus is the one he claims to be, then Scripture will have to be interpreted around him. This means that much of the Jewish interpretation of God's revelation regarding the nation, the land, the temple and the law itself will have to be rethought. John's Gospel is a sustained exposition of how Scripture actually bears witness to Jesus and against his opponents (Whitacre 1982:26-68).

The result of Jesus' clear teaching is division among the crowd (v. 43). This is the judgment that comes when the light shines. Such judgment is part of the job description Jesus spelled out in his keynote address (5:22, 30), as is evident throughout his ministry and as will be addressed more directly later at this feast (8:15-16, 26, 50).

Another attempt is made to seize Jesus (v. 44; cf. v. 30). Instead of receiving him as the Son of God whose word they should obey, they wanted to have him under their own will. This disordered desire is at the heart of human rebellion against God. But they do not act on their desire: *no one laid a hand on him* (v. 44). Again we see the contrast between the desire of rebellious humanity and the sovereign outworking of God's plan.

John shifts from the crowd and their chaotic reaction to the Jewish leadership, referred to as *the chief priests and Pharisees* (v. 45). Their settled opposition to Jesus is contrasted with a few of their associates' favorable response to Jesus—first their servants (vv. 45-49) and then Nicodemus, one of their own members (vv. 50-52).

The temple guards return empty-handed not because they had been rendered powerless by Jesus (cf. their later experience, 18:3-6), nor

---

7:42 The designation of Bethlehem as *the town where David lived* points to a focus on place and ancestry similar to that regarding Jacob's well earlier (4:12). The greatness of Jacob and David is not contested, but one greater than either of them is now present.

because they feared the crowds, for some among the crowds also wanted to seize him (contrast later, Mt 26:5 par. Mk 14:2 par. Lk 22:2, 6). Rather, they are struck by the uniqueness of Jesus' message (7:46). This probably accounts for the fact that they were gone for four days (cf. 7:14, 32, 37) instead of an hour or so, as the authorities might have expected! It is right that they should be struck by Jesus' teaching—here the eternal Word was speaking about himself, about God and about the salvation he had brought in fulfillment of the promises made through the prophets. Jesus' very way of speaking was unique, as befit his unique message: "The words I have spoken to you are spirit and they are life" (6:63). It is a mark of our own spiritual dullness if we can read the Gospels and be bored. Boredom is one response to Jesus we never find in the Gospels.

Their own servants have born witness to Jesus, but the authorities are rigid in their opposition. They accuse their servants of having been deceived, a view expressed earlier by some in the crowd (7:12). They knew their servants were learned in the Scriptures, so they were surprised that "even they" *(kai hymeis)* have been deceived. So they point to themselves as the ones learned in the Scriptures and capable of discerning the truth of religious teaching (v. 48), and then they contrast their secure assessment with that of the crowd, which was ignorant of the law (v. 49).

To speak of the crowd as ignorant of the law and under a curse corresponds to the rabbinic view of the *'am hā 'āres,* the people of the land. Prior to the exile this was a more positive term, referring simply to "the body of free men, enjoying civic rights in a given territory" (de Vaux 1961:1:70). Later it meant the people in distinction to various forms of leadership (de Vaux 1961:1:71). A tone of disdain begins in Ezra and Nehemiah, where the term sometimes refers to "the heterogeneous population which the returnees found in the land" (Healey 1992:169; cf. Ezra 9:1-2; 10:2, 11; Neh 10:30-31). For the rabbis the term is theological

---

7:45 These *temple guards (hypē retai)* could be servants of the Sanhedrin who were called upon for a variety of services, including, at times, police activity (Brown 1994:1:249) or Levites who formed a temple police force to keep order within the temple and, at times, outside the temple (Jeremias 1969:209-13). In either case they would have been highly trained in the law, hence the surprise of the Pharisees (v. 47).

and negative. The Pharisees' use in our passage corresponds to this rabbinic view and also probably reflects the power struggles within first-century Judaism (cf. Meyer and Katz 1967:589-90). This term is basically a code phrase for those who do not approach the law in the same way as the rabbis and the Pharisees, who study the law constantly and work out meticulous interpretations for how to fulfill its commandments. Since one cannot keep the law if one does not know it, such ignorance implies law breaking and thus God's curse (cf. Deut 27:15-26). Rabbi Hillel (20 B.C.) said, "An uneducated man does not fear sin, and an Am ha-aretz is not pious" (*m. 'Abot* 2:5). This does not mean the '*am hā 'ā reṣ* were ignorant of the Scriptures or immoral. It means they did not try to keep the form of ritual purity promoted by the scribes and Pharisees. From the debates in all four Gospels it is clear that Jesus was as learned in the law as the rabbis were, yet he rejected their understanding of faithfulness to the Torah.

The opponents' ignorance or deceit is revealed in their response to the guards (vv. 45-49). First, they say that not one *(mē tis)* of the rulers or Pharisees has believed in Jesus when in fact Nicodemus, who was both a Pharisee and a ruler (3:1), had acknowledged that Jesus was a teacher come from God and, by implication, certainly not a deceiver (3:2). Second, they take their stand on the law in contrast to *this mob that knows nothing of the law* (v. 49). But their whole way of handling the situation is contrary to the law, as Nicodemus points out (v. 51). The Old Testament does not contain an explicit text that makes Nicodemus's point, but the law's exhortation to make a thorough investigation when passing judgment (Deut 17:2-5; 19:15-19) would include hearing the accused, as later rabbinic teaching makes clear (*m. Sanhedrin* 5:4; *Exodus Rabbah* 21:3). This principle was recognized at the time of Jesus, otherwise Nicodemus's response would carry no weight. The text also implies that they knew of this principle because they do not dispute Nicodemus's point.

7:52 The reading *a prophet* should probably be accepted, as it is in the NIV, since the opponents are rejecting Jesus from being a prophet in any sense. Early scribes are more likely to have included a definite article here under the influence of verse 40 (where it is clearly original) than to have left it out in this place.

Instead, they choose to defend their judgment using a different supposed teaching of Scripture: *a prophet does not come out of Galilee* (v. 52). The NIV margin note indicates that two early manuscripts (**p**[66] and **p**[75]) read "the Prophet" instead of *a prophet*. A reference here to "the" prophet fits the context well (v. 40) and has been accepted by a number of scholars. Since, however, Scripture does not say where the prophet like Moses is to arise, the opponents' rejection of Galilee is based more on prejudice against that region than revelation.

This prejudice is even stronger if the reading *a prophet* is accepted, as it probably should be. On this reading the evidence of their perversity is further heightened because Scripture reveals that in fact prophets had arisen in Galilee; for example, the prophet mentioned in 2 Kings 14:25 was Jonah, son of Amittai from Gath Hepher, which was about three miles northeast of Nazareth. Indeed, rabbinic sources from the late first-century A.D. speak of prophets having arisen from every tribe of Israel (*b. Sukka* 27b). Thus, whether we read "the prophet" or *a prophet,* there is great irony in their false claim to scriptural authority for their view regarding Galilee. Indeed, their very response to Nicodemus's accusation that they are acting contrary to the law reveals yet more clearly the truth of his charge.

On a deeper level this passage provides a vivid example of part of John's primary assessment of these opponents. They are judging by appearances (7:24) and are concerned more with human opinion than God's truth (5:44). When their servants bear witness to Christ they do not consider the authority of Jesus that the servants had experienced. Instead, they assume the servants were swayed by the crowd, and they contrast their own response to this response. They are weighing one set of human voices against another. In this they are acting as though they are in a trial: they attend to the witnesses, as it were, but they do not confront the evidence of Jesus himself. As Jesus will make clear, they are judging by weak and faulty human standards (8:15).

Nicodemus, unlike his peers, had undertaken an investigation of the sort he here refers to (v. 51). He had come to a conclusion based on Jesus' deeds (3:2), but when he then went to Jesus and heard him Nicodemus came away confused. Thus, he had already learned for himself the truth of the servants' report that *no one ever spoke the way this man does* (v. 46). Our present passage shows that Nicodemus is still inclined toward Jesus; he is even willing to stick up for him in the face of severe opposition. He is not a full disciple, but he is a supporter. This passage reveals that the Pharisees are at the heart of the opposition to Jesus. Given the strong dualistic language John uses throughout his Gospel, it is important to see that he realizes that even the most negative group, the Pharisees, contains a person who is open to Jesus. John focuses on groups, but he also keeps sight of individuals.

As Jesus continues to act and speak it is increasingly clear that one must either receive him and his message on his own terms or utterly reject him. This is no less true today, not only for non-Christians considering the claims of Jesus, but also for those who call themselves his followers. Like these Pharisees it is all too easy to mistake our interpretations of God's revelation for reality. We should hold firmly to what has been revealed in Scripture under the guidance the Spirit has given the church, but we must do so in an abiding relationship with the living God in whose presence we live. We must hold firmly to him in his objectively real presence and allow him to correct our personal, faulty understandings of him and his ways. The truth is in Jesus in perfection, but our apprehension of him is not yet perfect.

In this section, then, we have a striking picture of the opponents' rejection of Jesus. We are at the low point in Jesus' ministry; most of his disciples have abandoned him, and he is moving about like a marked man. Even in this setting, some are open enough to respond by recognizing him as one sent from God in some sense (vv. 40-41). The division among the crowd and the positive response of the leaders' servants and of Nicodemus serve to highlight just how strong the opponents' rejection of Jesus is. This absolute rejection prepares us for Jesus' teachings in the next chapter, in which he will reveal the true identity of these opponents who claim to speak for God.

Jesus Forgives a Woman Taken in Adultery (7:53—8:11) This story, beloved for its revelation of God's mercy toward sinners, is found only in John. It was almost certainly not part of John's original Gospel. The NIV separates this passage off from the rest of the Gospel with the note, "The earliest and most reliable manuscripts and other ancient witnesses do not have John 7:53—8:11." That is, the earliest Greek manuscripts, the earliest translations and the earliest church fathers all lack reference to this story. Furthermore, some manuscripts place it at other points within John (after 7:36, 7:44 or 21:25), others include it in the Gospel of Luke (placing it after Luke 21:38), and many manuscripts have marks that indicate the scribes "were aware that it lacked satisfactory credentials" (Metzger 1994:189). Furthermore, it contains many expressions that are more like those in the Synoptic Gospels than those in John.

It appears to have been a well-known story, one of many that circulated orally from the beginning yet that none of the Gospel writers were led to include. But some in the later church thought this one was too good to leave out. The controversy with *the teachers of the law and the Pharisees* (v. 3) is similar to stories found in the Synoptics, as is the theme of God's mercy mediated by Jesus.

Those who believe that authorship is a primary criterion for canonicity will suspect or even reject this passage. Most of Christendom, however, has received this story as authoritative, and modern scholarship, although concluding firmly that it was not a part of John's Gospel originally, has generally recognized that this story describes an event from the life of Christ. Furthermore, it is as well written and as theologically profound as anything else in the Gospels.

What we have here, then, is a bit of Synoptic-like material stuck in the middle of John's Gospel. Its presence highlights some of the similarities and differences between John and the Synoptics. The setting is one of controversy in the temple, though the way this is introduced in 7:53—8:2 is much more like Luke's style (cf. Lk 19:47; 20:1; 21:37) than John's. Furthermore, the theme of judgment also corresponds to the theme of the larger section in John (7:24; 8:15-16). This setting and theme probably led to its inclusion in John at this point.

Most importantly, however, this story highlights the similarities and differences between John and the Synoptics regarding Jesus identity. The clarity of Jesus' self-revelation, typical of John and central to this larger passage (chaps. 7—8) is missing from this story. Jesus has spoken

---

8:1-2 The reference to the Mount of Olives and Jesus' coming to the temple is more like Luke than John. So also is the reference to Jesus sitting to teach, found only here in John, but more frequently in the Synoptics.

clearly and openly of himself by his invitation to come to himself as the source of living water (Jn 7:37-38). Our present story is immediately followed by another clear self-revelation of Jesus as the light of the world (8:12). Thus, Chrysostom, who does not comment on this story of the adulteress (no one in the East does so before the twelfth century), notes this larger theme (*In John* 52.2), whereas Augustine, who does comment on the text, does not make these connections (*In John* 33.2-3).

It is usually said that this story interrupts John's flow of thought, as though a patch of a different pattern has been sewn onto a piece of cloth. On the contrary, while the style of Jesus' self-revelation is quite different in John, this added story contains an example of the Synoptic form of revelation, which shows that Jesus is more than a human prophet. So although there is a patch, the patch is of the same pattern as the whole, albeit less bright. While the style of the material is very different, the substance is quite similar. This specific story is a case in point of what is generally true of the relation between the Synoptics and John. The Synoptics have as high a Christology as John does, though they express it differently.

The story unfolds in four stages. The first stage sets the scene (7:53—8:2). The meeting of the chief priests and Pharisees with their servants, the "temple guards" (7:45-52), presumably took place on the last (and seventh) day of the feast (see note on 7:37). As this passage stands in this context, Jesus is coming early to the temple to teach on the morning of the added eighth day of the feast, which was a day of rest (Lev 23:39).

The second stage of the story (8:3-6) describes the challenge presented to Jesus by the Jewish leaders. Their treatment of the woman is callous and demeaning. If she had committed adultery the previous evening (which is perhaps more likely than around dawn, v. 2), then we can assume these opponents had been holding her during the night and waiting for Jesus to show up in order to use her to test him. Her fear would have been great. Putting her in the midst of the crowd would have added public humiliation. A certain attitude of male-chauvinism

---

8:3 The designation of the opponents as *the teachers of the law* (*hoi grammateis,* "scribes") *and the Pharisees* is a common way of referring to Jesus' adversaries in the Synoptics, but this is the only time this designation is found in John.

comes across in their statement that the law of Moses commands the stoning of *such women* (v. 5). More precisely the law speaks of the death of both the man and the woman involved (Lev 20:10; Deut 22:22-24).

These opponents have a commendable zeal for righteousness, but theirs is a shallow righteousness that shows no concern for the soul of this woman. They are also being rather deceitful. There is no evidence that this law was carried out with any regularity, so they are raising a question in the name of loyalty to Moses, using a part of Moses' teaching that they themselves most likely have not kept. Furthermore, since the law says both the man and the woman who commit adultery are to be killed, we are left wondering why the man was not brought in as well. It may be that he had escaped, but the fact that only the woman is brought raises suspicions and does not speak well of their zeal for the law of Moses; for if they were really committed, they would have brought the man as well. Indeed, the law makes it clear that stoning could only take place after a careful trial, which included the chance for the condemned to confess his or her wrong (*m. Sanhedrin* 6:1-4). The hypocrisy of the opponents is evident.

This situation is apparently just an attempt to entrap Jesus (v. 6). If he is lax toward the law, then he is condemned. But if he holds a strict line, then he has allowed them to prevail in their ungodly treatment of this woman and has opened himself up to trouble from the Romans, for he will be held responsible if the stoning proceeds. The leaders of Israel are putting God to the test in the person of his Son, repeating the Israelites' historical pattern on more than one occasion in the wilderness at Meribah and Massah (Ex 17:2; Num 20:13; cf. Deut 6:16; Ps 95:8-9; 106:14).

The third stage, Jesus' response to the opponents (vv. 6-9), is very memorable. While remaining seated he bends over and writes with his finger on the ground. This act of writing on the ground is itself very significant. Kenneth E. Bailey has pointed out (in unpublished form)

8:5 Stoning is the punishment for sleeping with "a virgin pledged to be married" (Deut 22:23-24), but it is not the specified form of death for other forms of adultery (Deut 22:22; Lev 20:10). But Ezekiel 16:38-40 suggests stoning was applied to adultery in general (Brown 1966:333), so there is no need to insist that this woman is betrothed but not married. At some point stoning was reserved for adultery with a betrothed and strangulation for other

that it was unlawful to write even two letters on the sabbath but that writing with dust was permissible (*m. Šabbat* 7:2; 12:5). If this were the eighth day of the feast, which was to be kept as a day of rest, then Jesus' writing on the ground would show that he knows well not only the law but also the oral interpretations.

Furthermore, his writing echoes an Old Testament passage, thereby turning it into a symbolic action (Jeremias 1972:228): "O Lord, the hope of Israel, all who forsake you will be put to shame. Those who turn away from you will be written in the dust because they have forsaken the Lord, the spring of living water" (Jer 17:13). Here "written in the dust" probably means the opposite of being written in the book of life (Ex 32:32; Dan 12:1); those who have turned away are consigned to death because they have rejected the one who is the source of the water of life. Thus it appears that Jesus is associating his opponents with those whom God condemns for forsaking himself and whom he consigns to death. The judgment that they suggest Jesus execute on this adulterous woman is in fact the judgment that he visits upon them for their rejection of him—the one who has offered them God's living water (7:38-39). In rejecting Jesus, they are forsaking God, and thereby committing a most shameful act. Adultery is shameful, certainly, but they themselves are acting in a shameful way worthy of death.

All of this is conveyed simply by Jesus' action of writing on the ground, which alludes to this passage from Jeremiah. This action could have this meaning whatever it was he wrote. Not surprisingly, many people have proposed theories of what he actually wrote on the ground. Perhaps the most common suggestion is still the most likely—that he wrote out some form of condemnation addressed toward them. This interpretation has been strengthened in recent years by the publication of a papyrus fragment from 256 B.C. (Zenon Papyrus 59) that uses the verb found here *(katagraphō)* in the sense of writing out an accusation against someone (Bauer, Gingrich and Danker 1979:410). So perhaps

---

forms of adultery (*m. Sanhedrin* 7:9)

8:6 The attempt to find some charge to bring against him after they had just sent their servants to arrest him (7:32) is probably further evidence that this story was added later. Cf. also 5:16-18.

Jesus cited commands he knew them to be guilty of breaking, or it could be he cited Jeremiah 17:13 putting, as it were, a caption under his symbolic act. Or maybe he enacted Jeremiah 17:13 by actually writing out the names of the accusers. Since they did not get his point right away, perhaps first he cited Jeremiah and then, as they persisted, he began to write their names. Such suggestions are obviously speculative, but they indicate possible explanations of what is happening.

When Jesus calls for the one without sin to cast the first stone he accomplishes several things: it relieves him from the charge of having instigated a stoning; it ensures there will not be a stoning, since none of the accusers will want to take responsibility for it; and it causes them to reflect on their own sinfulness before God. It has often been suggested that the eldest accusers were the first to leave (v. 9) because they recognized their own sinfulness more readily. However, leaving in this order may simply reflect the custom of deferring to the elders. In any case, their withdrawal was in fact a confession of sin. Those who came to condemn ended up condemning themselves by not casting a stone.

Jesus is left alone, sitting on the ground, bent over and writing, with the woman standing before him. As Augustine says, "The two were left alone, misera et misericordia" ("a wretched woman and Mercy"; *In John* 33.5). This prepares for the fourth and final stage of this story—Jesus' response to the woman (vv. 10-11). He straightens up and asks for a report of what happened, as if he had been totally oblivious to what took place as he concentrated on his writing. He does not ask her about the charges but rather about that aspect of the situation most heartening to the woman: *Where are they? Has no one condemned you?* (v. 10). They had of course condemned her in their accusations, but by not following through on the charge they had thrown out her case.

But there is one left who could still execute the judgment—the only one present who was without sin and thus could throw the first stone. Is she hopeful at this point or still quite frightened? We can only speculate as to whether the woman was familiar with Jesus and his embodiment of the mercy of God. In any case, she becomes a memorable example

---

8:11 Jesus is revealed in this Gospel as the one who delivers from sin (for example, 1:29;

of the fact that "God did not send his Son into the world to condemn the world, but to save the world through him" (3:17). Jesus says to her, "Neither do I condemn you. Go, and from now on no longer sin" (8:11). By adding *then* to the beginning of this sentence the NIV allows the most unfortunate suggestion that Jesus' response was caused by the response of the teachers of the law and the Pharisees. The translation of the end of the verse is also unfortunate, since *leave your life of sin* "almost paints the woman as an habitual whore (though the Greek bears no such overtones)" (Carson 1991:337).

Jesus grants pardon, not acquittal, since the call to leave off sinning shows he knew she was indeed guilty of the adultery. His noncondemnation is quite different from theirs. They wanted to condemn but lacked the opportunity; he could have done so, but he did not. Here is mercy and righteousness. He condemned the sin and not the sinner (Augustine *In John* 33.6). But more than that, he called her to a new life. The gospel is not only the forgiveness of sins, but a new quality of life that overcomes the power of sin (cf. 8:32-36; 1 Jn 3:4-6).

This story raises very significant pastoral issues. The first issue is the nature of the commandments of Scripture. We see Jesus upholding the law's teaching that adultery is sin while also setting aside the specific regulations concerning the community's enforcement of that law. The implication is that the law contains revelation of right and wrong, which is true throughout history, as well as commandments for embodying that revelation in the community of God's people, which are not true for all times and places. To understand this distinction we must understand that the law as revelation of right and wrong is not an arbitrary set of rules that God made up to test our obedience. Rather, the law is the transposition into human society of patterns of relationship that reflect God's own character. Adultery is wrong because it violates relationships of faithfulness, and such violation is wrong, ultimately, because God himself is characterized by faithfulness. The morality of Scripture is a pattern of life that reflects God's own life. This aspect of the law is unchanging, but the law's prescription for how the community

---

8:32-36), but nowhere is it said that Jesus forgives. The word *forgive* only occurs in 20:23 regarding the ministry of the disciples.

is to embody and enforce the revealed vision of relationships may vary.

This story also illustrates another pastoral issue. As Augustine noted (*In John* 33.8), we are in danger from both hope and despair. That is, we can have a false optimism that says "God is merciful so I can do as I please" or a despair that says "there is no forgiveness for the sin I have committed." This story shows we should keep these two inclinations in balance. There is no sin that God does not forgive. Christ's death atoned for all sin. The only sin that remains unforgiven is the one that is not repented of. But, on the other hand, God's call to us is to intimacy with himself, and sin cannot be in his presence any more than darkness can be in the presence of light. Christ's atonement cleanses us from sin as we repent day by day, and his Spirit is working in us a transformation so that in the end we will come out pure, though not in this life (1 Jn 1:8). But sin must be cut off. We must take it seriously. Jesus himself often tells us to fear God and his judgment.

While addressing these pastoral issues, this passage also contains extremely significant revelation of Jesus' identity. The fact that it comes in this Synoptic style and yet fits so well in this context in John makes it all the more remarkable. The opponents challenged Jesus regarding the law of Moses by saying, essentially, Moses tells us to stone such a person, but you—what do you say? (v. 5, *you* is emphatic in the Greek). Jesus sets aside Moses' clear command, albeit one that few ever acted on in Jesus' day. He does not follow through on Moses' command even when challenged to do so, which leads us to believe that he is more than just a prophet (see comment on 9:34).

Jesus does not say explicitly that he forgives the woman, but such is the implication of his saying he does not condemn her and then telling her to not sin again. So here we seem to have another occasion when Jesus mediates the forgiveness of God (cf. Mt 9:1-8; Mk 2:3-12; Lk 5:18-26; 7:36-50). In doing so, he is bypassing the temple and acting in a divine role. This revelation of Jesus' divinity is as profound as other such revelations in this Gospel, though it is expressed in the form it takes in the Synoptics. This patch of cloth sown onto John's Gospel has the same pattern as the whole, even if the colors are somewhat different.

Jesus Reveals Himself as the Light of the World (8:12-20) Jesus has

dramatically called people to come to him for God's living water (7:37-38) and now he *again* (*palin,* 8:12) refers to himself in a most startling way, saying, *I am the light of the world* (v. 12). This claim, like the claim to give living water, also corresponds to events at this feast. A lamp-lighting ceremony took place in the temple every evening of the feast, during which large lamps were set up in the Court of Women. The lamps' light, it was said, filled every courtyard in the city (*m. Sukka* 5:3). In the light of these lamps there was great singing and dancing all evening in celebration of God's salvation, especially his deliverance at the exodus as he lead his people with his presence in a pillar of fire by night. In the sight of these great lamps in the Court of Women (8:20), perhaps even in the evening while they blazed, Jesus proclaims himself to be the light of the world.

Light is a universal religious image (cf. Barrett 1978:335-37; Conzelmann 1974a: 310-43). The primary context for John's use of this image is the Old Testament, but readers from virtually any background would find meaning in these words. In the Old Testament the motif of light is used to refer to God's presence (Num 6:25; Ps 4:6; 104:2; Ezek 1:4, 27-28), his salvation (Ps 27:1; 44:3; 67:1-2; 80:1, 3, 7, 19; Is 60:19-20) and his revelation (Ps 119:105, 130; Prov 6:23; cf. Conzelmann 1974a:319-22). Thus, in the setting of this festival, which celebrates the Israelites' deliverance, Jesus is claiming to be the divine presence that saves God's people from their bondage. He is the saving presence for the whole world, not just for the Jews. He has already spoken of his mission to the world (Jn 6:33, 51; cf. 1:29; 3:16-17), and now he reiterates it in terms that remind us of the role of the suffering servant, who was to be a "light to the nations" (Is 49:6).

Israel followed the presence of the Lord in the pillar of fire as they escaped Egypt and journeyed to the Promised Land (Ex 13:21; Neh 9:12; Ps 78:14; 2 Esdras 1:14). Now Jesus says that those who follow him *will never walk in darkness, but will have the light of life* (Jn 8:12). Here is a promise of salvation much greater than the salvation Israel experienced, for it is deliverance not just from a national enemy, but from the forces of rebellion against God that lie behind every form of evil in the world. And this deliverance is not just a rescue from darkness and a glimpse of the light, but an ongoing life apart from darkness through possession of *the light of life*. This pregnant phrase refers to "the light which both springs from life and issues in life; of which life is the essential principle and the necessary result" (Westcott 1908:2:3). The world lies in darkness and death because it has rebelled against God and thus broken contact with the one source of light and life. Jesus claims to be the light that brings light and life back to the world and sets it free from its bondage to sin. All the salvation that went before, such as the deliverance celebrated at this feast, was a type of this deepest and truest salvation that Jesus now offers.

The Pharisees do not yet realize the enormity of Jesus' claims regarding himself, so they do not respond with a charge of blasphemy. Instead, they challenge the form his self-proclamation takes, charging him with bearing witness to himself and therefore lacking sufficient witnesses (8:13). The need for two or three witnesses is laid down in the law (Deut 19:15), and the later tradition, reflected here, said that "none may be believed when he testifies of himself" (*m. Ketubot* 2:9).

Jesus says his testimony is *valid* (*alēthēs*, "true") because he knows where he is from and where he is going, even though they do not (v. 14). That is, he really does know the truth about himself because he knows the Father and is conscious of his relation to the Father. They cannot see this truth about him because they are judging *by human standards* (v. 15; *kata tēn sarka,* "according to the flesh"). It is as though they are trying to evaluate the straightness of a line and their only tool is a crooked yardstick, or as if they are in an art gallery trying to evaluate the paintings when they have been blind from birth, never having seen shape nor color. Their judgment is limited to the human sphere and "breaks down when applied to anything which puts this sphere in question" (Bultmann 1971:281).

Jesus contrasts their inability to judge with his own ability (8:15-16). They judge by human standards, he says, but *I pass judgment on no one* (8:15). He does not pass judgment like they do, that is, according to "mere appearances" (7:24) and "according to human standards" (8:15).

8:14 In saying he knows where he is from and where he is going, Jesus speaks as the true gnostic. "Through the Johannine Christ's use of this language the false claim of Gnosis is refuted and Jesus again confirmed as the true light which enlightens every man (1:9)" (Schnackenburg 1980b:193).

Instead, he passes judgment in keeping with reality, because he does so in oneness with the Father (8:16). He judges simply by revealing the truth and pointing out one's distance from that truth. That is why he says he will not judge but his words will judge (12:47-48). Such revelation carries implicit condemnation of that which is untrue, and Jesus makes that condemnation explicit. So what does he mean when he says he not condemn (3:17-18)? The Pharisees have determined Jesus is in error, and they have condemned him in the sense of writing him off. Jesus, on the other hand, has determined they are in error and has shown that they are culpable for their rejection of him and for the alienation from God which lies behind this rejection. But he has not condemned them in the sense of dismissing them, for he still bears witness to them, offering them revelation and thereby offering them salvation.

These distinctions regarding judgment are important within the church. Jesus says, "Do not judge, or you too will be judged" (Mt 7:1). Clearly this does not mean we should not distinguish good from evil or truth from error, for Jesus calls us to do just that a few verses later in his teaching on false prophets (Mt 7:15-20). But it is one thing to recognize evil and error and quite another to conclude that an individual is totally lost to God. The final state of a person's soul is known only to God. Therefore we should write off no one, yet all the while we should discern the teaching and behavior to see whether it is of God. Such discernment can only come from Christ through the Spirit, for our judgments, like Jesus' (Jn 8:16), can only be right if they are in union with the Father.

Jesus brings up the need for two witnesses (8:17) in order, it seems, to bring home the point that when he bears witness his is not the witness of a single person but of two persons, himself and his Father (8:18; cf. 5:31-32). Since the two witnesses required by the law do not include the accused this would not be a valid legal argument. So Jesus seems to use the law in a nonlegal way to bear witness to his relationship with the Father. The Father is known as the one *who sent me* (v. 18); in other

---

8:17 The phrase *your law* is similar to Samuel's phrases "your fathers" in his reference to Israel under Moses (1 Sam 12:6-8, 15) and "your God" (1 Sam 12:11) when he speaks to the people about their desire for a king. The context in 1 Samuel, as well as the context here in the Gospel, is conflict among coreligionists.

words, Jesus is identified by his relationship to the Father, and the Father, likewise, is known by his relationship to Jesus.

When the Pharisees ask *Where is your father?* (v. 19), they reveal that they do not realize Jesus is talking about God. It is as if they want to locate this Father so they can interrogate him, as they will the parents of the blind man in the next chapter. It would not do them much good, since those who are not open to God cannot hear him even when he speaks directly to them (12:28-30). They do not realize that in Jesus they are seeing the clearest revelation of the Father himself: *If you knew me, you would know my Father also* (v. 19; cf. 14:9-11). To know Jesus is to know God—such is the core proclamation of this Gospel. Their question points up once again their alienation from God.

Jesus' revelation of himself as the light of the world and this ensuing discussion take place in the temple *near the place where the offerings were put* (v. 20), which is, most likely, in the Court of Women (Carson 1991:341). In the temple Jesus has revealed himself as the fulfillment of what the temple itself was about—the presence of God on earth. And "in the temple itself they gave proof of their being closed to the Revealer!" (Bultmann 1971:283). John suggests that the opponents wanted to seize him (v. 20). Just as Jesus' every action is under the direction of the Father, so are the circumstances of his life. They were not able to act against him *because his time had not yet come* (v. 20). Thus, these opponents are ignorant of both Jesus and his Father (v. 20), a point already made clear at this feast (7:28, 34) and driven home over and over in this chapter.

Jesus Reveals Himself as the One from Above (8:21-30) John introduces this section as he did the last (*palin,* translated *once more;* cf. 8:12), indicating a progression as the Light of the World shines ever more brightly, revealing himself, his Father and his opponents' true condition. Jesus returns to the theme of his departure, but now he connects it with his opponents' sinfulness. His departure has implications for them, for they will look for him, presumably for help, but they will die in their sins. His conclusion—*Where I go, you cannot come* (v. 21)—seems to give the reason they will die in their sins: they will die in their sins because they are not able to go with him to the Father. Jesus is the way to the Father (14:6), the one who takes away the sin of the world (1:29), who enables sinful mankind to be united with the Father. In rejecting him the opponents are cutting themselves off from the presence of the Father.

They speculate that Jesus may be contemplating suicide. According to Josephus, the Jews viewed suicide as consigning a person to "the darker regions of the nether world" because it was a crime "hateful to God" as an act of "impiety toward our creator" (*Jewish Wars* 3.375-79). So when Jesus says they will die in their sins because they cannot go where he is going, they think he is saying that he himself will die in a sinful way. Their interpretation of his words shows that either they are missing entirely what he is saying or they are hardheartedly rejecting his message. This reference to suicide ironically applies to them, for there is a sense in which their unbelief is suicide in that they are choosing to reject his offer of the light of life.

Jesus does not pick up on their reference to suicide. We see here the mercy of God refusing to be deflected by human perversity or hardness of heart. Instead, he repeats his witness in different language: *You are from below; I am from above. You are of this world; I am not of this world* (v. 23). What was implied earlier in the charge that they "judge by human standards" (v. 15) is now expressed quite clearly: Jesus and the Jews are not in the same sphere. Jesus has come from God and is bringing God's own presence into our midst, but they have no openness to God (1:10-11). Jesus is speaking of states of being, of core realities. He has come into this world in the fullness of humanity (1:14; cf. Thompson 1988), but unlike them, he is not of this world, that is, of human society as it exists apart from God. Indeed, it is because he is above this world that he is able to help the world.

In saying that he is from above Jesus contrasts himself with every other agent of revelation. He is not simply a human being who has achieved enlightenment and now has come to share what he has learned. His point of origin is not this world to begin with. He is a human being just as we are, but there is more to him than that. This claim, in the light of Jesus' use of "I am" (vv. 12, 24, 58), reveals the two natures of Christ, as the church later came to express it—fully God as well as fully man.

Jesus concludes by spelling out his identity, their peril and the remedy: *I told you that you would die in your sins; if you do not believe that I am [the one I claim to be], you will indeed die in your sins* (v. 24). Jesus says they must believe that "I am" *(egō eimi)*. The NIV takes this use of *egō eimi* as a recognition formula (see comment on 6:20). This may be correct, but John always intends Jesus' uses of this formula to echo the divine name, as becomes clear at the end of this chapter (v. 58). Indeed, *the one I claim to be* (to use the NIV's paraphrase) is the I AM. The people are trying to figure out whether he is the Prophet or the Messiah, but they still need to believe his identity is much more profound than anything they mean by these titles.

Without faith in Jesus as God's divine Son who has come from above, they will die in their sins. By repeating this warning Jesus is shining as the light of the world, revealing their true condition and its consequences. If we cannot see God in the clearest and most accessible revelation of him ever given—the clearest it is even possible to give—then how can we see him in any lesser manifestation? How are we going to recognize the cryptic, invisible God whom nobody has seen (1:18; 6:46) if we cannot recognize his Son incarnate?

Sin is separation from God and therefore a state of death, since God is the source of all life. Jesus says they are *in their sins,* which means they are alienated from God and thus under the wrath of God (cf. 3:36). Human beings apart from God are not in neutral territory. They are in a state of rebellion against God that began at the first rebellion (Gen 3) and is characterized by death (Gen 2:17). The people Jesus addresses are as ignorant of their own condition as they are of his identity.

Jesus' lucid statement leads them to ask the right question: *Who are you?* (v. 25). Jesus does not respond with a fresh statement right away (though he will do so in what follows immediately in vv. 28-29) but instead points them back to what he has already told them. This question, after all, has been raised throughout this festival. They are

---

8:24 Augustine says of Jesus' call to believe that he is the I AM, "Well, God be thanked that He said, 'If ye believe not,' and did not say, 'If ye comprehend not' " *(In John* 38.10).
8:25 Jesus' reply *(Just what I have been claiming all along)* has been called "the most obscure sentence in the Gospel" (Beasley-Murray 1987:125). Although there are half a dozen possible translations, they boil down to either a statement, such as in the NIV, or a question

viewing him according to human standards (v. 15), so he makes no sense to them. Until they are willing to open themselves to his message and accept him on his own terms they will make no headway.

Unfortunately, they are not close to doing so. Jesus warns them that he will need to spell out further their own condition: *I have much to say in judgment of you* (v. 26). This judgment is not just Jesus' own assessment. Here, as always, he is passing on what he has heard from the Father, who is himself *reliable* (*alēthēs*, "true"). He pronounces his judgment in what follows in this chapter.

They still do not *understand that he was telling them about his Father* (v. 27), so he speaks yet more clearly. They will know his identity when the Son of Man is lifted up (v. 28). Again, *egō eimi* can be used here as a recognition formula, as the NIV takes it (cf. v. 24), or as a reference to the divine name, as will be the case at the end of the chapter (v. 58). In either case, the Son of Man's death at their own hands (*When you have lifted up*) will reveal both his unique identification with the Father and his dependence on the Father as one distinct from the Father. They may be confused now, but they will know then. Whether this knowledge will result in salvation or judgment is not said. The idea is probably that they will at that point see the revelation shining at its brightest and have their hearts revealed as, in the light of that revelation, they either embrace or reject Christ and the God he reveals (cf. Schnackenburg 1980b:203).

Jesus concludes by repeating his witness to the Father's presence: *The one who sent me is with me; he has not left me alone, for I always do what pleases him* (v. 29). He had just spoken of not being alone but standing with the Father (v. 16), though the way he expressed himself could have merely suggested that he has the Father's backing. Now he repeats his claim that he is not alone, but here he makes it clear that he is talking about the Father's personal presence with him at all times, including right at that moment. Most of his disciples may have left him

---

something like, "Why do I talk with you at all?" Either way the general effect is the same—these folk have already been told quite enough. He will go on to speak further with them, but if they were really open to God and his Son, they have already heard enough.

at this point (6:66), but he has not been deserted by his Father. Here we get a glimpse into the mystery of the relations between the Father and the Son, for the Father sends the Son and yet is present with the Son. The sending refers to the incarnation and the presence to the eternal relations (cf. Augustine *In John* 35.5; 36.8; 40.6; Chrysostom *In John* 53.2).

By saying this presence is due to his always doing what is pleasing to the Father, Jesus reveals the primacy of the Father. Not only the created order but the eternal Son of God is at one with the Father through sharing in the Father's will. That will is simply life itself—Reality. All else in existence, even the Son and the Spirit in their eternal, uncreated being, are dependent upon the Father as the source of all life. All life is an expression of the Father's one life. To *do what pleases him* is not simply a matter of morality but of sharing in his life itself. It is another way of saying that Christ does what he sees the Father doing and speaks what he hears from the Father. As such he is the model of all discipleship. The life Jesus is offering involves being taken up into the one life of the Father himself.

As Jesus thus speaks clearly, *many put their faith in him* (v. 30). Earlier in the Gospel such faith was tested and so also this faith will now be tested through more scandalous teaching by Jesus. This testing will reveal whether this faith is genuine or whether it is like that of an earlier crowd at an earlier feast in Jerusalem, which proved false (2:23-25).

In this section we have Jesus' very clear statement of his divine identity, of the necessity to have faith in him and of how the cross will reveal most clearly his identity as I AM. We also see the opponents asking the right question, but their ignorance of the Father is evident. The rest of this chapter will spell out as clearly as anywhere in the Gospel the truth about these opponents.

Jesus Clearly Reveals Both His True Identity and His Opponents' Identity (8:31-59)

Jesus' critique of his opponents here reaches its clearest expression, revolving around the theme of Abraham's children. Jesus makes it clear that they do not have the freedom they claim as children of Abraham nor do they reveal the characteristics of the children of Abraham. Instead, their attitudes and actions reveal that they are really children of the devil (v. 44). This is the deepest glimpse into the heart of his opponents, and it occurs in the context of Jesus' clearest revelation of his own identity. He is the unique Son of God who can use the divine I AM of himself, even though he is also distinct from God.

Many are now putting their faith in Jesus (v. 30), and his following seems to be growing again after its low point (cf. 6:66). Whenever people put their faith in Jesus he immediately tests that faith. In this case he begins by explaining what is behind such testing. Those who are really his disciples *hold* to his teaching, they remain in it (*meinēte*, v. 31). Jesus tests his disciples by giving them further revelation that stretches them and requires them to put their trust in him, rather than in their understanding of all he is saying and doing. They need to understand him well enough to recognize that he is from God, but the very fact that he is from God means he is going to speak and act in ways that are not in keeping with this world. Being able to humbly remain in Jesus' teaching is a sign of a true disciple because it is evidence of openness and loyalty to Jesus.

Jesus promises that if they do remain in his teaching, *you will know the truth and the truth will set you free* (v. 32). This is surely one of the most abused texts in the Bible, for it is often cited with no regard for either the condition attached (remaining in Jesus' teachings) or the sort of freedom in view, namely, freedom from sin (v. 34). In Judaism it was the study of the law that set one free (Ps 119:45; *m. 'Abot* 3:5; 6:2), so Jesus is claiming for his teaching that which is recognized as true of God's own teaching. This implicit claim to divinity will be spoken clearly when he uses the divine I AM of himself at the end of this chapter. To know Jesus is to be liberated from all error and evil, for it is to know God himself, who is truth and purity and life.

In Jesus' teaching and in the teaching of Judaism obedience to God is true freedom. This truth is quite different from the thinking of most people today, for it takes God, rather than our own personal feelings and ambitions, as the one good. The freedom in view is not a freedom to do whatever we wish according to the dictates of our own fallen selves, but a freedom from our fallen selves and the power and guidance to act in accordance with God himself, the source of all goodness and life.

The Jews who have believed in Jesus do not respond as true disciples. Instead of receiving with docility, they question see note on 2:20). They do not react to the implications of Jesus' identity (although they will do so before too long) but to the implications concerning their own condition (v. 33). At first their claim to *have never been slaves of anyone* (v. 33) seems delusory, since they probably said it within sight of Roman soldiers. In addition to Rome, Israel at one time or another had been subject to Egypt, Philistia, Assyria, Babylon, Greece and Syria. Yet though these nations had ruled over them, they "had never accepted the dominion of their conquerors or coalesced with them" (Westcott 1908:2:15). They had maintained their national identity as children of Abraham throughout, so their claim is not entirely groundless.

Their response is a typical example of their misunderstanding. They think Jesus is speaking of national freedom, but he is speaking of inner freedom, which he now makes clear (v. 34). Spiritual freedom is the freedom from sin, and sin, at its heart, is an alienation from God. This alienation is caused by sin in the sense of both error and evil. The antidote, faith, corresponds to both of these aspects since it is the appropriation of knowledge of God (which replaces the error) and of forgiveness for our rebellion against God (which overcomes the evil). Jesus is offering a restored relationship of intimacy with God, which brings life in place of death.

Jesus continues to work with them and give them revelation despite their misunderstanding, just as he did with the woman of Samaria (4:13, 16). As always in this Gospel, the focus comes back to Jesus' own identity: *Now a slave has no permanent place in the family, but a son belongs to it forever. So if the Son sets you free, you will be free indeed* (vv. 35-36). Jesus clearly contrasts his status in the family of God with that of the rest of humanity, which is enslaved to sin. Given this unique status he is the one who has freedom in God's household and is able to offer it to others. Only God can liberate us from sin, yet here Jesus says that he, the Son, can do so. Once again we see the implied claim regarding his unique oneness with the Father (cf. Chrysostom *In John* 54.2).

After he says the truth will liberate (v. 32), he says that he, the Son, will liberate (v. 36). In fact the Son is the truth, and as such he is the way to the Father (14:6). The freedom he is offering is, precisely, union with the Father, the source of all true life. The way to receive this life, with its freedom from sin's alienation and death, is to remain in his teaching. This involves an actual remaining in the Son himself, which includes remaining in his commands (15:1-17). In order to receive the power to become children of God we must receive the Son of God (1:12). We share in the Son's own relationship with the Father (17:20-26), a thought that Paul develops (Gal 4:6) with the same implications regarding freedom (Gal 5:1).

Jesus then returns to their claim to have Abraham for a father. They are indeed *Abraham's descendants* (*sperma,* v. 37), but they are not *Abraham's children* (*tekna,* v. 39) because they are seeking to kill Jesus (vv. 37, 40). Jesus is telling them what he has *seen in the Father's presence* (v. 38) and *heard from God* (v. 40), but they are not receptive because, he says, *you have no room for my word* (v. 37). In other words, once again we understand that they reject Jesus because of their inner disposition. Their problem is a form of spiritual heart disease. Their heart has no room for Jesus' revelation; there is no room at their inn, as it were. Since he is telling them what he has seen and heard from the Father, their inability to accommodate his word means they have no room for God himself in their lives. Yet again, we see their alienation from God.

The Great Physician is diagnosing their disease, and they are not happy about it. They have put faith in Jesus (v. 30), yet they rebel as he tries to help them become true disciples. When confronted with their inner disease they should have accepted his assessment and repented. This is what each of us must do as a disciple of Jesus, for each of us has inner disease that he desires to cure and that must be cured. His diagnosis is perfect, and he knows how to heal us. He does not have to leave us waiting while he goes in the next room to consult his medical books. Nor does he lack the resources to effect our cure. He lacks nothing except our signature on the permission slip to get on with the process. Discipleship includes allowing Jesus to deal with our inner brokenness and deadness. He will not be satisfied until we come out entirely clean and whole, a fact that is part of the good news. To be a disciple one needs not only the humility to receive what Jesus reveals about himself but also the ability to receive what he reveals about oneself. He always reveals in order to redeem. The judgment the light brings is meant to lead us to salvation, not condemnation. The sin is condemned in order to reveal it as sin and lead us to repentance. If we reject the diagnosis or the cure, then the light does indeed bring condemnation, for we have chosen to remain in our state of alienation from God, who is the one source of life.

Jesus sets his revelation of what he has seen in the Father's presence in opposition to their own activity of doing *what you have heard from your father* (v. 38). This obviously creates a contrast between his Father and theirs. They claim Abraham as their father (v. 39), to which Jesus responds by comparing their attempt to kill him with what Abraham did (vv. 39-40). This refers, most likely, to Abraham's reception of the heavenly visitors (Gen 18), since in this interchange Jesus is addressing his would-be disciples' receptivity.

The imitation of Abraham was discussed within Judaism in terms very similar to what we find in John. For example, the disciples of Abraham are said to have "a good eye and a humble spirit and a lowly soul," while disciples of Balaam have "an evil eye, a haughty spirit, and a proud soul" (*m. 'Abot* 5:19 [5:22 in some editions]). These descriptions correspond to John's description of the characteristics of Jesus' disciples and Jesus' opponents. Furthermore, at a later date some of the rabbis seem to explicitly compare Jesus to Balaam (*b. Sanhedrin* 106a-b). Thus, it is possible that the charges Jesus brings against these Jewish opponents are the same charges the Jewish opponents bring against Jesus and his followers. Both are claiming humbleness of heart in loyalty to Abraham and God, and both see in their adversaries those who are haughty and false to God, like Balaam, the archetypal false prophet in the Old Testament (Num 22—24; 31:16, Deut 23:5-6; Josh 24:9-10; Mic 6:5; 2 Pet 2:15; Jude 11; Rev 2:14; cf. Kuhn 1964a).

Behind the claim to have Abraham for a father is the claim to have God as a father, which becomes clear as we now approach the heart of the polemic. After Jesus says these folk are not behaving like Abraham, he adds, *You are doing the things your own father does* (v. 41). This obviously suggests someone besides Abraham is their father, and they take this, rightly, as an attack on their loyalty to God. They reject the charge, saying, *We are not illegitimate children* (v. 41). Literally, they say they are not born "from unchastity" *(ek porneias)*. Instead, they claim that *the only Father we have is God himself,* which indicates their reference to unchastity alludes to the Old Testament notion that the covenant with God is like a marriage, and, correspondingly, idolatry is like unchastity (Deut 31:16; Jer 3:14; Hos 1:2; 2:1-13; 5:3; Philo *De Migratione Abrahami* 69; *Numbers Rabbah* 2:15-16). Central to the covenant was the idea that Israel was God's son (Ex 4:22) and that the Lord was Israel's father (Deut 32:6), "a theme reiterated constantly in the prophetic preaching (Isa lxiv 8; Mal ii 10)" (Brown 1966:364).

Jesus proceeds to attack precisely his opponents' claim to have God for a father (Jn 8:42-47). Here is the heart of the polemic between Jesus and these Jewish opponents: Jesus is one with God the Father, expressed here once again in terms of his origin and obedience (v. 42). It follows that anyone who rejects him is rejecting God the Father who sent him and to whom he is obedient. The rest of this section (vv. 43-47) works out the implications of this point. Jesus has said the opponents have no room for his word (v. 37), and now he says that they are not able to hear his word (v. 43). This inability *(ou dynasthe)* indicates that something is radically wrong with them. The next verse is the central accusation: they have the wrong father—they are of their father, the devil. The centrality of this verse is signaled by its place at the center of a chiasm:

A The Jews and God (v. 42a)

  B The Jews and Jesus (vv. 42b-43)

    C The Jews and the devil (v. 44)

  B′ The Jews and Jesus (vv. 45-46)

A′ The Jews and God (v. 47)

The reason Jesus gives for their rejection of him and their alienation from God is their relation to the devil.

John portrays the devil as exactly the opposite of Jesus. Here the devil is described with respect to a *beginning* (v. 44), as is Jesus also (1:1). But Jesus is life (14:6) and has life in himself and gives life (1:4; 5:26), whereas the devil is *a murderer* (v. 44). Furthermore, the devil was *not holding to the truth* (more literally, "did not stand in the truth," *en tē alētheia ouk estēken*), because *there is no truth in him* (v. 44).

In John's thought "truth" *(alētheia)* "means eternal reality as revealed to men—either the reality itself or the revelation of it" (Dodd 1953:177). These two aspects of truth are united in Jesus who both is the truth (14:6) and speaks the truth (8:40). Just as it is Jesus' very nature to be the truth, so it is the devil's very nature to lack the truth and speak lies, for *he is a liar and the father of lies.* So John depicts the devil as the personification of what is the exact opposite of Jesus.

The three main characteristics of the devil in this verse move from the exterior to the interior, as it were. The first description is of the devil's external activity as a murderer. This is followed by a general reference to his alienation from the truth. The description concludes with the assertion that this alienation from the truth is thorough; to his very core there is no truth in him, but rather lies. Thus, John is pointing to the inner core of the devil just as he points to the heart of the opponents.

When the devil lies he *speaks his native language;* more literally, he speaks "from his own things" *(ek tōn idiōn)*. Since this expression is the equivalent of *ex heautou,* "from himself," again we have the exact opposite of Jesus, for he never speaks from himself: "For I did not speak of my own accord" ("from myself," *ex emautou;* 12:49). This chapter has emphasized that Jesus always speaks from the Father (8:38) and that his activity and teaching are dependent on the Father (8:28, 38, 42, 50). In this context the conclusion that the devil *is a liar* is a statement of his very being. He speaks lies (that which is contrary to God and his revelation, especially his revelation in Jesus, the truth) because he is a liar (one whose being is characterized by separation from God, who is the truth). This contrast between Jesus' dependence on the Father and the devil's independence from the Father is the crucial distinction between them. Indeed, Jesus' dependence and the devil's independence are their chief characteristics.

What does it mean that the devil is the father of Jesus' opponents? Many scholars think this refers to their origin in the sense that a father

---

8:44 The devil as *a murderer* probably refers to his introduction of death into the world through the temptation of Adam and Eve, since in this way he "robbed Adam of immortality" (Barrett 1978:349; cf. Gen 3; Wisdom of Solomon 2:24; Sirach 25:24; Rom 5:12; Irenaeus *Against Heresies* 5.23; Augustine *In John* 42.11; Chrysostom *In John* 54.3). Some, however (for example, Brown 1966:358), suggest it refers to the first murder when Cain killed Abel (Gen 4:8; cf. 1 Jn 3:12). But this was "only one manifestation of the ruin wrought by

is one you "draw your being from, and so reproduce in your character" (Westcott 1908:2:21). On this interpretation the devil begets children in a sense analogous to the begetting of Christians by God. But the devil does not have a spiritual power at work in the lives of individuals analogous to God's power. The danger to avoid here is a concept of cosmic dualism that includes a strict determinism. John uses dualistic language and has a strong view of divine sovereignty (for example 1:13; 6:37, 44), but he also affirms a role for people (for example, 1:12; 6:40, 45). The opponents have not been forced to reject Jesus; it is something they themselves will—they *want [thelete] to carry out* the devil's desire (8:44). A simplistic dualism that sees people as mere puppets who only act when prompted by God or the devil is not a Christian worldview. In fact, such fatalistic determinism characterized much of pagan thought (cf. Dillon 1992) and was one of the reasons the good news was good.

The NIV gives Jesus' words to the opponents as *You belong to your father, the devil* (v. 44), but a more literal translation reads, "you are of your father, the devil" *(hymeis ek tou patros tou diabolou este)*. In John's language, to "be of" speaks of both "origin and type of being" (Schnackenburg 1980a:371). Instead of the devil being the source of sin in some deterministic sense in the lives of individuals, he is the source of sin in a more general sense, as the first sinner. And he is father in terms of providing a type of being; that is, he provides the pattern of sin. So there is a spiritual relationship, a unity of mind, in that sinners, including these opponents, imitate the devil (cf. Augustine *In John* 42.10). Indeed, it is possible that the first part of verse 44 means, "you are of your father, the devil; that is, you will to do his desires" (epexegetic *kai*).

The crucial point is that in seeking to kill Jesus the opponents show that their wills are in tune with the devil, who is a murderer, and in rejecting the one who has told them the truth of God they show that their wills are in tune with the devil, who is a liar. The devil was a murderer from the beginning and has no truth in him, which is to say,

---

selfishness (see 1 Jn 3:8ff.)" (Westcott 1908:1:21).

Calling the devil the *father of lies* suggests he originated lying; saying he does not stand in the truth suggests a fall away from the truth. Thus, this verse has been taken as pointing to the mystery of the fall of Satan (for example, Augustine *In John* 42.11-13; *The City of God* 11.15.13-15).

he is thoroughly alienated from God, evil to the very core. By saying that he is the opponents' father Jesus implies that they are at heart alienated from God as well. It is loyalty to God as they know him that leads them to reject Jesus. Because their rejection is based on what is deepest within them Jesus asserts that at heart they are not related to God at all but to the devil. They have nothing in common with God. In a sense they are being accused of "unchastity" in its religious sense of idolatry. But they do not have to remain in this alienation. Paul was a Jewish opponent similar to these people when Jesus met him. But whereas Paul accepted the revelation, these earlier Jewish opponents do not do so.

Many people today, at least in Western cultures, find the language Jesus uses here rather extreme. It leads many to see the Gospel of John as anti-Jewish (see comment on 19:11). There is no doubt that John and other parts of the New Testament have led members of the church to hate and vilify Jews. This is a cause for genuine grief on the part of the church, for such hatred is certainly not God's view! Such ungodly views and passions are not derived from sharing in Christ. But what are we to make of such language? Three considerations might help interpret this language aright. First, though the opponents are often referred to in this Gospel as "the Jews," this is not a reference to all Jews of that time, let alone throughout history afterwards. Jesus was a Jew, as were John and all the first disciples. "The Jews" is a summary title for the opponents of Jesus, and it probably reflects the conflicts with the synagogue in John's own day and may also be associated with Judea (see comment on 1:19). There were quite a few forms of Judaism before the destruction of the temple in A.D. 70, but after that time, especially later in the first century, the Pharisees, in the name of Judaism, were trying to eliminate all forms of Judaism other than their own. Thus, the use of "the Jews" in John has the insinuation "the supposed true Jews."

Second, while this language may seem extreme to many of us it was quite common in the first century. This is simply how people talked about their opponents (cf. Johnson 1989). And third, although this polemic goes back to the time of Jesus himself, John is most likely telling

---

8:48 The charge of being a Samaritan could mean Jesus is taken to be a magician (M. Smith

the story of Jesus late in the first century at a time when the relations between followers of Jesus and their fellow Jews were coming to a breaking point. The passionate witness of Jesus and his first followers is all the more intense late in the first century as the expulsion from the synagogue of Christians is more widespread and settled. With these considerations in mind we can distinguish the substance of what is being said from its form. There is no doubt that John used strong words to convey the deep differences between Jesus' followers and his opponents. But Jesus' condemnation is not addressed to all Jews, and the language he uses should not be read as expressing hatred. Indeed, he uses very strong language in an effort to break through their closed minds and hearts. He had spoken in gentler terms before, with great patience (for example, v. 49). But there are times when a jarring intervention such as this language represents is the best way to effect change, as Paul might testify given his experience on the road to Damascus.

On a different level, Jesus' use of language teaches us very valuable lessons in meekness and zeal. Jesus uses forceful language here where he is attacking their false pride and perilous position. But when they call him demon possessed (v. 48) he responds not with vehemence but with gentle correction, "thus teaching us to avenge insults offered to God, but to overlook such as are offered to ourselves" (Chrysostom *In John* 55.1). This pattern may be traced all the way through the Gospels. In the present situation Jesus and his opponents both believe the truth of God is being challenged by the other.

After revealing the opponents' situation, Jesus returns to their relation to himself and his Father. Unlike the devil, Jesus speaks the truth and is not guilty of any sin (vv. 45-46). When Jesus asks, *Can any of you prove me guilty of sin?* (v. 46) they could have responded that, according to their interpretation of the law, he had broken the sabbath and that he was a false prophet at best (v. 48) or a blasphemer at worst (v. 59). They would charge him with such sins, but he claims to have the better case and in fact be innocent.

Since he is telling them the truth, why do they not believe (v. 46)?

1978:21, 33-34, 81-82).

He answers his own question: *He who belongs to God hears what God says. The reason you do not hear is that you do not belong to God* (v. 47). This is a clear statement summarizing the flow of his argument up to this point. They do not *belong to God,* or, more literally, they are not "of God" *(ek tou theou)* but of the devil (v. 44). Their identity is clear. Jesus' identity is also clear in that he said one who belongs to God hears "what God says," not "what I say." When Jesus teaches, God is speaking.

Instead of accepting his testimony to himself and his judgment of them and then repenting, they accuse him of what he has just accused them. In saying he is *a Samaritan and demon-possessed* (v. 48; cf. 7:20) they are saying that he, not they, is the one who is a foreigner to the covenant with God and is in fact in league with the devil. Similar charges are thrown back and forth.

Jesus rejects their charge and continues to insist on his relationship with his Father: *I honor my Father and you dishonor me* (v. 49). In failing to honor Jesus they are disobedient to God's will, which is that "all may honor the Son just as they honor the Father" (5:23). The Father himself is seeking the glory of the Son (v. 50), just as the Son is seeking the glory of the Father. Jesus and his opponents have traded accusations, and now he warns them that the one who will pass judgment in this dispute is the very Father to whom he is bearing witness and whom they are rejecting (v. 50).

Then, as he frequently does, Jesus increases the scandal by saying, *if anyone keeps my word, he will never see death* (v. 51). This simply follows from the fact that Jesus' word is in fact God's own word, as we have just seen (v. 47). It recalls his earlier word that asked them to hold to his teaching and be set free from sin (vv. 31-32). The idea of abiding or remaining in his teaching (v. 31) is now complemented by the motif of keeping it. This refers to remaining watchful, attentive and focused so as not to disregard it (Westcott 1908:2:24) but rather to continue to obey it (Louw and Nida 1988:2:468). These verses indicate that it takes work to keep in touch with Jesus' teaching. The disciple must expend energy to remain true to his teaching.

8:53 When they say Abraham is *our* father they may be implying he is not Jesus' father,

The promise that the faithful disciple will not die (v. 51) is a theme already introduced in John (5:24; 6:40, 47) and one that will be developed more fully (chap. 11). It does not mean the disciple will not physically die; it means that he or she will not enter that state of "selfish isolation which is the negation of life" (Westcott 1908:2:25). The very fact that the disciple remains in contact with Jesus, the source of life, suggests such communion, with its death to self and life to God.

Just as Jesus' promise of life had scandalized an earlier group of would-be disciples (6:60), so it does here as well: *Now we know that you are demon-possessed!* (v. 52). They have heard something that they cannot understand. Instead of receiving it with humility and awaiting further insight, they question and reject it. They question whether Jesus is claiming to be greater than their father Abraham (v. 53), a question similar to the Samaritan woman's question of whether Jesus is greater than their father Jacob (4:12). Jesus' claim to offer life goes beyond anything that Abraham or the prophets could offer or even had experienced themselves, since they had all died (vv. 52-53). So the question once again boils down to who Jesus is making himself out to be (v. 53). The translation *Who do you think you are?* misses the point of the question, which is literally, "Who are you making yourself out to be?" In other words, the issue is not just what Jesus thinks, but what he is promoting. Since only God is the giver of life, they are beginning to perceive the enormity of Jesus' claims. In asking for clarification they are almost acting like a jury, giving the defendant a chance to be condemned with his or her own words. Jesus is happy to oblige since this is what he has come for—to bear witness. So Jesus, as he did with the woman of Samaria, goes on to answer their question.

First, he speaks plainly of the Father. He refuses to glorify himself but says his Father will do so. He clearly and explicitly identifies his Father: *My Father, whom you claim as your God, is the one who glorifies me* (v. 54). Earlier they did not know he was referring to God (v. 27), but Jesus has now said it plainly. God is focused upon Jesus, seeking to glorify him (vv. 54, 50). This is the truth revealed in dramatic form in

---

an example of the exclusive use of the first-person pronoun (Wallace 1996:397-98), which would correspond to their calling Jesus a Samaritan (v. 48).

the Synoptics, for when the Father speaks from heaven at the baptism he speaks of his Son; he repeats this at the transfiguration and adds a call to pay attention to him: "This is my Son, whom I love; with him I am well pleased. Listen to him!" (Mt 17:5; see also Mt 3:17; Mk 1:11; 9:7; Lk 3:22; 9:35).

Second, Jesus continues to speak plainly of their ignorance of God. He had spoken of the devil as a liar (v. 44), and now he calls these opponents liars (v. 55), since they claim to know God when in fact they do not.

Third, he speaks of his relationship to God. The language used at the end of verse 55 is striking: *I . . . keep his word*. This phrase had just been used by Jesus as he spoke of his own disciples (v. 51), so this repetition indicates that Jesus is our model of discipleship. The idea of keeping God's word picks up many of the themes of discipleship developed in this Gospel, such as docility, humility, receptivity, perseverance, loyalty and obedience. Here, in a passage where Jesus is about to claim divine prerogatives in the clearest terms, we have this reminder that he is both distinct from God and submissive to God. As disciples, we are to share in his relationship with the Father through the Spirit. As we keep his word we are joining him in his own keeping of the Father's word.

Finally, we also have a clear word about his own divine identity. The topic has been the identification of the true children of Abraham. Now Jesus spells out clearly what he has already implied in many ways, namely, that his own identity is far beyond such a category. This revelation comes in two parts. First, Jesus says, *Your father Abraham rejoiced at the thought of seeing my day; he saw it and was glad* (v. 56). The *day* that Jesus refers to is his whole advent, ministry, death, resurrection and ascension—the total event of salvation that he has brought.

It is uncertain which of Abraham's experiences is referred to here. It could be something Abraham experienced during his lifetime or something that he has experienced in heaven. Either view would resonate

---

8:57 According to Irenaeus, Jesus was over fifty years old when he died (*Against Heresies* 2.22.5). This fact is said to be attested to by John (through those who had heard him) and

with Jewish traditions. Some traditions spoke of Abraham's seeing the future during his own lifetime (*Genesis Rabbah* 44:25). In this case the joy of Abraham would most likely refer to his experience at the promise of Isaac's birth (Gen 17:17), which was joy at the goodness of God and in anticipation of the fulfillment of his promises. Philo stresses the anticipation evident in Abraham's laughter (*De Mutatione Nominum* 154-165), and *Jubilees* 16:15-19 (second century B.C.) says that Abraham and Sarah "rejoiced very greatly" when the divine messengers made the promise to Abraham and spoke explicitly of a "holy seed" who would come from the line of Isaac and produce for God a people from among the nations. According to this tradition the joy was linked to the fulfillment of God's promises through one who would come through Isaac. Jesus would be claiming to be the ultimate fulfillment of that promise.

The alternative, the idea of a heavenly rejoicing, might be similar to *Testament of Levi* 18:14 (second century B.C.), which speaks of Abraham's rejoicing at the coming of the eschatological priest who brings God's salvation. Perhaps Jesus is saying Abraham rejoiced in the recent past, as he saw from heaven the coming of the Word made flesh, the dawning of the light of salvation.

In saying, *You are not yet fifty years old . . . and you have seen Abraham!* (v. 57), the opponents focus on Jesus' vision of Abraham, not Abraham's of him. It could be that they are simply pointing out that Jesus is not several thousand years old. This seems to be a stupid response to Jesus' cryptic saying, but the opponents are not the only dull ones in this Gospel, for similar responses are given even by Jesus' true disciples (for example, 11:12). But it could be that they are saying that Jesus "cannot have seen Abraham in paradise because he is too young for such a (mystical) vision" (Schnackenburg 1980b:223). Rudolf Schnackenburg objects that the tense of *have seen* (*heō rakas,* a perfect) suggests "a long-standing relationship between Jesus and the ancestor of the Jews" (Schnackenburg 1980b:223). Yet the perfect tense need not suggest this at all, and, on the other hand, such an interpretation would

---

other apostles. Such an age for Jesus does not contradict the fixed points we have for dating (Westcott 1908:2:28).

fit quite well with the concern throughout this Gospel with the claims of the Jewish mystics.

In any case, not only has Abraham seen Jesus' day (whether during his lifetime or from heaven), but Jesus is aware of this fact, which means he has seen Abraham either in heaven or during Abraham's lifetime, whether by mystical vision or through his existence at the time of Abraham.

Jesus' reference to Abraham sounds to the opponents like an incredible claim to spiritual experience. His reply to their incredulity pushes his claim far beyond the idea of vision whether mystical or otherwise, whether of the past or through ascents into heaven: *I tell you the truth . . . before Abraham was born, I am!* (v. 58). He is not just making a statement of his age, for then he would have said something like, "Before Abraham was born, I was" (Carson 1991:358). Rather, he is now using in an unambiguous way the divine I AM (Harner 1970:26-30). The I AM was the name of God revealed to Moses, though the Greek expression *(egō eimi)* is not that used in the Septuagint in Exodus 3:14 *(ho ōn)*. The phrase *egō eimi* is used of the divine name in Isaiah (41:4; 43:10, 25; 45:18; 46:4; 47:8, 10; 51:12; 52:6). Isaiah 43:10 is a particularly significant passage since it includes a reference to the Lord's chosen servant *(pais)* who is his witness, "so that you may know and believe and understand that I am he *[hoti egō eimi]*. There was no other god before me nor will there be after me." This strong statement of monotheism is the very thing the opponents think Jesus' claim is denying.

By using the I AM Jesus is claiming to have existed not just at the time of Abraham, but from eternity. This is not only a statement about his salvific work, though that is implied here as it was in God's self-identification at the bush (Schnackenburg 1980b:224). Rather, he is saying that his words and deeds are not *about* God; they are in fact God's *own* words and deeds. He speaks in language of oneness, though he has just clearly expressed distinctness also (vv. 54-55). Jesus is God, though not

---

8:58 Some scholars deny there is an affirmation of deity here since "John never simply identifies Jesus with God" (Lindars 1972:336). But in fact, John does identify Jesus with God in many ways, not least through the confession of Thomas: "My Lord and my God" (20:28). Certainly the opponents are represented as understanding Jesus to have made such

simply by way of identification with Yahweh, for there is also distinction. He is not simply a human being who has been taken up into the divine counsels and made an agent of God unlike any other, but neither is he simply God in a suit of flesh. Rather, as the later church counsels said, he is fully God and fully man. Such formulations are based on revelation such as found in this passage.

Clearly this is the climax of the revelation that has been unfolding during the Feast of Tabernacles. People have been wondering if Jesus is the Prophet or the Messiah. "But messianic categories are transcended when Jesus offers Himself as the source of living water, and as the light of the world, and finally pronounces the *egō eimi* which affirms the mystery of His own eternal being, in unity with the Father" (Dodd 1953:351).

The opponents have understood nothing Jesus has said about himself or his Father. They seek to stone him (v. 59), presumably for the same reason they do so at other times (5:18; 10:31-33)—on a charge of blasphemy (cf. Lev 24:16; *m. Sanhedrin* 7:4). But they are not able to carry out their desires, the desires of their father, who was a murderer from the beginning (v. 44). Jesus slips away from the temple, leaving it secretly, as he came at the beginning of this section (7:10). This hiddenness has a double significance. Jesus is still a marked man. He came to the temple secretly because of death threats, and now this danger has intensified. On another level, his approach to the temple and now his departure from it in a hidden fashion, corresponds to the emphasis in these chapters that the opponents do not know where he comes from or where he goes, meaning the Father. The main points of these two chapters have been Jesus divine identity, his role as the bringer of God's salvation as water and light and the opponents' utter alienation from God. This alienation has been stated explicitly, depicted dramatically in their questions and behavior and is now expressed symbolically in Jesus' leaving in hiddenness. Jesus has claimed to be I AM, the divine presence. So when he leaves the temple it is nothing less than "the

---

a claim (5:18; 10:31-33), an impression Jesus does not correct. Jesus is identified with God but, as we have seen, not simply as God (cf. Lindars 1972:615), for that would confuse the distinctions of the Father and the Son (see comment on 1:1).

departure of the Divine Presence from the old 'Holy Space' " (Davies 1974:296). He will not return again to the temple; he will come only to its outer precincts (10:23). His formation of a community apart from the temple will now become more apparent.

□ Jesus Forms a Community Around Himself Over Against Official Judaism (9:1—10:42)

Jesus has just revealed himself as the light of the world and has passed judgment on the leaders among the Jews and, indeed, on the temple itself (chap. 8). Now he heals a man born blind, thus giving a sign that bears witness to his claim to be the light of the world. He also continues to condemn the opponents by accusing them of being blind spiritually, a far worse condition than the physical blindness of the man he has healed.

In the midst of these continuing themes a new element is added. When the Jewish authorities cast the healed blind man out of the synagogue, Jesus begins to form a body of disciples that are clearly separate from the synagogue. Thus the break between Jesus and the Jewish authorities (chap. 8) is now seen to characterize his followers also. This separation brings to a head the crisis that has been building for several chapters. Chapter 5 revealed Jesus as the true referent of the law, while chapters 6 through 8 showed Jesus to be the fulfillment of Judaism as represented by its feasts and temple. Now Jesus is forming a new community apart from the institutions of Judaism, with himself as its center and guide.

Thus, the story of the man born blind provides a sign regarding not only Jesus, but also his opponents and the community of those believing in Jesus. All three of these themes are continued in chapter 10, when Jesus teaches that he is the Good Shepherd in contrast to the evil shepherds who have gained power in Jerusalem. In a climactic confrontation at the end of chapter 10 Jesus declares that the Jewish opponents are not members of his flock. He concludes with a clear claim to a unique oneness with God, and he grounds that claim in the Scriptures. This

---

9:2 The idea of a person's sinning before birth could suggest that the person sinned in a previous life. The Greek idea of the soul's immortality is present within Judaism at this time

forms the culmination of his public ministry and prepares for the greatest of his signs—the raising of Lazarus—and the fulfillment of all the signs in his own death, resurrection and ascension.

Jesus, the Light of the World, Opens the Eyes of a Man Born Blind (9:1-41)

It appears that Jesus is still in Jerusalem (since the man is sent to wash in Siloam), but Jesus is no longer in hiding (contrast 8:59). Perhaps some time has elapsed since his confrontation with the authorities in the temple, though as the story reads he could be coming straight from their debate. Certainly John intends us to connect this healing with the previous chapter, as the references to Jesus as the light of the world indicate (8:12; 9:5).

Jesus Heals a Man Born Blind (9:1-7) Jesus, taking the initiative, notices a man blind from birth. It is not said how Jesus and his followers know that he has been blind from birth. Perhaps the Lord knew preternaturally, or maybe he simply asked him. Once this information is known the disciples treat the man's condition as a theological problem. People commonly assumed that disease and disorders on both the personal and national level were due to sin, as summarized in the rabbinic saying from around A.D. 300 that "there is no death without sin and there is no suffering without iniquity" (*b. Šabbat* 55a). But the case of a person born blind raises the question of whose sin caused this condition, that of his parents or of the person himself while in the womb. The idea that the parents' sins can affect their children finds support in the Old Testament itself (Ex 20:5), as does its antithesis (Ezek 18:20). Likewise the rabbis debated whether fetuses could sin, some arguing they could (for example, *Genesis Rabbah* 63:6) and others that they could not (*Genesis Rabbah* 34:10). Obviously, such issues were matters of debate within Judaism (cf. Schrage 1972:290-91), including the time during Jesus' ministry, as our text indicates.

The disciples' question was a request that Jesus comment on this debate. Jesus shifts the focus, and instead of addressing the cause of the man's blindness he speaks of its purpose: *so that the work of God might*

(cf. Schürer 1973-1987:2:391; 3:886-87), but John does not use *psychē* ("soul," "life") in a Greek sense (Schnackenburg 1980b:496 n. 7).

be displayed in his life (v. 3). We should not be concerned with assigning blame. Trying to figure out the source of suffering in an individual's life is futile given our limited understanding, as the book of Job should teach us. Rather, here is one in whom Jesus can manifest God's works and thus reveal something of God himself and his purposes on earth. Jesus is being led by his Father to provide a sign that he is indeed the light of the world. In this sign he continues to reveal the Father's glory, that is, his love and mercy. For the ultimate truth about Jesus' works is that the Father, living in him, is doing his own works (14:10). This is what it means that his works are done from the Father (10:32) and in the Father's name (10:25, 37), revealing that Jesus is in the Father and the Father in him (10:38; cf. 10:30). As is always the case in John, Jesus' identity and his relation to the Father are at the heart of what is being said and done.

Jesus' statement touches on the theme of suffering. There is a sense in which every aspect of our lives, including our own suffering, is an occasion for the manifestation of God's glory and his purposes. Scripture describes four types of suffering viewed in terms of causes or purposes (cf. John Cassian *Conferences* 6.11): first, suffering as a proving or testing of our faith (Gen 22; Deut 8:2; Job); second, suffering meant for improvement, for our edification (Heb 12:5-8); third, suffering as punishment for sin (Deut 32:15-25; Jer 30:15; Jn 5:14); and fourth, suffering that shows forth God's glory, as here in our story and later in the raising of Lazarus (Jn 11:4). To these should be added a fifth form of suffering, that which comes from bearing witness to Christ, illustrated by what happens to this former blind man in being cast out of the synagogue.

Suffering is connected to sin (see comment on 5:14), at least generally if not always directly. But the present passage develops this connection further. Our sufferings are opportunities for God's grace. If our suffering is indeed a punishment for sin, then it becomes an occasion for repentance and thus the manifestation of God's grace as we are restored to fellowship with God. If our suffering is not a direct punishment for sin, then it is something God allows to happen in our lives, usually for reasons beyond our knowing, which nevertheless can help us die to self and find our true life in God. God does not allow anything to enter our lives that is not able to glorify him by drawing us into deeper intimacy with him and revealing his glory. When we cling to self and our own comfort we are led to resentment. When we trust in God's goodness and providence we are able to find comfort in God himself and not in our circumstances. Consequently, we can genuinely "give thanks in all circumstances" (1 Thess 5:18). This is not to say that misfortune and evil are God's will in general, but they are part of what it takes to live with him and unto him in this mess we have made through our rebellion against him and his rule over us. Our rebellion has brought disorder to every aspect of our existence, and the way back to the beauty and peace and order of his kingdom leads through suffering, as the cross makes clear. So we should not deny or avoid the reality of our suffering, but we should ask God to use it to further his purposes in us and through us. Some lessons only become ours in reality through suffering and the relationship with God that results from these tests. We can help others with the truths we learn in this way (cf. 2 Cor 1:3-11), and we can identify with the blind man and reflect on ways the Lord might display his works in us in the midst of our own sufferings.

In his keynote address Jesus said he does what he sees the Father doing, which includes in particular giving life and judging (5:19-30). Both features are evident here. In giving sight to his man Jesus reveals himself as the Messiah who brings the new quality of life that the prophets promised, seen now in terms of a relationship with himself. He brings light into this man, both physically and spiritually. In the conflict that erupts as a result of this act of divine grace and mercy, the other aspect of the coming of the light, judgment, is also clearly seen.

Jesus includes his disciples in such work when he says, *we must do the work of him who sent me* (9:4). Such involvement on the disciples' part has been hinted at earlier (3:11; 4:32-38; cf. 6:5) and will be developed more later (chaps. 13—17; 20:21). Jesus' disciples are to share in his relationship with the Father and thereby in the revelation of the Father's glory through doing the work of the Father and in the judgment of the world.

The fact that Jesus' disciples will do such works in the future—indeed, even greater works (14:12)—makes Jesus' next statement puzzling. He says this work is to go on *as long as it is day* for *night is coming, when no one can work* (9:4). Clues appear later in the Gospel as to when this *night* occurs. As Jesus approaches his Passion he will warn the people, "You are going to have the light just a little while longer" (12:35). When Judas leaves to betray Jesus it is said, "And it was night" (13:30). This is the beginning of the Passion, when Jesus will be taken from them for three days (cf. also Lk 22:53). When the light is absent it is night, and the *night* for John is when Jesus is absent, as Jesus himself says in verse 5: *While I am in the world, I am the light of the world.* Thus, the *night* seems to be the time when Jesus is absent from the world between his death and resurrection, since thereafter the Spirit will be present (20:22) who will continue Jesus' work through the disciples. Through this strong warning, which regards such a limited period of time, we are led to see the enormity of the darkness of those three days in salvation history.

Thus, Jesus' somewhat cryptic statement tells us that what is about to occur is a work of God made possible because Jesus, the light of the world, is present. The glory of God continues to be manifested in Jesus' activity, as it has from the outset (2:11).

Jesus' identity is revealed by the very act of healing a blind man, for a sign of the messianic age was the healing of blindness, both physical blindness (for example, Is 35:5) and spiritual blindness (for example, Is 42:18-19; cf. Westcott 1908:2:31). It is quite striking that the only references to healing of blindness in the Bible other than in Jesus' ministry are Tobit (Tobit 2:10; 11:7-13) and Paul (Acts 9:8, 17-19). Tobit may not have actually been blind, since his loss of sight resulted from getting bird droppings in his eyes. In the case of Paul it was Jesus who both blinded and restored him. So Jesus' healing of the blind stands out as a major sign of his identity and the significance of his coming.

Although the healing reveals Jesus as Messiah, the way Jesus goes about healing suggests his identity as Messiah goes beyond anyone's conception of the Messiah. The use of saliva for medicinal purposes was common in the ancient world (Barrett 1978:358), and Jesus himself uses

---

9:4 Augustine interprets this *night* as a reference to hell, the time "when no man can work, but only get back what he has wrought before" (*In John* 44.6). This interpretation is theologically appropriate and worthy of reflection, but it does not seem to be what is directly in view in the text.

9:5 The Greek here for *I am the light of the world (phōs eimi tou kosmou)* does not include the expression *egō eimi* as in 8:12. This "perhaps underlines the significance of that form when it does occur; pronouncements can be made without it" (Barrett 1978:357).

it in his healings at times (Mk 7:33; 8:23). Clay also could have associations with pagan healing practices, in particular with the cult of Aesculapius (Rengstorf 1968:118-19). But for the healer to make clay out of spittle and use it for healing is unusual. John emphasizes this mud in the repeated recounting of the event by the former blind man (9:6, 11, 15) and also by including it where it is unnecessary (v. 14). K. H. Rengstorf suggests that this emphasis may be intended to draw a contrast with Aesculapius, but more likely the allusion is to the biblical picture of God as a potter and human beings as clay (for example, Job 10:9; Is 45:9; 64:8; Jer 18:6; Sirach 33:13; cf. Rom 9:21). Irenaeus picks up this allusion when he interprets this story in the light of the creation of man from the ground (Gen 2:7), for "the work of God [cf. Jn 9:3] is the fashioning of man" (*Against Heresies* 5.15.2). Thus, "that which the artificer, the Word, had omitted to form in the womb, [namely, the blind man's eyes], He then supplied in public, that the works of God might be manifested in him" (Irenaeus *Against Heresies* 5.15.2). In this way Jesus revealed his own glory, "for no small glory was it that He should be deemed the Architect of the creation" (Chrysostom *In John* 56.2). This story illustrates the truth revealed in John's prologue that Jesus, the Word, is the one through whom all things were made, having in himself the life that is "the light of men" (1:3-4). While many modern scholars would agree with C. K. Barrett that Irenaeus's interpretation is "improbable" (Barrett 1978:358), the association with the prologue actually makes it likely—all the more so as this story follows directly Jesus' clear expression of his claim to divinity (8:58).

The healing was not effected until the man obeyed Jesus' command: *Go . . . wash in the Pool of Siloam* (9:7). Why didn't Jesus just heal him on the spot, as he did others? Why send a *blind* man, in particular, on such a journey? There must be something involved here that contributes to the revealing of God's work. Perhaps the man's obedience is

---

9:6 Much in Jesus' teaching and miracles would have come across to outsiders as evidence that he was a magician (M. Smith 1978). Such use of spittle would be a case in point (M. Smith 1978:128).

9:7 Others have interpreted the significance of *Sent* as a reference to the Spirit (7:39; cf. Michaels 1989:164), who will be sent by the Father (14:26) and the Son (15:26; 16:7). This association is less likely, given the focus on Jesus in the context.

significant, revealing that he shares a chief characteristic of Jesus' true disciples. Like Naaman the Syrian (2 Kings 5:10-14), this man obeys God's command to go and wash and is healed. Also like Naaman, he is able to bear witness to God as a result (2 Kings 5:15). But John's parenthetical note that Siloam means *Sent* (v. 7) suggests more than the man's obedience is involved. References to Siloah, the stream associated with the pool of Siloam (Shiloah in Gen 49:10 [NIV margin]; Shiloah in Is 8:6), were seen as messianic (*Genesis Rabbah* 98:8; Gen 49:10 in *Targum Onqelos; b. Sanhedrin* 94b; 98b). This fits with the emphasis in John's Gospel on Jesus as the one sent from the Father, including such an emphasis in the immediate context (8:16, 18, 29, 42; 10:36). Thus, both the healing itself and the details involved point to Jesus as the Messiah. Here is an example of the triumph of the light over the darkness (1:5).

The Man's Neighbors Raise Questions (9:8-12) The crowd had a hard time identifying Jesus (chaps. 7—8), and now they are divided in their recognition of this one whom he has healed (9:8-9). The man uses the same language Jesus has used to identify himself, *egō eimi,* though here it does not allude to the divine name but is used as an identification formula: *I am the man* (v. 9; see comment on 6:20).

Once they have established that he is indeed the blind beggar they had known, they ask the obvious question of how he came to have his sight (v. 10), and he recounts what happened (v. 11). This question will be asked four times in this story, stressing that something highly unusual has taken place, something that cannot be explained in the categories of this world (Beasley-Murray 1987:156). Unlike the man by the pool of Bethesda, this man does realize from the beginning that Jesus is the one who has healed him (v. 11; cf. 5:12-13), but he does not know where Jesus is (v. 12). This ignorance will be resolved soon enough. The deeper ignorance of the opponents, who do not know where Jesus is from (v. 30), does not improve as a result of this act of mercy and glory on Jesus' part. The man's admission of ignorance is an attribute of a true disciple, revealing him to be honest and humble. He stands in marked contrast to the Jewish opponents in this story, for they claim to know what in

---

9:15 The Greek includes the word *again (palin)*—"Therefore again the Pharisees also

fact they realize they do not really know (v. 24; cf. v. 16). It is precisely this lack of integrity and self-awareness that Jesus criticizes in his conclusion to this story (vv. 39-41).

The Pharisees Interrogate the Man (9:13-17) The neighbors bring the man to the Pharisees, presumably because something unusual has taken place and they are the recognized experts on the things of God. There does not seem to be anything sinister in their going to the Pharisees, unlike the contact between the Jewish opponents and the man at the pool of Bethesda (5:15).

The fact that this healing took place on the sabbath is mentioned in dramatic fashion midway in the story (v. 14; so also 5:9). In healing the blind man Jesus broke the sabbath rules in several ways, at least as they appear in later texts. Healing was permitted on the sabbath since "whenever there is doubt whether life is in danger this overrides the Sabbath" (*m. Yoma* 8:6; cf. *b. Yoma* 84b-85b; Lohse 1971:14-15). But, as in the case of the man at the pool of Bethesda, Jesus again heals what is not a life-threatening condition. Furthermore, just as his command to the man to carry his mat violated sabbath rules (5:11), so now Jesus' own activity of making mud violated the prohibition of kneading on the sabbath (*m. Šabbat* 7:2). It is possible that his use of spittle also violated sabbath rules, since later at least "painting" the eye, that is, anointing it for healing, was clearly prohibited (*b. 'Aboda Zara* 28b), and some included the use of spittle in this prohibition (*y. 'Aboda Zara* 14d; cf. Beasley-Murray 1987:156-57). Finally, it was unlawful to take a journey of more than 2,000 cubits (1,000 yards) on the sabbath (cf. *m. 'Erubin* 4-5). A trip to Siloam and back from the nearest wall of the temple, for example, would be about 1,300 yards. It is perhaps likely that the trip to and from Siloam was further than was allowed, though we cannot be sure since we do not know where the healing took place. Jesus may be not just breaking the sabbath, but trampling on it, at least according to the views of these Jewish opponents!

The former blind man has to tell the story a second time, this time speaking to a new audience and adding the dramatic note that it was the sabbath. The crowd had wanted to know how the healing had

---

asked him"—emphasizing how repetitive the man's experience was.

happened out of understandable curiosity. The Pharisees now ask the same question but with different intent, for they want to determine whether any sabbath laws have been broken. The man recounts his healing with great brevity (v. 15). Many scholars see in this brevity an exasperation with having to retell his story, but this is only the first time he has told it to these people. Perhaps he senses their displeasure and sticks to the bare facts, as peasants have a tendency to do when interrogated by the junta—not an inappropriate image for this story, as we will see.

The Pharisees are divided over the man's witness (v. 16), a common occurrence when the light shines (cf. 7:43). The division among his opponents bears witness to Jesus' identity as the light of the world (cf. Lohse 1971:28). But here the light is shining through this man's testimony, providing an example of what all disciples are to do in the future (20:21).

The Pharisees face a dilemma for Jesus' sabbath breaking suggests he is not of God whereas his extraordinary power to heal suggests he is of God. Some of the Pharisees ask, *How can a sinner do such miraculous signs?* (v. 16). The plural, *signs,* indicates a larger familiarity with Jesus' activity. Perhaps we may assume that we are hearing the voice of Nicodemus, who has already said the same thing to Jesus himself (3:2). If so, then the one who came to Jesus at night is now sticking up for him once again (7:50-51) while it is day.

Divided amongst themselves, the Pharisees ask the blind man for his opinion of Jesus, given that it was his eyes Jesus had opened (v. 17). It is ironic that these Jewish leaders, who are so proud of their possession of the law and their ability to evaluate religious claims, are asking this man for his opinion on a religious matter. The Christians in John's own day would have loved this verse, since they were being persecuted by these same authorities for their loyalty to Jesus. This scene is like an underground political cartoon that deflates the self-important persecuting officials.

The man responds that Jesus is a prophet. This is true as far as it goes, though it is not in itself adequate. He clearly thinks Jesus is on the side of God, despite such supposed abuse of the sabbath. The crowd has also viewed Jesus as a prophet (7:40), as have those so misguided as to want to make Jesus king (6:14). But the Samaritan woman also held this view (4:19), and Jesus went on to lead her into a deeper understanding of himself. Jesus will lead this man in the same way.

The Pharisees Interrogate the Man's Parents (9:18-23) Jesus' disregard for their sabbath regulations is so blatant the opponents cannot accept the idea that God would honor such lawlessness. So to reconcile what has happened to their presuppositions, they assume that the man must not have been blind. Not only do they reject the man's evaluation of Jesus as a prophet, they don't even accept his testimony about his own former condition! Instead, they investigate. They call in the parents and ask them to identify the man, confirm whether or not he was born blind and explain how he gained his sight (v. 19). The parents clarify that he is indeed their son who was born blind, but they refuse to speculate on how he gained sight. This is now the third time the question of "how" has been asked. But here the parents understand the question to be asking for more than what mechanism enabled him to receive his sight, because they say they know neither how nor by whom this happened. The issue now is by what or whose power this unheard of event took place. To answer this more serious "how" question would require a confession regarding Jesus and his relationship to God, as the explanation makes clear (v. 22). Such a confession has implications for one's life within the community, and the parents are not willing to be put out of the synagogue for the sake of Jesus. The parents fail to stand up for Jesus in the face of the Jewish opponents, so it is clear they do not model discipleship. Their son is of age, that is, thirteen years old or older, so he must answer such a question for himself.

This scene is full of tragedy, for these parents are not allowed to give thanks to God for the great thing he has done for their son. They must have agonized over his blindness and the begging he was forced into. Now he has been miraculously healed, and they must put aside the overwhelming parental joy and knuckle under to the goons from the committee for the investigation of un-Jewish activity, as it were. The parents' agony would have been very great, given the guilt over the possibility that it was their sin that had been responsible for their son's blindness. In such a situation Jesus' healing would have had far-reaching implications concerning God's gracious acceptance of sinful humanity.

Not only was their son released from the bondage of his blindness and its related life of begging, but they and their son would see themselves in a new relation to God. Yet they had to stifle all of these feelings of joy and gratitude when they were called in by the authorities for questioning.

The parents' fear stems from the threat that *anyone who acknowledged that Jesus was the Christ would be put out of the synagogue* (9:22). Such exclusion was used in the Old Testament (Ezra 10:8), and later sources speak of different degrees of exclusion that were exercised, from a week-long exclusion from the congregation, to a thirty-day exclusion, to an unlimited exclusion from the congregation with avoidance of all contact, to an exclusion from the entire community of Israel (Schrage 1971:848-49). At the time of Jesus one of the lighter forms may have been exercised, and this continued to be the case for some time, as Paul's example indicates: he was thrown out of local synagogues (for example, Acts 13:50; cf. 1 Thess 2:14-16) but was not viewed as outcast from the people of Israel.

Later in the first century, as the gulf between followers of Jesus and the synagogue widened, the harshest form of exclusion came into force. Many scholars see this reference to being *put out of the synagogue* (*aposynagōgos poieō,* v. 22; 12:42; 16:2) as reflecting changes in the synagogue liturgy late in the first century. A curse against heretics, known as the Twelfth Benediction, or the *birkat ha-minim,* was added to the liturgy (cf. *b. Berakot* 28b-29a). This is taken as a way of smoking out the Christians and thus causing the separation between church and synagogue. John is probably writing late in the first century, and although such a separation was taking place then, it is unclear whether John is referring specifically to this addition to the liturgy and whether the addition had such an intent (Robinson 1985:72-80; Beasley-Murray 1987:lxxvi-lxxviii, 153-54; Carson 1991:369-72). After a careful study William Horbury concludes that the addition "was not decisive on its own in the separation of church and synagogue, but it gave solemn liturgical expression to a separation effected in the second half of the first century through the larger group of measures to which it belongs" (Horbury 1982:61; cf. Lindars 1981:49-54). Given such separation, this story would have particular relevance for John's first readers.

Under this threat of expulsion we can see the nucleus of a community gathering around Jesus, clearly distinct from these officials who represent what emerges after A.D. 70 as official Judaism. Jesus has withdrawn from the temple (8:59), and now he is gathering a group around him over against the structures and leadership of Israel. Jesus will set this process in place as this story continues (9:35). The full expression of this split will not emerge for some years, but its seed was planted, John says, by Jesus himself.

The Pharisees Interrogate the Man a Second Time (9:24-34) When the Jewish authorities put the "how" question to the man himself they get a very different response than they got from the parents, and the fur flies. They begin their interrogation on a solemn, formal note: *Give glory to God* (v. 24). This is not an invitation to sing a hymn of praise for his healing! The expression means the man is being exhorted to confess his guilt (cf. Josh 7:19; *m. Sanhedrin* 6:2). The man has told them the truth, but they don't really want the truth, they want their own answer. These people, whom Jesus called liars (8:55), are trying to force this man to lie, and they are doing so in the name of truth. (Double talk is not an invention of the twentieth century.) The terms they use are full of irony. These people who care only for the glory of men, not God (12:43; cf. 5:44), are telling him to *give glory to God*. They are demanding that he give glory to God by confessing his sin, but the man has given glory to God by bearing witness to Jesus.

They are being deceptive when they say, *We know this man is a sinner* (v. 24). Jesus has clearly broken their sabbath rules and thus could be labeled a sinner, but we have just been told they are divided over this very question (v. 16). John is showing us the deception and bullying of these ideologues who are in power. The Christians in John's day could identify with this man. Indeed, John himself had such an experience with some of these very same individuals (Acts 5:17-41). Those Christians in the world today who are persecuted for their faith can also identify with this man.

The authorities say Jesus is a sinner, but the man does not pick up on that. Instead he points to the one certain fact of the case—he was blind and now he sees (v. 25). Their supposed knowledge about Jesus is pitted against his certain knowledge of his healing. With this fact thrown in their faces again they are stymied. They can only repeat once more their questions of what happened (v. 26). They are at a loss, and the man pushes them. His reply is very cheeky: *I have told you already and you did not listen. Why do you want to hear it again? Do you want to become his disciples, too?* (v. 27). Here he reveals much about them and himself. They didn't listen, which Jesus has already pointed out (8:43, 47). And by asking if they want to become Jesus' disciples *too* he reveals that he himself has such a desire (cf. Michaels 1989:169). The man has progressed yet further in his Christology, for he here implies "that Jesus is his master" (Talbert 1992:160).

The man may simply be being cheeky when he asks whether they want to become Jesus' disciples, but in effect he is doing the work of an evangelist. Here is another offer of God's grace to those most deeply opposed to Jesus and alienated from God. In their furious reply they comment again that they are disciples of Moses (v. 28; cf. 5:45-47). The Pharisees insist that a choice must be made between being a disciple of Jesus and being a disciple of Moses, at least as they understand Moses. It is one of John's purposes to show how Moses and the Scriptures actually witness against the opponents and to Jesus (cf. 5:46). This story is preparing us for an important example of such a witness in the next chapter (10:34-36).

The Pharisees once again condemn Jesus by saying they do not *know where he comes from* (v. 29), a major theme of chapter 7. But now someone stands up to them and uses what they think is a charge against Jesus as a condemnation of themselves. He focuses on their ignorance. It is *remarkable* (v. 30) that those who know God and his ways so well would not be able to recognize one who is able to do what is unheard of—open the eyes of a man who had been blind from birth (v. 32). For a man *born* blind would have defective eyes, not just damaged eyes. A person born blind had no hope of sight, as this man well knew from experience. He picks up the very misgiving some of the Pharisees were having (v. 16) and drives it home: God listens to those who are godly and who do his will, not to sinners (v. 31). *If this man were not from*

9:31 The idea that God does not listen to sinners is very common; cf. Deuteronomy 1:45; Job 27:8-9; 35:12-13; Psalm 66:18; 109:7; Proverbs 1:28-29; 15:29; 28:9; Isaiah 1:15; 59:2; Jeremiah 11:11; 14:12; Ezekiel 8:18; Micah 3:4; Zechariah 7:13; James 4:3; *b. Sanhedrin* 90a;

God, he could do nothing (v. 33). Earlier the man refused to say whether Jesus was a sinner (v. 25), but now he makes it very clear what he thinks.

The authorities do not deal with his argument. Instead, they cast him out, saying, *You were steeped in sin at birth; how dare you lecture us!* (v. 34). Literally they say, "would you teach us," revealing again their unteachable spirit. Instead of facing up to the evidence the once-blind man has presented they throw back at him his blindness as evidence of his sinfulness. They refuse to entertain the possible implications of his healing, that is, that he is accepted by God. These who had asked him for his opinion earlier (v. 17) now show their true contempt for him. We get the impression that if he had gone along with them and attributed his healing to someone other than God, then they might not have thrown this in his face. But four times in this story Jesus has been referred to directly or indirectly as a sinner. This is the only place in John that this word occurs. So we have the Master referred to as a sinner and the one who confesses him suffering the same fate. Such a fate awaits all of Jesus' disciples, as he will make clear later (15:18-25). Again we see this man as a model disciple (cf. Chrysostom *In John* 58.3-4).

So the issue comes down to who is the real sinner, Jesus and his disciple or the Jewish authorities. The impasse these leaders face is the same that faced Saul of Tarsus when Jesus appeared to him on the road to Damascus. To accept Jesus means a complete rethinking of the law for a Pharisee. The reality of the law and the reality of Jesus come up against one another, and one of them has to budge. Jesus' approach to the law is only appropriate if he is God himself. This has been illustrated by the modern rabbi and prolific scholar Jacob Neusner. In his book *A Rabbi Talks with Jesus,* Neusner puts himself back in the days of Jesus and watches and listens to him as Matthew's Gospel records his life. He asks himself whether he would have been a follower of Jesus and concludes he would not. The reason is Jesus' use of the Torah. He would part from Jesus, saying, "Yours is not the Torah of Moses, and all I have from God, and all I ever need from God, is that one Torah of Moses" (Neusner 1993:3). The main problem is that "Jesus has asked for what

---

and *b. Berakot* 20a. For evidence of the corresponding truth—that God hears the godly—cf. Genesis 18:23-32; Psalm 34:15; 145:19; John 14:13-14; 15:7; 16:23-26; James 4:3; 5:13-18; 1 John 3:21-22; *b. Berakot* 6b; and *Exodus Rabbah* 21:3.

the Torah does not accord to anyone but God" (Neusner 1993:32; cf., e.g., pp. 53, 74). Neusner illustrates that the main sticking point, as we've seen in John's Gospel, is Jesus' view of himself.

With these implications regarding the law this story continues the development of the theme in chapter 5 that the law bears witness to Jesus. In chapters 6—8 we find Jesus replacing the temple and its festivals with himself. Now we see that the law as regulation is also superseded in Jesus. "The Law in condemning Jesus had condemned itself (Gal. 3.10-14); this theme forms the theological basis of the present chapter. The Law condemns itself, and so do its exponents, when they try and condemn Jesus" (Barrett 1978:362). Here is the great divide between Jesus and his Jewish opponents, with each side claiming loyalty to the Torah rightly interpreted.

On the surface this story may look like a showdown between personal experience and Scripture, but it is more complicated than that. The man's statement that if Jesus *were not from God, he could do nothing* (v. 33) is not true, strictly speaking. The works of the Egyptian magicians show as much (Ex 7:11, 22; 8:7). Indeed, Jesus warns against false Christs and false prophets who "will appear and perform great signs and miracles to deceive even the elect" (Mt 24:24) and speaks of those who prophesy in his name, cast out demons in his name and do many mighty works in his name, whom he does not know at all (Mt 7:22-23). So much for experience being an infallible guide! But then the Scriptures, in and of themselves, are not an infallible guide either, as the example of the Jewish opponents reveal. It depends on one's interpretation. The Christian claim is that the Scriptures are an organic whole that make sense when interpreted in the light of Jesus the Christ under the guidance the Spirit has provided the church (Jn 14:26; 15:26). The bottom line is that we need God to guide our understanding of both the Scripture and our experience. Once again we see the importance of humility and openness to God as a core attribute of true discipleship. If the opponents of Jesus had really been loyal to God, open to him and holding to his truth, then they would have been able to see him when he came, as did Nathanael, the true Israelite (1:45-49).

Jesus Leads the Man to Faith (9:35-38) Jesus finds the one who has been thrown out, acting like the Good Shepherd he will soon claim to be. Here is the tenderness and mercy of God in action, but such love is never sentimental in this Gospel. When Jesus finds the man he confronts him with another of his testing questions, *Do you believe in the Son of Man?* (v. 35). Some Jews at this time associated the Son of Man of Daniel 7 with the Davidic Messiah (J. Collins 1995:189), so the man could think Jesus was asking whether he believed in the Messiah. He obviously would not understand the more specific meaning of the Son of Man in John, namely, the Messiah from heaven who brings God's life and judgment, especially through the cross (see comments on 3:13-14 and 5:27).

The man responds in a way that reveals his desire to believe (v. 36). He does not ask what the *Son of Man* is, he asks *who* he is. Belief is not merely an intellectual assent to a proposition, but an attachment of trust to an individual as the one who comes from God. Such an expression of a "longing and inquiring soul" (Chrysostom *In John* 59.1) does not go unanswered any more than the openness and desire of the Samaritan woman did (4:25-26). Jesus responds, *You have now seen him; in fact, he is the one speaking with you* (v. 37), a particularly poignant way of speaking to one who has only been able to see anything at all for a very short time. Here is a crucial step in the development of this relationship: Jesus has cured him and found him, but he now reveals something of his identity to the man. The man has spoken of Jesus as a prophet (v. 17), but will the man accept Jesus on Jesus' own terms? True faith requires such a humble acceptance, as John emphasizes throughout this Gospel.

The man responds with faith: *Then the man said, "Lord, I believe,"* *and he worshiped him* (v. 38). The word for *Lord (kyrios)* could simply mean "sir," (cf. 4:11; 12:21). Likewise, the word for *worshiped* *(proskyneō)* means to fall down and do homage to either God or a human being (Greeven 1968:758-63), and thus could refer to homage due to a man of God rather than God himself. But H. Greeven has argued that the word is always used in the New Testament for adoration of "something—truly or supposedly—divine" (Greeven 1968:763). Certainly the other uses in John signify worship of God (4:20-24; 12:20). Jesus has been presented in divine categories with increased emphasis at the end of chapter 8. But the title "Son of Man" would not convey such a notion in Jewish ears. So while the language used in the man's response to Jesus continues the presentation of the man as a model disciple, it is unclear how much of all this he grasped at the time. He has been progressing as a true disciple, moving from knowledge of Jesus' name (v. 11), to confession of him as a prophet (v. 17), to bearing witness that Jesus is one come from God (v. 33) and finally to accepting his claim to be the Son of Man (vv. 35-38; cf. Brown 1966:377; Westcott 1908:2:37). So even if he does not understand the full significance of his confession and homage to Jesus, he is accepting Jesus on Jesus' own terms and thus placing himself in the position to receive further revelation and grow in his understanding of Jesus and his relationship with him. None of the disciples have understood with any real depth the identity of Jesus or the nature of the salvation he brings. But here in this former blind man we have the anticipation of Thomas' dramatic confession of Jesus as Lord and God (20:28).

Jesus Comments on the Healing and Its Aftermath (9:39-41) We have seen a man go through the stages of becoming a disciple of Jesus, but we have also seen Jesus' opponents' actions progress from debate and division (v. 16) to judgment (v. 24) and on to expulsion of one who would be a disciple of Jesus (v. 34; cf. Westcott 1908:2:36). Jesus' concluding comment puts both of these results in perspective: *For judgment I have come into this world, so that the blind will see and those who see will become blind* (v. 39). Here, in a key definition, Jesus says his judgment both enlightens and blinds. He has not come for judgment in the sense of condemnation (3:17), but such condemnation does take place as he who is the light of the world is revealed. When the light shines, judgment takes place; however, salvation comes as well, for when the light of the world dawns hearts are revealed and the truth about individuals' relationships with God is brought into the open. The same sun that melts wax, hardens clay (Origen *On First Principles* 3.1.11). The opponents have hard hearts—they reject God's offer of mercy and his call to repentance that come through his chastisement (cf. Jer 5:3; 7:25-26; 19:15; Zech 7:11-12; Rev 9:20-21; 16:9-11). Such hardness of heart darkens their minds and alienates them from the life of God (Eph 4:18). The sight they think they have must be taken from them if they are to receive true sight, which sees the true light (Jn 8:12; see comments on 10:1, 8).

That Jesus is using this healing of physical blindness to speak of spiritual conditions is clear to some of the Pharisees who were near Jesus. They are not physically blind, but they ask, *What? Are we blind too?* (v. 40). Here is revealed their self-perception as those who are spiritually illumined with the knowledge of God. They are the ones who think they know (3:2; 8:52; 9:24, 29), but they have a knowledge that does not recognize Jesus for who he is. So Jesus responds with words of great grace—hard words, but words that can break through and lead them into the true light: *If you were blind, you would not be guilty of sin; but now that you claim you can see, your guilt remains* (v. 41). Clearly, it is their claim to have knowledge that is the dilemma. They do not recognize their need; there is no poverty of spirit (Mt 5:3).

We again see the great need for humility, openness and recognition of need. The man has emphasized his ignorance (vv. 25, 36), while they have emphasized their knowledge (vv. 16, 22, 29). Those who settle into blindness without a disposition of openness to God are "incurable since they have deliberately rejected the only cure that exists" (Barrett 1978:366). In a similar situation Jesus refers to blasphemy against the Holy Spirit (Mk 3:29), since in that case Jesus' opponents were seeing his gracious acts and saying they were the work of the Beelzebub, the prince of demons. Such a sin is unforgivable precisely because the person is looking at the character and work of the one who is all good and calling it evil. This perception prevents one from turning to God. For, on the one hand, if one does turn to Christ while thinking Christ represents evil, then that person in his or her own mind is choosing evil and thus sinning (cf. Rom 14:23). If, on the other hand, one refuses to embrace evil but thinks that Jesus is evil, then obviously one cannot turn to him. Either way one has precluded repentance and thereby shut oneself off from forgiveness. God offers forgiveness for all sin. The only sin that cannot be forgiven is the unrepented sin. Thus, until one has a right view of Jesus and comes to him for forgiveness, one remains in one's sin, not because God will not forgive, but because such a one refuses to accept the forgiveness in accordance with God's reality in Christ.

So here at the end of the story we see that spiritual blindness is the real sin, not physical blindness, as the disciples and the Pharisees had thought (vv. 2, 34; cf. Chrysostom *In John* 56.1). Jesus has given sight to a man born blind, but this is a sign of the more significant spiritual light that he provides for those who are spiritually blind. In the very act of mercy, the giving of physical and spiritual sight to this blind man, Jesus continues to reveal the glory of God, that is, his love. Ironically, as earlier (5:1-18), the very brightness of the light that is shining brings a reaction from those who see such signs but do not get it. In their judgment and condemnation of Jesus they stand self-judged and self-condemned.

But even this judgment reveals God's glory. It does so, first, because it is indeed an offer of mercy that they are rejecting. Second, his mercy is seen in the care he provides to those who do receive him, for in condemning their opponents he is protecting his people. As in the case of Pharaoh, God's hardening of one who rejected his call to repentance revealed God's own glory as the one greater than Pharaoh and as the one who redeems his people from evil (Ex 7:3, 14; 14:4, 17). The evil in the present story is the blindness of Jesus' opponents, which is alienation from God. There is a veil over the opponents' hearts (cf. 2 Cor 3:15). But there is also evil in their preventing people from recognizing Jesus and believing in him. God must condemn such evil not only because it is not in keeping with his reality, but also because it is opposing his work in the lives of those who are open to him.

Jesus' condemnation of the Pharisees at the conclusion of this story reveals their alienation from God more clearly, and it also says something about those who, like the blind man, do come to faith in Jesus. This story is an encouragement to stand up and bear witness, as we have seen, and it also illustrates the experience of everyone who becomes a true disciple. Every human being is in the condition of this man spiritually—born blind and in need of enlightenment. It is not surprising, therefore, that the ancient church saw in this story a depiction of baptism, since baptism was known as enlightenment. Some modern scholars continue to find such allusions here (Brown 1966:380-82) or, in a similar way, to conversion (Michaels 1989:160, 168). This story describes one who is in the process of being born from above, becoming capable of seeing the kingdom of God present in the presence of the King (Jn 3:3).

We are all in need of the faith that is itself an organ of spiritual perception similar to what Paul refers to as the "eyes of the heart" (Eph 1:18; cf. Schnackenburg 1980b:255). Unless God opens our eyes we will not see, but he is offering sight to all who will receive it—such is the biblical antinomy of divine sovereignty and human responsibility.

This coming to faith is the crucial point of this story. In the physical healing of the man's eyes we see the agent of creation at work within his world. But the even more astounding work takes place as Jesus leads the man to faith in himself, for this is not just a creative work on the man's body, but the bringing of that essential life that was lost in Eden. That life had existed by virtue of the relationship of intimacy between Creator and created, and now in this man's worship of God in Jesus we see the return to the proper relationship that had been severed by the rebellion. The worship of the man who has found God in Christ is his entrance into eternal life (17:3).

There is also a corporate dimension to this story. Jesus has departed from the temple (8:59), and now a new society is being formed around him in separation from what will become official Judaism. He has revealed himself to people earlier in the Gospel and has accepted spontaneous expressions of faith, but now he takes it a step further and "proposes a test of fellowship" (Westcott 1908:2:43); that is, he offers himself as an object of faith with a specific confession attached: *Do you believe in the Son of Man?* (v. 35). This is a new development in the process of the light shining and the polarization which that causes. "The separation between the old and the new was now consummated, when the rejected of 'the Jews' sank prostrate at the feet of the Son of man" (Westcott 1908:2:44). Jesus is the Good Shepherd of a flock that is distinct from official Judaism, a theme developed in the next chapter.

So this story offers many challenges. We need to realize our own utter poverty, blindness and need apart from Christ. We need to see with his eyes the desperate condition of all who have not been illumined by him, the light of the world. We need to consider before God whether there are ways we reject the evidence of our own experience because we have a faulty understanding of him and his ways. We need to consider before God whether we have God too figured out—or, in this day, whether we have the opposite tendency to think that everything is up for grabs and there is no objective truth or that the Scriptures are not clear and coherent when interpreted in the light of the guidance the Spirit has given to the church. Finally, among many other connections that might be made, we need Jesus to be our center of reference, like this blind man did, so that we are stable, secure and bold no matter what hassles come to us due to our relationship with Jesus, for we have experienced the goodness and mercy of God in Jesus.

Jesus Is the Good Shepherd Who Is Gathering His Flock (10:1-21)

Jesus now puts the events of chapter 9 into perspective by contrasting himself, the Good Shepherd, with the Pharisees, whom he identifies with the evil shepherds of Ezekiel 34. "The 'Pharisees' have expelled from God's flock the man whom Christ Himself enlightened. They are scattering the sheep whom Christ came to gather" (Dodd 1953:359). In this way, Jesus' estrangement from official Judaism is further developed as he calls into being a people who follow him rather than the leaders of Israel.

Jesus Contrasts the Good Shepherd with the Thieves and Robbers (10:1-6) Jesus has used divine language when speaking of himself (8:58) and backed it up with a healing unheard of since the world began (9:32), thereby revealing himself as the agent of creation. By referring to himself as the shepherd of the flock he is appropriating further divine language. In the Old Testament, the leaders of the people are called shepherds, especially Moses (Ps 77:20) and David (Ps 78:70-72; Ezek 34:23). But God is the shepherd par excellence (for example, Ps 80:1; cf. Jeremias 1968:488-89; Barrett 1978:373-74). Jeremiah and Ezekiel in particular develop the shepherd motif to express how God cares for his people and his condemnation of false and evil rulers. God will condemn the false shepherds (Jer 23:1-2; Ezek 34:1-10) and appoint faithful shepherds to tend his flock after the manner of his own heart (Jer 3:15; 23:4). Indeed, the coming Davidic Messiah will be God's shepherd for his flock (Ezek 34:23-24), a prophecy given in the

---

10:2 The word for *robber (lēstēs)* is often used by Josephus for revolutionaries or Zealots (Rengstorf 1967:258-59). But it is unlikely that this usage was widespread (cf. Schnackenburg 1980b:504 n. 22), and, in any case, it is not the meaning in this passage. Here it is combined with *thief* to apply to a single individual, literally, "that one is a thief and a

context of God's announcement that he himself will come to shepherd his flock. He will search for his scattered flock, gather them from the nations and lead them to good pasture on the mountains of Israel. He will tend to the weak and injured but will judge those sheep who only look after themselves and harm the others (Ezek 34:11-22).

In these passages God shepherds through his designated leaders. Jesus is claiming such a role for himself, but in a way unlike anything seen before. He has made clear claims to divinity and messiahship, which will be repeated shortly (Jn 10:22-39). So when he claims to be the shepherd he is claiming that Messiah has come and in him God himself has come to shepherd his people.

Jesus begins with a scene from everyday life, though the exact nature of this scene is uncertain. Kenneth Bailey (1993) suggests the background is from village life where each family owns a couple of sheep for personal use. The animals stay at night in the courtyard of the family's house (*aulē*, paraphrased in the NIV as *sheep pen,* v. 1). Families on a given street agree as to who will shepherd their combined flock, often designating one or more of the children. In the morning this shepherd goes down the street to gather the sheep. The person at the door recognizes the shepherd and opens the door for the sheep to pass through. The shepherd has a distinct call or whistle, sometimes using a small flute, which the sheep recognize and follow. When several flocks end up at a watering place at the same time and mingle together, they are easily separated again by the shepherd, who gives his call as he starts to walk away. In addition to their own distinctive call, some shepherds also give their sheep names (Bailey 1993:10; cf. Beasley-Murray 1987:168).

This interpretation assumes there is a single flock composed of the sheep from several families that have been gathered from the courtyards of the various houses. However, the presence of a *watchman* (v. 3; literally, "doorkeeper," *thyrōros*) seems unlikely in the home of a village family, and later in Jesus' application he speaks of a single courtyard (v.

---

robber" *(ekeinos kleptēs kai lēstēs)*, thus focusing on the idea of theft, not guerrilla activity. This is also the case later in the chapter where a reference to "thieves and robbers" (v. 8) is developed only in terms of "the thief" (v. 10).

16). So instead of several courtyards and a single flock, the picture seems to be of a larger courtyard or enclosure (possibly a *sheep pen* as the NIV suggests) in which the sheep of several flocks are kept. In the morning a shepherd comes to collect the sheep of his flock and is able to do so in the way Bailey describes.

Jesus contrasts those who enter through the gate and those who do not (vv. 1-2). The one who has legitimate business and authorization enters in the proper fashion, while those without authorization use underhanded means. These thieves and robbers do not have in mind the good of the sheep but rather selfish ends of their own. The shepherd is recognized by the one who guards the fold, and so his entrance is natural, out in the open, without forcing. Such has been Jesus' entrance into this world and amongst his own people. He has come in the appropriate manner, having been sent by the Father, in contrast to the Jewish leaders who are rejecting Jesus.

Jesus' call is a fulfillment of Wisdom's crying out in the streets to see if anyone hears and responds (Prov 1:20-21). The focus here, however, is not on a general call, for he calls *his own sheep by name* (v. 3). Each particular sheep is known by this shepherd. They are "not simply units in a flock" (Westcott 1908:2:51).

Jesus refers to bringing out *all his own* (v. 4). The word for *brought out (ekballō)* is the same word used to describe the leaders' throwing the man out of the synagogue (9:34-35). The picture of the shepherd who *leads them out* (v. 3) to find pasture and water thus interprets what has just occurred to the man born blind. Jesus goes on ahead of his sheep, calling them as Bailey has described, and they follow him *because they know his voice* (v. 4). They don't follow strangers; indeed, they flee from them, *because they do not recognize a stranger's voice* (v. 5). The word for *know* and *recognize* are the same word in Greek *(oida),* so the sheep will be known by whom they know. Here is a beautiful picture of both divine sovereignty in the shepherd's call and the human response in the hearing, knowing and following by the sheep. We also find the theme of discernment, since there are more voices calling to them than just their own shepherd's. Following Jesus means refusing to follow others who are claiming to be shepherds. Put in this perspective, the expulsion from the synagogue is no great hardship—indeed, Jesus' sheep will actually *run away* from strangers.

Jesus spoke this *figure of speech* to the Pharisees (v. 6, *autois;* ["to them"], left out of the NIV), but they did not get it. These are people who claim to be able to see (9:40-41), but their inability to understand Jesus is yet another example of their spiritual blindness. The word for *figure of speech (paroimia)* refers to an obscure saying that needs to be interpreted (cf. Jn 16:25, 29, Hauck 1967a:856). It is not just a figure of speech or a comparison, but a saying that is loaded with significance—the verbal equivalent of Jesus' signs. Little that Jesus says in this Gospel is not conveyed in this manner, as he will admit at the end of his teaching (16:25).

Jesus uses the shepherd motif to interpret what has just taken place with the former blind man. Judaism is described as a sheep pen, but not all the sheep in the pen belong to Jesus' flock. They are separated out as they recognize his voice and follow him out from the sheep pen. Jesus is gathering his flock together from the pen of official Judaism.

Jesus Is the Gate for the Sheep (10:7-10) Because these Jewish leaders did not understand what Jesus was saying he goes back over it again from a different perspective. In this repetition we see God's graciousness, the same graciousness that caused the word of the Lord to come a second time to Jonah (Jon 3:1) and suffered with Israel's waywardness throughout her history. It is the same graciousness we each depend on every day of our lives.

In this second statement Jesus says, *I am the gate for the sheep* (v. 7). The scene has shifted from the village to the open field. In the summer sheep are sometimes kept out in the pasture overnight. The pen used is simply an enclosure made of piled rocks. There is neither roof nor door, but thorns along the top of the rock walls protect the sheep from wild animals, and the shepherd himself sleeps in the entrance, providing a door (cf. Bailey 1993:11; Beasley-Murray 1987:169). So when Jesus says he is *the gate for the sheep* (v. 7) he is still using the image of a shepherd, but applying it directly to himself. From this picture of a shepherd sleeping in the entrance we would expect Jesus' role to be the protector of the sheep. Jesus does indeed protect his own (cf. 6:39; 17:12), but the image is developed here in a surprising way. The sheep are to *enter through* Jesus (v. 9), something not true of the shepherd sleeping in the entrance of a summer shelter! So the image is not that of a door as a barrier for protection, but of a door as a passageway.

Jesus also refines his earlier reference to the thief and robber (v. 1), saying, *All who ever came before me were thieves and robbers* (v. 8). This is a sweeping generalization. If it were not for references to Moses, the prophets and John the Baptist as witnesses to Jesus (for example, 1:17, 19-36; 5:39), then they would seem to be included in the category of *all who ever came before me*. But the context of our passage is the condemnation of the Jewish rulers, some of whom have rejected Jesus and others who have faith in him. This sweeping statement shows that these leaders are members of a much larger group. Jesus, the one mediator of salvation, contrasts himself with all others who would claim to be "mediators of salvation" (Beasley-Murray 1987:170). The reason Moses, the law, the prophets and John the Baptist are not included in this condemnation is precisely because they bear witness to Jesus. All who do not bear witness to Jesus, who alone has seen the Father and makes him known (1:18), are not of the truth. They do not bring blessing but rather take it away, like a thief or a robber.

So we see the contrast between different ways of salvation. The Jewish leaders have rejected Jesus on the basis of their knowledge of God and his ways. They have expelled the man healed in chapter 9 from the people of God on the basis of his confession of Jesus. They believe they have consigned the former blind man to death, that is, to separation from God and his people. But Jesus has found him and incorporated him into his own company.

Jesus says the one who enters through him (*through me* is emphatic in the Greek) *will be saved. He will come in and go out, and find pasture* (v. 9). This is said to be true of each individual, as just illustrated by the former blind man—the shepherd knows each sheep by name (v. 3). The salvation spoken of refers to protection from the sheep's enemies, here understood to be false teachers as typified by the Jewish opponents. Such teachers threaten death by keeping people from a true knowledge of God, who is himself the sole source of life.

The one who enters by Jesus has the liberty *to come in and go out.* This is an Old Testament expression often used in political and military contexts to refer to leadership (for example, Deut 31:2, paraphrased in the NIV as "to lead you"), but it is also used elsewhere in a more general sense to refer to the entirety of one's daily activities (Deut 28:6, 19; Ps 121:8; cf. Acts 1:21). Jesus' sheep have the freedom to live their lives in his presence. Both their going out and their coming in is through him. In this way he fulfills the type of Joshua as described by Moses (Jesus is actually the name Joshua in Greek): "Moses said to the Lord, 'May the Lord, the God of the spirits of all mankind, appoint a man over this community to go out and come in before them, one who will lead them out and bring them in, so the Lord's people will not be like sheep without a shepherd' " (Num 27:15-17; cf. Jn 10:18). The freedom of Jesus' sheep to go out and come in reflects Jesus' own freedom, for their going out and coming in are not on their own but are a part of their following him.

As he brings them into the safety of his fold and leads them out to find food and water they find *pasture* (v. 9). The Good Shepherd will make them "lie down in green pastures" and lead them "beside quiet waters," preparing a table in the presence of their enemies (Ps 23:2, 3, 5). Through Jesus they receive their "daily bread" (Mt 6:11; Lk 11:3), that which is needed for life with God, for he offers the bread of life (Jn 6:35-58) and living water (7:38). Jesus has spoken repeatedly of the provision of life as the purpose of his coming (3:15; 4:14; 5:21, 24, 40; 6:27, 33, 35, 40, 47, 51, 54; 8:12), and now he focuses this key theme when he says, *I have come that they may have life, and have it to the full* (10:10). In the next section (vv. 11-18) he will explain further this life he has come to offer, which will be illustrated in the raising of Lazarus (chap. 11).

In contrast to the protection, freedom and pasture that come from entering through Jesus are the stealing, death and destruction brought by the thief (v. 10). One has a positive effect on the sheep, whereas the effect of the other is negative. The thief acts for his own selfish ends and to the detriment of the sheep. Jesus, however, serves the sheep by providing for them the way of life, which he will do, we learn in the next section, at the cost of his own life. Thus, the contrast with the thief is complete.

Those who enter through Jesus find life, which means we all begin on the outside and need to enter through him. We are all sheep in need of a shepherd, just as we all, like the man born blind, are in need of the light. Jesus is declaring that he "mediates membership of the Messianic community and reception of the promised blessings of salvation, that is, deliverance from judgment, . . . citizenship in the divine community of salvation . . . and eternal life" (Jeremias 1965:180). The salvation he brings is personal but not merely individual: he knows each sheep by name, but salvation is membership in a community, the community that is called and guided and provided for by Christ. The flock of Christ is neither an aggregate of isolated, autonomous individuals nor a faceless corporation, but a community in which each member is taken up into the life of God to form with others a single whole as branches on a vine (15:1). By referring to himself as the shepherd Jesus is claiming to be the leader of this new community.

When Jacob had his vision he said, "How awesome is this place! This is none other than the house of God; this is the gate of heaven" (Gen 28:17). John wants us to have the same response. How awesome is this place—and the place is now this person in our midst, Jesus, the Son of God, the gate leading to God.

The Good Shepherd Lays Down His Life for His Sheep (10:11-18) Jesus says, *I am the good shepherd* (v. 11), an "I am" saying that, like the others, ultimately concerns the issue of life. He has just promised life *to the full* (v. 10), and he now says this life comes through his death (vv. 11, 15, 17-18). Once again he starts with a familiar image in his audience's life, since shepherds commonly had to deal with the problem of wild animals (cf. Gen 31:39; 1 Sam 17:34-37). A good shepherd, one who is worthy of admiration *(kalos),* would risk his life to protect the sheep. But Jesus does not merely risk his life; he consciously gives his life for the sake of his sheep (vv. 15, 17-18; cf. Jeremias 1968:496 104).

The idea of a voluntary and vicarious death for the sheep is not found in the Old Testament nor elsewhere (Jeremias 1968:496-97; Barrett 1978:374). The closest conceptual background is that of the suffering servant of Isaiah 53 (Brown 1966:398; Westcott 1908:2:57). While this servant is likened to a sheep rather than a shepherd (Is 53:7), it is said of him that "the Lord makes his life a guilt offering" (Is 53:10). The expression in John 10, *lays down his life (tithē mi tē n psychē n),* could be taken as a translation of "makes his life" (*śî m na p š ô,* Is 53:10;

Jeremias 1967c:710). *For the sheep (hyper tōn probatōn)* does not in itself necessarily speak of sacrifice, but in John it does (Barrett 1978:375). In every place the preposition *hyper* ("for") is used in John (6:51; 10:11, 15; 11:50-52; 13:37-38; 15:13; 17:19; 18:14), with two exceptions (1:30; 11:4), it is used of sacrifice in which "the death envisaged is on behalf of someone else" (Carson 1991:386). So again Jesus' death is seen to be central to his task.

Another part of the conceptual background comes from the prophet Zechariah, who contrasts two shepherds. One is the messianic shepherd-king who is rejected by the people, which, in turn, results in their condemnation (Zech 11:4-14). The second is the worthless shepherd who deserts the flock (Zech 11:4-17). God's messianic shepherd will be struck down, causing the sheep to be scattered and leading to the judgment and refining of God's people (Zech 13:7-9). This rejection by the leaders of the people and their own condemnation is echoed in John, as is the striking of the shepherd, though with a different effect. It will indeed lead to the scattering of Jesus' flock for a brief time, but it will also be central in the gathering of his own flock from among the nations: "But I, when I am lifted up from the earth, will draw all men to myself" (Jn 12:32).

This death makes him the shepherd that is *good (kalos)*. This word refers in such a context to that which is beautiful, noble, honorable, worthy of praise. In other words, Jesus is fulfilling his job as a shepherd in an exemplary fashion so that such goodness is able to be perceived (Grundmann 1965:548). He is the admirable shepherd, and there is something admirable, heroic and attractive in his death. Consequently, it is in his death that he will draw all men to himself (12:32). The beauty of the Lord's character attracts those whose hearts are able to receive divine beauty. This is far more than an admirable death of a martyr. For in this death we see the beauty of God himself, since God is love, and love, as John says (1 Jn 3:16), is the laying down of life. It is precisely because he was in the form of God that he poured himself out and laid down his life (Phil 2:6-8; cf. C. F. D. Moule 1972:97). In Jesus we see the divine character, and what we see is beautiful. When we are able to really see God as Jesus has revealed him we cannot help praising him if we have hearts that are open to God. Such a vision of God's beauty is at the heart of all true worship.

Jesus goes on to contrast the shepherd who will risk his life for the sheep with a hireling who runs from the wolf and leaves the sheep behind to be attacked (*harpazei,* literally, "snatched" or "carried off") and scattered. They are not his sheep, and he does not care about them (Jn 10:12-13). This picture is not so much an allusion of Ezekiel 34 as a development from it. In Ezekiel the danger from wild animals arises after the sheep have been scattered (Ezek 34:5, 8), and the false shepherds are indeed shepherds, though like the hireling they care nothing for the sheep. So there are some general associations with Ezekiel, which may suggest that Jesus is continuing his condemnation of the leadership of Israel. But the main point seems to focus on the character of the Good Shepherd, specifically, his care for the sheep.

His care for the sheep addresses two problems, the lack of care on the part of the hireling and the threat of scattering by the wolf. Elsewhere the wolf is an image of false teachers who come both from outside the community and from within (Mt 7:15; Acts 20:29-30). Such a problem was present in John's day in Ephesus, since Paul's prediction to the Ephesian elders (Acts 20:29-30) was already coming to pass in Paul's own day (cf. 1 Tim 1:3) and continued in John's time (cf. 1 John). Likewise, the problem of hirelings continued in the church, as seen in Peter's exhortation to the elders to shepherd God's flock willingly and not just for money (1 Pet 5:2).

The themes introduced in a general way (Jn 10:11-13) are then personalized and developed (10:14-18). Jesus' knowledge of his flock and their knowledge of him (v. 14) are compared to the knowledge the Father and the Son have of one another (v. 15). The conjunction translated *just as (kathōs)* is most often used as a comparative, but it can have a causal sense (Wallace 1996:674). Both senses are true here, for "the relationship between God the Father and his Son is the original model and reason for Jesus' fellowship with his own" (Schnackenburg 1980b:297). As always, Jesus' identity as the Son and his relationship with the Father are crucial for understanding what is being said.

10:14 A neuter plural subject usually takes a singular verb, but here the neuter plural *my (ta ema) sheep* has a plural verb, *know (ginōskousi).* This occurs when "the author wants

This knowledge is not simply a knowledge about one another or merely the knowledge of an acquaintance. Rather, it is an intimacy that is love. The intimacy of the Father and the Son is so close it is described as a oneness (10:30), and a similar oneness of life is affirmed between Jesus and his disciples (for example, 15:1-7). The believer is not stirred into some cosmic soup, as in false forms of mysticism, but rather there is a radical oneness that does not obliterate the distinctness of the person. As the holy Trinity is both One and Three, so the believer is one with God and yet distinct from God. This theme of intimacy has been introduced earlier, for example in Jesus' teaching that his followers must eat his flesh and drink his blood (see comments on 6:53-57), and it will be unpacked in detail in the discourse in the upper room (chaps. 13—17). Its inclusion here provides important clarification regarding the nature of the new community Jesus is bringing into existence. This closeness includes the most intimate of relations between Jesus and each of his followers, and it is part of the union with God that they enter into in Christ through membership in his flock.

This new community is based in his death (10:15). The very pattern of life in this new community is that of life laid down for one another, a cruciform life. The possibility of such a life and the power for such a life come through the life of the Son of God poured out on the cross, thereby uniting God and mankind by taking away the sin of the world and revealing the glory of God.

Before revealing more about his death, Jesus mentions that he has other sheep not of this sheep pen who must be brought also, so *there shall be one flock and one shepherd* (v. 16). The most natural reading, accepted by most commentators, is that Jesus is referring to sheep from outside the fold of Judaism. There are Gentiles who will listen to his voice and be joined to his flock. Thus, in this section that speaks of Jesus' founding a community apart from official Judaism, Jesus himself speaks to one of the greatest points of controversy in the earliest church. He does not clearly specify on what terms the Gentiles are to be included, and so the church later had to discern his will whether or not

---

to *stress* the individuality of each subject involved in a neuter plural subject" (Wallace 1996:400).

Gentiles must become converts to Judaism in order to join his flock. But the present context, which describes a follower who has been expelled from the synagogue, hints at the answer. Most recent scholars think John is simply giving Jesus some lines that would address the later situation, but the potential ambiguity of the figure is typical of Jesus himself (cf. 21:22-23).

They are already his sheep because they have been given to him by the Father (v. 16; cf. 10:29; 6:37-39; 17:2, 6, 24; Beasley-Murray 1987:171), yet they must hear his call and respond. So once again we see both divine sovereignty and human responsibility at play. In saying that he must *bring them also* he speaks of the love that goes in search of the lost, which is a theme running throughout this Gospel and indeed the New Testament. He *must (dei)* do this; it is a divine necessity (cf. Grundmann 1964:22-24) that comes from the very character of God as love.

But how will he bring the Gentiles? When Gentiles do come to him it signals his hour has finally arrived (12:20, 23), but Jesus himself is not seen going to the Gentiles. He will bring the Gentiles into the flock by the ministry of his disciples, whom he will send (20:21). Jesus will continue his own ministry through his people, which will be accomplished through the presence of the Spirit. They are the ones who will bring the Gentiles, but Jesus is saying it is he himself who is doing so. This is an example of the oneness between the shepherd and his flock.

Similarly, the one shepherd unites the flock (Morris 1986-1988:380). The oneness comes from sharing the life of the one God in his Son by his Spirit. This flock is thus a spiritual entity yet not in the sense of being nonhistorical or only invisible any more than the incarnate Son who is its shepherd is such. This community has identifiable marks as a recognizable entity within history. Several marks are referred to in the New Testament, but the main ones mentioned in this passage are the centrality of Christ, the confession of him as exemplified by the former blind man and the fact that this community is to be composed of both Jews and Gentiles. The centrality of Christ is especially strong, given his

---

10:17 The conclusion of this verse is more likely a purpose clause, "so that *(hina)* I may take it again." "He died that the power of his resurrection might be manifested and released"

exclusivist claims. "The text does not suggest that this Good Shepherd will one day join a series of other shepherds who will then form a cooperative 'shepherds' union' " (Bailey 1993:17). Thus, the oneness of the flock corresponds to the thought found throughout this Gospel that Jesus is the only way to the Father.

Jesus concludes this teaching by revealing more fully the mystery involved in the shepherd's laying down his life for the sheep (vv. 17-18). He says he lays down his life *of my own accord* (literally, "from myself," *ap' emautou*), which makes it clear that his life is not simply taken from him by his opponents. At no point in this Gospel are his actions determined by human agenda, and his death will be no different. It may look like the triumph of darkness over light, but it is not. Pilate may think he has the authority (19:10, *exousia,* "power" in the NIV), but Jesus tells him, "You would have no power *[exousia]* over me if it were not given to you from above" (19:11). This does not mean that the human agents of God's power, both Pilate and Caiaphas, are without sin (19:11) but rather that there is an antinomy between divine sovereignty and human responsibility.

Jesus' statement that he has the authority to lay down his life stretches the imagery of the shepherd. He next proceeds to transcend it altogether by saying he has the authority not only to lay down his life, but also to take it back again. This cryptic teaching will become clearer in the next chapter, when he speaks of resurrection. The theme of life has been central throughout John's Gospel, and soon it will be the focus of the climax of Jesus' public ministry in the raising of Lazarus (Jn 11). The abundant life that this shepherd has come to give (v. 10) is something far beyond anything ever before available. Those in the story cannot even begin to grasp what he is talking about.

Despite this talk about having authority and acting from himself, the hallmark of his life is dependence on the Father. So he concludes by grounding all that he has said in this truth (v. 18). In laying down his life and taking it back he is obeying his Father. He knows his Father's voice and obeys, just as we are to hear his voice and obey.

(Barrett 1978:377). The death is not complete without the resurrection (cf. Brown 1966:399).

It is in this light that we must understand his statement that *the reason my Father loves me is that I lay down my life—only to take it up again* (v. 17). This statement seems to imply that the Father's love is based on the Son's obedience, but it is clear that the Father's love for the Son is from all eternity (17:24; cf. 3:35; 5:20; 15:9; 17:23, 26). Furthermore, the Father loves the world, which is certainly not obedient (3:16), so the Father's love is not conditioned by obedience. Some commentators resolve this problem by looking at the character of the love between the Father and the Son and concluding that it is "eternally linked with and mutually dependent upon the Son's complete alignment with the Father's will and his obedience even unto death" (Barrett 1978:377; cf. Carson 1991:388). Others point to the effects of the obedience, either in terms of its revelation of the love between the Father and the Son (Bultmann 1971:384; Beasley-Murray 1987:171) or in terms of its accomplishment of the salvation of the world (Hoskyns 1940b:440; Beasley-Murray 1987:171). Rudolf Schnackenburg says the Father's love for the Son is mentioned here "to throw the Son's deed into relief" (Schnackenburg 1980b:301).

Each of these efforts touch on Johannine themes, but what does it mean that *the reason* the Father loves the Son is that he lays down his life? The Father simply *is* love (1 Jn 4:8), and as a part of his very character his love is not contingent on the loveliness of the objects of his love. But it is possible to fall out of "the sphere of His active love" (Hoskyns 1940b:440), which is the condition of the world upon whom God's wrath abides (3:36). His wrath is his settled opposition toward that which disrupts the harmony of relations between himself and his creatures and which corrupts and destroys those whom he loves. In the case of Christ, his sinless obedience maintains the harmony of relationship between himself and his Father—therefore God's love remains fulfilled toward him. Jesus refers to this when he says, "If you obey my commands, you will remain in my love, just as I have obeyed my Father's commands and remain in his love" (15:10). Such obedience is the expression of love (14:15, 21) and is the condition for intimacy (14:23). Thus, in our

---

10:22 Charles H. Talbert (1992:164-65) has drawn attention to the correspondence between major themes in John 10 and 11 and themes associated with the Feast of Dedication

passage Jesus would be saying that the Father is able to fulfill his love for the Son because the Son does the Father's will. In this way, as the commentators have suggested, we see both the character of God's love and the effects of the Son's love, which is shown in obedience.

The Jewish Opponents Remain Divided over Jesus (10:19-21) Jesus has addressed this profound teaching to "some Pharisees who were with him," who were surprised at the idea that they might be blind (9:40). These are the same folks who had been divided over Jesus due to his healing of the blind man (9:16), and they continue to be divided over him (10:19). For some, Jesus' teaching reinforces the idea that he is *demon-possessed* (v. 20; cf. 7:20; 8:48-52). To this they now add that he is *raving mad,* "since madness was thought to be the result of demonic possession (Brown 1966:387; cf. Mk 3:20-30; 5:1-20). Others counter the Pharisees' assertion, saying that a person who is demon-possessed does not speak like this and cannot open the eyes of the blind (v. 21). Thus, both Jesus' words and deeds combine to bear witness to him, but the revelation simply increases the division. The more light, the greater the polarization.

Jesus Claims to Be the Messiah and to Be One with God (10:22-42)
We now come to the climax of Jesus' public ministry. In a sense his ministry remains public until chapter 13, but this encounter is the last public teaching before the triumphal entry into Jerusalem, which is the beginning of his Passion. Here he speaks as clearly as possible about himself and his opponents. This exchange is his last effort to get them to understand who he is. Later, when they try to raise the issue again he simply calls upon them to respond to the light he has already given them (12:34-36).

This teaching occurs at the Feast of Dedication (v. 22), about two months after the Feast of Tabernacles. This feast commemorates the rededication of the temple in 164 B.C. (1 Macc 4:36-59; 2 Macc 10:1-8; Josephus *Antiquities of the Jews* 12.316-26). The Seleucid king Antiochus IV Epiphanes had forbidden Jews to continue to practice their religion

---

according to the first-century B.C. book of 2 Maccabees. This strengthens the point that Jesus is the replacement of this festival and the temple it commemorates.

and had tried to force them to worship Zeus. He had an altar set up in the temple in Jerusalem and sacrifice was offered on this altar on the 25th of Chislev, 167 B.C. This led to a revolt known as the Maccabean Revolt. It was initiated by a priest named Mattathias and then carried on under the leadership of his son Judas, known as Maccabeus, "the hammer" (1 Macc 1—3; 2 Macc 5—9; Josephus *Antiquities of the Jews* 12.248-315). The revolt was successful, and the temple was restored and rededicated, with proper sacrifice being offered once again, beginning on the 25th of Chislev, 164 B.C. An eight-day feast was held and has continued each year from that time, and it is known today as Hanukkah. A hallmark of the festival is the lighting of lamps and a sense of joy.

Jesus has withdrawn from the temple (8:59) and begun to gather around him a community distinct from official Judaism (chap. 9). He has interpreted his activity as the divine shepherd's gathering the flock of God (10:1-21) and has concluded with a reference to the authority God has given him to lay down his life and take it back again (10:18), echoing what he had said in his first public teaching to these Jewish leaders concerning his body, the temple (2:19-22). Now he returns to the vicinity of the temple, though not to the temple proper. Solomon's Colonnade (10:23) was an open, roofed 45-foot walkway with double columns that were 38 feet tall. It was situated along the east side of the Court of Gentiles (Westerholm 1988:772). Although it was part of the temple complex, it was not considered to be part of the actual temple (Brown 1966:402), as evidenced by the fact that Gentiles were not allowed into the temple but they could be present in Solomon's Colonnade. Thus, Jesus' departure from the temple at the end of chapter 8 was final. But now, right next to the temple, at a feast commemorating the rededication of the temple, Jesus gives his clearest teaching about his own identity. It is this identity that is the grounds for his replacement of the temple as the place where forgiveness of sins is available and God is to be met. "Christ in fact perfectly accomplished what the Maccabees wrought in a figure, and dedicated a new and abiding temple" (Westcott 1908:2:64). Jesus also clearly spells out the separation between himself and the Jewish leaders.

10:27 As in verse 14, we have here a neuter plural, *ta probata ta ema (my sheep)*, with a plural verb, *akouousin* ("hear"), emphasizing that each of the sheep hears his voice (cf. Wallace 1996:400).

These leaders surround Jesus in the colonnade (v. 24), perhaps so he could not escape as he had before (8:59) or perhaps just out of intense earnestness. They keep asking him (*elegon,* an imperfect), *How long will you keep us in suspense? If you are the Christ, tell us plainly* (v. 24). They are tired of the figures of speech (cf. 10:6). Jesus realizes he has not been speaking plainly (16:25) in that he hasn't said simply, "I am the Messiah." But he also can reply, *I did tell you* (v. 25), for if one puts his words and deeds together, the message is plain enough. The problem lies not in his lack of clarity, but in their lack of faith (v. 25), for they are not his sheep (v. 26). In this way Jesus continues to work with the imagery of sheep and shepherd, and now he applies it to his opponents. He is speaking more plainly, for earlier he had not actually said these opponents were not of his flock, though the thought was expressed rather clearly through the images he used.

After saying that these Jewish leaders are not his sheep Jesus describes something of the blessings of those who are his sheep. He repeats his earlier teaching that each of his sheep hear his voice, are known by him, follow him (v. 27; cf. vv. 3, 4, 14, 16) and have eternal life (v. 28; cf. vv. 9-10). He concludes with a dramatic emphasis on the security of his sheep: *no one can snatch them out of my hand* (v. 28). In the light of the danger to the sheep from thieves, robbers and wolves this comes as a great comfort. The security of the sheep rests on the shepherd. Jesus' reference to himself as the one able to protect his flock from all dangers is yet another aspect of the incredible claims he is making in this chapter. As always, however, he is not acting on his own apart from the Father: *My Father, who has given them to me, is greater than all; no one can snatch them out of my Father's hand* (v. 29). Again we see the primacy of the Father, the one who these opponents think is their God. In threatening Jesus and his followers they are up against God himself.

In this passage of infinite comfort this Gospel touches once again upon the mysteries of divine sovereignty and human responsibility. We

---

10:29 The clause *who has given them to me, is greater than all* follows the reading of the majority of manuscripts (the Byzantine text) as well as one of the earliest manuscripts ($\mathbf{p}^{66}$). This reading makes the most sense, but then why would the text have been changed if this

have both the call of God and the response of faith on the part of the sheep. B. F. Westcott captures the balance well when he says we must distinguish between

> the certainty of God's promises and His infinite power on the one hand, and the weakness and variableness of man's will on the other. If man falls at any stage in his spiritual life, it is not from want of divine grace, nor from the overwhelming power of adversaries, but from his neglect to use that which he may or may not use. We cannot be protected against ourselves in spite of ourselves. He who ceases to hear and to follow is thereby shown to be no true believer, 1 John ii.19. . . . The sense of the divine protection is at any moment sufficient to inspire confidence, but not to render effort unnecessary. (Westcott 1908:2:67)

His sheep are safe in his hand (v. 28) and his Father's hand (v. 29). The implication of such a juxtaposition comes with Jesus' climactic claim, *I and the Father are one* (v. 30). What is this oneness? In the context Jesus is speaking of God's love, care and power and his own claim to share in these. Such a claim to oneness with God is not a claim to deity, since the same unity with God is true of Christians, who share in God's very life and are participants in his will, love, activity and power. Thus Jesus is one with the Father in the same way believers are. But even when this language is used of Christians it is made clear that their oneness with God is mediated to them by Christ (17:22-23). Jesus' own oneness with the Father includes these aspects, but it also is of a completely different order (cf. 8:58). The Father not only gave Jesus life, as he has done for believers, but has made him the giver of life (5:21), a divine attribute illustrated in what Jesus says about the bread (chap. 6) and the water (chap. 7) and which will be climactically demonstrated in the raising of Lazarus (chap. 11). So this figure of the hand is not just about sharing in God's power or exercising God's power; it is part of his claim to equality with God. It implies a oneness in essence since "infinite

---

were the original meaning (Metzger 1994:198)? Of the other readings (cf. Beasley-Murray 1987:165), the main alternative to the NIV is "what has been given to me is greater than all." This could mean that the flock that the Father has given to Jesus is greater than all, which would comment on the superiority of the community Jesus is gathering around him. Or this reading could mean that the power the Father has given to Jesus is greater than all (cf. Grundmann 1967:537), thus reinforcing his claim that *no one can snatch them out of*

power is an essential attribute of God; and it is impossible to suppose that two beings distinct in essence could be equal in power" (Westcott 1908:2:68; cf. Chrysostom *In John* 61.2; Augustine *In John* 48.7). Here, then, is a powerful claim to deity. The opponents take it as such (v. 33), and Jesus does not deny that interpretation.

The word used here for *one* is the neuter form, *hen,* rather than the masculine, *heis.* If the masculine had been used, it could have suggested that the Son is the Father, thus losing the distinctness of each, a heresy known later as Monarchianism or Sabellianism (Tertullian *Against Praxeas* 25; Augustine *In John* 36.9). But the Gospel throughout has been true to the insight revealed in the first verse of its first chapter: the Word is God, yet it is "with God," distinct from God. This truth is also found in this verse in the plural form of the verb *are.* "He did not say, 'I and the Father *am one,*' but *are one*" (Hippolytus *Against Neotus* 7; Augustine *In John* 36.9). So although this passage is not expressed in philosophical categories, it is clear, as the church has understood and given expression in the creeds, that "some kind of metaphysical unity is presupposed, even if not articulated" (Carson 1991:395; cf. Pollard 1957).

The opponents have asked Jesus about his identity as the Messiah, and in reply he has continued his claim to deity. If they had accepted Jesus' identity as somehow divine, as at least some sort of agent of God, then they would have been able to receive him as Messiah. Jesus does not claim to be Messiah in their understanding of that term, but all of his words and deeds have been those of the Messiah in truth. But the Jews were not expecting a messiah who shared in God's divinity, and thus these opponents could not see his messiahship and were scandalized by his claims to equality with God. So, as before, they *picked up stones to stone him* (v. 31; cf. 8:59). But this time instead of slipping away (8:59), he discusses his claim with them.

This is a most amazing scene. They are standing there with stones

---

my hand (v. 28). Thus, any of the major readings could fit the present context.
10:33 The NIV translation *claim to be God* misses part of the force of the original, which more literally is "make yourself God" *(poieis seauton theon).* The opponents miss Jesus' point. "Jesus never makes himself anything; everything that he is stems from the Father. He is not a man who makes himself God; he is the Word of God who has become man" (Brown 1966:408).

and are ready to kill him, and he calmly tries to help them see their error. Here is sovereign calmness that comes from being centered in God's will, the will of the Father who is greater than all. And by continuing to try to help them come to faith even as they are seeking to stone him Jesus manifests amazing grace. He is graciously calling them to reconsider, for they know not what they do. These men are seeking to kill the one who is offering them life—offering it to them even in the midst of their attack against him. The glory of God, which is his grace, continues to shine brightly at this point.

He appeals to them on the basis of their own experience and the Scriptures. He begins with the deeds he has done: *I have shown you many great miracles from the Father. For which of these do you stone me?* (v. 32). These deeds (*erga*, "works") are from the Father, from the one they claim as their God. They are *great (kalos)*, the same word used to described the shepherd as "good" (10:11, 14). His deeds are not just great, they are admirable. "It is impossible to find a single English word equivalent to the Greek, which suggests deeds of power and moral excellence, resulting in health and well-being" (Barrett 1978:383). These are deeds that should have provoked awe and admiration and praise, not anger and hostility. They are *kalos* precisely because they are from the Father. Nothing is truly *kalos* except that which proceeds from the Father, the source of all that is good and true and worthy.

The opponents have been divided over what to make of Jesus, but a sufficient number of them have decided his scandalous claims are clear enough, whatever might be the explanation of the miracles, to warrant putting his followers out of the synagogue and stone Jesus himself: *We are not stoning you for any of these . . . but for blasphemy, because you, a mere man, claim to be God* (v. 33). The understanding of blasphemy in later sources has to do with pronouncing the divine name, the Tetragrammaton (YHWH; *m. Sanhedrin* 7:5). In Jewish literature the only case of calling oneself God reflects fairly clearly the debates between church and synagogue over the claims of Jesus (*y. Ta'anit* 2; 65b; 59; *Exodus Rabbah* 29:5; cf. Barrett 1978:383-84). Presumably there would not need to be a law for such a thing—it is unthinkable that one would make such a claim. But if such a claim were made, it would not take a lot of deliberation to determine that this was blasphemy against the one God. The tradition may speak of the Torah and Wisdom as divine and even hypothesize them (see comment on 1:1-2), but it would be something quite different for a human being to claim such status.

Jesus defends his claim using language they should be able to understand, through an appeal to the law. He cites a text that uses the word *god* of those who are not God: *Is it not written in your Law, "I have said you are gods"?* (v. 34). It is unclear who is being referred to in Psalm 82:6. Of the several proposals made by scholars (cf. Beasley-Murray 1987:176-77), the most likely takes this as a reference either to Israel's judges or to the people of Israel as they receive the law. The latter is a common understanding among the rabbis (for example, *b. 'Aboda Zara* 5a; *Exodus Rabbah* 32:7), but the former is also represented in Jewish interpretation (*Midraš Psalms; b. Sanhedrin* 6b; 7a; *b. Soṭa* 47b). Jesus' explanation that these *gods* are those *to whom the word of God came* (v. 35) might point to the Israelites receiving the law. In this case the contrast between these *gods* and Jesus would be that Jesus is the one who both fulfills the law and is greater than the law. But this expression *to whom the word of God came* could also refer to the judges (as suggested by the rest of Ps 82) who have received a commission from God to exercise the divine prerogative of judgment on his behalf. The psalm is actually a condemnation of the judges for not exercising their responsibility faithfully, thus corresponding both to the condemnation of these Jewish leaders in John and to Jesus as the true judge.

To make his point Jesus uses an argument from the lesser to the greater, a very common form of argument in the ancient world, not least among the rabbis. He compares the people who are called *gods* to himself, the Son of God. They merely received the word of God, whereas he is *the one whom the Father set apart as his very own and sent into the world* (v. 36). Here is a succinct summary of the central truth of his identity, which has been emphasized throughout this Gospel. He is using the language of an agent (see note on 5:21), but the implication is that he existed with the Father before coming into the world. Thus, he is putting himself in the category of the law that was given by God rather than in the category of one of the recipients of that law. By saying he was *set apart* ("consecrated," *hagiazō*) he is claiming a status similar to the temple, whose reconsecration these opponents are celebrating at this feast.

What he means by the title Son of God goes beyond anything they had thought before, but it is not a denial of the truths of Scripture. Indeed, the Scripture itself, as illustrated by Psalm 82:6, contains hints of such a revelation, and *the Scripture cannot be broken* (v. 35); the Scripture cannot be kept from fulfillment (Brown 1966:404). This parenthetical comment spoken by Jesus shows how important this line of argument is for Jesus and John. But, as with all other arguments, it only makes sense if the listener is open to entertaining the truth of who Jesus is.

So the Scriptures indicate that they should not be put off by his claims and therefore should be open to the evidence of the deeds he has done. Jesus presses this line of evidence: *Do not believe me unless I do what my Father does. But if I do it, even though you do not believe me, believe the miracles* (vv. 37-38; cf. 5:19-28). His deeds are like the deeds of God, both in power and in graciousness. Miracles alone are not enough to confirm the truth of one who speaks for God (see comment on 9:33). But the point of these signs is not simply that they are powerful or awesome or supernatural but that they are in keeping with God's own character—they manifest his gracious love.

His conclusion again transcends the category of agent: *that you may know and understand that the Father is in me, and I in the Father* (v. 38). They are standing there with rocks in their hands (though perhaps not, since the rocks used for stoning were large; cf. *m. Sanhedrin* 6:4), and he is appealing to them to accept the evidence of their senses, as witnessed to by the Scriptures, that he is uniquely related to God. Again we see the antinomy between divine sovereignty and human responsibility. These are the folk Jesus said could not believe because they were not of his sheep (v. 26), but here he is appealing to them to believe. The Gospel is to be shared with everyone, even persecutors, for who knows—one may turn out to be a Saul (Acts 9:1-19).

But the appeal is in vain at this point: *Again they tried to seize him, but he escaped their grasp* (v. 39). They had not grasped his message so they tried to grasp him to kill him. "They failed to apprehend Him,

---

10:38 The expression *know and understand* actually contains two forms of the same verb. "Awareness of Jesus' living fellowship with the Father is the commencement (*gnōte:*

because they lacked the hand of faith" (Augustine *In John* 48.11). The Father who is greater than all will protect those who believe in Jesus (v. 29), so how much more will he protect Jesus himself.

Jesus leaves Jerusalem and goes back *across the Jordan to the place where John had been baptizing in the early days* (v. 40; cf. 1:28). John's witness was reported extensively in chapter 1 and then referred to a couple of times 3:23-30; 5:33-36). This reference ties together the first ten chapters and therefore signals the conclusion of a major section of the Gospel. Jesus' next great deed, the raising of Lazarus, reveals the heart of what his whole ministry has been about, but it takes place in a semiprivate setting. Thus the public ministry of Jesus now concludes— "the narrative of the Lord's ministry closes on the spot where it began" (Westcott 1908:2:73).

The opponents in Jerusalem have rejected him, but now, across the Jordan, many come to him and believe in him (vv. 41-42). They have received John's witness concerning Jesus: *Though John never performed a miraculous sign, all that John said about this man was true* (v. 41). No miracles are associated with John in the New Testament, Josephus (*Antiquities of the Jews* 18.116-19) or any other source (Bammel 1965:183-88). This is striking because "the praise of a man of God who did *not* perform miracles was completely unknown in Jewish sources" (Bammel 1965:191). This makes John's witness to Jesus stand out even more as the great accomplishment of his ministry. From a Christian point of view, such witness *is* a great work for it enables people to do the work of God, to believe in the one sent from God (6:29).

The people say that *all that John said about this man was true* (v. 41). The focus here is not so much on Jesus' deeds, since not all that John said had yet been accomplished, for example, taking away the sins of the world or baptizing with the Holy Spirit (1:29, 33; cf. Brown 1966:411). Rather, the focus is on Jesus' identity as the one who was to come (1:26-27, 30-31), as summarized in John's testimony: "I have seen and I testify that this is the Son of God" (1:34). Now, in the light of all Jesus has said and done, the truth of this testimony has been

---

ingressive aorist) and the abiding task (*ginōskēte:* enduring present) of faith's journey" (Schnackenburg 1980b:313).

made evident to those who are able to see.

□ Jesus' Revelation as Life and His Reception as King Lead to His Death (11:1—12:36)

Jesus' public witness has climaxed in his declaration of oneness with God, which he supported from Scripture (10:30-38). Now, in a semiprivate setting, the raising of Lazarus reveals plainly what all the signs have been about—Jesus as the resurrection and the life. But this action galvanizes the opponents to seek his death, so now we come to the beginning of the end. Instead of seeing Jesus doing signs, we see signs occurring through what others do to him. First, Mary anoints Jesus at Bethany in a private setting (12:1-8). Second, there is the public outpouring at the triumphal entry into Jerusalem, as a great crowd receives him as the king of Israel (12:12-15). Third, after the awaited king has entered his city the Gentiles come to him, which signals that the long expected hour has arrived. Jesus announces the coming of his hour and speaks of his death (12:20-26). This is followed by a fourth and final sign offered to the crowd not by Jesus but by the Father himself, who bears witness to Jesus (12:27-28). The crowd, however, does not receive the Father's witness any more than it has Jesus' (12:29). Jesus interprets the voice for them, but the crowd only raises further questions (12:30-34). So Jesus adds no further teaching; he only warns them to receive what they have already been given and then hides himself from them once again (12:35-36).

Jesus Raises Lazarus (11:1-54) In this transitional story there are many connections with earlier chapters. The motif of light found in chapters 8 and 9 continues (11:9-10), the purpose given for the illness of the blind man is similar to that given for Lazarus' death (9:3; 11:4), and the healing of the blind man is referred to (11:37), as is the conflict with the Jewish authorities in chapter 10 (11:8). We have another example of Jesus, the Good Shepherd, calling his own and gathering his flock (11:54). There

---

11:1 Mary and Martha are mentioned in Luke 10:38-42, though without reference to Lazarus. There are several accounts of Jesus' being anointed by a woman (Mt 26:6-13; Mk 14:3-9; Lk 7:37-50), but these are not references to this Mary (cf. Smalley 1996:737). There is no reason to identify this Lazarus with the character of that name in Jesus' parable (Lk 16:19-31), since

are also larger connections, for the raising of Lazarus is the last of a series of Jesus' signs that began in chapter 2; both the first and last of the signs in this series (2:11; 11:4) are explicitly linked with the revelation of God's glory. All of the signs were revelations of who Jesus is and what he offers. The final sign, the raising of Lazarus, points most clearly to what has been at the heart of the revelation all the way through and what was emphasized in Jesus' keynote address (5:19-30)—that Jesus is the one who gives life. The irony, of course, is that he gives life by giving up his own life on the cross. A further irony is that by giving life to Lazarus, Jesus sets in motion his own death. The raising of Lazarus, then, is the final sign before the event that actually accomplishes what all the signs have pointed toward—the provision of life through the death of the Son of God.

This story also continues to develop the theme of faith. Jesus has just made a very clear statement of his unity with the Father (10:30, 38), and many have believed in him (10:42). Often in this Gospel Jesus reacts to faith by doing or saying something scandalous or cryptic. Although these folk who have faith are not present at the raising of Lazarus, the raising can perhaps be seen as a further revelation in response to their faith, as they represent a general turn upward in his popularity.

Lazarus Dies (11:1-16) John does not say exactly when this event took place, only that it was sometime during the four months, roughly, between the Feast of Dedication and Passover. John is, however, careful to describe the place. This Bethany is a little less than two miles southeast of Jerusalem on the road to Jericho (cf. v. 18). It is to be distinguished from the Bethany where John had been baptizing (1:28) and to which Jesus had just returned (10:40), which is either in Perea at the Jordan a few miles north of the Dead Sea, about a day's journey from Jerusalem, or up north in Batanea, several days journey away (Riesner 1992; cf. Carson 1991:147, 407).

The sisters send a message to Jesus: *Lord, the one you love is sick* (v. 3). Clearly, Jesus had a special relationship with this man and his sisters

---

Lazarus is an abbreviation of Eleazar, one of the most common names among Palestinian Jews at this period (Bauckham 1996:678).

11:2 Mary is identified by reference to an event that has not yet been recounted, suggesting this Gospel is written for those who already know the story.

(v. 5). Yet chapters 11 and 12 are the only reference to Lazarus in the New Testament. We are alerted, once again, to how little we know of the life of our Lord (cf. 21:25).

This request is very similar to Jesus' mother's request at the wedding of Cana (2:4). It presents a need but does not dictate to the Lord how he should respond. In these requests we have a model of intercession that makes a need known to the Lord with humility and a recognition that it is his will that should be done. Such humility and submission are key characteristics of true disciples.

Jesus had responded to his mother by saying it was not yet his hour, a reference to the cross (2:4). Now, however, his hour is fast approaching. Mary and Martha must have known how dangerous it had become for Jesus to be in the vicinity of Jerusalem. They might have known that Jesus could heal at a distance (cf. 4:49-53), yet they seem to want him to come to heal Lazarus (11:21, 32). Perhaps their anxiety for their brother led them to summon Jesus. But love is the laying down of life (cf. 1 Jn 3:16), and the sisters seem to think that Jesus would be willing to risk his life for the sake of their brother, whom he loves. Whatever they may have been thinking, we see that Jesus, the Good Shepherd, was indeed willing to risk his life for his friend (cf. 10:11, 15), though he was under no real danger since he was doing the Father's will and under his protection (10:39; cf. 10:29).

Jesus' love for Lazarus and his sisters teaches us that our faith in God's love, even in the midst of adversity, is well grounded. Even those especially dear to God must endure such things (cf. Chrysostom *In John* 62.1). "The one sick, the others sad, all of them beloved: but He who loved them was both the Savior of the sick, nay more, the Raiser of the dead and the Comforter of the sad" (Augustine *In John* 49.7).

When Jesus heard the message he said, *This sickness will not end in death. No, it is for God's glory so that God's Son may be glorified through it* (v. 4). This response sets the agenda and provides the approach to what will take place. Just as the man's blindness in chapter 9 was an

---

11:3 This description of Lazarus as *the one you love* has led some to identify him as the Beloved Disciple (cf. survey in Charlesworth 1995:185-92), but verse 5 "suggests that we should think of the 'beloved family' and not simply of the beloved brother" (Beasley-Murray 1987:183). The language in verses 1-2 suggest Mary was the best known of the three due

opportunity for the work of God to be manifested (9:3), so the purpose here is the glorification of God and his Son through this sickness. In both cases we see a revelation of the divine activities of life-giving and judgment, though here they are more intense for we are close to the cross and resurrection, the ultimate glorification (12:23; 13:31).

In all that Jesus does we see the glory of God (1:14), for we see God's love and life-giving power. Now, in the raising of Lazarus, we will have the most spectacular manifestation of this glory. God is the one who brings life to the dead out of his love for those in such need. This is the heart of the Gospel. God's glory is thus seen in his victory over death—indeed, it is "possible *only* through death—first the death of Lazarus, and then the death of Jesus himself!" (Michaels 1989:195).

The close connection between Jesus and the Father clearly presented in chapter 5 and chapters 8—10 is evident here as well. This is one of the few times Jesus refers to himself explicitly as God's Son (cf. 5:25; 10:36, perhaps 3:18). The Son of God will be glorified through this illness and thereby the glory of God himself will be manifested. The Father will be glorified as the source of life, and the Son will be glorified as the one who acts in obedience to the Father and shares in his identity as the source of life (cf. 1:3-4, 10; 5:21, 26; cf. Michaels 1989:195).

When Jesus' mother appealed for help in Cana he put her off with a statement that seemed abrupt or even harsh (2:4). Now, when the most powerful sign is about to be performed, Jesus behaves in an especially shocking manner. John prepares us for this by emphasizing Jesus' love for Lazarus and his sisters (v. 5). Jesus loved them and "therefore" (*oun*, translated in the NIV as *yet*) *when he heard that Lazarus was sick, he stayed where he was two more days* (v. 6). Jesus acts only in accordance with his Father's will (2:4; 7:3-9), not the will of his family or, as we see now, his closest friends. His activity is scandalous, as Mary and Martha will show by their responses (11:21, 32), because he is concerned with God's glory (v. 4), with doing God's will and, as "therefore" indicates, with love for these friends. His love does not feel like love but it is love,

---

to her anointing of Jesus for his burial (12:7).
11:6 *Oun* in this context can signal contrast (as in NIV's *Yet*) or "an action in response to a previous action or utterance" (Young 1994:191), "so," "therefore." Either option points up the strangeness of Jesus' action, though the second suggests his motivation is love.

and it is for the best in their lives. His delay leads to a greater blessing.

There are two possible ways to understand the sequence of events that follow, depending on whether one believes the Bethany where Jesus is staying is in the south or the north. If Bethany is in the south, as most scholars believe, then it would take the messengers one day to reach Jesus and one day for Jesus to reach Lazarus. Since Jesus stayed put for two days and Lazarus has been dead for four days when Jesus does arrive, that means Lazarus must have died on the same day as the messengers set out (cf. Barrett 1978:391). If Bethany is a reference to Batanea in the north the timing would be different. It takes four days to travel from Batanea to where Lazarus is. Since Jesus arrives when Lazarus has been dead for four days, Jesus had waited until Lazarus died before he set out. In either case the two-day delay does not cause the death of Lazarus, since Jesus could not have gotten to him before he died, either because he was dead before the messengers arrived with their message (southern view) or because Jesus would only be halfway there (northern view). In either case the two-day delay does, however, insure that Lazarus will have been dead for four days when Jesus arrives.

When Jesus announces that they are to return to Judea (v. 7), his disciples remind him that the Jewish opponents had just been trying to stone him there (v. 8). The disciples are taking their cues from their circumstances rather than from the Father. They are very aware of the danger their opponents present, but they are not in tune with the voice of the Father. Jesus responds with a cryptic saying, which, as usual, directly addresses the issue at hand but is not able to be understood (vv. 9-10). He uses the imagery of light to put things into perspective for them. In the natural realm one is able to walk without stumbling while there is light, and there is light for a set period of time. One need not worry about stumbling while it is day. The point is that they need not worry about what will happen to them for they have the Light of the World with them (8:12), for with him they are able to get on with the work of the Father (9:4). With the psalmist they can say, "The Lord is my light and my salvation—whom

11:9 Although the amount of daylight in Israel varies between 14 hours, 12 minutes and 9 hours, 48 minutes, the period of daylight was always divided into 12 hours (Strack and Billerbeck 1924:543).

11:10 The verse reads, more literally, "because there is no light in him." It has been

shall I fear?" (Ps 27:1). They should stick with Jesus even when he seems to lead them into danger, for no matter what happens it will work out for the best, even as Lazarus's illness will work for the glory of God. Here is a word of assurance and a call to all believers to take their bearings from God and not from their circumstances.

From this cryptic saying, which goes over their heads, as Thomas' response will soon indicate (v. 16), Jesus spells out why they must now return to Judea: *Our friend Lazarus has fallen asleep; but I am going there to wake him up* (v. 11; cf. Mt 9:24). The use of the metaphor of sleep to refer to death is common in the ancient world, including ancient Jewish thought (Balz 1972:548-53), but the disciples nevertheless misunderstand and think Jesus is referring to *natural sleep* (v. 13). This misunderstanding is quite amazing. Who could think that Jesus was concerned about Lazarus's merely falling asleep? And even if this were an acceptable concern—perhaps they think Jesus means Lazarus is now sleeping peacefully after his illness—who could think Jesus would need to be informed that Lazarus would wake up, especially since it would take Jesus up to four days to get to Lazarus, depending on where one thinks Jesus was when he received the news about Lazarus? So it appears the disciples are thinking that Jesus had preternatural knowledge that Lazarus had fallen asleep and that he wanted to go wake him up! There must have been no dull moments with Jesus. He was doing incredible miracles, he was a marked man in the eyes of the authorities, and one never knew what he would say next. The disciples are very disoriented, which should be of some encouragement to us when we feel the same way. Jesus' patience with them is a manifestation of God's grace for which we can only be thankful. "Christ's kindness in putting up with such stupidity in the disciples was remarkable" (Calvin 1959:5).

Jesus has spoken of death as a sleep from which he will awaken the sleeper. Such language has profound implications concerning our Lord's power over death and the continuity of the person in death. Even in death Lazarus is still *our friend* (v. 11; cf. Westcott 1908:2:84), and he is able to

---

suggested that ancient people understood that sight was made possible from an inner light and, indeed, that the eyes send forth light (Allison 1987). On this interpretation this verse continues the natural imagery, even as the language also suggests its spiritual application (cf. Schnackenburg 1980b:325).

be restored even after his body has begun to decay, which happens by the fourth day. He may have died (v. 14), but they are still going *to him* (v. 15), that is, "He speaks of the body 'sleeping' in the tomb as the man himself" (Westcott 1908:2:86).

It is no wonder, then, that sleep becomes the main way of referring to death in Christian thought beginning with the postapostolic fathers (cf. Balz 1972:555-56). Indeed, our word *cemetery* comes from the Greek word *koimētērion,* a place of sleep. Chrysostom says that since Christ died for the life of the world, we no longer call death *thanatos* (death) but *hyptos kai koimēsis* (two words for sleep) (Chrysostom *On the Cemetery and the Cross* 1; cf. Balz 1972:556). As he says elsewhere, "What is death at most? It is a journey for a season; a sleep longer than usual! So that if you fear death, you should also fear sleep!" (Chrysostom *Concerning the Statues* 5.11; cf. 7.1).

Since the disciples do not understand that Jesus is speaking of Lazarus' death, he has to explain it to them (v. 14) and thereby give them his perspective on this opportunity: *for your sake I am glad I was not there, so that you may believe* (v. 15). He has no doubt that he could have cured Lazarus if he had been there, but something even more helpful for their faith is now going to take place. "It is sometimes expedient for disciples that Jesus should be absent from them; cf. 16.7" (Barrett 1978:393). To have faith in the Son of God is far more important than to have health and comfort in this life. Such faith leads to eternal life (20:31), as this miracle will symbolize. This faith is a progressive thing, for here Jesus is talking to those who have believed in him already, and yet he says this miracle is *so that you may believe.* Faith must be exercised in the face of each new revelation, and each new revelation is taking the disciples nearer to the ultimate revelation in the most extremely scandalous event, the cross—the ultimate revelation of God's light and life and love and thus the ultimate manifestation of God that faith must grasp hold of. As God reveals more of himself and his ways to us we must likewise have a faith that both grasps firmly

---

11:14 Jesus' cryptic sayings usually are with regard to himself, but here they refer to Lazarus and his condition. This correspondence is continued in Lazarus himself becoming a stimulus to faith in Christ (12:9).

11:17 The rabbis taught that death itself was, for those who were penitent, a means of cleansing from one's sins (Büchsel and Herrmann 1965:312-13). Thus when Lazarus began

onto him as he is revealed in Jesus and also is able to be stretched and deepened. Faith enables us to rest in God, but God himself also keeps us on the move as we continue to grow closer to him for ever.

Jesus may be rejoicing, but Thomas, and presumably the other disciples, is not. We usually think of Thomas as "doubting Thomas" from his reactions after the resurrection of the Lord (20:24-28). In the present story we see another facet of Thomas—his loyalty. This is the response of a true disciple. Just as Peter sticks with Jesus even though he does not understand what Jesus is talking about regarding eating his flesh and drinking his blood (6:68), so Thomas is willing to go with Jesus to death (v. 16). He is still fixated with the evident danger (v. 8), and he does not understand the encouraging words Jesus has just spoken (vv. 9-10), but he is attached to Jesus and is going to stay with him, even though he does not see how Jesus' decision makes any sense. Here is an incredible picture of faith. He is not following because he sees how it all fits; he is following out of loyalty to Jesus himself. He is a model disciple at this point. As Thomas follows Jesus into what he thinks is death he is answering the call, expressed in the Synoptics, that "if anyone would come after me, he must deny himself and take up his cross and follow me. For whoever wants to save his life will lose it, but whoever loses his life for me and for the gospel will save it" (Mk 8:34-35).

Jesus Reveals Himself to Martha as the Resurrection and the Life (11:17-27) The scene now shifts to Bethany, near Jerusalem, as Jesus arrives and finds that Lazarus has been in the tomb for four days. Burials normally took place on the day of the death (cf. Acts 5:6-10), so he has been dead for four days. For Jews this probably signifies that Lazarus is clearly dead and beginning to decay (cf. *m. Yebamot* 16:3). A later Jewish text that cites an authority from the early third century A.D. says the mourners should continue to come to the tomb for three days because the dead person continues to be present. Mourning is at its height on the third day, presumably because it is the last time the dead person will be present there. "Bar Kappara taught: Until three days [after death] the soul keeps on

---

to decompose some might have seen this as the beginning of his expiation for his sins. If Jesus raises him, then he must deal with the expiation of his sin. The life Jesus gives is eternal life, which is only possible when sin has been dealt with.

11:19 The word *Jews* here seems to have the sense of Judeans (see comment on 1:19).

returning to the grave, thinking that it will go back [into the body]; but when it sees that the facial features have become disfigured, it departs and abandons it [the body]" (*Genesis Rabbah* 100:7; cf. *Leviticus Rabbah* 18:1; *Ecclesiastes Rabbah* 12:6). Thus, the reference to the fourth day may be quite significant for setting the scene for another dramatic miracle. The healings in this Gospel have taken place in response to desperate needs (cf. Talbert 1992:172) from the son of the royal official who was close to death (4:49), to the man who was paralyzed for thirty-eight years (5:5), to the man born blind (9:1). Now we come to the climax of this sequence.

John spells out that Bethany is quite near Jerusalem (v. 18). This note heightens the drama. Jesus had said he was returning to Judea (v. 7), which the disciples recognized as the place of hostility. Now John makes sure we understand that Jesus has come back to the region of Jerusalem itself, the very heart of the opposition. Jerusalem is also the key place for revelation, and the greatest of all revelations is now starting to unfold.

As Jesus approaches, Martha comes out to meet him. It is unclear why Jesus halted and met her in this way. Some have suggested the desire for relative privacy, but perhaps more likely this reflects the danger he is in by returning to the suburbs of Jerusalem. The crowd of mourners may well contain those who would inform the authorities of Jesus' presence, as indeed does happen after the raising of Lazarus (v. 46).

Martha says, *Lord, . . . if you had been here, my brother would not have died. But I know that even now God will give you whatever you ask* (v. 21). It is difficult to know how to understand this statement. It is possible to find in her first sentence a rebuke of Jesus (Wallace 1996:703) and in her second sentence a very defective view of Jesus: "She regards Jesus as an intermediary who is heard by God (22), but she does not understand that he is life itself (25)" (Brown 1966:433; cf. Chrysostom *In John* 62.3). The fact that she says, literally, "I know that whatever you ask of God, God will give you" suggests a distance between Jesus and God through the repetition of the word God (not evident in the NIV). Also, the word she uses for *ask (aiteō)* is not the word used by Jesus for his own prayer to the Father but the word he uses of the disciples' prayer (Westcott 1908:2:89). Thus, there is no doubt that her view of Jesus is defective. Indeed, in this very interchange Jesus is revealing himself more perfectly to her, as he revealed himself to the Samaritan woman, despite her defective views.

But we should also see here a genuine, though defective, faith. Her initial statement (v. 21) need not imply a rebuke. It could simply be a lament (see, for example, Beasley-Murray 1987:190). And although her knowledge of Jesus is defective, nevertheless, she does believe Jesus could have healed Lazarus. And her belief that Jesus' prayers are answered does pick up on the truth of Jesus' dependence upon the Father, as will be illustrated later in this story (vv. 41-42). So there is more here than simple unbelief or defective belief.

Indeed, her statement in verse 22 is actually a profound statement of faith: *But I know that even now God will give you whatever you ask.* It might be that she believed Jesus even now could ask God to raise Lazarus, but her reaction when he actually does raise Lazarus indicates that is not part of her thinking (v. 39). Rather, the greatness of her faith is seen in the words *even now (kai nyn).* She continues to believe in him even though Lazarus' death seems to call into question the messengers' report that Jesus had said, *This sickness will not end in death* (v. 4). Moreover, even though Jesus has delayed coming to help, she continues to believe that Jesus is the agent of the gracious God—despite the fact that this graciousness was not present to heal her brother. Her trust in God's love for one that Christ clearly loved (v. 3) is not shaken by what seems like indifference or disregard (cf. Job 13:15; Hab 3:16-19). In this way Martha is an example of stellar faith, which should encourage all believers who face situations in which God seems to be absent or uncaring. The hard parts of life are occasions for learning about God and drawing closer to him.

Jesus' response, *Your brother will rise again* (v. 23), comes across as a common consolation among those Jews who believed in the future resurrection. That is how Martha takes it (v. 24), which is another case of misunderstanding. Not that her belief in the future resurrection is wrong—indeed, it is confirmed by what takes place. But Jesus is speaking of something more profound, the very foundation upon which the future resurrection itself rests. As almost always in John's Gospel, the key to unlocking Jesus' cryptic sayings is Jesus' own identity.

Martha has expressed her faith in the future resurrection and her brother's place in it (v. 24). Jesus responds to this statement of faith by challenging her with a deeper revelation of himself: *I am the resurrection and the life. He who believes in me will live, even though he dies; and whoever lives and believes in me will never die* (vv. 25-26). All of the "I am" sayings have to do with Christ as the life-giver, as is clearly the case here where we see that he does not just give life, but is life itself. As is made evident in some of the other "I am" sayings, he gives life by becoming our life (for example, 6:51; 15:1).

The main point is that Jesus' own identity spans the gap between the already and the not yet: "The resurrection *because* the life" (Augustine *In John* 49.14). Life is the more basic term, and the life Jesus is talking about even encompasses the resurrection life of the world to come (cf. Howard 1943:106-28; Beasley-Murray 1991:1-14). This "already" and "not yet" was met earlier (6:54; cf. 5:24-29). So we have in the raising of Lazarus a revelation of Jesus' authority and his identity as life-giver because he is life itself. Jesus' role goes far beyond our earthly existence.

The two terms Jesus uses, *resurrection* and *life,* are unpacked in the statements that follow (Dodd 1953:365). "I am the resurrection": *He who believes in me will live, even though he dies* (v. 25). This statement addresses Martha directly in the situation she is experiencing with the death of her brother. Jesus' claim is mind-boggling. He says it is faith in him that brings one back to life at the resurrection at the last day. He is the ground of eschatological hope. But then he goes even further. "I am the life": *and whoever lives and believes in me will never die* (v. 26). The life that comes through believing in Jesus is not interrupted by physical death. "The topic is the nature of the life that the believer has, namely one that death cannot destroy since the believer is in union with him who is the Life" (Beasley-Murray 1987:191). "By taking humanity into Himself He has revealed the permanence of man's individuality and being. But this permanence can be found only in union with Him. Thus two main thoughts are laid down: Life (resurrection) is present, and this Life is in a Person" (Westcott 1908:2:90).

Martha has confessed her faith in the resurrection (v. 24), and now Jesus has revealed himself to be the source of resurrection and life itself. He asks her, *Do you believe this?* (v. 26). She, like the former blind man (9:35-38), is given the opportunity to make a confession of faith. She does so in a statement that "echoes earlier confessions in the Gospel (1:42, 49) and anticipates the statement of its purpose in 20:30-31" (Beasley-Murray

---

11:27 It is possible that *who was to come into the world* is not modifying *Son of God* but is

1987:192). She responds, *Yes, Lord, I believe that you are the Christ, the Son of God, who was to come into the world* (v. 27). She does not repeat the terms Jesus has used, but she combines two of the most common titles used for Jesus in this Gospel. It would seem that she does not really grasp what Jesus is saying, as will be clear from her response when he does raise Lazarus (v. 39). So her use of more common titles may be a sign that she has not understood him. But her faith is still genuine and solid, for it is in Jesus himself. She is not grasping all that he is saying about himself, but she is sticking with him and confessing as much as she knows, which is what faith is all about. As the events of the raising of Lazarus unfold Jesus will instruct her in what he has just claimed, thus bringing her step by step in her knowledge of who he is and what he is offering so she may respond in faith. "The relevance of faith lies not in the power of faith as such, but in the fact that faith creates communion with Jesus and that through Jesus believers receive the gift of life" (Schnackenburg 1980b:332). This example of patient progress in our Lord's dealing with Martha should be a great encouragement to those of us who are not always quick on the uptake when it comes to God's revelation of himself to us.

While Martha's use of terms may suggest her lack of comprehension, the effect her statement has in the unfolding revelation in this Gospel is more positive. Jesus' language of resurrection and life is combined with a common Jewish term, Christ, and John's favorite title for Jesus, Son (of God). This combination brings together several strands of thought and makes them interpret one another. The most fundamental category in John is life. At this point, when Jesus most clearly speaks of himself as life, other major terms are brought in, thus suggesting that they should be interpreted in the light of this theme of life as well. Thus, Martha's confession and Jesus' claim provide a major point of revelation in this Gospel.

Jesus Meets with Mary (11:28-32) After Martha made her confession of faith Jesus apparently sent her to call her sister Mary, since she tells Mary, *The Teacher is here . . . and is asking for you* (v. 28; more literally, "he is calling you," *phōnei se*). The designation of Jesus as *teacher* is interesting after the more exalted terms of Martha's confession. But it is appropriate since he had just given her a teaching.

itself a third title (cf. 1:9; 3:31; 6:14; Barrett 1978:397).

Mary runs to Jesus (v. 29), as had Martha (v. 20), showing that they had a great attachment to Jesus, which reciprocated his love for them. In coming to Jesus in the midst of suffering the sisters provide a model for all believers.

John tells us that Martha gives her message secretly (v. 28) and that Mary and Jesus meet apart from the crowd (v. 30) so it would seem Jesus desires privacy, perhaps, as noted above, because he is a marked man in this region. But his cover is blown when those who were mourning with Mary follow her, thinking she was going to wail at the tomb (v. 31). So all the mourners in the house gather at the tomb, providing witnesses to what is about to happen and thus giving them the opportunity to believe—and others as well through their testimony.

When Mary reaches Jesus, she falls *at his feet and said, "Lord if you had been here, my brother would not have died"* (v. 32). This is exactly what her sister had said (v. 21). It would seem the sisters had been sharing this thought with one another (Westcott 1908:2:94). Whether her statement is rebuke or lamentation is unclear, as it is in the case of Martha. It could have elements of both, though the fact that she is wailing (v. 33) suggests lamentation is her main response. Mary does not add an expression of faith as Martha had (v. 22), though falling at Jesus' feet may suggest a similar attitude.

Jesus Calls Lazarus Back from the Dead (11:33-44) The wailing of Mary and those with her provokes a strong emotional reaction in Jesus. The NIV translation, *he was deeply moved in spirit and troubled* (v. 33), is common among English translations, but it does not do justice to the language. The word for *deeply moved (embrimaomai)* can be used of snorting in animals (for example, Aeschylus *Seven Against Thebes* 461) and in humans refers to anger (Beasley-Murray 1987:192-93). The second word, *troubled (tarassō),* is literally "troubled himself" *(etaraxen heauton).* So a better translation would be, "became angry in spirit and very agitated" (Beasley-Murray 1987:192-93).

Clearly the wailing provokes his response, but there are two very different ways to understand the nature of this reaction. Some would see Jesus as upset over their obtuseness and lack of faith, which is evident in

---

11:31 It would appear that the Jewish mourners were both men and women since *the Jews,*

their wailing (Schnackenburg 1980b:336; Beasley-Murray 1987:193). In this case we would have an occasion similar to his upbraiding of the disciples for their little faith at the stilling of the storm in the Synoptics. As Matthew tells that story, Jesus upbraids them before he stills the storm, while they are still being tossed about (Mt 8:26; contrast Mk 4:39-40; Lk 8:24-25)! There is not, however, a clear note of anger in those stories such as we find here (though see Mt 17:17 par. Mk 9:19 par. Lk 9:41).

Others suggest Jesus is angry at death itself and the pain and sadness it causes evident in the wailing (Westcott 1908:2:96; Brown 1966:435; Michaels 1989:203). This could be a parallel with the emotion Jesus felt in the Garden of Gethsemane (Mk 14:33), "prompted by the imminence of death and the struggle with Satan" (Brown 1966:435; cf. Chrysostom *In John* 63.2), though there it is more like sadness.

Either interpretation gets at a truth. Since the focus of this chapter is the theme of life, death is the more likely object of his anger. In a Gospel in which life is one of the primary themes, death is clearly the great enemy. Also, anger at their lack of faith would not be appropriate since they have not been faithless, though theirs is an imperfect faith. And he has no reason to expect the Jews present to trust in him, especially since they did not hear his revelation to Martha. Thus, his anger is most likely not at their imperfect faith, but at death itself and the reign of terror it exercises.

Jesus asks where they have laid Lazarus, and they reply, *come and see, Lord* (v. 34). Their wailing had triggered anger; now their invitation triggers weeping (v. 35). Jesus has not yet come to the tomb (v. 38), so he is not weeping over Lazarus. There would be no reason to do so anyway, at least on his part. It is their invitation that wrings his heart. He does not wail *(klaiō)* like them. Rather, he weeps *(dakryō)*, that is, sheds tears. He is not in anguish over the death of Lazarus, but rather saddened by the pain and sadness they feel. He is weeping with those who weep (Rom 12:15) because he loves them. The grief caused by death is one facet of death's evil that caused his anger. He is angry at death and saddened at grief. In both cases the reason is the same, namely, his love for his friends. The love of God for us and his wrath toward that which corrupts and destroys us are two sides of a single coin.

---

hoi Ioudaioi, here and in verse 33 is in the masculine, unless this is simply a set term for John.

Though Jesus' weeping was not over the death of Lazarus itself, his weeping—not wailing—has rightly been taken as a model of Christian mourning. Paul says we should not "grieve like the rest of men, who have no hope" (1 Thess 4:13). "He wept over Lazarus. So should you; weep, but gently, but with decency, but with the fear of God. If you weep thus, you do so not as disbelieving the resurrection, but as not enduring the separation. Since even over those who are leaving us, and departing to foreign lands, we weep, yet we do this not as despairing" (Chrysostom *In John* 62.4). But for believers, the separation is only for a while. Jesus' raising of Lazarus shows that his death was not final and that Jesus has the power over death. We may miss the one who has died and thus be saddened, but perfect love casts out wailing.

The Jewish mourners take note of how much Jesus loved Lazarus. They have interpreted his tears correctly. But then some of them go on to say, *Could not he who opened the eyes of the blind man have kept this man from dying?* (v. 37). This is often taken as a statement of unbelief, which then provokes Jesus' anger again (v. 38; for example, Schnackenburg 1980b:337). But something much more profound is going on. This link back to the healing of the blind man is relevant, for that miracle was unheard of and actually bore witness to Jesus as the agent of creation (see comment on 9:6). If one has such powers, then it is reasonable to ask whether he could have prevented this death. This is not so much unbelief as it is puzzlement. It looks like death is stronger than Jesus despite the implications of his healing the man born blind.

So Jesus' anger in verse 38 is not at their lack of faith as such, but again at death and its challenge to him as life-giver. Jesus came to the tomb in this state of anger (*embrimōmenos,* present participle; see comment on 11:33), ready to exercise his power over death and thereby initiating the process that will lead to his own death and decisive victory over death. "Christ does not come to the sepulchre as an idle spectator, but like a wrestler preparing for the contest. Therefore no wonder that He groans again, for the violent tyranny of death which He had to overcome stands before His eyes" (Calvin 1959:13).

Jesus orders the mourners to take the stone away from the entrance of the tomb (v. 39). Martha's objection that there would be a stench due to decomposition highlights the greatness of this sign. Jesus is raising someone who should already have begun to decay. There is no indication in the story that Lazarus comes out bearing marks of decay. Here we should see, as we saw with the giving of sight to the blind man, a revelation of Jesus' power and authority as the agent of creation. He does not just bring the person back to life by reuniting soul and body, he also restores the body itself. Thus, not only is the raising of Lazarus a sign of Jesus' identity and authority as life-giver, it also reflects the reality of the resurrection of the body. God is able to restore physical bodies after decay. The analogy is not complete, since Lazarus is not raised as an imperishable, spiritual body, as will be the case at the resurrection of the dead (1 Cor 15:42-44). But there is a continuity between the spiritual body and the physical body: it is a bodily resurrection. The overcoming of corruption in the raising of Lazarus thus provides, in part, a sign of the future resurrection.

The messengers had reported that Jesus said this illness *is for God's glory* (v. 4), and when Jesus met with Martha he presented himself to her as the object of faith. Now Jesus refers back to that conversation, though not in exactly the same words, at least as reported by John (cf. also 6:36, Schnackenburg 1980b:338). Jesus does not say that his ability to raise Lazarus is dependent on her faith. Rather, seeing God's glory depends upon her faith. Since she does indeed benefit from this sign it seems that her faith, defective as it may be, is nevertheless sufficient at this stage in God's eyes for her to see his glory. The repetition of the theme of God's glory at this point, just before the raising, keeps our focus on what is most significant. Here is the most powerful sign of Jesus' power and authority, but it does not point to him except as evidence that he is doing what he sees the Father doing. He is here to glorify God, not himself.

This dependency upon the Father is further emphasized in Jesus' prayer. Indeed, prayer itself is the form of speech that directly corresponds to the most significant thing about Jesus—his relationship with God, his Father. Each part of this prayer reveals something about that relationship. He *looked up,* or, more literally, he "lifted up his eyes" (v. 41; cf. Ps 123:1; Lam 3:41; 1 Esdras 4:58; 4 Maccabees 6:26; Mt 14:19 par. Mk 6:41 par. Lk 9:16; Jn 17:1), a gesture of looking away from self and toward God. It implies otherness and transcendence. But this gesture of transcendence is immediately juxtaposed with a word of intimacy, *Father,* the main title for God in this

Gospel. Indeed, for Christians, God is now known primarily as the Father of Jesus. Our language for God as Father has its source in Jesus' own revelation of God. It is his relationship with God that a Christian enters into and thus comes to know God as Jesus knows him, within the limitations of human nature.

We do not hear an actual petition but rather Jesus' thanksgiving that the Father heard him (v. 41). The communication between the Father and the Son regarding Lazarus had taken place much earlier, since he already announced what would take place when the messengers arrived with the news (v. 4). We here see the Son as subordinate to the Father, bringing a request to the Father. But far more is involved, for he goes on to say, *I knew that you always hear me* (v. 42). The clear teaching of the Old Testament is that God listens to the righteous, not the unrighteous, except for prayers of repentance (see note on 9:31). Thus, Jesus is claiming to be righteous before God and in unbroken fellowship with him. He knows he is heard; he has utter confidence in this relationship. "Jesus lives in constant prayer and communication with his Father. When he engages in vocal prayer, he is not entering, as we do, from a state of non-praying into prayer. He is only giving overt expression to what is the ground and base of his life all along. He emerges from non-vocal to vocal prayer here in order to show that the power he needs . . . for the raising of Lazarus . . . depends on the gift of God. It is through that prayer and communion and constant obedience to his Father's will that he is the channel of the Father's saving action. That is why the prayer is a thanksgiving rather than a petition" (Fuller 1963:107).

He vocalizes his prayer for the sake of the crowd: *I said this for the benefit of the people standing here, that they may believe that you sent me* (v. 42). In other words, it is not enough for people to be impressed with Jesus. They must believe in him as the one sent from God. It is precisely because Jesus is sent from God and does as God directs him that he is heard by God. The Father as the sender is primary. Jesus is not a wonderworker who is able to get God to do what he wants him to do. He is the obedient Son sent by the Father to do the Father's will. The Father's will and the Son's petition coincide exactly. Later Jesus will say that his followers are to share in this same relationship through their union with him, and thereby they will also be heard by the Father (14:11-14; 15:7, 16; 16:24). In such prayer, as also in the case of Jesus' prayer, "It is not the setting up of the will of self, but the apprehension and taking to self of the divine will, which corresponds with the highest good of the individual" (Westcott 1908:2:101).

In saying the purpose of this prayer is that they might believe, Jesus is again acting with divine graciousness and mercy. Such belief brings eternal life. Thus, this miracle is not just for the sake of Lazarus and his sisters, who already do have such faith and the life it brings, but for others that they may have life. The miracle reveals Jesus as the life-giver sent from the Father, and one receives life from him as one has faith in him. We see the grace of God evident in several ways in this story. This last miraculous sign continues to reveal the glory of God as have all the others.

After the prayer comes the deed: *Jesus called in a loud voice, "Lazarus, come out!"* (v. 43). Jesus could have healed Lazarus when he was still sick with a word of command, even across the miles. But now he utters a mightier word across a much greater distance—that between the living and the dead. The voice at the end of the age is heard here ahead of time (cf. 5:28; 1 Thess 4:16). The Word through whom all was made (1:1-3) here speaks forth life. Those standing around were given tasks to do, such as taking away the stone and unbinding Lazarus. The physical contact helped drive home the reality of what was happening. But for Jesus, his work is his word.

Perhaps, as is often suggested, he had to include Lazarus' name or all the dead would have come forth! The dead man still existed as Lazarus and could be called by name, for those who believe in Christ never die (v. 26). Jesus does not actually say something like "Rise" (contrast Mk 5:41 par. Lk 8:54; Lk 7:14). Rather, it seems the very calling of his name brought Lazarus back, and the call to come out that followed was "the command to use the new-given life" (Westcott 1908:2:102).

Lazarus *came out, his hands and feet wrapped with strips of linen, and a cloth around his face* (v. 44), presumably hopping or perhaps shuffling. It is unclear what was involved in burial in the first century (Brown 1994:2:1243-44; Green 1992:89). The NIV assumes we should picture Lazarus as a mummy, with strips of cloth passing around and around his body. This interpretation may be correct (cf. Brown 1994:2:1264), but there is evidence for the use of a single large sheet as the main covering (Brown 1994:2:1244-45). So it has been suggested that the Jewish custom was not to wind the corpse like a mummy, but rather to use a cloth like that of the Shroud of Turin. "The corpse would have been placed on a strip of linen, wide and long enough to envelop it completely. The feet would be placed at one end, and the cloth would then be drawn over the head to the feet, the feet would be bound at the ankles, and the arms secured to the body with linen bandages, and the face bound round with another cloth to keep the jaw in place" (Sanders 1968:276). The separate cloth used to bind up the jaw is mentioned in later sources (*m. Šabbat* 23:5; cf. Safrai and Stern 1974-1976:2:773), though this cloth in verse 44 may refer rather to a covering for the face (Beasley-Murray 1987:195).

Jesus gives yet another command, *Take off the grave clothes and let him go* (v. 44). This is a cry of victory. The grave has been defeated and liberty achieved. It is only a partial sign of the coming victory of Jesus' resurrection, since Lazarus will need to die again and enter the grave until the final resurrection. But it is a great sign of the life that is stronger than death, which those who believe in Jesus share. And it is a graphic sign of Jesus' own power and authority.

The call to loose Lazarus and let him go picks up "the biblical imagery of 'loosing' for victory over death and the powers of evil (for example, Matt. 16:19; Luke 13:16; Acts 2:24; cf. John 8:32-36)" (Michaels 1989:207). As such, this story speaks to all Christians bound by the fear of death and, on another level, bound by various sins. The Christian is in union with the one who himself is resurrection and life. As Christ offers freedom from the power of sin (8:32-36), so faith in Christ as resurrection and life brings freedom from the fear of death (cf. Heb 2:14-15).

Few would deny the theological and spiritual power of this story, but many would question whether the raising of Lazarus ever in fact took place. Some would say miracles do not happen, so therefore this could not have happened. This perspective derives more from prejudice than scientific observation and seems to be on the wane. But even those who believe such a thing could happen are suspicious of this story since it is not recounted in the Synoptics. If this event is so climactic, as John suggests, then this omission is striking. But neither John nor the Synoptics are trying to tell the whole story. John leaves out similar miracles in the Synoptics: the raising of Jairus's' daughter (Mt 9:18-19, 23-26 par. Mk 5:21-24, 35-43 par. Lk 8:40-42, 49-56) and the raising of the widow's son at Nain (Lk 7:11-17). So the omission is not that unusual. John includes this story because he sees in it the theological climax of Jesus' public ministry. It is also, from John's perspective, the key factor in the Jewish leaders' decision to have Jesus eliminated (11:53). John is fitting the pieces together to highlight the truth of what takes place in Jesus' ministry. That is very different from saying he is making up stories to illustrate his theology. "He who wrote the Gospel of the Word *made flesh* viewed history as of first importance; he would never have related a story of Jesus, still less created one, that he did not have reason to believe took place" (Beasley-Murray 1987:199). Thus, while the story of Lazarus looks suspicious to some, its historicity can be accounted for (cf. further Westcott 1908:2:77-79; Beasley-Murray 1987:199-201; Harris 1986:310-17).

Both Faith and Rejection Arise from the Raising of Lazarus (11:45-54) As a result of this miracle there is again a variety of responses. Many put faith in Jesus (v. 45), but others inform the authorities (v. 46). John does not make clear whether their trip to the authorities is innocent or a betrayal of Jesus. At an earlier stage the crowd was well aware of the authorities' concerns over Jesus (7:13, 25), and their animosity deepened significantly at the Feast of Dedication (10:31-39), leading Jesus to withdraw from the area (10:40-42). So it may well be that this is another betrayal of Jesus, similar to the lame man's betrayal earlier in Jesus' ministry (5:15).

The report alarms the Pharisees, and so *the chief priests and the Pharisees called a meeting of the Sanhedrin* (v. 47). The Sanhedrin was the supreme Jewish court in Jerusalem, which, under Roman oversight, "had both religious and political powers and comprised the elite (both priestly and lay) of society" (Moulder 1988:331). Both Sadducees and Pharisees were part of the Sanhedrin. Which of the two was the dominate part is uncertain (Schürer 1973-1987:2:213), though John implies it was the *chief priests* (7:45, 48; cf. 12:10). The *chief priests* were members of high-priestly families, along with others from prominent priestly families (cf. Acts 4:6), including, perhaps, temple officers like the treasurer and captain of police (Hubbard 1996:961; cf. Jeremias 1969:160-81; Schürer 1973-1987:2:235-36). Of the fifty-four references to *chief priests* in the Gospels, all of them are associated with Jerusalem, and almost all of them concern Jesus' final conflict (the exceptions are Mt 2:4; Jn 7:32, 45). In John's Gospel the Pharisees are also closely associated with Jerusalem. When John mentions opponents outside Jerusalem or its environs he uses the term "the Jews" (6:41, 52; see comment on 1:19).

Thus the two chief components of the Sanhedrin now call the Sanhedrin together. Both the Pharisees and the chief priests had attempted to apprehend Jesus earlier (7:32, 45), but now the situation is reaching a crisis, as they see his popularity rising. The low point after the feeding of the five thousand, at which almost everyone deserted Jesus (6:66), is now past and many are believing in him. Like many religious leaders since, Jesus is accused of being a threat to national security. Jesus' popularity could look like a popular uprising that would require calling in the Roman legions (cf. Acts 19:23-41, especially 19:40), who would *come and take away both our place and our nation* (Jn 11:48). As the NIV footnote indicates, *place* here refers to the temple (cf. H. Koester 1972:204). The position of the word *our* is emphatic. In fact, this could be translated, "will come and take away from us both our place and our nation." While they seem concerned for the nation, John says they are actually concerned about their own self-interests, as are the hirelings Jesus condemned earlier (10:12; cf. Westcott 1908:2:105). The irony is that they do destroy the temple of Jesus' body (cf. 2:19, 21), but this does not prevent the Romans from destroying their temple and their nation, nor does it prevent increasing numbers of people from believing in Jesus. Their plot prevented neither of the things they feared, even though they succeeded in getting Jesus killed.

Caiaphas, who ruled as high priest for a very long time by the standards of the day (A.D. 18-36), speaks up: *You know nothing at all! You do not realize that it is better for you that one man die for the people than that the whole nation perish* (vv. 49-50). Here again the self-interest is evident *(for you)*. This is a very significant statement for John, as is evident from his dwelling on it (vv. 51-52). Unknown to Caiaphas, he had in fact *prophesied that Jesus would die for the Jewish nation* (v. 51). Caiaphas is thinking of Jesus' death in place of the destruction of the nation by Rome, but John sees the divine intent that Jesus die in place of the nation for their sin. Here,

11:49 High priests did not hold the office on a yearly basis. The fact that he repeats *that year* in verse 51 shows his emphasis on that one year. "What he means is 'that fateful year.' That was the year when the world's salvation was wrought out. In that year of all years it was Caiaphas who was the high priest" (Morris 1971:566).

11:51 The idea that someone could prophesy without knowing it was recognized in Judaism (for example, *b. Soṭa* 12b, regarding Pharaoh's daughter; Philo *De Vita Mosis* 1.277,

along with 1:29, is the clearest expression in this Gospel of Jesus' death as dealing with sin. John focuses on the cross as revelation (Forestell 1974), but here we see that he also affirms the cross as atonement. The cross as revelation alone leads to Gnosticism, as John discovered in his own communities, hence the emphasis in 1 John on the atonement aspect (1 Jn 2:2; 4:10, cf. Whitacre 1982:156-57). But those members of the community who headed off in gnostic directions were not true to John's teaching in its fullness. John's experience in his community is a cautionary tale. Each aspect of the Gospel needs to be in place, or some deformed shape will emerge. The period of the New Testament saw the articulation of a variety of ways to express the Gospel, with the Holy Spirit guiding and protecting. The unity and diversity we now have in the canon provides a composite shape to the faith that is a guide to the truth of the Gospel—that is what "canon" means.

Caiaphas refers to the *people (laos)* and the *nation (ethnos),* but in the next verse John only uses *nation.* The word *laos* was not used frequently in classical Greek, but it occurs more than two thousand times in the Septuagint, having become "a specific term for a specific people, namely, Israel, and it serves to emphasize the special and privileged religious position of this people as the people of God" (Strathmann and Meyer 1967:32). Thus, John's refusal to use *laos* may be significant in the light of the theme of Jesus' departure from the temple and the formation of the core of the new community around him (see comments on 8:59 and 10:1-21). "The Jews at this crisis had ceased to be 'a people.' They were a 'nation' only, as one of the nations of the world. The elements of the true 'people' were scattered throughout the world, as Jews, and Jews of the Dispersion, and Gentiles" (Westcott 1908:2:107).

Caiaphas is only thinking of the Jewish nation, but John sees the significance of Jesus' death to extend to all of humanity (v. 52). Jesus death is also *for the scattered children of God, to bring them together and make them one.* The idea of gathering together God's scattered people is a hope

---

regarding Balaam). Indeed, the *Mekilta* on Exodus 15:17 says, "All prophets who have prophesied have not known what they prophesied; only Moses and Isaiah knew it" (cf. Strack and Billerbeck 1924:546). Philo associates prophesy with the priesthood (*De Specialibus Legibus* 4.192), and Josephus cites examples of high priests who prophesy (*Jewish Wars* 1.68-69; *Antiquities of the Jews* 11.327-28; 13.299-300). Cf. further Dodd 1968:63-68.

found extensively in the Old Testament (for example, Is 11:12; Jer 31:8; Ezek 11:17; Mic 2:12-13; 2 Macc 1:27). Now this gathering will begin to take place in the most unusual way—through the death of the Messiah. Jesus' work as the Good Shepherd (10:16) is accomplished through his death, as he himself will emphasize shortly (12:32). So even in this passage, which touches on the atoning significance of his death, other aspects are developed as well. The oneness with God that the atonement accomplishes is complemented by the oneness of the people of God drawn from the whole of the human race. They are already referred to as *children of God* since each one who enters Christ's community has been given to him by the Father (6:37) and has responded in faith and has been born again (1:12). John places great stress on the individual, but here we see his appreciation of the corporate whole (cf. Brown 1966:443). The nature of this unity will be brought out soon (chaps. 14—17), but for now we see that it is Christ, especially Christ crucified, that unites the people of God.

The Sanhedrin comes to the decision to kill Jesus (v. 53). There had been attempts to take his life already (5:18; 7:1, 19 ; 8:59; 10:31), but now the decision had been reached in an official manner by the central authority for the Jewish people. "Jesus is formally devoted to death by a vote of the competent authority. This is, in fact, the act by which, in its historical or 'objective' aspect, the death of Christ is determined" (Dodd 1953:367). *They plotted* in the NIV does not do justice to the Greek *ebouleusanto,* which means, rather, that they "resolved," "determined" or even "passed a resolution" (Bammel 1970:30). Thus, by giving life to Lazarus, Jesus has sealed his own death. In what follows we see the even greater irony that through his death comes life for the world.

Jesus knows of this increased danger, though we are not told whether he knows this through an informant, preternatural knowledge or just common sense. He goes back into seclusion once again, this time to *Ephraim* (v. 54; cf. 10:40). It is not certain where *Ephraim* was located, though it was probably four miles to the northeast of Bethel, which places

11:57 This searching by the authorities presents a striking contrast to the search of the Greeks (12:21).
12:1 The story of the anointing reminds one of similar events in the Synoptics (Mt 26:6-13 par. Mk 14:3-9; Lk 7:36-38; cf. Brown 1966:449-54). The anointing recounted in Matthew and Mark at the house of Simon the leper is probably this same event, while that in Luke,

it some fifteen miles north-northeast of Jerusalem (cf. Barrett 1978:408; Brown 1966:441). His movement in and out of seclusion shows him working around the intentions of his enemies as he works out the intentions of his Father. There is a similar pattern in his work in the lives of his followers today. He moves in and out of seclusion in our lives, not because his life is threatened but as part of his love for us, to wean us from false attachments, even false views we may have of God himself.

Jesus Is Anointed at Bethany (11:55—12:11) It is almost time for Passover, and people are going to Jerusalem to prepare for the feast by undergoing ritual purification (v. 55; cf. Westerholm 1992). They are standing in the temple, speculating whether or not Jesus will come to the feast, aware that the chief priests and Pharisees are seeking his arrest (v. 57). Again we see the interested crowd and the antagonistic authorities (cf. 7:11-13, 32, 47-49). But Jesus has already departed from the temple (8:59) and will not be standing where they are standing as they ask such questions. He will come up to this feast, but he will not be coming to the temple. Rather, the one true sacrifice is about to take place in the temple of his body.

This description of Jesus' danger adds a dramatic touch to the fact that he returns to Bethany again (12:1). He is back with Lazarus and his sisters in a relatively private setting. There is a party in his honor *six days before the Passover* (v. 1), probably on Saturday night after the conclusion of sabbath. It is not said where the party takes place, but from the account in Matthew and Mark it would be at the house of Simon the leper (Mt 26:6 par. Mk 14:3). Lazarus is also an honored guest, while Martha helps with the serving (v. 2), true to the picture of her elsewhere (Lk 10:38-42).

The picture of Mary is also true to that in Luke (10:38-42); that is, she is a devoted disciple who ignores the taboos of her society in her commitment to Jesus. Sitting at his feet as a disciple (Lk 10:39) was not the place for a woman, but she is commended by Jesus (Lk 10:42). Now she acts in an even more scandalous manner in anointing Jesus' feet with extremely

which takes place in Simon the Pharisee's house and is done by a sinful woman, is a different one. The account in John can be harmonized with that in Matthew and Mark (Carson 1991:425-27). But some of the details in John's account correspond also with details in Luke, in particular the anointing of the feet and wiping with the hair, which will be discussed below.

expensive perfume and then wiping them with her hair (Jn 12:3).

Both aspects of her action—the extravagance and the method—were disturbing. The *pure nard* she uses was imported from northern India (Brown 1966:448). Judas says, no doubt correctly, that it was *worth a year's wages* (v. 5). The text literally reads "three hundred denarii" (cf. NIV note). Since a denarius was a day's pay for a day laborer, the NIV paraphrase is accurate, taking into account feast days and sabbaths when one would not work. A rough equivalent would be something over $10,000, the gross pay for someone working at minimum wage for a year. No wonder the disciples (Mt 26:8), Judas in particular, respond with dismay at such a waste.

In the accounts in Matthew and Mark, she anoints Jesus' head, while in John it is his feet. Obviously, it could have been both, and with twelve ounces to work with (not a full pint, as in the NIV) she could have anointed his whole body. Indeed, since he interprets this as an anointing for his burial (v. 7) it seems she did anoint more than his head and feet, as Matthew and Mark suggest (Mt 26:12 par. Mk 14:8; cf. Carson 1991:426).

The other part of her action that would have been quite disturbing was the wiping of his feet with her hair. Jewish women did not let down their hair in public. This is an expression of devotion that would have come across as extremely improper and even somewhat erotic, as indeed it would in most cultures. There is no indication of why Mary did this act. The most obvious possibility was her sheer gratitude for what Jesus had done for her brother and the revelation it brought to her of Jesus' identity, power, authority and grace. John's focus on her anointing Jesus' feet points to Mary's great humility. As she has come to realize a bit more of the one who has been a friend to her and her brother and sister, her faith deepens and she recognizes her unworthiness. The humility of her act prepares us to be all the more scandalized when Jesus himself washes his disciples' feet in the next chapter.

Whatever Mary's intentions and reason for her action, Jesus sees it in reference to his coming death (v. 7). Jesus sees cryptic significance in another person's actions instead of making his more usual cryptic explanation of his own activity. There is no reason to think Mary knew the full

---

12:7 The most natural translation of this text would be "leave her alone so she might keep it for the day of preparation for my burial." But verses 3 and 5 imply all the perfume has been used up (cf. also Mk 14:3). A number of grammatical solutions have been proposed,

import of what she was doing, any more than Caiaphas knew what he was saying (11:49-51). The people around Jesus are being caught up in the climax of all of salvation history. They are acting for their own reasons, yet they are players in a drama that they do not understand, doing and saying things with significance beyond their imaginings. "Mary in her devotion unconsciously provides for the honour of the dead. Judas in his selfishness unconsciously brings about the death itself" (Westcott 1908:2:112).

Judas' shock at the waste of such costly ointment (vv. 4-5) makes us more aware of Mary's extravagance. According to the Synoptic accounts (Mt 26:8-9 par. Mk 14:4-5), Judas is simply expressing what others were also thinking. Being the treasurer of the group, it would not have surprised anyone to hear him express this concern. So, at the time, Judas' remarks would not have stood out as unusual. But with hindsight John knows there was more motivating him. If Caiaphas and Mary reveal more about Jesus in their actions than they realize, Judas is revealing something deeper about himself. John says Judas used to steal from the common fund (v. 6). It is doubtful that this was known at the time, for if it was Judas would have been relieved of his duties, at the least. But such embezzlement reveals a heart in love with self and in love with money, neither of which have a place in the life of a disciple (cf. Chrysostom *In John* 65.3). But beyond even this, the deepest sin, of course, was Judas' betrayal of the Lord (v. 4). Every time John mentions Judas he refers to his betrayal (6:71; 13:2, 26-29; 18:2-3, 5). Judas may have thought he was acting for God's glory, as did also the opponents of Jesus, but he, like them, was in fact alienated from God. God's glory will indeed be manifest, but not as Judas thinks.

Judas' heart is thus fundamentally different from the heart of Mary as she lavishes her love and respect upon Jesus. This Gospel provides a great many examples of the difference between faith and unbelief through descriptions of true disciples on the one hand and, on the other, both would-be disciples and Jesus' opponents. But here we have the contrast between a true disciple, Mary, and one of the Twelve, which shows that privilege of position is no substitute for faith and obedience. Chrysostom says that Jesus, even though he knew Judas' heart (6:64), "bare with him,

---

none of them very convincing (cf. Barrett 1978:413-14). The NIV rendering is probably the best approach. "The idea is not that she is to keep the perfume for some future use, but that (unknowingly) she was keeping it until now to embalm Jesus" (Brown 1966:449).

desiring to recall him" (*In John* 65.2). But Judas, like the Jewish opponents, resisted God's grace.

Jesus' statement in verse 8, *You will always have the poor among you, but you will not always have me,* must be understood in its context both within Judaism and salvation history. On one level Jesus is simply reminding Judas and the others of priorities as understood within Judaism. He is alluding to the Scripture "There will always be poor people in the land" (Deut 15:11) and perhaps also to the notion that acts of kindness, such as burial, are higher than works of charity, which would include giving alms to the poor (*b. Sukka* 49b). This view is based, in part, on the fact that kindness can be shown to the living and the dead (through funerals and burials), whereas charity can only be shown to the living (cf. Brown 1966:449; Barrett 1978:415). So the fact that Jesus is about to die (cf. 12:35-36) justifies Mary's action. But on another level, the identity of Jesus also justifies this action. In the Synoptics even the burying of one's father is put second to responding to Jesus and the call of the kingdom (Mt 8:22 par. Lk 9:60). So this anointing also makes sense given who Jesus is and the awesome events unfolding in salvation history.

Care for the poor is a sacred duty because it is the concern of God's own heart. Those who share in his life will share in his concern for the poor and will act appropriately as he guides. This diversion of funds from the poor for the sake of Jesus' burial implies that there are times for such exceptional use of funds. But it also implies that the funds would usually go to the poor and that this is the proper thing to do. John's "suggestion that Judas did not care about the poor (v. 6) has implied in passing that Christians *should* care" (Michaels 1989:218).

This section concludes with a description of a *large crowd* seeking out Jesus there at the party, attracted also by Lazarus' presence (v. 9). Many Jews were putting their faith in Jesus because of Lazarus, so he was included in the authorities most-wanted list (vv. 10-11). Obviously, Jesus' popularity is rising once again. Lazarus was a living sign of Jesus' identity as life and life-giver, victor over death.

The crowd's faith in Jesus makes prominent the authorities' rejection of

---

12:12 The story of Jesus' entry into Jerusalem is one of the few stories told in all four

Jesus. It also points up the weakness of the authorities' control at this point. Things were getting out of hand for them because their control was slipping. "In not going directly to the chief priests, the crowd was defying the Sanhedrin and protecting two fugitives rather than one" (Michaels 1989:216). But this slip in their control is in fact quite true to the circumstances, for the whole effort of the Sanhedrin is quite futile. They seek to kill Lazarus, but if Jesus raised him once why could he not do it again (cf. Augustine *In John* 50.14)? Their great weapon of control is useless against the Lord of life and his followers.

The statement *many of the Jews were going over to Jesus* (v. 11) in the Greek is simply "many were going." But the NIV captures the correct sense that "many Jews left their former Jewish allegiance and way of life to become disciples" (Barrett 1978:415). Jesus' alternative community continues to grow as people shift their allegiance from the Jewish authorities to him.

Jesus Enters Jerusalem as King of Israel (12:12-19) The scene now shifts from a private setting to a public setting. Given the tensions and expectations that have been growing (cf. 10:39-42; 11:46-57; 12:11), Jesus' entry into Jerusalem is very dramatic. By openly entering the city where he is a marked man he takes the first step toward the final confrontation.

Passover was one of the three feasts that Jews were supposed to attend in Jerusalem, and consequently the population of Jerusalem swelled enormously at this time. As this great crowd is beginning to gather from around Israel and the larger world of the diaspora, news about Jesus is spreading, and people are wondering whether he will come to the feast (11:55-56). On Sunday, the day after the party in Bethany at which Mary anointed Jesus, news arrives that Jesus is *on his way to Jerusalem* (v. 12), and a crowd of pilgrims, presumably those who had been wondering if he would come, goes out to meet him. Mary's private expression of emotion is now matched by the crowd's public outpouring of enthusiasm.

They shout *Hosanna! Blessed is he who comes in the name of the Lord!* (v. 13). These are lines from one of the Psalms of Ascents (Ps 118:25-26) sung as a welcome to pilgrims coming up to Jerusalem. As such, this is an

Gospels (Mt 21:1-11; Mk 11:1-11; Lk 19:28-38). For detailed comparisons of the accounts see especially Brown 1966:459-61 and Carson 1991:431-35.

entirely appropriate thing to do as Jesus is coming up to Jerusalem. But there is more involved here. The cry of *Hosanna!* is a Hebrew word *(hôš î'āh-nā)* that had become a greeting or shout of praise but that actually meant "Save!" or "Help!" (an intensive form of imperative). Not surprisingly, forms of this word were used to address the king with a need (cf. 2 Sam 14:4; 2 Kings 6:26). Furthermore, the palm branches the people carry are symbolic of a victorious ruler (cf. 1 Macc 13:51; 2 Macc 10:7; 14:4). Indeed, in an apocalyptic text from the Maccabean era, palms are mentioned in association with the coming of the messianic salvation on the Mount of Olives (*Testament of Naphtali* 5). The cry of *Hosanna!* and the palm branches are in themselves somewhat ambiguous, but their import is made clear as the crowd adds a further line, *Blessed is the King of Israel!* (v. 13). Clearly they see in Jesus the answer to their nationalistic, messianic hopes. Earlier a crowd had wanted to make Jesus king (6:15), and now this crowd is recognizing him as king in the city of the great King. Here is the great dream of a Davidic ruler who would come and liberate Israel, establishing peace and subduing the Gentiles (cf. *Psalms of Solomon* 17:21-25).

Jesus responds by finding a *young donkey* to sit on (v. 14), thereby making a mess of the picture they were creating. He should have found a horse to ride on or made use of some other symbol of power. Instead he paints from a different palette. His action undercuts their nationalism and points in a different direction, evoking an image from the Prophets: *Do not be afraid, O Daughter of Zion; see, your king is coming, seated on a donkey's colt* (v. 15; from Zech 9:9). He is indeed king, but not the sort of king they have in mind.

John says the disciples did not make the connection with the passage from Zechariah at the time: *At first his disciples did not understand all this. Only after Jesus was glorified did they realize that these things had been written about him and that they had done these things to him* (v. 16). The word translated *realize* is *emnēsthēsan,* "remember," the same word used to describe their recollection and insight into the cleansing of the temple (2:22). At the time they were caught up in the swirl of events and did not really understand what was going on. From what we know of them elsewhere, they probably shared the nationalistic hopes of the crowd (for example, Acts 1:6). The disciples and the crowd thought they were honoring Jesus, and they were. But they did not really understand the true meaning of what was happening nor even what they were saying. They did not put the events of Jesus' entry into Jerusalem and the Scripture together, so they did not grasp what had taken place until after Jesus had been glorified. They needed to see the revelation at it greatest in the death and resurrection of Jesus and to have the help of the Spirit who was not available to them until after the glorification (7:39) before they understood the significance of these events (cf. 15:26; 16:13-14).

The meaning of what takes place is conveyed through both the Scripture shouted by the crowd at the time and the Scripture that occurred to the disciples later. The crowd shouted, "Help!" and "Save!" and Jesus has come precisely to help and save them, though it will not be through the political liberation the crowd expects. The crowd chants a line from a Psalm of Ascent: *Blessed is he who comes in the name of the Lord!* (v. 13, from Ps 118:26). This line applies to Jesus in a way it never had to anyone else before. Jesus is the one who makes known the Father and has come in the Father's name (5:43), and he desires that the Father's name be made known (17:6, 26). So of him it is uniquely true that he comes in the name of the Lord. This expression is one way of summarizing his whole mission.

The crowd, in their messianic, nationalistic fervor, adds another line not found in the Psalm of Ascent: *Blessed is the King of Israel!* (v. 13). This acclamation ties together the whole of Jesus' ministry up to this point, signaled by the word *Israel*. Apart from this verse, the words *Israel* and *Israelite* occur only in the first three chapters. John the Baptist's witness to Israel (1:31) finds its initial response in the confession of Nathanael, a true Israelite (1:47), when Nathanael confesses Jesus to be the Son of God, the King of Israel (1:49). Nathanael stands in marked contrast to Nicodemus, a teacher of Israel (3:10), who is unable to understand earthly things, let alone heavenly things. So the first three chapters are characterized by a concern with the initial witness to Israel, and this motif now finds its fullness in this crowd's acclamation of Jesus as the King of Israel. Jesus is indeed King of Israel, and this motif now comes to the fore as the story nears its end (cf. 18:33-39; 19:3, 12-15, 19-21). His kingdom, however, far transcends Israel's boundaries. "What honor was it to the Lord to be King of Israel? What great thing was it to the King of eternity to become the King of men?" (Augustine *In John* 51.4). Augustine's language is too dismissive to be true to John at this point, but he does help us keep the Johannine perspective on the identity of the one entering Jerusalem.

The crowd is probably not aware that the line they have added to the acclamation is an echo of another passage that further contributes to the depth of revelation concerning Jesus in this story: "The Lord, the King of Israel, is with you; never again will you fear any harm" (Zeph 3:15). The context in Zephaniah is of the future time of peace when Jerusalem is no longer at war—the lame and the scattered have been brought home, and even the Gentiles have been purified so that they might call on the name of the Lord (3:9-20). The hallmark of this time is the Lord's own presence (3:15, 17). For Zephaniah, as for this crowd, such a scene was the anticipated outcome of the final battle with the Gentiles, which would liberate Israel once and for all. But John has shown that the realities described by Zephaniah are already taking place in the midst of Israel through the ministry of Jesus, though in a very different manner. Key themes in Zephaniah's description are heard also in the previous chapters in John. In particular, the bringing together of both Jew and Gentile was said to be the work of the Good Shepherd (10:4, 16), and the picture of life in the messianic kingdom is alluded to in Jesus' promise of abundant life (10:10), which was then further revealed in the raising of Lazarus (chap. 11). Thus, the crowd's nationalistic agenda is thrown into relief. "They should not be acclaiming him as an earthly king, but as the manifestation of the Lord their God who has come into their midst (Zeph 3:17) to gather the outcast" (Brown 1966:462). If they had eyes to see what Jesus was doing and ears to hear what he was saying they would find in him the fulfillment of their desires, though without the nationalistic element.

The Scripture passage that occurs to the disciples later is also, like the acclamation of the crowd, a composite text. The first part, *Do not be afraid, O Daughter of Zion* (v. 15), probably comes from the passage we have just examined in Zephaniah (3:16). The exhortation not to fear is very common in Scripture, but the Zephaniah passage is the closest to the full expression in John (Brown 1966:458). Thus, the crowd's acclamation and this later Scripture are tied together in John through Zephaniah, though not in the thinking of those in the midst of the event. The magnificent picture of eschatological peace in Zephaniah is behind this lack of fear. The fulfillment of this promise of peace is taking place right before the eyes of this crowd, though they do not know it.

The rest of the quote comes from Zechariah: "Rejoice greatly, O Daughter of Zion! Shout, Daughter of Jerusalem! See, your king comes to you, righteous and having salvation, gentle and riding on a donkey, on a colt, the foal of a donkey" (Zech 9:9). As with the Zephaniah passage, this verse from Zechariah foresees the coming of the messianic age of peace, when the war-horses are taken from Jerusalem and the king will reign "from sea to sea and from the River to the ends of the earth" (Zech 9:10). John has abbreviated the citation, and he probably did this for the sake of simplicity rather than in an effort to exclude the themes of righteousness, salvation and gentleness. Donkeys and mules were used by important persons and kings in the Old Testament (for example, Judg 10:4; 12:14; 2 Sam 13:29; 18:9), including David himself (1 Kings 1:33), but the contrast in this context in Zechariah 9 is between the warhorses (v. 10) and the donkey on which the king rides (v. 9) is a striking image of humility. The king is righteous, blameless in the eyes of the law, which reminds one of the controversies in this Gospel over who is the true disciple of Moses. The "having salvation" is a form that could be either passive or reflexive (Niphal, *nôšā'*). This means that this king has himself been delivered by God (passive) or that he shows himself to be a deliverer (reflexive)—either sense is true of Jesus as revealed in this Gospel. Thus, by riding on a donkey, Jesus connects with a rich picture of the messianic king, thereby providing insight for interpreting his own identity and plans as he enters Jerusalem on this particular Sunday at the time of Passover.

John gives us a report on both the crowd and the opponents, as he does elsewhere in this Gospel. The repetition of the word "crowd" *(ochlos)* is a little awkward (Jn 12:17-18). Verse 18 reads literally, "Because of this the crowd went out to meet him, because they heard he had done this sign," which makes it sound like what was described in verse 12. The NIV has the right sense—the number of people gathering around Jesus was continuing to grow, spurred on by the report by those who had seen the raising of Lazarus (vv. 17-18). Despite the awkward expression, this is an important note for John to add, for it continues to connect the raising of Lazarus to what is now going on. John does not let us forget that the one who is heading toward his death is the Lord of life.

While the crowds build, the Pharisees, on the other hand, are getting more and more upset. The translation *See, this is getting us nowhere* (v. 19) is too weak. The verbs are in the second-person plural, capturing the mutual condemnation they are throwing at one another: "You guys see that you are doing no good." The crowd around Jesus is so large that they conclude, *Look how the whole world has gone after him!* (v. 19). This exaggeration expresses their dismay and frustration, but of course it is also yet another example in John of people's words being more significant than they realize.

A series of different people are coming to Jesus. First, we heard just before the triumphal entry that "many of the Jews were going over to Jesus and putting their faith in him" (12:11). Second, the Pharisees speak of the *world* (v. 19) probably because they are seeing even Jews from the diaspora, who are in town for the feast, being attracted to Jesus. But the world that God loves and for which he sent his Son (3:16) includes all humanity. Representatives of the third group, the Gentiles, appear in the next section as some Greeks who are seeking Jesus arrive. The Good Shepherd is indeed gathering his flock from the whole world (10:16) in fulfillment of the prophecies of the universal messianic kingdom such as those found in Zechariah and Zephaniah. Jesus continues to form his community apart from the official structures of Judaism. The same witness to Jesus that disturbs the leaders might have instead encouraged them to reconsider their rejection of Jesus and come to him for life. But they continue in their hardened position against Jesus, rejecting his love for them.

Jesus' Hour Arrives (12:20-36) Some Greeks now come to see Jesus, signaling to him that his long awaited hour has arrived (vv. 20-23). Jesus speaks of the mystery of life coming through death, applying this to his own death (vv. 24-33). In the midst of this teaching the Father himself bears witness to Jesus from heaven, but the crowd has a mixed response to the Father's voice, just as they have had to Jesus, the Father's Word (vv. 28-30). The section concludes with the crowd's raising further questions about the identity of the Son of Man, but Jesus does not engage them in discussion. His teaching to the world has been completed. He simply exhorts them to receive the light while they still can (vv. 34-36).

John has already called our attention to the crowds gathering for Passover and their interest in whether Jesus would come to the feast (11:55-56). Then the crowd welcomed Jesus with great acclamations (12:12-18). Now from among this Passover crowd one particular group comes forward to meet Jesus. These *Greeks* are not Greek-speaking Jews but rather Gentiles, whether from Greece or elsewhere (Barrett 1978:421). The fact that they *went up to worship at the Feast* (v. 20) suggests they were proselytes. Josephus says there were many such foreigners who would come up to the feast, though they could not actually partake of the sacrifice (*Jewish Wars* 6.427-28), since they had not fully entered Judaism. These were pious Gentiles who were attracted to Judaism. They had come to the feast to worship God, suggesting an openness of heart to God. Their interest in the things of God leads them to Jesus.

It is not clear why they approach Philip (v. 21). Perhaps they heard someone call Philip by name and thought because he had a Greek name he might be more responsive to them. Perhaps Philip dressed in a Greek style. In any event, they come to Philip and say, *Sir, . . . we would like to see Jesus* (v. 21). Earlier, Philip had told Nathaniel to come and see Jesus (1:46), and now these Greeks have come and want to see Jesus, thus signaling that a new stage has been reached in Jesus' ministry (see comment on 12:23). When they say they want to *see Jesus* they are simply asking to meet with him, but the motif of sight is a major expression for revelation in this Gospel. Indeed, their request sums up the right attitude of any disciple and the core focus of any ministry. This request, "Sir, we would see Jesus," has been attached to more than one pulpit as a guideline for the preacher.

Philip does not go straight to Jesus with the Greeks' request, but rather to Andrew, who was from Philip's town (1:44). This may bear witness to Philip's humility, but more likely it shows how unusual the situation was. Jesus has had contact with non-Jews (cf., probably, 4:43-53), but very rarely. He has taught much about the universal scope of God's love, but the full implications of this were not grasped by his followers until later. The nationalism stirred up during Jesus' entry into Jerusalem might make the disciples uncertain about such a request, though these Greeks were proselytes. It seems Philip simply needs some encouragement to approach the Lord when faced with this new and stretching situation. He goes to Andrew, who seems to have been a trusting person who was willing to speak up even when it seemed foolish (6:8-9). If we are stymied by a situation, it helps to have a friend with whom to go to the Lord, not to demand of the Lord but simply to lay before him the situation.

Quite often Jesus has responded to questions and situations with cryptic sayings, and this is no exception. When Andrew and Philip announce the coming of the Greeks something wondrous happens. It triggers the moment the reader has been anticipating since the story began: *Jesus replied, "The hour has come for the Son of Man to be glorified"* (v. 23). As with all his cryptic sayings, this response addresses the issue, but it does so in ways incomprehensible at the time. He does not speak directly to the Greeks, but he speaks of their place in his community in the future. For he reveals that it is time for his death to take place, through which a great crop will be produced (v. 24) as he draws *all men* to himself (v. 32). Thus, verse 24 answers the Greeks indirectly, for through his death he "will become accessible for them as the exalted Lord" (Bultmann 1971:424).

It may seem strange to refer to Jesus' death as a glorification. But the death is at the heart of the Son's revelation of the Father, for God is love and love is the laying down of one's life (cf. 1 Jn 4:8; 3:16). So in the cross the heart of God is revealed most clearly. Selflessness and humble self-sacrifice are seen to be divine attributes. Throughout his life Jesus has done the Father's will, and such selflessness is a key component in the eternal life he offers. God's own life is a life of love that denies self for the sake of the beloved, and therefore such love is the very nature of life itself, real life. "Sacrifice, self-surrender, death, is the condition of the highest life: selfishness is the destruction of life" (Westcott 1908:2:123). Thus, the cross is not just a one-time event that atones for sin, though it is certainly that. It is the most dramatic case in point of the pattern of divine life that exists for all time.

Jesus proceeds to speak of the mystery of life coming through death. He uses the image of a seed that must fall into the ground and die in order to produce "much fruit" (v. 24, *polyn karpon;* the NIV *many seeds* is unjustified). The contrast between remaining "alone" (*monos;* NIV, *only a single seed*) and bearing much fruit indicates that the fruit Jesus speaks of are people, the fruit of evangelism. But a second meaning of *fruit* is also present: through his death fruit will be produced in the lives of his followers, namely, the very quality of life, divine life, revealed in the death (cf. 15:1-8). The next verses spell out this connection between fruit and discipleship.

Jesus begins speaking in general terms: *The man who loves his life will lose it, while the man who hates his life in this world will keep it for eternal life* (v. 25). Here is the call to radical discipleship, similar to those found earlier in Jesus' ministry in the Synoptics (Mt 16:24-26 par. Mk 8:34-37 par. Lk 9:23-25; Mt 10:39 par. Lk 17:33; cf. Brown 1966:473-74). The word for *life (psychē)* does not only refer to physical life; it is more comprehensive than that, taking in one's whole being, one's "self." The self was not created to be an autonomous center of being, but rather to be in union with God and receive life from him. "*Psychē* is the life which is given to man by God and which through man's attitude toward God receives its character as either mortal or eternal" (Schweizer 1974:644). The love of this self as such is at the heart of all sin, beginning with the rebellion in the Garden of Eden. That rebellion brought death and continues to bring death. When Jesus says the one who loves this self will *lose* it he does not mean "misplace" it but rather "destroy" it *(apollyei)*.

What is needed is a detachment from this self, and this is what is meant in verse 25 by *hates* (Michel 1967:690-91). When Jesus says the disciple must hate father and mother (Lk 14:26) he does not mean despise, reject and abominate in an absolute sense. He is speaking about choices and attachments. He means the devotion and obedience to himself must be so thorough that nothing else is distracting. The same language is used when he teaches that one can only serve one master (Mt 6:24 par. Lk 16:13). So Jesus is not speaking of a hatred of the "self" itself but rather of a rejection of the self's claims to autonomy and control. Indeed, rejecting the false claims of the self *in this world* is actually a way of caring for one's true self, for thereby one *will keep it for eternal life* (v. 25). Thus, this passage is not referring to self-destruction or masochism; it calls one to reject the way of rebellion and live in the light of eternity. At the heart of discipleship is love, and at the heart of love is sacrifice.

Such denial of self opens one to receive the divine life that never dies (11:25-26), which comes through union with Christ by the Spirit, as Jesus will soon go on to teach his followers privately. Already now, while he is still teaching publicly, he refers to this reality in more general terms: *Whoever serves me must follow me; and where I am, my servant also will be. My Father will honor the one who serves me* (v. 26). He has been speaking of his death and now says the servant must follow the master. So we continue to hear the Synoptic theme of taking up one's cross and following Jesus.

The reward of such obedience, even through death, is twofold: to be with Jesus and to be honored by the Father. Jesus has been living in the presence of God and is returning to the presence of God, so this is a promise of being with Christ in the presence of God. The honor we receive from the Father comes from our union with Christ, the one whom the Father honors throughout. Such union with God in Christ and such honor from the Father are what we were created for and what we rejected in the rebellion in the Garden of Eden. It is only through a death to the false, rebellious self that we can receive such life and return to our true humanity in union with God. In a sense, then, these two verses contain the core description of discipleship. "Self must be displaced by another; the endless, shameless focus on self must be displaced by focus on Jesus Christ, who is the supreme revelation of God" (Carson 1991:439). This death to the false self is a form of suffering. Christ's call may also include actual physical suffering as well: like master, like disciple (cf. 15:18—16:4). "Christ draws men to fellowship with himself, alike in suffering and in the presence of God" (Beasley-Murray 1987:212).

Jesus is under no delusion that hating yourself is easy. After saying what is necessary for his servants to follow him, he reveals the agony he himself is experiencing: *Now my heart is troubled, and what shall I say? "Father, save me from this hour"? No, it was for this very reason I came to this hour* (v. 27). In John's Gospel, there is a greater emphasis than in the Synoptics on Jesus' calmness and control as he faces various difficulties. This verse is John's allusion to the agony of Gethsemane, which shows us that John realizes Jesus' death did not cost him nothing. Indeed, the parallel between this verse and the scene in Gethsemane may be closer than the NIV suggests. The statement *Father, save me from this hour* could be taken as Jesus' actual prayer, rather than as a hypothetical prayer he is considering (cf. Carson 1991:440). In this case, Jesus actually prays to be saved from the hour and then immediately rejects this prayer, as he does in the Synoptics (Mk 14:36, toned down in Mt 26:39 par. Lk 22:42).

When Jesus says *my heart is troubled (hē psychē mou tetaraktai)* he is quoting from Psalm 6, in which David says, "My soul is in anguish" (Ps 6:3; cf. LXX: *hē psychē mou etarachthē sphodra*). But although David then prays for salvation (*sōson me,* Ps 6:4 and Jn 12:27), Jesus does not have that option if he is to fulfill the will of his Father. The majority of Old Testament references in John's account of the Passion, beginning here, are taken from psalms referring to a righteous sufferer.

This verse gives us a glimpse into the reality of the incarnation. John has revealed as clearly as anyone the fullness of Christ's deity, but he has also stated clearly that the Word became flesh (1:14). In becoming flesh, the Word did not empty himself of his divine attributes, as many have wrongly inferred from Philippians 2:7. But in Jesus' becoming fully man, his divine attributes worked within the confines of true humanity, somewhat like a Mozart symphony being played on a kazoo. Human nature in its true, unfallen state is capable of expressing much more of the divine nature than we could have dreamed based on our experience, which is limited to fallen, rebellious, spiritually dead human nature. (This is why, in passing, all attempts to do Christology "from below" are doomed to failure.) But true, sinless humanity is here seen to be tempted with rebellion against God and his will. We are back to the Garden, but this time the one who represents us chooses wisely.

In Jesus' struggle we see that temptation itself is not a sin. We also see the real agony involved in dying to self. But there is a great difference between what we face and what Jesus faced. The actual form this death to self takes for us is the exact opposite from what Jesus faced here. In our case, we must die to our false self, which is in rebellion against God. We must detach from "all the vain things that charm me most." Many of these may even be good in themselves, but they are idols we worship. They are attachments and addictions that give us pleasure; they are centered in self and disruptive of relationship with God and our fellow human beings. In Jesus' case, this dying to self is the reverse: he is living in union with God and must give that up to fulfill the role of Lamb of God, "who takes away the sin of the world" (1:29). He must die by taking upon himself our alienation and the effects of our rebellion. His agony is the agony of a death to self, and so it is like ours, but it is far more profound and painful. Yet it is precisely his union with God as the Son that enables him to go through with it, for in that union he shares in the divine love that leads inexorably to such a sacrifice.

As Son of God in union with the good and loving Father, Jesus responds, *Father, glorify your name!* (v. 28). The concept of the name is very important (see comment on 1:12; cf. Bietenhard 1967). The name is the person himself or herself as made accessible to others. It is the handle by which one is known. It represents the person and thus their character, their honor or dishonor. To glorify is to turn the spotlight on someone or something and to reveal that which is worthy of praise. In the cross the heart of God is revealed more clearly than anywhere else, and those who grasp what the cross reveals about God cannot help but be awestruck.

In verse 23 Jesus had said it was time for the Son of Man to be glorified, and now he calls upon the Father to glorify his own name. This connection is yet another indication that Jesus' closeness to the Father transcends the association of a mere human agent (see comment on 5:21). These two verses "are perhaps an indication of the equation of Jesus with the name of God" (Bietenhard 1967:272 n. 195; cf. 13:31-32).

Jesus' whole life has been about glorifying the Father's name, as the heavenly voice testifies: *I have glorified it, and will glorify it again* (v. 28). This confirms Jesus' past revelation of the Father and the revelation that is to come in the future. Throughout the story "the glory of the One and Only, who came from the Father, full of grace and truth," (1:14) has been revealed, and now the Father himself bears witness to this fact. The future glory includes the cross, the scandalous event that seems furthest from God's glory.

When the Father himself speaks from heaven within the crowd's hearing the people are divided over what has happened, with some saying it thundered and others saying an angel spoke with Jesus (v. 29). There is ambiguity to everything divine in this world, and this ambiguity tests hearts. The opponents have never heard God's voice (5:37), and now when God himself speaks it does them no good. The responses to this voice, therefore, are similar to the responses to Jesus' cryptic sayings. Some relate the voice to the divine realm and thus at least put it in the right perspective, even if they do not understand it. The others hear only noise. The voice testifies to the Father and the Son, but to no avail.

They have not understood this voice, but Jesus says this voice is for their benefit (v. 30). In saying this he is giving them the opportunity to realize they are missing something; perhaps they "might be led to inquire what the words meant" (Chrysostom *In John* 67.2). It is an invitation to become open and receptive to him. Jesus affirms that a message has been transmitted and

---

12:28 There was much teaching in Judaism about the heavenly voice, known as the *bat qôl* (cf. Betz 1974:288-90). In the second half of the first century there was a sudden change of opinion concerning the value and authority of the heavenly voice, perhaps due in part

that if they did not get it then something is wrong with their receivers. Indeed, he goes on to spell out that they are not missing just any message. He indicates that they are in the midst of the most significant events in human history: *Now is the time for judgment on this world; now the prince of this world will be driven out. But I, when I am lifted up from the earth, will draw all men to myself* (vv. 31-32). The cross will look like the defeat and the end of Jesus, but in fact it will be his glorification (v. 23), the defeat of the evil one and the drawing together of Jesus' community from among all humanity. The phrase *lifting up* echoes the description of the Suffering Servant in the fourth of the Servant Songs in Isaiah (Is 52:13—53:12; cf. Brown 1966:478). The description of the Servant being "raised and lifted up and highly exalted" is followed by a description of people being appalled at him because he was disfigured and marred (Is 52:13-14). This strange combination is seen in the lifting up of Jesus on the cross. The Servant is rejected and despised as he takes on the transgressions of the world (Is 53:3-12). This Servant Song will be directly quoted in John 12:38, but already its imagery is evident.

The *judgment* is a revelation of the true state of affairs and a division among humanity (cf. Jn 3:19-21; 5:22-30), a work that the Spirit will continue after the departure of Jesus (16:8-11). *World* here and in the rest of the Gospel refers to that which is in rebellion against God, especially in the religion of God's own people. There may be much talk of God and much activity for him that essentially is motivated by a love of self and has nothing to do with God. The cross exposed this terrifying reality and condemned it. The only true religion is complete submission to God, as we see in Jesus' submission to the Father. The cross exposes and condemns all that does not have the Father as its source.

The reference to *the prince of this world* being *driven out* (v. 31) probably does not refer to the devil's being cast out of heaven (Rev 12) or his being cast out from this world, since John is well aware that Satan's influence continues after the cross (1 Jn 5:19). Satan is not yet destroyed (cf. Rev 20), but clearly his power has been broken. It is now possible to live free from his control. Augustine writes,

---

to the claims of the Jewish mystics and the Christians. Rejection of claims based on the voice coincide with an increased emphasis on the Torah, as is reflected in John.

Where is he cast out from? From heaven and earth? From this created universe? No, he is cast out of the hearts of believers. Since the invader has been cast out, let the Redeemer dwell within, because the same one who created was also the one who redeemed. The devil now assaults from without but does not conquer the Redeemer who now has taken possession within the believer. The devil assaults from without by throwing various temptations into the believer, but the person to whom God speaks within, and who has the anointing of the Spirit, does not consent to these temptations. (Augustine *In First John* 4.1)

Thus, it is precisely the victory of the cross that enables the believer to hate *his life in this world* and *keep it for eternal life* (v. 25). Believers can claim the defeat of Satan at the cross, and they can effectually break his spell through union with Christ (which the Lord will speak of in coming chapters) and, by God's grace, through focusing attention on God and detaching attention from that which is not of God. As one is united to Christ one comes to share in his own life of sacrifice, which includes, as Paul says, the fact that "our old self was crucified with him so that the body of sin might be done away with, that we should no longer be slaves to sin" (Rom 6:6).

For Jesus' talk about *judgment on this world* and the driving out of *the prince of this world* (v. 31) is the language of warfare (cf. Heb 2:14-15). He has come into enemy-occupied territory, defeated the ruler who had usurped the region, revealed the true state of bondage that had existed under this false ruler and reclaimed it for its rightful ruler. As a returning king might set up his flag to rally his subjects to him after defeating the one who had taken over his realm, so Jesus speaks of a rallying point: *But I, when I am lifted up from the earth, will draw all men to myself* (v. 32). Here is the banner Isaiah spoke of when he wrote, "In that day the Root of Jesse will stand as a banner for the peoples; the nations will rally to him, and his place of rest will be glorious" (Is 11:10; cf. Is 11:11-12). Here is the fulfillment of the messianic prophecies that the tribes of the earth will gather on Mt. Zion to worship God (for example, Is 2:1-5; Mic 4:1-5; Zech 14:16-19). But the gathering place is not the temple, for Jesus has replaced the temple. The one sacrifice on the cross will fulfill the function of the sacrifices of the temple, and in Jesus' own person *(to myself)* is the presence of God, whom they went to the temple to worship. The new community is grounded in the work of the cross (cf. Pryor 1992:172).

The language used *(all men)* is very sweeping. It could refer to the nations, which fits with the coming of the Greeks in this context (cf. Chrysostom *In John* 67.3; Barrett 1978:427). B. F. Westcott, however, says the phrase "must not be limited in any way" (1908:2:129), for God's love for the whole world is revealed on the cross. Christ is "the atoning sacrifice for our sins, and not only for ours but also for the sins of the whole world" (1 Jn 2:2). Indeed, some manuscripts, versions and church fathers (most notably $\mathbf{p}^{66}$, followed by all Latin versions; cf. Irenaeus *Against Heresies* 4.2.7; Augustine *In John* 52.11) read not *all men (pantas)* but "all things" *(panta),* pointing to the cosmic implications of Christ's death (cf. Rom 8:19-22; Eph 1:10; Col 1:20). John does not suggest, however, that everyone will in fact be drawn to Jesus. The present text shows folk rejecting him or simply being confused, and the next section is a reflection on the mystery of unbelief (12:37-43). Satan, the jailer, has been mortally wounded, and Jesus, the liberator, is standing in the cell, but many prisoners prefer to remain in bondage!

This prediction of his death shows *the kind of death he was going to die* (v. 33). On one level this reveals Jesus' role as a prophet and how all is working out according to God's sovereign purposes. But more is involved, since in Judaism not knowing the day of one's death was considered part of the human condition (for example, *Mekilta* on Ex 16:32). Thus, John "is deliberately setting Jesus alongside God when he has Him know the manner of His own death" (Rengstorf 1971:265).

John writes next about the crowd's response to this teaching (v. 34). This is the last time the crowd speaks to Jesus in this Gospel. They were not able to understand the voice of the Father, and now we see they are not able to understand the Son either. They pick up on Jesus' reference to being lifted up and try to make sense of it by fitting it into their own framework derived from the law. This use of the law has been a stumbling block throughout this Gospel, so it is fitting to see one more example of it at the end of Jesus' public ministry.

They say, *We have heard from the Law that the Christ will remain forever, so how can you say, "The Son of Man must be lifted up"?* (v. 34). Some Jews expected a messiah who would reign for a limited time (2 Esdras 7:28-30; perhaps *2 Apocalypse of Baruch* 30:1), but others expected an eternal reign

(*Testament of Reuben* 6:12; *Sibylline Oracles* 3:48; *1 Enoch* 49:2; *Psalms of Solomon* 17:4; cf. Talbert 1992:187). There is, however, no text in the Old Testament that says *the Christ will remain forever.* Perhaps the allusion is to the eternal reign itself, which could be derived from some passages (Ps 72:17; 89:35-37; Is 9:7; Ezek 37:25). More likely the crowd is referring to a Targum, a rendition of an Old Testament text in the synagogue. Perhaps the best candidate is *Targum of Isaiah* 9:5: "The prophet saith to the house of David, A child has been born to us, a son has been given to us; and he has taken the law upon himself to keep it, and his name has been called from of old, Wonderful counselor, Mighty God, He who lives for ever, the Anointed one (or, Messiah), in whose days peace shall increase upon us" (cf. McNeil 1977: 23-24). Here the Messiah is explicitly called "He who lives for ever." Since the peaceful reign of the Messiah is also referred to here, perhaps this passage occurred to some of the people when they saw Jesus riding a donkey, which signaled peace rather than war (Jn 12:14-15). With this text in mind they are then confused by Jesus' statement that he, whom they are taking to be the Messiah, must be lifted up and (apparently) not live for ever.

John's editing of the material here is a bit awkward because he does not report that Jesus used the term *Son of Man* (v. 32), though the Johannine reader realizes Jesus had used this exact expression earlier (3:14). This awkwardness could be due to the way the sources have been edited (see, for example, Bultmann 1971:354) or simply due to the way John is telling the story—what B. F. Westcott refers to as "the compression of the narrative" (1908:2:130). Bringing in the *Son of Man* at this point juxtaposes the term *Christ* with the term *Son of Man.* In this way the messianic expectations of the crowds, as seen in the triumphal entry, are confounded by Jesus' more distinctive language for himself, which refers to the Messiah from heaven who brings God's life and judgment, especially through the cross (cf. comments on 3:13-14 and 5:27). Messiahship must be understood in terms of the cross, and this confuses the crowd.

They ask the right question—*Who is this "Son of Man"?*—for the key to all their questions is Jesus' identity. Jesus appears to avoid their question,

---

12:34 It could be the crowd thinks that "lifting up" refers to exaltation and their confusion is with Jesus' use of the term *Son of Man,* but it is more likely that "lifting up" means death (cf. Michaels 1989:228).

instead issuing an admonition for them to pay attention to what they have already seen and heard. But in fact he answers them in a profound way, for he implies that he is the light (v. 35). The fact that this light will be with them only a short time longer corresponds to his earlier reference to being lifted up. In calling upon them to *walk while you have the light* he is calling upon them to become his disciples and follow him (cf. v. 26). If they do not walk while they have the light then the darkness will overtake them. The image may be of sunset: if they do not keep moving with the sun they will end up in the darkness, and one *who walks in the dark does not know where he is going*. In other words, they will only become more confused if they do not put their faith in Jesus and become his disciples.

If they do put their trust in the light they themselves will become *sons of light* (v. 36). The expression "son of" is a Hebrew expression that points to an important characteristic of the one described. For example, Judas is called a "son of perdition" (17:12, RSV). The expression "sons of light" was used by the Qumran community of themselves (for example, *Rule of the Community* 1.9; *War Scroll* 1.1) and is found in Paul's writings (1 Thess 5:5; Eph 5:8). In the Christian context, however, especially in this passage in John, more is involved than just the description of a characteristic of the believer. The term *son* must be viewed in light of the teaching regarding the filial relationship with God that is offered in Jesus. For faith in Christ gives believers "the right to become children of God" (Jn 1:12). Jesus' followers share in his own life through their faith in him, and because Jesus himself is the light, they are *sons of light* as they share in his light. Just as believers need not fear death because they have life itself in their relation with the one who is himself resurrection and life (11:25-26), so also they need not fear the darkness because they have light through their relationship with him who is the light. "Those who believe in Jesus themselves take on the quality of light and so never walk in darkness" (Barrett 1978:429).

Jesus is inviting this crowd to become his disciples. This teaching is an example of the judgment of the world and the shining of the light because it contains both revelation and judgment. Jesus' very admonition and warning are also an invitation. He did not come to condemn but to save,

---

12:35 The translation *before* is unjustified and misses the fact that this is not a temporal clause but a negative purpose clause in the Greek *(hina mē skotia hymas katalabē)*.

so even his condemnations have the potential for leading to salvation. This is a consistent theme in Scripture—one must take advantage of the opportunity to repent because there will come a time when it will not be possible to do so.

When he had finished speaking, Jesus left and hid himself from them (v. 36). He had hidden himself before (8:59), signaling a departure from the temple. Now he departs from the people themselves. This is a further development of the theme of judgment, and it leads to John's own reflections on the rejection the Son of God encountered when he entered the world.

□ John Concludes the Revelation of Jesus' Ministry (12:37-50)

John brings his account of Jesus' public ministry to a close by showing how the unbelief Jesus has met is a fulfillment of Scripture (12:37-43). Then he adds a general appeal given by Jesus without indicating when or where it is spoken. It sums up many of the themes Jesus has taught throughout his ministry and provides an introduction to the section that follows: his private teaching to his disciples.

John Reflects on the Tragedy of Unbelief (12:37-43) John summarizes the unbelief of Jesus' fellow Jews in words that express how tragic and inexcusable is this rejection by "his own" (1:11): *Even after Jesus had done all these miraculous signs in their presence, they still would not believe in him* (v. 37). While this rejection was tragic and inexcusable, it was not completely surprising to those who understood the Scriptures. These opponents, who have taken such pride in Moses, have in fact repeated the pattern of those Israelites Moses condemned. "With your own eyes you saw those great trials, those miraculous signs and great wonders. But to this day the Lord has not given you a mind that understands or eyes that see or ears that hear" (Deut 29:3-4; cf. Brown 1966:485).

Furthermore, their rejection was actually a fulfillment of Isaiah: *This was to fulfill the word of Isaiah the prophet: "Lord, who has believed our message and to whom has the arm of the Lord been revealed?"* (v. 38). The text comes from the fourth of the Servant Songs of Isaiah, already alluded to in verse 32. The Servant Song begins by saying that the Servant will be lifted up and exalted but that many will be appalled at him because he is disfigured (Is

52:13-14). It is said "many nations and kings will shut their mouths because of him" because they were not prepared for what they saw (Is 52:15). It is at this point that Isaiah says, "Who has believed our message and to whom has the arm of the LORD been revealed?" (53:1). In other words, the prophet is saying the message he has been given is very difficult to believe. For "the arm of the Lord" is a metonymy for the strength of God, seen especially in great acts of deliverance such as the exodus (for example, Ex 6:6; 15:16; Deut 4:34; 5:15; cf. Schlier 1964). But now this strength has been revealed in one who is despised, stricken and crushed (Is 53:2-12). Finding God's strength in one who is crushed is such a reversal of normal thinking that those who hear it can only stand mute in disbelief. Thus, the same pattern is repeated in the ministry of Jesus. God's strength, his "arm," has been revealed in ways that defy normal religious sensibilities and has been met with shocked disbelief. The reference to the Servant Song prepares us for the intensification of this shock, which is to come as Jesus repeats the pattern of Isaiah 52:13—53:12 in detail in his Passion.

But for now, John's emphasis is on the unbelief of those who have witnessed the Lord's Servant. John further develops this explanation of unbelief by appealing to another passage in Isaiah: *For this reason they could not believe, because, as Isaiah says elsewhere: "He has blinded their eyes and deadened their hearts, so they can neither see with their eyes, nor understand with their hearts, nor turn—and I would heal them"* (Jn 12:39-40, quoting Is 6:10). John's quote does not follow exactly either the Hebrew or the Greek forms of this passage, and his changes help highlight the significance he sees in this text. First, in both the Hebrew and the Greek of Isaiah, people are affected in their hearts, ears and eyes, in that order. Thus, John leaves out the ears and reverses the order so the eyes are first. In this way he focuses on the signs of Jesus (cf. v. 37) and moves from the outer to the inner, as he has done before (see comment on 8:44). The interior disposition plays a major role, as verse 43 will emphasize. Second, along with this clarification on the human side he also clarifies the divine side. In the Hebrew, Isaiah is commanded to "make the heart of this people fat," and in the Greek it is put in the passive, "the heart of this people has been made thick" *(epachynthē)*. While the Isaiah passage refers to God's action, this passage in John shows more clearly God as the agent of the blinding and "hardening" *(epōrōsen;* cf. *pōros,* "stone" or "callus"). Similarly, at the end of the verse the Hebrew has a passive ("and be healed") whereas in John and the Septuagint a future active verb is used for God's action ("I would heal them"). Thus, God's activity is spoken of more directly in John's version of the text.

John says people were not able to believe because God had blinded their eyes and hardened their hearts, as revealed by Isaiah. How does God go about blinding and hardening? The clue is in the next verse: *Isaiah said this because he saw Jesus' glory and spoke about him* (v. 41). More literally, Isaiah said "these things," that is, both quotes from Isaiah are in view. "Isaiah could report on Christ's saying concerning the predestined unbelief of the Jews because he had in his vision [in Isaiah 6] seen the glory of the crucified Son of God" (Dahl 1976:108). Isaiah *spoke about him,* and thus the verbs that have God as their subject in Isaiah are taken here as referring to Jesus (cf. Carson 1991:450). This would be in keeping with John's earlier statement that no one has ever seen God (1:18), but we have beheld the glory of the only Son (1:14) so that those who have seen the Son have seen the Father (14:9). For the glory of God revealed in Jesus is the self-sacrificing love evident in the Suffering Servant. The scandal of the arm of the Lord revealed in the Suffering Servant corresponds to the scandal of the love of God revealed in Jesus. And as the revelation of the arm of the Lord produced mute disbelief in Isaiah 52:12—53:1, so the glory of the Lord revealed in Jesus has produced disbelief. God's revelation of his glory has caused the blindness and the hardness (cf. Jn 9:39-41). The same sun that melts wax, hardens clay (Origen *On First Principles* 3.1.11). The hardness of heart found in these opponents is that which rejects God's offer of mercy. Specifically, it is his offer of healing that they reject. This offer of healing, which has blinded and hardened, has come from God through Christ.

After making this blanket statement about unbelief John adds that *yet at the same time* [*homōs mentoi,* "yet nevertheless," a strong adversative] *many even among the leaders believed in him* (v. 42). Even among those least likely to be open to the revelation of this strange and disturbing grace of God, some did in fact believe (cf. 1:11-12). But they feared expulsion from the synagogue by the Pharisees and therefore *would not confess their faith*

12:41 The Targum of Isaiah 6 makes the connection between Isaiah's vision and glory. Instead of "I saw the Lord" (v. 1), the Targum has "I saw the Lord's glory." And instead of "my eyes have seen the King, the LORD Almighty" (v. 5), the Targum has "I have seen the

(v. 42). Consequently, they provide yet another example of false profession of faith that has been described from the outset (2:23-25). As Chrysostom remarks, such fear means that "they were not rulers, but slaves in the utmost slavery" (*In John* 69.1). "Such ineffective intellectual faith (so to speak) is really the climax of unbelief" (Westcott 1908:2:136).

As with other forms of false faith (cf. 2:25), the problem goes back to the condition of their hearts, *for they loved praise from men more than praise from God* (v. 43). The word translated *praise* is the same word translated *glory* in verse 41. Isaiah saw God's glory and proclaimed it despite its scandalous nature, but these would-be believers prefer human glory for God's glory. The issue is a matter of the heart, for the problem is in their love. They have received the revelation of the Son but are not willing to live in the light of the truth they have seen (cf. 12:47).

Thus, once again both the divine and the human sides of the drama of salvation are addressed (cf. Westcott 1908:2:134-38; Carson 1981; 1991:448-50; Talbert 1992:181). From the outset of the Gospel, John has spoken clearly of both divine sovereignty and human responsibility (1:12-13) without trying to explain rationally how both are true. It is one of the antinomies of this Gospel, which are inevitable in dealing with a revelation of reality that goes beyond our common, limited, four-dimensional perceptions. But these two aspects of reality are not opposed to one another; God's sovereign action is never a violation of our moral responsibility, for such determinism would turn us into robots and preclude love and relationship. "The divine predestination works through human moral choices, for which men are morally responsible" (Barrett 1978:431), as is made clear in the next section (12:47-48). But the human responsibility never violates the necessity of divine grace. "Let no one dare to defend the freedom of the will in any such way as to attempt depriving us of the prayer that says, 'Lead us not into temptation'; and, on the other hand, let no one deny the freedom of the will, and so venture to find an excuse for sin. But let us give heed to the Lord, both in commanding and in offering His aid; in both telling us our duty, and assisting us to discharge it" (Augustine *In John* 53.8).

Salvation is by grace from first to last. To use Pauline terms, we are saved

---

radiance of the glory *ĭšᵉkĭnaṯ* of the King of the ages." This reference to glory may also allude to the Jewish mystics' views (Kanagaraj 1998:224-26).

by grace and not works. But we are not saved without works because salvation is a matter of life and relationship, which means it is more than an intellectual assent or an emotional experience. These would-be believers are a prime example of the fact that faith without works is dead, for such faith is only a thought or an emotion and not a relationship of love in a true sense on the level of the heart. At the end of the day what matters is where our love is placed, for where our treasure is, there will our heart be also. And the love of our heart is evident not just from our thoughts and emotions, though these are involved, but from the commitments of our lives.

John's reflection at the end of the first half of his Gospel presents Isaiah's seeing the glory of the rejected graciousness of God offered to Israel by the Son of God. Understood in this way, it is clear how this vision of Isaiah draws together some of the major themes in the first twelve chapters of this Gospel. By focusing on the tragedy of the would-be disciples John also offers a challenge to all who claim to be disciples of Jesus.

Jesus Gives a Final Summarizing Pronouncement (12:44-50) Now that the public ministry is complete and John has reflected on the rejection Jesus has met, a final statement from Jesus is given. It is not located either in place or time (the NIV's *then,* v. 44, is misleading; the conjunction *de* is much weaker here). The statement weaves together many major motifs from the first twelve chapters, the main theme being the salvation and judgment that have come through Jesus and that are all grounded in the Father.

Jesus begins by emphasizing his oneness with the Father. Faith is not just in him but in the one who sent him (v. 44). Putting it this way places the emphasis on the Father in such a way as to include the Son, since the Father is described as *the one who sent me* (cf. Westcott 1908:2:138). Likewise, to see him is to see the one who sent him (v. 45). Here again is the language of agency, drawing on the Jewish notion that an agent is to act in accordance with the intentions of the one who has sent the agent, though Jesus far transcends the category of agent (see note on 5:21). Isaiah was privileged to have seen the Lord in his glory (v. 41), and now it is said

---

12:44 Major motifs from earlier in the Gospel that are gathered in these verses include faith (vv. 44, 46), Jesus and the one who sent him (vv. 44-45, 49), light versus darkness (v. 46), judging (vv. 47-48), saving the world (v. 47), Jesus' not speaking on his own accord (v. 49) and eternal life (v. 50). Some of the vocabulary in these verses is found only here in

that all who have seen Jesus have also seen this glory. Because faith in Jesus is faith in God the cowardice of the would-be believers in the previous section (vv. 42-43) is heinous. This unity between Jesus and the one who sent him grounds this section, as it has the whole Gospel.

Jesus next speaks of the salvation he has brought, using the image of light (v. 46; cf. 1:4-5, 9; 3:19-21; 8:12). He has come into the world as the light. The world is dark precisely because it is alienated from God, who is light. Because Jesus has brought the light of God everyone who believes in him no longer remains in the darkness.

After speaking of the believer Jesus describes two forms of unbelief (Westcott 1908:2:140), described as two responses to his teaching (vv. 47-48). First, there are those who hear his words but do not *keep them* (v. 47). Such people will listen, but they will not take the teaching into their life and live according to it. The would-be believers in verses 42-43 are one example of such folk. Jesus says he will not judge such a person since he came to save the world, not condemn it (cf. 3:17; 8:15). However, his very presence as the light (v. 46), revealing God, is an exposure and thus condemnation of the darkness. So in fact judgment does take place through him (cf. 5:22, 27; 8:16, 26). "Justification and condemnation are opposite sides of the same process; to refuse the justifying love of God in Christ is to incur judgment" (Barrett 1978:434). Although judgment takes place it is still of the utmost importance to understand that God's intent is salvific. Without this fundamental truth our view of God will go rotten quite quickly.

The second sort of unbeliever is one who out-and-out rejects Jesus by not receiving his teachings (v. 48). To refuse to receive Jesus' word is to reject Jesus himself, just as to refuse to receive the Father's Word, Jesus, is to reject the Father himself. Jesus says, *that very word which I spoke will condemn him at the last day.* In other words, the judgment will be on the basis of that which had been made available to the person. "The same word which was to save him judges him" (Schnackenburg 1980b:423). The condemnation begins with the rejection (cf. 3:18) and, if one persists in rejecting him, it will lead to condemnation *at the last day.*

John (for example, *phylassō* instead of *tēreō* for *keep*, v. 47; *atheteō* for "reject," v. 48; and *ex emautou* instead of *ap' emautou* for "from myself," v. 49). John is not gathering bits from his earlier chapters, but he probably is using additional material that has addressed these same themes (cf. Michaels 1989:235).

The condemnation works out in this way "because" *(hoti),* says Jesus, *I did not speak of my own accord, but the Father who sent me commanded me what to say and how to say it. I know that his command leads to eternal life. So whatever I say is just what the Father has told me to say* (vv. 49-50). In other words, the teaching that these unbelievers reject comes from the Father and offers eternal life. Indeed, the text is even more graphic than the NIV suggests, for it says "his command is eternal life" *(hē entolē autou zōē aiōnios estin,* v. 50). The command has to do with a relationship with God himself and a sharing in his life. It is not just a description of a pattern of life and a demand to conform to it. It is a life that expresses the pattern of God's own character. Since Jesus' teachings come from God and offer eternal life, a rejection of these teachings is itself condemnation, for it is a rejection of God and his offer of life.

This final section has emphasized the words of Jesus, just as the previous section had emphasized his deeds (vv. 37-41). What is said about Jesus and his teachings in this final section echoes sections of Deuteronomy regarding the prophet like Moses who was to come (Deut 18:18-19) and the conclusion of Moses' own ministry (cf. Brown 1966:491-93). "When Moses finished reciting all these words to all Israel, he said to them, 'Take to heart all the words I have solemnly declared to you this day, so that you may command your children to obey carefully all the words of this law. They are not just idle words for you—they are your life' " (Deut 32:45-47). The theme of Jesus' superiority to Moses thus returns here at the end of the public ministry (cf. 5:46).

The final words of the public ministry emphasize that the foundation for Jesus' statements, and for his whole ministry, is his oneness with the Father. He has not spoken on his own accord, or, more literally, "from myself" *(ex emautou,* v. 49). Here is the divine humility of the Son (cf. Chrysostom *In John* 69.2). "In the first part of the gospel, which here closes, Jesus lives in complete obedience to the Father; in the second part he will die in the same obedience" (Barrett 1978:435).

□ Jesus Meets Privately with His Disciples Prior to His Crucifixion (13:1—17:26)

13:1 This reference, *It was just before the Passover Feast,* is vague. It could mean that this meal took place before Passover and thus was not the Passover meal, although the

The third section of John's Gospel, which follows the prologue (1:1-18) and the account of Jesus' public ministry (1:19—12:50), is characterized by Jesus' being alone with his disciples before his betrayal and arrest. While there may have been others present, such as those who were serving the meal, the focus is on the Twelve (so also Mt 26:20 par. Mk 14:17 par. Lk 22:14). The section begins with an account of Jesus washing the disciples' feet and the prediction of Judas' betrayal (13:1-30). Then there is a lengthy section known as the farewell discourse, which consists of teachings (13:31—16:33) and a concluding prayer by Jesus (17:1-26).

Jesus Washes His Disciples' Feet (13:1-20) The opening verse of chapter 13 sets the scene for the whole of chapters 13—17. *Love* is one of the key terms in chapters 13—17, occurring thirty-one times in these five chapters as compared to only six times in chapters 1—12. Jesus now shows his disciples *the full extent [eis telos] of his love. Full extent* could also be translated *to the last* (cf. NIV note). The ambiguity is probably intentional, for the two meanings are related. Love is the laying down of one's life, and therefore to love completely means to love to the end of one's life (cf. 1 Jn 3:16). The love that has been evident throughout continues right up to the end. At the end, in the crucifixion, we will see the ultimate revelation of that love, that is, its *full extent.*

This is now the third or fourth Passover mentioned (2:13; 6:4; perhaps 5:1). The shadow of the cross has been evident from the very outset through the references to Jesus' hour *(hōra).* Jesus now knows that his hour has arrived (translated *time* in the NIV). John emphasizes the context of the Passover, for the lamb is about to be sacrificed for the sins of the world (1:29). That is part of the story, but it is also the occasion for Jesus to pass over *(metabē;* NIV, *leave)* from this world to the Father. This theme of departure and return to the Father will be developed at length in the teachings that follow.

While this first verse introduces the whole section through chapter 17, it also introduces the account of the footwashing in particular. For the love that is evident in the laying down of life at the crucifixion is also

Synoptics speak of the final meal as a Passover meal (Mk 14:12; Lk 22:15). See coment on 18:28.

demonstrated in the laying down of life in humble service in the footwashing. In the footwashing we have "an acted parable of the Lord's humiliation unto death" (Beasley-Murray 1975:154; cf. D. Wenham 1995:15).

The next three verses (13:2-4) introduce the footwashing itself. Jesus *got up from the meal, took off his outer clothing, and wrapped a towel around his waist* (v. 4). The verb used for *took off (tithēmi)* is not the usual word for this idea *(apotithēmi)*. Perhaps John intends an allusion to Jesus' imminent laying down of life, since this verb is used for that idea elsewhere (10:11, 15, 17-18; 13:37-38). Similarly, the word used for taking up his garments *(lambanō,* v. 12) was used to describe his taking up his life again (10:17-18, cf. Brown 1970: 551). So perhaps through the language he uses, John is connecting these two events of great humility.

John notes that *the devil had already prompted Judas Iscariot, son of Simon, to betray Jesus* (v. 2). This is the first of several references in this section to the betrayal (vv. 11, 18-20), which will be the focus of the next section (vv. 21-30). It is extremely important to realize that Jesus is going to wash the feet of one who is considering betraying him. Judas has not yet given in to the temptation (cf. v. 27), but the devil has *prompted* him, or more literally, "put it into his heart." This is the first step in a sequence that temptation follows, according to the teachers of the ancient church (Nikodimos and Makarios 1979:364-66). This is known as "provocation," the initial idea. It is wise to reject the thought at this point because the temptation is at its weakest and one is not yet guilty of sin. If this salesman is at the door, it is best to ignore the knocking.

Jesus' own awareness is also an important part of the context of the footwashing. He *knew that the Father had put all things under his power* (literally, "into his hands") *and that he had come from God and was returning to God* (v. 3). Here in Johannine language is the description of Jesus' identity in his relation to the Father. This knowledge does not simply give Jesus the security to wash the disciples feet—his sharing in the divine essence is what leads him to wash their feet. Jesus said that he only does what he sees the Father doing (5:19), and this footwashing is not said to be an exception to that rule. John's introduction to the event ensures that we understand God's glory is revealed in Jesus in this sign. This is what God himself is like—he washes feet, even the feet of the one who will betray him! Thus, the footwashing is a true sign in the Johannine sense, for it is a revelation of God.

Having taken off his outer garment *(himation),* Jesus was left with his tunic *(chitōn),* a shorter garment like a long undershirt. Slaves would be so dressed to serve a meal (cf. Lk 12:37; 17:8). Jesus tied a linen cloth around his waist with which to dry their feet, obviously not what one would expect a master to do. A Jewish text says this is something a Gentile slave could be required to do, but not a Jewish slave *(Mekilta* on Ex 21:2, citing Lev 25:39, 46). On the other hand, footwashing is something wives did for their husbands, children for their parents, and disciples for their teachers *(b. Berakot* 7b; cf. Barrett 1978:440). A level of intimacy is involved in these cases, unlike when Gentile slaves would do the washing. In Jesus' case, there is an obvious reversal of roles with his disciples. The one into whose hands the Father had given all (13:3) now takes his disciples' feet into his hands to wash them (cf. Augustine *In John* 55.6).

Slaves were looked down upon in the ancient world (cf. Rengstorf 1964b), and Peter cannot stand the thought of his teacher doing the work of a slave (13:6). It would have been appropriate for one of the disciples to have washed Jesus' feet, but the reverse is intolerable. In the Greek both pronouns, *you* and *my,* are emphatic. This response expresses Peter's love (cf. Chrysostom *In John* 70.2), but his is a defective love. It lacks humility, which is one of the essential attributes of discipleship according to this Gospel. Indeed, humility is the very thing illustrated in Jesus' present action. In Peter's response we see the pride and self-will that is at the heart of all sin and that is the very thing for which the cross will atone and bring healing. Peter is working from a worldly point of view, and not for the first time (cf. Mt 16:22 par. Mk 8:32).

Jesus realizes this act is scandalous and mystifying, given their current ignorance: *You do not realize now what I am doing, but later* (literally, "after these things") *you will understand* (v. 7). On one level, Jesus' act is an example of humility, and they are expected to grasp this point (vv. 12-20). But as with most of what Jesus has said and done, they will fully understand this event only after the cross and resurrection and the coming of the Spirit, who will lead them into all truth (cf. 2:22; 12:16; 13:19, 29; 16:4, 13, 25).

In response to Peter's rejection (v. 8) Jesus says cryptically, *Unless I wash you, you have no part with me* (v. 8). The word for *part (meros)* can be used of one's share in an inheritance (cf. Lk 15:12), though other words are more commonly used for this idea *(meris, klēros* and *klēronomia)*. If Peter is to have a share with Jesus in his community and the eternal life that comes through faith in him, then he must be washed by Jesus. Since this is Peter's greatest desire he responds, *Then, Lord, . . . not just my feet but my hands and my head as well!* Again we see his love, but again there is still a strong element of self. He is not simply receiving with humility what the Lord is saying and doing. Peter at this point is an example of religious enthusiasm that is really a manifestation of the unregenerate self rather than of genuine discipleship. He has not discovered the depths of his own brokenness and selfishness and thus does not have a solid foundation in reality to build on. His denial of Jesus, soon to be predicted by Jesus (vv. 31-38), will tear down his pride and clear the way for the genuine humility that is necessary for any real spiritual life (see comments on 21:15-19).

So Jesus must further correct Peter and thereby give more insight into his scandalous act: *A person who has had a bath needs only to wash his feet; his whole body is clean. And you are clean, though not every one of you* (v. 10). People would bathe before going to a special meal, but their feet would get dirty on the way since they wore sandals. Here, as in verse 8, Jesus is addressing Peter as an individual, but by implication he is also addressing each of the disciples. Jesus must wash him, or else he is not clean and has no share with him. What does this washing refer to? Some think it is a reference to his death, which will make possible a sharing in eternal life with Christ. The footwashing would then be a symbol of the cross (cf. Brown 1970:566). Others think that the bathing (v. 10) is the cleansing from sin on the cross and that the footwashing would refer to the forgiveness of one's daily sins (Carson 1991:465; Talbert 1992:192). Many, both in the ancient church (cf. Brown 1970:566-67) and today (for example, Oepke 1967a:305-6), note that the word *wash (louō)* is from a word family commonly associated with baptism (Acts 22:16; 1 Cor 6:11; Eph 5:26; Tit 3:5; Heb 10:22) and thus take this washing as baptism.

But how can these disciples be said to be clean when the sacrifice for sin has not yet been offered and the Spirit has not yet been given (Chrysostom *In John* 70.2)? Perhaps Jesus is speaking as if the crucifixion and resurrection have already been accomplished (see comment on v. 31). Or perhaps Jesus is referring to being made clean by his word (cf. 15:3).

Such cleansing would refer to their receiving the light of revelation that Jesus has offered, accepting him and his teaching as having come from God (cf. 17:6-8) and thereby becoming one with him to the extent that this is possible before the cross, resurrection, ascension and coming of the Spirit. They are "with him" (cf. v. 8) as members of his community, though Peter's attitude in this very passage shows they are not yet fully of Jesus' spirit. The footwashing would then symbolize further teaching. Indeed, the footwashing would itself convey something of the further teaching of which it was the symbol: they have received him as the one come from God, and now he reveals more clearly the love that characterizes the Father.

Although Jesus is speaking to Peter he is also speaking to the disciples as a group. They have formed a community with him as their head. It is as if, as Paul spells out, they are his body and his own body needs to have its feet washed. He has cleansed his body of disciples through his teaching and deeds that have attracted some and scandalized others (cf. Michaels 1989:239). But his body is not yet entirely clean (v. 10): *For he knew who was going to betray him, and that was why he said not every one was clean* (or "not all are clean"; v. 11). Judas was unclean himself in the sense that he has not received Jesus with true faith, and he is himself an unclean presence among the body of believers that has yet to be cleansed. Judas's cleansing from the body of believers is about to take place.

Jesus' reference to his betrayal is an act of judgment toward Judas, who must know he is the one referred to since the thoughts are already in his mind (v. 2). As such it is also an act of grace. It reveals clearly the nature of the deed he is contemplating, thereby perhaps giving him a chance to think again.

After Jesus finishes washing their feet, he puts his outer garment back on and returns to his place, asking, *Do you understand what I have done for you?* (v. 12). They will not completely understand until they have seen the cross (v. 7), but they can at least grasp his act as an example of humility. The cleansing word that they have received includes the recognition of Jesus as *Teacher* and *Lord* (v. 13). Jesus affirms that this is indeed his identity. The humility he is exemplifying is not a false humility. True humility is always grounded in the truth. But although they have grasped something of Jesus' identity, they now need the further cleansing that comes through a revelation of the nature of Jesus, whose authority they recognize. Jesus' understanding of the characteristics of a teacher and a lord (or the Lord) are quite different from those of the disciples and their culture.

While they are reeling from this embarrassing event, Jesus spells out the implications for their own lives of what he has done: *Now that I, your Lord and Teacher, have washed your feet, you also should wash one another's feet. I have set you an example that you should do as I have done for you* (vv. 14-15). What does Jesus have in mind? Some have established a footwashing ceremony, either as a separate service or as part of the Maundy Thursday service. Jesus, however, does not say to do "what" he did but "as" he did. The cleansing and the further footwashing are symbolic of the revelation that Jesus gave of the Father, and thus the disciples are called upon to embody this same revelation. The disciples are to pass on the same teaching that he, their teacher and Lord, has done by conveying as he has, both in word and deed, the selfless love of God (cf. Barrett 1978:443; Michaels 1989:241-42). The community Jesus has brought into being is to manifest the love of God that he has revealed through serving one another with no vestige of pride or position. There will be recognized positions of leadership within the new community, but the exercize of leadership is to follow this model of servanthood.

If Jesus takes the role of *servant* (*doulos,* better translated "slave"), then the slave of such a master should expect to do the same (v. 16). Jesus adds *nor is a messenger greater than the one who sent him,* bringing in the theme of mission (cf. Michaels 1989:243-44). Jesus is the one sent by the Father, and the disciples will be sent by Jesus. Jesus has been submissive to the Father, and the disciples are to be under the authority of Jesus. The pattern of life exemplified in the footwashing is true blessedness, contrary to what the world, which is centered in pride and selfishness, thinks. Accordingly, he says, *Now that you know these things, you will be blessed if you do them* (v. 17). The Gospel is a life to be lived and not just an ideal to be contemplated.

Jesus then makes another allusion to his betrayer: *I am not referring to all of you; I know those I have chosen* (v. 18). Some think Jesus is referring to the election to eternal life (Calvin 1959:61-62), but he is referring to his

---

13:13 The titles *"Teacher" and "Lord"* could simply be ways of referring to Jesus as rabbi.

historical choice of the Twelve (cf. Barrett 1978:444). John shows us that the betrayal need not raise doubts about Jesus' identity for he knows the character of each one. The betrayal is not going to catch him by surprise. Indeed, it has been spoken of in Scripture: *But this is to fulfill the scripture: "He who shares my bread has lifted up his heel against me"* (v. 18, quoting Ps 41:9). As with most fulfillment texts, this is not an explicit prophecy that has now been fulfilled; rather we have a pattern from the Old Testament now repeated. The figure of David as the sufferer in Psalm 41 is seen as a pattern, or type, of Jesus (cf. Carson 1991:470). The psalm describes betrayal by a close friend. Lifting up the foot to expose the sole is an especially offensive gesture even today in the Middle East. Not only does the betrayal by Judas not cast doubts on Jesus' identity, it actually affirms that he is a fulfillment of the Davidic type.

The betrayal itself does not begin until verse 27, so the psalm is given by Jesus as a prophecy (v. 19). Jesus' foreknowledge of the event is emphasized (cf. 14:28, 31) and is even evidence of his divinity, that he is the I AM (*egō eimi; I am He*, v. 19). The common Old Testament idea that God and his true prophets are known by their ability to foretell events (for example, Is 48:5) is seen to be true of Jesus. He continues to give the word that cleanses his disciples by revealing himself to be the revealer of God. Thus the betrayal story itself bears witness to Jesus in three ways, namely, through his preternatural knowledge of his disciples, through the witness of Scripture and through his own prediction.

After his use of the divine name in reference to himself, his return to the theme of mission is striking: *I tell you the truth, whoever accepts anyone I send accepts me; and whoever accepts me accepts the one who sent me* (v. 20). To accept the messenger is to accept the sender, following the principle that "a man's agent is like to himself" (*m. Berakot* 5:5; see note on 5:21). Jesus gives his own mission and that of his followers "an absolute theological significance; in both the world is confronted by God himself" (Barrett 1978:445). Seen in the context of the footwashing, this statement of the dignity of the Christian witnesses is not an expression of power and authority in any worldly sense. The one who represents Christ by bearing

---

But "it is unthinkable that a Christian author writing at the end of the first century should mean no more than this" (Barrett 1978:443).

the same self-sacrificing love of God will meet with the same response Jesus met (cf. 15:18—16:4) but will also be the agent of the same eternal life that comes through knowledge of the Father in the Son by the Spirit. Each disciple should walk through his or her day with a consciousness of being on such a mission, which is only made possible through the closest intimacy with Jesus (15:1-17).

In the story of the footwashing, then, we have the most profound revelation of the heart of God apart from the crucifixion itself. We also learn more of the relation between Jesus and his disciples, the relation of the disciples with one another in humble service and the mission of the disciples to the world. These themes are similar to those of the Eucharist developed earlier (see comments on 6:52-59). The community that Jesus has been forming here takes more definite shape, revealing more clearly "the law of its being" (Bultmann 1971:479), which is humble, self-sacrificing love.

Jesus Predicts His Betrayal (13:21-30) The betrayal is all the more horrendous coming after the footwashing in which the depth of Jesus' divine love is revealed. Once again we see Jesus deeply agitated as he bears witness: *I tell you the truth, one of you is going to betray me* (v. 21). He has been agitated with anger at death (11:33) and in anguish over his own coming death, which will mean separation from his Father for the first time (12:27). In both cases love causes the disturbance—the love for his friends at Lazarus's tomb and the love for his Father. Here also his anguish is caused by great love—the love he has for his disciples, including his betrayer. In his anguish we see revealed the effects of our sin on the heart of God, from the first rebellion in the Garden right up to the most recent sin you and I have committed today. All sin is a rejection of God's great love.

The disciples *stared at one another, at a loss to know which of them he meant* (v. 22). They did not all swing around and look at Judas. They could not imagine who would do such a thing. Indeed, according to other accounts each of them asked, "Is it I, Lord?" (RSV, Mt 26:22 par. Mk 14:19). We are all quite capable of the worst sin. If we think otherwise, we are deluded and have no real idea how much we owe to the grace of God.

13:23 The fact that they were reclining suggests this was the Passover meal. Reclining was not the normal way to eat a meal, though it was used for special meals. However, it was required at Passover as a symbol of freedom (Jeremias 1966a:48-49).

With such a statement hanging in the air, everyone wondering to whom he could be referring, we can imagine Peter bursting to ask Jesus. But he has just been rebuked at the footwashing so instead of speaking up he motions (literally, "nods," *neuei*) to *one of them, the disciple whom Jesus loved* (vv. 23-24; cf. Chrysostom *In John* 72.1). This person is said to be *reclining next to* Jesus (v. 23; more literally, "on/at his breast/bosom," *en tō kolpō*). Three couches or mats are arranged in a U shape around a table. The men are reclining on their left arms with their right hands free to get at the food. Most likely there are three at the head couch and five at each of the side couches. Jesus is at the center of the head couch, the place of honor. The second most honorable position is to the back of the place of honor, that is, to Jesus' left when looking from behind them. The third place of honor is in front of Jesus, that is, to his right (*t. Berakot* 5:5). The one to whom Peter nods is in this third place of honor, for he leans back against Jesus to ask him, *Lord, who is it?* (v. 25). Since Peter is able to catch his eye, presumably Peter is along the couch on the right at some distance. Since the ranking alternated from left to right, Peter's place would have been in the second half of the disciples, perhaps even at the very end. This reconstruction is somewhat uncertain, however, not least because of the unconventional views Jesus had about rank (cf. Mt 20:26 par. Mk 10:43 par. Lk 22:26; Mt 23:11; Mk 9:35; Lk 9:48), exemplified par excellence in the present story of the footwashing.

Jesus says, *It is the one to whom I will give this piece of bread when I have dipped it in the dish* (v. 26). Since Jesus is able to give the bread to his betrayer it is likely that Judas was in the second place of honor. This would also fit with the custom of the host's giving food in this way to one he wishes to honor (Westcott 1908:2:156; Brown 1970:578; Talbert 1992:195-96). In the face of such honor and intimacy we see the heinousness of Judas' deed (cf. Ps 55:12-14). Jesus is pouring out his love and grace upon Judas. He is trying to win Judas over, but to no avail (Chrysostom *In John* 72.2). Early in the Gospel Jesus healed one who turned around and betrayed him, a Judas figure (5:1-16). That healing was the climax of a series of revelations of the divine grace, which then triggered the conflict. The conflict itself is now coming to its climax, and we are seeing brighter and brighter

---

13:26 The word translated *bread* is *psō mion,* a diminutive of *psō mos,* which means a "fragment," "bit" or "morsel." This could refer to the dipping of the bitter herbs in *ḥaroset* sauce during the Passover feast (cf. Barrett 1978:447).

revelations of the divine grace, first in the footwashing and now in Jesus' treatment of his betrayer. All of this is leading up to the grand climax of glory in the cross.

Presumably, this exchange is spoken quietly (Beasley-Murray 1987:238). Peter is too far away to hear what was said, so only this disciple to Jesus' right knows the identity of the betrayer. This is the first we hear of the Beloved Disciple in this Gospel. He is referred to several times in the coming account of the Passion and the postresurrection appearances of Jesus (19:26-27, 35; 20:2-10; 21:7, 20-23; probably 18:15-16), and it is his testimony that is represented in this Gospel (21:24). In the present story we see him as Jesus' confidant, one who is said to be *en tō kolpō* to Jesus, the very description of Jesus' own relation to the Father—"at the Father's side" (1:18)—suggesting "the Disciple is as intimate with Jesus as Jesus is with the Father" (Brown 1970:577). This intimacy is borne out in the special knowledge this disciple has. "As Jesus' most intimate disciple and eye-witness he is allowed to know by whom Jesus will be betrayed (13:13-21) and to understand the meaning of the empty tomb (20:2-10). He witnesses Jesus' suffering and death and because he saw blood and water coming out of Jesus' side he is able to state beyond doubt that Jesus died a real death" (de Jonge 1979:104). His insight regarding Jesus' death and resurrection means, in Johannine language, that he understands Jesus' glorification through which the Father is revealed. He also has insight concerning the betrayer, which is to say, Jesus' enemies. Thus, his special knowledge enables him to present both the positive and the negative sides of the case: he can both testify to the truth and identify the error. In this way he shares in the Holy Spirit's functions of bearing witness to Jesus and judging the world (14:16, 26; 15:26; 16:7-11). In writing this Gospel this disciple is himself the prime example of the Spirit's leading into all truth, teaching all things and bringing to remembrance what Jesus said.

The very anonymity of the Beloved Disciple may be a reflection of his humility, though we should not assume that John is carefully calculating to produce such effects. If he is calling himself the Beloved Disciple perhaps it is because he *is* the beloved disciple, the one whose heart, whose inward

_____

13:29 If this were a meal earlier in the week, as many assume, there would seem to be no

disposition, is particularly open and sensitive to Jesus. John presents himself in a way that actually has certain similarities to his Master because he *is* humble. John has no false humility; he exalts in what he has heard, seen and touched, and he knows his place of authority. But in his humility he keeps pointing to Jesus in the same way Jesus keeps pointing to the Father.

When Judas receives the bread he seals his fate: *As soon as Judas took the bread, Satan entered into him* (v. 27). Earlier Satan had put the idea of betraying Jesus into Judas' heart and mind (13:2). Indeed, the Synoptics tell us that Judas had already gone to the chief priests to plan the betrayal (Mt 26:14-16 par. Mk 14:10-11 par. Lk 22:3-6). But now we have the point of decision. Just as faith is a progressive sequence, so acceptance of the devil's will also follows a sequence (cf. Nikodimos and Makarios 1979:364-66). "His acceptance of the morsel without changing his wicked plan to betray Jesus means that he has chosen for Satan rather than for Jesus" (Brown 1970:578). Satan has found in Judas a willing agent (cf. 8:44), who serves as a counterexample to Jesus, the willing agent of his Father.

The contest now begins in earnest. There is no doubt as to the outcome, for Satan and his agent are under Jesus' command: *What you are about to do, do quickly* (v. 27). Jesus is not commanding Judas to sin but rather commanding him to get on with what he is going to do, one way or the other. "No man in all history was more truly 'put on the spot' than Judas in that moment" (Beasley-Murray 1987:238). It is very ironic that this gesture of friendship—the sharing of bread—is the point of decision to betray, an irony matched only by the use of a kiss to accomplish the betrayal itself (not mentioned by John; cf. Mt 26:49 par. Mk 14:45 par. Lk 22:47-48).

The disciples could not imagine which of them would betray Jesus (v. 22), and they are ignorant of why Jesus is telling Judas to act quickly. *No one* (v. 28), not even the Beloved Disciple, knew the betrayal was upon them even then. It is one thing to know who is going to betray Jesus; it is another to know how and when it will take place. They figured Jesus must be *telling him to buy what was needed for the Feast, or to give something to the poor* (v. 29). There is debate over whether they are eating the Passover meal or not (see comment on 18:28). If they are eating the Passover meal,

---

need for haste to purchase something for the feast. Thus, this detail may point to the meal they are eating as the Passover (Jeremias 1966a:53).

the feast referred to would be the Feast of Unleavened Bread, which began that night and lasted for seven days. While purchases on the evening of Passover were not impossible, they would not be possible for the next two days of the high feast and the sabbath, which, some of the disciples thought, explained the urgency (Jeremias 1966a:53; cf. Carson 1991:475). The setting of Passover might also give rise to the disciples' other explanation that Jesus has sent Judas to give alms, since this was a custom on the eve of Passover (Jeremias 1966a:54). If Jesus is not referring to the Feast of Unleavened Bread, then he is referring to the Passover itself, which means the meal they are now sharing occurs just before Passover.

Again we see that the disciples have no special suspicion of Judas. Indeed, they think he is being sent forth on an errand for Jesus and his band. That is, they think Judas is acting as a servant, as Jesus has just modeled. There is great irony in their thinking that he has gone on an errand of service or piety (cf. Michaels 1989:252). He is indeed going to buy what is needed for the feast—the Lamb of God who will take away the sin of the world. Instead of giving to the poor he is selling the archetypal Poor Man, though in doing so he provides eternal wealth to the poor, all of us made beggars by sin.

At the beginning of the footwashing John notes that the hour for which we have been waiting since the beginning of the Gospel has now arrived (13:1). At the end of this section we reach another benchmark: now comes the night (v. 30) in which people do not know where they are going (12:35-36). It is time for the ultimate contest between light and darkness.

Jesus Introduces Major Themes of His Farewell Discourse (13:31-35)
Jesus now begins what is commonly called his "farewell discourse" (13:31—17:26). This section follows a literary form common in the ancient world, not least within Judaism (Brown 1970:598; Talbert 1992:200). There are numerous examples of a great man or woman giving a final speech to those who are close to him or her: for example, Jacob (Gen 47:29—49:33), Moses (Deut; Josephus *Antiquities of the Jews* 4.309-26), Joshua (Josh 23—24), Samuel (1 Sam 12), David (1 Chron 28—29), Tobit (Tobit 14:3-11), Noah

13:31 There has been much speculation regarding the composition of the farewell discourse (cf. Brown 1970:582-97). Like the rest of the Gospel this text seems to derive from the Beloved Disciple's preaching and teaching at various times and places, brought

(*Jubilees* 10), Abraham (*Jubilees* 20—22), Rebecca (*Jubilees* 35), Isaac (*Jubilees* 36), Enoch (*1 Enoch* 91), Ezra (2 Esdras 14:28-36), Baruch (*2 Apocalypse of Baruch* 77) and the twelve sons of Jacob (*Testament of the Twelve Patriarchs*). These accounts, though diverse, have several common elements (Brown 1970:598-601; Talbert 1992:200-202). The great man or woman tells of his or her impending death and in some cases offers comfort in the face of the grief this announcement produces. He or she predicts what will come in the future, including, in different cases, evil or God's care. This is in keeping with the belief that one about to die is given prophetic powers (cf. Josephus *Jewish Wars* 7.353; Plato *Apology* 39C; cf. Talbert 1992:200-201). These farewell discourses also contain instruction on how those left behind should behave, and at times the discourses conclude with a prayer for those left behind.

Although Jesus' farewell discourse fits this pattern, there is the notable exception that the one who is about to leave will continue to be present through the Spirit and will return at the end of the age (cf. Brown 1970:582; Carson 1991:480). Indeed, the way Jesus speaks in this section transcends time, for he speaks in oracular style and often as if the glorification has already taken place. "He is really speaking from heaven; although those who hear him are his disciples, his words are directed to Christians of all times" (Brown 1970:582).

The keynote of these chapters is assurance and comfort in the face of two difficulties coming upon the disciples, Jesus' death and their own persecution. He prepares them for his death and the coming of the Spirit, now called the Paraclete. He speaks of the opposition between the world and them as his disciples, and he prepares them for hardships to come (cf. Tolmie 1995:228-29). He does this by showing them that this opposition comes from their union with himself.

In the course of offering assurance and comfort, Jesus develops various themes that have been introduced earlier in his ministry, including in particular glory, mutual indwelling and love. His main point is the experience of life in God the disciples have and will continue to have. The relation between the Father and the Son, which has been revealed in the first twelve

---

together by him or his disciples with little editing to smooth out rough connections (e.g., see comments on 14:31; 16:5; cf. 13:36).

chapters, is now "declared to be realized in the disciples" (Dodd 1953:397). The relations between the Father, the Son and the Spirit are described in more detail here than anywhere else in the Bible. In these chapters, therefore, is the most profound teaching on God and discipleship in the Bible—the life of believers described in relation to the persons of the Godhead.

The teaching in these chapters is expressed in typical Johannine terms, distinct from the language in the Synoptic Gospels. Yet many of the specific topics included here reflect those discussed in the Synoptics at various points. C. H. Dodd has summarized these as (1) precepts, warnings and promises for the disciples, (2) predictions of the death and resurrection of Jesus and (3) eschatological predictions (1953:390-91). Two items found in the Synoptics, however, are missing from these themes in John, namely, the discussion of signs of the end and detailed ethical instructions (Dodd 1953:391). Instead of rehearsing Jesus' predictions of the end, John concentrates on the coming of the Paraclete. This is part of his emphasis on realized eschatology, the notion that, although there will be a future return of the Lord, already he is present through his Spirit. Likewise, instead of giving Jesus' ethical instructions, John focuses on their substance, which is the love command. Thus, John is touching on some of the themes found in the Synoptics, but he emphasizes different aspects. The same is true for this Gospel's more obvious difference from the Synoptics—the omission of the institution of the Eucharist. The account of the footwashing along with the teaching in chapter 6 provide profound reflections on the significance of the Eucharist without ever describing the institution itself.

In these chapters there is much repetition and an interweaving of themes, which is a characteristic of Hellenistic style. "We shall not repeat the same thing precisely—for that, to be sure, would weary the hearer and not elaborate the idea—but with changes" (*Rhetorica ad Herennium* 4.42.54, an anonymous treatise from c. 86-82 B.C.; cf. Talbert 1992:202). Instead of simply discussing a particular idea in a linear-sequential fashion, the thought is developed in a more poetic way through repetition. Accordingly, the section can be outlined in a number of ways, though three main parts are fairly clear. The first part (13:31—14:31) focuses on Jesus' departure and discusses the disciples' relation to Jesus and their conflict with the world. The second part (15:1—16:33) develops these same themes, moving from the relationship of Jesus to the disciples, using the figure of the vine and the branches (15:1-17), to the conflict between the disciples and the world (15:18—16:15), and on to a promise to the disciples of joy in the future after the sorrow of this time of separation (16:16-33). In the third major part Jesus prays to his Father (17:1-26). Throughout, the overall theme is the Father's presence with the disciples and the Son's and Spirit's roles in mediating his presence.

The first major section of the farewell discourse (13:31—14:31) is characterized by a series of questions by various disciples and Jesus' responses. An initial statement by Jesus gets the sequence started: he speaks of glorification (vv. 31-32), his departure (v. 33) and love (vv. 34-35). These themes are developed in the rest of the farewell discourse in reverse order, thereby forming a chiastic structure, moving from love (15:1—16:4a), to departure (16:4b-33), to glorification (17:1-26; cf. Westcott 1908:2:159; Michaels 1989:253). While there are other important themes in these chapters as well and all the themes are quite interwoven, generally speaking these five verses contain the major themes of the entire farewell discourse.

Judas' departure, like the coming of the Greeks (12:20-23), signals to Jesus that a new stage of the glorification has been reached. The betrayal has begun, and so *now is the Son of Man glorified and God is glorified in him* (13:31). Glorification can refer to either the giving of praise or the manifestation of that which is worthy of praise. When Jesus says *now* he is referring to the manifestation of God now taking place rather than the praise it will bring forth in the future.

What is this manifestation? In general the glory of God refers to his "own essential worth, greatness, power, majesty, everything in him which calls forth man's adoring reverence" (Caird 1969:269). This glory has been manifested throughout Jesus' ministry, but now it comes to a climax on the cross (cf. 12:23-33). For the chief characteristic of God revealed in Jesus is his love, a self-sacrificial love. Thus, *God is glorified in him* through his death, "for in the cross of Christ, as in a splendid theatre, the incomparable goodness of God is set before the whole world" (Calvin 1959:68).

The Son of Man is the one to be glorified (v. 31), that is, the Messiah from heaven who brings God's life and judgment, especially through the cross (see comments on 3:13-14 and 5:27). The cross is itself the revelation of divine glory and the way for Jesus to share the divine life with his followers. It is also the way for God to *glorify the Son in himself* (v. 32), which he will do *at once* as Jesus returns to his presence (17:5). Just as Jesus' keynote address focused on the relation between the Father and the Son (5:19-27), so also his farewell discourse begins from that same fundamental point. This relationship is central to this Gospel.

Jesus next addresses the immediate impact of the cross on the disciples: *My children, I will be with you only a little longer. You will look for me, and just as I told the Jews, so I tell you now: Where I am going, you cannot come* (v. 33). By calling them *children* (using the diminutive form *teknia*, "little children," which the NIV tries to capture by adding *my*) he is putting them in a relation to himself that is analogous to his relation to the Father (cf. 14:20; 17:21, 23; cf. Westcott 1908:2:161). This term would be in keeping with the Passover meal setting since "small groups that banded together to eat the paschal meal had to pattern themselves on family life, and one of the group had to act as a father explaining to his children the significance of what was being done" (Brown 1970:611).

This term of endearment expresses his love for them and is a poignant introduction to his announcement that his departure is imminent. The term *a little longer (eti mikron)* is imprecise (cf. 7:33), so they could not be sure how soon this separation would take place, but given the announcement of the betrayal they might suspect that it would be very soon. Jesus seems to refer not just to the time of separation between his death and resurrection, but also to the time thereafter. For he says they will look for him, which they did not do after his death, but which they did do after the resurrection. Just as the first disciples sought him out (1:38), so will they continue to seek for him after his departure. Part of the purpose of the farewell discourse is to tell them of the new ways in which they will find him in the future.

The departure had been a theme in the controversy with the Jewish opponents (7:34; 8:21), as Jesus reminds the disciples. While it is impossible for either group to follow Jesus where he is going, there is a big difference between the groups' relationships to Jesus. For the opponents are alienated from God and can never follow Jesus into the Father's presence as long as they remain in that condition. The disciples, on the other hand, have been

---

13:32 As the NIV footnote indicates, some manuscripts leave out *If God is glorified in him,* including important manuscripts p^{66}, $\aleph^*$, B, C* and D. Because of the repeated phrases in the passage, either exclusion or inclusion of the text could be the result of scribal error or

cleansed (v. 10). They are *little children* who will indeed follow Jesus later (v. 36). As the following chapters will make clear, they first need to receive the Spirit, the Paraclete, to share in the Father's life and love and to accomplish his works, as Jesus himself has done.

The crux of this new quality of life with God is found in the love command: *A new command I give you: Love one another. As I have loved you, so you must love one another. By this all men will know that you are my disciples, if you love one another* (vv. 34-35). On one level, there is nothing new about the command to love. While there are different understandings of love, the love command, or ideal, is already known widely in Judaism (for example, Lev 19:18; *Rule of the Community* 3.13; *m. 'Abot* 1:12) and the Greco-Roman world (for example, Pliny *Natural History* 2.17.18; Marcus Aurelius *Meditations* 7.13, 22; Porphery *To Mark* 35; cf. Klassen 1992:382-84). But on another level, this love is new in that it is in keeping with Jesus' own love for them. The love of God has now been mediated in a radically new way, through the incarnation. And the possibility of sharing in that divine love now becomes possible in a manner and to a degree unlike anything up to this point. The disciples are called to enter into the relation of love that exists between the Father and the Son (10:18; 12:49-50; 14:31; 15:10; cf. Barrett 1978:452). This love also is not new; it has existed from all eternity. But it has not been manifested or made available until the incarnation. Such love is the fruit of the disciples' union with Jesus and, in Jesus, with the Father (cf. chap. 15). The disciple, therefore, is one who is characterized by love, which is the laying down of life. The disciple, like the Master, reveals the Father.

This love command focuses on relations within the new community rather than toward outsiders, a focus that has led many to view John as a narrow sectarian with no concern for outsiders. Such a view, however, misses the larger picture. John is quite clear that this divine love, in which the disciples are to share, is for the whole world (3:16; 4:42; 17:9). Indeed, their love for one another is part of God's missionary strategy, for such love is an essential part of the unity they are to share with one another and with God; it is by this oneness of the disciples in the Father and the Son that the

---

improvement. The main point of mutual glorification of the Father and the Son is clear whether or not the longer reading is adopted.

world will believe that the Father sent the Son (17:21). Jesus' attention here in the farewell discourse, as well as John's attention in his epistles, is on the crucial stage of promoting the love between disciples. The community is to continue to manifest God as Jesus has done, thereby shining as a light that continues to bring salvation and condemnation (cf. chaps. 15—16). Without this love their message of what God has done in Christ would be hollow.

John was known in the ancient church for his concern for love. Jerome tells of John in his extreme old age saying, whenever he was carried into the assembly, "Little children, love one another."

When his disciples got tired of this, they asked, "Master, why do you always say this?"

"It is the Lord's command. If this alone be done, it is enough" (Jerome *Commentary on Galatians* at Gal 6:10).

The story of John and the conversion, fall and restoration of a brigand (Clement of Alexandria *Who Is the Rich Man That Shall Be Saved?* 42 par. Eusebius *Ecclesiastical History* 3.23.5-19) is another beautiful story that illustrates the love revealed in this Gospel. For when John finds this fallen Christian he entreats him to repent, saying, "If it must be, I will willingly suffer your death, as the Lord suffered for us; for your life, I will give my own."

In the earliest centuries of the church divine love was indeed the hallmark of the community of Jesus (for example Ignatius of Antioch *Letter to the Ephesians* 4.1; Justin Martyr *1 Apology* 1.16; Minucius Felix *Octavius* 9). Tertullian reports that the pagans said of the Christians, "See, they say, how they love one another . . . how they are ready even to die for one another" (*Apology* 39). E. R. Dodds (not to be confused with C. H. Dodd), himself not a Christian (Dodds 1965:5), thinks that the genuine love and unity among Christians was "a major cause, perhaps the strongest single cause, of the spread of Christianity" (Dodds 1965:138). "Love of one's neighbour is not an exclusively Christian virtue, but in our period [from the second century A.D. to Constantine, early in the third century] the Christians appear to have practised it much more effectively than any other group" (Dodds 1965:136-37).

Such cohesiveness is part of what made Christianity attractive to Constantine, for he saw that it would help unify the empire. Before Constantine, when one became a Christian there was no question but that a death to self was involved in being a Christian. But this changed after Constantine, and so it is not surprising to find Chrysostom, preaching in the fourth and early fifth century, chastising his congregation for their lack of love. In contrast to the earlier age, he now must say, "There is nothing else that causes the Greeks [that is, the non-Christians] to stumble, except that there is no love. . . . We, we are the cause of their remaining in their error. Their own doctrines they have long condemned, and in like manner they admire ours, but they are hindered by our mode of life" (*In John* 72.5). In parts of the world today the church continues to be the greatest obstacle to people's coming to believe that the Son has come into the world, sent from the Father.

The love that Jesus is speaking of is not simply a feeling. One cannot really command a feeling. It is willing and doing the best for the other person (1 Jn 3:11-18). Since God's will alone is that which is truly good in any situation, love acts in obedience to God's will, under the guidance of the Spirit. Jesus has revealed such a life—only doing what he sees the Father doing and only speaking what he hears from the Father. The same pattern is to be true of the disciple, because "whoever claims to live in him must walk as Jesus did" (1 Jn 2:6). Feelings of compassion and concern will be present as the disciple more and more perfectly shares in God's own love for those around him or her, but such feelings are not the source nor the evidence for this love that Jesus demands of his followers (cf. 15:1-17).

Jesus Predicts Peter's Denial and Speaks of His Own Departure (13:36—14:4) Having heard all the profound things that Jesus has just said, Peter zeros in on that which is clearest and most disturbing, Jesus' coming departure. He asks Jesus, *Where are you going* (v. 36), presumably so he will be able to follow him. Jesus will answer Peter's question, but first he focuses on a point he has already made, namely, Peter's inability to follow him. This inability is due in part to Peter's own unreadiness, as his coming denial exhibits. But Peter is also unable because the way has not yet been opened through the death and resurrection of Jesus.

Jesus encourages Peter by saying that this inability is temporary and that he *will follow later.* This promise will be fulfilled after Peter's death, but it will also be fulfilled after the resurrection of Jesus and the coming of the

Spirit (for example, 12:26; 14:23; 17:24), as will be developed in the next section.

Peter continues to protest, wanting to know why he cannot follow now (v. 37). As he did at the footwashing, Peter again evidences his love for Jesus along with his lack of humility in accepting Jesus' word. His response comes more from his own self will than from true discipleship that acts in accordance with the will of the Father. Thus, it is an imperfect love. Possibly, he is even clinging to Jesus, trying to prevent him from departing in accordance with the Father's will (Ridderbos 1997:478).

He claims he would lay down his life for Jesus (v. 37). But he does not know his own heart, for Jesus says, *before the rooster crows, you will disown me three times!* (v. 38). If Peter were to lay down his life for Jesus that night, it would be his own selfish act of martyrdom rather than an act of obedience to the Father. But in fact he is not really able to lay down his life for Jesus at this point. Despite his own estimate of his devotion, his love is still too selfish and he does not yet have the guidance of the Spirit. The Lord will bring him to a new stage of maturation after the resurrection, though even then there is evidence that yet further maturation is needed (see comments on 21:15-19).

The poor showing of Peter, Judas and the other disciples at this point can be an encouragement to us in our immaturity. The Lord is incredibly patient. Indeed, he is love, a will to all goodness in our own lives. But God alone is good, and we are not the ones to define goodness. So we should find in Judas's and Peter's experience a warning to be loyal to Jesus as he is rather than as we would like him to be. Only he can guide and correct our mistaken notions, as we see him doing in this Gospel repeatedly. We should be asking him to do so in our lives, receiving the guidance he has given to the church through the Spirit.

Jesus has been speaking directly to Peter, but now he broadens his focus to include the other disciples. *Do not let your* (plural) *hearts be troubled* (14:1). He has just revealed to Peter that his heart is not nearly as loyal as he thinks. Peter has it on the best authority that there is plenty that could justify his disturbed state! The prediction of Peter's denial would have shaken all of them. Peter did not always have the right answers, but his fierce loyalty to Jesus was very clear. If he is going to deny Jesus, what hope was there for the rest of them? Jesus' talk about departure and denial gave them much to be disturbed about.

Such disturbance, however, does not take into account all the relevant facts of the situation. First, while Jesus has made it clear that they cannot trust in their own loyalty to him, this is not a cause of despair but an invitation to true security. They can only find real hope and confidence by focusing on God rather than on themselves. So Jesus tells them to *trust in God; trust also in me* (v. 1). The form of the word *trust* (*pisteuete,* present tense) often has the nuance of continuing on in an activity or state, as it does here. They have had such faith, and now they are to continue in that faith. Although *trust* could be a simple statement of fact (see NIV note), the context suggests that Jesus is commanding them to trust. They are to stop letting their hearts be disturbed and hold firm their trust in God and in Jesus.

By claiming it is right to trust in himself as well as in God, Jesus continues to act and speak as one who is divine as well as human. In one sense, to believe in the Son is to believe in the Father (12:44; cf. Brown 1970:625). This puts Jesus in a unique and exclusive position (cf. 14:6).

The command to stop being disturbed requires that the disciples change their feelings. They are to do so not by focusing on their feelings, which would simply trap them in self-preoccupation, but by focusing on objective reality, namely, the Father and the Son. The disciples are to continue to hold on to their confidence in the Father and the Son despite all the feelings that will come as they see Jesus killed and as they are confronted with their own weakness. Despite all the evidence to the contrary in what is about to happen, God remains the loving, just, sovereign Father that Jesus has revealed, and Jesus remains his Son, beloved by God, and the disciples themselves remain loved by the Father. Their confidence is in God as revealed by Jesus, not in their circumstances nor in themselves. Only by being thus grounded in God do they have a stable center to focus on and to calm their hearts. By living from God's reality rather than their own feelings and the appearances of this world, they are engaging in the battle that Jesus himself is waging. Jesus' death is central to his victory over the world (16:33) and its ruler (12:31). By their faith the disciples also conquer the world (1 Jn 5:4). Thus, "Jesus' demand that they have faith in him is more than a request for a vote of confidence" (Brown 1970:624)!

Jesus has already provided them with an example of what he here commands. When his heart was "troubled" (a form of *tarassō,* the word used here in v. 1) he focused on the Father and the accomplishment of his will (12:27). Such remains the only source of peace and security. Given the presence of fear and worry in epidemic proportions among people, including Christians, the lesson Jesus is teaching his disciples at this point is greatly needed today as well. Only a trust in the revelation of the beauty, goodness and power of the Father and the Son will bring healing. It is perfect love that drives out fear (1 Jn 4:18).

Second, if their troubled state fails to take God into account, it also does not reckon with the purpose of Jesus' departure: *In my Father's house are many rooms; if it were not so, I would have told you. I am going there to prepare a place for you. And if I go and prepare a place for you, I will come back and take you to be with me that you also may be where I am* (vv. 2-3). Peter's question is now answered—Jesus is going to his Father's house. He is going there for their sake, in order that their relationship with him may continue. This revelation speaks directly to their concerns. If they can take hold of it in trust, their hearts will indeed no longer be troubled.

The language used here—*Father's* (God's) *house* and *rooms (monai)*— is used in many Jewish sources when speaking of heaven (for example, *1 Enoch* 39:4-5; *2 Enoch* 61:2; 2 Esdras 7:80, 101; Philo *On Dreams* 1.256; cf. Schnackenburg 1982:60-61). Jesus' main point is that he is going to God and will return for them; Jesus is talking about heaven and his second coming (cf. Brown 1970:626; Ridderbos 1997:490-92). This is one of the few places in this Gospel where Jesus speaks of the future hope (cf. especially 5:28-29).

The word *room (monē)* is related to the verb to stay (or to "remain," "abide"; *menō*), which is used forty times in this Gospel. It can be used of either a permanent dwelling place or a temporary stopping place (cf. Liddell, Scott and Jones 1940:1143). "Mansion," the older translation, has led to very unfortunate misunderstandings. At the time of William Tyndale and the King James Version "mansion" also, like *monē,* meant a dwelling place or stopping place. It could also be used of the physical dwelling place or of the manor house of a lord, but these seem to be secondary to the earlier uses as in the Greek. Now, however, we understand a mansion as being limited to a physical dwelling and having specific socioeconomic implications. This has contributed to very materialistic views of heaven, which are quite foreign to John's language. It is indeed an objective "place" but not in the material sense many have in mind. Perhaps the most helpful language we have at present to speak of such a reality is to refer to it as another "dimension." The exact relation between the present physical universe and the new heavens and new earth is unclear, but the idea that someone could reach heaven in a spaceship misunderstands the language of Scripture.

The phrase *my Father's house* (v. 2) was used earlier to refer to the temple in Jerusalem and Jesus' own body (2:16, 19-22). Therefore, the dwelling place of God is now to be identified with Jesus. Also of significance is the earlier saying, "The slave does not continue [or "dwell," *ou menei*] in the house [*oikia*, the same word used in 14:2] forever; the son continues [or "dwells," *menei*] forever" (8:35 RSV). "This special house or household where the son has a permanent dwelling place suggests a union with the Father reserved for Jesus the Son and for all those who are begotten as God's children by the Spirit that Jesus gives" (Brown 1970:627). The word *monē* itself suggests "the permanence, indestructibility and continuation of this union" (Hauck 1967b:580). So the dwelling places would refer to "possibilities for permanent union *(monē/menein)* with the Father in and through Jesus" (Brown 1970:627, following Schaefer 1933). The idea is "not mansions in the sky, but spiritual positions in Christ" (Gundry 1967:70; cf. Brown 1970:627). "His body is his Father's house; and wherever the glorified Jesus is, there is the Father" (Brown 1970:627). Therefore, he prepares a place for them by his death, resurrection and ascension, for these enable them to be united to him and, in him, with the Father; his going to the Father is itself part of the preparation of a place for them. Heaven is experienced even now through the believer's union with the Father and the Son and the Spirit. However, this present union with God that occurs as the Father, Son and Spirit abide in the believer only comes to its complete fulfillment at the second coming, when the believer is taken by Jesus to be where he is (v. 3). While the ultimate goal is the Father, this passage (and in fact the whole Gospel) is centered on Christ—it is his Father's house, and Jesus says he will come again to take them *to be with me* (v. 3; more literally, "I will take you to myself," *pros emauton*).

In saying there are *many rooms* (v. 2) Jesus lets the disciples know it is not only he who has a place in the Father's house, nor just Peter (cf. 13:36), for there is room for all of them and many more (cf. 17:20). He emphasizes the certainty of this fact by saying *if it were not so, I would have told you* (v.

2). He here speaks of the thoroughness of his revelation, for, as he will say shortly, "everything that I learned from my Father I have made known to you" (15:15). He has not been stringing them along with his revelation of God's love, only to pull the carpet out from under them at the last minute. What is about to take place may look like this is what Jesus has done, but it is not. It is all part of the plan. Their greatest desire will be fulfilled, for they will be where Jesus is (v. 3).

After speaking of himself as the agent of their future access to the presence of God, he throws out a statement that steers them toward the next stage of his revelation: *You know the way to the place where I am going* (v. 4). This could be taken as a question: "Do you know the way to the place where I am going?" Whether or not he is asking a question, Jesus seems to be alluding to his earlier teaching about being the gate through whom the sheep "will come in and go out, and find pasture" (10:9; cf. Talbert 1992:204). If he is alluding to this, the disciples miss it. Indeed, all of Jesus' teaching in these chapters is mystifying to the disciples (cf. 16:25). But he is walking them through it so the Spirit will be able to unpack it for them later (14:26). This statement (or question) triggers the next question by a disciple, which leads Jesus to further develop the thoughts he has already expressed in very condensed fashion.

Jesus Declares Himself to Be the Way to the Father (14:5-7) Jesus has spoken of going to his Father's house and has said the disciples know the way there (14:1-4). Thomas, speaking for all the disciples, responds, *Lord, we don't know where you are going, so how can we know the way?* (v. 5). Here is the response of a true disciple. He asks rather than demands, which conveys a sense of humility (cf. Chrysostom *In John* 73.2). He is also honest, admitting his ignorance. Without such humility and honesty real discipleship is impossible. Thomas seems to understand Jesus' reference to his Father's house on a "this world" level, not unlike the way others in this Gospel, such as the woman of Samaria (chap. 4), have misunderstood. Thomas says, in effect, If we don't know the address, how are we supposed to know the route? Such a misunderstanding may seem amazing to those familiar with this Gospel, but all of us continue to have patches of such dullness, no

14:6 Since *way, truth* and *life* are associated with the Torah in Judaism, the theme of Jesus'

matter how far we have traveled with God.

Jesus condemned the Jewish opponents' ignorance of his destination (for example, 8:19-27), but because these disciples have been loyal to Jesus even in their ignorance, Jesus' response is encouraging. He does not upbraid Thomas but rather proceeds to offer further enlightenment. Always in John the clue to Jesus' cryptic sayings is his own identity and his relation to the Father, and this case is no exception: *I am the way and the truth and the life. No one comes to the Father except through me* (v. 6). Here we have "a culminating point in Johannine theology" (Schnackenburg 1982:65). All of John's thought could be expounded from this one verse.

This "I am" saying, like the others, is grounded in Jesus' divine identity and expresses something of his saving action. The three terms *way, truth* and *life* are simply linked together with "and" in the Greek *(kai)*. But the central term is *way* because that was the subject of the question (vv. 4-5) and the second half of the verse speaks of coming to the Father *through* Jesus. Throughout the Gospel we hear of Jesus' coming *from* the Father, revealing God, bringing new life and then returning to the Father. But now the focus is on Jesus' role as the one who leads people *to* the Father. The Father is seen as distant; one must undertake a journey to reach him. Perhaps, then, the text should be translated "No one *goes* to the Father . . ." For it seems the primary focus is still on heaven and the future, though we will see a shift beginning to take place.

The other two terms explain how Jesus is the *way;* "Jesus is the way inasmuch as He is the truth and the life" (Michaelis 1967:81). *Truth* and *life* correspond to Jesus' roles in this Gospel as revealer and life-giver. God alone is truth and life, and when our rebellion separated us from God, we plunged into ignorance and death. It follows that the way to the Father requires both revelation, because of our ignorance, and life, due to our death. This idea is clear in the Old Testament, and it was addressed by the giving of the Torah and the activity of law-givers, prophets and sages. But this verse brings out how Jesus' fulfillment of the roles of revealer and life-giver is unique. Jesus' unity with the Father means he is not just a law-giver, prophet or sage who conveys God's truth, but, like God, he *is*

---

fulfillment of the Torah is continued here.

the truth. Similarly, he is not simply one through whom God rescues his people. Rather, he was the agent of the creation of all life (1:3-4), and the Father has given to him to have life in himself, like God himself (5:26). Here Jesus, like God himself, *is* truth and life, and yet he remains distinct from God and is the way to God. As a fourteenth-century writer put it, "He Himself is the way, and in addition He is the lodging on the way and its destination" (Cabasilas 1974:48).

The second half of the verse clearly speaks of Jesus as the only way to the Father. This fact simply flows from who he is and what he has accomplished through his incarnation and upcoming death, resurrection and ascension. This verse scandalizes many people today since it seems to consign to hell large numbers of people who have never heard of Jesus, let alone those who have heard but have not come to believe in him. There are a variety of views on this topic among Christians. Some views deny the uniqueness of Jesus and have a too optimistic view of human nature, while others have a too restricted idea of God's ways of dealing with this world, which he loves. Only through Christ can we "apprehend God as the Father, and so approach the Father. . . . It does not follow that every one who is guided by Christ is directly conscious of His guidance" (Westcott 1908:2:170-71). This verse does not address the ways in which Jesus brings people to the Father, but what it does say is that no one who ends up sharing God's life will do so apart from Jesus, the unique Son of God who *is,* not just who conveys, truth and life.

Jesus' next statement shifts from speaking of coming (or going) to God to knowing God, thereby beginning the shift from speaking of the future and heaven to speaking of God's presence here and now: *From now on, you do know him and have seen him* (v. 7). This translation refers to future knowledge, but the words translated *from now on (ap' arti)* can also mean "now already" or "assuredly." Such a statement of their present knowledge of the Father would be more in keeping with how the conversation progresses in the next section, for Jesus' affirmation that they *have seen* the Father introduces a new term to the discussion, which triggers the next question and the next stage of his teaching.

14:7 The NIV reads like a reproach: *If you really knew me, you would know my Father as well.* Equally weighty manuscripts read, "If you really have known me, you will know" (see NIV note), which is more a promise, based on their knowledge of Jesus. Clearly

Jesus Speaks of Both His Relation to the Father and His Disciples' Relation to the Father (14:8-21) In response to Jesus' assertion that they know the Father and have seen him (v. 7), Philip says, *Lord, show us the Father and that will be enough for us* (v. 8). It *will be enough for us*—one would hope so! Here is the great desire of people throughout the ages—the vision of God. In saying it *will be enough for us* perhaps Philip simply means such a vision would take care of their troubled hearts (v. 1). In any case, Philip's request focuses on what has been central to Jesus all the way through, namely, the Father. Philip has the right focus, though he has much to learn concerning his master.

What in particular does Philip have in mind? His request echoes that of Moses when he said to God, "Show me your glory," which the Septuagint translates, "Show me yourself" (Ex 33:18). The Old Testament has accounts of people who have seen God, yet also warns that such a vision would bring death (see comment on 1:18). Philip seems to have in mind an experience such as Moses or Isaiah had. He has a very exalted view of Jesus since he thinks Jesus can enable such an experience. But his view is not nearly exalted enough, as Jesus makes clear.

Philip has not really known Jesus (v. 9) because at the center of Jesus' identity is his relation to the Father, a relation of such intimacy that Jesus can say *anyone who has seen me has seen the Father* (v. 9). Again we have the language of agency, reflecting the idea that one's representative is "like to himself" (*m. Berakot* 5:5; see note on 5:21). But the way Jesus describes this relationship goes far beyond the notion of an agent, for he speaks of a mutual indwelling: *I am in the Father, and . . . the Father is in me* (v. 10). He does not simply represent the Father, he presents him. Such complete union means that Jesus' words and deeds have their source in the Father (v. 10; cf. 5:36; 8:28; 10:38). Jesus may be the Father's agent, but the Father is also the agent at work through Jesus. Jesus does not say, however, that he *is* the Father. Throughout the gospel Jesus maintains a careful distinction between his oneness with God and his distinctness from him (see comments on 1:1 and 10:30).

Thus, elements of all three of the forms of sight mentioned above (see

---

they are still quite ignorant, but this second reading is more in keeping with Jesus' affirmation that in fact they do know far more than they realize (cf. vv. 4-5).

comment on 1:18) are included in Jesus' response to Philip. The incarnation points to the value of these first two types of sight, the physical and the intellectual, but in themselves they do not go deep enough. Physical sight is involved in observing Jesus, but this form of seeing is the least significant element, since even the opponents had that. Intellectual insight is important, because Philip is supposed to draw out the implications of what he has seen and heard in Jesus. But again this is not enough, for even the opponents have seen the implications but have rejected them (for example, chap. 9). The third type of sight is needed, that which comes through faith. Jesus asks Philip whether he believes that the Father and the Son dwell within one another (v. 10). Then he addresses all the disciples, saying, *Believe* [*pisteuete,* plural] *me when I say that I am in the Father and the Father is in me; or at least believe on the evidence of the miracles themselves* (v. 11). They should trust his claim or, if need be, go to the evidence of the deeds he has done. These deeds have manifested "his glory, the glory of the One and Only, who came from the Father, full of grace and truth" (1:14). "The faith at issue is the faith that man really encounters God in his encounter with Jesus, that Jesus and the Father are one" (Bultmann 1971:609). Until they grasp this aspect of Jesus' identity they cannot really understand anything else about him.

With Jesus about to depart, he speaks of greater things, which the disciples themselves are to accomplish (v. 12). Those who will do *greater things* are not just the disciples to whom Jesus is speaking but *anyone who has faith in me.* Each believer *will do what I have been doing* (v. 12), or more literally, "will do the works *(ta erga)* that I do." Some people find it odd to join together faith and works. Scripture is clear that salvation comes from God's grace, which we appropriate by faith. Our works do not produce life in us, but faith itself includes works because faith is not just a response of the intellect or the feelings but of the whole person, especially of the will. Salvation itself is a matter of sharing in God's own life, and that life is very active. As Paul will say, "The only thing that counts is faith expressing itself [or "working" *energoumenē*] through love" (Gal 5:6).

What are these *greater things* of which Jesus speaks? Some think he is referring to spectacular miracles, but what would top the raising of Lazarus? Others think it refers to the missionary activity of the disciples, their bringing more converts to faith. Such activity is an important focus for the disciples, but the meaning here is more specific. These *greater things* are possible *because I am going to the Father* (v. 12). That is, Jesus' greatest work has yet to occur: his death, resurrection and ascension. After he is glorified, the Spirit will be given (7:39), and believers can then receive the full benefits of the salvation Jesus has accomplished through the union that comes through the Spirit. The disciples' works are greater in that they are "the conveying to people of the spiritual realities of which the works of Jesus are 'signs' " (Beasley-Murray 1987:254). So *greater things* refer to our having a deeper understanding of God and sharing in his own life through actual union with him, which is now possible as a result of Jesus' completed work (cf. 14:20). It is not just a matter of more disciples; it is a matter of a qualitatively new reality in which the disciples share.

Even though Jesus is departing, these *greater things* are not accomplished by the disciples apart from Jesus (cf. Bultmann 1971:611), but rather through prayer to him (vv. 13-14). Even though he will be gone, they can still ask him. Such a claim may mean merely that Jesus will be a heavenly mediator, but given the clear teaching throughout the Gospel that affirms Jesus' deity we should see much more involved here. Like the Father, he is an appropriate one to whom to pray.

Jesus assures them that *I will do whatever you ask in my name* (v. 13), a theme that will be repeated throughout the farewell discourse (15:7, 16; 16:23-24, 26; cf. 1 Jn 3:22; 5:14-15). Praying "in Jesus' name" does not refer to some magic formula added to the end of a prayer. It means to pray in keeping with his character and concerns and, indeed, in union with him. The disciples, through their union with Christ, are taken up into his agenda. This agenda, as throughout his ministry, is to *bring glory to the Father* (v. 13). This verse has been understood by some Christians to be a blanket promise that Jesus will give them whatever they want. Such idolatry of the self is the very opposite of eternal life. "Whatsoever we ask that is adverse to the interests of salvation, we do not ask in the name of the Savior" (Augustine *In John* 73.3). Rather, the promise is made to those who will pray in Jesus' name and for the glory of the Father. As such it is a great promise for the advance of God's purposes in oneself, in the church and in the world.

That which is called for on the part of the disciple is love: *If you love me, you will obey what I command* (v. 15), or, more literally, "you will keep my commands" *(tas entolas tas emas tērēsete)*. Again Jesus describes himself in a role commonly, though not exclusively, associated with God, the giver of commands. This statement is not so much a promise that the one who loves him will keep his commands as it is a definition of love itself. Jesus is referring not only to his ethical instructions, which are very few in this Gospel, but to the whole of his teaching (vv. 23-24), including his way of life. Accordingly, John will instruct his disciples later, saying, "Whoever claims to live in him must walk as Jesus did" (1 Jn 2:6; cf. 1 Cor 4:17). Now the hallmark of Jesus' "ways," his "walk," was complete dependence on and obedience to the Father, only doing and speaking what he received from the Father. Such a life is itself an expression of love, since love, for John, is the laying down of one's life (1 Jn 3:16). Thus Jesus himself has modeled the life of love he describes here in terms of obedience (cf. 8:29; 14:31). Love, like faith, is the engagement of the whole person, especially the person's will.

Faith and love unite disciples to God and take them up into God's work, but these "greater things" will require God's own resources. So Jesus promises that *I will ask the Father, and he will give you another Counselor to be with you forever* (v. 16). Here is the first of several references in the farewell discourse to the Paraclete *(paraklētos)*, translated in the NIV as *Counselor* (14:16-17, 26; 15:26; 16:7-11, 13-15). This word is a verbal adjective meaning "called alongside," related to the verb *parakaleō,* "call to one, summon." Outside the New Testament it is used in legal contexts to mean "a legal assistant, advocate" (Liddell, Scott and Jones 1940:1313; Behm 1967:800-803). Johannes Behm, among others, tries to argue that this is the meaning in John as well (1967:811-14) but has to conclude "subsidiary senses were interwoven into the primary sense of 'advocate,' so that no single word can provide an adequate rendering" (1967:814). Actually, even the sense of advocate, as either a defense attorney or a spokesman, is not present in John (Brown 1970:1136). Rather, in John the functions of the Paraclete are mainly "teaching, revealing and interpreting Jesus to the disciples" (Turner 1992:349). While the Paraclete's activity of testifying to Jesus (15:26) and convicting the world (16:7-11) are like legal activities, they

---

14:16 Many suggestions have been made for the background of the Paraclete (Burge 1987:10-31), but it most likely comes from the Johannine transformation of Old Testament themes of advocacy and wisdom (Burge 1987:30-31; Witherington 1995:251). The strong

are not specifically activities of a defense attorney but rather of a prosecuting attorney, toward the world, and a witness, toward the disciples. Thus, "the title and the tasks ascribed to the Paraclete seem to be out of step" (Burge 1987:7), and there is no comprehensive title that does justice to "the variety of traits given to the Paraclete" (Burge 1987:9). It is best to use the transliteration "Paraclete" and examine the Gospel itself to see how John uses the term.

John speaks of the Paraclete in relation to the Father, the Son, the disciples and the world. The Father is the source of the Paraclete (14:16, 26; 15:26), and Jesus is the one who sends the Paraclete by asking the Father to send him (14:16, 26; 15:26; 16:7). Thus both the Son and the Paraclete have the same source, the Father, but the Son has a role in the historical sending of the Paraclete. Both Jesus and the Paraclete play distinct but related roles in the revelation of the Father and the giving of life. Indeed, Gary Burge has counted sixteen similarities between Jesus and the Paraclete (1987:141), which we will note as they appear in the text. For instance, in our present text the Paraclete is called "another Paraclete" (14:16), which implies that Jesus himself is *the* Paraclete. In 1 John the term itself is actually used of Jesus: "But if anyone does sin, we have one who speaks to the Father in our defense [the NIV's paraphrase of *paraklētos*]—Jesus Christ, the Righteous One" (2:1). In 1 John the role does seem to be in a legal setting. Jesus, in his humanity as the Righteous One, is our advocate before God when it comes to dealing with our sin. But in the Gospel, Jesus says the Paraclete will take up the role Jesus himself has already been fulfilling during his ministry. Perhaps the most fundamental aspect of Jesus' ministry has been to mediate the divine presence, so it is tempting to find the general idea behind the usage of the word Paraclete, both in John's letter and in the Gospel, to be "presence." Jesus is a human presence ("the Righteous One") in heaven, and he is the divine presence on earth. The Paraclete (who is himself distinct from Jesus and not simply Jesus' presence) is to continue that divine presence among the disciples.

The various terms used to translate *paraklētos,* such as Counselor, Advocate and Comforter, get at different aspects of what he accomplishes

---

trial motif in John, including the Paraclete's functions as witness, may explain why John adapted the word *paraklētos,* which is used mostly as a legal term in secular Greek (Turner 1992:350).

through his presence. The Paraclete is called "the Spirit of truth" (14:16; 15:26; 16:13) and "the Holy Spirit" (14:26), which may help explain why the world does not see or know him (14:17), since the world is neither holy nor of the truth. His dwelling is with the believers, for he is in them and is known by them (14:17). By his presence with the disciples, not with the world, and by his witness to Jesus who was rejected by the world, the Paraclete judges the world through the believers (16:7-11). As the divine presence among believers the Paraclete enables them to be God's presence in the world. He is with them and in them glorifying Jesus by revealing the truth about him to believers (14:16-17; 14:26; 16:13-15). In this way, the community, by the presence of the Paraclete, bears witness to Jesus and thus continues Jesus' own mission of judgment and life-giving. Most commentators think that the Paraclete actually mediates the presence of Jesus to the community. This is true (see comment on 16:25), though John does not say this directly (see comment on 14:23-27).

Thus, we understand that much of John's theology is captured in this term *paraklētos*, especially when we realize it is used of both Jesus and the Spirit. Jesus as the divine presence on earth and the human presence in heaven speaks of the mystery of the incarnation, of the divine-human being who is "presence" both before God and humanity. Jesus and the Spirit together reveal the Father within history—Jesus within his own person and the Spirit through testimony to Jesus within and through the community of God, those who have received Jesus and been given power to become children of God (1:12) and have become witnesses to Jesus (15:26-27). The Spirit is the divine presence within believers, bringing about the transformation of human beings so they live the life of God in the form that such divine life takes within and among us creatures, though John does not use the term Paraclete when referring to this role of the Spirit. Rather, the role of the Spirit as Paraclete is similar to that of the Spirit of prophecy in the Old Testament, that is, "the Spirit acting as the organ of communication

---

14:17 The word *Spirit* in Greek *(pneuma)* is in the neuter gender, whereas the word *Paraclete (paraklētos)* is in the masculine. It is often said that in this verse John observes the neuter gender of the word Spirit in his use of pronouns *(ho, auto)*, but in later passages he will use masculine pronouns with the word *Spirit* (14:26; 15:26; 16:8, 13-14), suggesting that this Spirit is not simply an impersonal force or atmosphere. However, in each case the antecedent is the masculine word *paraklētos* (Paraclete), so no such significance is attached to the masculine pronouns (Wallace 1996:331-32). The personhood of the Spirit is conveyed

between God and a person" (Turner 1992:342; see also p. 351). He bears witness to Jesus, thereby leading the disciples into all truth and convicting the world for their rejection of Jesus. This theme of bearing witness is part of the larger motif of a legal trial that runs through the Gospel: Jesus reveals the Father, which brings about the world's judgment, and the world in turn condemns Jesus.

Returning to our present passage (14:16), we see that the Paraclete, like the Son, comes from the Father as a gift of the Father, for Jesus says the Father will *give* them the Paraclete at the Son's request. In contrast to Jesus, who is now departing, the Paraclete will be with them *forever*. As we will soon learn, it is only Jesus' visible presence that will be absent from them; Jesus himself will remain in union with them. Thus both Jesus and the Paraclete will be with the believers. Further connection with Jesus is evident when he refers to the Paraclete as *the Spirit of truth,* since Jesus is the truth, as he has just affirmed (14:6). The Paraclete's relation to the world is like Jesus', since the world *cannot accept him, because it neither sees him nor knows him* (v. 17), as has been the case with Jesus.

Jesus contrasts the disciples to the world: *But you know him, for he lives* (*menei,* "remains," "abides") *with you and will be in you* (v. 17). This present tense, *you know him,* seems strange, since Jesus has yet to request the Spirit (v. 16; 16:7) and the disciples have not yet received the Spirit. Although Jesus says this Paraclete *will be in you,* he already remains among them (v. 17; *par' hymin menei,* translated in the NIV as *lives with you*). The Spirit is not absent before the glorification. Indeed, he is present "without limit" in Jesus (3:34; cf. Burge 1987:83-84) and must be at work in the disciples in order for them to have the faith and love that Jesus mentions (vv. 12, 15; cf. Augustine *In John* 74.1-2). But the Paraclete has not yet been sent to the disciples and received by them in the new way Jesus is opening up. Both Jesus and this Paraclete have been present to the disciples already, even though the coming level of intimacy with both will be so much deeper that

in these texts by what is said about the Paraclete, not by the grammar.
    A footnote in the NIV mentions that some manuscripts have a present tense rather than a future at the end of this verse and thus say that the Spirit "is in you" rather than "will be in you." The support is fairly evenly divided between the two. If the present tense is accepted, then the preposition would not mean "in" (since this will only be true after the resurrection) but "among," as in he "is among you."

it is the difference between death and life (see comment on 20:22; cf. Gen 2:7).

Having promised that the Paraclete would be given to the disciples, Jesus next speaks of his own return to them (v. 18). Some suggest that *orphans* is "simply used in a figurative sense for 'abandoned'," with "perhaps a hint of the defenselessness of the orphan: 'I will not leave you unprotected' " (Seesemann 1967:488). But more is involved, for Jesus is the only way to the Father (v. 6), and apart from him we *are* in fact orphaned. Only his coming to us overcomes this condition. But which coming does Jesus refer to? The fact that the disciples will see him (v. 19) suggests his coming spiritual presence with them is not in view, and the fact that the world will not see him rules out the second coming. So, most likely, he is speaking of his appearance after the resurrection (Beasley-Murray 1987:258), at which time he will impart the Spirit to them (20:22).

Not only will they not be abandoned, with Jesus' return after the resurrection they will enter into the new kind of life he has been revealing throughout his ministry (v. 19). The phrase *before long,* literally, "yet a little while" *(eti mikron),* comes from the Old Testament (for example, Ps 37:10 par. 36:10 LXX; Is 10:25; 26:20; 29:17; Jer 51:33 par. 28:33 LXX; Hos 1:4; Hag 2:6), where it is used "to express optimistically the shortness of time before God's salvation would come" (Brown 1970:607). When Jesus uses the expression it is indeed only a little while, a matter of a couple of days, until the salvation that is the beginning of the fulfillment of all the hopes will come. This salvation is a matter of life: *Because I live, you also will live* (v. 19). They *will live* because they will be united to him by the Spirit and thus come to share in the life of him who is resurrection and life. All of this is made possible by Jesus' own death and resurrection.

These connections are brought out in the next verse: *On that day you will realize that I am in my Father, and you are in me, and I am in you* (v. 20). The day referred to is the day of resurrection that inaugurates on earth a qualitatively new form of life, eternal life. The phrase *on that day,* like the phrase *before long,* echoes Old Testament hopes, for it is used 111 times in the Prophets to refer to the day of God's great acts of judgment and salvation. Here the salvation is expressed in terms of knowledge and union. The intimacy that exists between the Father and the Son has been the subject of Jesus' revelation. Jesus has called upon the disciples to accept this truth about him in faith (vv. 10-11), and now he promises that after the resurrection the disciples will come to *realize* it *(gnōsesthe),* they will know it. Like faith, this knowledge is not just an intellectual grasping of a truth. It comes from a participation in the divine reality itself, for it is said they will share in that relationship because they will be in the Son and he in them. Thus, what was just said of the Paraclete (v. 17) is now said of the Son. The Son and the Paraclete will both indwell the disciples, key themes that will be developed in the rest of the farewell discourse.

This indwelling is what will enable them to accomplish the task of doing "greater things" (v. 12). What has been true of Jesus will now be true of them—not that they will become unique sons and daughters of God as Jesus is the "One and Only" (1:14, 18), but rather that they, continuing as creatures, will share in the divine life by being taken up into the Son, just as Jesus took up into himself humanity at his incarnation. For Jesus "was much more than one individual among the many. He was the true self of the human race, standing in that perfect union with God to which others can attain only as they are incorporate in Him; the mind, whose thought is truth absolute (14:6), which other men think after Him; the true life of man, which other men live by sharing it with Him (14:6, 20; 6:57)" (Dodd 1953:249).

Jesus then ties this teaching together by repeating his description of the disciples of whom all of this will be true: *Whoever has my commands and obeys them, he is the one who loves me* (v. 21). This union is not simply a matter of shared ideas or feelings but of shared life. The love is reciprocal: *He who loves me will be loved by my Father, and I too will love him and show myself to him* (v. 21). This verse does not deny the love God has for all his creatures, but rather speaks of the fulfillment of that love in a qualitatively new way for those who are in the Son. Believers are those who "have entered into the same reciprocity of love that unites the Father and the Son" (Barrett 1978:465).

Jesus says that he himself will *love* such a disciple and will *show* himself to him or her (v. 21). Thus, Jesus himself will remain in personal contact with his disciples. He may be departing, but he will remain in relationship with them although the relationship will exist in a new form (see comment on 20:17). The showing he mentions could refer to his resurrection appearances, but the shift from the plural (v. 20, *you*) to the singular (v. 21, *he who*) suggests more is intended (Ridderbos 1997:507). The reference to resurrection presence slides over into a reference to the ongoing presence mediated by the Spirit, as becomes clear from the further discussion raised by this statement.

Jesus Contrasts His Disciples' Relation to God with the World's Relation to God (14:22-31) Jesus has said he will show himself to the one who loves him (v. 21), so Judas (not Judas Iscariot) asks, *But, Lord, why do you intend to show yourself to us and not to the world?* (v. 22). The term used for *show (emphanizō)* is used in the Septuagint for the theophany Moses received on Sinai (Ex 33:13, 18). Judas seems to be confused because he is "looking for another theophany that will startle the world" (Brown 1970:647), but Jesus is only speaking of showing himself to his disciples.

As is often the case, Jesus does not seem to address the question directly, yet in fact he goes to the heart of the issue. Judas has spoken of the contrast between *us* and *the world,* and Jesus describes the disciple as one who loves him (v. 23): *If anyone loves me, he will obey my teaching* (v. 23; or "keep my word," *ton logon mou tērēsei).* Jesus is referring not to simply holding onto his teaching, but to actually acting in accordance with it, as he himself has responded to the Father (v. 31). His teaching is not just interesting thoughts about God and the world. Rather, he has revealed God and opened the way to share God's own life. To obey his teaching is to adopt God's pattern of life. But the condition for such obedience is love for Jesus. The commands of Jesus are not a set of rules like a traffic code; they are a description of a pattern of life that reflects God's own life transposed into human circumstances. Love for Jesus involves both an attachment to him and a oneness with him and his interests, which naturally leads one to obey him and walk as he walked (1 Jn 2:6). One obeys what one loves. Indeed, our patterns of obedience reveal what we really love.

After describing the one to whom he will show himself, Jesus speaks of the showing itself: *My Father will love him, and we will come to him and make our home with him* (v. 23). Instead of describing a spectacular theophany, Jesus speaks of dwelling with his disciples. The word for *home (monē)* is the same used earlier of the "rooms" in the Father's house (v. 2). The future intimacy in heaven will begin already here on earth. The great prophetic hope of a time when God would dwell with his people (Ezek

37:26-27; Zech 2:10) has come to pass in the incarnation and the dwelling Jesus here mentions.

In this passage, as throughout the Gospel, we have the dependency of the Son upon the Father. The Father, in love, sent the Son, and so those who receive the Son in love will receive this love of the Father. For the word that they obey in love is not the Son's but that of the Father himself (v. 24). Jesus' word is not the word of a mere human teacher that can be debated and modified; it comes from the Father and thus *is* and expresses ultimate reality. Those who do not love and obey the Son reject the Father himself (v. 24; cf. 1 Jn 2:23). The opponents are not able to hear Jesus' word from the Father (8:43), but the disciples receive the Father's word through the Son and take into their lives that which is of God, thus sharing in his love. The Son does not come to the disciples on his own, but, just as with the incarnation itself, this new mode of dwelling with them will be initiated by the Father's love. The Son continues to do what he sees the Father doing, and together he and the Father come to the disciple. The divinity of the Son, his oneness with the Father, again underlies what is being said (cf. Westcott 1908:2:181).

While in the future the Father and the Son will make their dwelling *with (para)* the true disciple (v. 23), in the meantime Jesus is still *with (para)* them, giving them further words to receive and obey (v. 25). He realizes that there is no way they can understand what he has just been explaining to them, so he comforts them with the promise of an interpreter: *But the Counselor, the Holy Spirit, whom the Father will send in my name, will teach you all things and will remind you of everything I have said to you* (v. 26). Here is the second of the Paraclete passages (cf. v. 16). Jesus has just referred to himself as one sent by the Father (v. 24), and now he says the same of the Paraclete. This is the only place the Paraclete is identified with the Holy Spirit, which indicates that the Paraclete passages convey only part of the larger teaching about the Holy Spirit, focusing mainly on the role of witness and instruction. Earlier it was said the Paraclete is sent at Jesus' request (v. 16), and now it is said that he is sent *in my name*. This expression, as we have seen elsewhere (see comment on v. 13), includes the idea of union. As the disciple's prayer is to be in conformity with Jesus' character and actually in union with Jesus' own intent (v. 13), so the Paraclete himself is in union with Jesus and in conformity with his character and mission. "Jesus bore God's name (17:11, 12) because he was the revelation of God to men; the Spirit is sent in Jesus' name because he unfolds the meaning of Jesus for men" (Brown 1970:653). Thus, the Paraclete will bear witness to Jesus just as Jesus has borne witness to the Father, having come in his Name (5:43; 10:25).

Specifically, the Paraclete will teach and remind. In John, to remember something means both to recall it and understand it (see comment on 2:22; Mussner 1967). Teaching and reminding probably should not be seen as two separate activities but instead as two ways of speaking of the same thing (the *kai* would be epexegetic; cf. Schnackenburg 1982:83), so verse 26 is perhaps better translated as "that one will teach you everything, that is, he will remind you of everything which I said to you." The *all things* that the Paraclete will teach the disciples does not refer to knowledge of all sorts, such as the height of Mount Everest or the general theory of relativity. God is indeed the God of all creation, but the *all things* spoken of here is the revelation of himself that has come in Jesus (see comment on 16:14). The Spirit understands all about Jesus and will clarify all that he has taught (cf. 1 Cor 2:11-12). This word "all" (*panta,* translated *all things* and *everything* in the NIV) speaks of the comprehensiveness of the Spirit's work; he will leave out nothing of what Jesus has taught. Later we will learn that Jesus himself has left out nothing of what he has learned from the Father (15:15), and all that belongs to the Father is his (5:20; 16:15; 17:10). Thus, Jesus is the fullness of the revelation of the Father. No further revelation is needed, nor would it be possible. What is called for is an understanding of the revelation that has come in Jesus, and this is what the Paraclete will provide.

The promise that the Father and the Son will dwell with believers is in close proximity to the promise of the Spirit. This has led many to understand the presence of the Father and Son as being mediated by the Spirit (cf. Turner 1992:349-50), though others point out that the text does not say as much (Beasley-Murray 1987:258, 260). It is clear that the Father and the Son are personally present with the believers and that the Spirit has a role clearly distinguished from, though in union with, the Father and the Son. The Paraclete's teaching role is focused on the historical Jesus, as indicated by the reference to *all things* and *everything* (v. 26) and the use of the past tense *(eipon,* translated *I have said).* This focus on the Son is further emphasized by the inclusion of the emphatic personal pronoun "I" *(egō,* in

v. 26: *everything I have said to you*) though the manuscripts vary at this point. Later passages will also indicate that Jesus himself continues to instruct the disciples, which suggests the Spirit mediates Jesus' presence (see comment on 16:25).

The other distinctive is the gift of peace that Jesus gives them: *Peace I leave with you; my peace I give you. I do not give to you as the world gives* (v. 27). Here is the fulfillment of the prophets' promise of peace (for example, Is 9:6-7; 52:7; Ezek 37:26; cf. Beasley-Murray 1987:262). The peace Jesus is talking about is not the cessation of hostilities from enemies, but rather the gift of calmness and confidence that comes from union with God and faith in him and his purposes. The world's idea of peace is something that comes through destroying of enemies and consists of physical and emotional comfort. The peace that Jesus gives is grounded in God and not in circumstances. It is the peace that Jesus himself has exhibited in this Gospel and is exhibiting in this farewell discourse, even while he knows he is about to be killed. Soon he will speak of the continued trouble his disciples will experience in the world (15:18—16:4), but they will simply be living out what he himself has already been experiencing. They will share his troubles, but they will also have his peace, for they will share in his own relationship with the Father.

This promise of the gift of his own peace serves as the foundation for the command he now gives: *Do not let your hearts be troubled and do not be afraid* (v. 27). He repeats exactly the command that began this chapter (v. 1), adding now a reference to fear *(mēde deiliatō)*. This word family is always used of fear in a negative sense, as the opposite of courage. Those with a settled disposition of such fear evidence a lack of faith in God and a denial of his presence, his goodness and his power. Those who experience such fear, which includes virtually all of us to some degree, may take comfort that as God's life grows within us and as our hearts are healed, we enter into the inheritance of Jesus' peace, which replaces our sinful fear. Jesus here calls us to receive his peace. The grounds of this peace is the "perfect love" that "drives out fear" (1 Jn 4:18). This love is ultimately a sharing of the relationship between the Father and the Son, of which Jesus now goes on to speak.

His announcement that he is departing to the Father should fill them with joy instead of disturbance and fear (v. 28). The construction in Greek of the phrase *If you loved me* indicates that Jesus' view is that they have not done so. So their response shows that they have not yet come to love him in the truest sense. They think they love him, but in fact they are more focused on themselves than on him (Westcott 1908:2:185). Fear in itself is focused on self and circumstances rather than on God. Focus on God is central to all Jesus does and says, as it is here: *If you loved me, you would be glad that I am going to the Father, for the Father is greater than I* (v. 28). Jesus' great love and focus is the Father; thus the prospect of returning to him fills Jesus with joy. If the disciples shared this focus and really loved Jesus, that is, willed the best for him, they also would share this joy.

Jesus' statement that *the Father is greater than I* is very important for understanding the relation between the Father and the Son. Arius, who lived in the fourth century, and others who have held views similar to his since then have taken this verse as proof that Jesus is not divine. The teachers of the church rejected this notion, and indeed it is not compatible with other material in this very Gospel. It has been clear from the first verse that the Son is one with God yet distinct from God (especially 1:1-18; 8:58; 10:30; 20:28). In fact, this distinctness is now further clarified by Jesus' saying the Father is greater. From the time of the early church this verse has been the focus of much thought (cf. Westcott 1908:2:191-96; Pollard 1970). There have been two main ways to understand this verse that do justice to the oneness of the Father and the Son.

First, some say that the verse's focus is on Jesus' historical mission. The Father is greater in that he is the source and goal of Jesus' mission (for example, Calvin 1959:89-90; Brown 1970:655; Schnackenburg 1982:85-86; Ridderbos 1997:512). Others hold another form of this first view, which says the Father is greater than the Son in reference to his incarnate state (for example, Cyril of Alexandria, Ambrose, Augustine; cf. Westcott 1908:2:195). Such focus on the incarnation as such or on Jesus' historical mission are quite compatible with "the belief in the unity of the divine Nature, and therefore with the belief in the equality of the Godhead of the Son with the Godhead of the Father" (Westcott 1908:2:191). Indeed, many of the fathers of the church accepted more than one view. But some also said that while the incarnate Son may be in view here, by itself this interpretation is inadequate. After all, it is no big deal to say that God is greater than a man (Basil *Letter* 8.5; Gregory of Nazianzus *Oration* 30.7).

While the words "Father" and "Son" are obviously taken from our human context, they refer, according to the second main interpretation of this verse, to realities within the Godhead itself. Fatherhood is not our projection onto God; rather it is from him that our fatherhood derives (cf. Eph 3:14-15). His fatherhood transcends our limited ideas and experience, but it is not less than that which is reflected amongst us, and indeed it provides a standard of true fatherhood. Now, to be a father one must have an offspring. Jesus is eternally Son; he is not just Son at his incarnation. Such was the faith of the ancient church, as expressed in the Nicene Creed, which refers to Jesus Christ as "the only Son of God, eternally begotten of the Father, God from God, Light from Light, very God from very God." So the Father is understood as the source of Jesus not just in his incarnation and mission, but in his eternal being as Son. "What else does the word Father signify unless the being, cause and origin of that which is begotten of him?" (Basil *Against Eunomius* 1.25; 3.1). The Father is greater in that he is the origin (eternally) of the Son, but he and the Son are equal in that they share the same nature (Gregory of Nazianzus *Oration* 30.7). To say that the Father is greater than the Son does not in the least mean that the Son does not share in the deity, since "comparisons are made between things of the same species" (Basil *Letter* 8.5). As D. A. Carson says, if he were to say, " 'Her Majesty Queen Elizabeth the Second is greater than I,' no one would take this to mean that she is more of a human being than I" (1991:507). Thus, this passage gives a further glimpse into the relations within the Godhead without denying the oneness of the Father and the Son.

Given the focus in this Gospel on the relation between the Father and the Son it seems likely that the passage addresses this deeper issue. This does not mean that John himself was thinking in the categories the later church used to express the relation between the Father and the Son. But the fundamental mystery, the reality itself, is here revealed. The fact that the deeper relation is in view does not mean the reference to the incarnation is not also appropriate. C. K. Barrett stresses the incarnation view, but he actually captures nicely the two thoughts together in one sentence: "The Father is *fons divinitatis* [fountain/source of divine nature/Godhead] in which the being of the Son has its source; the Father is God sending and commanding, the Son is God sent and obedient" (1978:468).

The issues raised by this verse are matters of significant debate today.

The false teaching of Arius is still quite prevalent, and thus the issue of Jesus' deity continues to be debated. But even among those who accept his oneness with God there is dispute over the nature of this relationship. Since the life of the church derives from and is to reflect the pattern of the life of God the question of hierarchy and equality within the Godhead has significant implications for our view both of God and of the life to which he calls us. Unfortunately, most of the debate seems to be between those promoting hierarchy on the one side and equality on the other. Few are wrestling with what seems to be the biblical picture of both hierarchy and equality. Fallen human society can understand hierarchy and equality separately, but to have them both at the same time is a concept found rarely if ever in fallen humanity. But then Jesus is quite clear that his kingdom is not of this world (18:36; cf. 8:23; 14:30). The patterns of kingdom life proposed by both hierarchicalists and egalitarians are altogether too much of this world. We need to take more seriously the otherworldly revelation John is passing on to us. We need now as much as ever the Paraclete to instruct us.

Jesus concludes this short section on peace by saying the very fact that he is telling them all of this ahead of time is itself a part of his message of assurance and peace (v. 29). Jesus knows what is about to occur, so therefore these events, as devastating as they will seem, should strengthen their faith in him rather than undermine it (cf. 13:19; 16:4).

After emphasizing his present teaching (vv. 25, 29), Jesus concludes by saying the time for talk is over—now come the final deeds (vv. 30-31). The reason he will not speak with them *much longer* is that *the prince of this world is coming* (v. 30). This passage has dealt mainly with the distinction between the disciples and the world, and now at its conclusion we have the fundamental contrast between Jesus and the world. Behind Jesus' human opponents is the one primary opponent who has led the rebellion that transformed the world as the created order, which was good, to the world in opposition to the loving Father. According to the NIV Jesus says this *prince . . . has no hold on me*. This verse may reflect a Hebrew expression (*'ayin lô 'ālî*) that was used in a legal sense of having no claim over a person (Beasley-Murray 1987:263). So Jesus would be making again the point that no one takes his life from him; rather he lays it down of his own accord (10:18). The expression *has no hold on me* could also be translated "has nothing in me" *(en emoi ouk echei ouden)*. With this reading, the text would give us the reason the prince has no hold or claim on Jesus—there is nothing of his rebellion in Jesus; Jesus is not of this world (8:23).

The NIV takes Jesus' next expression as an imperative: *but the world must learn that I love the Father* (v. 31). The construction here (a *hina* clause) more often conveys purpose, and this reading would be more in keeping with the flow of thought. There is nothing in Jesus that gives the ruler of this world a hold or claim on him, but Jesus is going to go through with the Passion in order that the world may know that he loves the Father. This love for the Father is then explained in the next clause (taking the *kai* as epexegetic; cf. Brown 1970:656): ". . . that I love the Father, that is, that I do just what the Father commanded me to do." The command, of course, is to lay down his life, which itself *is* love (1 Jn 3:16).

This obedient love Jesus has for the Father is the ultimate contrast between himself and the devil. As the disciples share in this love by their own obedient love for Jesus they also will no longer be of this world (17:14). In the Passion that is about to take place, the prince of this world will be driven out, and the world will be judged (12:31). But more is involved than just condemnation. Another side of the Passion, as verse 31 reveals, is its witness to Jesus. The cross itself will demonstrate what everything else in his life has also testified, that he loves the Father and is obedient to him. Here is a manifestation for the world, and it is meant for the salvation of the world (12:32). The cross is both God's judgment and his evangelism, and both are expressions of his love. Witnessing to this revelation of the cross will be the job of the disciples, enabled by the Paraclete, as the next two chapters will explain. While Jesus will not manifest himself to the world (v. 22), the disciples' union with the Father, the Son and the Paraclete and their sharing in the divine life and peace and joy will be a witness to the world. They will bear witness both verbally and in their life to the love of God manifest in the cross.

Jesus concludes, *Come now; let us leave* (v. 31). These words are puzzling, because Jesus and his disciples do not seem to leave until later: "Having said these things, Jesus departed with his disciples" (18:1; obscured in the NIV, which paraphrases *eipōn,* "having said," as "when he had finished praying"). Some commentators take the end of chapter 14 quite literally and assume the next three chapters were spoken en route, with 18:1 referring to the departure from Jerusalem (Westcott 1908:2:187). Others suggest, as commonly happens, that they stood to leave but lingered to talk further. In this case the end of verse 31 would signal a new stage in the teaching (Morris 1971:661). Others, such as C. H. Dodd, spiritualize the leaving referred to in verse 31: "There is no physical movement from the place. The movement is a movement of the spirit, an interior act of will, but it is a real departure nevertheless" (Dodd 1953:409). The majority of recent commentators believe this is a clear seam in the fabric of the Gospel, which indicates that chapters 15—17 were added to an earlier version of the Gospel. They point to the fact that 13:31—14:31 forms a coherent whole, whereas the material in chapters 15—17 shares the same style and theology and for the most part covers the same ground. Some would say, therefore, that these chapters formed an alternative version of the farewell discourse. But the fact that new angles are explored in this material (for example, through the theme of abiding and through an increased emphasis on the conflict with the world) suggests rather that this material was a supplement to the material in 13:31—14:31 and not an alternative version. This material could have been composed by later disciples, but one would expect them to have done a better job of editing. More likely it came from John, comprising further material that he was used to including as he recounted the story of Jesus but that he had left out of his draft of the Gospel. These chapters were added later either by him or by his disciples. If they were added by John's disciples, then the fact that they did not modify these last words of verse 31 to make the transition smoother may point not to their incompetence but to their reverence for their master's teaching. Thus, while there is debate about the exact nature of this inclusion (cf. Beasley-Murray 1987:223-24; Carson 1991:476-80; Paschal 1992:231-32), some such theory seems likely. Further work on ancient literary and oral forms will probably add new insight to this puzzle.

Jesus Calls the Disciples to Remain in Him, the True Vine (15:1-17)

We now come to one of the most powerful descriptions of the eternal life to which John is bearing witness. Jesus has spoken of the cleansing of the

---

15:1 The vine includes an allusion to the Eucharist (Brown 1970:672-74; Barrett 1978:470; Beasley-Murray 1987:269), especially since the sacrament and the image of the vine both

disciples (13:10-11), the coming intimacy with him and his Father (14:20-21, 23), the coming of the Paraclete (14:16-17, 26) and the love command (13:34-35). Each of these themes, among others, is further developed in chapter 15. Jesus begins with the themes of intimacy and cleansing using the figure of the vine (15:1-6), and then he interprets and applies that teaching, tying it in with themes found throughout the farewell discourse (vv. 7-17).

Jesus Declares He Is the True Vine and His Disciples Are the Branches (15:1-6) Jesus begins with the Gospel's final "I am" saying. The earlier sayings had focused on Jesus as the life-giver and had included an invitation to come to him and to believe in him (6:35; 8:12; 10:9; 11:25-26; 14:6). Now, however, Jesus is speaking to those who have already come to him, and so his charge is that they remain in him (cf. Michaels 1989:271). The earlier theme of life is now developed in terms of intimate union with Jesus, a sharing in his own life. Thus, this is a fitting conclusion to the "I am" sayings.

The image is not a parable, since it is not a story, but rather an extended metaphor (Carson 1991:513), that is, basically an allegory, for all the details have significance. The main point of the image is clear enough: the intimate union of believers with Jesus. The disciple's very life depends on this union. As branches, believers either bear fruit and are pruned to bear more fruit or do not bear fruit and are thrown away and burned.

The image of the vine, and the closely associated term *vineyard,* were commonly used throughout the Mediterranean world (cf. Barrett 1978:472; Brown 1970:669-72). Most significant for our passage is their frequent use in the Old Testament and in Judaism to symbolize Israel (Barrett ibid.; Brown ibid.; Behm 1964:342). Isaiah has an extended use of this image in his "Song of the Vineyard" (5:1-7), and there are many other less developed uses (for example, Jer 5:10). The image of the vineyard frequently shifted to the vine, as here in John (for example, Jer 6:9). On the temple there was a "golden vine with grape clusters hanging from it, a marvel of size and artistry" (Josephus *Antiquities of the Jews* 15.395), and the vine was used to represent Jerusalem on coins made during the first Jewish revolt (A.D. 66-70), so the

---

speak of intimacy, of relationship, indeed, of union. This reference, however, is not explicitly developed.

vine was clearly a symbol of Israel. Furthermore, even the notion of a true vine shows up in the Old Testament: "I planted you as a fruitful vine, entirely true *[alēthinos]*. How have you become a wild vine, turned to bitterness" (Jer 2:21 LXX). Here, as also in Isaiah's Song of the Vineyard, God, the gardener, cared for his vineyard but got sour grapes. Consequently he will destroy the vineyard. This theme of judgment accompanies virtually every use of this imagery in the Old Testament.

Therefore, when Jesus refers to himself as the *true vine* (v. 1) he is once again taking an image for Israel and applying it to himself. Jesus himself is true Israel (cf. Hoskyns 1940b:560; Pryor 1992:124-31). This claim corresponds to his break with the temple at the end of chapter 8 and his forming a renewed people that began in chapter 9 and came clearly to the fore in chapter 10. Israel's place as the people of God is now taken by Jesus and his disciples, the vine and its branches. This is not a rejection of Judaism as such, but its fulfillment in its Messiah. The identification of the people of God with a particular nation is now replaced with a particular man who incorporates in himself the new people of God composed of Jews and non-Jews. Israel as the vine of God planted in the Promised Land is now replaced by Jesus, the true vine, and thus the people of God are no longer associated with a territory (Burge 1994). Jesus' corporate significance has been included throughout the Gospel in his use of the term Son of Man, so it is perhaps significant that the image of the vine and that of the Son of Man are identified together in Psalm 80:14b-16: "Watch over this vine, the root your right hand has planted, the son [*bên;* cf. LXX: *hyion anthrōpou,* 'son of man'] you have raised up for yourself."

Given this strong association of the vine with Israel, when Jesus refers to himself as the vine that is *true* he signals a contrast between himself and the official Judaism as represented in the Jewish leaders who have rejected him and thus cut themselves off from him and his Father. The role of the Father as the *gardener* (v. 1) continues the theme of Jesus' dependence on and subordination to the Father (cf. 14:28) and also emphasizes again the contrast between Jesus' relationship with God and that of his opponents. The specific focus, however, is on the branches, who are in intimate contact with Jesus (v. 2). There is no real parallel to this specific use of the image of the vine and the branches elsewhere (cf. Behm 1965). This passage, then, uses imagery that speaks of Jesus' identity over against official Judaism, but it uses the imagery to address issues within the new community rather than between the community and their Jewish opponents.

The new community has been established and now must bear fruit for God, in contrast to Israel and its fruitlessness. As among the people of Israel, so among Jesus' disciples, there are those who bear fruit and those who do not (v. 2). What is this fruit? Some scholars suggest Jesus is referring to the fruit that comes from bearing witness to Jesus, that is, converts, the fruit of evangelism. At least twice in John the image of bearing fruit is used with something like this meaning (4:35-38; 12:24). Other scholars interpret this fruit as being the ethical virtues characteristic of the Christian life (for example, Morris 1971:670). But something more basic, something that underlies both missionary work and ethical virtues, seems to be intended. The development of the image in the next section (vv. 7-17) suggests that bearing fruit refers to the possession of the divine life itself and especially the chief characteristics of that life, knowledge of God (cf. 15:15) and love (15:9-14). Jesus says when they bear much fruit they demonstrate that they are his disciples (15:8), and elsewhere he states love the evidence that one is a disciple (13:35; 14:21, 23) and is in union with God and with one another (17:21-23). Thus, the image of fruit symbolizes that which is at the heart of both Christian witness and ethics—union with God.

As it is the Father who draws people to Jesus (6:44), so it is the Father who *cuts off (airei)* those who do not bear fruit and who *prunes (kathairei,* "cleans"; cf. the NIV footnote) those who do bear fruit. In a sense, these two activities summarize chapter 13, with the cutting off of Judas (13:21-30) and the cleansing of the disciples (13:10; cf. Michaels 1989:271). All judgment is in the hands of the Father, both among Christ's disciples and those outside that community. Indeed, some would see the persons referred to in verse 2 as ones outside the community of Christ. Those who believe that "true disciples are preserved to the end" (Carson 1991:515, citing Jn 6:37-40; 10:28) assume that the disciple in verse 2 is not a true disciple, since a true disciple will persevere to the end (Carson 1980:97-98). "Many are reckoned by men's opinions to be in the vine who in fact have no root in the vine" (Calvin 1959:94). But Jesus does not say "those who appear to be in me" but every branch *in me.* It will not do to collapse the antinomies of Scripture. "How a man can be 'in Christ,' and yet afterwards separate himself from Him, is a mystery neither greater nor less than that involved in the fall of a creature created innocent" (Westcott 1908:2:198). The believer's assurance is not in the decision to follow Jesus, but in the graciousness and faithfulness of the Father and the Son (see comment on 6:37). Though God allows us to reject him, his own disposition toward us is love, a love that continues to pursue even those who reject him (see comment on 13:26). Those who are worried about the assurance of their salvation should find comfort in the character and actions of God. Our fretting over ourselves is itself a preoccupation with self that must be pruned away, for it inhibits our relation with God, our bearing of the fruit of eternal life.

Since fruit refers to sharing in the life of God and the activities that naturally come to expression when that life is present, this cutting off follows by definition. It is impossible to be united to God and remain ignorant of him and not manifest his own characteristic love. In such a case the branch is cut off and cast out to be burned (v. 6). The reference to being cast out (*eblēthē exō; thrown away* in the NIV, v. 6) may point to excommunication from the community, but the actual practice in 1 John does not seem to present active excommunication on the part of the community—the antichrists seem to leave on their own (1 Jn 2:19). Obviously they would not leave without reason. Most likely John showed clearly the errors of their ways and wanted them to accept his teaching, but they eventually withdrew instead. Thus, the way the cutting off appears to take place in the Johannine community is the same way the judgment takes place in the Gospel, namely, the light shines and does its own work of separation.

Jesus' disciples have been cleansed by his word, and they will be cleansed in the future (15:2-3). This word refers to all that Jesus taught, his entire message *(logos),* conveyed by both word and action. This revelation centers on the same two foci mentioned with regard to bearing fruit—knowledge of God in the Son and the love command—the foci being united, for God is love. This knowledge and this love do not characterize the disciples right then, but will "on that day" (14:20-21), after the glorification of Jesus. But something related to this later state must now characterize them since Jesus has already said they are all clean except Judas (v. 3; cf. 13:10). Indeed, if they were not clean, they could not come into the divine

---

15:4 The theme of indwelling may include an allusion to views of the Jewish mystics (Kanagaraj 1998:264-81).

presence, yet it is said that they are in Christ. Perhaps what they have is the vague outline of this knowledge and love, which will later be filled in by the Spirit. They certainly believe Jesus is come from God, even though their continued ignorance is quite evident here in the farewell discourse. More obvious is their love for Jesus, mostly evidenced in their willingness to lay down their lives for him. That they came to Jerusalem is evidence of this willingness (11:16), and it is stated explicitly by Peter (13:37). They are not yet capable of such love when things get bleak, but at least they have the desire to be loyal. Such adherence to Jesus on a social level is analogous to the coming internal co-inherence referred to in this figure of the vine. Their humility in accepting Jesus, along with his cryptic sayings and deeds, and their willingness to die with him, even though this willingness is weaker than they realize, manifest the love that is crucial for remaining in Jesus. They still have much in their lives that is not in keeping with the life of God. Such false growths need to be pruned away so God's eternal life might grow and increase in their lives. Part of the good news is that the Father undertakes such pruning in the life of each disciple. The discipline may be painful (cf. Heb 12:4-11) as the life of self and rebellion is cut away, but the result will be untold blessing for the disciple and for others through him or her. The Father's pruning is for the sake of growth, which suggests the eternal life is a very dynamic reality.

Jesus stresses the impossibility of producing this fruit apart from him (vv. 4-5). People are able to produce much without God, including converts, good deeds and even prophesies, exorcisms and miracles (cf. Mt 7:22-23; Ridderbos 1997:517). But the divine life such as we see in Jesus is dependent on God's own character, power and guidance at work in the life of the disciple. Jesus did not will nor speak nor act from himself; neither is the branch capable of bearing fruit "from itself" (v. 4, *aph' heautou;* NIV reads *by itself*). Hence Jesus' command to *remain in me* (v. 4).

The second part of this sentence is probably also a command. The Greek simply says, "Remain in me, and I in you"; the verb is left out of the second half. The NIV supplies a future *and I will remain in you,* which is a valid option. But the parallelism in verse 5 suggests that here also the two sides

---

15:6 The verbs *is thrown away (eblēthē)* and *withers (exēranthē)* are in the aorist tense, which is used here "to emphasize the suddenness and completeness" of the action (C. F. D. Moule 1959:12).

are balanced, and thus the dwelling of Christ in the believer is also an imperative (Barrett 1978:474). "In one sense the union itself, even the abiding of Christ, is made to depend upon the will of the believer" (Westcott 1908:2:199). At this point the vine imagery breaks down, since branches do not have consciousness and will. But the point is clear enough, for throughout this Gospel the human and the divine work together. The Father prunes and cleanses, and the Son has cleansed by his word, showing the Son's oneness with the Father (cf. Chrysostom *In John* 76.1). But the disciples themselves must make an effort to *remain*. Remaining is not simply believing in him, though that is crucial, but includes being in union with him, sharing his thoughts, emotions, intentions and power. In a relationship both parties must be engaged. The divine must take the initiative and provide the means and the ability for the union to take place, but it cannot happen without the response of the disciple.

The consequence of remaining is the bearing of much fruit (v. 5), but the consequence of not remaining is being cast out, withered, gathered and burned. This may be a reference to eschatological judgment (cf. 5:29), using imagery common in the Old Testament and Judaism (cf. Lang 1968:936-40) and in the Synoptics (for example, Mt 3:10 par. Lk 3:9; Mt 7:19; 13:40; Mk 9:43; cf. Lang 1968:942-46). Ezekiel 15 is especially relevant because it speaks of God's judgment against Jerusalem, his vine. The wood of the vine is useless except as fuel for a fire (Ezek 15:1-8). As Ezekiel shows, the image can refer to God's judgment whenever it takes place, not just at the end of time. Since John does not use such imagery elsewhere to refer to the final judgment, the reference here is probably not to the final judgment and hell (Beasley-Murray 1987:273). For John "it was punishment enough to be separated from Christ and God and therefore exposed to 'withering' and death" (Schnackenburg 1982:101). The casting out "happens simultaneously with the cessation of the vital union with Christ. It is not a future consequence, as at the last judgement, but an inevitable accompaniment of the separation" (Westcott 1908:2:200). Such separation from God, the source of all light and life and love, is the essence of all judgment, whether eschatological or not. The ones who are so judged in this passage are those who have refused to remain in Christ. Like the opponents throughout the Gospel, they have rejected Jesus and thereby turned their backs on God and thus life itself. Their former intimacy with Jesus, such as it was, makes their rejection all the more worthy of judgment.

Jesus Applies His Teaching on the Vine and the Branches (15:7-17)
Jesus now explains more of what it means to remain in him (v. 4). This
section forms a chiastic pattern (Brown 1970:667), with Jesus' teaching (vv.
7, 17) and the promise of answered prayer (vv. 7, 16) forming the two ends
and Jesus' joy at the midpoint (v. 11). Themes from throughout the farewell
discourse are woven together within this carefully constructed exposition
of the image of the vine (Brown 1970:666).

The first section (vv. 7-10) draws out once again the relation between
love and obedience (cf. 14:21, 23-24) and views this relation in light of the
theme of mutual indwelling. Jesus' dwelling in the believer is now referred
to as his words remaining in them (v. 7). If they remain in him and his
words in them, Jesus promises their prayers will be answered (v. 7; cf.
14:13-14; 15:16; 16:23-24, 26). To have his words remaining in them means
to share his mind and his will. They are to be caught up into his own focus
on the doing of God's will. Accordingly, they will pray for his purposes
rather than for their own selfish desires. Jesus' purposes have been to reveal
God and share his life and love so people will be brought into union with
him in his new community. Such will be the concerns also of the disciples
who have Jesus' words in them, and God will answer their prayers as they
live according to their life in Christ and his life in them.

They bear the fruit of this shared life, which is evidence that they are
Jesus' disciples (v. 8), unlike others who claim to believe but do not (2:23-24;
8:31). Since the fruit refers to the knowledge and love of God, it follows
that as the disciples produce fruit the Father is glorified (v. 8; cf. 13:31-32;
14:13; 17:1, 4). The glory of the Father is Jesus' chief delight and has been
the focus of all he has said and done. Since the disciples are now going to
live in union with Christ, the Father's glory will be the goal of their lives as
well.

The other side of the mutual indwelling is the disciples' remaining in
Christ (vv. 4, 7), which is now described as their remaining in his love (v.
9). Jesus describes this love as like the love with which his Father has loved
him (v. 9; cf. 17:23). The Father is the source and pattern of all love, so, as
always, Jesus is doing that which he receives from the Father. Jesus' disciples
must remain in his love (cf. 13:1, 34; 14:21), and they do this by obeying
his commands (v. 10). In part this means they are to remain in Jesus' love

for them, but further it means they must remain in his own love for the Father. Jesus' own love for the Father was seen in his obeying the Father's commands and remaining in his love (v. 10). For the disciples to remain in Jesus' love for the Father, therefore, they must share in Jesus' obedience. Their obedience is itself the fruit of their remaining in Jesus because it is a characteristic of his love (1 Jn 2:5-6).

Jesus has spoken about love and obedience that they might share in his own joy (v. 11). As his word remains in them through their obedience they are actually sharing in his life with the Father, which is characterized not only by obedience, but also by joy. The Jewish delight in God's law (Ps 1:2; 119:14) is here fulfilled in sharing in Jesus' own obedience to the Father. Indeed, the joy in God's salvation, both in past events and in the future, ultimate salvation, referred to in the Old Testament and later Jewish texts (Conzelmann 1974b:362-66), finds its completion here in Jesus' joy. But joy is not what springs to mind for many people when they think of obedience. They see obedience as conforming to rules, which produces drudgery or chaffing. Rules often induce guilt in those not keeping them and a prideful delight in those who do obey. But the obedience Jesus is talking about is an obedience not to societal rules, but to the Father who is all love. To obey him is to conform one's life to the very pattern of God's own life. Such obedience shares in his life, which is characterized by harmony, grace, goodness and beauty. We are in intimate union with him and swept up into his dance for which we were created and which brings the deepest fulfillment and deepest joy to our lives. Jesus' joy came from such intimacy with the Father and his delight to do that which pleases the one who is all love and goodness. Jesus is showing how our *joy may be complete*. If we have no joy in obeying the Father, then we should consider whether we know him as Jesus knows him and whether we understand his will as the description of our true freedom (8:31-36) and joy. Indeed, we might ask ourselves what does bring us joy. The answer will reveal to us our own hearts.

Jesus loves just as the Father loves (v. 9), and he commands his disciples to love one another just as he has loved them (v. 12). Thus, the community is characterized by divine love. If this love were just a feeling, such a command would be impossible to fulfill. But the love Jesus refers to is an act based in a certain state of heart. Specifically, it is the laying down of one's life based on willing the good of the other. By God's grace we can indeed choose to will the good of the other, and we can choose to act accordingly. This is the love Christians are called to in Christ, for Jesus says we are to love one another just as he has loved us, which he immediately defines in terms of laying down of one's life for one's friends (v. 13; cf. 10:14-15, 18; 13:34, 37; 14:31).

The word for *friends, philoi,* is related to a verb meaning "love" *(phileō)* and conveys a greater sense of intimacy than does our modern use of *friend,* though our word is actually related to the Anglo-Saxon verb *frēon,* "to love" (Brown 1970:664). The idea that one should lay down one's life for one's friends was well known in the ancient world (for example, Aristotle *Nicomachean Ethics* 9.8; cf. Stählin 1974:153). Jesus reveals that this human ideal is in accord with the divine ideal. It might be thought that laying down one's life for one's enemies is a greater love. Jesus does indeed have such love for his enemies (see comments on 5:5; 6:51; 13:21-26), but the focus in the present setting is on the disciples and their change of status from slaves to friends.

Jesus says his friends are those who obey him (v. 14). This is not a definition of friendship itself, but it follows in this instance given who Jesus is; just as love for the Father and the Son involves obedience, so does friendship. All this talk about obedience seems more fitting for a master-slave relationship, but Jesus no longer calls them slaves *(douloi)* but friends (v. 15). This does not mean that the relation of slave is not also appropriate for Jesus' disciples (cf. 13:16; 15:20). Paul refers to himself as a slave *(doulos)* five times, though he also notes that in some senses the Christian is no longer a slave (Gal 4:7). Even the worshipers in the heavenly city at the end, who will reign for ever and ever, are called God's slaves (Rev 22:3, 6). So although the idea of slave is valid, it is limited. Jesus' point here is intimacy.

His disciples are his friends because he has made known to them *everything* he heard from his Father (v. 15). The disciples thereby fulfill the ideal of Abraham and Moses. Abraham was called God's friend (2 Chron 20:7; Is 41:8), and he was one from whom God did not keep secret his plan for Sodom and Gomorrah (Gen 18:17). Moses likewise was God's friend, for "the Lord would speak to Moses face to face, as a man speaks with his friend" (Ex 33:11; cf. Deut 34:10). The opponents in this Gospel have exalted ideas of Moses and Abraham (chaps. 5, 8), based in part on such texts. But such intimacy with God is now open to all in Christ. For Jesus fulfills the role of Wisdom, which "passes into holy souls from age to age and produces friends of God and prophets" (Wisdom of Solomon 7:27).

Jesus says he has kept nothing hidden (v. 15), an important claim for the all-sufficiency of Jesus' revelation of the Father. All that belongs to the Father belongs to Jesus (16:15; 17:10), and he has passed it all on to his disciples. There is nothing more to be known about the Father apart from Jesus and his revelation. We await no new revelation to reveal more of God, nor do we need to search the world's religions and philosophies to fill in gaps in Jesus' revelation. Study of other religions and philosophies can be valuable, but all the truths of God present in them, such as the ideal of self-sacrifice just noted, are recognized to be true by their congruence with Jesus. Here we have the exclusivist claims of Christianity at full strength.

Jesus has been discussing love and intimacy, but that does not mean that his disciples' relationship with him has somehow become that of equals (rightly, Bultmann 1971:544; Haenchen 1984:132). The relationship between Jesus and his disciples includes friendship, but is far more intimate than friendship. Nevertheless, he is always the Lord. They did not choose him, but he chose them (v. 16; cf. 6:70; 13:18; 15:19). This is not a reference to salvation, but rather to service, since the rest of the verse speaks of being *appointed . . . to go and bear fruit* (Beasley-Murray 1987:275). If this fruit is eternal life, which is knowledge of God and sharing in his love (cf. comment on 15:2), then Jesus is saying he chose and appointed his disciples to go and manifest the life of God. The primary expression of this fruit that Jesus speaks of here is the love within the Christian community. The fruit that remains is thus the love that flows from, and bears witness to, life in union with God. This love has come into the world in Jesus and now is to remain in the world in the community of his disciples. This divine love manifested within the church will bear witness to Jesus before the world (17:21, 23), which will enable some to find eternal life and will also reveal the judgment of those who reject it.

The result of such fruit bearing, of living in union with God and sharing in his love, will be answered prayer (v. 16). Prayer in Jesus' name is prayer

---

15:16 The NIV translation of *hina* as *then* is too weak. *Hina* probably signals the result; that is, bearing fruit (sharing in the divine life) results in answered prayer.

that is in union with him and in keeping with his character and his purposes (see comment on 14:13). Thus, while the disciples themselves must go and bear fruit or risk being cut off (v. 6), they have the assurance that Jesus has chosen and appointed them for this activity and that the Father will answer their prayers. These assurances correspond to the fact that apart from Jesus the disciples can do nothing (v. 5). A person's sharing in the divine life begins and continues only by God's gracious activity. The grace of God that has characterized Jesus' life and ministry will continue to characterize the life and ministry of his disciples.

The reference to Jesus' command in the final verse (v. 17) picks up the reference both to Jesus' words (v. 7) and to his command (v. 12), thus tying the unit together. Obedience to Jesus' command is the evidence that we love him (vv. 9-10), and the content of his command turns out to be love. This final reference to love for one another ties together this passage and provides a striking contrast to what immediately follows—Jesus' description of the world's hatred of the disciples. Jesus has been speaking of the enormous blessings of knowing and loving God in a community of love. However, the church is not to be an isolated hothouse, but a garden in the midst of the world.

Jesus Speaks of Conflict with the World and of the Paraclete (15:18—16:15) Jesus' love for his disciples (15:1-17) is now contrasted with the world's hatred of Jesus and his disciples. Jesus has confronted his opponents repeatedly with the fact that their rejection of him reveals their alienation from God. Now Jesus says that their alienation will lead them to reject his disciples as well.

Jesus Explains the Source of the World's Hatred of His Disciples (15:18-25) Jesus relates what he has experienced to what the disciples will now experience (vv. 18-20). The rejection of Jesus by his opponents has been based in their alienation from God. Jesus now refers to them as *the world,* since the world is that which is in rebellion against God. The disciples would face rejection by Gentiles as well (cf. Tacitus *Annals* 15.44; Suetonius *Nero* 16), but at the moment Jesus has Jewish opposition in mind (16:2).

15:18 Instead of saying the world hated him *first,* Jesus could be saying the world hated him most, since *prōtos* can have either meaning.

Since the disciples are members of Christ like branches are members of a vine, they receive what he receives—both the sunshine and rain of the love of the Father and the storms of the hatred of those who are in rebellion against the Father.

The disciples are included in the world's hatred of Jesus because, like him, they are not of this world (v. 19; cf. 8:23; Neyrey 1988). They are Jesus' friends *(philoi,* 15:14-15), and thus they are not loved *(ephilei)* by the world. Jesus has chosen them *(exelexamēn)* and appointed that they to go bear fruit (15:16), and this commission was based on a more fundamental act that he now refers to as choosing them *(exelexamēn) out of the world.* They have been transferred to Jesus' kingdom, which is not of this world (18:36). The world's hatred of them, therefore, is an encouragement to the disciples since it is due to the difference Jesus has made within them. This does not mean the world has no hatred for others besides Christians. Nor does it mean that someone who is hated by the world is necessarily being true to God. But Jesus does say that those who are his disciples are quite distinct from all that is in rebellion against God and should not be surprised when opposition arises.

Jesus refers his disciples back to his saying, *"No servant is greater than his master"* (v. 20; cf. 13:16). Earlier Jesus was referring to his example of humility in washing their feet. Now this saying applies to his humility in undergoing persecution by the world, even to the point of death. Here we see the incredible humility of the master, who is Lord of all. If humility is appropriate for a slave, how much more for a slave of such a master. Jesus concentrates on two items of comparison in particular—persecution and obedience to his teaching. While Jesus' statement *if they obeyed my teaching* could refer to those who did in fact do so, the present context is focused on rejection (vv. 20, 21), so the idea is probably more like "they will follow your teaching as little as they have followed mine" (NEB). Thus, the disciples are rejected not only because they are not of this world, but also because they are proclaiming a message (cf. v. 27). The present text shows the disciples in the role of prophets, meeting the prophets' fate. As the Lord

---

15:22 Such a text could be taken as saying that those who have never heard of Christ are without sin (or guilt). Jesus is not addressing the question of whether those who have not seen or heard him are guilty, but rather whether those who have seen and heard and yet have rejected him are guilty. The word translated *excuse (prophasis)* can also mean

told Ezekiel, "The house of Israel is not willing to listen to you because they are not willing to listen to me, for the whole house of Israel is hardened and obstinate" (Ezek 3:7). There has been plenty of such hardness within the church as well.

Jesus summarizes his point thus far by saying, *They will treat you this way because of my name* (v. 21). His *name* refers to his identity and his character as it is made manifest (see comment on 1:12). But Jesus cannot be understood apart from the Father, so he concludes that the reason they reject him is their ignorance of *the One who sent me*. Here is the core problem (cf. 5:37-38; 7:28; 8:19, 47, 55), which introduces the main point of the rest of this section (vv. 22-25). Jesus has been speaking of the connection between the treatment he has experienced and that of his disciples. Now he focuses on his own ministry and its relation to the Father.

His central assertion is that this ignorance of the Father is culpable because of the witness he has borne in word and deed. He has spoken to them the words of the Father himself (14:10-11) and shown them the deeds of the Father (5:19, 30), deeds unlike anyone else's (v. 24). If he had not spoken and acted thus *they would not be guilty of sin* (vv. 22, 24). The text says literally, "they would not have sin" *(hamartia). Hamartia* can refer to guilt, but here the reference is more likely to sin itself. For in John's Gospel sin is understood as lack of faith in Jesus, that is, hatred of him and his Father (Michaels 1989:276). The opponents do not think they hate God, but such is the case given their hatred of Jesus (vv. 23-24). "This hatred is the human 'no' to the divine 'yes' expressed in the mission of his Son" (Ridderbos 1997:525).

The disciples are actually experiencing the deep-seated rebellion of sinful humanity against the Father himself. The conflict they experience is a part of something much bigger than themselves. Sometimes Christians today say they are being persecuted for the sake of God, when in fact they are being rejected merely because they are obnoxious. But many Christians are indeed undergoing the most horrid persecution and suffering for the Name. Jesus' words of encouragement here speak directly to his disciples

---

"pretext." So Jesus could be saying his revelation has taken away their rationalizations for remaining in their sin. They cannot continue to justify their crookedness now that straightness has been revealed, as it were.

in such situations. He gives them the larger perspective, helping them understand that what they are going through is part of the world's rejection of the Father and the Son.

Such suffering is not outside God's providential care. It corresponds to a pattern found in Scripture, which is what *fulfill* means here (v. 25). The rejection of Jesus and his disciples is found in the very law to which those rejecting them claim to be loyal, thus further demonstrating their culpability. The passage cited, *They hated me without reason,* is probably either Psalm 35:19 or 69:4. The latter may be more likely because it is referred to so often in the New Testament, being quoted or directly alluded to seventeen times in all. In either case the innocent psalmist is complaining to God about his persecutors. So Jesus is not just using a convenient proof text but making connection with an important type. He is using Scripture to assure his disciples that they should not be surprised by what he is experiencing nor by what they themselves will experience. God is in control.

Thus Jesus is giving the disciples two grounds for assurance, himself and the Scriptures. They should look to him for his example and for what he has said to them. They also gain confidence through what they find in the Old Testament, understood in relation to Jesus (v. 25). The Scriptures in general, and the Gospels in particular, continue to play such a role in the lives of faithful disciples today.

Jesus Says the Paraclete and the Disciples Will Bear Witness to Him (15:26-27) From his own witness and that of Scripture Jesus now returns to the witness of the Paraclete and his disciples. The witness of the Paraclete and the disciples stands in marked contrast to the rejection by the world, confirming the fact that Jesus and those associated with him are not of this world. Referring to the Paraclete as *the Spirit of truth* (v. 26) provides yet another contrast with the world, which has rejected Jesus out of error.

Jesus says he will send the Paraclete *from the Father* (v. 26), thus affirming both that the Paraclete is associated in a primary way with the Father and that the Son is involved in his historical mission (14:26; 16:7). Then Jesus refers to the Paraclete as the one who *goes out from the Father* (v. 26). The meaning of this line has been the source of enormous

---

15:26 The Spirit is indeed a person, but the use of the masculine pronoun here is not due to that fact. See note on 14:17.

Some in the Western church recognize that speaking of the Spirit as proceeding from

controversy right down to today. Many Western Christians would say the going out is another way of referring to the historical mission of the Paraclete. The Eastern church, on the other hand, sees this as referring to the eternal relations within the Godhead: this procession of the Spirit is not into history; it is the coming forth of the Spirit from the Father from all eternity. The Son is God begotten, the Spirit is God proceeding, and the Father is the one source of both.

The Father as the one ultimate source of all is true to the thought of this Gospel and the rest of Scripture, but it is doubtful that this verse is dealing in its primary sense with the eternal relations between the Father and the Spirit. The word used for *from (para)* does not denote source in this sense. Indeed, the line in the Nicene Creed referring to the eternal relations is "I believe in the Holy Spirit . . . who proceeds from *(ek)* the Father." The Greek fathers who refer to the eternal procession use *ek* and even change *para* to *ek* when referring to verse 26 in this connection (Westcott 1908:2:213). Furthermore, the language in our verse *(para)* is used elsewhere in John to describe Jesus' coming forth from the Father on his mission within history, though with a different verb (16:27; 17:8). Thus, the going out probably also refers to the historical mission of the Spirit. Jesus repeats the thought in this way to emphasize that the Spirit is from the Father—that is, like Jesus himself, he is not of this world.

The Paraclete is going to *testify* about Jesus (v. 26). Because he is being sent to the disciples—*whom I will send to you*—it would seem his testimony is to the disciples, who in turn will testify before the world. Further details about the Paraclete's testimony will be given shortly (16:8-15), but first the testimony of the disciples themselves is introduced.

The disciples were chosen out of the world (v. 19) and are now said to be witnesses because they have been with Jesus *from the beginning* (v. 27), referring to the beginning of his ministry. This implies Jesus is speaking primarily to the eleven in these chapters. They have been along for the whole trip so they can tell the whole story (cf. Acts 1:21-22). Because the Gospel is not just an abstract message but an account of what God himself has done and said as he was incarnate, history matters enormously and the

---

the Son as well as from the Father does not deny that the Father is the ultimate source, for the Son is not "an Origin independent of the Father" (H. C. G. Moule 1890:125).

role of eyewitnesses is crucial. "The New Testament is . . . neither a collection of thoughtful essays nor an attempt to construct a system of ethics. It bears witness to a unique history, and it discovers the truth in the history. . . . The fourth Gospel persuades and entices the reader to venture a judgement upon the history" (Hoskyns and Davey 1947:181). The Gospel of John is itself a primary example of the witness referred to in verse 27. The eyewitness testimony is now available through the New Testament, which is foundational and is the criterion of all claims to bear witness to Christ.

These two verses, then, introduce the offense which the disciples are to wage in the face of the world's hatred and persecution, with the disciples' giving voice to the Paraclete's witness against the world (Brown 1970:698).

Jesus Refers Directly to the Jewish Persecution of His Disciples (16:1-4) The general description of conflict (15:18-27) is now spelled out more specifically, beginning with the topic of persecution. Jesus warns that expulsion from the synagogue and even death awaits the disciples (16:2; cf. Mt 10:17, 21 par. Mk 13:9, 12 par. Lk 21:12, 16). Such martyrdom began with Stephen (Acts 7:54-60) and continued on a local basis (Acts 12:1-2; 14:5, 19; 18:12; 22:4; 26:10; 2 Cor 11:23-25; Rev 2:13; Josephus *Antiquities of the Jews* 20.200; Justin Martyr *Dialogue with Trypho the Jew* 95.4, 133.6; *Martyrdom of Polycarp* 13.1). The expulsion from the synagogue also occurred on a local basis and then more widely late in the first century (see comment on 9:22).

Jesus' opponents are about to put him to death for the sake of what they believe to be God's truth and honor. The same fate awaits his followers, since the one who kills his disciples *will think he is offering a service to God* (v. 2). The word *service (latreia)* refers to religious service. A later Jewish text says, "if a man sheds the blood of the wicked it is as though he had offered a sacrifice" (*Midrash Rabbah* on Num 21:3; cf. *b. Sanhedrin* 9:6). Such a view is quite understandable among those who believe they have received the revelation of the truth, which includes most, if not all, the major religions. Such killing is against the teaching of Jesus and the New

---

16:2 The word *time* is literally "hour" *(hōra),* which echoes Old Testament references to the hour of God's action, either of blessing or judgment (fifteen times in Jeremiah, three times in Amos; also 1 Sam 2:31; 2 Kings 20:17 par. Is 39:6). Jesus' own hour is the time of his glorification through the cross (12:23). Their death, like his, is under God's control.
16:4 The word *time* here is literally "their hour" *(hē hōra autōn).* "Their" could refer either to *such things* (v. 3) or to the opponents who are doing *such things.* As with Jesus'

Testament, but this has not stopped such activity in the name of Christ.

The opponents' zeal is itself commendable (cf. Rom 10:2), but because it is directed against Jesus and his followers, it simply bears further witness to their alienation from God. That is, Jesus and John agree with their Jewish opponents that God has revealed himself—there is revealed truth to live and die for, truth that distinguishes those who are of God and those who are against him. But they disagree about the locus of this truth. Jesus says they are doing these things *because they have not known the Father or me* (v. 3; cf. 15:21, 23). So the knowledge of the Father and the Son, which is the very source of the disciples' joy and peace, is also the cause of their troubles in the world.

Jesus tells them about these troubles ahead of time so they *will not go astray* (v. 1; cf. 13:19). This verb *(skandalizō)* does not refer to making a mistake but to something preventing one's progress, in this case a falling away (Stählin 1971:345). Earlier, when the disciples had grumbled over a hard saying, Jesus used this same word when he said, "Does this offend you?" (6:61). The teaching did offend them, and "many of his disciples turned back and no longer followed him" (6:66). Such a falling away is what Jesus wants to prevent by warning them of persecution. When the hard times come they should stick with him, just as these eleven did when the hard sayings hit them (6:67-68). These are the ones who have received Jesus' words, and they are to remember these words (16:4) so they do not fall away.

Disciples today also need to receive deeply the teachings of Christ and his apostles in order to be ready for times of persecution or temptation. Jesus here provides an example of pastoral care. It is part of the pastor's duty to ensure that God's people receive such preparation so they will continue on the pilgrim way and not fall away or otherwise get blocked along the way.

Jesus Explains the Twofold Work of the Paraclete in More Detail

(16:4-15) Jesus now comes to his final teaching about the Paraclete. Jesus'

---

own hour, this hour will look like defeat, but in fact it is part of the defeat of those opposing Jesus and his disciples (cf. Carson 1991:532).

The NIV has *I did not tell you this,* giving the impression that Jesus is only referring to the persecution by the synagogue. But the word used is plural, as in "I did not tell you these things" *(tauta),* thus probably referring also to his departure and the coming of the Paraclete.

departure, the talk of which has caused the disciples so much distress, is necessary in order that the Paraclete might come (vv. 4b-7). When the Paraclete does come he will continue the work of revelation begun in Jesus, both his judgment of the world (vv. 8-11) and the revelation of God to the disciples (vv. 12-15).

Jesus has been speaking of his departure, the persecution the disciples will soon meet and the coming of the Paraclete. These topics were not part of his teaching from the beginning because he was still with them (v. 4). His revelation has unfolded as was appropriate at the various stages of his ministry. Now that he is about to depart to the Father he is preparing them for what comes next, both the blessing and the danger.

He upbraids them for not asking where he is going (v. 5). This is puzzling because Peter had already done exactly that (13:36) and Thomas also had expressed ignorance of where Jesus was going (14:5). This could be a seam in the garment of the Gospel (see comment on 14:31; Brown 1970:710). If this is not a seam, then there must be some distinction between Peter's question and what Jesus is referring to here. Perhaps Peter's earlier question was not really a serious one, since he was immediately distracted from it and did not follow up on it (Morris 1971:695-96). Or perhaps the clue is in the present tense—none of them *asks* him. They had asked earlier, but now they are grieving instead of asking (v. 6; Barrett 1978:485). Perhaps Jesus is saying that they lack trust, that they are grieving when they should be taking into account where he is going (Calvin 1959:115).

Whatever the solution, the main point as it now stands is the disciples' focus on themselves rather than on Jesus. Earlier Jesus had said it is a blessing for him to return to the Father (14:28). Now he adds that it is also for their good that he is going away, for then he will send the Paraclete (v. 7). The Spirit is already present (see comment on 16:25), but Jesus cannot send the Spirit in his role as Paraclete until he himself has returned to the Father. Why is this? Earlier John had explained that the Spirit was not yet given because Jesus "had not yet been glorified" (7:39). Jesus' glorification is his death, resurrection and ascension to the Father, and these provide both the climax of his revelation and a testimony to the truth of his life and teaching. The role of the Spirit is to interpret and bear witness to Jesus and his revelation of the Father (vv. 12-15). So until Jesus has completed his revelation, the Spirit is not able to do his job, for he does not have the full revelation to work with.

Thus it is better for the disciples that Jesus go, because this will be the completion of his own work on their behalf (and on behalf of the whole world) and because he will then send the Paraclete, who will lead them into all that Jesus has revealed. But more is involved since this work of the Paraclete is not simply intellectual. The Paraclete is the Spirit of God, and union with God is accomplished by being born of the Spirit (3:5). Thus, the Spirit will deepen their knowledge of the Father through the Son in the sense of both understanding and relationship. Through the Spirit the disciples will share in the very life of God that they have seen in Jesus. Their intimacy with Jesus himself will be far deeper than before. This union with God is accomplished by Jesus' glorification, and thus the glorification must take place before the sending of the Paraclete.

The coming of the Paraclete is not some automatic, impersonal response. He is personally sent by Jesus, and he is sent not to the world but to the disciples (v. 7; 14:17). Before explaining further what the Paraclete will do for the disciples, Jesus describes the effect that the Paraclete's presence among and within the disciples will have on the world (vv. 8-11). When the Paraclete comes to the disciples he will *convict the world* (v. 8). In the New Testament this word *(elenchō)* means "to show someone his sin and to summon him to repentance" (Büchsel 1964:474). The emphasis can be on either exposing (cf. 3:20) or condemning and convicting (cf. 8:46). As we will see, the exposure of the the truth about the world is clearly in view in our present passage. Whether Jesus is also saying that the world will be convicted by this revelation is not clear, though certainly some within the world will be convicted since the disciples' witness will be received by at least some (17:20).

There are three parts to the exposure of the world's errors (v. 8). First, the world is wrong about sin because it does not believe in Jesus (v. 9). Here, as throughout this section (15:18—16:15), the Jewish opponents are understood as representing the world. The opponents had condemned Jesus as a sinner, which is both explicitly stated (9:16, 24) and implicit in all their accusations. But they are really the ones who are guilty before God, because the work of God is to believe in the one whom he sent (6:29) and rejecting Jesus is the most basic sin (1:11; 3:19; 5:45-47; 8:24; 15:22).

Second, the world is wrong about righteousness because Jesus is going to the Father (v. 10). The word *righteousness (dikaiosynē)* probably includes its sense of "justice." His opponents did not judge with right judgment (7:24), and this is seen especially in their condemnation of Jesus for his claim to be God's Son (19:7). Jesus' return to the Father will expose their justice as unjust. Jesus adds, "And you will no longer see me" (paraphrased in the NIV), which reinforces it is to the disciples advantage that Jesus go to the Father (v. 7).

Third, the world is wrong about judgment because *the prince of this world now stands condemned* (v. 11). The opponents had condemned Jesus, but the Paraclete will reveal that it was the evil one who was judged and condemned at Jesus' glorification. This judgment in turn condemns the world itself (12:31), since they have the devil for a father (8:44).

Each of these terms—*sin, righteousness* (or "justice") and *judgment*—were quite familiar to the Jewish opponents. But now they are redefined around Jesus: "Sin is rejecting Jesus; justice is what God has done for Jesus; judgment is what Jesus has accomplished already by his death" (Michaels 1989:283). The conflict with the Jewish opponents is therefore put in perspective. These opponents represent the world itself, that which is in rebellion against God. The conflict reflected in this rebellion is here seen in cosmic terms, with the Son of God and the prince of this world as the leading actors, each desiring the allegiance of the world. The main characteristics of each actor in the drama are here revealed: the world consists of all who fail to believe in Jesus, Jesus is known as the just or righteous one (cf. 1 Jn 2:1), and the devil is judged. Thus the Paraclete will reveal the verdict of the trial that has been in session throughout the Gospel.

The Paraclete exposes these realities to the disciples and to the world itself through the disciples (15:26-27). This witness will be through oral and written proclamation, of which this Gospel is itself a supreme example. But the primary witness will be in the quality of life that the Paraclete produces within the community as the new birth brings them into union with God. First (cf. v. 9), faith in Jesus brings a new freedom from sin (8:32-36; 1 Jn 1:5—2:2; 3:4-10), though not sinlessness apart from the cleansing of Jesus' blood (1 Jn 1:7-10). Second (cf. v. 10), they are able to live the pattern of righteousness and justice that was present in Jesus because they have his Spirit, which he sent to them after his return to the Father. The world may not see Jesus, but the disciples continue to be close to him (16:19). Third (cf. v. 11), the defeat of the evil one by Jesus is now evident in the lives of his disciples, who also overcome the evil one (1 Jn 2:13-14; 5:4).

More generally speaking, it is primarily the community's life together that witnesses to Jesus and, by the same token, exposes and condemns the world, in particular by their love (13:35) and unity (17:21). Such love and unity reveal that they are sharing in God's own life, and, consequently, their rejection and persecution show that the opponents are acting against God. The very judgment that Jesus brought into the world continues through his disciples and elicits the same hatred (7:7).

Jesus has been speaking to them of matters that were not appropriate to share earlier because the time was not right (vv. 4-5). Now he says there are still more things he has to say to them, but they are not yet ready to hear them (v. 12). Their grief makes it hard enough for them to follow what Jesus is saying. But on a deeper level, until the Spirit comes and they receive the new birth they will not be able to understand Jesus or the things of his otherworldly kingdom (3:3; 18:36; cf. 1 Cor 2:10-16). Jesus himself is passing on to them all that he has received from the Father (15:15), but they are not yet able to grasp it.

So the Paraclete will take over as their teacher and will enable them to grasp the richness of the revelation of Jesus. Jesus said earlier that the Paraclete will teach the disciples "all things" by reminding them of "everything I have said to you" (14:26). Now he develops this thought further when he says *the Spirit of truth . . . will guide you into all truth* (v. 13). Such guidance by God's Spirit is mentioned in the Old Testament (Ps 24:5 LXX; 142:10 LXX; Is 43:14 LXX) and is also associated with God's Wisdom (*Wisdom of Solomon* 9:11; 10:10, 17). But although the Spirit guides (*hodēgeō*), it is Jesus who is the way (*hodos*) itself, indeed, the truth itself (14:6). So the Spirit will focus on the Son and *will not speak on his own* but *will speak only what he hears* (v. 13). The Son has done exactly the same with respect to the Father (3:32-34; 7:16-18; 8:26-29, 40; 12:47-50; 14:10; 15:15). The Son has revealed the Father, and now the Spirit will reveal the Father by revealing the Son.

When Jesus says *all truth* he does not appear to be referring to truth in all areas of knowledge, though indeed all truth is God's truth (see comment on 14:46). Rather, the Spirit is going to guide them into all the truth in Jesus, for he is going to glorify Jesus *by taking from what is mine and making it known to you* (v. 14). The reference is to insight regarding the historical ministry of Jesus (cf. 2:22; 12:16; 13:7; Brown 1970:714) and to a deeper understanding of who Jesus is and of his revelation of the Father. For *all that belongs to the Father is mine* (v. 15), and "everything that I have learned from my Father I have made known to you" (15:15). Jesus' knowledge of the Father is complete (cf. also 5:20; 17:10), and he has held back nothing from his disciples.

But the disciples cannot grasp much of this at this point, both because the ultimate revelation has not yet occurred, namely the crucifixion and resurrection and ascension, and because they have not yet entered into the divine life, the eternal life, through the new birth by the Spirit. But when the revelation is complete and when they do receive the Paraclete, he will guide them into all the truth that is in Jesus, which means all the truth of the Father. As always in this Gospel, the Father is the ultimate source and focus (v. 15). The Spirit will focus on the Son, who is focusing on the Father. Jesus' staggering claim to have complete knowledge of God is the foundation for the Christian claim that Jesus is the unique and only way to the Father. But how are we mere mortals to appropriate such knowledge of God? Jesus provides the way by sending the Spirit of God. The "all" of Jesus' revelation is matched by the "all" of the Paraclete's instruction, an instruction that is not merely cerebral, but that involves a sharing of the very life of God.

The passage's focus on Jesus helps us understand what Jesus means when he says the Paraclete *will tell you what is yet to come* (v. 13). This is often taken as a promise that the Paraclete will give the disciples predictions of the future, presumably at least what will take place in and through the church. Such prediction is indeed a divine activity (for example, Is 42:9; 44:7; 46:10; 48:14; see comment on Jn 13:19), but it is probably not what is referred to here since the idea of prediction does not fit this passage. The expression *what is yet to come* is paralleled in the next two verses by the phrase *what is mine,* suggesting the future events have to do with Jesus. The reference would be to the glorification—the crucifixion, resurrection and ascension—which still lies in the future at this point. This complex of events forms the climax of Jesus' revelation and thus will play a central role in the Paraclete's instruction of the disciples; he will glorify Jesus (v. 14) in large measure by declaring to them the truth revealed in Jesus' glorification.

So Jesus' promise is not of new revelation but of insight into the one revelation found in him. Throughout the history of the church, leaders within the church as well as groups on the fringes of Christianity have appealed to this passage to justify new teachings. Any such new teaching must, however, be true to the revelation received in Jesus. The flower will continue to unfold, but it must be the same flower—the genetic code must be the same. The Scriptures, including the apostolic witness of the New Testament, has been the touchstone for this continuity throughout the life of the church. Indeed, the present passage speaks primarily of that apostolic witness, since Jesus is promising this work of the Paraclete to those who have been with him from the beginning (15:27), whom the Paraclete can remind of what Jesus has done and said (14:26). The idea of further revelation to others besides the eleven is not here addressed (cf. Carson 1991:542).

Jesus Predicts Joy and Suffering (16:16-33) The final part of the discourse directs the disciples' attention to what they are about to experience as a result of Jesus' crucifixion and resurrection. Soon their grief will be turned to joy (vv. 16-21) as they see him again (v. 22) and enter into a new level of intimacy in their relationship with the Son and the Father (vv. 23-28). The disciples respond with an affirmation of faith (vv. 29-30), but it is premature, for they have not yet encountered the greatest revelation or the greatest suffering (vv. 31-32). Jesus does not conclude on this down note, but instead he assures them of peace because he has conquered the world (v. 33).

Jesus Promises That After a Little While the Disciples' Grief Will Turn to Joy (16:16-21) Earlier Jesus told the disciples he would be with them only a little longer (13:33) and encouraged them not to mourn. Now he points to the time in the future when their grief will be turned to joy. Earlier Jesus' statements had triggered questions by the disciples (13:36—14:8). His teaching on the Paraclete also raises questions, but instead of asking Jesus what he means, the disciples question one another (vv. 17-18). They want to ask him (v. 19) but hold back. Perhaps they despair of getting an answer that makes any sense. Throughout the Gospel Jesus has spoken cryptically, as he is about to admit (v. 25). And here in the farewell discourse he has piled on more lessons that are beyond their understanding at this point, as he is well aware (v. 12). The word used for *asking* (*zēteō,* v. 19) means to seek. The disciples are seeking insight in the wrong place, for they have no answers to offer one another.

He has been speaking of the Paraclete who will come to them, but he has also spoken of his own coming to them (14:3, 18-19, 23, 28). His focus on his going to the Father, combined with his statement that *in a little while you will see me no more, and then after a little while you will see me* (v. 16), confuses them, especially the phrase a *little while* (*mikron,* v. 18). This Greek word is repeated seven times in these four verses (vv. 16-19), giving it great emphasis. This adds to the disciples' anxiety because they do not know what he is talking about, but it is clear that whatever he is speaking of is imminent. All they know is that something very big is about to happen that involves Jesus' departure from them.

Jesus is referring to his death and resurrection. A number of interpreters think the coming of the Spirit and Jesus' second coming are also included in his meaning, but the context suggests Jesus is describing the climactic events of his revelation, which will indeed literally take place in *a little while*. Jesus has just said that the Paraclete will tell the disciples "what is yet to come," which is a reference to his crucifixion and resurrection (v. 13). Now the explanation he offers (vv. 20-22) indicates that the resurrection will be the point at which he sees them again, the time when he inaugurates for the disciples a qualitatively new life and relationship with God (vv. 23-26).

Jesus' explanation begins with the solemn *I tell you the truth* (v. 20), literally, "amen, amen" (see note 1:51). It is certain that the disciples will *weep and mourn* (v. 20). The word *mourn (thrēneō)* clearly refers to grief at a death (cf. *thrēnos,* "dirge"). Weeping need not refer to grief at a death, but in John it is only used in such a context (11:31, 33; 20:11, 13, 15). Thus, Jesus is referring to the grief they suffer at his death. The world thinks it has conquered its enemy and rejoices. The disciples' grief will only last a little while and then will be turned to joy. The world and the disciples are utterly opposed, which means one will be grieved and the other filled with joy. These responses clarify which "coming" Jesus is referring to. Both the joy of the world and the grief-turned-joy of the disciples are more appropriate in response to Jesus' death and resurrection than in response to the coming of the Spirit or Jesus' second coming.

Before applying his point directly to the disciples Jesus uses an image to interpret their grief and its cause (v. 21). The pain a woman experiences at childbirth is predictable, brief (though it may not feel that way at the time) and followed by joy. It is predictable because it is following an established order. Jesus refers to the time of birth and its pains as her "hour" coming upon her (*hōra;* NIV, *time*). Jesus has spoken throughout this Gospel of his own hour, meaning his death and the resurrection and new life that follows. So the theme of birth pangs and of new life entering the world speaks powerfully of the significance of what is now taking place in him and his disciples.

The disciples might have grasped something of this significance because the image of childbirth is used in the Old Testament to refer to God's actions. In particular it is used, with both its pain and joy, to refer to God's decisive future act of salvation (for example, Is 66:7-14; Brown 1970:731; Beasley-Murray 1987:285-86). Isaiah 26:16-21 even includes reference to resurrection of the dead and mentions the phrase "a little while," which itself is often used in such eschatological material (for example, Is 10:25; Jer 51:33; Beasley-Murray 1987:285-86). Such Old Testament material is also echoed in Jesus' reference to the woman's *anguish*, since that word (*thlipsis*) is often used of the tribulation that will come when God acts decisively (for example, Dan 12:1; Zeph 1:14-15, Brown 1987:285-86). So Jesus' imagery and language speak of God's climactic act of salvation. He is providing an interpretive framework in which the disciples can make sense out of what he and they are about to experience (Jn 16:33). They are in the midst of the event for which so many within Judaism were longing (cf. Lk 2:25, 38; 23:51; 24:21). The pain will be intense but limited. It will be what J. R. R. Tolkien labeled a "eucatastrophe," "the sudden joyous 'turn' " in the midst of catastrophe, which is at the heart of the Gospel story (1965:68-73).

Jesus Describes the Reasons for the Joy That the Disciples Are About to Experience (16:22-28) While the grief is already beginning, the joy is coming, for *I will see you again* (v. 22). Earlier Jesus had said that they would see him (vv. 16, 19), and now he says it is also he who will see them. Such a statement makes it clear that what they see will not be the result of some sort of inner experience with no objective grounds in Jesus himself, though it is not clear whether this is the intention of Jesus' words. At the least it encourages the disciples that they will once again be of interest and concern to him. This restored relationship is the cause of their joy. Because the relationship is secure so is the joy, even in the midst of the suffering that Jesus says is awaiting them (15:18—16:4). There will be those who want to take this joy from the disciples, but they will not be able to do so.

Their joy is primarily rooted in their restored relationship with Jesus, but there will be changes in that relationship. Something of these changes will become clear in the postresurrection encounters, but already Jesus refers to a change in their patterns of asking (vv. 23-26). There are two different Greek words translated *ask* in verse 23. One, *erōtaō*, can be used of asking for something but often is used for asking questions. The other, *aiteō*, usually refers to petitions. The NIV captures this distinction nicely, though the distinction is easily missed if one is not paying attention: *you will no longer ask [erōtaō] me anything. I tell you the truth, my Father will give you whatever you ask [aiteō] in my name.* By adding the words *no longer* (not found in the Greek) the NIV draws out the connection that exists with the context. The disciples have been asking Jesus a lot of questions in the farewell discourse, but they have not been petitioning him. Because *erōtaō* can refer to petitions it is possible that Jesus is only referring to this kind of question. But the context of the disciples' questions, combined with the solemn "amen, amen" that separates the two halves of the verse and the "and" *(kai)* that connects verse 23 to verse 22 (omitted in the NIV), suggests there are two types of asking in view.

Thus the first change of relationship that will be a source of joy is reflected in their no longer needing to ask Jesus questions (v. 23). This does not mean the disciples will have no questions in the future. We believers have plenty of them even now. But the things the disciples have been asking about will become clear once they see the Lord's death and resurrection and receive the help of the Paraclete to sort it all out (cf. 1 Jn 2:20). That is, the disciples will have an understanding of Jesus that gives them the heart of the truth. They may come up with interesting questions, some of which are inappropriate and thus not answered (21:21-22), but they will have all they need to live the divine life now made available.

The second change of relationship will be their sharing in Jesus' work

---

16:25 Jesus' promise to speak *plainly* to the disciples echoes God's description of how he speaks to Moses (Num 12:8). Jesus' assurance to his disciples is relevant to his controversy with his Jewish opponents: they have rejected Jesus, including his claims to deity, on the

as his friends (vv. 23-24). This is the reality behind Jesus' reference to asking the Father in his name (cf. 14:13; 15:7, 15). They have not asked in his name up to this point because they have not dwelt in him and he has not dwelt in them. This will soon change, and then they will share in the eternal life that Jesus has with the Father, which includes being taken into the work of God in the world. Such prayer is based on the love that is obedience (15:7-17; 1 Jn 3:22) and therefore is directed toward God's will being done and not toward one's own will apart from God (1 Jn 5:14-15). This work is the same as seen in Jesus and as described in regard to the Paraclete, namely, the revelation of the love of God in word and deed. This revelation will be manifest in each disciple's life and especially in the quality of life of the community as a whole. John later promotes such life in the community through sharing in the life that has been revealed, which brings fullness of joy (1 Jn 1:1-4).

These two types of asking, then, speak of the new intimacy with God that the disciples are about to experience. The communication will go both directions. The disciples will be able to hear from God with understanding, and they will be able to pray to God in accord with his own purposes (cf. Michaels 1989:287). The key to both types of communication is listening. Unless the disciple listens he or she will neither receive the insight into Jesus and his revelation nor be able to enter into God's purposes in prayer. Thus, at the center of the disciples' intimacy with God is the humility depicted throughout this Gospel. This humility is a docility and openness toward God that receives life from God and all the outworkings of that divine, eternal life.

Jesus then expounds on these aspects of the coming intimacy, returning first to the theme of future insight and knowledge. He says he has been *speaking figuratively* (v. 25). He is not referring merely to the image of the woman in childbirth (v. 21), but to the general cast of most of his teaching throughout the Gospel. His subject has always been the Father. Even when he has spoken of himself it has been as the Son who is revealing the Father. Jesus has said that his opponents' inability to understand him is due to their lack of faith and their alienation from God. But his own disciples have had

---

basis of their loyalty to Moses, but Jesus is saying his disciples will experience what Moses himself experienced—with Jesus himself in the role of God.

a hard time keeping up also, as Jesus has recognized (6:60-69; 16:12). Jesus has promised to them the Paraclete, who will instruct them (14:26; 15:26; 16:13-15), but now he says that he himself will also speak to them (16:25). Because Jesus has been speaking of his resurrection, this plain speaking could refer to his teaching after his resurrection and before his ascension. But the references to prayer in his name (vv. 23-24, 26) extend beyond the resurrection period, so this further instruction probably does so as well. But if the Son himself will continue to teach the disciples, then it seems that, although the Son and the Paraclete are distinct from one another, the presence of Jesus with the disciples will be mediated by the Paraclete (see comment on 14:16, 23-28). Jesus' teaching will become clear to the disciples because the revelation will be complete, with the cross and resurrection giving the deepest insight into Jesus' identity and the significance of his ministry. But even these climactic events would not be clear without the new birth through the Spirit that enables them to share (as much as is possible for human beings) in the very life of God that Jesus shares (17:21-23). Thus, these verses speak of Jesus' resurrection and the new life there begun.

Jesus returns to the theme of asking in his name (v. 26; cf. vv. 23-24), adding a very powerful point. Asking in his name is not a matter of their asking him and then his asking the Father on their behalf. He is indeed a paraclete before the Father (1 Jn 2:1) and the one who intercedes (Rom 8:34; Heb 7:25). But such texts "deal not with petitionary prayer but with the status of the Christian before God, a status which rests entirely upon the eternal consequences of the priestly work of Christ" (Barrett 1978:496). The very fact that Jesus is our mediator means we have direct access in him to the Father. So in him we can pray to the Father, and at the same time Jesus himself prays for us. He prayed for Peter (Lk 22:32), and we will hear in the next chapter his amazing prayer for the apostles, and all disciples, spoken as if he were already in heaven.

The fact that we need a mediator could imply that the Father is aloof or hateful toward us. But Jesus makes it clear that such is not the case. Jesus need not pass on our requests to the Father, "for" (*gar,* left out of the NIV) *the Father himself loves you* (v. 27)—here we have the key revelation of the whole Gospel in a bumper sticker. Everything Jesus has been about reveals this Father and this love.

The reason the Father loves the disciples is because they have loved Jesus and believed he came from God. This does not mean God's love is dependent on our initiative or that it is not universal (see comment on 14:21). "We love because he first loved us" (1 Jn 4:19). This speaks instead of the fulfillment of that love in those who love and believe in the Son. Both the love and the belief are significant. The Son must be received as he is in truth, as the one who has come from God. John must deal later, in his first letter, with those who claim to know and love the Father and the Son but who do not receive the Son as he truly is. Neither love for a Christ of human invention nor a mere correct rational assessment of Jesus are in view here. A right relationship includes both the right understanding of who Jesus is and an attachment of love.

If the crucial revelation of the Father is his love, the key revelation of the Son is his relation to the Father, summarized in the fact that he has come from God (cf. 1 Jn 4:14, 16). Jesus unpacks this core affirmation in a four-line chiasm (v. 28; cf. Brown 1970:725):

A *I came from the Father*

   B *and entered the world*

   B' *now I am leaving the world*

A' *and going back to the Father*

This chiasm connects the belief the disciples already have—that Jesus came from the Father—to the point that has been causing them grief—his return to the Father. The chiasm's focus is the Son's relation to the Father and his mission to the world: his incarnation and ascension are viewed in the first and last lines in relation to the Father and in the middle lines in relation to the world (Brown 1970:725). This statement is "at once a summary of Johannine Christology and the heart of this Gospel" (Beasley-Murray 1987:287).

Thus, in verses 27 and 28 we have the fundamental grounds for the climactic salvation Jesus has been speaking about. At the heart of this salvation is the Father's love, the relation between the Father and the Son and the Son's entrance into the world. On the human side the response that brings one into intimacy with God is love and faith toward the Son as sent from God. The centrality of this view of Jesus as the one sent from God has been evident throughout the Gospel (especially 8:42-47) and is seen again in its repetition by the disciples (16:30) and its affirmation by Jesus in his concluding prayer (17:8).

Jesus Prepares the Disciples for Their Imminent Desertion of Him
(16:29-33) Jesus has promised to speak plainly, and the disciples think he
has now done so (v. 29). The climactic affirmation in verses 27-28 is indeed
quite clear. Jesus has just said that they believe that he has come from God
(v. 27), and they affirm that faith, basing it on their knowledge *(oidamen,*
"we know"; NIV, *we can see)* that *you know all things and that you do not
even need to have anyone ask you questions* (v. 30). Their reference to
questions may seem backward. If someone knows something, then we
would say he or she does not need to *ask* questions. The idea here, however,
is that "the ability to anticipate questions and not to need to be asked is a
mark of the divine" (Brown 1970:725-26; cf. Mt 6:8; Josephus *Antiquities of
the Jews* 6.230). As the one sent from God, Jesus' knowledge is complete;
thus one can trust him and not fret over the questions one might have. His
revelation has validated his claim to be the one sent from God. Our
knowledge of his identity grounds our faith in him, both in the sense of
belief about him and trust in him.

Earlier, in the face of very cryptic teaching, Peter had made essentially
the same statement: "We believe and know that you are the Holy One of
God" (6:69). Despite this affirmation the disciples have been full of
questions until now, when they think they finally get it. But they have not
yet seen the cross, and therefore they do not yet know the Father's heart
of love revealed in the laying down of the Son's life. So in fact their
expression of knowledge reveals their ignorance. How often even today,
with the new birth and the Spirit, we think we have something figured out,
only to have God reveal to us yet further riches about himself and the life
he shares with us.

So Jesus, in his love for them, must give them a reality check. His
statement *You believe at last!* (v. 31) could actually be a question, "Now
you believe?" But Jesus is not doubting their faith. Instead he is telling
them they have not yet taken the final exam for this course, so their
celebrations are premature. Their faith will be tested and deepened
enormously in the next few days. Everyone of them, without exception,
will be scattered (v. 32; cf. Zech 13:7). John himself will return to Jesus
and be at the cross, but he, like Peter, will not remain close enough to
Jesus to be in harm's way (see comments on 18:12-14; cf. Carson
1991:549). They will all be scattered until they are gathered again beyond

the cross by the resurrected one, after the "little while."

They will all abandon Jesus, but the Father will still be with him (v. 32). How does this correspond to Jesus' cry of abandonment on the cross, "My God, my God, why have you forsaken me?" (Mt 27:46; Mk 15:34)? When Jesus took our sin upon himself on the cross, he who had always known complete intimacy with the Father experienced, for the first time, the gulf that separates God from sin, light from darkness. But something deeper was also at work. This abandonment and its experience do not mean Jesus lacked faith in God. In fact, the cry of abandonment is a quote from the beginning of Psalm 22, "and the whole meaning of the Psalm is that God does not desert His suffering servants" (Hoskyns 1940b:582). His cry expresses both the reality of what he was undergoing and his faith in its outcome. If Abraham could offer up Isaac in the hope of resurrection (Gen 22; Heb 11:17-19), how much more could Jesus have confidence in God, whom he knew far better than Abraham did, and in the power of God's life, which he understood far better than Abraham did. Rather than contradicting the Synoptic accounts, Jesus' statement in verse 32 helps us interpret them correctly (cf. Hoskyns 1940b:582).

While Jesus must warn the disciples that the suffering is far from over, he does not end on that note. Now, as he has throughout the farewell discourse, Jesus warns them ahead of time so they will be prepared. He has told them not to let their hearts be troubled (14:1) but to receive his peace (14:27). This peace, as he now emphasizes (v. 33), is found in him, not in the world. The world will give them *trouble,* that is, the opposition that comes from those who are in rebellion against God (*thlipsis;* cf. v. 21). But they can *take heart* because he has *overcome* the world; he has met it in battle and conquered it *(nenikēka).* The theme of conflict has been present throughout the Gospel, since the beginning of the prologue (1:5), but this is the only place this word occurs. The peace and salvation spoken of throughout the Gospel all depend on his having conquered. His conquest, in turn, enables the disciples themselves to conquer the evil one, as John stresses in his first letter (1 Jn 2:13-14; 4:4; 5:4-5; cf. Rev 2:7, 11, 17, 26; 3:5, 12, 21; 21:7). Thus, this is indeed a fitting line for the conclusion of Jesus' teaching.

Until death itself becomes a revelation of God the disciples can be troubled in the world, the place of death. Their joy cannot be stable and secure until they see him again (v. 16, 19) and he sees them (v. 22). Then will they reap the benefits of his conquest by becoming one with him as he pours out the Spirit. They will not ask him, but rather they will be one with him, asking the Father in his name. So their joy will be full—the joy of union with God in Christ by the Spirit. They will know God's glory and will manifest his glory as they, in union with the living Christ by the Spirit, bear fruit as Jesus did, asking for what Jesus did. Their focus and source will be God, and thus they will have peace no matter what the world may throw at them.

Jesus Concludes His Time Alone with His Disciples by Praying to His Father (17:1-26) This chapter contains the most extensive and profound prayer of Jesus we have. When Jesus prayed at Lazarus's tomb he made it clear that he had no need of expressing prayer because he is one with God in his whole life, the union true prayer expresses. Nevertheless, he prayed for the benefit of those present (11:41-42), and the same is true here as well (17:13). Jesus' whole life has been a revelation of the Father, based on Jesus' union with him, so it is appropriate that his teaching concludes in the form of prayer, the genre most closely associated with union with God. Other farewell discourses also conclude with prayers (for example, *4 Ezra* 8:19b-36; Beasley-Murray 1987:293), but in Jesus' case prayer is itself related to the essence of his message.

As Jesus turns to address the Father his speech implies that he is taken up into the eternal presence (cf. Brown 1970:747). He speaks as if his work were already complete (for example, v. 4). Indeed, he even says, "I am no longer in this world" (v. 11, completely obscured in the NIV). But right after that he says, *I say these things while I am still in the world* (v. 13). He is right there with his disciples just before his death, but he is praying from the realm of eternity. Just as the book of Revelation reveals from a heavenly perspective the certainty of God's unfolding will, so this prayer of Jesus shows that he is completely confident in the outworking of that will.

Jesus' intercession for his disciples from within God's presence antici-pates his role after his ascension (cf. 1 Jn 2:1). Because this intercession corresponds to the role of the high priest elsewhere in the New Testament (Rom 8:34; Heb 7:25-26) and because Jesus uses sacrificial language when he refers to sanctifying himself (17:19), this prayer has been known as the High Priestly Prayer. In the fifth century Cyril of Alexandria saw these two activities as fitting for the one who is "our great and all-holy High Priest" (*In John* 11.8).

This chapter completes the chiasm of the farewell discourse spelled out in 13:31-35, with a return to the glory mentioned in 13:31-32 (see comment on 13:31). This passage concentrates on the relation of the Father and the Son and the glory they share. The Father is seen as the one who "gives" (used thirteen times of the Father in this chapter), highlighting his grace and his role as source of all. Jesus focuses specifically on the Father's gift to the Son of disciples. The Son continues to show himself to be the revealer sent from the Father, but he is seen also as a giver—he gives his disciples the Father's word, glory and eternal life.

This prayer gathers many of the key themes found throughout the Gospel. Indeed, "almost every verse contains echoes" (Dodd 1953:417). The Son's work in the disciples is developed through the themes of faith, knowledge, love, indwelling, oneness and God's name. There is also an emphasis on the world, including its separation from God, God's love for it and the disciples' mission to it.

As with much of the farewell discourse, this material is complex and can be outlined in several ways (cf. Brown 1970:748-51; Beasley-Murray 1987:295-96). Jesus begins with a petition for the glorification of the Father and the Son (vv. 1-5), after which he prays for the disciples gathered around him, first describing their situation (vv. 6-11) and then praying that they be protected and sanctified by God (vv. 11-19). Jesus then prays for all who will become believers through the witness of the eleven, that they may share in the divine oneness (vv. 20-24). He concludes with a summary of his past and future work (vv. 25-26).

Jesus Prays for the Glorification of the Father and the Son (17:1-5) Jesus begins his prayer where his keynote address began, with the relationship between the Father and the Son (5:19-23). The oneness-yet-distinctness continues here as Jesus "lifts up his eyes toward heaven" (v. 1, obscured in the NIV) to the Father who is distinct from him and to whom he is obedient.

In his prayer Jesus will speak of the past and the future from an eternal perspective, but it is all grounded in the present, at this particular climactic point in salvation history: *Father, the time* ["hour," *hōra*] *has come* (v. 1). This hour has cast its shadow over the whole story (2:4; 7:6, 8, 30; 8:20), and its arrival has already been signaled (12:23), with its implications for glory (12:27-28), judgment (12:31-32) and Jesus' return to the Father (13:1). Jesus now addresses the theme of glory, asking the Father to glorify the Son so that the Son may glorify the Father (v. 1). Thus, even in asking on behalf of himself his ultimate goal and delight is the Father. In general, to glorify someone means to hold him or her up for honor and praise. So on one level the Son is asking that his own honor be revealed, namely, that he is one with God; Jesus in turn will glorify the Father as he continues to reveal him as one worthy of all praise and worship. In John, however, glorification also has a more specific meaning: the death of the Son of God. Throughout the Gospel, Jesus has revealed the Father's glory by manifesting his characteristic gracious love. In the death of the Son this same love is revealed most profoundly, for God is love, and love is the laying down of one's life (cf. 1 Jn 4:8, 16; 3:16). Thus, in his death Jesus will reveal his own character and his Father's character to be gracious love.

In verse 2 Jesus expands this request for glorification, though following his exact train of thought requires careful attention. According to the NIV, Jesus' request for his glorification is grounded on *(for)* the *authority* that the Father already gave him over *all people (pasēs sarkos,* "all flesh"). But *for (kathōs)* could also be translated "just as," indicating that the previous granting of authority is not the grounds for the glorification, but, rather, comparable to the glorification. We will soon see reason to prefer this alternative.

What *authority* is Jesus referring to? Earlier in the Gospel Jesus spoke of his *authority* from the Father to give life and to judge (5:20-27). Now he is speaking of the role the Father gave the Son as agent of creation. While "all flesh" commonly means "all people," the expression can also mean "all life on earth" (for example, Gen 7:15-16, 21; Alford 1980:875), which would be in keeping with the Son's being the one through whom "all things were made" (1:3).

The last part of verse 2 refers to the Son's giving *eternal life to all those*

17:2 The second use of *all* is the word *pan,* a neuter singular. This form has the effect of stressing the group as a whole, a significant nuance in the light of the emphasis on unity later in the chapter. This word is set alongside the masculine plural pronoun *autois,* which *you have given to him.* The NIV takes this as the purpose *(that)* of the Father's granting Jesus *authority over all people.* This is possible grammatically, but it does not do justice to the distinctions between the two halves of the verse. It is better to take the second half of verse 2 as parallel to *that your Son may glorify you* in verse 1. In other words, the Son will glorify the Father through giving eternal life to those the Father gives him. And the Father's glorification of the Son is in keeping with his having given him authority over all flesh.

Thus, the flow is from creation to new creation. In both cases the Father is the ultimate source, and the Son is God's agent. The Son has given life to all creation, and now it is time for him to give eternal life to those within creation given him by God. As with the Son, so with the disciples—the Father is their source (cf. 6:37, 39; 10:29; 17:6; 18:9). He gives them to the Son, and the Son gives them eternal life. The Father acts while they are still dead (cf. Eph 2:1-10); all is of his grace. Both divine sovereignty and human responsibility have been stressed throughout this Gospel, but there is never any doubt that all depends on the Father's grace. "In the contrast between *all flesh* and *whatsoever thou hast given* is expressed the inevitable tragedy of the mercy of God; it is offered to all, but received by the few, and those the elect" (Hoskyns 1940b:590; cf. H. C. G. Moule 1908:32-36).

Jesus pauses to reflect on the meaning of the term *eternal life* (v. 3). This verse is commonly viewed as a parenthetical statement added by John, like a footnote (Barrett 1978:503). But it flows quite naturally even when understood as Jesus' comment on what he has just said, much as verses 6-8 will comment on verse 4. Jesus' reference to himself in the third person seems strange, but the Old Testament contains examples (e.g., 2 Sam 7:20). The phrase *only true God* is not attributed to Jesus elsewhere, but it is similar to John's own language (1 Jn 5:20). Likewise, nowhere else does Jesus refer to himself as *Jesus Christ,* but this expression is very common outside the Gospels. Indeed, this double reference to the one true God and to Jesus is similar to texts in Paul contrasting the Christian faith with pagan polytheism and idolatry (1 Thess 1:9-10; 1 Cor 8:6). So the language probably comes from a later date (though cf. Mt 11:27). Most scholars today would say the

reflects the individuals of which this group is composed. So verse 2b reads, "that he might give eternal life to them *(autois),* namely, the whole group *(pan)* that you have given him."

thought itself is from the later church, but this begs the question of Jesus' identity and how much of the later church's understanding derives from Jesus himself (cf. C. F. D. Moule 1977). B. F. Westcott is probably closer to the truth when he says John is giving "in conventional language (so to speak) the substance of what the Lord said probably at greater length" (1908:2:244). Such is the case throughout this Gospel.

The Son's ultimate mission is to give eternal life, that is, knowledge of the Father and the Son (v. 3). "The notion that knowledge of God is essential to life (salvation) is common to Hebrew and Hellenistic thought," though knowledge does not mean the same thing in every source (Barrett 1978:503). For John, this knowledge is closely associated with faith (which enables the appropriation of eternal life; 6:47; 20:31) and includes correct intellectual understanding, moral alignment through obedience and the intimacy of union (cf. Dodd 1953:151-69). That is, it refers to shared life, and because it is the life of God that is shared it is eternal life. *Eternal (aiōnios)* means unending or timeless, but it refers to not just the quantity but also a certain quality of life. In Hebrew *eternal life* is literally "life of eternity, age" (*ḥayyê ʿôlâm*, Dan 12:2), a expression used in contrast to temporal life and also in the contrast between this age and the age to come. Indeed, the word *eternal* is related to the word "age" *(aiōn)*. This association with the age to come is most significant in John. For in Jewish thought, life in the age to come is characterized by a restored relationship with God, and that is precisely what Jesus speaks of here. The life of the age to come is already present in Jesus and made available to his disciples, and at the heart of it is an intimate relation with God. "The only life is participation in God, and we do this by knowing God and enjoying his goodness" (Irenaeus *Against Heresies* 4.20.5).

This stress on knowledge sounds Gnostic. In a sense it is, and early Christians believed they had the true knowledge, as opposed to that which is "falsely called knowledge" *(tēs pseudōnymou gnōseōs,* 1 Tim 6:20). Clement of Alexandria (died in A.D. 220), for example, constantly referred to Christians as the true gnostics, and his view of knowledge at core was very much in keeping with our verse. While some of the language and thought of this Gospel is similar to Gnosticism in its various forms (for which see Rudolph 1992), the fact that this knowledge comes through the historical deeds of Jesus, the incarnate Son of God, that it is grounded in faith, that it is available already now within history and that it is not concerned with self-knowledge and cosmic speculation sets it off from Gnosticism itself (cf. Schmitz and Schütz 1976:403-5). Any revealed religion will be gnostic—the issue is whether the knowledge claimed is true or false.

The statement in verse 3 is also strikingly similar in form to the central affirmation of Islam, "There is no god but Allah, and Mohammed is his Prophet." Both religions claim to honor the *only true God,* a theme from the Old Testament as well (e.g., Ex 34:6 LXX; Is 37:20), and both speak of the great revealer of God. But they differ radically in what is said of this revealer. Jesus *is* a prophet—indeed, the revealer of God par excellence. But this verse, in keeping with the whole of this Gospel, says Jesus is far more than just a prophet. For eternal life is not just a knowledge of God as revealed by the Son; it includes a knowledge of the Son himself. Thus he shares in deity, since "the knowledge of God *and a creature* could not be eternal life" (Alford 1980:875). This amazing statement, therefore, affirms both the equality of the Son with the Father and his subordination as son and as the one sent.

Jesus has prayed that he might glorify God in the future, but now he speaks of the glorification of the Father he has already accomplished in his ministry (v. 4). His work is not complete before his death (10:18; 19:28, 30), but he says, "I glorified [*edoxasa,* aorist] you on earth, having completed [*teleiōsas,* aorist] the work. . . ." The NIV translation is grammatically possible, but it misses the eternal, confident perspective evident in Jesus' statement that his work is already over. The glorification of the Father has been the distinguishing feature of his life throughout the Gospel, a glory characterized by grace and truth (1:14). The work was given to him by the Father. So the character of the works revealed the character of him who gave them to the Son to do, and in this way the words and deeds of Jesus revealed the Father's glory. But also in the Son's obedience itself is seen the glory of God, since his humility, obedience and sacrifice reflect the love that is the laying down of one's life.

Having prayed for the glorification of the cross and its provision of life (vv. 1-2) and having mentioned the glorification evident in his ministry (v. 4), Jesus concludes with yet another aspect of the glory: *And now, Father, glorify me in your presence with the glory I had with you before the world began* (v. 5). Here language used of Wisdom (Prov 8:23; Wisdom of

Solomon 7:25; Brown 1970:754) is taken up by the incarnate one, who is about to die. Glory now seems to refer to the shining splendor of the divine presence, the "unapproachable light" that Paul mentions (1 Tim 6:16). Nevertheless, it still retains the element of love. For the Son is asking that, through the glorification of the cross, resurrection and ascension, he may return to where he was before, beside *(para;* NIV, *with)* the Father (cf. vv. 2, 24; 1:18, H. C. G. Moule 1908:40-42). The ineffable mystery of the loving unity of the Godhead is here revealed to us once again.

Jesus Begins His Prayer for the Eleven Disciples by Describing Their Situation (17:6-11) The opening verses have focused on the glory of the Father and the Son, but they have also included the disciples, and to them Jesus now turns more directly. He comments on his work among them, their response and the relation they now have with the Father and the Son in contrast to the world's.

As in verse 4, Jesus again speaks as if his ministry is complete: "I revealed [*ephanerōsa,* aorist] your name [cf. NIV margin] to those whom you gave me out of the world" (v. 6). Revealing the name could point specifically to Jesus' use of the I AM (Dodd 1953:417; Brown 1970:755-56), but in any case it certainly means to make manifest the person and character of God (cf. 1:12). Thus, revealing the name is similar to revealing the glory, and, like the glorification, it will not be complete before Jesus' death. The manifestation through teaching has been completed, but the climactic revelation through death and resurrection yet remains.

The disciples were given to Jesus by the Father from the world, another reference to the amazing grace of God. The Father is the ultimate agent in the disciples' lives just as he is in Jesus' life. Jesus states the pattern of relations very succinctly: *They were yours; you gave them to me and they have obeyed your word* (v. 6). What does it mean that they were God's? Some would see here a reference to predestination (Barrett 1978:505)—they were the Father's through "the eternity of election" (Calvin 1959:139). But Paul, who develops this specific theme, writes that the election "before the creation of the world" is in Christ (Eph 1:4). If our text referred to this election it would seem to drive a wedge between the Father and the pre-existent Son, a false inference from this text (vv. 9-10; cf. Chrysostom *In John* 81.1; Augustine *In John* 106.5). Jesus is probably speaking not of an eternal relation but of a relation within salvation history, that is, the relation the disciples had with God through the covenant with Israel (Westcott 1908:2:246; Ridderbos 1997:551-52). Those true Israelites (1:47), who had an affinity with God (8:47), were already God's and were awaiting his Messiah, who would bring them to the fulfillment of that relationship. The Father gave them to the Son for this purpose; and through their faith and obedience, as they were drawn by God to the Son and his teaching (6:44-45, 60-66), they demonstrated that they were God's. This relationship is about to be changed radically, for the disciples are now on the brink of the birth from above. Thus, the disciples were already of the Father—there was an affinity—just as the opponents were of their father, the devil (8:42-47). This interpretation leads us to ask why some had (and have) an affinity for God and some do not, why some, but not others, have hardness of heart that alienates them from the life of God (cf. Eph 4:18). Since both divine grace and human responsibility are mentioned together in this Gospel, the answer probably lies in some combination of the two, a combination that eludes our full understanding.

The point here, however, is that true Israelites whom God has shepherded have been handed over by him to Jesus, and the sheep have recognized his voice and have received Jesus as come from God. In doing so *they have obeyed* ["kept," *tetērēkan*] *your word* (v. 6). This is the only such reference in John to keeping the Father's word. Most interpreters think this refers to keeping Jesus' word, which is God's word. Jesus will speak of that soon (vv. 8, 14), but here he is probably saying that the disciples obeyed the Father's voice, which was drawing them to Jesus, and that Jesus in turn passed on to them the revelation of the Father.

Jesus does then address the disciples' response to himself (vv. 7-8). These disciples, who are of God and are given by God to the Son, have been able to recognize and receive as from the Father all that the Son has received from the Father and passed on to them (v. 7). The specific reference is to Jesus' teaching, which they have received. Jesus' words are God's words, and these bring life and judgment (3:34; 6:63, 68; 12:48; 14:24; 17:14). Thus, Jesus' teaching has been grounded on his own identity as the Son sent from the Father. Accordingly, these disciples have been given *to the Son;* the focus is on him and their acceptance of him. They knew for certain that he came from the Father, and they believed that the Father sent him. So they knew and believed the truth about both the Son and the Father in their mutual relation.

Jesus picks up the affirmation spoken by disciples (16:30) just minutes before he began his prayer. Their knowledge and faith are not as complete as they think it is, but Jesus affirms they have reached a decisive point. They have believed in him and hung in with him, even when most of his followers abandoned him (6:60-69). There is still an enormous amount they do not know, and Jesus told them as much when he promised them the Paraclete to instruct them (14:26; 16:13). But the foundation has been laid, and it is secure. They have been receptive, the fundamental attitude of a true disciple, and now they have grasped the crux of the revelation—the identity of the Son in relation to the Father. The grace of revelation has been met with by human response of humble openness, faith and obedience. Jesus' affirmation of these disciples should be tremendously encouraging to present-day disciples. Here we see God's acceptance of believers despite their great ignorance and weakness.

The disciples' relation to God has enabled them to recognize the Son and believe in him. It is for these believers—and not the world, which has rejected Jesus—that he is now praying (v. 9). Jesus' frank statement *I am not praying for the world* may sound as though he has nothing to do with the world, and it has even led some to think he only ever prays for the elect (Calvin 1959:140-41). But, in fact, he does go on to pray for the world (vv. 21, 23)! So here he means the petitions that follow about protection, sanctification and union with God are prayers only for the disciples (cf. Alford 1980:877). None of these petitions are applicable to the world, to the system and those beings in rebellion against God. Since it is through the disciples' witness that the world will continue to be challenged with God's love and call, Jesus' prayer for his disciples is actually an indirect prayer for the world (Beasley-Murray 1987:298).

Jesus repeats his earlier description of the disciples (v. 6) but changes it subtly. These disciples are those the Father has given the Son—*for they are yours*. They were the Father's before he gave them to the Son, and they remain the Father's after he gives them to the Son. The next verse (v. 10) explains how this can be: *All I have is yours, and all you have is mine.* Here is the fundamental truth of this Gospel—the oneness of the Father and the Son—expressed in terms of possession. The disciples' very relations with the Father and Son bear witness to this foundational truth. They have been given to the Son and yet remain the Father's because of the divine oneness.

Here, as throughout this Gospel, Jesus' deeds and words make no sense unless one realizes he is God. Indeed, this very statement bears witness to this claim. For anyone can, and should, truthfully say to the Father, *all I have is yours.* But the reverse, *all you have is mine*—"this can no creature say before God" (Alford 1980:878). The *glory* that Jesus says *has come to* him *through them* comes from both the Father and the disciples. In the Father's giving the disciples to Jesus, the Father bore witness to this relation of oneness; and the disciples, who were of the Father, recognized him and believed in him.

So we see that the mutual glorification between the Father and the Son for which the Son is praying (v. 1) has already occurred on one level. But now Jesus looks to the time when the Son is taken from them and they are left in the world (v. 11a). The relation that has begun must now be maintained in this new situation; and the glory that has begun must come to completion in divine oneness (v. 22) and then eventually, in yet another stage, in the fullness of the revelation of the glory of Son (v. 24). The world and the evil one would like to thwart these plans, so Jesus now turns to pray for his disciples in the situation they are about to face.

Jesus Prays for the Eleven Disciples (17:11-19) Jesus prays first for God to protect the disciples by his name, which he has given to Jesus (v. 11; the NIV adds *power*). Many interpret this as referring to Jesus' revelation of the Father, and therefore the petition is that they remain loyal to what Jesus has revealed of God (for example, Beasley-Murray 1987:299). This is certainly true, and, indeed, Jesus' very address to God in this verse, *Holy Father,* captures much of that revelation. While God is commonly known as the Holy One, the expression *Holy Father* is not found anywhere else in the Bible. Holiness refers to divine otherness, the realm of the divine in contrast to the mundane. Thus, this phrase captures beautifully God's "purity and tenderness" (Westcott 1908:2:250), the "transcendence and intimacy characteristic of Jesus' personal attitude to God and of his teaching about God" (Beasley-Murray 1987:299).

But more is involved than just the revelation of God, for the goal of keeping them in the Father's name is *that they may be one as we are one* (v. 11). This oneness, as will be made clear soon (vv. 21-23), is not merely a unity of thought among those who receive the teaching of Jesus. It is a matter of shared life. So *name* here refers not just to the revelation, but to the reality that has been revealed—the Father himself. The *name* is the point of contact between Christ and his disciples in the Father. "God's Name is His revelation of Himself" (Lloyd 1936: 230). When he says (again speaking from an eternal perspective) *while I was with them, I protected them and kept them safe by that name you gave me* (v. 12), he is referring to the protection they had by his own divine presence among them as the I AM. Jesus is asking God to continue to protect them by his powerful presence, a presence that will be mediated by himself and the Spirit, as he has taught in the farewell discourse (13:31—17:26).

If Jesus protected them, why did Judas fall away into *destruction* (v. 12)? Judas's failure to find life would raise questions for the disciples about Jesus' ability to protect them. Jesus points to two explanations for what happened to Judas. First, his action fulfilled the scriptural pattern of the enemy of the righteous sufferer (for example, Ps 41:9, which was referred to in Jn 13:18 regarding Judas). This does not mean Judas was locked into some deterministic plan but rather "Jesus knew himself to be one with, and had to go the way of, the threatened people of God in the world to fulfill their God-given task" (Ridderbos 1997:553-54). Thus, Jesus finds an assurance in the Scripture of the same sort he is offering his disciples, for they also are the threatened people of God.

The other explanation regarding Judas concerns Judas's own character as "the son of destruction" (NIV, *the one doomed to destruction*). While this expression can have the sense of indicating one's destiny, as the NIV takes it (cf. Beasley-Murray 1987:299), its basic idea is "to denote one who shares in this thing or who is worthy of it, or who stands in some other close relation to it" (Bauer, Gingrich and Danker 1979:834). In Ephesians, for example, the expression "sons of disobedience" (2:2, RSV) is explained in terms of actions that flow from an inner disposition (2:3). So also here the reference is primarily to Judas's own character. The text reads, literally, "no one was destroyed *[apōleto]* except the son of destruction *[apōleias]*." Judas had heard the words and seen the deeds and even been the recipient of special signs of love from Jesus (see comment on 13:26), but in his heart he was not of the Father (cf. 17:6) and so did not receive with humility, faith and obedience the one sent from the Father. When one rejects the offer of life one is left only with destruction. The tree became known by its fruit. Jesus offered life to Judas, but he did not force Judas to accept it, for he does not force anyone's acceptance (cf. Chrysostom *In John* 81.2). The disciples have confidence because this same offer is made to them, as it is to everyone, and they have responded and received. Jesus is saying these things in the world, that is, in the arena of conflict, so that his disciples can have *the full measure of* his *joy within them* (v. 13). This joy comes from total confidence in the Father and in his protection as well as in the intimate communion with him such as Judas lacked.

While he was with the disciples Jesus kept and guarded them (v. 12) and gave them God's word (v. 14). This is the word that both comes from God and is about God. The same expression was used earlier (v. 6) to refer to the Father's own word, but here it is his word as expressed through Jesus (cf. vv. 7-8). This word of God sets them apart from the world and causes the world to hate them, *for they are not of the world any more than I am of the world* (v. 14), a point he repeats for emphasis (v. 16). Again, Jesus is speaking from the eternal perspective, for the disciples' removal from the world is not complete until they have received the birth from above (1:13; 3:3-8). Already they are hated by the world because of their association with Jesus, and the world's hatred will only increase as their association becomes union.

Having spoken of what he has done for the disciples while with them Jesus returns to his request that the Father keep them (v. 11b), which he now specifies in two ways. First, this protection is to be in the midst of the world, not through removal from it (v. 15). In their identification with Jesus they draw upon themselves the world's hatred of him, but they also share in his mission to the world, as will be spelled out shortly (v. 18). Second, the protection is *from the evil one* (v. 15). Behind this world, which hates them, is the evil one, for "the whole world is under the control of the evil one" (1 Jn 5:19). The warfare motif runs throughout Scripture (cf. Boyd 1997) and is fundamental in Jesus' own understanding of reality.

Although Jesus is about to complete his work of salvation, God's warfare with the world will continue. Neither the Father nor the Son is going to abandon the world; rather they will continue to engage it, confront it and call it to repentance. "The disciples' place in the world is not something that they can give up because the world is not something that God can give up" (Ridderbos 1997:558). In some Christian circles today there is a healthy sense of this antagonism between the world and the people of God, though sometimes believers need to bring to this antagonism more of God's love for the world. Also, some forms of monasticism can be a direct contradiction to the Lord's will as it is expressed here, though at its best monasticism is a confrontation with the world. In other Christian circles this view of the world is unpopular, for there human culture is seen as an expression of God's word through his immanent Spirit. While God is active in culture, this latter view often leads to new revelations that contradict the revelation in Jesus and in the Scriptures as the Spirit has instructed the church. A passage such as the present one has "a message for an era that becomes naively optimistic about changing the world or even about affirming its values without change" (Brown 1970:764).

Jesus' second great petition is that the Father *sanctify* the disciples (v. 17). Sanctifying is not the same as the cleansing (13:10; 15:3), but it is related to the pruning (15:2). The word used here *(hagiazō)* is related to the word "holy" *(hagios)* that Jesus has just used of the Father (v. 11). It means to consecrate, to set apart. It is used for the preparation necessary for entering the presence of God (Ex 19:10, 22) and for the commissioning for a divine task, for example, that of a priest (Ex 28:41; 40:13) or a prophet (Jer 1:5; Sirach 49:7). The whole people of God are set apart for God as a holy nation (Ex 19:6), answering the call to be holy as God is holy (Lev 11:44), in contrast to the foreign nations (2 Macc 1:25-26; 3 Macc 6:3). All three of these nuances are relevant to Jesus' prayer. This sanctification is *by the truth,* that is, God's *word.* Such is a common thought in Jewish sources (Schnackenburg 1982:185), but here this *word* is Jesus' revelation of God in word and deed (cf. 15:3). Jesus is himself the Word (1:1), as he is the truth (14:6). God's word and truth correspond to what has already been referred to in this prayer as God's glory and name. They are all manifestations of God that point to and actually enable contact with him in and through Jesus. As the disciples share in God's glory (v. 22) and are in his name (v. 11), so here this sanctification means being drawn "into the truth, into the unity between Father and Son, and into salvation in such a way that the Father's being, his holiness, permeates them" (Tolmie 1995:225).

Because the disciples have God's truth they are set apart and sent into the world, just as Jesus was (v. 18). Like him they are to be in the world but not of it, judging and calling the world by being the presence of God's light, bearing witness to his love and offering his life in the midst of the world. They share in the very life of God in the Son of God through the Spirit of God, and thus they do the work of God as Jesus has done, revealing God's love and life and light. In this way, all three aspects of sanctification are evident: they are set apart to enter God's presence, indeed, to have his presence enter them; they are commissioned for holy service; and they constitute the holy people of God, restored Israel, who are distinct from all others in the world because of the divine presence.

Jesus concludes this section of his prayer with another reference to sanctification (v. 19), which draws out yet another nuance of the term and takes us to the heart of his work and the life to which he calls his disciples. When he says *for [hyper] them I sanctify myself*, he alludes to the consecration of sacrificial animals (Ex 13:2; Deut 15:19, 21) and so speaks of his coming death as a sacrifice (see comment on 10:11; cf. 1:29; 10:11, 15; 15:13; 1 Jn 3:16, Hoskyns 1940b:595-99; Schnackenburg 1982:187). It is the same theme as that found in the accounts of the Last Supper when Jesus says, "My body . . . for *[hyper]* you" (Lk 22:19; 1 Cor 11:24) and "My blood . . . for *[hyper]* many" (Mk 14:24; cf. Beasley-Murray 1987:301). Thus sanctification, like glorification, includes a reference to the cross, the moment of revelation when the truth of God—his heart of sacrificial love—is most clearly seen. The cross is the ultimate revelation of the truth, and thus his sacrificial death is necessary if the disciples are to be *truly sanctified,* an expression that could also be translated "sanctified in the truth" *(en alētheia;* cf. v. 17, *en tē alētheia).* The cross is also the final and supreme act of Jesus' humility, obedience and death to self that have characterized his whole ministry and are at the heart of his relation with God. So his sacrificial death not only takes away the sins of the world (1:29) and reveals God; it also completes the pattern of life that he will share with them. For the disciples are to have their life in Christ, as branches are in a vine, thus sharing in his very life with the Father, which includes a death of self. They will live out the life of Christ by receiving life from the Father and by dying to self and the world (cf. Rom 12:1). And at the end, after walking as Jesus walked (1 Jn 2:6), their deaths, like Jesus', will also be a glorification of the Father (cf. Jn 21:19). Both sacrificial living and dying, whether by martyrdom or not, are part of the disciples' sanctification (cf. Chrysostom *In John* 82.1).

As the disciples bear witness to God in this way they will produce followers of God, just as Jesus has done. So the themes of consecration and sending lead naturally to the next section of the prayer, Jesus' petition for those who will believe as a result of the disciples' witness.

Jesus Prays for All Who Believe in Him Through the Witness of the Eleven (17:20-24) Jesus now prays for all believers that which he has prayed for the eleven (vv. 20, 22a). His ultimate purpose in his requests is that all may be one (vv. 21a, 22b-23a) so, in turn, the world may believe (v. 21b) and know (v. 23b) that the Father sent the Son. Jesus then adds the request that all believers may be with him in heaven to see his glory (v. 24).

Jesus' disciples are described by him as *those who will believe in me through their message* (v. 20). All later belief, Jesus implies here, is to come through the apostolic word (Alford 1980:880), thereby showing that the apostolic foundation of the church (cf. Mt 16:18; Eph 2:19-20; Rev 21:14) was the will of Christ himself. This Gospel does not speak much of the twelve apostles as such (6:67), but important truths about them are conveyed, especially in the farewell discourse, which is addressed to them. Most importantly, they are the chief witnesses to Jesus (cf. 15:27), as we see here.

What follows is usually seen as the content of Jesus' prayer for all disciples—*that all of them may be one* (v. 21)—as it is in the NIV. The word *that (hina)* is used this way quite often, but it also frequently signals purpose. Jesus uses this same language in two other places in this prayer (vv. 11, 22), both times clearly indicating purpose, which suggests he intends this meaning here as well (Ridderbos 1997:559; cf. Alford 1980:880). The content of Jesus' prayer for all believers, then, would be the same as the content of his prayer for the eleven, namely, that they be kept and sanctified by God (vv. 11-19), through God's name (vv. 11-12), word (v. 14) and truth (v. 17), which they have received through Jesus. He now summarizes using yet another parallel term when he says *I have given them the glory that you gave me* (v. 22; cf. Schnackenburg 1982:192). Like the other terms, *glory* refers to the revelation of God in all his beauty of being and character. But, also like the other terms, *glory* is a manifestation of God

---

17:20 The present tense can function as a future, so the NIV translation of the present

himself—not just a revelation about him, but his actual presence (cf. Ex 33:18-23). Jesus shares in this glory as the eternal Son (vv. 5, 24), and he has now given (*dedōka,* perfect tense, another pointer to the eternal perspective of Jesus in this prayer) this glory to his disciples. In part this refers to his revelation of the Father, which he has made known to his disciples; but this revelation brings them the knowledge that is a participation in God's own eternal life (v. 3). Accordingly, Jesus says he has done all of this, here summarized as his giving of the divine glory, in order that they might share in the divine oneness.

In the first century there was a widespread belief among Jews, Greeks and Romans in the unity of humanity. Various sources for this unity were suggested, including the concept of one God, the recognition of one universal human nature, the recognition of a universal law and the notion of one world (Taylor 1992:746-49). Efforts were made to embody this unity. For example, Alexander the Great had set out to unite the inhabited world, and later the Romans picked up the same goal. On a smaller scale, the members of the community at Qumran referred to themselves as "the unity," which included a unity with the angels, thus linking heaven and earth (Beasley-Murray 1987:302). So Jesus' prayer would speak to an issue of great interest, but the oneness he refers to is distinctive in its nature from other notions of unity. It is grounded in the one God, as were some other views of unity (Taylor 1992:746), but also in himself and his own relation with the one God. He claims to offer the unity that many were desiring, but this unity is grounded in his own relation with his Father. Furthermore, he says that the band of disciples there in the room with him is the nucleus of the one unified humanity.

Jesus speaks of the oneness of all believers (*that all of them may be one,* v. 21) and then links this with the mutual indwelling of the Father and the Son. The NIV has this indwelling as the model for the relationship among believers: *just as you are in me and I am in you.* The word translated *just as (kathōs)* can signal not only comparison but cause. Both of these two meanings are appropriate here, for the mutual indwelling of the Father and the Son is both the reason that all may be one and the pattern for such

---

pisteuontōn as *will believe* is not impossible, but it obscures another instance of Jesus' eternal perspective in this prayer.

oneness. This becomes clearer when Jesus adds "that they themselves also may be in us" (v. 21; the NIV makes this a new sentence). The oneness of believers is to be found *in us,* in their relation to the Father and the Son. The same twofold thought occurs when Jesus repeats *that they may be one as [kathōs] we are one* (v. 22). The oneness of the Father and the Son is both the cause of and the model for the believers' unity.

The Father and the Son's oneness has been mentioned earlier (10:30) and has been implicit in all that Jesus has said and done. This oneness includes both a unity of being and a distinctness of person, and it has been seen especially as a oneness of will and love. These are also the characteristics of the oneness that Jesus desires for his disciples to have in their relationship with one another in God. The picture of the relation believers have with one another and with God becomes clear when the various expressions are compared (see figure 1). This oneness is made possible through two types of mutual indwelling—the believers in the Son and the Son in them (14:20; 15:4-5) as well as the Son in the Father and the Father in the Son (10:38; 14:10-11; 17:21). These two types are combined to explain the believers' living in God: on the one hand, the believers are in the Son, who is in the Father (14:20; cf. Col 3:3); on the other hand, the Father is in the Son, who is in the believers (Jn 17:23). The believers' point of contact in both cases is the Son. Nowhere in this Gospel is it said that the Father is in believers or that believers are in the Father. The believers have a mutual indwelling with the Father, but only by the Son, for no one comes to the Father except through the Son (14:6). So the oneness of the Son with the Father is unique (1:14, 18), for Jesus shares in the deity of the Father. But in the Son believers have access to the Father and share in his very life, the eternal life.

Jesus seems to suggest that the actual outworking of the believers' oneness with one another in the Father through the Son is a process that will take some time, for he adds, *may they be brought to complete unity* (v. 23). More literally, he says, "may they have been perfected into one." The perfect tense is used, suggesting once again Jesus' eternal perspective as he prays. He is speaking, in part, about the oneness that is further perfected as the "other sheep" (10:16) and the "scattered children of God" (11:52) are gathered in. But this oneness must also refer to the oneness that is present throughout the life of the community as the community makes "every effort

Believers in the Son and the Son in the believers (14:20; 15:4-5).

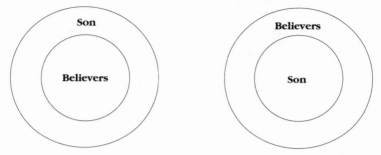

The Son in the Father and the Father in the Son (10:38; 14:10-11; 17:21).

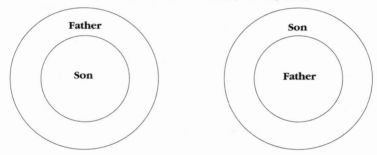

The two types of mutual indwelling combined (14:20; 17:23).

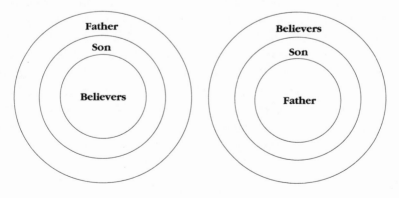

Figure 1. Mutual Indwelling

to *keep* the unity of the Spirit through the bond of peace" (Eph 4:3), for it is something that the world can notice. So this is a spiritual oneness that comes from God, but it has to do with how the community of believers lives in the world.

Indeed, Jesus says the purpose of this oneness is *that the world may believe that you have sent me* (v. 21). Such belief is the key response Jesus has received from his disciples (v. 8), so this is a reference to those who are still in the world yet are becoming believers. To believe that the Father sent Jesus is to accept that the Father is as Jesus has revealed him to be and that Jesus is the one way to the Father. When Jesus repeats this purpose he changes the term from *believe* to *know* (v. 23), again echoing his earlier description of the disciples (v. 8). Because this knowing is parallel to believing, Jesus does not refer to some mere intellectual recognition of the fact that the Father sent the Son, but rather to the knowledge that is eternal life (v. 3).

Thus, the disciples are sent on mission just as Jesus was sent (v. 18), and the very purpose of their life together is to bear witness to the Father and the Son. This oneness flows from a common life that is characterized chiefly by love, and thus the world will see that the Father has loved the disciples as he has loved the Son (v. 23). In other words, the amazing transcendent love evident between the Father and the Son is not an exclusive glory that humans must be content only to admire from afar. The love the Father has for Jesus is the same love he has for believers, indeed for the whole world (3:16). For "God is love" (1 Jn 4:8, 16), and "there is only one love of God" (Brown 1970:772). The believers are to embody this love and thereby provide living proof of God's gracious character, which is his mercy, love and truth. They will be an advertisement, inviting people to join in this union with God. The love of God evident in the church is a revelation that there is a welcome awaiting those who will quit the rebellion and return home. Here is the missionary strategy of this Gospel—the community of disciples, indwelt with God's life and light and love, witnessing to the Father in the Son by the Spirit by word and deed, continuing to bear witness as the Son has done.

17:23 This same Christocentric focus is evident in Paul's prayer that his readers "be filled with all the fullness of God" (Eph 3:19 NRSV), for this fullness is to be found in Christ (Col 2:9), as the context of Paul's prayer suggests (Eph 3:18-19a). The reference in 2 Peter to

A great deal has been written about this passage regarding the meaning and implications of this oneness for the church (cf. Staton 1997). The main points in the text seem to be that this oneness is a spiritual reality, derived from sharing in the divine life of the Father and the Son and embodied in a particular community of human beings such that it can be evident to unbelievers. In other words, it is a sacrament, a reality in the human sphere participating in the divine sphere. So this is not simply some invisible church, although the actual institutional structure of this community is not discussed beyond the reference to the apostles' word (v. 20). The actual lack of unity among Christians throughout history, both between groups of Christians and within groups, tempts a believer to despair and holds Christ up to contempt by the world. Jesus' prayer shows that there can be no oneness apart from him, yet Christians disagree on who Jesus is and how one is to relate to him! This oneness clearly must come from God and is not something people of goodwill can manufacture. It is predicated on sharing in the divine glory (v. 22) and name (v. 26). Oneness can only come through being born from above, hearing the voice of the Good Shepherd and accepting the witness of the Paraclete, thereby revealing the glory of the Father within history.

This oneness is to take place in history in order that the world can continue to be confronted with a witness to the Father. Jesus' last petition, however, looks beyond this life to heaven (v. 24). Jesus is returning to the Father, and now he prays for *those you have given me,* repeating again the fact that these are his disciples only because of the Father's will (cf. vv. 2, 6, 9). This expression is more literally translated as "that which you have given me," another use of the neuter singular to speak of his disciples as a unit (see note on v. 2; cf. 6:37, 39; perhaps 10:29), which is particularly appropriate after his referring to their oneness. But the band of disciples is not a faceless group; it is composed of beloved individuals who each are indwelt by the Son (15:5), and so he immediately uses the masculine plural pronoun for them (*kakeinoi;* left out of the NIV). In this way the grammar captures both the oneness of the community and the distinct individuals within the one community.

---

our being partakers of the divine nature (1:4) refers, as the context makes clear, to sharing in God's moral holiness and immortality (1:3-4), using terms very similar to those in this Gospel.

He whose will is one with God's will now expresses that will when he says *I want*. What he wants is this community of individuals to be with him where he is. So those who are "in" him are also to be "with" him, again recognizing the distinction of persons. Union with God is not homogenization. Jesus' request that they be with him raises interesting questions, since as divine Son he is present everywhere (cf. Augustine *In John* 111.2). But the connection with Jesus' earlier teaching about returning to take them to be with him where he is (14:1-3) suggests strongly he is referring to heaven. This being the case, his prayer takes in the whole span of the believers' life, from then on into eternity. Specifically, he wants them *to see my glory, the glory you have given me because you loved me before the creation of the world*. We have already seen his glory (v. 22; 1:14; cf. 2 Cor 3:18; 4:6), but there is a yet more complete vision of his glory awaiting believers. John later says that at his coming "we shall be like him, for we shall see him as he is" (1 Jn 3:2; cf. Col 3:4). What begins at his second coming will continue on, for Jesus is talking not about his coming itself but about that which takes place afterwards. He has promised Peter, and, through him, his other disciples that they will follow him later (13:36), and here is what they will meet, the glory of the Lord—the glory that comes from the Father, who is the source of all, and that is a gift of love. That which Jesus has revealed in his earthly ministry is a mere glimpse of an eternal reality that existed before creation. In his prayer, Jesus has been speaking of the future from an eternal perspective. Here in his final petition he looks on ahead to the ultimate future.

Jesus Concludes His Prayer with a Summary and a Pledge (17:25-26) Having looked ahead to the glory of heaven, Jesus returns to the present situation, though he sees it from his eternal perspective. Jesus summarizes the results of his ministry thus far: both his rejection by the world and his acceptance by the disciples. All the verbs in verse 25 are in the aorist tense, which, in the form used here, usually refers to the past. The NIV adopts a rarer use of the aorist and translates them in the present tense, a translation that is possible but that misses Jesus' eternal perspective.

Jesus begins with the bad news: the world did not know, or recognize, the Father. In contrast *(though, kai)*, the good news is Jesus knew the Father and his disciples knew that the Father sent the Son. In contrast with the world's ignorance of the Father is not the disciples' knowledge of the Father, but their knowledge of the Son as sent by the Father. Again we see the primacy of Jesus' role. It is precisely in and through the Son that they know the Father, for the Son has made known (*egnōrisa,* aorist) to them the Father's name (v. 26). Earlier in the prayer (vv. 6, 11-12) the name was an expression for the revelation brought by the Son that actually brings contact with God and not just information about him.

Jesus then pledges to continue to make the Father's name known to his disciples in the future. On one important level he refers here to his imminent Passion and resurrection, for these events are the climax of his revelation of the Father, which shows most clearly the love of God. On another level he is speaking of his continued presence among the believers and his continued revelation of the Father to them after his ascension. He is repeating his promise to be with them in his resurrection appearances (14:18-20) and beyond (14:21). His continued revelation parallels the activity of the Paraclete (16:12-15, 25).

The purpose of Jesus' making God's name known to them is not that they would have information about God, but that they would have intimacy *in order that the love you have* (*ēgapēsas,* another aorist) *for me may be in them and that I myself may be in them* (v. 26). In his ministry he revealed the Father's love for them (v. 23), and in the future he will continue to help his disciples actually receive this love within each of them and amongst them as a community. But again, he himself is the point of contact. It is precisely by his being in them that they will receive the love of the Father, for it is the Father's love for the Son that they are enabled to share. The Son's coming to earth brought the presence of God's love, and his coming into the lives of believers also brings that love, for God is love. Our relationship with the Father will always be mediated through the Son, even in eternity. Meditation on such truths begins to give us a faint glimpse of the Father's glorifying the Son and the Son's glorifying the Father (v. 1). It also helps us understand why, in this final section of the prayer, Jesus addresses his Father as *righteous* (v. 25). All that Jesus has done and all that he will continue to do are in response to God's righteous will. He is *righteous* because he is truth itself and does only what is right. His purposes are perfect, reflecting his own characteristic life and light and love.

□ The Climax of the Glorification Begins: Jesus' Passion and Death (18:1—19:42)

As John begins to tell of the Passion of our Lord he continues to focus on the manifestation of the glory of God. At each point in the story thus far, the key to understanding all that Jesus does and says has been his identity as the Son of God. His suffering might call his identity into question, but instead his identity is revealed even more clearly, for as Jesus is crucified he conquers the enemy and is enthroned as King. Furthermore, the glory of this victory is matched by the glory of his obedience. Throughout his humiliation, pain and suffering we see Jesus confident in his Father and set upon fulfilling his will. As he does so his death reveals the very heart of God—God is love, and love is the laying down of one's life (1 Jn 4:8, 16; 3:16). In these chapters we see Jesus as the king of love who completes his mission of revealing the Father and providing eternal life.

John's Gospel is a literary masterpiece (cf. Culpepper 1983), and this is nowhere more evident than in his account of the Passion. But John is not giving us just a story—he is giving us history. Each of the four Gospels recounts the events of the Passion in the same order, but each leaves out some material and includes items not found in the other accounts (for a convenient list see Westcott 1908:2:262-63). John's Gospel is distinct from the Synoptics, offering important elements to the whole story. The reliability of John's historical account here, as elsewhere in this Gospel, has been called into question by many. Some of the important historical issues will be touched on as we go through this section, but more thorough discussion will be left to others, particularly the brief, insightful introduction by William Horbury (1972) as well as the major studies by John A. T. Robinson (1985:238-87) and Raymond E. Brown (1970:785-962; 1994). B. Corley (1992) provides a helpful survey of the four accounts of Jesus' trial.

Jesus Is Arrested (18:1-11) Jesus and his disciples go out of the city to the east, crossing the Kidron, which John refers to as a wadi (*Valley,* NIV; *cheimarros,* literally, "winter-flowing," since winter is the rainy season). This same word is used of the Kidron in the account of David's flight from

---

18:1 The Synoptics describe Jesus as going out of the city straight from the Upper Room. John has already described their departure from the room (14:31), so in the Gospel as we now have it the material in chapters 15—17 is spoken either at the doorway or along the

Absalom (2 Sam 15:23 LXX), and John may well be alluding to that story (Westcott 1908:2:264; Brown 1994:1:125, 291). David was betrayed by his counselor Ahithophel, who later hangs himself (2 Sam 17:23), the only person in Scripture apart from Judas who does so. Thus David's sorrow and humiliation may be echoed in Jesus', though in Jesus' case he is actually in control, and this humiliation is part of his great victory (Hendriksen 1953:376, 383).

They go to a familiar place, an *olive grove* where Jesus *often met* with his disciples (vv. 1-2). In this way he is accepting the coming betrayal, since *Judas . . . knew the place* (v. 2). In the Synoptics it is called Gethsemane, meaning "oil press," which suggests an olive grove. While it is an olive grove, John does not actually call it an *olive grove* (despite the NIV); he calls it a garden *(kēpos)*. John notes that Jesus' death and resurrection also took place in a garden (19:41; 20:15). "The Passion and resurrection which effected the salvation of the world are contrasted with the Fall in the *garden of Eden*" (Hoskyns 1940b:604). Modern commentators express doubt that John would have the Garden of Eden in mind. However, the fact that he mentions the garden setting several times in the Passion and resurrection accounts suggests he does want to draw attention to this connection.

The group that came to arrest Jesus was composed of Roman soldiers, Jewish servants and an apostate apostle (v. 3). John will make it clear that both Jew and Gentile are guilty of the death of the Son of God. Jesus is about to die for the life of the world, and the whole world needs it. The Jewish forces that were sent were the same as those sent to arrest Jesus once before (7:32, 45-46). They were not a police force as such but "court servants at the disposal of the Sanhedrin when necessary for police purposes" (Brown 1994:1:249). The *detachment of soldiers (speira)* refers to a cohort, a group of 600 soldiers under a military tribune *(chiliarchos,* vv. 3, 12; NIV, *commander).* The entire cohort would not have been deployed on this mission, but there would have been a significant force. The festivals in Jerusalem were always politically volatile, and after the welcome Jesus had received there was good reason to expect trouble—or so it would have seemed to the Roman and Jewish authorities who understood Jesus so

---

route. In an earlier draft, it seems 18:1 followed right after 14:31, chapters 15—17 having been added later (see comment on 14:31).

poorly. They bring torches and lanterns to search for the Light of the World; they bring weapons against the Prince of Peace (Hendriksen 1953:378).

They may well have expected to have to search in dark corners and meet with armed resistance once they had cornered the accused. But Jesus knows what is coming upon him (v. 4; 13:1), that he is going to engage the prince of this world one-on-one (cf. 14:30). So he goes out to meet them (v. 4) and asks, *Who is it you want?* This is not a question from ignorance, seeking an answer. Rather, it is like other questions asked by God that are intended to reveal a situation and bring people to action.

John does not mention Judas's kiss, which would have taken place just before or after Jesus' question. Judas here takes his place with those who have come out against Jesus (v. 5). The awkward statement that tells us where Judas is, which the NIV puts in parentheses, is an eyewitness detail branded into John's memory. We sense his shock at seeing Judas *with them*. John's continual reference to Judas as the betrayer all stems from this event. John makes it clear that Judas is not the revealer but rather that Jesus will identify himself. Enemies had not been able to lay their hands on Jesus before (7:30, 44-45; 8:59; 10:39; 12:36), and it is not Judas's presence that now brings success. Rather, it is now the Father's will.

They say they are looking for *Jesus of Nazareth,* and Jesus responds, *I am he* (v. 5, *egō eimi*). Here the most humble and human of Jesus' names is juxtaposed with the most exalted and divine. The two together are the cross hairs that target Jesus' identity: he is the human being from an insignificant, small town in Galilee who is also God. Jesus' self-identification has been at the heart of this Gospel, and this public act of identification produces dramatic effects. When he uses the divine I AM *they drew back and fell to the ground* (v. 6). People falling to the ground in the presence of God are mentioned elsewhere (for example, Ezek 1:28; Dan 10:9; Rev 1:17), but here the ones falling are his enemies rather than his worshipers. This reaction is closer to that of Pharaoh, who fell down as though dead when Moses said the name of God, as told by Artapanus, a pre-Christian Jewish apologist (Eusebius *Preparation for the Gospel* 9.27; Talbert 1992:233). This reaction is a reflection not of their hearts, but of Jesus' majesty. Here is a little preview of the moment in the future when every knee will bow to Jesus (Phil 2:10) and all things be brought into subjection to him (1 Cor 15:27; Phil 3:21), even those who do not own allegiance to him and thus for whom this submission is hell.

Jesus puts the question to them again (v. 7). The impression given by this passage is that they have been completely neutralized and that he must allow the events to proceed and give them permission to take him (cf. Talbert 1992:234). Amazingly, they answer the same as before: *Jesus of Nazareth*. They have just experienced the numinous, and it has not spoken to them at all. They are just doing their job, like those sent to investigate John the Baptist at the beginning of the Gospel (1:19-27). This repetition of the question "Whom do you seek?" emphasizes its importance, for it focuses on Jesus. It is also a question that searches the soul. The very first thing Jesus said in this Gospel was, literally, "What are you seeking?" (1:38), his question for the two disciples of John the Baptist, and their reply indicated they wanted to be with him. Now we see people seeking Jesus, but they do so not for their soul's sake. They have their own agenda, as many people do today. There are ways of seeking Jesus that do not bring life.

Jesus repeats the I AM but now allows the proceedings to continue by telling them to let his followers go (*aphete,* an imperative). He issues orders to those arresting him! Their power has just been shown to be insignificant compared to the power of his word, and now the fulfillment of his word is the operative force, not their designs (v. 9). The formula used to speak of the fulfillment of Scriptures from the Old Testament is now used of Jesus' own words. The Word himself, who created all that exists, has spoken of his protection for those the Father has given him (6:39; cf. 10:28; 17:12), and now he fulfills that word. The protection Jesus spoke of earlier referred to eternal salvation, and now we see that such protection includes occasions of temptation that threaten to overwhelm the disciples' faith (cf. Bultmann 1971:640). Here is Jesus as the Good Shepherd caring for his flock, a glimpse of the grace that is at work throughout the Passion as it has been throughout the ministry. The temptation the disciples face here is an extreme case of what all temptation represents. And the Lord's protection is as necessary in the day to day assaults as it is in this great test. It is not without reason that our Lord commanded us to pray daily not to be led into temptation (Mt 6:13 par. Lk 11:4; cf. Mt 26:41 par. Mk 14:38 par. Lk 22:46).

Jesus has demonstrated that he has complete power over these adversaries, and he has expressed his will that the disciples be let go, but Peter still thinks he has to resist with force (v. 10). The Synoptics tell us there were only two swords, and we might have guessed that Peter would have one of them. He may have been emboldened by their having fallen to the ground. But he does not go after one of the soldiers or one of the Jewish force, but rather the slave *(doulos)* of the high priest. He takes off the man's right ear! John does not mention that Jesus healed the slave's ear (Lk 22:51), though this would account for Peter's not being arrested or killed on the spot. John does, however, add that the man's name was Malchus. John was known to the household of the high priest (v. 16) and knew this man and his family (v. 26). We do not know how well John knew these men, but such connections add poignancy to the scene.

The fact that Peter only got the man's right ear suggests several possibilities: that Peter was left-handed, or that he attacked the man from behind, that the man moved or that Peter simply had bad aim. In any case, Peter's boldness is as great and as obvious as his misunderstanding. He is not at all in sync with God's will, and this isn't the first time he is out of step (cf. 13:6-9; Mt 16:22-23 par. Mk 8:32-33). Jesus says, *Shall I not drink the cup the Father has given me?* (v. 11). Jesus is willing to receive all that the Father gives him, both the disciples (v. 9) and the suffering.

The image of the cup is used in the Old Testament to denote suffering (Ps 75:8) and, in particular, the wrath of God (Is 51:17, 22; Jer 25:15-29; 49:12; Lam 4:21; Ezek 23:31-34; Hab 2:16; cf. Rev 14:10; 16:19). John has not included the prayer of agony in the garden in which Jesus asked that, if possible, the cup be removed from him (Mt 26:39 par. Mk 14:36 par. Lk 22:42). But John includes this later reference to the cup, which reveals the conclusion of the earlier agony. "The struggle in Gethsemane is over. Jesus no longer prays that the cup . . . may pass from him" (Hendriksen 1953:382). The Son's humility and obedience continue to manifest the glory of God and his pattern of life with God.

Jesus Is Confronted by Annas; Peter Is Confronted by People in the Courtyard (18:12-27) Throughout John's story the world has been judged by the presence of Jesus, and the world has in turn judged him. The whole Gospel is thus a description of a trial (cf. Harvey 1976), a theme that reaches a climax as Jesus is brought before the authorities. As he is put on trial we see revealed both his own identity as King and his confident trust in his Father.

The force that came out to arrest Jesus was composed of both Jews and Romans, and Jesus will now be arraigned before both Jewish and Roman officials. In the Synoptics Jesus is brought first before Caiaphas and the Sanhedrin and then before Pilate. Luke adds a further appearance before Herod Antipas (23:6-12). John begins, here in our present text, with Jesus' earlier appearance before Annas, an interrogation not mentioned in the Synoptics. John will then move on to the interrogation by Pilate, leaving out a description of the appearances before Caiaphas and the Sanhedrin and before Herod. It is clear that he knows of the trial before Caiaphas (v. 24) but has chosen not to include it in his account.

John weaves together the confrontation between Jesus and Annas and the confrontation going on at the same time between Peter and the people in the courtyard. This textured scene, which shifts between what is going on inside with Jesus and what is going on outside with Peter, is paralleled in the scene that follows by Pilate's encounter with Jesus inside the governor's palace and his dealings with the Jewish opponents outside. Such juxtaposition enables John to make comparisons between Jesus and the other characters in the story. The inner and outer scenes in the story also reflect John's purpose to show us here, as throughout his Gospel, the inner and outer dimensions of the events themselves—the eternal reality being manifested in the midst of the world as the Word comes to his own and the eternal significance of the events that unfold.

Jesus Is Taken to Annas, the High Priest (18:12-14) John describes Jesus' arrest and binding as the activity of the whole party that has come out against him, both Gentile and Jew (v. 12). John will make it clear that the Jewish authorities have special responsibility for Jesus' death (19:11), but the Gentiles have a share as well. Here we have the shocking sight of the one who brings freedom to mankind (8:31-36) being bound by representatives of the whole human race.

They took Jesus first to Annas, probably the most respected and powerful of the Jewish authorities at that time. He had held the office of high priest earlier (A.D. 6-15), and his influence continued through his son-in-law Caiaphas, the current high priest (v. 13) and through his five sons, who had also been high priest for various lengths of time (Josephus *Antiquities of the Jews* 18.2.1-2; 20.9.1; cf. Chilton 1992:257). Annas was the head of a dynasty, which probably accounts for John's reference to him as high priest

(vv. 15-16, 19, 22, cf. Acts 4:6), even though John is clear that Caiaphas is the one holding that office at the time (vv. 13, 24).

There seem to be both historical and theological reasons why John includes this scene of Jesus' questioning before Annas. John mentions "another disciple" who is "known to the high priest" (v. 15) and his household (vv. 16, 26). As with the references to the Beloved Disciple, this is most likely a reference to himself. Like the Beloved Disciple, this other disciple is unnamed, closely associated with Peter and characterized as having special knowledge. It is unclear whether John is saying that he knew the high priest personally or that he knew just some in his household. He is not described as speaking to Annas himself, but he does have personal knowledge of the servants. Perhaps he had contacts through marketing fish, though in that society this would not itself imply limited social contact (cf. Brown 1970:823; Carson 1991:582).

Whatever the nature of his familiarity with Annas, John had other contact with him later when he himself was on trial (Acts 4:6). John had to bear witness before this man, and his bearing witness is the main theme that comes through in this story. He can bear witness to the Passion because he was there (cf. Ridderbos 1997:581). John does not narrate the scattering of the disciples (cf. 16:32), but presumably it took place here at the arrest. John was separated from Jesus at that point, but we now discover it was only for a brief time. He and Peter recover and return to see what transpires. In this way, John has not missed much of the action and thus is able to bear witness to the whole story. Unlike Peter, he is inside the high priest's palace and witnesses the whole of the Passion. This theme of witness is also the focal point of Jesus' exchange with Annas (vv. 20-23). Thus this particular story is important for John, both personally and for the theme it brings out.

John concludes his introduction to Jesus' interrogation by Annas by identifying Annas as the father-in-law of Caiaphas (v. 13). John refers back to an earlier meeting of the Sanhedrin (11:47-53) and in particular to Caiaphas' prophetic statement that *it would be good if one man died for the people* (v. 14). This allusion reminds the reader of the reason for Jesus' death. John uses Caiaphas' own statement as a caption under this picture of the Passion, providing the interpretation of the cross as surely as does the title that Pilate will require to be nailed above the head of Jesus (19:19-22). This death is for the sake of the very people who are causing it.

Peter Denies He Is a Follower of Jesus (18:15-18) Peter and John follow as Jesus is brought before Annas. John's familiarity with the high priest, or at least with his household, enables him to enter with Jesus and to get Peter admitted also (vv. 15-16). The one who reclined next to Jesus a few hours earlier at the meal (13:23) continues to be close to him. But his going back out to bring Peter in shows that he, like his master, is also concerned for others, in particular this fellow believer. The love evident in this gesture reveals John's character as a true disciple and as one to whose care Jesus can entrust other disciples, indeed even his mother (19:27).

Presumably John returns to the room where Jesus is being questioned, which leaves Peter in the courtyard with the servants and others. It is not said whether Peter was unable to enter the room with John or whether he chose to remain outside. The latter seems unlikely, given Peter's character, but the arrest has shaken him. He is now sifted, beginning with a question from the woman who attended the door (v. 17). She asks, literally, "You also are not one of the disciples of this man, are you?" Her expression "this man" (*tou anthrōpou toutou,* left out of the NIV) seems to suggest some disdain, as does the use of *mē* ("not"), here with the sense, "surely not you too." But, of course, there would be little other reason for a stranger to be there in the courtyard in the middle of a cold night. Furthermore, the fact that she says "you also" (*kai sy,* also missing from the NIV) most likely indicates that she knows John is a disciple of Jesus.

In this account, therefore, it seems to be Peter's association with John, the unnamed disciple, that draws attention to his relation to Jesus. John himself shows no concern about her feelings regarding his discipleship, for he not only was admitted by her, but also came back to get Peter in. While Peter's attack with the sword (18:10) may have made him fearful of being recognized, he is not in a position of legal difficulty, since there is no warrant for his arrest. Nor is there indication that he was physically threatened by this woman or the others. He has no such excuses for his denial. He who a few hours earlier had said he would die for Jesus (13:37) now denies any association with him purely out of fear of what people would think. John, like Luke, is gentle in his account of Peter's denials, leaving out the curses and oaths he used (Mt 26:74 par. Mk 14:71); and John will give prominence to Peter's restoration (21:15-19). But this does not mean that John takes the denial less seriously than Matthew or Mark do. The very terms of the restoration ("Do you love me?") show the enormity of the denials and also stand in contrast to the love that John shows in this scene as he sticks close to Jesus even in his disgrace.

After Peter's first denial, John's narrative switches back to what is going on inside between Annas and Jesus. Peter is outside warming himself at a charcoal fire (*anthrakia,* v. 18). A charcoal fire gives off warmth but little light. This dim fire, along with the darkness in the garden, helps account for Peter's not being recognized immediately by the relative of the man whose ear Peter had cut off (v. 26). The darkness of the courtyard may also have a symbolic significance, for it means Peter is outside in the half-light while John is inside with the Light of the World. Peter is not denigrated in this Gospel, but he does "serve as a foil for the behavior of another disciple who is never deflected from his following of Jesus" (Brown 1994:1:623). In the half-light, separated from Jesus, Peter encounters temptation for which he does not have the resources to resist. The only hope for any of us in the time of temptation is to remain close to Jesus.

Annas Questions Jesus (18:19-24) Back inside, Annas is beginning his interrogation. This is not an actual trial; John has not confused this encounter with the meeting with the Sanhedrin. Here there are no witnesses, no jury and no sentence. This is more like "a police interrogation of a newly arrested criminal before any formal trial procedures are begun" (Brown 1970:834; cf. 1994:1:412, 423-25; Robinson 1985:248-50). Annas asks Jesus about his disciples (v. 19), reflecting the Sanhedrin's earlier concern over Jesus' popularity (11:48), a popularity that can have only increased after Jesus entered Jerusalem attended by a great crowd. Indeed, some of the Pharisees said it looked like the whole world had gone after him (12:19).

Annas also asks Jesus about his teaching (v. 19). He seems to want Jesus to incriminate himself as a false prophet (Beasley-Murray 1987:324-25) or at least as a false teacher (Robinson 1985:259; Brown 1994:1:414). But Jesus will not be trapped in this way. Indeed, in later law it was illegal to have "an accused person convict himself" (Brown 1970:826), and this rule may have applied at this time also. Furthermore, Jesus has already completed

---

18:20 The word *world* refers in particular to Jesus' Jewish hearers, as the second half of his public teaching regarding himself (see comment on 12:34-35). Only one last statement of Jesus' teaching remains, but that is reserved for the Gentile Pilate (18:33-37; 19:11). So Jesus tells Annas to check with those who have heard him, since he has taught quite openly (v. 20-21). In this way he heightens Annas' anxiety. The very fact that Jesus has spoken openly and that there are plenty of people who are familiar with his teaching is what concerns Annas. That Jesus does nothing to assure Annas that his teaching is kosher would also increase the high priest's fears. Indeed, Jesus shows chutzpah at this point, which is so unlike the way others come cringing before the Sanhedrin (cf. Josephus *Antiquities of the Jews* 14.172), showing Annas that Jesus is indeed a danger.

Jesus' appeal to the witness of those who had heard him is essentially a demand for a fair trial (Brown 1970:826), since in Jewish law the witnesses are questioned, not the accused (see comment on 5:31; cf. Beasley-Murray 1987:324). Jesus has completed his witness by word. There remains only the climax of all his ministry as he witnesses to the Father through his death, resurrection and ascension. It is now up to those who have heard him to bear witness to him. Such remains the case today. His abiding presence remains with believers, but those who abide in him are to bear witness to him before the world. "The author insists that the teaching of Jesus must be known through attention to His disciples, who by the guidance of the Spirit preserve and interpret His words (cf. 2:22; 14:25; 16:4ff.). A true judgement of the world upon the Christ depends upon the fidelity of His disciples" (Hoskyns 1940b:610).

One of the *officials* (a "servant," *hypēretēs*) hits Jesus and says, *Is this the way you answer the high priest?* (v. 22). Since Jesus is still bound there is no way for him to defend himself. The more severe abuse that Jesus suffers later before the Sanhedrin (Mt 26:67-68 par. Mk 14:65 par. Lk 22:63-65) is not recounted by John. This blow was more an insult than it was physically damaging (Brown 1970: 826). It highlights Jesus' dignity and boldness as well as his respect for the truth, rather than for mere office holders. His reply to the servant stresses this issue of truth: *If I said something wrong . . . testify as to what is wrong. But if I spoke the truth, why did you*

the verse indicates. But on another level there may be an allusion also to Jesus' more universal audience.

strike me? This question applies to all the opposition he has experienced throughout his ministry (cf. 8:46).

In essence, Jesus' question is a final act of grace extended toward a representative of his opponents. But Annas does not accept the offer to consider the truth of Jesus. Instead he sends Jesus, still bound, to Caiaphas (v. 24). From the Synoptics it seems there was a preliminary phase in which Jesus was taken before Caiaphas and a quorum of the Sanhedrin at night (Mt 26:57-75 par. Mk 14:53-72 par. Lk 22:54-65) and then a more formal trial at dawn before the full Sanhedrin (Mt 27:1 par. Mk 15:1 par. Lk 22:66-71). John signals where all of this fits in his account (vv. 24, 28), but he does not recount it, presumably having assumed it was familiar to his readers. In John's Gospel, therefore, this scene before Annas is the final encounter between Jesus and his Jewish opponents. A high priest, as Annas is known in this Gospel, has rejected the true high priest. From this point on, all contact between Jesus and his opponents is mediated through Pilate.

Peter Denies Jesus Two More Times (18:25-27) Jesus has stood up to this powerful leader, but when John's narrative switches back to Peter at the fire we find him continuing to deny that he is a disciple of Jesus. "They said to him, 'You also are not one of his disciples are you?' " (v. 25). "They said" *(eipon)* refers either to an unspecified group or, as in the NIV, to an unspecified individual (cf. Wallace 1996:402-3). When this unspecified group or individual confronts him he denies any connection with Jesus. Then there comes a very specific accusation from a relative of the man whose ear Peter had cut off: *Didn't I see you with him in the olive grove?* (v. 26). Here an eyewitness testifies to what he has seen—the very thing Peter is supposed to be doing with regard to Jesus. Instead of bearing witness to Jesus, he will not even admit to being Jesus' disciple. Just then the rooster crows, bringing to fulfillment Jesus' prediction that "before the rooster crows, you will disown me three times!" (13:38). John does not write of Peter's grief at this point (cf. Mt 26:75 par. Mk 14:72 par. Lk 22:62), waiting instead to recount the grief Peter experiences at his restoration later (21:17).

The main points of the story of Peter's denial are the same in all four Gospels, but the Gospels differ in detail (cf. Brown 1970:836-42). One main difference is the place of Peter's denials (Beasley-Murray 1987:235-36): the Synoptics have Peter in Caiaphas' courtyard (Mt 26:57-58 par. Mk 14:53-54 par. Lk 22:54) whereas in John it is Annas' courtyard. Unless one or more of the accounts is inaccurate, it would seem Annas and Caiaphas either lived in the same place or at least did official business in the same place (Alford 1980:888).

The other main difference is the timing of Peter's denials. In the Synoptics it is during the session with the Sanhedrin, yet in John it is earlier, in association with Jesus' meeting with Annas. Efforts to harmonize such differences have produced suggestions that Peter denied Jesus more than three times or that the two denials in our present passage are actually a complex account of the third denial, John having left out the second denial. Such solutions do not do justice to John's account, in particular to the prediction that speaks of three denials (13:38). Instead, these differences reflect the different emphases of the evangelists and their own form of precision, which differs from that of most North Americans, among others. In particular, their reordering of material in order to bring out nuances of significance—for example, the difference in the sequence of Jesus' tempta-tions (cf. Mt 4:1-11 with Lk 4:1-13)—is jarring to some folk. It would seem, however, that the case at hand has John juxtaposing Peter's denials and Jesus' own response to Annas. "By making Peter's denials simultaneous with Jesus' defense before Annas, John has constructed a dramatic contrast wherein Jesus stands up to his questioners and denies nothing, while Peter cowers before his questioners and denies everything" (Brown 1970:842). The foil Peter provides helps highlight Jesus' regal strength and authority, the hallmark of John's portrait of Jesus in his passion.

Pilate Interrogates Jesus (18:28—19:16) John's account of the trial before Pilate is much more extensive than the accounts in the Synoptics. The literary power is evident here as John presents seven scenes in a chiastic pattern that alternates between the Jewish opponents on the outside and Jesus inside, with Pilate going back and forth between them (Brown 1970: 859, from which the following diagram is adapted):

 A Outside (18:28-32) The Jews demand Jesus' death
  B Inside (18:33-38a) Pilate questions Jesus about kingship
   C Outside (18:38b-40) Pilate finds Jesus not guilty; Barabbas choice
    D Inside (19:1-3) Soldiers scourge Jesus
   C′ Outside (19:4-8) Pilate finds Jesus not guilty; "Behold the man"
  B′ Inside (19:9-11) Pilate talks with Jesus about power
 A′ Outside (19:12-16a) The Jews obtain Jesus' death

Inside Jesus exhibits a royal calmness while outside the opponents are greatly agitated (Brown 1994:1:758-59). "Pilate must shuttle back and forth, for he is the person-in-between who does not wish to make a decision and so vainly tries to reconcile the opposing forces" (Brown 1994:1:744). Jesus is no more cowed by Pilate than he was by Annas. Just as he offered Annas a chance to accept him (v. 23), so will he confront Pilate with the claims of his identity and demand a decision. He reveals himself as king of an otherworldly kingdom and as witness to the truth—terms that transcend Jewish categories in Jesus' addresses to this Gentile. But Pilate in his own way rejects Jesus as decisively as had Annas. Both Jew and Gentile collaborate in the Passion of Jesus. Both Jew and Gentile are graciously offered a chance even now to accept Jesus rather than reject him.

The glory of the love of God shines forth, as it has throughout the story, in the way Jesus relates to everyone with whom he comes in contact as he suffers through this humiliating and painful climax to his ministry.

Jesus Is Handed Over to Pilate by the Jewish Opponents (18:28-32)
Jesus is brought to Pilate at the praetorium (NIV, *the palace of the Roman governor,* v. 28), which was located either at the Antonia Fortress at the northwest corner of the temple or, perhaps more likely, at Herod's old palace to the west of the temple, near the Jaffa gate (Pixner 1992; Brown 1994:1:705-10). The opponents bring him early in the morning, which would not have inconvenienced Pilate because it was common for Roman officials to begin work very early and complete their business by ten or eleven in the morning (Sherwin-White 1963:45).

The Jewish opponents refuse to enter the praetorium *to avoid ceremonial uncleanness* (v. 28). There is no law in the Old Testament against entering a Gentile's home, but in later teaching it is laid down that "the dwelling-places of gentiles are unclean" (*m. Oholot* 18:7; cf. Brown 1994:1:745; Beasley-Murray 1987:327). The opponents sought to avoid defilement because they *wanted to be able to eat the Passover* (v. 28). Since Jesus has already eaten with his disciples a meal that the Synoptics say was the Passover (Mt 26:17 par. Mk 14:12 par. Lk 22:8; 22:15), this verse raises questions. Many interpreters argue either that John has shifted the chronol-

---

18:28 This verse shows John knows of the appearance before Caiaphas, even if he does not give an account of that meeting here. Some suggest he leaves out the account because

ogy in order to have Jesus dying at the very time the Passover lambs are being sacrificed—making the point dramatically that he is the Lamb of God who takes away the sin of the world (for example, Lindars 1972:444-46; Barrett 1978:48-51)—or that his chronology is historically accurate (especially Brown 1994:2:1351-73; cf. Robinson 1985:147-51) and therefore the meal he shared with his disciples was not Passover.

Others have attempted to maintain that the meal in all four Gospels is the Passover. One solution suggests that John is referring here not to the Passover meal itself, but to the Feast of Unleavened Bread, a week-long celebration that took place in conjunction with it. This longer celebration can be referred to as Passover, as it is, for example, in Luke: "Now the Feast of Unleavened Bread, called the Passover, was approaching" (22:1; cf. Josephus *Antiquities of the Jews* 14.21). These Jewish opponents, then, wish to be able to take part in the seven-day feast about to begin (cf. Carson 1991:589; Ridderbos 1997:457). Alternatively, some suggest that "John has in mind the lunchtime meal known as the *chagigah,* celebrated during midday after the first evening of Passover" (Blomberg 1987:177). But although the term Passover may be applied to the whole sequence, including the Feast of Unleavened Bread, the expression "eat the Passover" is not a natural way to refer to keeping the whole feast nor to eating the *chagigah,* but rather a way to refer to the Passover meal specifically. For example, the references in the Synoptics just cited use exactly the expression here *(esthiō to pascha)* to speak of sharing in the Passover meal. Furthermore, there is no evidence the term Passover was used to refer to the Feast of Unleavened Bread apart from the Passover itself (Morris 1971:778-79, but cf. Blomberg 1987:177 n. 2).

Another solution to the discrepancy is that different calendars were followed. The main calendar used was a lunisolar calendar, but some groups, apparently including the community at Qumran, used a solar calendar of 364 days (cf. Schürer 1973-1987:1:587-601; Vanderkam 1992). The main drawback to this solution is the lack of evidence for Jesus' having followed the solar calendar (cf. Vanderkam 1992:820). The other main proposal is that the Galileans and the Pharisees reckoned days from sunrise

---

he views the earlier decision of the Sanhedrin under Caiaphas (11:47-53) as the official sentence of death (cf. Brown 1970:833-34; Robinson 1985:249-50).

to sunrise, while Judeans did so from sunset to sunset. This means the Judeans, including these opponents, would slaughter their lambs late Friday afternoon, whereas Jesus and his disciples had theirs slaughtered late Thursday afternoon (Hoehner 1977:83-90; cf. Morris 1971:782-85). It has also been suggested that the slaughtering of the lambs actually took place over two days because of the volume of lambs involved (Hoehner 1977:84). According to these solutions, Jesus has already eaten Passover, but the opponents have yet to do so. A major drawback to theories of different days for celebrating Passover is "the lack of any hint of such a distinction in the gospels themselves" (Blomberg 1987:176-77).

Whatever the solution to this puzzle, the irony of the opponents' concern is evident. They wish to remain ritually pure even while seeking to kill someone by the agency of the Romans. They avoid defilement while bringing about the death of the Lamb of God who takes away the sin of the world (1:29), the root defilement that prevents one from intimacy with God and sharing in his life. Perhaps most ironic is the fact that their very act is a sin that defiles in this deep sense yet contributes to the cleansing of their sin and the sin of the whole world.

Pilate asks for the charges against Jesus (v. 29), and from the Jewish leaders' response it seems they were upset by this request: *If he were not a criminal . . . we would not have handed him over to you* (v. 30). They wanted Pilate simply to take their word for it and not begin his own investigation. Pilate is not inclined to do them such a favor and tells them to judge Jesus by their own law. In other words, if none of the charges mentioned are relevant to Roman rule, then this case is a matter for their own legal proceedings. A reluctance to get involved in matters of Jewish law was common among Roman governors (Sherwin-White 1965:112-13). It is unclear whether or not Pilate knew the opponents had already judged Jesus. John has omitted a description of the Jewish trial, but judging Jesus by their law is exactly what they have been doing throughout the Gospel.

Long before now they had come to the conclusion that Jesus had to be eliminated (7:19-20; 8:40, 44, 59; 10:31; 11:8, 16, 50). This is still their aim, and their specific request of Pilate now becomes clear when they respond that they do not have the right to execute people (v. 31). This could refer to Old Testament prohibitions against killing (Ex 20:13, Hoskyns 1940b:616;

Michaels 1989:314), but more likely it refers to limitations imposed by the Romans (Brown 1994:1:747-48). Among the Romans, "the capital power was the most jealously guarded of all the attributes of government, not even entrusted to the principal assistants of the governors" (Sherwin-White 1963:36). There were occasions when Jews did put people to death through mob violence (for example the stoning of Stephen, Acts 7:58-60). And they were given permission to execute any Gentile, even a Roman, who entered the temple's inner courts (Josephus *Jewish Wars* 5.193-94; 6.124-26). But mob violence has not succeeded against Jesus, and his case is not one for which Rome has given permission for execution. Presumably they could request permission to kill Jesus themselves, but this would limit them to the methods of stoning, burning, beheading and strangling, at least according to later law, which may have been in effect in the first century (*m. Sanhedrin* 7:1). They seem set, however, on having Rome execute Jesus, for then it would be by crucifixion. They probably want him crucified (19:6, 15) not only because it was a particularly brutal and painful form of death, but also because it would signify that Jesus is accursed by God (Deut 21:23; cf. Gal 3:13, Robinson 1985:257 n. 147; Beasley-Murray 1987:328). In John's Gospel the focus is on Jesus as the revealer of God. His opponents have rejected that claim and desire his death in order to vindicate their conclusion.

John, however, sees this desire as a fulfillment of Jesus' statement that he would die by being lifted up from the earth (v. 32; 12:32-34). "Both Jewish accusers and Roman judge are actors in a drama scripted by a divine planner" (Brown 1994:1:748). John's note reminds us both of Jesus' identity as the Word whose words are God's words, which will be fulfilled, and of the significance of this death: "I, when I am lifted up from the earth, will draw all men to myself" (12:32). Even the actions of his enemies are used to bear witness to the glory of his identity and of what he is in the process of accomplishing.

Pilate Questions Jesus (18:33-38) In this second of the seven scenes (see introduction to 18:28—19:16) we have the heart of the Roman interrogation. In a series of four questions Pilate probes the key topic of this Gospel—the identity and mission of Jesus. Here is Jesus' final teaching concerning himself before his resurrection.

We are not told what charges the Jewish opponents brought against Jesus to induce Pilate to consider condemning him to death. In the Jewish trial

Caiaphas had asked, "Are you the Christ, the Son of the Blessed One?" and Jesus said yes (Mt 26:63-64 par. Mk 14:61-62 par. Lk 22:67-70). John does not recount this exchange, although its substance is central to his revelation of Jesus throughout the Gospel and John does seem to allude to the exchange itself later (19:7, Beasley-Murray 1987:329). Presumably the opponents translated the matter for Pilate, saying that Jesus claimed to be the king of the Jews. This was obviously a political title and had even been used of Herod the Great (Josephus *Antiquities of the Jews* 14.385; 16.311). It was a claim that Pilate would have to take seriously, especially given the revolutionary setting in Israel, in which many desired the overthrow of Rome.

Many think Pilate's question expresses incredulity: Are *you* the King of the Jews? But more likely he is simply doing his job by putting the charge to the accused, using direct questions in keeping with Roman procedure (Sherwin-White 1965:105). What would he have expected to hear in response? Perhaps either cringing denial or stormy denunciations of Rome. The answer he gets is something quite different from either of these responses. Jesus neither affirms nor denies his identity as king, but he responds like a king. He speaks of his kingdom and quite calmly focuses the attention on Pilate, asking a question that tests Pilate's heart (v. 34). He is speaking to him as a human being, not as the Roman governor. Is he personally engaged, or is this just a formality? Such a question should signal to Pilate that he is dealing with someone who is not speaking merely on a political level. As seen earlier (e.g., see comments on 1:19-28), such personal interest is necessary to be able to recognize one come from God and to respond appropriately.

Pilate does not see how this question could be of interest to him since he is not a Jew (v. 35). He has not gone looking for Jesus, but rather Jesus has been handed over to him by his own nation and the high priests. Like the woman of Samaria and other people who have encountered Jesus, Pilate does not understand the full meaning of what Jesus says because he does not realize whom he is speaking with. And as he did with others earlier, Jesus now helps Pilate understand who he is and what he is offering.

Pilate asks what Jesus has done (v. 35). Jesus follows his common practice in this Gospel, for he does not directly address the question put to him, but in fact he gives a profound answer. Instead of speaking of what he has done he speaks of his kingdom (v. 36). This word only occurs one other place in John (3:3, 5), unlike in the Synoptics, where "kingdom" is Jesus' major theme. In Jewish thinking "kingdom" does not refer to a territory; it is an active concept referring to rule. "Kingdom of God," then, means God is king (cf. Kuhn 1964b:571-72). In the Gospels it includes also the realm of God's rule, in the sense not of a territory but of the community under his rule. While Jesus has not used this word much in this Gospel, all that he has done and said have been manifestations of God's rule and Jesus' own kingship. In this sense, "the whole Gospel is concerned with the kingship of God in Jesus" (Beasley-Murray 1987:330). Jesus has said a spiritual rebirth is necessary to even see the kingdom—the resources of this world are not sufficient (3:3, 5). Now Jesus continues this emphasis by saying his kingdom is *not of this world*. His kingdom is otherworldly because he himself is not of this world and neither are his followers (17:14, 16). He and his disciples have their source in God and reflect God's own life and character.

Both the divine source and the quality of his kingdom are evident, he says, in the fact that his disciples did not *fight to prevent my arrest by the Jews* (v. 36). Peter, of course, did try to do so and was out of step with Jesus' and the Father's will, as Jesus told him (18:11). Jesus' response to the opposition from the Jewish leaders had a divine source for it was determined by God's rule. Also, his response manifested God's characteristic gracious love. "Jesus' kingdom is based on something other than . . . power or protection. It is based on his self-surrender, on his offering of himself for the sin of the world" (Ridderbos 1997:595).

Thus, Jesus is working on a different level, one not of this world. Throughout the Gospel it is seen that he does not respond merely to stimuli from the environment; rather he acts in accordance with his Father's direction. So in a sense Jesus does answer Pilate's question about what he has done not by describing his teachings and signs, but by referring to his acceptance of suffering. If one does not realize who he is and why he has allowed himself to be handed over by his Jewish opponents, however, his glory is not evident. Nevertheless, his arrest, and everything else about him, bears witness that his kingdom is "not from here" *(ouk estin enteuthen,* paraphrased in the NIV as *from another place).* It is from the Father. If Pilate had an open heart he would have picked up this hint and asked where

Jesus' kingdom is from, but he does not.

Instead, he focuses on Jesus' reference to *my kingdom*. *My kingdom (hē basileia hē emē)* is repeated three times (one of them omitted in the NIV), and the expression *my servants* uses the same Greek construction that is used to emphasize the pronoun *my (hoi hypēretai hoi emoi)*. His kingdom is quite distinct from other kingdoms, but he does indeed have a kingdom. Pilate picks up on this emphasis and presses his earlier question, again in keeping with the Roman practice of questioning the defendant three times (Sherwin-White 1965:105), and says, *You are a king, then!* (v. 37).

The grace and humility evident in the Passion itself comes through also in the gentleness of Jesus' dealing with this Roman politician (cf. Chrysostom *In John* 84.1). Jesus replies, "You say that I am a king" (v. 37). This is often taken as an affirmative, almost as if Jesus were saying, "You said it!" (cf. NIV). This interpretation is possible (Beasley-Murray 1987:317); however, it is more likely that Jesus is saying, "That's your term." He is clearly claiming kingship, but he does not commit to the label of "king," probably because it is loaded with misunderstanding (6:15; cf. 1:49; 12:13). It is very much a term "of this world"! His reticence here is similar to his attitude toward other titles, such as "Messiah," elsewhere in the Gospels.

Jesus' further explanation reveals that he is king in a sense that transcends all other kings: *for this reason I was born, and for this I came into the world* (v. 37). Given what this Gospel has revealed of Jesus' identity, this is a profound statement of pre-existence (for example, 1:1-18; 3:13; 9:39). But if Pilate thought about what Jesus said at all, he would probably hear it only on a human level, that Jesus was claiming to be like any other child who was born a prince, in line to become king. Even this would be striking, since there was no such dynastic line functioning in Israel. But Pilate may not have gotten that far in his thinking, for Jesus says that he came into the world not to be king of the Jews, but *to testify to the truth*. This language makes obvious the contrast between his identity and mission on the one hand and the falsehood of his opponents on the other. "He is the king of Truth, and He manifests His royal power not by force, but by the witness He bears to the Truth (3:32; 5:33; cf. 3 Jn 3)" (Hoskyn 1940b:619). The truth he refers to is the truth of God.

By using the term "truth" rather than "God," Jesus is using language less likely to be misunderstood by Pilate. For he is still dealing here with Pilate himself: *Everyone on the side of truth listens to me* (v. 37), he says—everyone, whether Jew or Gentile. Jesus continues to walk through this trial on his own terms. Pilate thinks of Jesus as a defendant, but Jesus is taking the part of a witness (see comment on 5:31; cf. 1 Tim 6:13), who "has come to testify against the rule of the lie and for 'the truth,' that is, for God and for God's claim on the world" (Ridderbos 1997:596). So Jesus is asking for Pilate to pass judgment not on him as king of the Jews, but on him as the revealer of truth. And he puts pressure on Pilate, for if he does not decide in favor of Jesus, he will judge himself as not being *on the side of truth*. This expression is, more literally, "of the truth" *(ek tēs alētheias)*; it refers to one's inner disposition as tuned to the truth, able to hear the voice of truth (cf. 8:47; 10:3). "Absolute truth is a very uncomfortable thing when we come in contact with it" (Ward 1994:30).

Pilate's response, *What is truth?* (v. 38), is probably not a great philosophical remark, but a dismissal of the whole subject as irrelevant. Pilate has heard enough to determine that Jesus is not a political threat, and, therefore, he has gotten from the interview what he was after. Jesus has sown seed, but it has fallen on a beaten path. Pilate does not listen to Jesus, so, according to what Jesus has just said, he is not of the truth. The judge has been judged and found self-condemned through his response to Jesus. The Jewish opponents had come to this same place during the course of Jesus' ministry. So now both Jew and Gentile have been given a chance to respond to the one come from God, and they have rejected him.

Jesus' statement that his kingdom is not of this world does not mean that it has no impact in this world. Throughout the Gospels Jesus makes it clear that his kingdom is both otherworldly in its source and quality and present here in this world. Its focal point is the body of believers, who, through their union with the Father in the Son by the Spirit, are not of this world (cf. Augustine *In John* 115.2). Because it is a kingdom, it has to do with relationships, relationships inspired by God's own presence and manifesting his characteristic love. And because this network of relations is embodied in a community present in this world, it is expressed institutionally. Our passage does not indicate the shape of this institution, but it is clear that it is not of this world and that it is centered in the truth of God revealed by Jesus. These two criteria stand in judgment of much of the life of the church throughout the ages. All should be evaluated in the light of the pattern of life manifested in Jesus and revealed by him regarding the Godhead of the Father, the Son and the Spirit.

Pilate Finds Jesus Innocent (18:38-40) In scene three (see introduction to 18:28—19:16) Pilate returns outside and announces that he finds Jesus innocent, that, as the NIV well expresses it, he finds *no basis for a charge against him* (v. 38). Luke tells us that the crowd at this point insists Jesus has been causing trouble all over Judea, beginning in Galilee (Lk 23:5). This gives Pilate an excuse to send Jesus to Herod, an occasion that only Luke records (Lk 23:6-12). This additional material is helpful because with just John's account it is not clear why Pilate does not simply release Jesus once he finds him innocent. John seems to refer to the crowd's shouting at this point when he says, "therefore, *again (palin)* they cried out saying" (v. 40). The crowd's insistence leads Pilate to offer to release Jesus, in keeping with *your custom for me to release to you one prisoner at the time of the Passover* (v. 39). There is no other evidence for this custom (Brown 1994:1:814-20), but there is "no good reason for doubting it" (Robinson 1985:261; cf. Horbury 1972:66-67).

Pilate's use of the term *king of the Jews* (v. 39) is obviously sarcastic since he has just said Jesus poses no political threat. As is so often the case with sin, when one is succumbing to temptation one is given opportunities to come to one's senses and turn back (cf. 1 Cor 10:13; Ward 1994:44-50). Pilate's question can be seen as a chance for the opponents to renounce this determination to eliminate Jesus. But, of course, it is far too late. The Jewish opponents are rejecting Jesus precisely as their king.

So the crowd cries out again (or *shouted back,* NIV) that they want Barabbas, not Jesus (v. 40). Such dispute between a crowd and a Roman governor might seem strange, but it was not that unusual. Indeed, "Roman jurists expressly warn magistrates against submitting to popular clamour" (Horbury 1972:67). The picture of Pilate in Josephus and Philo is of a violent man who hated the Jews, which would lead one not to expect him to make any such offer to the crowd. But their picture of Pilate is probably overdrawn (cf. Brown 1994:1:693-705). Both authors, in fact, cite an instance when

---

18:40 The irony deepens in that Barabbas's personal name, according to some manuscripts of Matthew 27:16-17 (for example, Θ, f^1), was Jesus. This reading is not found widely but is probably original (Brown 1994:1:798-99), for scribes would be more likely to leave it out than add it in. "Jesus" *(Iēsous)* is simply the Greek word for Joshua, which in Hebrew

Pilate did give in to Jewish pressure (Josephus *Antiquities of the Jews* 18.55-59 par. Josephus *Jewish Wars* 2.169-174; Philo *Legatio ad Gaium* 302). The present occasion, of course, will play out the same way.

John describes Barabbas as a *lēstēs,* which the NIV renders by saying he was one who *had taken part in a rebellion.* There were many sorts of revolutionary leaders in Israel in the first century (cf. Brown 1994:1:679-93; Horsley and Hanson 1985; Horsley 1992). The term *lēstēs* is not used to refer to such people during the time of Jesus, but it is so used later in the century, after the revolt of A.D. 66 (Brown 1994:1:687). However, two of the other Gospels mention that Barabbas was indeed involved in an insurrection (Mk 15:7; Lk 23:19), so this is probably how John is using the term. The crowd demands the release of one under arrest for his threat against Rome. Their decision is very much "of this world."

There is a stark contrast between Barabbas, a violent man concerned with this world's politics, albeit religious politics, and Jesus, whose kingdom is not of this world, though it is active in this world. There is also irony in the name Barabbas itself, since it means "son of Abba"—the word Abba, "father," was used as a proper name (Brown 1994:1:799-800), but, especially in John's Gospel, Jesus is known as the Son of the Father. The crowd was choosing between two different approaches to liberation as represented by two men identified, in different ways, as "son of Abba." Here is the deceptiveness of sin that has been evident since the Garden of Eden. There is a path that looks right and seems to be of God, yet it is actually against him and his ways. The people choose their own path of liberation rather than God's, and they therefore choose "not the Savior, but the murderer; not the Giver of life, but the destroyer" (Augustine *In John* 116.1). Every time we choose sin we do the same, whether the sin is blatant or deceptive.

Pilate has rejected Jesus, his otherworldly kingdom and the truth, so he is left responding to the demands of the pressures of this world. He does not like the alternatives offered him by either Jesus or the opponents, but he is being forced to decide. Here is a picture of John's dualism, indeed, the dualism found throughout the Scriptures. God and Satan are both putting

---

($y^{e}hôšua'$) means "God saves" (the Greek following the Aramaic form *yešu'*). So the crowd had to choose between two men, both of whom were named Jesus and were identified as "son of Abba" yet who represented two different understandings of God's salvation. None of our Gospels put all of these elements together, but the composite picture is striking.

pressure on. Both desire us, though for very different purposes. "There is no neutral ground in the universe: every square inch, every split second, is claimed by God and counterclaimed by Satan" (Lewis 1967:33). Each of us faces the same challenge Pilate here faces. Even though we are able to avoid the crunch for now, we will not be able to do so forever. The Mercy would not allow that.

The Soldiers Mistreat Jesus (19:1-3) The theme of kingship continues as we now see the Roman soldiers dress Jesus up like a king, revere him and greet him as king of the Jews. They are doing so in cruel mockery, but they speak the truth. This may be another example of John's use of irony in having people speak truth that they themselves do not realize, providing "a sign that the Gentiles will ultimately confess the kingship of Jesus" (Brown 1970:889). This little section is at the center of a chiasm (see introduction to 18:28—19:16), which adds weight to this suggestion, since the center point of a chiasm is usually the main point.

Pilate turns Jesus over to the soldiers to be *flogged* (v. 1). In other Gospel accounts Jesus is flogged right before he is handed over for crucifixion (Mt 27:26 par. Mk 15:15), whereas here Pilate will make another effort to get Jesus released before he is eventually handed over (v. 16). Luke, like John, mentions several efforts made by Pilate to release Jesus (Lk 23:13-22), but Luke does not refer to the flogging itself, beyond Pilate's threat to punish Jesus (Lk 23:16, 22). Some think that Jesus was flogged once and that John has separated that event from the handing over (Sherwin-White 1965:104; Brown 1994:1:852-53), but more likely there were two floggings (Carson 1991:597). The Romans had several degrees of punishment (Brown 1994:1:851-52), with the lightest form being a beating that was both a punishment and a warning (Sherwin-White 1963:27). The more severe forms were used in interrogations to extract information from people or in connection with other punishments (Sherwin-White 1963:27). Since the punishment at this point in John's account was neither of these severe forms, the reference would fit the lighter form better. Pilate, who considers Jesus innocent, may have wanted to satisfy Jesus' opponents with this relatively light punishment. The later flogging, referred to by Matthew and Mark in connection with the sentence of crucifixion, would have been the more severe form. This type of flogging employed a whip made of leather thongs with pieces of bone or lead attached, which chewed up the flesh. Such flogging could itself result in death. Jesus' own flogging, while brutal and inflicting great suffering, was not carried out to this extreme, since he did not die from it. Indeed, Pilate was surprised he died so quickly on the cross (Mk 15:44; cf. Blinzler 1959:226). Pilate, however, did not know the whole story, for he did not know of the spiritual wounds Jesus suffered as he took away the sin of the world (1:29), being "pierced for our transgressions" and "crushed for our iniquities" (Is 53:5).

In addition to beating Jesus, as ordered by Pilate, the soldiers mocked him. The *crown of thorns* (v. 2) was most likely made from the date palm (Hart 1952), the same plant that had supplied the fronds laid on Jesus' path as he entered Jerusalem a short time before (12:13). The spikes on this plant can reach twelve inches long and were notorious for inflicting pain (cf. *Midrash Rabbah* on Num 3:1). Such long spikes would give the effect of a starburst around Jesus' head, in imitation of the likeness of deified rulers on coins of the period and much earlier. (H. Hart's article includes photos of such coins and the spikes from a date palm.) The *purple robe* (v. 2) and the greeting *"Hail, king of the Jews!"* (v. 3)—an imitation of the greeting to Caesar, "Ave, Caesar"—furthered the sick entertainment. As they lined up and came forward to greet him (cf. Bruce 1983:358), instead of giving him the kiss of greeting, they *struck him in the face* (v. 3).

This scene presents a powerful picture of Christ's glory, since this caricature of Christian worship, as E. C. Hoskyns calls it 1940b:621), actually speaks of Jesus' true identity as King of the Jews and, indeed, Lord of all. But throughout the story we have seen the chief characteristic of the glory of God revealed in Jesus to be his love. Jesus really is a king beyond the wildest imaginings of these soldiers. When we realize the power Jesus had we understand more of his humility and see God's brilliant glory. "Thus the kingdom which was not of this world overcame that proud world, not by the ferocity of fighting, but by the humility of suffering" (Augustine *In John* 116.1).

Pilate Again Declares Jesus Innocent (19:4-8) This second declaration of Jesus' innocence forms the fifth section of the chiasm (see introduction to 18:28—19:16), corresponding to the third section in which Pilate went out to the Jewish opponents and said he found no basis for a charge against Jesus (18:38b-40). This time he brings Jesus out with him—Jesus wearing the mocking signs of kingship and bearing the marks of the violence done against him. This very presentation of Jesus, with Pilate's dramatic words, *Here is the man!* (v. 5), could itself be a continuation of the mockery, as though Jesus is coming forth to be presented to his subjects as on some state occasion. But while Pilate is mocking Jesus and his fellow Jews he is also making the point that there is *no basis for a charge against* such a figure. Jesus may be dressed up as a king and a god (Hart 1952:75), but in Pilate's eyes he is only a man.

Once again we have an "unconscious prophet" (Westcott 1908:2:299), like Caiaphas (11:49-52) or the centurion in Mark's Gospel (Mk 15:39; cf. Bruce 1983:359). Several proposals have been made for the significance of Pilate's calling Jesus *the man* (cf. Barrett 1978:541; Brown 1994:1:827-28). One of the more likely proposals is Jesus' identity as the Son of Man, since Jesus had said, "When you have lifted up the Son of Man, then you will know that I AM" (8:28). Another possibility is an emphasis on Jesus' humanity: Jesus is indeed *man (anthrōpos),* for the Word became flesh (1:14). Since the real reason his opponents are against him is his claim to deity (19:7), we would have in Pilate's phrase references to both the humanity and the deity of Jesus. John may also see here allusions to Jesus as the last Adam, to use Paul's language (1 Cor 15:45), in keeping with similar possible allusions through the motif of the Garden (see comment on 18:1). This association with Adam is true, but since John does not make an explicit reference to him, we can't be sure he had it in mind here.

Pilate's bid to release Jesus is once again soundly rejected (v. 6a). The heart of the opposition to Jesus comes from *the chief priests and their officials,* and John singles these folk out as the ones crying, *Crucify! Crucify!* They want Jesus not merely dead, but crucified. The reason, most likely, is that this form of death was associated with the curse in the law against "anyone who is hung on a tree" (Deut 21:23, see comment on 18:32).

Pilate's little plan failed, so in exasperation he tells the leaders to take Jesus and crucify him themselves, since, as he says for the third time, he finds no charge against Jesus (v. 6). Pilate is trusting in political games rather than standing in integrity for what he knows to be true. When such people cannot control a situation they get frustrated and angry. He is not really

---

19:8 Up to this point John has not mentioned Pilate's being afraid, so the expression *even more afraid (mallon ephobēthē)* is puzzling. This may be an indication that John, or the later disciples, has left out material (cf. 18:40) that did refer to Pilate's fear. Or *mallon* may

offering them a chance to crucify Jesus themselves, and they understand that, as their actions show.

Pilate and the Jewish leaders are very agitated, but the appeal they both make is to law. According to Roman law Jesus is innocent, as Pilate has now said three times. But the leaders now assert that according to Jewish law (v. 7), Jesus must die *because he claimed to be the Son of God* (v. 7). This was the charge that was brought against Jesus at the trial before Caiaphas, though not recorded by John (Mt 26:63-66 par. Mk 14:61-64 par. Lk 22:67-71). The law they seem to have in mind says "anyone who blasphemes the name of the LORD must be put to death" (Lev 24:16). Later in the Mishnah blasphemy refers to pronouncing the divine name (*m. Sanhedrin* 7:5), but the concept was broader in the first century (cf. Robinson 1985:263). The claim to be a "son of God" is not necessarily a blasphemous claim to deity since the phrase was used in the Old Testament to describe beings other than God, in particular heavenly beings (Gen 6:2; Ps 29:1, obscured in the NIV) and the king of Israel (2 Sam 7:14; Ps 2:7; 89:26-27; cf. Wülfing von Martitz et al. 1972:347-53). Since "son of God" was used of the king, the opponents are not now shifting away from the charge that Jesus claims to be king, as seen in their repetition of this charge later (v. 12). Rather, they are helping Pilate understand that there is a religious as well as a political dimension to the kingship of Jesus, and the religious aspect is the crucial one. Throughout the Gospel they have rejected Jesus' claims to a special relationship with God, and they have already threatened his life because of such claims (5:18; 8:58-59; 10:33, 36). It is his claim to be God's Son in a special sense that constitutes the blasphemy (10:36).

The opponents had not introduced this underlying problem to Pilate at first but rather couched it in its political form to get him to act. Even now their expression allows Pilate to read his own content into it. For they say Jesus claims to be "a son of God" *(hyion theou)*. For a Roman, as for a Jew, this could be a political claim since the emperor could be referred to as "son of God" *(theou hyios, divi filius)*. But Pilate does not treat it as such but rather, it seems, as a claim to be a "divine man" *(theios anēr,* Dodd

---

have its other common meaning, "rather": "he became afraid rather (than complied with their desire)" (Bruce 1983:361).

1953:250-51). These "divine men" were Hellenistic religious philosophers who were "characterized by moral virtue, wisdom and/or miraculous power so that they were held to be divine" (Blackburn 1992:189).

Pilate's response is fear (v. 8). Some think this fear is due to his realization that the situation is getting out of his control and that "he will not be able to escape making a judgment about truth" (Brown 1994:1:830; cf. Ridderbos 1997:602). But John says it was this saying *(touton ton logon)* about Jesus as *Son of God* that caused Pilate's fear (v. 8) and led him to ask Jesus where he is from (v. 9). So he is probably experiencing a fear of the divine, on top of all the other problems this situation entails for him. The discussion Pilate had just had with Jesus about his kingdom now begins to make more sense to Pilate. He must take Jesus back inside and explore this new dimension to his case.

Jesus Speaks of Power and Guilt (19:9-11) In Pilate's earlier discussion with Jesus, which forms the corresponding section in the first part of the chiasm (see introduction to 18:28—19:16), Jesus had clearly said he was not from this world (18:36-37). This obviously raises the question of where he is from. Now that Pilate knows Jesus claims to be a son of God he investigates more closely, asking Jesus, *Where do you come from?* (v. 9). From the context this is clearly not an inquiry about what country he is from, "but it is as if he had said, 'Are you an earth-born man or some god?' " (Calvin 1959:172). Pilate's question gets at the central issue regarding Jesus—that he is from the Father in heaven. Jesus' origin was a major topic during his ministry (7:27-29; 8:14; 9:29-33), and now it comes to the fore at the end.

Jesus does not speak about his origin to Pilate. According to the Synoptics, Jesus has been silent already during his Passion, both before Pilate, when the chief priests and elders were accusing him (Mt 27:12-14 par. Mk 15:3-5), and before Herod, with the same opponents accusing him (Lk 23:9-10). Now he is also silent before Pilate in private (Jn 19:9). His silence echoes the silence of the Suffering Servant of Isaiah (53:7; cf. Acts 8:32; 1 Pet 2:22-23). He is silent, it seems, because Pilate has already revealed that he is not a man of truth and thus would not benefit from an answer to his question (see comment on 12:34-36).

Pilate has been exasperated by the Jewish leaders, and now he finds Jesus exasperating also. No one is cooperating with him! He threatens Jesus by referring to his power, though his threat comes across as a little lame given his obvious lack of power over the Jewish leaders: *Don't you realize I have power either to free you or to crucify you?* (v. 10). In Roman law it was said, "No one who has power to condemn is without power to acquit" (Justinian *Digest of Roman Law* 50.17.37; cf. Bruce 1983:361-62). Pilate had a clear understanding of his legal power, that is, his authority *(exousia)*. But he is thinking only in terms of this world.

Often in this Gospel we see people who are mistaken about Jesus and his teaching because they are viewing reality solely in this-worldly categories, for example, the woman of Samaria (chap. 4). Jesus has used their misunderstandings to help these people come to a better view of reality, and that is what he now does with Pilate also: *You would have no power over me if it were not given to you from above* (v. 11). Pilate well understands that his power is dependent on the one who is over him, the emperor. He could understand Jesus to be saying nothing more than this. But now that Pilate realizes Jesus is claiming to be a son of God he has a chance to interpret Jesus correctly, to understand that God is the source of this power. Indeed, Jesus' reference to *from above* gives Pilate a hint as to the answer to his question of where Jesus is from (cf. 3:31; 8:23). Thus this is a saying that tests Pilate's heart. Will he hear it correctly?

There are further hints as well about Jesus and his Father. The word for *power (exousia)* is in the feminine, whereas the verb *it were . . . given (ēn dedomenon)* is in the neuter and thus refers to more than just the *power:* "You would not have any power over me if something had not been given to you from above." In other words, this expression puts all the emphasis on the verbal idea of giving, a reference to the Father who is the source of all—the one who gives. Jesus' point is that Pilate, like all of us, is a recipient. So Jesus is saying, in part, that the power of government has been given by God (3:27; Rom 13:1-7). Jesus speaks for this God upon whom Pilate himself is dependent, thereby further hinting as to his identity and the character of his Father.

In addition to making this general point, Jesus also refers specifically to the power Pilate has *over me.* No one has power over Jesus except the Father. And, in particular, no one takes Jesus' life from him, but rather he lays it down of his own accord in obedience to his Father (10:17-18). Here is yet another hint for Pilate: he may have power over everyone else in

Israel, but not over Jesus. If Pilate realized who was standing before him, he would have a chance of making sense out of this situation and much more.

And he needs to make sense out of Jesus and this trial and his own relation to the Father because he is sinning. He should get this message from the conclusion of Jesus' statement that *therefore the one who handed me over to you is guilty of a greater sin* (v. 11). Pilate's fear is quite justified. He will be held accountable to God for how he exercises his authority. His sin may not be as great as someone else's, but he is in fact sinning. Furthermore, this indictment of Pilate implies something about Jesus' own identity and role, for he is claiming to know God and God's will. Indeed, Jesus himself is the point of reference for sin in that to reject him is sin (16:9) and to receive him is to obey God (6:29). When Jesus used a similar indirect exposure of the sin of the woman of Samaria she was able to perceive something of what Jesus was saying about himself and respond to him (4:16-19). Pilate, however, does not pursue the issue further. He feels the pressure Jesus has exerted and thus tries all the harder to release him (v. 12), but he does not turn toward the light. He is still trying to be neutral and stay in control.

If Pilate's sin is great, who is the one who has a *greater sin?* The reference would not be to Judas, since he did not hand Jesus over to Pilate. Rather, as Pilate said to Jesus earlier, it was "your people and your chief priests who handed you over to me" (18:35). Now Jesus uses the singular, *the one who,* collecting all his opponents into a unit, perhaps in the person of the high priest, Caiaphas. All has been given from above, *therefore* there are degrees of sin in keeping with the differences in what has been given. If Pilate sins by not administering justice to a man he knows is innocent, how much more sinful are the leaders of God's people who have received not merely laws of justice but the divine law that bears witness to the Father and the one whom he has sent. To whom much is given, much is required (Lk 12:48).

Thus, both Jew and Gentile share in the sin, and therefore the guilt, of Jesus' death. Indeed, "each of us is as guilty of putting Jesus on the cross as Caiaphas" (Carson 1991:575) or Pilate, for that matter. But John clearly says the Jews' sin is greater, not because John is anti-Jewish, but precisely because of the greater gifts of God within Judaism. The problem is not

Judaism as such but the rejection of their own Messiah by these particular leaders and their followers, despite what was available within Judaism. Thus, these members of the people of God are of this world, not of God (8:23).

Unfortunately, this Gospel has been read in anti-Jewish ways and thus has contributed to hatred of Jews and violence committed against them—all completely contrary to the teachings of Jesus. Although this Gospel reflects the conflict between the church and the synagogue late in the first century, it should not be seen as anti-Jewish (see comment on 8:44; cf. Brown 1994:1:383-97; Beasley-Murray 1987:308-10; Robinson 1985:271-75). It is, instead, anti-world. The Jews had a greater witness to the Light, so they should have embraced the Light more readily when he came. Accordingly their sin was greater than that of the Gentile Pilate. But from this perspective there is now a group whose sin is much greater yet. For from all appearances a great many Christians throughout the ages—and not least in our day— have been of the world as much as these Jewish opponents were, despite having not only the Old Testament but the Holy Spirit, the New Testament and the witness of the saints throughout the ages. Indeed, violence done against the Jews has itself been evidence of being of the world. Anyone, whether Jew or Gentile, who is of the world is allied with the evil one over against the Son of God (cf. 8:44). This spiritual contest is the real significance of what is taking place in the Passion (cf. 12:31; 14:30; 16:11).

Pilate and the Jewish Opponents Reject Jesus as King (19:12-16)
This final section of the chiastic account of the trial before Pilate (see introduction to 18:28—19:16) corresponds with the first section (18:29-32), in which Pilate was also outside the praetorium and the opponents called for Jesus' death. Jesus has just borne witness to the truth about himself, his Father, Pilate and the opponents. He has made Pilate even more uncomfortable, so Pilate begins to make further efforts to release him (v. 12; *ezētei,* NIV *tried,* is in the imperfect tense, here signifying repeated action). The Jewish leaders counter these efforts with a decisive move—they bring in the issue of Pilate's loyalty to Caesar (v. 12). A later emperor, Vespasian (A.D. 69-79), had a specific group of people whose loyalty and importance were recognized by the title *friend of Caesar*. It is possible that Tiberius also had such a group and Pilate was a member (Bammel 1952), though this is uncertain. In either case, the threat is to Pilate's position, and this settles

the issue. Pilate has already revealed that he is a man of this world, insensitive to the truth of God. A threat to his political position is an attack upon the heart of what he knows and cares about. Such a choice between Jesus and other ultimate concerns in our lives faces each of us, for Jesus really is King and insists on complete loyalty as strongly as Tiberius. Pilate is faced with a choice of kings, and he does not choose wisely.

It is, of course, highly ironic that Pilate's loyalty to Caesar should be threatened by Jews, members of the most disloyal and unruly section of the empire. Pilate is being humiliated by them. He knows he must give in to their wishes, but he is wily enough to humiliate them also in the process. Upon hearing their threat, he brings Jesus out and sits on the judge's seat *(bēma)* to pass judgment. This is the climax of the trial and, indeed, of the ministry of Jesus.

John underscores the importance of this moment by specifying the place and time, though, unfortunately, the precise meaning of both is uncertain today. The place where the trial before Pilate occurred is uncertain (see comment on 18:28), and the addition of the term *Gabbatha* does not help. This Aramaic word does not mean *Stone Pavement* but is a different word for the same place, probably meaning something like "elevated" (McRay 1992). The location would have been well known in the first century because it was the place of judgment.

The reference to *the day of Preparation of Passover Week, about the sixth hour* (v. 14) is problematic when compared to the Synoptics. If *Passover (pascha)* refers to the Passover meal itself, then John has the trial and the crucifixion happening a day earlier than the Synoptics do (see comment on 18:28). This would mean that this dramatic point before Pilate's *bēma* occurs just as the lambs are beginning to be slaughtered in the temple. Jesus' death then took place while they were continuing to be killed. This setting would tie in with Jesus' identity as the Lamb of God (1:29) and the several allusions to the pascal lamb in the Passion narrative (see comments on 19:19, 33-34, 36). On the other hand, if *pascha* refers to *Passover Week,* as in the NIV (cf. Torrey 1931; Carson 1991:603-4), then John's account is not in conflict with the Synoptics. If the word *preparation (paraskeuē)* regularly referred to the

---

19:13 The grammar allows the possibility that Pilate placed Jesus upon the judge's seat rather than sitting upon it himself. This would add to the mockery of the scene and would touch on the theme in this Gospel of Jesus as the judge. Early sources take it this way

day before the sabbath, that is, Friday, this would lend support to the latter interpretation (Ridderbos 1997:456). For then both John and the Synoptics would present Jesus as eating Passover on Thursday evening, the beginning of Friday according to Jewish reckoning in which days begin at sundown. This usage, however, is contested (cf. Zeitlin 1932; Brown 1994:1:846). Alternatively, the suggestion that two different calendars were used (see comment on 18:28) would also account for the differences, since for some it would still be the period of preparation for the Passover meal. In this way Jesus ate the Passover and also died while the Passover lambs continued to be killed. There is no clear solution to this quesstion.

The *sixth hour* would be noon, which seems to conflict with Mark's statement that Jesus was crucified at the third hour, that is, 9 a.m. (Mk 15:25). Again there is a division of opinion, with some assuming the two accounts simply contradict one another (Robinson 1985:268), perhaps due to a corruption in the text (Alford 1980:897-98; Barrett 1978:545) or because both John and Mark cite an hour that has symbolic significance for them (Barrett 1978:545; Brown 1994:1:847). Others think the imprecision of telling time in the ancient world accounts for the discrepancy (Augustine *In John* 117.1; Morris 1971:800-801).

Whatever the solution to these puzzles, John emphasizes this particular moment because Jesus is now presented to his people as king: *Here is your king* (v. 14). Pilate may be making one last bid to get them to change their minds, but given their threat to him regarding his loyalty to Caesar this is unlikely. Rather, Pilate mocks the Jews by saying this battered, weak man dressed in sham regal trappings is their king. Pilate is perhaps imitating a ceremony formally recognizing a ruler, somewhat similar to what takes place today at the coronation of a British monarch (cf. Bruce 1983:365). Jesus is indeed their king, and here is their one last chance to receive him as such, but they will have nothing of it. Pilate thereby "makes the moment of *his* decision the moment of decision *for the Jews*" (Beasley-Murray 1987:342).

The Jewish opponents have trapped Pilate, and now he springs on them a trap of his own. When they once more reject Jesus as their king and call

(*Gospel of Peter* 3:7; Justin Martyr *1 Apology* 35.6), as do some modern scholars, but this is not the most natural reading of the grammar and would be highly unlikely historically (Brown 1994:2:1388-93).

for his crucifixion, Pilate replies, *Shall I crucify your king?* (v. 15). What they should have said in return was, "We have no king but God," but in order to force Pilate's hand with their threat regarding his loyalty to Caesar the chief priests instead say, *We have no king but Caesar* (v. 15). Like Pilate, they are forced to choose which king they will serve, and they also fail to choose wisely. Here are the spiritual leaders of Israel denying the very faith they are claiming to uphold in their rejection of Jesus. God alone was Israel's king (Judg 8:23; 1 Sam 8:4-20). The human king was to be in submission to God as a son is to his father (2 Sam 7:11-16; Ps 2:7). These ancient attitudes found expression in one of the prayers these chief priests prayed every day: "May you be our King, you alone." Every year at this very feast of Passover they sang, "From everlasting to everlasting you are God; beside you we have no king, redeemer, or savior, no liberator, deliverer, provider, none who takes pity in every time of distress and trouble; we have no king but you" (Talbert 1992:241). The hope was for a redeemer to come, the Messiah, who would be a king like David. "But now hundreds of years of waiting had been cast aside: 'the Jews' had proclaimed the half-mad exile of Capri to be their king" (Brown 1970:895; cf. Westcott 1908:2:306). These opponents stand self-condemned.

Jesus is indeed the King of Israel, and that means true Israel is found among those who owe allegiance to him. Jesus had already withdrawn from the temple (8:59) and formed the nucleus of the renewed people. Now the leadership of the nation completes this judgment, for "in the breaking of the covenant whereby God or his Messiah was Israel's king, the movement of replacement comes to a climax, for 'the Jews' have renounced their status as God's people" (Brown 1970:895). The light is shining brightly at this point, and the darkness's rejection of the light is equally strong (cf. 3:20).

Pilate then hands Jesus over to them to crucify (v. 16). They themselves did not carry out the crucifixion, but this way of putting it completes the cycle of guilt. They had handed Jesus over to Pilate, and now he hands Jesus over to them. Both Jew and Gentile have rejected Jesus, and the way is now prepared for the ultimate revelation of the glory of God. This rejection of the Son of God is the essence of sin, and Jesus will now die to take away the sin of the world.

Jesus Is Crucified (19:16-30) Jesus is led to the place of crucifixion and nailed to the cross (vv. 16-18). While his enemies continue to squabble with one another (vv. 19-22) and divide his clothes (vv. 23-24), Jesus himself continues to love his followers and direct their own sharing in his love (vv. 25-27). Then he dies (vv. 28-30).

Jesus Is Hung on the Cross (19:16-18) John's description of the actual crucifixion is amazingly brief. People in the ancient world would not need a description, since such executions were not rare (Hengel 1977:38). Although crucifixion could take a variety of forms (cf. Hengel 1977:25-32; Brown 1994:2:945-52), it was common to have the victim carry the crossbeam to the place of crucifixion where the upright was already in place. Occasionally the victim was tied to the crossbeam with leather thongs, but most often nails were used, as in the case of Jesus. The nails were five to seven inches long and were driven through the feet and wrists, not the hands (Edwards, Gabel and Hosmer 1986:1459). Crosses in the shape of an X or a T were used, but since the title was attached over Jesus' head (Mt 27:37) we know the style used for Jesus' cross was the shape we usually imagine, a †, which was also a common form. The person was laid on the ground and nailed to the crosspiece, which was then hoisted into place. Often the person was only a short distance off the ground, though the fact that a stick was needed in order to offer Jesus a drink (v. 29) suggests his head was higher than arm's length above the people on the ground. The nail wounds would cause a great deal of bleeding, but death often took place through suffocation. A little seat rest was attached to allow the person to maintain a position in which it was possible to breathe, thus prolonging the agony.

It is not known why the place was called Skull (v. 17; *calvaria* in Latin, hence the name Calvary), but the fact that Joseph had a tomb close by suggests this was not a place of public execution (Brown 1970:900). The notion that the landscape had the appearance of a skull is possible, as evidenced by the hill near Gordon's Calvary today, though the shape of this particular hill is more recent than the first century. The traditional site at the Church of the Holy Sepulchre, not the Garden Tomb at Gordon's Calvary, is most likely authentic (R. H. Smith 1976; Brown 1994:2:937-40, 1279-83).

John mentions the other two victims crucified with Jesus (v. 18), but he does not describe them as fully as the Synoptic writers do. John also leaves out mention of Simon of Cyrene helping carry Jesus' cross. This comparison with the other Gospels helps us appreciate how John's account is very focused, very spare. In what follows he will not dwell on Jesus' own agony, except for his thirst just before his death (v. 28). Instead, John describes the activity swirling around Jesus, showing how it all relates to the glory. While John directs our attention to various people around the cross, we must not lose sight of the one on the cross. That which is not described is actually what dominates the scene.

Pilate and the Jewish Leaders Fight over the Title (19:19-22) It was common practice to have those sentenced to crucifixion carry signs indicating the cause of their punishment or to have others carry the signs for the accused (Brown 1994:2:963). The title Pilate has written, JESUS OF NAZARETH, THE KING OF THE JEWS (v. 19), continues to goad the Jewish leaders, as their reaction demonstrates (v. 21). They insist that he change it, but for the first time he stands firm against them. Now that their threat against him has passed he can afford to be strong (cf. Westcott 1908:2:310), which only serves to portray his pathetic weakness all the more clearly. His famous line—*What I have written, I have written* (v. 22)—sounds, in the context, merely petulant and childish.

Pilate earlier announced Jesus as "the man" (v. 5) and as "your king" (v. 14), and now he combines these themes in the title for Jesus' cross. Designating Jesus as being from Nazareth focuses on his humble humanity, while giving him the title of king speaks of his grandeur (see comment on 18:5-6). It was written in the three major languages of the region and read by *many of the Jews* since it was *near the city* (v. 20). The Romans did what they could to make crucifixions gruesome and public for the purpose of deterrence. But John seems to suggest this title over the cross was itself a form of witness to Israel and the world. Pilate unwittingly made such a proclamation, of course, as was the case with his having chosen the title itself. Such features fit with John's theme that all is working out according to God's will, even despite some of the participants. Indeed, "the two men who were most responsible for the death of Jesus became the unwitting prophets of the death of Jesus: the one declaring it as the means of redemption for Israel and the nations (11:49-50) the other proclaiming it

---

19:21 The NIV obscures their proposal for the title, which more literally reads, "This man said, 'I am King of the Jews.' " This term, in fact, is never used of Jesus or by Jesus in this Gospel. Others refer to him as King of Israel (1:49; 12:13), but his own claims go far deeper.

the occasion of his exaltation to be King of Israel and Lord of all" (Beasley-Murray 1987:346).

So here we have another irony: the man who does not have a clue about the truth (18:38) proclaims, unwittingly, the truth about Jesus. And we have the tragedy of the representatives of the one true God, who should have recognized the truth, continuing to reject it.

The Soldiers Divide Jesus' Clothes (19:23-24) Normally the victim would be led naked to the place of crucifixion. The fact that Jesus' clothes were not taken from him until the point of crucifixion may suggest that he was allowed to retain some form of covering while on the cross itself (Brown 1994:2:953), perhaps out of deference to Jewish objections to nudity. Since, however, the normal undergarment was either a tunic or a loincloth, and Jesus' tunic was taken from him (v. 23; Brown 1970:902), it is perhaps more likely he was naked. Early Christian tradition is divided on the subject (cf. Brown 1994:2:953).

It is this *undergarment* (*chitōn,* the garment worn next to the skin) that is of most interest to John. It is seamless, and therefore to prevent its being torn the soldiers decide to draw lots for it (v. 24). The fact that it is seamless probably does not indicate that it was unusual or an item of luxury (Brown 1970:903). John's focus on this feature has led many to find symbolism in this garment (cf. Brown 1994:2:955-58). The two main proposals for John's detail have been that it is a symbol either of Jesus as high priest, since the high priest's *chitōn* was seamless, according to Josephus (*Antiquities of the Jews* 3.161), or of the unity of the church (for example, Cyprian *On the Unity of the Church* 7), that is, the community as brought together by the death of Christ (Barrett 1978:550, 552).

Such thoughts are true and edifying, but they are not John's primary focus. The significance of the garment's being seamless is that the soldiers are led to draw of lots for it, which in turn echoes Psalm 22:18 (v. 24). This is the first of four Old Testament passages cited as being fulfilled in Jesus' Passion, all of which refer to particular details of what takes place (vv. 28, 36-37). John marshals these texts around this most central, and most scandalous, event in order to show that the death of God's Son was in fact

---

His "I am" statements point to an identity that includes such kingship, but it is a kingship not merely of Israel and not merely as a human monarch.

the will of God the Father. Behind the idea of fulfillment is the notion of God's sovereign control, which weaves repeating patterns: Scripture expresses God's will, and Jesus is submissive to God's will, so his activity fulfills the Scripture because it flows from the same source and is controlled by the same Father.

Psalm 22 is a psalm of King David in his role as a righteous sufferer. The title above Jesus' head is proclaiming him to be king of the Jews, and John sees Jesus as replicating a pattern of the greatest king in Israel's past. Thus, this reference is not a gratuitous proof text, but a link with a type. Fulfillment of Scripture, in this sense, is the replication of a pattern, and Jesus is the ultimate fulfillment, the center of all the patterns. The Synoptics also allude to this connection regarding the garments (Mt 27:35 par. Mk 15:24 par. Lk 23:34) as well as the connection through Jesus' cry from the cross, "My God, my God, why have you forsaken me" (Mt 27:46 par. Mk 15:34), which is Psalm 22:1. The figure of the righteous king who suffers is embodied in Jesus par excellence. If the opponents understood King David better they might have recognized King Jesus.

Jesus Cares for His Mother and the Beloved Disciple (19:25-27)

John now turns to another distinct group at the cross (*men . . . de,* vv. 24-25), namely those who are there out of love for Jesus. It was not unheard of for friends and relatives to be near the one crucified or for enemies to come to jeer (cf. *t. Gittin* 7:1, 330; *y. Gittin* 7; 48c; 39; *b. Baba Metzia* 83b; Stauffer 1960:136, 229). Mark tells us there was quite a crowd of women present (15:41), but John focuses on a handful near the cross. The list of women most likely refers to four individuals (Brown 1994:2:1014-15). Mark, in his Gospel, lists three women in particular who were present, "Mary Magdalene, Mary the mother of James the younger and of Joses, and Salome" (15:40). It has been assumed from early times that the mother of James and Joses is the one referred to in John as *Mary the wife of Clopas* and that Salome is the one John calls *his mother's sister.* Salome, in turn, is further identified with the mother of the sons of Zebedee, as mentioned in Matthew's account (27:56). Accordingly, the sons of Zebedee were Jesus' cousins. Raymond Brown considers this identification "dubious" (1994:2:1017), and the texts admittedly do not allow certainty, since, as Mark says, there were a number of women present. However, if the Beloved Disciple, whom I take to be John, the son of Zebedee, is Jesus' cousin, then Jesus' commending his mother to his care corresponds a little more with normal family patterns, though much more is involved as we will soon see. Furthermore, it is striking that neither Jesus' mother nor his aunt are named, a trait they share with the Beloved Disciple (cf. Carson 1991:616).

With these supporters standing near him, Jesus focuses on his mother and the Beloved Disciple (vv. 26-27). Jesus says to his mother, "Woman, behold your son," and to the Beloved Disciple, "Behold your mother." Similar language was used in connection with betrothal (Tobit 7:12) and thus seems to signal some change of relationship. Jesus' mother is now brought under the care of the Beloved Disciple (v. 27). In this Gospel there is a symbolic role for both the mother of Jesus and the Beloved Disciple, for they are both examples of true discipleship (see comments on 2:1-11 and 13:23). So in changing the relationship they have to one another, Jesus is completing the formation of the community gathered around him—gathered around him precisely as he is on the cross (C. Koester 1995:214-19). The new community is now seen to be a new family (cf. 20:17; Newbigin 1982:255).

A great deal has been made of this text. Many have understood Jesus' mother to be a symbol of Eve, the mother of the living, or a symbol of the church (cf. Brown 1970:923-27). Quite often it has been assumed that the disciple is given into the care of the mother, which has contributed to the development of views regarding Mary's role in the lives of Christians, who are symbolized by the Beloved Disciple. Such symbolism is a further development of John's own focus, which is on the new family formed among the disciples of Jesus, with the Beloved Disciple, who is the witness to Jesus par excellence, as the one exercising care (cf. Ridderbos 1997:611-15). The mother and the Beloved Disciple together symbolize the new community.

Here at the very end we see Jesus still exercising love and care (cf. 13:1). This loving concern is the glory that his death itself reveals most powerfully, since love is the laying down of one's life (cf. 1 Jn 3:16). In the course of his ministry Jesus was forming a new community around himself, and in the farewell discourse (13:31—17:26) he described how that community is to share in his own relation with the Father and to participate in the divine life, which is characterized by love. Now he has completed the formation of this community, at least for the stage prior to the sending of the Spirit and his own dwelling with them in a new way. This community is the fruit of his death, for it will be the locus of the divine life on earth. The divine life is characterized by love and therefore requires a community to express itself. The life of the community derives from Jesus' own giving of himself, and in turn such self-giving is to typify the community itself. Jesus' death is both a revelation of the love of God and an example of such self-giving love. Such love is only really possible when sin has been taken away, since the essence of sin is a false self-love that prevents one from sharing in the life of God, which is love.

Jesus Dies (19:28-30) The significance of the formation of the community that has just taken place is further underscored when John says Jesus knows *that all was now completed* (v. 28). This is what he came to do—to form a community that can share in his own relation with the Father. With the work completed he can now finalize the completion through his death, so he says, *I am thirsty* (v. 28). John notes he said this in order to fulfill the Scripture—not that he was consciously thinking of texts and doing things to echo them, but rather that Scripture reveals God's will and Jesus perfectly accomplishes God's will (see comment on v. 24). The text he echoes (Ps 69:21) is another passage featuring King David as the righteous sufferer, and thus bears witness to Jesus' identity.

John shifts from *plēroō,* the word usually used to speak of the fulfillment of Scripture, to *teleioō,* the same word in the first part of the verse, there translated *completed,* and in Jesus' final cry, *It is finished* (v. 30). Jesus' own life, including his death and resurrection, is the primal pattern that Scripture itself replicates. He is the sun whose rays create shadows both backward and forward in time. Accordingly, he not only fulfills Scripture in the sense of replicating its patterns, he brings Scripture itself to completion by being its central referent.

John does not say who soaked a sponge in some cheap wine and lifted it to Jesus' lips with a stalk of hyssop (v. 29). The Synoptics also leave this indefinite, but they say a *kalamos* was used (Mt 27:48 par. Mk 15:36), that is, a reed, a staff or a stalk. Perhaps John has referred specifically to a hyssop

---

19:29 It is often said that a hyssop branch would not be long enough or strong enough to lift a sponge to Jesus. This depends on how high up he was and how big the sponge. A sponge could be supported on a bunch of hyssop.

19:30 The spirit referred to here is Jesus' human spirit, not the Holy Spirit, as 20:22 indicates.

stalk to interpret what is taking place, since hyssop was used to sprinkle the blood of the lamb on the doorposts just before the Exodus (Ex 12:22) and later was used for other purifying rites (Lev 14:4, 6; Num 19:18; Ps 51:7). John would be drawing out the juxtaposition of Jesus as king and Jesus as lamb, similar to the description in heaven of the Lion of the tribe of Judah who turns out to be "a Lamb, looking as if it had been slain" (Rev 5:5-6).

There seems to be something particularly significant about Jesus' thirst, since once Jesus receives the wine he says, *It is finished,* and dies (v. 30). On one level this thirst is the only reference in this Gospel to Jesus' actual physical suffering on the cross. But the idea of thirst may also have spiritual significance. Earlier Jesus had said, "My food . . . is to do the will of him who sent me and to finish *(teleioō)* his work" (4:34). And when he was arrested he told Peter to put his sword away, saying, "Shall I not drink the cup the Father has given me?" (18:11). "Hunger and thirst become images for Jesus' desire to fulfill the Father's will to the end" (Schnackenburg 1982:283). Since the cup represents wrath and suffering (see comment on 18:11), Jesus' taking of this drink may suggest the completion of that experience, as the Lamb of God now takes away the sin of the world. The work he has come to do is now complete. The great significance John attaches to the saying *I am thirsty* would then make sense because it would symbolize both Jesus' commitment to obey God's will and the fulfillment of the suffering of the one who is the righteous sufferer par excellence.

Jesus had said that no one takes his life from him but that he lays it down of his own accord (10:18), and his death is indeed described as a voluntary act: *he bowed his head and gave up his spirit* (v. 30). The order of Jesus' actions is important (Chrysostom *In John* 85.3). John does not say that Jesus died and then his head slumped over, but rather that he bowed his head, an attitude of submission, and then gave over *(paredōken)* his spirit. "At his own free will, he with a word dismissed from him his spirit, anticipating the executioner's work" (Tertullian *Apology* 21). The very form of his death continues to reveal him as the obedient Son, the key theme regarding his identity throughout his ministry. As the obedient Son, submissive to the

---

But the actual giving of the Spirit after the resurrection is somewhat complex (see comment on 20:22). So perhaps this way of describing his death is also part of that complexity, drawing the connection between his death and the giving of the Spirit (cf. 7:37-39) through a double meaning of the word *spirit.*

Father, he fulfills the type of the true King, confirming the message of the sign over his head.

Enemies and Friends Attend to Jesus' Body (19:31-42) John finds the events immediately following Jesus' death to be highly significant. He begins with Pilate and the Jewish opponents (v. 31), then the soldiers (vv. 32-37) and finally Jesus' friends (vv. 38-42). This is the same sequence he followed in the previous section (cf. vv. 19-27). The opponents are still trying to discredit Jesus even after his death; the soldiers unwittingly produce a witness to Jesus through their actions, as do Jesus' friends. The striking new feature is the witness of Jesus himself. The way in which he died was a witness to the truth about himself (see comment on v. 30), but now, even after he has died, his body produces a witness both to the truth about his identity and to the truth about what his death has accomplished (vv. 34-37).

The Jewish Leaders Ask Pilate to Mutilate Jesus' Body (19:31) Death by crucifixion could take a very long time, but the Romans did not mind this because it added to the deterrent value. But sometimes the Romans would smash the victim's legs with a heavy hammer, which prevented the person from pushing up in order to breathe and thereby caused death from suffocation within minutes (Edwards, Gabel and Hosmer 1986:1461). The Jewish opponents ask Pilate to have the soldiers speed up the dying process in this way in order to get the bodies disposed of before *the next day,* which was *a special Sabbath*. In the law it says the body of a person put to death and hung on a tree must not be left on the tree overnight. "Be sure to bury him that same day, because anyone who is hung on a tree is under God's curse. You must not desecrate the land the LORD your God is giving you as an inheritance" (Deut 21:23). This law applies to any day of the year, so how much more to a special feast day. These Jewish leaders continue to be greatly concerned with ritual purity (cf. 18:28), but more may be involved as well. They might intend that such mutilation would emphasize the point already made clear by the crucifixion itself—that Jesus

---

19:31 The sabbath was special either because Passover coincided with the sabbath that year (Brown 1970:934) or because the sabbath coincided with the second day of the feast, which was the dedication of firstfruits (Lev 23:11; Carson 1991:622; Ridderbos 1997:618). This puzzle is part of the larger question of dating the crucifixion (see comments on 18:28 and 19:14).

was accursed (Beasley-Murray 1987:354).

The Soldiers' Actions Provide Further Witness to Jesus (19:32-37)
The soldiers break the legs of the other two men being crucified, perhaps working in toward Jesus from the two sides (v. 32; Bruce 1983:375). When they come to Jesus they find him already dead and therefore do not break his legs (v. 33). In this way, although the opponents attempted to further discredit Jesus, they unwittingly bear witness to what he has accomplished. Jesus has drunk the cup of God's wrath and indeed has become accursed (cf. vv. 28-29; Gal 3:13). But as the Lamb of God, Jesus has taken away the sin of the world. The opponents' attempt to have Jesus' legs broken ends up drawing attention to the fact that they were not broken. Thus, another pattern of Scripture is echoed: *Not one of his bones will be broken* (v. 36). The allusion is to the Passover lamb (Ex 12:46; Num 9:12) and to King David as the righteous sufferer (Ps 34:20), thereby continuing the juxtaposition of themes that John has emphasized in his account of the Passion. In this way, the body of Jesus continues to bear witness to his identity and his accomplishment even after he has died.

His body also bears witness in another way, which is emphasized by John. For when the soldiers find Jesus dead one of them stabs him to be sure he is dead, and out comes *a sudden flow of blood and water* (v. 34). The word *pierce (nyssō)* can be used of either a jab or a deep stab. Medical explanations of this flow of blood and water differ according to the depth of the wound. One theory is that the scourging produced "a bloody accumulation" in the chest, which separated into layers as he hung on the cross, with the heavier blood on the bottom. The wound from the spear entered below the level of separation, so the liquid came out first red and then more clear (Sava 1960). The other main theory is that Jesus was stabbed in the heart, so the blood came from the heart while the water came from the pericardial sac around the heart (Edwards, Gabel and Hosmer 1986:1463).

There have been many suggestions over the centuries for the significance

---

19:34 It was a common belief in the Hellenistic world that the gods did not have blood in their veins but rather had a clear liquid known as *ichōr* (cf. Talbert 1992:245-46). For such folk, the fact that blood and water both flowed could suggest Jesus is both god and man.

of this flow (cf. Westcott 1908:2:328-33), and John may see a very complex web of associations. It is possible, in the light of later rabbinic thought, that the flow of blood and water mingled together is yet another allusion to Jesus as a Passover sacrifice. The blood of a sacrifice had to flow at the moment of death so it could be sprinkled (*m. Pesaḥim* 5:5, 8). Thus, this description may suggest that Jesus was a valid sacrifice (cf. Ford 1969; Brown 1970:951).

Jesus used both blood and water as important symbols in his teaching, and this gives us guidance for their import here. Water has been associated with cleansing (1:26, 31, 33; 2:6; 13:5), the new birth (3:5) and the Spirit (7:38-39). The reference to living water in chapter 4 is probably a comprehensive image for the Spirit, revelation and salvation (see comment on 4:10). Blood has referred to Jesus' sacrificial death, which brings life to the world (6:53-56). From these associations it would seem that in this flow of blood and water "John saw a symbol of the fact that from the Crucified there proceed those living streams by which men are quickened and the church lives" (Barrett 1978:557; cf. Dodd 1953:428; Schnackenburg 1982:294).

The fact that water symbolizes purification, the Spirit and the new birth provides a connection with baptism. The fact that blood symbolizes the sacrificial death of Christ, which gives life to the world, provides a connection with the Eucharist. These are "the ideas which underlie the two Sacraments" (Westcott 1908:2:320) and thus support the allusion to the sacraments that Christians have found here throughout the centuries (cf. Hoskyns 1940b:635-38).

As with the unbroken bones, so with the piercing: it is not only rich in symbolism but also a fulfillment of Scripture (v. 37). The passage cited is Zechariah 12:10, in which God says, "They will look on me, the one they have pierced." Here God seems to be identified with the leader of his people, a shepherd who is raised up by God (11:16) and yet will be struck by the sword (13:7). This passage, therefore, picks up the theme of the Good Shepherd who is one with God, laying down his life. Again, Jesus' identity and his fulfillment of God's will is conveyed through the replication of a Scriptural pattern.

The piercing is the point of interest for John (Barrett 1978:557), but

---

19:35 Both here and at 20:31 the manuscripts vary in their form of the verb for *believe*.

perhaps there is also significance in those who look upon the pierced one. In Zechariah, the ones who look at him are "the house of David and the inhabitants of Jerusalem" upon whom God has poured out "a spirit of grace and supplication" (Zech 12:10). Accordingly, they do not look upon him in fear, but rather "they will mourn for him as one mourns for an only child, and grieve bitterly for him as one grieves for a firstborn son" (Zech 12:10). Given the focus in the Passion account on the salvation Jesus has accomplished, perhaps "the salvation aspect is to the fore here also. Naturally the obverse of judgment for those who persist in looking on the Redeemer in unbelief is not excluded" (Beasley-Murray 1987:355; cf. Schnackenburg 1982:292-94). If this is the case, then this echo of Scripture speaks not only of Jesus' identity and work, but also of the fruit of that work as he is lifted up and draws all to himself (Jn 12:32). Indeed, the next scene shows us the first two examples of this fruit.

Between John's description of these events and their fulfillment in Scripture, there is a parenthetical comment on the truthfulness of his witness to the flow of blood and water: *The man who saw it has given testimony, and his testimony is true. He knows that he tells the truth, and he testifies so that you also may believe* (v. 35). This could be John's own statement of the trustworthiness of his testimony, but it is not like the other comments he has added to his account (for example, 2:22; 6:64, 71; 12:6, 16, 33; 18:9, 32; cf. Schnackenburg 1982:291). Instead, it reads very much like the testimony of the later disciples at the end of the Gospel: "This is the disciple who testifies to these things and who wrote them down. We know that his testimony is true" (21:24). Possibly, then, verse 35 was added by John's disciples to underscore his witness to the death of Jesus. They might have added this because there were members of the community at a later stage, as reflected in the letters, moving in a Gnostic, or proto-Gnostic direction. Much of the argument against these views centered on the nature and significance of Jesus' death (cf. Whitacre 1982:121-51). Since these false teachers claimed to be true to the Johannine tradition, this note could have been added, perhaps originally only in the margin, "underlining the key text of the Gospel that belies this claim by the later opponents" (Whitacre 1982:213 n. 217).

The aorist *(pisteusēte)* could suggest coming to faith, and the present *(pisteuete)* continuing

Joseph and Nicodemus Bury Jesus' Body (19:38-42) John's account of the burial may continue to develop the theme of Jesus' royal identity. The large amount of spice used (v. 39) obviously expresses their love for Jesus, as had the extravagance of Mary's gesture earlier (12:3). Such excessive amounts of spice were a feature of at least some royal funerals (2 Chron 16:14; Josephus *Antiquities of the Jews* 17.199). Further associations with royalty may be implied from the fact that Joseph's tomb is a garden tomb (v. 41), since the kings of Judah were buried in garden tombs (2 Kings 21:18, 26), including King David (Neh 3:16 LXX; cf. Brown 1994:2:1270). Plenty of people besides kings had extravagant funerals and were buried in garden tombs, but given all the emphasis in the Passion account on Jesus as king, such details may continue the theme here at the burial.

The fact that it is *a new tomb* is emphasized by John (v. 41). Some think John's point is that Jesus would not be brought into contact with corruption (Westcott 1908:2:324), or that there would be no question of mistaken identity when the tomb was empty (Chrysostom *In John* 85.4; Brown 1970:959). John may have been conscious of these notions, but it would seem the main point is simply that a new tomb is a token of appropriate honor given to a king. It may also tie in with the theme of the creation of the new community: Jesus has reordered the lives of his mother and the Beloved Disciple (vv. 26-27), in keeping with the new order of relationships of those who are united to him (cf. Mt 12:46-50 par. Mk 3:31-35 par. Lk 8:19-21). Jesus has no ancestral tomb but rather has begun a new family of those born from above who will never die (11:26).

Indeed, in this story we see this family gaining two new members. For the two men who bury Jesus had not publicly associated with him before. Joseph of Arimathea was indeed a disciple, but he was so *secretly because he feared the Jews* (v. 38). And Nicodemus, though not actually called a "disciple," nevertheless had *visited Jesus at night* (v. 39) and had affirmed at that time that Jesus was a teacher come from God (3:2). Thus, these are two of the people referred to earlier, who were secret believers, "for they loved praise from men more than praise from God" (12:42-43). Now, at Jesus' death, they are no longer under this condemnation; they have passed from hiding in the darkness to coming into the light.

in faith. See comment on 20:31.

From the Synoptics we learn that Joseph was a wealthy member of the Sanhedrin who was looking for the coming of the kingdom and who had not consented to the Sanhedrin's condemnation of Jesus (Mt 27:57; Mk 15:43; Lk 23:50-51). Nicodemus, who is not mentioned in the Synoptics, was also a member of the Sanhedrin (Jn 3:1) and, presumably, was wealthy, given the amount of spice he provides for Jesus' burial (v. 39). John A. T. Robinson considers Nicodemus to be from a well-established family of Jerusalem, while Joseph is "the *nouveau riche* country cousin with his brand-new tomb [cf. v. 41; Mt 27:60], which may suggest the lack of an established family mausoleum in the city" (1985:287). In any case, these are both men of power, privilege and wealth. Although Joseph, and presumably Nicodemus, had dissented from the vote, as members of the Sanhedrin they were indeed those who pierced Jesus and now they are looking upon him and mourning (see comment on v. 37). Jesus has been lifted up and is now beginning to draw all people to himself (12:32), beginning with these hidden disciples, who were members of the very group that insisted on Jesus' death.

It is ironic that these two men come out of hiding and clearly associate themselves with Jesus at his death, since they would have thought his movement had come to an end. They had nothing to gain and everything to lose. This action makes the extent of their dissent evident to their fellow Jewish leaders. Their request for the body was also a very courageous act. The Romans would often leave the body on the cross for days, though they might allow the family to take down the body for burial. They would not do this, however, in the case of treason (Beasley-Murray 1987:358). Thus, Joseph had no claims on the body and, depending on how Pilate viewed the case, would have been putting himself in considerable danger. But Pilate had clearly said three times that Jesus was innocent, which may account for his allowing Joseph to take the body. In addition, by allowing Jesus to have a decent burial Pilate would be able to further annoy the Jewish leadership.

The men did not have time to give Jesus a proper burial, which would include washing the body, anointing it with oil and then clothing and wrapping it (Brown 1994:2:1261). Instead, the seventy-five pounds of

---

19:41 This garden may echo the Garden of Eden (see comment on 18:1).

spices, which were probably in granular or powder form, could be packed under and around the body and in the *strips of linen* with which they wrapped the body. This would offset the smell of decay and help preserve the body until it could be properly attended to after the sabbath (v. 42; Robinson 1985:282-83). The meaning of the word for *strips of linen (othoniois)* is unclear. There does not seem to be evidence that Jews wrapped corpses in strips, as Egyptian mummies were wrapped (Brown 1994:2:1265), and the Synoptics say a single sheet was the main covering (Mt 27:59 par. Mk 15:46 par. Lk 23:53). Upon his being raised from the dead, Lazarus came out with "his hands and feet wrapped with strips of linen, and a cloth around his face" (11:44), but the word for "strips of linen" *(keiria)* in that verse is not the same word used here *(othonion)*. Though the plural is used here, it may refer to a single sheet (cf. Brown 1994:2:1265) or be used generically for "grave clothes" (Robinson 1985:291). Thus, it is not clear how exactly they wrapped the body.

The action taken by Joseph and Nicodemus signals a change in their own discipleship as they clearly break with the rest of the Jewish leadership. By handling the body they have made themselves ritually unclean and are thus disqualified from participating in the feast. According to some accounts of the dating (see comment on 18:28; 19:14), this means they would miss the Passover itself, in which case Christ has replaced the Passover for them in keeping with John's focus on Jesus as the Lamb of God and the fulfillment of the Jewish feasts in general.

□ The Climax of the Glorification Continues: Jesus Is Raised and Meets with His Disciples (20:1—21:23)

John's account of the resurrection appearances is highly structured. The first part (chap. 20) describes a series of encounters in which the disciples are brought to faith in the risen Lord. The chapter concludes with a statement of purpose that summarizes the whole Gospel (vv. 30-31). The second part (chap. 21) uses the symbolism of fish and fishing to speak of the community's fruitful labor and the symbolism of sheep and shepherding to speak of the community's leadership. The Gospel ends with a testimony to the reliability of the Beloved Disciple's witness in this Gospel and a reflection on the greatness of Jesus' deeds (vv. 24-25).

Jesus Appears to His Disciples (20:1-29) In his resurrection appearances Jesus continues to reveal the glory of God by manifesting the grace and love that characterize God. This love is seen in the gentleness, care and humility with which he deals with his disciples. This section contains a series of encounters with Christ that show him overcoming a variety of barriers to faith, including ignorance, grief, fear and doubt (Westcott 1908:2:334, 336-37). Five occasions of faith are mentioned, forming a chiasm. In the first and last, Jesus himself is not seen. In the first, the Beloved Disciple' faith is based on the evidence of the grave clothes; in the last, Jesus says future believers will have the witness of those who did see him (cf. vv. 30-31). The other three occasions are actual sightings of the resurrected Jesus. Mary sees both angels and Jesus but only believes when she hears him call her name. Thomas also requires something more than sight to believe—to touch Jesus' wounds. Between these two individuals, at the center of the chiasm, is Jesus' appearance to the disciples as a group, who recognize him by seeing his wounds and in whose presence Jesus imparts the Holy Spirit.

This chiastic structure makes it clear that John has chosen his material and arranged it with care, as have the other Evangelists. A comparative study of the different Gospel accounts yields valuable insight (cf. Osborne 1984), though coordinating the details is difficult (but see J. Wenham 1992; Westcott 1908:2:335-36). Only occasional reference will be made in what follows to the Synoptic accounts, and even fewer references will be made to the issues of composition and sources (see surveys in Brown 1970:966-78; Schnackenburg 1982:300-307; Beasley-Murray 1987:367-70; Carson 1991:631-34). The philosophical issues raised by the resurrection will also be left to others (for an introduction see Craig 1995).

Mary Magdalene and Two Disciples Visit the Tomb (20:1-10) All of the Gospels agree that Mary of Magdala was the first of the disciples to go to the tomb. The Synoptics mention she was accompanied by other women (Mt 28:1; Mk 16:1; Lk 24:1, 10), and her use of the pronoun *we* in verse 2 could imply the same. All accounts mention that she went when it was very early in the morning, though John goes further and states that it was *still dark* (v. 1). Earlier the image of darkness symbolized the period of deadly conflict with the prince of this world (cf. 13:30), but now Jesus has been victorious. So if this darkness at the tomb is symbolic, it would reflect Mary's condition and that of the other disciples rather than the period of salvation history. This chapter shows the great light breaking in on a series of disciples who are in various forms of darkness.

The Synoptics mention that Mary came with other women and actually looked in the tomb (Mk 16:5; Lk 24:3) and encountered the angels. John mentions such details in the next section, so if his account is coordinated with the Synoptic accounts, then presumably this visit by Mary happened earlier at the tomb, while it was still dark. Perhaps Mary had hurried on ahead of the other women. She does not look into the tomb at this point. Since it was dark, she would not have been able to see anything even if she had.

Mary assumes someone has taken Jesus' body because the tomb is standing open. Tomb robbery was not uncommon. Indeed, one of the caesars of the first century A.D. (it is unclear whether it was Augustus, Tiberius or Claudius) made the disturbance of graves and tombs a capital offense (cf. Barrett 1987:13-15). Mary, however, may not have had such hostile activity in mind (see vv. 13, 15). In any case, she runs to the two apostles with her disturbing news. A little later in the morning she goes to the disciples with a much different message (v. 18). One can only pass on what one knows.

The grammar may suggest the disciples were staying in two different places (repetition of *pros,* not represented in the NIV; cf. v. 10), though not necessarily far apart from one another. If she knows of Peter's denial of the Lord, then her fetching him is quite striking. Certainly the Beloved Disciple knows of the denial, but there is no suggestion he rejects Peter because of it. They had all deserted the Lord that night.

The focus now shifts to Peter and the Beloved Disciple and to their race to the tomb (vv. 3-4). There has been much speculation regarding the significance of the Beloved Disciple's outrunning Peter. The idea that this Gospel favors the Beloved Disciple at the expense of Peter has become popular, but is not supported by the text, for "in no place is Peter criticized or devalued" (Schnackenburg 1982:314; cf. Brown 1970:1006-7; Beasley-Murray 1987:373-74). The idea that the Beloved Disciple was spurred on by a greater love is possible, given that Peter's love must be reaffirmed later (21:15-17). But perhaps it was not a lesser love that slowed Peter, but rather a great love that was burdened by shame. But if the Beloved Disciple had so much love, why did he pause at the tomb entrance? And if Peter loved less or was ashamed, why did he charge on in? Others attribute the cause to Peter's being older. The text does not offer guidance for such speculations.

While there were a few different kinds of tombs in use at this period (cf. Meyers 1976:906-8), the details provided here (vv. 5-7) help indicate the type in which Jesus was buried. Most likely it had a low entrance and a step down into the central, rectangular pit, with shelves cut into the rock around the pit (see diagram in R. H. Smith 1976:414). If Jesus had been laid on the shelf either to the right or left of the entrance, then only part of the grave clothes would be visible from the entrance. If he had been positioned with his head toward the entrance wall, this would explain why the cloth for Jesus' head was not noticed until they actually entered the tomb.

Great attention is given to the grave clothes. The *strips of linen* (vv. 5-6; *othonia*) were the covering for the body, whether they consisted of strips, as in the NIV, or a shroud (see comment on 19:40) or both. Since Jesus' resurrected body was able to appear in a locked room (v. 19), it seems he simply passed through the grave clothes. With the body gone, the clothes were presumably collapsed, though perhaps retaining much of their shape due to the spices. The cloth for Jesus' head *(soudarion)* was either a face covering or a cloth tied around Jesus' face to hold his jaw in place (see comment on 11:44). If the latter, then perhaps John's description indicates the cloth was lying in place, still in the oval shape it had when around Jesus' head. Or it could be John means this cloth, however it had been used, was in a separate place, rolled or wrapped up (v. 7, *entetyligmenon*). Jesus' body passed through the grave clothes, presumably including the *soudarion,* so the fact that the *soudarion* was rolled up suggests Jesus tidied up before leaving! "There were no traces of haste. The deserted tomb bore the marks of perfect calm" (Westcott 1908:2:340). The royal calmness of Jesus throughout his Passion is also hinted at here in his resurrection.

When the Beloved Disciple entered, *he saw and believed* (v. 8). What is this faith, since the next verse says *they still did not understand from Scripture that Jesus had to rise from the dead* (v. 9)? Such faith, with only limited understanding, has been true of the disciples throughout this Gospel, beginning from the first sign (2:11). It is a true faith, for it is based in an openness and receptivity to God. With this faith one is able to recognize what is seen and heard in God's presence and activity, though often one does not understand much more than that. Here the Beloved Disciple sees an empty tomb and inside grave clothes neatly rolled up. If Jesus' body had been stolen, the thieves would not have left the grave clothes behind. If Jesus had revived and had somehow struggled out of the grave clothes (not likely since seventy-five pounds of spices held them together), then they would be torn to shreds and the *soudarion* would not be rolled up. So the Beloved Disciple sees that something very strange has happened. He has faith in that he recognizes God's fingerprints at the scene. But he still does not understand the full meaning of what he sees.

John does not say whether Peter also believed at this point. But he does say that neither of them understood the Scripture regarding resurrection, thereby admitting his own ignorance at this point. Several texts of Scripture have been suggested as the ones to which John is referring (Ps 16:10; Hos 6:2; Jon 1:17), but he may simply mean the Scripture's witness as a whole, as when Paul says Christ "was raised on the third day according to the Scriptures" (1 Cor 15:4; cf. Lk 24:44-47; Beasley-Murray 1987:373).

This confession of ignorance puts the Beloved Disciple in the same boat as Peter, contrary to views that play the two disciples off against one another. They are able to bear witness to the empty tomb and the grave clothes, though not yet to the resurrection. But they do not bear witness at all. Rather, they simply return to the places where they are staying (v. 10; see comment on v. 2). If they do speak to the other disciples, John does not mention it. This lack of witness is another sign that although the Beloved Disciple's faith may be significant, it is still lacking.

Jesus Appears to Mary Magdalene (20:11-18) John does not describe when Mary returns to the tomb; he simply picks up the story with her there. The emphasis is on her *crying* (vv. 11, 13, 15). Her great love is poured out in her grief. She thinks she is alone, though "like other sorrowful disciples since" (H. C. G. Moule 1898:48), she actually has angels in front of her and the Lord behind her. When she bends down to look in the tomb she sees the angels. They are sitting, presumably on the shelf, at the two ends of the grave clothes, that is, *where Jesus' body had been*. Such heavenly messengers appear at many of the significant points in salvation history. Like the grave clothes, their presence witnesses "that the powers of heaven have been at work here" (Beasley-Murray 1987:374).

Often in Scripture the person who encounters an angel is struck with terror. But if Mary felt such a reaction, John does not mention it. Indeed, there is no indication that she even recognizes them as angels, presumably due to is the depth of her grief. The angels speak to her with great compassion: *Woman, why are you crying?* (v. 13). This is in striking contrast with the angels' triumphant announcement of the resurrection recorded in the Synoptics (Mt 28:5-7 par. Mk 16:6-7 par. Lk 24:5-7). In the face of this grief the angels do not bombard her with good news but rather ask the question that can lead to the healing word.

Mary's answer (v. 13) shows that she is totally focused on the fact that Jesus' body is missing. He is still her *Lord* even though he is dead; her loyalty is still fixed on him. In saying she does not know where *they have put him* she seems to assume that Joseph of Arimathea had his workmen move Jesus to a more permanent site (H. C. G. Moule 1898:58).

Her answer gives the angels a perfect opportunity to proclaim the good news, but they are interrupted by the appearance of the Lord himself. Mary turns to see Jesus (v. 14). Perhaps she heard him or simply sensed a presence behind her, or perhaps, as Chrysostom suggests, "while she was speaking, Christ suddenly appeared behind her, striking the angels with awe" (*In John* 86.1). She saw him, *but she did not realize that it was Jesus* (v. 14). She had not been able to pick up on the clues provided by the grave clothes nor even recognize the angels who spoke with her. Now she sees the very object of her concern, but she is unable to recognize him. Such can be the blinding effect of profound emotions. In this case her inability to recognize him also seems to be due to the character of Jesus' resurrection body, since such failure is typical of encounters with him (cf. Mt 28:17; Mk 16:12; Lk 24:16, 37; Jn 21:4).

Jesus is well aware of her condition, and he comes to her with great love and gentleness. The good news is not just that Jesus arose but that the character of God is revealed in Jesus. He is life, and he is also love. He asks the same question asked by the angels, *Woman, . . . why are you crying?* but immediately he focuses it further: *Who is it you are looking for?* This question, the first thing the risen Jesus says, echoes the very first thing he said at the beginning of this Gospel (1:38). It is a question that reveals the heart.

Mary does not answer the question but assumes that Jesus is Joseph's gardener and that he knows whom she is looking for (v. 15). His appearance has given her hope—hope that she can now find Jesus' dead body. She wants to care for Jesus' corpse. "So she plans a second interment for Jesus, while the living Jesus is there, and just about to lift her in the embrace of His manifested power and love" (H. C. G. Moule 1898:59).

The sight of the grave clothes and of angels and of Jesus himself have not been able to pierce her darkness. But when Jesus calls her name she knows his voice, for she is a true sheep (10:3-4). *Rabboni* could mean "my dear teacher," and such endearment would be in keeping with Mary's attachment to Jesus. But the term is not always used so (cf. Mk 10:51), and John simply translates it *teacher*. Jesus calls her by the name he used for her before, and she responds with the title she used before. She would naturally assume that their relationship could pick up where it left off and continue on as before. Jesus' response, however, lets her know there has been a radical change in him and consequently in his relationship with his followers.

This change is indicated when Jesus tells her not to touch him (v. 17). The use of the present tense *(haptou)* suggests in this context that he is not forbidding her to touch him but telling her to stop that which she is already doing. Apparently, then, when Mary recognizes Jesus she approaches him and touches him. John does not describe what exactly happens. It is possible that she is touching him on the arm or hand, to be assured that he is really there (H. C. G. Moule 1898:64-66). In this case, Jesus would be saying, "You don't have to continue to touch me since *(gar)* I have not yet ascended to the Father—I really am here." Or perhaps she kneels before him and grabs his feet (Mt 28:9; cf. Beasley-Murray 1987:376), not just touching him, but holding onto him, as in the NIV. Such clinging may suggest she is not only trying to assure herself that he is really there, but expressing her desire that he not leave again. In this case, Jesus lets her know that she must not try to restrict him, for he has not yet ascended to the Father.

Jesus says he is still on the move, and he also sets Mary in motion to bear the news to the disciples. She has just found him, and now she is sent away, but she is sent with a commission. As the ancient church put it, she

---

20:17 Jesus is not saying Mary should not touch him until he has ascended, as if he were like wet paint that needed to dry. Such an interpretation has raised unnecessary difficulties with Jesus' later invitation to Thomas to touch him (v. 27), as though this implies that he

becomes an apostle to the apostles. The message she is given says a great deal about the new phase that has begun in the relations between the Father, the Son and the disciples. Indications of change begin with the commission itself: *Go instead to my brothers and tell them* (v. 17). This is the first time in this Gospel that Jesus refers to his disciples as his brothers (cf. Mt 12:50 par. Mk 3:35 par. Lk 8:21). This implies not only that Jesus has not put off his humanity in his resurrected state (Alford 1980:980), but that he has inaugurated a new level of intimacy between himself and his disciples. The new community he founded during his ministry became a new family at the cross (19:26-27), and now the disciples are to enter into this new form of relationship.

This new relationship is expressed in the message Mary is to convey: *tell them, "I am returning* [ascending, *anabainō*] *to my Father and your Father, to my God and your God"* (v. 17). It is perhaps surprising that his first message is not "I have risen from the dead." He does not focus on himself in this way; he focuses on himself in relation to his Father. Jesus had spoken of his going to the Father, both in his general teaching (7:33-36) and in the farewell discourse to his disciples (13:3; 14:2-4, 12, 28; 16:5, 10, 17, 28). The Father is his center of reference, and to return to him is his greatest joy and therefore the joy of his disciples (14:28). So the message *I am returning to my Father* expresses Jesus' great delight. He has finished the work (19:30) and can now return to the Father.

His returning to the Father is also good news for the disciples, not just because they share in his joy, but also for their own condition. For when Jesus returns to the Father he will send the Paraclete, who will teach them all things and complete their union with the Father and the Son (16:7; cf. 14:16-17, 28; 15:26). This new relationship has already been established through Jesus' death and resurrection, but the disciples will enter into it fully when the Spirit comes. The message Jesus gives Mary shows the christological basis of the new relationship. "Because God is Jesus' Father, he is also their Father; because he is Jesus' God, he is also their God. They are taken up into the fellowship that unites Jesus and the Father" (Ridderbos 1997:640). Jesus is the point of contact between the disciples and the Father

---

had ascended between the two meetings. Thomas will be invited to touch him to confirm the truth of his resurrection. Mary is not forbidden to touch him at all, but she is forbidden to continue to do so.

(see comment on 17:21-22). The Father is the Father of the disciples in this new intimacy precisely because he is Jesus' Father, for the disciples are now Jesus' brothers.

Jesus characterizes the time of his resurrection appearances as the time when he is ascending to the Father. He has received his orders, and he is about to ship out. This focus implies a contrast between "the passing nature of Jesus' presence in his post-resurrectional appearances and the permanent nature of his presence in the Spirit" (Brown 1970:1015). But it does not mean the resurrection and the ascension have somehow been blended into one another or that the one has been replaced by the other (Carson 1991:645). Jesus must return to the Father before the Paraclete can come (16:7). The fact that Jesus imparts the Spirit later this same day (v. 22) suggests to many that John does not view the ascension as a definite act as described by Luke (Lk 24:51; Acts 1:9-11). But we will see that the account of Jesus' breathing impartation of the Spirit suggests his giving of the Spirit, like his ascension, was not a simple event. John may not describe the ascension, but his account assumes it, as becomes evident in his description of the impartation of the Spirit and what follows.

Mary Magdalene goes off and announces to the disciples what she has seen and heard. John does not mention the poor reception that was given to her message (Mk 16:11 par. Lk 24:11), though the fearful, doubting state of the disciples in the next section implies as much. All a witness can do is share what he or she knows to be true. Christian witness should not attempt to share an experience; it should direct people to Jesus so people can encounter him for themselves. Mary's message could alert the disciples to the fact that Jesus was alive, but they had to come to faith for themselves. Jesus met Mary in a way that was best for her. Now he will do the same for the disciples as a group.

Jesus Appears to the Disciples as a Group (20:19-23) In the evening of the day of the resurrection the disciples were gathered together. They had heard the witness of Mary (v. 18) and perhaps also of the Beloved Disciple and Peter, as well as of other women mentioned in the Synoptics, though John does not mention any of these. Perhaps her witness has given them hope and expectancy or perhaps has just confused them; the only thing John mentions is their fear of the Jewish opponents. The Feast of Unleavened Bread was still in progress, but these disciples are isolated from the festivities. They have lost the feast of Israel and have not yet discovered the peace of Jesus. Their hearts were troubled before the crucifixion (14:1), and now, if anything, they are more so.

Despite the locked doors, Jesus appears in their midst and greets them with the greeting still common today in that part of the world—*Peace be with you* (v. 19). In his farewell discourse Jesus had given them peace and charged them not to fear (14:27), and now he will begin to lead them into that experience. This may be a common greeting, but in this context the full significance of the word *peace* is present. In the Old Testament peace is closely associated with the blessing of God, especially the salvation to be brought by the Messiah (cf. Ps 29:11; Is 9:6; 52:7; 55:12; Ezek 37:26; Zech 9:10; cf. Osborne 1984:166). Now indeed such peace has come, for "his 'Shalom!' on Easter evening is the complement of 'It is finished!' on the cross, for the peace of reconciliation and life from God is now imparted" (Beasley-Murray 1987:379).

The disciples, apparently did not receive peace from this greeting, for it is only after Jesus *showed them his hands and side* that they were filled with joy at the sight of him (v. 20). Jesus had said they would have joy when they saw him again (16:21-22), and now they do, once the wounds have certified it is really him. Such joy, like peace, was viewed as a mark of God's salvation, including the expected time of salvation in the future (Ps 96:11; 97:1; Is 49:13; 61:10; 66:10, 14; Joel 2:21-27; Hab 3:18; Zech 10:7). Both the peace and the joy come from the presence of Jesus himself, the very presence of God come to earth.

Jesus immediately speaks of a mission for these disciples, just as he did with Mary Magdalene. He repeats his blessing of peace. If peace prepares them to receive him, they also need it to receive his commission: *As the Father has sent me, I am sending you* (v. 21). Over forty times throughout the Gospel, Jesus is said to have been sent by God, and now that will become the characteristic of his disciples also. The Son has a role in the sending of the Paraclete (14:16; 15:26; 16:7), and he plays a role in the sending of the disciples. The Son, like the Father, sends. Mission is at the heart of discipleship.

Two different words are used here for sending: *As the Father has sent [apostellō] me, I am sending [pempō] you*. It is often said that *apostellō* denotes being sent with a commission with an emphasis on the sender whereas *pempō* focuses on the sending as such (Rengstorf 1964a:398-406). But this distinction is quite dubious (Köstenberger 1998b:97-106) and certainly the two words are used interchangeably in John (Barrett 1978:569). Of greater significance is the idea of comparison. The Son was sent as one completely dependent upon the Father and one with the Father, so he was the presence of God while yet remaining distinct from the Father. Such a relationship is also at the heart of the community of Jesus' disciples. This text, accordingly, has enormous implications for the nature and mission of the church. C. K. Barrett addresses this issue with great clarity:

> The sending of Jesus by God meant that in the words, works, and person of Jesus men were veritably confronted not merely by a Jewish Rabbi but by God himself (1:18; 14:9; and many passages). It follows that in the apostolic mission of the church . . . the world is veritably confronted not merely by a human institution but by Jesus the Son of God (13:20; 17:18). It follows further that as Jesus in his ministry was entirely dependent upon and obedient to God the Father, who sealed and sanctified him (4:34; 5:19; 10:37; 17:4, and other passages: 6:27; 10:36), and acted in the power of the Spirit who rested upon him (1:32), so the church is the apostolic church, commissioned by Christ, only in virtue of the fact that Jesus sanctified it (17:19) and breathed the Spirit into it (v. 22), and only so far as it maintains an attitude of perfect obedience to Jesus (it is here, of course, that the parallelism between the relation of Jesus to the Father and the relation of the church to Jesus breaks down). The life and mission of the church are meaningless if they are detached from this historical and theological context. (Barrett 1978:569)

Thus, in this Gospel, which focuses so much attention on the identity of Jesus, we also have a clear revelation of the core identity of the church. Unfortunately, the church has difficulty living up to this identity, despite the giving of the Spirit, which John now recounts.

If this community is to function in the way just described, then the gift of the Spirit is essential. Human beings in themselves are not capable of manifesting God's presence and doing God's will as Jesus did. Indeed, without the Spirit there is no spiritual life (3:3, 5). But Jesus now has been glorified, so the Spirit can be given (7:39; see comment on 16:7). At this point the life that has been in Jesus in his union with God is now shared with the disciples. The new state of affairs, described in the farewell discourse and hinted at already by the risen Christ (v. 17), begins to take effect among the disciples. They have been reunited with Jesus and now are given his very life by the Spirit—not only reunited with him, but beginning to be united to him. The word used for *breathed on (emphysaō)* is the same word used in the Greek Old Testament to describe God's action when he formed the man from the dust of the ground and "breathed into his face the breath of life" and the man became a living being (Gen 2:7; cf. Wisdom of Solomon 15:11; also Ezek 37:5-10, 14). This allusion implies there is now the new beginning of life, though, as George Beasley-Murray says, "Strictly speaking, one should not view this as the *beginning* of the new creation but rather as the beginning of the *incorporation of man* into the new creation which came into being *in the Christ* by his incarnation, death, and resurrection, and is actualized in man by the Holy Spirit (cf. 2 Cor 5:17)" (1987:381).

This imparting of the Spirit is clearly a climactic moment in the Gospel. Precisely because it is climactic one wonders how it is related to the coming of the Spirit at Pentecost (Acts 2). On the assumption that both John and Luke are describing the one giving of the Spirit a number of scholars think the accounts reflect different theological emphases (for example, Brown 1970:1038-39; Beasley-Murray 1987:381-82). Others would embrace a view condemned at the Fifth Ecumenical Council at Constantinople in A.D. 553, namely, that the imparting of the Spirit in John is symbolic of the later experience at Pentecost, "a kind of acted parable pointing forward to the full enduement still to come" (Carson 1991:655). Yet another position is that the two accounts describe two different events, though there is much variety in how the differences are understood (cf. Brown 1970:1038; Beasley-Murray 1987:381).

The evidence seems, in fact, to suggest that two different events are mentioned. The breathing of the Spirit by Jesus is certainly climactic, but the results do not fulfill the promises he made earlier in this Gospel. A week later they are not bearing witness but are back in the room with locked doors (v. 26). In the next chapter they are back fishing for fish, not for disciples. Furthermore, the conditions for the presence of the Spirit have not been completely met. The Spirit will be given after Jesus' return to the Father (14:16, 26; 16:7, 13). Jesus is in the process of returning but has not yet returned. Thus, it appears that Jesus' giving of the Spirit, like his ascending to the Father, is a complex process and not a simple, one-time event. John is filling in details not given by Luke regarding the beginning of the disciples' new life and ministry (though see the hint in Acts 1:2) just as he did regarding the outset of Jesus' ministry in his connection with John the Baptist and in the calling of the first disciples.

John's account describes a preliminary stage of preparation for ministry. "The mission is inaugurated, but not actually begun. . . . The actual beginning of the mission lies outside the scope of the Fourth Gospel. There remains, therefore, room for the Pentecostal outpouring, after which the disciples take up the mission in public in the power of the Spirit descending from Father and Son in heaven" (Hoskyns 1940b:653). Such preparation is clearly the point in Jesus' bringing the disciples to faith in himself and in the commissioning. But in what sense is the presence of the Spirit preparatory? A clue may be found in one of the strangest aspects of these first encounters: Thomas was not present when the Spirit was given (v. 24), yet he is the one who confesses Jesus as Lord and God, a confession which is the work of the Spirit. This suggests that the breathing of the Spirit was not simply directed at the individuals present, as if one had to be hit by the molecules coming from Jesus' mouth or nose in order to receive the Spirit. Rather, the Spirit is now unleashed into the world in a new way and begins to bring about new life where he finds faith. The disciples enter into a new phase in their life with God, but it is not yet the time of their active witness, as it will be from Pentecost on. Thus, it would seem John is describing the conception of the church, and Luke (in Acts), the birth.

Jesus then speaks further of his commission to them: *If you forgive anyone his sins, they are forgiven; if you do not forgive them, they are not forgiven* (v. 23). This is a surprising way to put the commission, since it is never said that anyone is "forgiven" in this Gospel. While the reality of forgiveness is depicted (e.g., see comments on 5:14 and 8:11), this is the only occasion where it is stated explicitly. The ultimate sin for which one needs forgiveness is the rejection of Jesus (9:41; 15:22-24; 16:9). The disciples are to bear witness to Jesus (15:26-27), not just by representing Jesus but by actually being the presence of Jesus through the Spirit. In this way they will be the agents of the Spirit's confrontation of the world (16:8-11), which is a continuation of Jesus' own confrontation. "The apostles were commissioned to carry on Christ's work, and not to begin a new one" (Westcott 1908:2:350). Through the disciples' witness to Jesus by word and by the life and love of the community, the world will be forced to choose for or against Jesus, just as they were during Jesus' own ministry. Those who repent and believe in Jesus can be assured of forgiveness, and those who refuse to repent can be assured that their sins are not forgiven. Such is the consequence of rejecting the Lamb of God who has taken away the sin of the world. This is how judgment takes place as people come in contact with the light (see comments on 3:19-21; 9:39-41; 12:44-50).

The ancient church understood this forgiveness and nonforgiveness as referring to admission to baptism (cf. Brown 1970:1042). Since baptism is associated with the forgiveness of sins (for example, Acts 2:38) this is certainly an important way in which this commission has been fulfilled, though it does not exhaust the commission. The text has also been applied to the matter of discipline within the community. Accordingly, the text has served to ground the sacrament of penance (cf. Brown 1970:1041). Such discipline was indeed necessary. The issue of cleansing and forgiveness among the disciples is of concern in the Gospel (13:3-11; 21:15-17; cf. Hoskyns 1940b:650). John's later reference to the sin unto death and the sin not unto death (1 Jn 5:16) seems to deal with matters that preclude membership in the community (cf. Whitacre 1982:136-40). The value and validity of the forms that developed over the centuries to embody such discipline is a separate matter, but such discipline in itself would be another way in which this commission has been fulfilled. This would be true whether or not the group gathered at this point is limited to the eleven (minus Thomas), though if this commission is given to the disciples in general, then presumably the exercise of discipline in the community was not limited to the leadership, as represented by the Twelve (cf. Mt 16:19; 18:15-17). John's first letter is an interesting study in the combination of a strong authority figure (John) and shared responsibility, as illustrated by 1 John 5:16 itself.

Both of these matters—entering into the community and maintaining the health of the community and its members—are a significant part of the missionary part of this commission. For the life of the community itself is a major aspect of the witness to the world (17:21, 23). It is through the disciples' unity with God and with one another that the world will be confronted with the truth about the Father and the Son. Such unity in God cannot include error and evil, for they are not of God, hence the need for discipline for the sake of the mission itself.

This encounter between Jesus and his band of disciples comes in the midst of a series of stories concerning individuals and speaks of the community Jesus has created. Both the imparting of the Spirit and the commission given reveal that the foundation of the church, its conception and its commissioning, was a concern to Jesus. "The foundation of the church is shown to be the actual words, actions, death and resurrection of Jesus who came in the flesh. And it is from him that the Spirit proceeds" (Hoskyns and Davey 1947:165). In Luke, Jesus' involvement is evident in his gathering the disciples together and charging them to wait for power from on high (Lk 24:48; Acts 1:4-5). In John we see Jesus' own giving of the Spirit. "What the Lord will do invisibly from heaven He here does visibly on earth" (Hoskyns 1940b:653).

Jesus Appears to Thomas (20:24-29) John now tells us that Thomas had not been present on that first day of the resurrection (v. 24). The disciples tell him they have seen the Lord, but he does not believe them. Perhaps they have only seen a ghost (cf. Mt 14:26 par. Mk 6:49). In fact, Luke tells of a meeting between Jesus and the disciples at which the disciples think they are seeing a ghost (Lk 24:37). So to convince them he is not a ghost, Jesus invites them to touch him and he eats a piece of broiled fish (Lk 24:39-43). Perhaps Thomas is simply saying he needs to see the same evidence that they have seen (Westcott 1908:2:353).

John's description of Thomas touching the wounds is quite dramatic (v. 25). Thomas wants to shove his hand *into* Jesus' side! On the assumption that the disciples have told Thomas about Jesus' wounds, some have taken Thomas's statement as evidence that Jesus' wound was large enough for one to put one's hand in and that it was not closed over. But more likely Thomas is simply being dramatic, as he was earlier in the Gospel (11:16). Similarly, the language he uses when he says he will not believe is very emphatic *(ou mē pisteusō)*.

A week later, the next Sunday after the resurrection, the disciples (including Thomas) were again in a locked room (v. 26). Jesus' appearances on Sundays, along with the timing of the resurrection itself, contributed to the church's making that the primary day of worship (cf. Beasley-Murray 1987:385). The expression John uses is literally "after eight days," since Jews counted the beginning and the ending of a period of time. This term itself was taking on special meaning at the time John is writing. In *Barnabas* (from about A.D. 96-100) the eighth day represents "the beginning of another world" (15:8). The author links it with Jesus' resurrection: "That is why we spend the eighth day in celebration, the day on which Jesus both arose from the dead and, after appearing again, ascended into heaven" (*Barnabas* 15:9).

Faith throughout the Gospel is depicted as progressive, renewed in the face of each new revelation of Jesus. The other disciples have moved on to the next stage, but Thomas has not been able to. To not move on when Jesus calls us to do so is to shift into reverse and move away. Both believing and unbelieving are dynamic—we are growing in one direction or the other. Thus, when Jesus appears in their midst he challenges Thomas to move on ahead in the life of faith, to *stop doubting and believe* (v. 27). The actual expression used may capture the dynamic quality, since *ginomai* often has the sense of "becoming" and the present tense "marks the process as continually going on" (Westcott 1908:2:355). Translated woodenly this reads, "Stop becoming unbelieving and get on with becoming believing" *(mē ginou apistos alla pistos)*. To get Thomas moving in the right direction again Jesus offers him the chance to feel his wounds. His offer echoes Thomas's own graphic language from verse 25, suggesting that Jesus was actually present when Thomas was making his protest or that he could at least perceive what was going on, an ability Jesus had even before he was raised from the dead (cf. 1:48).

John does not say whether Thomas actually did touch Jesus' wounds. The impression is that he did not, for John says, "Thomas answered and said to him . . ." That is, Thomas's confession is an immediate response to seeing Jesus and hearing his offer. Furthermore, in Jesus' response to Thomas he mentions seeing but not touching (v. 29).

Thomas's confession of Jesus as *my Lord and my God* is yet another climax in this Gospel. Jesus has invited him to catch up with the others in their new stage of faith, and he shoots past them and heads to the top of the class. His confession is climactic not only as part of the Gospel's story line, but also as an expression of the core of John's witness to Jesus in this Gospel. Thomas confesses Jesus as God when he sees that the crucified one is alive. It is in the crucifixion that God himself is made known, for he is love, and love is the laying down of one's life (1 Jn 4:8; 3:16). But God is also life. In John, this God is revealed perfectly in the death of the Son, but this death would be nothing without the life. When Thomas finds death and life juxtaposed in Jesus he realizes who the one standing before him really is.

Thomas has accepted the revelation, but he gets no commendation from Jesus. Rather, Jesus looks ahead to those who will believe through the witness of these disciples who have seen (cf. 15:27; 17:20): *blessed are those who have not seen and yet have believed* (v. 29). This beatitude, like others Jesus had spoken, is a shocking reversal of common expectations (cf. Mt 5:3-12; Lk 6:20-26). It suggests that if seeing is believing, as it was for Thomas, believing is also seeing. What matters is the relationship established by faith. But this faith is not a vague or general feeling, nor is it merely an intellectual assent to a position. It is openness and acceptance and trust directed toward God in Jesus. In John, as in the rest of the New Testament, the concern is not simply with various conceptions of God or various ideas, but with events in history that demand an interpretation and a response. If John is the "spiritual Gospel," as Clement of Alexandria said (Eusebius *Church History* 4.14.7), it is so not in the sense of being nonmaterial or ahistorical, for in John there is no sharp dichotomy between spirit and matter, though the two are not confused with one another. Rather, this Gospel is spiritual in the sense that it interprets historical events in the light of divine reality. As E. C. Hoskyns and Noel Davey have said, "The Fourth Gospel persuades and entices the reader to venture a judgment upon history" (Hoskyns and Davey 1947:263). Thomas's confession was such a judgment, and now Jesus challenges all who come after to venture a judgment upon this history, that is, upon his person, his presence through the Spirit in this particular community and through the life he offers. Peter later describes such believers: "Though you have not seen him, you love him; and even though you do not see him now, you believe in him and are filled with an inexpressible and glorious joy, for you are receiving the goal of your faith, the salvation of your souls" (1 Pet 1:8-9).

20:30-31 This section has been understood by many scholars as the conclusion to the

John Declares His Purpose in Writing This Gospel (20:30-31) John's statement of purpose is directly linked with Jesus' blessing upon those who have not seen and yet have believed (v. 29). John says, "therefore" (*oun,* left out of the NIV), while *(men)* Jesus did many other signs, these *(tauta de)* are written that you may believe. John refers to the Gospel as a whole, *this book,* and this entire sentence (vv. 30-31 are one sentence in the Greek) is appropriate for the whole Gospel, not just for the present chapter. The reference to *the presence of his disciples* is probably due to the crucial role their witness plays in the faith of those who come later. They had been with him from the beginning (15:27) and thus had received the full revelation. While many of Jesus' signs were done in the presence of others, the presence of his disciples is the crucial fact, for it is they who have believed and been enabled to, by the Spirit, understand their significance and bear witness to Jesus and Jesus' witness to the Father.

John's purpose is precisely to enable others to experience the blessedness that Jesus has just spoken of, which comes through faith. The two central titles for Jesus are *Christ* and *Son of God,* representing in this Gospel both the fulfillment of Jewish expectation and much more—the personal presence of God himself in our midst. The purpose (or result; *hina* can mean either) of this believing is to have *life in his name.* This life "belongs to the Father (5:26; 6:57) and the Son (11:25; 14:6), and is offered to men through Jesus' words (6:63; 10:10) and death (3:16; 7:39) on the basis of faith (3:16; 5:24; 20:31)" (Osborne 1984:176). Thus, it is the very life of God himself made available in the Son. It is *in his name* because it is in fellowship with him as he has made himself known (see comment on 1:12). He has brought life, but this life is not a gift separate from himself. Rather, it is a life in himself who, like the Father, *is* life itself (1:4; 5:26; 11:25; cf. Chrysostom *In John* 87.2). To live in his name is to live his own life, with its source in the Father, and therefore to live his pattern of life. This means to love as he loved (13:34; 1 Jn 2:6), obedient to God, totally trusting him and interpreting all the events in our own lives in the light of his divine presence. John expresses this same call—to share in God's life—at the beginning of his first letter.

Gospel, chapter 21 having been added as an epilogue either by John or by his disciples. See comment on 21:1.

"The life appeared; we have seen it and testify to it, and we proclaim to you the eternal life, which was with the Father and has appeared to us. We proclaim to you what we have seen and heard, so that you also may have fellowship with us. And our fellowship is with the Father and with his Son, Jesus Christ" (1 Jn 1:2-3).

There has been much discussion about whether John is writing for non-Christians, that they might come to faith, or for Christians, that they might continue and grow in the faith. This difference is perhaps reflected in the two main readings in the manuscripts for the word *believe*. Some texts have an aorist tense *(pisteusēte)* and some a present *(pisteuēte),* only one letter distinguishing them from one another. The aorist could be rendered "begin to believe," and the present, "continue to believe." The manuscript support is fairly evenly divided between the two. The Gospel as it now stands contains elements that clearly have in mind someone who has not heard the story before (1:38) as well as other elements that assume readers (or hearers) do know the story (11:2; cf. 12:3). Furthermore, given John's dynamic view of faith (20:29), there is a sense in which every believer is to continue to grow in his or her faith. While it appears John's primary purpose was to encourage believers, there was probably also an evangelistic concern. Certainly the Gospel has proved quite valuable for both purposes!

Jesus Appears Again to His Disciples (21:1-23) This chapter puzzles scholars. Why are the disciples fishing back in Galilee after having been commissioned by Jesus and having received the Spirit? Why don't they recognize him after having seen him more than once at this point? Why is this called the third appearance of Jesus when there were already three appearances in chapter 20? If the Gospel has prepared the disciples for the time of Jesus' absence and has come to a climax with a blessing on those who have believed without having seen, what place is there for these further stories about Jesus' presence? Such questions, among others (cf. Brown 1970:1077-82; Moloney 1998:545-47, 562-65), lead most scholars to conclude this chapter was added later, either by the same author or by one or more of his disciples.

This interpretation may be correct, but there are factors that suggest

---

21:1 Many words and some features of style in this chapter do not occur in the first twenty chapters, adding to the impression that it was added later. Such differences, however, are usually not taken as conclusive evidence in themselves since they may simply reflect the

chapter 21 was the intended conclusion and not an epilogue. To judge from the other Gospels, the telling of the life of Jesus normally concluded not just with faith in the risen Lord but "with a confident statement that this mission to the world, undertaken at His command and under His authority, will be the means by which many are saved" (Hoskyns 1940b:656). Of course, John may have his own way of ending a Gospel, as he has had his own way of telling it throughout. If he concluded with chapter 20, perhaps later disciples felt an ending such as chapter 21 was needed. But that John himself included chapter 21 is suggested by a second factor: there are several examples elsewhere in Johannine literature of summary conclusions occurring before the actual end of the material (12:36-37; 1 Jn 5:13; Rev 22:5; cf. Talbert 1992:258). So John's own practice earlier in this Gospel, as well as elsewhere (depending on one's views of the authorship of John, 1 John and Revelation), actually suggests the conclusion in 20:30-31 is not itself the end of the account. But what about the discrepancies noted above? We will see that these can provide insight into the story itself, rather than clues as to how this story came to us.

Jesus Appears to His Disciples While They Are Fishing (21:1-14)

After his appearances in Jerusalem that established the faith of the disciples, Jesus now appears in Galilee to a portion of the disciples. The seven disciples mentioned (v. 2) may be symbolic of the entire group, though John does not draw attention to the number. More important is the simple fact that they are *together*. Jesus had formed the nucleus of the new community during his ministry and had further established it at the cross and in the breathing of the Spirit. Now he reminds them of his lordship and their dependency upon him in the fulfillment of the commission he has given them (20:21-23). He does this by focusing on two of the leaders among the disciples, Peter and the Beloved Disciple.

John does not tell us why the disciples are back in Galilee, but in fact Jesus had told them to return there, where he would meet them (Mk 14:28; 16:7). They seem to have been sitting around, unsure of what to do, until Peter decides to go fishing and the others come along (v. 3). Peter is taking the lead, but what sort of lead is it? Some see this act as "aimless activity

---

particular subject matter in this chapter and, in any case, are balanced by a great many similarities with the earlier chapters (Brown 1970:1079-80 lists both; Lightfoot 1893:194-95 gives further similarities).

undertaken in desperation" (Brown 1970:1096) or even apostasy, that is, abandoning the Lord and returning to their former life (Hoskyns 1940b:660). Others think they went fishing simply because they needed to eat (Beasley-Murray 1987:399). The latter is probably true enough, but there is also a sense that Peter and the others, while not necessarily aimless and certainly not apostate, are doing what is right in their own eyes. The stories in this chapter reveal Jesus' bringing his disciples, especially Peter, more completely under his lordship. The disciples do not know what to do, so they do that which is necessary, and in taking this initiative they put themselves in a place where Christ meets them. Here is the simple truth, attested to by the saints, that when we are uncertain what to do we should simply do our duty and God will guide.

That night they catch nothing (v. 3), a graphic portrayal of barrenness. They have done what they thought was the right thing but experience utter failure. This prepares them to learn one of the central lessons of discipleship—apart from Jesus they can do nothing (15:5). Jesus has taught this lesson before, for "never in the Gospels do the disciples catch a fish without Jesus' help" (Brown 1970:1071)! But they need the lesson repeated, as we often do as well.

The turning point comes early in the morning, perhaps symbolizing the dawning of spiritual light. Jesus is described again as simply standing there, without a description of his arrival on the spot (v. 4; cf. 20:14, 19, 26). Also as earlier, they are not able to recognize him at first. Although some scholars take this as evidence that this chapter does not fit well after chapter 20, in fact this ignorance fits with the theme running throughout these chapters that there was something different about Jesus' body. John stresses in these descriptions both the continuity and discontinuity of Jesus' body.

Jesus takes the initiative and calls to them: *Friends, haven't you any fish?* (v. 5). The question is put in a form that expects a negative answer. This may be the common way of asking a hunter or fisherman whether they have had success (Brown 1970:1070), but in this case the one asking already knows the answer. The word translated *friends (paidiai)* is more literally

---

21:5 The word for *fish (prosphagion)* actually means a relish eaten with bread (Bauer, Gingrich and Danker 1979:710), but since such food was often made out of fish the word could simply signify fish. This seems to have been a colloquial way of referring to freshly caught fish (as was also, apparently, its synonym *opson;* cf. Liddell, Scott and Jones

"children" or even "little children." Many follow J. H. Moulton's suggestion (1908:170 n. 1), based on modern Greek, that this is an expression similar to the British "lads." While this usage would fit here, neither Liddell, Scott and Jones (1940), nor Bauer, Gingrich and Danker (1979) nor Oepke (1967b:638) site evidence for such a use in classical or Hellenistic Greek. In 1 John the word is used "as an affectionate address of the spiritual father to those committed to him" (Oepke 1967b:638; see 1 Jn 2:14, 18 and some manuscripts of 2:12; 3:7). This usage, unique to John, is probably the sense here in John 21 also (Oepke 1967b:638). Thus, this greeting was unusual and so would have sounded strange to the disciples, all the more so because they did not know who was calling them.

The disciples admit they have failed at fishing (v. 5), and Jesus tells them, *Throw your net on the right side of the boat and you will find some* (v. 6). They could hear this as the idle suggestion of a bystander. But he does not say, "Try over there and you might find some." He doesn't offer a suggestion; he gives a promise that in fact they will find fish where he directs them to cast. When they obey they cannot even get the net into the boat because there are so many fish enclosed in it (v. 6). Such abundance echoes the enormous provision of wine at the wedding in Cana (2:1-11) and of bread and fish at the feeding of the five thousand (6:1-13). Most commentators see these fish as symbolic of the missionary work of the disciples, similar to Jesus' original call, "Come, follow me . . . and I will make you fishers of men" (Mt 4:19 par. Mk 1:17; not given by John). Such symbolism may be included, but the primary point seems to be Jesus' lordship and the need to be obedient to him for any labor to be fruitful.

Earlier, Mary recognized Jesus when he called her name, and the disciples recognized him through his wounds. Now he is recognized through the abundance that comes through obedience to his word. It is the Beloved Disciple who is able to discern the identity of the stranger on the shore (v. 7). It is typical of the Beloved Disciple that he was not mentioned explicitly in the list of those present (v. 2) and also that he is the one able to recognize the Lord. If Peter had been the one to recognize Jesus, one

---

1940:1529, 1283; and cf. *opsarion* in vv. 9-10). Jesus could have been speaking to the disciples in Greek, though this is probably not likely. Assuming Jesus was speaking Aramaic or Hebrew, John uses words (for example, *paidion* and *prosphagion*) to capture the nuance of what Jesus said as well as the content.

suspects he would have thrown himself into the sea straight away. But when the Beloved Disciple receives this insight he bears witness to it. He speaks specifically to Peter, thus continuing the motif throughout the resurrection narratives of the close relationship between these two disciples.

Peter trusts the witness of the Beloved Disciple, and so he *wrapped his outer garment around him (for he had taken it off) and jumped into the water* (v. 7). This translation probably gives the wrong impression, since it suggests Peter was working with his undergarment on and added his outer garment before swimming to shore. This would be a good way to drown or at least slow oneself down. Perhaps, instead, he tied up the garment he was wearing so it would not hinder his swimming (Brown 1970:1072). The text, however, says that he was naked (*ēn gar gymnos,* paraphrased in the NIV), and this seems to have been typical for such work (Nun 1997:20-21). Most likely, then, he had been working naked and had put on a loincloth before swimming to shore (Nun 1997:23, 37). The other disciples follow in the boat, towing the catch (v. 8).

Peter's departure from the boat is mentioned, but his arrival on the shore is not. Some scholars think this omission is a sign that two stories have been joined together (cf. Schnackenburg 1982:345-47), but the story is coherent as it stands. The landing is told from the point of view of the Beloved Disciple and the other five disciples. There is no description of Peter talking with Jesus. The impression is thus given that his attempt to get to Jesus first did not do him much good. What the disciples notice is a charcoal fire with bread and fish already prepared (v. 9). The Lord has breakfast ready for them, another sign of his grace and provision, like the catch they have just taken. There is no indication of where Jesus got the bread and fish; the appearance of the food is as mysterious as his own.

The first one to speak is Jesus, and he tells them to bring some of the fish they have caught (v. 10). For the second time in this story Jesus gives them a command. Although Jesus addresses all the disciples (*enenkate, bring,* plural), it is Peter who brings the catch ashore, apparently by himself (v. 11). Peter's zeal to come to Jesus is now matched by his zeal to obey him.

A great many suggestions have been made over the years for the significance of the number 153 (cf. Beasley-Murray 1987:401-4), some suggestions more edifying than others. The emphasis in the story, however, is simply on how many fish there were and the fact that the net did not break. On the simplest level, these details speak of the abundance that the gracious God provides and how he also enables the abundance to be received. If more specific symbolism is present, perhaps the fish represent a large influx of converts from various nations and the unbroken net represents the unity of the church (for example, Brown 1970:1097).

At the feeding of the five thousand they had brought the bread and fish to Jesus, and he multiplied them (6:9-11). In this scene he already has food and invites them to add to it from their catch. Peter hauls up the fish, but there is no description of what is done with them. Rather, Jesus speaks yet another command—an invitation to have breakfast (v. 12). Throughout this encounter with Jesus the disciples have not said anything. The scene is one of great awe, with none of them daring to ask him, *Who are you?* (v. 12). There was something different about him, yet they were able to recognize him. The Lord Jesus is the focus of this story.

After inviting them to come and eat, he himself comes to the fire. He *took the bread and gave it to them, and did the same with the fish* (v. 13). This description echoes his action at the feeding of the five thousand (6:11) and provides the climax of this story. It answers their unasked questions— he is recognized in this breaking of the bread (cf. Lk 24:30-31). The master who commands them also serves them, continuing a theme found during the ministry (for example, 13:5, 13).

John concludes the story by saying, *This was now the third time Jesus appeared to his disciples after he was raised from the dead* (v. 14). Scholars see this note, like a similar note earlier (4:54), as evidence of poorly aligned sources, since this is in fact the fourth appearance recounted by John. But this conclusion misses the point because John is counting appearances to the *disciples* as a group, which would not include Jesus' appearance to Mary Magdalene. Jesus now appears to another partial gathering of the group, an appearance that reveals the same key characteristics as were manifested throughout the ministry, namely his lordship, his servanthood, his character as gracious giver of abundance and his love. He has met his disciples at a point of failure and revealed himself as the awesome Lord of creation who cares for them.

The fact that he provides a meal indicates that "lordship includes fellowship" (Osborne 1984:179). Such fellowship with Jesus at a meal reminds one of the many times he shared such fellowship during his ministry, especially at the Last Supper and also the theme of the new community he has now established (see comments on 9:1—10:42 and 19:25-27). This association, as well as the tie in with the feeding of the five thousand, brings echoes of the Eucharist (cf. Brown 1970:1098-1100). This meal itself is not a Eucharist, but it embodies a central aspect of what Eucharist itself is about—communion with the risen Lord in the midst of his people.

John's note in verse 14 indicates that the focus of the story to this point is on Jesus and his appearance. It also signals a transition. This story has focused on Jesus' love and lordship, but Peter and the Beloved Disciple have also been featured. Now we will see Jesus' love and lordship in action in their lives specifically.

Jesus Forms Peter as a Leader and as a Disciple (21:15-23) Jesus' inviting his disciples to share a meal signals his love and fellowship with them. But he has unfinished business with Peter, the one who denied him in a special way. After breakfast Jesus speaks to Peter. Throughout this story Peter has been referred to as Simon Peter (vv. 2-3, 7b, 11) or simply as Peter (v. 7a), the name Jesus had given him (1:42; cf. Mk 3:16 par. Lk 6:14). But now Jesus calls him by his former name, *Simon son of John* (v. 15), "as if he were no longer (or not yet!) a disciple" (Michaels 1989:359).

In the first part of this chapter Jesus began with a question that revealed the disciples' poverty (v. 5), and then he gave a series of commands (vv. 6, 10, 12). So also now he questions Peter and then gives a command, and he does so three times. His question is extremely searching, indeed, it is the ultimate question in life: *do you truly love me more than these?* (v. 15). What does *these* refer to? If it is the net and boat, then this question gets at the central point of discipleship and reveals a person's heart. What do we love the most? Have we abandoned all to follow Jesus? Every time we are faced with a temptation this question is raised. Every time we become preoccupied with even the good things God gives us this question is raised.

21:15 As elsewhere in the Gospel (for example, see note on 21:5) John is using Greek words to capture not just the content but also the nuances of what Jesus said.

This interview with Peter has been interpreted as giving an exclusive authority to Peter over all disciples. There is nothing in the context to warrant this (Beasley-Murray

But, while all of this is true, it is probably not the specific point here. By *these* Jesus probably means "these other disciples." According to the other Gospels, Peter had boasted that though all the others fall away, he would not (Mt 26:33 par. Mk 14:29; cf. Lk 22:33; Jn 13:37). John does not record this boast, but Peter's actions in swimming to shore and hauling up the net by himself reveal the same attitude. Jesus' question, therefore, goes even deeper than the issue of false attachments. He gets at the root of all sin, namely, pride.

Peter replies, *Yes, Lord, . . . you know that I love you* (v. 15). He does not claim to love Jesus more than the others do, which suggests he has benefited from having reflected on his shameful denials of the Lord. This response is typical of true discipleship, for it is humble and focuses on the Lord's own knowledge. According to the NIV it is also a humble response in that Peter does not claim to *truly love* Jesus, but only to *love* him. Behind this translation there are two verbs for love, *truly love (agapaō)* and *love (phileō)*. In the past it was common to find a great distinction between these two words, but in recent years the idea that they are close synonyms has come to prevail (for example, Carson 1991:676-77). The older idea that *agapaō* is divine love and *phileō* a lower, human love does indeed go too far. For both verbs are used of the love of the Father for the Son (3:35; 5:20), and *agapaō* can be used of false love, for example, the love of this world (2 Tim 4:10). So a simple distinction between the verbs is not justified, but this does not mean there is no distinction at all. For in this passage there is a pattern, with Jesus asking Peter twice whether he loves him *(agapaō)* and each time Peter responding that, yes, he does love him *(phileō)*. Then the third time Jesus switches to using Peter's word. Such a pattern suggests there is a distinction here (McKay 1985; H. C. G. Moule 1898:176), and since *agapaō* is used more often in John for God's love than is *phileō*, "it was likely that *agapaō* would be chosen for the higher meaning" (McKay 1985:322). The present context itself supports this view, for otherwise Peter would be claiming "the higher meaning" from the outset, which would not fit with his more chastened perspective. So the NIV seems justified in distinguishing these two terms in the present context.

1987:406-7), let alone the notion that such universal authority is then passed on through the bishop of Rome. Recent Roman Catholic commentators recognize that such issues are not the subject of this passage in itself (Brown 1970:1116-17; Schnackenburg 1982:366; Moloney 1998:555, 559).

Peter was not boastful when Jesus gave him the opportunity to be (v. 15), but by the third time Jesus asks whether he loves him, Peter is *hurt,* that is, deeply grieved (*elypēthē,* v. 17). Jesus' asking three times recalls the three denials, and Peter's pride is cut to the quick. Here we see the Great Physician performing painful but necessary surgery. The light is shining in the darkness of Peter's heart, bringing life. For this is what John of the Ladder (c. A.D. 570-649) refers to as "joy-producing sorrow" (*The Ladder of Divine Ascent,* chap. 7), the repentance that enables one to experience the Lord's love and salvation. Without such brokenness we are full of self and unable to hear and receive the guidance of the Chief Shepherd.

In response to this searing third question, Peter says, *Lord, you know all things; you know that I love you* (v. 17). Two different words for "know" are used here, although these are not distinguished in the NIV. But as with the two words for "love," these words are in a pattern. Each time Peter has responded *you know* (*sy oidas,* vv. 15-17), but now he adds *you know [sy ginōskeis] that I love you.* The pattern here suggests that there is a distinction between *oida* and *ginōskō,* with the latter perhaps meaning "you must be able to see" (McKay 1981:304). This shift of vocabulary, along with the reference to *all things,* reflects a view of the Lord that is more exalted and suggests that Peter's humility is deeper. "Do you see how he has become better and more sober, no longer self-willed or contradicting?" (Chrysostom *In John* 88.1). Peter is dying to self and finding his confidence only in the Lord. It is the Lord who knows (cf. 1:42, 47-48; 2:25). Despite the appearances, Peter does love Jesus.

After each profession of love Jesus gives a similar command, using different words. First he is to *feed [boske] lambs* (*arnia,* v. 15); then he is to *shepherd [poimaine] sheep* (*probata,* v. 16). The third command includes a word from both of the previous commands (v. 17, *boske/probata*), thereby tying the three commands together. While attempts have been made to find significant differences in these words, none are convincing (Brown 1970:1104-6; McKay 1985:332). Rather, this pattern suggests we have a comprehensive image of shepherding, a very familiar figure of speech for leadership over God's people. God himself was known as the shepherd of Israel (Gen 49:24; Ps 80:1; Is 40:11), and under him the leaders of his people were known as shepherds (2 Sam 5:2; Jer 23:4; Ezek 34). This motif continues in the New Testament (Acts 20:28; 1 Pet 2:25; 5:1-4). Jesus himself is the Good Shepherd (Jn 10:1-18), and now he commissions Peter to care for the flock that belongs to Jesus, for they are *my lambs . . . my sheep*. The community has already been established, and now Peter is given authority, though of a particular kind.

The key qualification for this task, as this chapter indicates, is a love for Jesus that is characterized by humility, dependence and obedience. Peter already had a devotion to Jesus, but he was still full of self will and was thrusting himself to the front. Such a proud attitude of heart would spell disaster for the community, as had already been evident in Israel's history right up to the opponents who had just had Jesus crucified and as has sadly been just as evident in the history of the church. But Peter himself learned his lesson, as is clear from his first letter. When he addresses the elders of the communities he does so as a "fellow elder" and encourages them to "be shepherds of God's flock that is under your care, serving as overseers . . . not lording it over those entrusted to you, but being examples to the flock. And when the Chief Shepherd appears, you will receive the crown of glory that will never fade away" (1 Pet 5:1-4). Here is authority exercised in humility and conscious of the Chief Shepherd. Such are marks of a true shepherd.

Jesus had predicted Peter's denials after Peter had said he was willing to die with him (13:37-38). Jesus told him, "Where I am going, you cannot follow now, but you will follow later" (13:36). Here now is the call to follow. After Peter professes his obedient love, Jesus spells out the cost of that love. He contrasts Peter's youth, his life up to this point, with what is coming. He has been able to go wherever he wanted, but when he is old, Jesus tells him, *you will stretch out your hands, and someone else will dress you and lead you where you do not want to go* (v. 18). Here is an explicit contrast between Peter's life of self will and his coming under the will of another. He has just submitted to Jesus and his will, and now Jesus says such submission is going to include being taken where he does not want to go.

John says this obscure saying is an indication of *the kind of death by which Peter would glorify God* (v. 19). The translation of the NIV (v. 18) could be a picture of death from natural causes after increasing senility. But according to tradition, Peter was crucified head down during the Neronian persecution in the midsixties A.D. (Eusebius *Ecclesiastical History* 2.25.5; 3.1.2-3). So John, late in the first century, knows that Peter's hands were stretched out and tied to a cross. The word *dress (zōnnymi)* is a play on words. It is used for getting dressed, but it specifically means to gird, that is, fasten a belt or rope around one's clothes. While this word is not used for the binding of prisoners (cf. 18:12, 24; Acts 21:11-13), this could be the significance of this image. More likely, however, it refers here to the binding of a person's arms to the crossbeam as they are led to crucifixion (Beasley-Murray 1987:408-9).

The Good Shepherd laid down his life for the sheep, and this shepherd will have to do likewise, though his death will not, of course, take away the sins of the world. He has submitted his will to God, and his death, like Jesus' death, will be in accordance with God's will and thereby glorify him (Moloney 1998:556). Furthermore, in the death of Jesus the glory of God is revealed since God is love and love is the laying down of one's life (1 Jn 4:8; 3:16). So now Jesus predicts that Peter also will glorify God by his death (v. 19).

Having spelled out his will for Peter, Jesus calls him to follow him (v. 19). Peter had answered such a call at the outset of the ministry, but now he understands much more about who Jesus is and what following him entails. He has also received a commission from the Lord for leadership in the community. So this is a call to recommit himself. Just as this Gospel shows that faith must be exercised in the face of each new revelation, so one's commitment to Jesus must be renewed as one learns more of Christ and his call.

Jesus has been teaching Peter many lessons in this encounter on the beach, but in what follows it is clear that Peter has more to learn. Peter has had his attention fixed on Jesus ever since the Beloved Disciple told him the person on the beach was Jesus, but now he takes his eyes off Jesus and looks at the Beloved Disciple, who is following (v. 20). Apparently Jesus and Peter have had this conversation while walking along the beach. The NIV says the Beloved Disciple *was following them,* but the word *them* is not in the text. The NIV thus obscures the connection, for right after Jesus commands Peter to follow him we hear of one who is following. The Beloved Disciple is identified as the one who leaned against Jesus and asked who would betray him (v. 20; 13:25). This note recalls that first explicit reference to the Beloved Disciple in the Gospel and the setting in which Jesus demonstrated his love and servanthood, key characteristics about which he has just been speaking to Peter. It also recalls the insight Jesus granted to the Beloved Disciple. Peter now tries to assume this same role and asks for insight regarding his friend (v. 21).

In response Jesus speaks strong words to Peter. Peter's old habit of lapsing into error right after experiencing truth is still present (cf. Mt 16:16, 22-23 par. Mk 8:29, 33). He is sure of the Lord's knowledge (cf. v. 17), but he has not learned what submission to his will entails (vv. 18-19). Jesus repeats his call: *If I want him to remain alive until I return, what is that to you? You must follow me* (v. 22). Jesus is indeed Lord, and his will shall be accomplished in the Beloved Disciple's life, but that is none of Peter's business. Peter can trust Jesus with the life of his friend.

Jesus' statement about the Beloved Disciple, like that about Peter (v. 18), is rather obscure. It includes a clear reference to Jesus' personal return, but what does it mean for the Beloved Disciple *to remain (menein)?* The NIV interprets it to mean *remain alive,* and certainly this is how the later disciples, *the brothers* (v. 23), took it. But since it is the word used for indwelling Christ, as in the image of the vine and the branches (15:4-7), a spiritual sense could be involved. John distinguishes carefully between what Jesus actually said and how it was interpreted (v. 23). Such lack of attention to the precise words of God has been a source of difficulty ever since the Garden of Eden (Gen 2:16-17; 3:1-5, 13). This misunderstanding highlights the need for the instruction of the Paraclete (14:26).

It is usually assumed that this correction (v. 23) implies that the Beloved Disciple has in fact died or is very near death. Such may be the case, but the text does not say as much. The Beloved Disciple could still be in the prime of life, and here he is simply trying to squelch an error he knows to be floating around among the disciples. Jesus' will is the crucial factor, whatever *remain* might mean.

A number of scholars think there is a rivalry between the Beloved Disciple and Peter, but this final chapter shows them to be friends of one another and to both have special roles in the community. Peter will be a shepherd, and the Beloved Disciple is able to discern the Lord and receive insight into his life and thought. Accordingly, the conclusion will focus on the Beloved Disciple as witness.

☐ Later Disciples Bear Witness to the Beloved Disciple's Witness (21:24-25)

The reference to the Beloved Disciple (vv. 20-23) leads right into an identification of him as *the disciple who testifies to these things and who wrote them down* (v. 24). As the author of this Gospel, the Beloved Disciple fulfills Jesus' commission to those who were with him to be witnesses to him (15:27). The word *wrote* does not necessarily mean John actually did the writing. Indeed, one tradition of the church names his scribe as Prochorus. Or perhaps there were a number of disciples involved. But *wrote* does mean the Beloved Disciple is at least directly responsible for what was written, just as Pilate was responsible for the title on the cross (19:22). This Gospel claims to be an eyewitness account.

Next is an attestation to this witness: *We know that his testimony is true* (v. 24). Some think this is the Beloved Disciple bearing witness to himself, but the editorial "we" is followed by a first-person plural pronoun (cf. 3:11; 1 Jn 1:2, 4), not a third-person singular as here *(his)*. So this is the testimony of John's disciples, probably the leaders within the churches or at least those who have helped with the production of the Gospel. It is not clear on what grounds they bear witness. Were some of them also eyewitnesses who can certify the accuracy of the information, or are they testifying that the Spirit has confirmed to them the truth of what John has said (cf. 1 Jn 2:27)? If it is the latter sense, then we today can join our testimony to theirs and to that of Christian brothers and sisters throughout the ages who have found the truth of this Gospel confirmed by the living Jesus through the Spirit.

This Gospel, which is so full of cryptic sayings and deeds, ends with one last enigma. After the *we* of verse 24, who is this *I* in verse 25? Are these the words of a further redactor, beyond the work of the disciples in view in verse 24? Or is this first-person singular pronoun merely part of the hyperbole (Brown 1970:1129)? Or is this the Beloved Disciple himself, who now "feels free to make an overt self-reference" (Carson 1991:686)? Or is this neither the Beloved Disciple himself nor the disciples who have helped with the Gospel but the scribe who has taken it down (cf. Rom 16:22, Michaels 1989:364)? It would be fitting for a scribe to conclude with a reference to all *the books that would be written!* One's view of the identity of this person will be determined in large part by how one thinks the Gospel came to be produced. For my own part, the last option mentioned is attractive, but there can be no certainty on this matter.

This final voice adds one last witness to the greatness of Jesus. Such hyperbole may be a literary convention (Talbert 1992:264; Moloney 1998:562), but in this case it is quite literally true, for there is no limit to the riches that are in Christ Jesus. Jesus is the very presence of God come into our midst. All authority has been given to him, and judgment is in his hands. He is quite strict regarding obedience, but he is full of mercy. He has revealed the Father, overcome the prince of this world and taken away the sin of the world. He also washed his disciples' feet and served them breakfast. No human being has ever dreamed up such a God—we have a hard enough time remaining true to the witness he has left us through his servants, in particular, through John, the Beloved Disciple.

Bibliography

Aalen, Sverre
1976   "Glory, Honour." In *New International Dictionary of New
                        Testament Theology,* 2:44-48. Edited by Colin Brown. 3 vols.
                        Grand Rapids, Mich.: Zondervan.

Abbott, Edwin A.
1906   *Johannine Grammar.* London: Adam and Charles Black.

Alford, Henry
1980   *Matthew—John.* Vol. 1 of *Alford's Greek Testament: An
                        Exegetical and Critical Commentary.* Grand Rapids, Mich.:
                        Baker. Reprint of the 7th revised edition of 1874.

Allison, Dale C.
1987   "The Eye Is the Lamp of the Body (Matt. 6.22-23 = Luke
                        11.34-36)." *New Testament Studies* 33:61-83.

Ashton, John
1991   *Understanding the Fourth Gospel.* Oxford: Clarendon Press.

Bailey, Kenneth E.
1993   "The Shepherd Poems of John 10: Their Culture and Style."
                        The Near East School of Theology Theological Review 14:3-21.

Balz, Horst
1972   "ὕπνος κτλ." In *Theological Dictionary of the New Test-
                        ament,* 8:545-56. Edited by Gerhard Kittel and Gerhard
                        Friedrich. 10 vols. Grand Rapids, Mich.: Eerdmans.

Bammel, Ernest
1952   "Φίλος τοῦ Καίσαρος." *Theologische Literaturzeitung*
                        77:205-10.
1965   "John Did No Miracles: John 10:41." In *Miracles: Cambridge
                        Studies in Their Philosophy and History,* pp. 181-202.
                        Edited by C. F. D. Moule. London: Mowbrays.
1970   "Ex illa itaque die consilium fecerunt. . . ." In *The Trial of
                        Jesus: Cambridge Studies in Honour of C. F. D. Moule,* pp.
                        11-40. Studies in Biblical Theology, Second Series 13.
                        Edited by Ernst Bammel. London: SCM Press.

Barnhart, Bruno
1993   *The Good Wine: Reading John from the Center.* New York:
                        Paulist.

Barrett, C. K.
1978   *The Gospel According to St. John: An Introduction with
                        Commentary and Notes on the Greek Text.* 2d ed. Philadel-
                        phia: Westminster Press.

1987   *The New Testament Background: Writings from Ancient*
               Greece and the Roman Empire That Illuminate Christian
               Origins. Rev. ed. San Francisco: HarperSanFrancisco.
Bauckham, R. J.
1996   "Lazarus." In *New Bible Dictionary,* pp. 678-79. 3d ed.
               Edited by I. Howard Marshall, A. R. Millard, J. I. Packer
               and D. J. Wiseman. Downers Grove, Ill.: InterVarsity Press.
Bauer, Walter, F. Wilbur
Gingrich and
Frederick W. Danker
1979   *A Greek-English Lexicon of the New Testament and Other*
               Early Christian Literature. 2d rev. and aug. ed. Chicago:
               University of Chicago Press.
Beasley-Murray, George R.
1962   *Baptism in the New Testament.* Grand Rapids, Mich.:
               Eerdmans.
1975   "Baptism, Wash." In *New International Dictionary of New*
               Testament Theology, 1:143-54. Edited by Colin Brown. 3
               vols. Grand Rapids, Mich.: Zondervan.
1987   *John.* Word Biblical Commentary 36. Waco, Tex.: Word.
1991   *Gospel of Life: Theology in the Fourth Gospel.* Peabody,
               Mass.: Hendrickson.
Behm, Johannes
1964   "ἄμπελος." In *Theological Dictionary of the New Testament,*
               1:342-43. Edited by Gerhard Kittel and Gerhard Friedrich.
               10 vols. Grand Rapids, Mich.: Eerdmans.
1965   "κλῆμα." In *Theological Dictionary of the New Testament,*
               3:757. Edited by Gerhard Kittel and Gerhard Friedrich.
               10 vols. Grand Rapids, Mich.: Eerdmans.
1967   "παράκλητος." In *Theological Dictionary of the New Testa-*
               ment, 5:800-814. Edited by Gerhard Kittel and Gerhard
               Friedrich. 10 vols. Grand Rapids, Mich.: Eerdmans.
Bernard, J. H.
1928   *A Critical and Exegetical Commentary on the Gospel Accord-*
               ing to St. John. 2 vols. The International Critical Commen-
               tary. Edited by A. H. McNeile. Edinburgh: T & T Clark.
Betz, Otto
1974   "φωνή κτλ." In *Theological Dictionary of the New Testa-*
               ment, 9:278-309. Edited by Gerhard Kittel and Gerhard
               Friedrich. 10 vols. Grand Rapids, Mich.: Eerdmans.
Bietenhard, Hans
1967   "ὄνομα κτλ." In *Theological Dictionary of the New Testa-*
               ment, 5:242-83. Edited by Gerhard Kittel and Gerhard
               Friedrich. 10 vols. Grand Rapids, Mich.: Eerdmans.

1976	"Name." In *New International Dictionary of New Testament Theology,* 2:648-55. Edited by Colin Brown. 3 vols. Grand Rapids, Mich.: Zondervan.

Blackburn, B. L.
1992	"Divine Man/*Theios Anēr.*" In *Dictionary of Jesus and the Gospels,* pp. 189-92. Edited by Joel B. Green, Scot McKnight and I. Howard Marshall. Downers Grove, Ill.: InterVarsity Press.

Blass, F., and A. Debrunner
1961	*A Greek Grammar of the New Testament and Other Early Christian Literature.* Translated and revised by Robert W. Funk. Chicago: University of Chicago Press.

Blinzler, Josef
1959	*The Trial of Jesus.* Translated by Isabel and Florence McHugh. Westminster, Md.: Newman Press.

Bloch, Abraham P.
1980	*The Biblical and Historical Background of Jewish Customs and Ceremonies.* New York: KTAV.

Blomberg, Craig L.
1987	*The Historical Reliability of the Gospels.* Downers Grove, Ill.: InterVarsity Press.

Boismard, Marie-Émile
1993	*Moses or Jesus: An Essay in Johannine Christology.* Translated by B. T. Viviano. Minneapolis: Fortress; Leuven: Peeters.

Borgen, Peder
1965	*Bread from Heaven: An Exegetical Study of the Concept of Manna in the Gospel of John and the Writings of Philo.* Supplements to *Novum Testamentum* 10. Leiden, Netherlands: E. J. Brill.
1968	"God's Agent in the Fourth Gospel." In *Religions in Antiquity: Essays in Memory of Erwin Ramsdell Goodenough,* pp. 137-48. Edited by Jacob Neusner. Leiden, Netherlands: E. J. Brill.

Boyd, Gregory A.
1997	*God at War: The Bible and Spiritual Conflict.* Downers Grove, Ill.: InterVarsity Press.

Breck, John
1991	*Origins of Johannine Pneumatology.* Vol. 1 of *Spirit of Truth: The Holy Spirit in Johannine Tradition.* Crestwood, N.Y.: St. Vladimir's Seminary Press.

Brown, Raymond E.
1966	*The Gospel According to John I—XII.* Anchor Bible 29. Garden City, N.Y.: Doubleday.
1970	*The Gospel According to John XIII—XXI.* Anchor Bible

	29A. Garden City, N.Y.: Doubleday.
1979	*The Community of the Beloved Disciple: The Life, Loves and Hates of an Individual Church in New Testament Times.* New York: Paulist.
1988	*The Gospel and Epistles of John: A Concise Commentary.* Collegeville, Minn.: Liturgical Press.
1994	*The Death of the Messiah, from Gethsemane to the Grave: A Commentary on the Passion Narratives in the Four Gospels.* 2 vols. Garden City, N.Y.: Doubleday.

Browne, Edward Harold
| 1998 | *An Exposition of the Thirty-Nine Articles of Religion: Historical and Doctrinal.* 1887. Reprint, Houston: Classical Anglican Press. |

Brownlee, William H.
| 1990 | "Whence the Gospel According to John?" In *John and the Dead Sea Scrolls*, pp. 166-94. Edited by James H. Charlesworth. New York: Crossroad. An enlarged edition of *John and Qumran*. London: Geoffrey Chapman, 1972. |

Bruce, F. F.
| 1983 | *The Gospel of John: Introduction, Exposition and Notes.* Grand Rapids, Mich.: Eerdmans. |

Büchsel, Friedrich,
| 1964 | "ἐλέγχω κτλ." In *Theological Dictionary of the New Testament,* 2:473-76. Edited by Gerhard Kittel and Gerhard Friedrich. 10 vols. Grand Rapids, Mich.: Eerdmans. |

Büchsel, Friedrich,
and Johannes Herrmann
| 1965 | "ἵλεως κτλ." In *Theological Dictionary of the New Testament,* 3:300-323. Edited by Gerhard Kittel and Gerhard Friedrich. 10 vols. Grand Rapids, Mich.: Eerdmans. |

Bultmann, Rudolf
| 1964 | "γινώσκω κτλ." In *Theological Dictionary of the New Testament,* 1:689-719. Edited by Gerhard Kittel and Gerhard Friedrich. 10 vols. Grand Rapids, Mich.: Eerdmans. |
| 1971 | *The Gospel of John: A Commentary.* Translated by G. R. Beasley-Murray. Edited by R. W. N. Hoare and J. K. Riches. Oxford: Blackwell. |

Burge, Gary M.
| 1987 | *The Anointed Community: The Holy Spirit in the Johannine Tradition.* Grand Rapids, Mich.: Eerdmans. |
| 1994 | "Territorial Religion, Johannine Christology and the Vineyard of John 15." In *Jesus of Nazareth: Lord and Christ. Essays on the Historical Jesus and New Testament Christology*, pp. 384-96. Edited by Joel B. Green and Max Turner. |

Grand Rapids, Mich.: Eerdmans.

Cabasilas, Nicholas
1974   *The Life in Christ.* Translated by Carmino J. de Catanzaro. Crestwood, N.Y.: St. Vladimir's Seminary Press.

Caird, G. B.
1969   "The Glory of God in the Fourth Gospel: An Exercise in Biblical Semantics." *New Testament Studies* 15:265-77.

Calvin, John
1959   *The Gospel According to St. John: Part Two, 11—21 and The First Epistle of John.* Calvin's New Testament Commentaries: A New Translation 5. Translated by T. H. L. Parker. Edited by David W. Torrance and Thomas F. Torrance. Grand Rapids, Mich.: Eerdmans (original ed., 1553).
1961   *The Gospel According to St. John: Part One, 1—10.* Calvin's New Testament Commentaries: A New Translation 4. Translated by T. H. L. Parker. Edited by David W. Torrance and Thomas F. Torrance. Grand Rapids, Mich.: Eerdmans (original ed., 1553).

Carson, D. A.
1980   *The Farewell Discourse and Final Prayer of Jesus: An Exposition of John 14—17.* Grand Rapids, Mich.: Baker.
1981   *Divine Sovereignty and Human Responsibility: Biblical Perspectives in Tension.* New Foundations Theological Library. Atlanta: John Knox Press.
1991   *The Gospel According to John.* Leicester, U.K.: Inter-Varsity Press; Grand Rapids, Mich.: Eerdmans.

Chambers, Oswald
1935   *My Utmost for His Highest: Selections for the Year.* Toronto: McClelland and Stewart.

Charlesworth, James H.
1983   *Apocalyptic Literature and Testaments.* Vol. 1 of *The Old Testament Pseudepigrapha.* Garden City, N.Y.: Doubleday.
1995   *The Beloved Disciple: Whose Witness Validates the Gospel of John?* Valley Forge, Penn.: Trinity Press International.

Chilton, Bruce
1992   "Annas." In *Anchor Bible Dictionary,* 1:257-58. Edited by David Noel Freedman. 6 vols. New York: Doubleday.

Collins, John J.
1987   *The Apocalyptic Imagination: An Introduction to the Jewish Matrix of Christianity.* New York: Crossroad.
1995   *The Scepter and the Star: The Messiahs of the Dead Sea Scrolls and Other Ancient Literature.* The Anchor Bible Reference Library. New York: Doubleday.

Collins, Raymond F.
1990   *These Things Have Been Written: Studies on the Fourth Gospel*. Louvain Theological and Pastoral Monographs 2. Louvain: Peeters; Grand Rapids, Mich.: Eerdmans.

Conzelmann, Hans
1974a   "φῶς κτλ." In *Theological Dictionary of the New Testament*, 9:310-58. Edited by Gerhard Kittel and Gerhard Friedrich. 10 vols. Grand Rapids, Mich.: Eerdmans.
1974b   "χαίρω κτλ." In *Theological Dictionary of the New Testament*, 9:359-72. Edited by Gerhard Kittel and Gerhard Friedrich. 10 vols. Grand Rapids, Mich.: Eerdmans.

Corley, B.
1992   "Trial of Jesus." In *Dictionary of Jesus and the Gospels*, pp. 841-54. Edited by Joel B. Green, Scot McKnight and I. Howard Marshall. Downers Grove, Ill.: InterVarsity Press.

Cory, Catherine
1997   "Wisdom's Rescue: A New Reading of the Tabernacles Discourse (John 7:1—8:59)." *Journal of Biblical Literature* 116:95-116.

Craig, William Lane
1995   "Did Jesus Rise from the Dead?" In *Jesus Under Fire*, pp. 141-76. Edited by Michael J. Wilkins and J. P. Moreland. Grand Rapids, Mich.: Zondervan.

Culpepper, R. Alan
1983   *Anatomy of the Fourth Gospel: A Study in Literary Design*. New Testament Foundations and Facets. Philadelphia: Fortress.

Dahl, Nils A.
1976   "The Johannine Church and History." In *Jesus in the Memory of the Early Church: Essays by Nils Alstrup Dahl*, pp. 99-119. Minneapolis: Augsburg.
1990   " 'Do Not Wonder!' John 5:28-29 and Johannine Eschatology Once More." In *The Conversation Continues: Studies in Paul and John in Honor of J. Louis Martyn*, pp. 322-36. Edited by Robert T. Fortna and Beverly R. Gaventa. Nashville: Abingdon.

Daube, David
1956   *The New Testament and Rabbinic Judaism*. London: Athlone Press.

Davies, W. D.
1974   *The Gospel and the Land: Early Christianity and Jewish Territorial Doctrine*. Berkeley: University of California Press.

de Jonge, M.
1979   "The Beloved Disciple and the Date of the Gospel of John."

In *Text and Interpretation: Studies in the New Testament Presented to Matthew Black,* pp. 99-114. Edited by E. Best and R. McL. Wilson. Cambridge: Cambridge University Press.

Demarest, Bruce A.
1978   "Seed, Plant, Grass, Flower, Harvest." In *New International Dictionary of New Testament Theology,* 3:521-27. Edited by Colin Brown. 3 vols. Grand Rapids, Mich.: Zondervan.

Derrett, J. Duncan M.
1970   *Law in the New Testament.* London: Darton, Longman and Todd.

de Vaux, Roland
1961   *Ancient Israel.* 2 vols. New York: McGraw-Hill.

Dexinger, Ferdinand
1989   "Samaritan Eschatology." In *The Samaritans,* pp. 266-92. Edited by Alan D. Crown. Tübingen: J. C. B. Mohr/Paul Siebeck.

Dillon, John M.
1992   "Fate, Greek Conception of." In *Anchor Bible Dictionary,* 2:776-78. Edited by David Noel Freedman. 6 vols. New York: Doubleday.

Dodd, C. H.
1952   *According to the Scriptures: The Substructure of New Testament Theology.* London: Nisbet.

1953   *The Interpretation of the Fourth Gospel.* Cambridge: Cambridge University Press.

1963   *The Historical Tradition in the Fourth Gospel.* Cambridge: Cambridge University Press.

1968   "The Prophecy of Caiaphas: John 11:47-53." In *More New Testament Studies,* pp. 58-68. Grand Rapids, Mich.: Eerdmans.

Dodds, E. R.
1965   *Pagan and Christian in an Age of Anxiety: Some Aspects of Religious Experience from Marcus Aurelius to Constantine.* New York: W. W. Norton.

Dunn, James D. G.
1991   "Let John Be John: A Gospel for Its Time." In *The Gospel and the Gospels,* pp. 293-322. Edited by Peter Stuhlmacher. Grand Rapids, Mich.: Eerdmans.

1992   "Prayer." In *Dictionary of Jesus and the Gospels,* pp. 617-25. Edited by Joel B. Green, Scot McKnight and I. Howard Marshall. Downers Grove, Ill.: InterVarsity Press.

Edwards, William D.,
Wesley J. Gabel and
Floyd E. Hosmer
1986   "On the Physical Death of Jesus Christ." *Journal of the
                       American Medical Association* 255:1455-63.
Ellis, Peter F.
1984   *The Genius of John: A Composition-Critical Commentary
                       on the Fourth Gospel.* Collegeville, Minn.: Liturgical Press.
Ford, J. Massingberd
1969   " 'Mingled Blood' from the Side of Christ (John 19:34)."
                       New Testament Studies 15:337-38.
Forestell, J. Terence
1974   *The Word of the Cross: Salvation as Revelation in the Fourth
                       Gospel.* Analecta Biblica 57. Rome: Pontifical Biblical Insti-
                       tute.
Fortna, Robert Tomson
1970   *The Gospel of Signs: A Reconstruction of the Narrative
                       Source Underlying the Fourth Gospel.* Society for New
                       Testament Studies Monograph Series 11. Cambridge: Cam-
                       bridge University Press.
1988   *The Fourth Gospel and Its Predecessor: From Narrative
                       Source to Present Gospel.* Philadelphia: Fortress.
Friedrich, Gerhard
1968   "προφήτης κτλ." In *Theological Dictionary of the New
                       Testament,* 6:828-61. Edited by Gerhard Kittel and Gerhard
                       Friedrich. 10 vols. Grand Rapids, Mich.: Eerdmans.
Fuller, Reginald, H.
1963   *Interpreting the Miracles.* London: SCM Press.

Goppelt, Leonhard
1972   "ὕδωρ." In *Theological Dictionary of the New Testament,*
                       8:314-33. Edited by Gerhard Kittel and Gerhard Friedrich.
                       10 vols. Grand Rapids, Mich.: Eerdmans.
Goulder, M. D.
1991   "The Visionaries of Laodicea." *Journal for the Study of the
                       New Testament* 43:15-39.
Gowan, Donald E.
1982   *Bridge Between the Testaments: A Reappraisal of Judaism
                       from the Exile to the Birth of Christianity.* Pittsburgh Theo-
                       logical Monograph Series 14. 2d and rev. ed. Pittsburgh:
                       Pickwick.
Green, J. B.
1992   "Burial of Jesus." In *Dictionary of Jesus and the Gospels,*
                       pp. 88-92. Edited by Joel B. Green, Scot McKnight and

I. Howard Marshall. Downers Grove, Ill.: InterVarsity Press.

Greeven, Heinrich
1968   "προσκυνέω κτλ." In *Theological Dictionary of the New
            Testament*, 6:758-66. Edited by Gerhard Kittel and
            Gerhard Friedrich. 10 vols. Grand Rapids, Mich.: Eerdmans.

Grese, William C.
1988   " 'Unless One Is Born Again': The Use of a Heavenly
            Journey in John 3." *Journal of Biblical Literature* 107:677-93.

Gruenwald, Ithamar
1980   *Apocalyptic and Merkavah Mysticism*. Arbeiten zur
            Geschichte des antiken Judentums und des Urchristentums,
            Band 14. Leiden, Netherlands: E. J. Brill.

Grundmann, Walter
1964   "δεῖ κτλ." In *Theological Dictionary of the New Testament*,
            2:21-25. Edited by Gerhard Kittel and Gerhard Friedrich.
            10 vols. Grand Rapids, Mich.: Eerdmans.
1965   "καλός." In *Theological Dictionary of the New Testament*,
            3:536-50. Edited by Gerhard Kittel and Gerhard Friedrich.
            10 vols. Grand Rapids, Mich.: Eerdmans.
1967   "μέγας κτλ." In *Theological Dictionary of the New Testa-
            ment*, 4:529-44. Edited by Gerhard Kittel and Gerhard
            Friedrich. 10 vols. Grand Rapids, Mich.: Eerdmans.

Gundry, Robert H.
1967   "In My Father's House Are Many *Monai* (John 14:2)."
            Zeitschrift für die neutestamentliche Wissenschaft 58:68-72.

Gutbrod, Walter
1965   "'Ισραήλ κτλ." In *Theological Dictionary of the New Testa-
            ment*, 3:356-91. Edited by Gerhard Kittel and Gerhard
            Friedrich. 10 vols. Grand Rapids, Mich.: Eerdmans.

Haacker, Klaus
1978   "Samaritan, Samaria." In *New International Dictionary of
            New Testament Theology*, 3:449-67. Edited by Colin Brown.
            3 vols. Grand Rapids, Mich.: Zondervan.

Haenchen, Ernest
1984   *John 2: A Commentary on the Gospel of John Chapters
            7—21*. Hermeneia. Translated by Robert W. Funk. Edited
            by Robert W. Funk and Ulrich Busse. Philadelphia: Fortress.

Harner, Philip B.
1970   *The "I Am" of the Fourth Gospel: A Study in Johannine
            Usage and Thought*. Facet Books, Biblical Series 26. Phila-
            delphia: Fortress.

Harris, Murray J.
1986   " 'The Dead Are Restored to Life': Miracles of Revivification
            in the Gospels." In *The Miracles of Jesus*, pp. 295-326.

Vol. 6 of *Gospel Perspectives*. Edited by David Wenham and Craig Blomberg. Sheffield, U.K.: JSOT Press.

Hart, H. St. J.

1952   "The Crown of Thorns in John 19.2-5." *Journal of Theological Studies* n.s. 3:66-75.

Harvey, A. E.

1976   *Jesus on Trial: A Study in the Fourth Gospel*. London: SPCK.

Hauck, Friedrich

1967a   "παροιμία." In *Theological Dictionary of the New Testament*, 5:854-56. Edited by Gerhard Kittel and Gerhard Friedrich. 10 vols. Grand Rapids, Mich.: Eerdmans.

1967b   "μένω κτλ." In *Theological Dictionary of the New Testament*, 4:574-88. Edited by Gerhard Kittel and Gerhard Friedrich. 10 vols. Grand Rapids, Mich.: Eerdmans.

Healey, Joseph P.

1992   "Am ha'aretz." In *Anchor Bible Dictionary*, 1:168-69. Edited by David Noel Freedman. 6 vols. New York: Doubleday.

Hendriksen, William

1953   *New Testament Commentary: Exposition of the Gospel According to John*. Grand Rapids, Mich.: Baker.

Hengel, Martin

1974   *Judaism and Hellenism: Studies in their Encounter in Palestine During the Early Hellenistic Period*. 2 vols. Translated by John Bowden. London: SCM Press; Philadelphia: Fortress.

1977   *Crucifixion in the Ancient World and the Folly of the Message of the Cross*. Translated by John Bowden. London: SCM Press.

1981   *The Charismatic Leader and His Followers*. Translated by James Greig. New York: Crossroad.

1989   *The Johannine Question*. Translated by John Bowden. London: SCM Press; Philadelphia: Trinity Press International.

Hoehner, Harold W.

1977   *Chronological Aspects of the Life of Christ*. Grand Rapids, Mich.: Zondervan.

Horbury, William

1972   "The Passion Narratives and Historical Criticism." *Theology* 75:58-71.

1982   "The Benediction of the *Minim* and Early Jewish-Christian Controversy." *Journal of Theological Studies* n.s. 33:19-61.

Horsley, Richard A.

1992   "Messianic Movements in Judaism." In *Anchor Bible Dic-*

tionary, 4:791-97. Edited by David Noel Freedman. 6 vols. New York: Doubleday.

Horsley, Richard A.,
and John S. Hanson
1985   *Bandits, Prophets and Messiahs: Popular Movements at the Time of Jesus.* Minneapolis: Winston.

Hoskyns, Edwyn Clement
1940   *The Fourth Gospel.* 2 vols. Edited by Francis Noel Davey. London: Faber & Faber.

Hoskyns, Edwyn,
and Noel Davey
1947   *The Riddle of the New Testament.* 3d ed. London: Faber & Faber.

Howard, W. F.
1943   *Christianity According to St. John.* London: Duckworth.

Hubbard, David A.
1996   "Priests and Levites." In *New Bible Dictionary,* pp. 956-62. 3d ed. Edited by I. Howard Marshall, A. R. Millard, J. I. Packer and D. J. Wiseman. Downers Grove, Ill.: InterVarsity Press.

Hurtado, Larry W.
1988   *One God, One Lord: Early Christian Devotion and Ancient Jewish Monotheism.* Philadelphia: Fortress.

Jeremias, Joachim
1965   "θύρα." In *Theological Dictionary of the New Testament,* 3:173-80. Edited by Gerhard Kittel and Gerhard Friedrich. 10 vols. Grand Rapids, Mich.: Eerdmans.
1966a   *The Eucharistic Words of Jesus.* London: SCM Press.
1966b   *The Rediscovery of Bethesda.* Louisville, Ky.: Southern Baptist Theological Seminary Press.
1967a   "λίθος κτλ." In *Theological Dictionary of the New Testament,* 4:268-80. Edited by Gerhard Kittel and Gerhard Friedrich. 10 vols. Grand Rapids, Mich.: Eerdmans.
1967b   "νύμφη κτλ." In *Theological Dictionary of the New Testament,* 4:1099-1106. Edited by Gerhard Kittel and Gerhard Friedrich. 10 vols. Grand Rapids, Mich.: Eerdmans.
1967c   "παῖς θεοῦ." In *Theological Dictionary of the New Testament,* 5:677-717. Edited by Gerhard Kittel and Gerhard Friedrich. 10 vols. Grand Rapids, Mich.: Eerdmans.
1968   "ποιμήν κτλ." In *Theological Dictionary of the New Testament,* 6:485-502. Edited by Gerhard Kittel and Gerhard Friedrich. 10 vols. Grand Rapids, Mich.: Eerdmans.

| 1969 | *Jerusalem in the Time of Jesus: An Investigation into Economic and Social Conditions During the New Testament Period*. Philadelphia: Fortress. |
| 1972 | *The Parables of Jesus*. New York: Charles Scribner's Sons. |

Johnson, Luke T.

1989   "The New Testament's Anti-Jewish Slander and the Conventions of Ancient Polemic." *New Testament Studies* 108:419-41.

Kanagaraj, Jey J.

1998   *"Mysticism" in the Gospel of John: An Inquiry into its Background*. Journal for the Study of the New Testament Supplement Series 158. Sheffield, U.K.: Sheffield Academic Press.

Kim, Seyoon

1985   *"The 'Son of Man' " as the Son of God*. Grand Rapids, Mich.: Eerdmans.

Kirk, K. E.

1932   *The Vision of God: The Christian Doctrine of the Summum Bonum*. 2d ed. London: Longmans, Green and Co.

Kittel, Gerhard

1967   "λέγω κτλ." In *Theological Dictionary of the New Testament*, 4:100-143. Edited by Gerhard Kittel and Gerhard Friedrich. 10 vols. Grand Rapids, Mich.: Eerdmans.

Klassen, William

1992   "Love (NT and Early Jewish Literature)." In *Anchor Bible Dictionary*, 4:381-96. Edited by David Noel Freedman. 6 vols. New York: Doubleday.

Koester, Craig

1995   *Symbolism in the Fourth Gospel: Meaning, Mystery, Community*. Minneapolis: Fortress.

Koester, Helmut

1972   "τόπος." In *Theological Dictionary of the New Testament*, 8:187-208. Edited by Gerhard Kittel and Gerhard Friedrich. 10 vols. Grand Rapids, Mich.: Eerdmans.

1982   *Introduction to the New Testament*. 2 vols. Philadelphia: Fortress.

1990   *Ancient Christian Gospels: Their History and Development*. Philadelphia: Trinity Press International; London: SCM Press.

Köstenberger, Andreas J.

1998a   "Jesus as Rabbi in the Fourth Gospel." *Bulletin for Biblical Research* 8:97-128.

1998b   *The Missions of Jesus and the Disciples According to the*

Fourth Gospel. Grand Rapids, Mich.: Eerdmans.

Kuhn, Karl Georg

1964a   "Βαλαάμ." In *Theological Dictionary of the New Testament,* 1:524-25. Edited by Gerhard Kittel and Gerhard Friedrich. 10 vols. Grand Rapids, Mich.: Eerdmans.

1964b   "βασιλεύς κτλ." In *Theological Dictionary of the New Testament,* 1:571-74. Edited by Gerhard Kittel and Gerhard Friedrich. 10 vols. Grand Rapids, Mich.: Eerdmans.

Kümmel, Werner Georg

1975   *Introduction to the New Testament.* Rev. ed. Translated by Howard Clark Kee. Nashville: Abingdon.

Kysar, Robert

1975   *The Fourth Evangelist and His Gospel.* Minneapolis: Augsburg.

1983   "The Gospel of John in Current Research." *Religious Studies Review* 9:314-23.

Lang, Friedrich

1968   "πῦρ κτλ." In *Theological Dictionary of the New Testament,* 6:928-52. Edited by Gerhard Kittel and Gerhard Friedrich. 10 vols. Grand Rapids, Mich.: Eerdmans.

Lee, Edwin Kenneth

1962   *The Religious Thought of St. John.* London: SPCK.

Lewis, C. S.

1967   *Christian Reflections.* Edited by Walter Hooper. Grand Rapids, Mich.: Eerdmans.

Liddell, H. G., R. Scott
and H. S. Jones

1940   *A Greek-English Lexicon, with a Supplement 1968.* Oxford: Clarendon.

Lightfoot, J. B.

1893   *Biblical Essays.* London: Macmillan. Reprint, with an introduction by Philip E. Hughes, Grand Rapids, Mich.: Baker, 1979.

Lindars, Barnabas

1972   *The Gospel of John.* New Century Bible. London: Oliphants; Greenwood, S.C.: Attic.

1980-1981   "John and the Synoptic Gospels: A Test Case." *New Testament Studies* 27:287-94.

1981   "The Persecution of Christians in John 15:18—16:4a." In *Suffering and Martyrdom in the New Testament: Studies Presented to G. M. Styler by the Cambridge New Testament Seminar,* pp. 48-69. Edited by William Horbury and Brian McNeil. Cambridge: Cambridge University Press.

1983   *Jesus Son of Man: A Fresh Examination of the Son of Man Sayings in the Gospels in the Light of Recent Research.* Grand Rapids, Mich.: Eerdmans.

Lohse, Eduard
1971   "σάββατον κτλ." In *Theological Dictionary of the New Testament,* 7:1-35. Edited by Gerhard Kittel and Gerhard Friedrich. 10 vols. Grand Rapids, Mich.: Eerdmans.

Louw, Johannes P.,
and Eugene A. Nida
1988   *Greek-English Lexicon of the New Testament Based on Semantic Domains.* 2 vols. New York: United Bible Societies.

Loyd, Philip
1936   *The Life According to S. John: Eighty-four Meditations.* London: Mowbray.

MacDonald, John
1964   *The Theology of the Samaritans.* London: SCM Press.

MacRae, George W.
1970   "The Fourth Gospel and *Religionsgeschichte.*" *Catholic Biblical Quarterly* 32:13-24.

Manson, T. W.
1946-1947   "The Fourth Gospel." *Bulletin of the John Rylands University Library of Manchester* 30:312-29.

Marshall, I. Howard
1992   "Son of Man." In *Dictionary of Jesus and the Gospels,* pp. 775-81. Edited by Joel B. Green, Scot McKnight and I. Howard Marshall. Downers Grove, Ill.: InterVarsity Press.

McKay, K. L.
1981   "On the Perfect and Other Aspects in New Testament Greek." *Novum Testamentum* 23:289-329.
1985   "Style and Significance in the Language of John 21:15-17." *Novum Testamentum* 27:319-33.

McNeil, Brian
1977   "The Quotation at John XII 34." *Novum Testamentum* 19:22-33.

McRay, John
1992   "Gabbatha." In *Anchor Bible Dictionary,* 2:862. Edited by David Noel Freedman. 6 vols. New York: Doubleday.

Meeks, Wayne A.
1967   *The Prophet-King: Moses Traditions and the Johannine Christology.* Supplements to *Novum Testamentum* 14. Leiden, Netherlands: E. J. Brill.
1972   "The Man From Heaven in Johannine Sectarianism." *Journal of Biblical Literature* 91:44-72.

Meier, John P.
1991   *The Roots of the Problem and the Person.* Vol. 1 of *A Marginal Jew: Rethinking the Historical Jesus.* The Anchor Bible Reference Library. New York: Doubleday.

Metzger, Bruce M.
1994   *A Textual Commentary on the Greek New Testament.* 2d ed. Stuttgart: Deutsche Bibelgesellschaft/German Bible Society.

Meyer, Rudolf,
and Peter Katz
1967   "ὄχλος." In *Theological Dictionary of the New Testament,* 5:582-90. Edited by Gerhard Kittel and Gerhard Friedrich. 10 vols. Grand Rapids, Mich.: Eerdmans.

Meyers, E.
1976   "Tomb." In *The Interpreter's Dictionary of the Bible: An Illustrated Encyclopedia, Supplementary Volume,* pp. 905-8. Edited by Keith Crim. Nashville: Abingdon.

Michaelis, Wilhelm
1967   "ὁδός κτλ." In *Theological Dictionary of the New Testament,* 5:42-114. Edited by Gerhard Kittel and Gerhard Friedrich. 10 vols. Grand Rapids, Mich.: Eerdmans.

Michaels, J. Ramsey
1989   *John.* New International Biblical Commentary. Peabody, Mass.: Hendrickson.

Michel, Otto
1967   "μισέω." In *Theological Dictionary of the New Testament,* 4:683-94. Edited by Gerhard Kittel and Gerhard Friedrich. 10 vols. Grand Rapids, Mich.: Eerdmans.

1978   "Son, etc." In *New International Dictionary of New Testament Theology,* 3:607-53. Edited by Colin Brown. 3 vols. Grand Rapids, Mich.: Zondervan.

Minear, Paul S.
1977   "The Audience of the Fourth Gospel." *Interpretation* 31:339-54.

Moloney, Francis J.
1978   *The Johannine Son of Man.* Biblioteca di scienze religiose 14. 2d ed. Rome: LAS.

1998   *The Gospel of John.* Sacra Pagina 4. Collegeville, Minn.: Liturgical Press.

Morris, Leon
1969   *Studies in the Fourth Gospel.* Grand Rapids, Mich.: Eerdmans.

1971   *The Gospel According to John: The English Text with Introduction, Exposition and Notes.* Grand Rapids, Mich.: Eerdmans.

| 1986-1988 | *Expository Reflections on the Gospel of John*. Grand Rapids, Mich.: Baker. |
| 1989 | *Jesus Is the Christ: Studies in the Theology of John*. Leicester, U.K.: Inter-Varsity Press; Grand Rapids, Mich.: Eerdmans. |

Motyer, Stephen

| 1997 | *Your Father the Devil? A New Approach to John and "the Jews."* Paternoster Biblical and Theological Monographs. Carlisle, U.K.: Paternoster. |

Moulder, W. J.

| 1988 | "Sanhedrin." In *International Standard Bible Encyclopedia*, 4:331-34. Rev. ed. Edited by Geoffrey W. Bromiley. 4 vols. Grand Rapids, Mich.: Eerdmans. |

Moule, C. F. D.

1959	*An Idiom-Book of New Testament Greek*. Cambridge: Cambridge University Press.
1972	"The Manhood of Jesus in the New Testament." *Christ, Faith and History: Cambridge Studies in Christology*, pp. 95-110. Edited by S. W. Sykes and J. P. Clayton. Cambridge: Cambridge University Press.
1977	*The Origin of Christology*. Cambridge: Cambridge University Press.
1995	" 'The Son of Man': Some of the Facts." *New Testament Studies* 41:277-79.

Moule, H. C. G.

1890	*Outlines of Christian Doctrine*. London: Hodder and Stoughton.
1898	*Jesus and the Resurrection: Expository Studies on St. John 20, 21*. 3d ed. London: Seeley. Reprinted in *The Resurrection of Christ* by H. C. G. Moule and James Orr, with a foreword by Cyril J. Barber. Minneapolis: Klock & Klock, 1980.
1908	*The High Priestly Prayer: A Devotional Commentary on the Seventeenth Chapter of St. John*. London: The Religious Tract Society.

Moulton, James Hope

| 1908 | *Prolegomena*. Vol. 1 of *A Grammar of New Testament Greek*. 3d ed. Edinburgh: T & T Clark. |

Mussner, Franz

| 1967 | *The Historical Jesus in the Gospel of St. John*. Quaestiones Disputatae 19. Translated by W. J. O'Hara. London: Burns & Oates. |

Neusner, Jacob

| 1993 | *A Rabbi Talks with Jesus: An Intermillennial, Interfaith Exchange*. New York: Doubleday. |

Newbigin, Lesslie
1982   *The Light Has Come: An Exposition of the Fourth Gospel.*
               Grand Rapids, Mich.: Eerdmans; Edinburgh: Handsel.
Neyrey, Jerome H.
1988   *An Ideology of Revolt: John's Christology in Social-Science*
               Perspective. Philadelphia: Fortress.
Nikodimos and Makarios
1979   *The Philokalia, Volume I: The Complete Text.* Compiled by
               St. Nikodimos of the Holy Mountain and St. Makarios of
               Corinth. Translated by G. E. H. Palmer, Philip Sherrard and
               Kallistos Ware with the assistance of the Holy Transfigura-
               tion Monastery (Brookline), Constantine Cavarnos, Basil
               Osborne and Norman Russell. London: Faber & Faber.

Nun, Mendel
1997   "What Was Simon Peter Wearing When He Plunged into
               the Sea?" *Jerusalem Perspective* 52:18-23, 37.

Nuttall, A. D.
1980   *Overheard by God: Fiction and Prayer in Herbert, Milton,*
               Dante and St John. London: Methuen.

O'Day, Gail R.
1986   *Revelation in the Fourth Gospel: Narrative Mode and Theo-*
               logical Claim. Philadelphia: Fortress.

Odeberg, Hugo
1965   "'Ἰακώβ." In *Theological Dictionary of the New Testament,*
               3:191-92. Edited by Gerhard Kittel and Gerhard Friedrich.
               10 vols. Grand Rapids, Mich.: Eerdmans.
1968   *The Fourth Gospel Interpreted in Its Relation to Contempor-*
               aneous Religious Currents in Palestine and the Hellenistic-
               Oriental World. Chicago: Argonaut (original ed., 1929).

Oepke, A.
1967a   "λούω κτλ." In *Theological Dictionary of the New Testa-*
               ment, 4:295-307. Edited by Gerhard Kittel and Gerhard
               Friedrich. 10 vols. Grand Rapids, Mich.: Eerdmans.
1967b   "παῖς κτλ." In *Theological Dictionary of the New Testa-*
               ment, 5:636-54. Edited by Gerhard Kittel and Gerhard
               Friedrich. 10 vols. Grand Rapids, Mich.: Eerdmans.

Osborne, Grant R.
1984   *The Resurrection Narratives: A Redactional Study.* Grand
               Rapids, Mich.: Baker.

Painter, John
1993   *The Quest for the Messiah: The History, Literature and*
               Theology of the Johannine Community. 2d ed., rev. and
               enlarged. Nashville: Abingdon.

Pamment, Margaret
1985   "The Son of Man in the Fourth Gospel." *Journal of Theological Studies* n.s. 36:56-66.

Paschal, R. W., Jr.
1992   "Farewell Discourse." In *Dictionary of Jesus and the Gospels*, pp. 229-33. Edited by Joel B. Green, Scot McKnight and I. Howard Marshall. Downers Grove, Ill.: InterVarsity Press.

Pixner, Bargil (Virgil)
1992   "Praetorium." In *Anchor Bible Dictionary*, 5:447-49. Edited by David Noel Freedman. 6 vols. New York: Doubleday.

Pollard, T. E.
1957   "The Exegesis of John X.30 in the Early Trinitarian Controversies." *New Testament Studies* 3:334-349.
1970   *Johannine Christology and the Early Church*. Cambridge: Cambridge University Press.

Pryor, John W.
1992   *John: Evangelist of the Covenant People: The Narrative and Themes of the Fourth Gospel*. Downers Grove, Ill.: InterVarsity Press.

Rengstorf, Karl Heinrich
1964a   "ἀποστέλλω κτλ." In *Theological Dictionary of the New Testament,* 1:398-447. Edited by Gerhard Kittel and Gerhard Friedrich. 10 vols. Grand Rapids, Mich.: Eerdmans.
1964b   "δοῦλος κτλ." In *Theological Dictionary of the New Testament,* 2:261-80. Edited by Gerhard Kittel and Gerhard Friedrich. 10 vols. Grand Rapids, Mich.: Eerdmans.
1967   "λῃστής." In *Theological Dictionary of the New Testament,* 4:257-62. Edited by Gerhard Kittel and Gerhard Friedrich. 10 vols. Grand Rapids, Mich.: Eerdmans.
1968   "πηλός." In *Theological Dictionary of the New Testament,* 6:118-19. Edited by Gerhard Kittel and Gerhard Friedrich. 10 vols. Grand Rapids, Mich.: Eerdmans.
1971   "σημεῖον κτλ." In *Theological Dictionary of the New Testament,* 7:200-269. Edited by Gerhard Kittel and Gerhard Friedrich. 10 vols. Grand Rapids, Mich.: Eerdmans.
1976   "Jesus Christ, etc." In *New International Dictionary of New Testament Theology,* 2:330-48. Edited by Colin Brown. 3 vols. Grand Rapids, Mich.: Zondervan.

Ridderbos, Herman
1997   *The Gospel of John: A Theological Commentary*. Translated by John Vriend. Grand Rapids, Mich.: Eerdmans.

Riesner, Rainer
1992   "Bethany Beyond the Jordan." In *Anchor Bible Dictionary,*

1:703-5. Edited by David Noel Freedman. 6 vols. New
York: Doubleday.

Robinson, John A. T.
1976   *Redating the New Testament*. London: SCM Press; Philadel-
               phia: Westminster Press.
1985   *The Priority of John*. Edited by J. F. Coakley. London: SCM
               Press; Oak Park, Ill.: Meyer Stone Books, 1987.

Rowland, Christopher
1982   *The Open Heaven: A Study of Apocalyptic in Judaism and
               Early Christianity*. New York: Crossroad.

Rudolph, Kurt
1992   "Gnosticism." In *Anchor Bible Dictionary*, 2:1033-40.
               Edited by David Noel Freedman. 6 vols. New York:
               Doubleday.

Safrai, S., and M. Stern
1974-1976   *The Jewish People in the First Century: Historical Geog-
               raphy, Political History, Social, Cultural and Religious Life
               and Institutions*. In cooperation with D. Flusser and
               W. C. van Unnik. 2 vols. Assen: Van Gorcum.

Sanders, J. N.
1968   *The Gospel According to St. John*. Black New Testament
               Commentaries. Edited and completed by B. A. Mastin.
               London: Adam & Charles Black.

Sava, A. F.
1960   "The Wound in the Side of Christ." *Catholic Biblical
               Quarterly* 19:343-46.

Schaefer, O.
1933   "Der Sinn der Rede Jesu von den vielen Wohnungen in
               seines Vaters Hause und von dem Weg zu ihm (Joh 14:1-7)."
               Zeitschrift für die neutestamentliche Wissenschaft 32:210-17.

Schlier, Heinrich
1964   "βραχίων." In *Theological Dictionary of the New Testa-
               ment*, 1:639-40. Edited by Gerhard Kittel and Gerhard
               Friedrich. 10 vols. Grand Rapids, Mich.: Eerdmans.

Schmitz, Ernst Dieter,
and Eduard Schütz
1976   "Knowledge, Experience, Ignorance." In *New International
               Dictionary of New Testament Theology*, 2:390-409. Edited
               by Colin Brown. 3 vols. Grand Rapids, Mich.: Zondervan.

Schnackenburg, Rudolf
1980a   *The Gospel According to St. John*. Vol. 1. New York:
               Crossroad.
1980b   *The Gospel According to St. John*. Vol. 2. New York:
               Crossroad.

| 1982 | *The Gospel According to St. John.* Vol. 3. New York: Crossroad. |

Schneider, Walter,
and Colin Brown
| 1978 | "Tempt, Test, Approve." In *New International Dictionary of New Testament Theology,* 3:798-808. Edited by Colin Brown. 3 vols. Grand Rapids, Mich.: Zondervan. |

Schrage, Wolfgang
| 1971 | "συναγωγή κτλ." In *Theological Dictionary of the New Testament,* 7:798-852. Edited by Gerhard Kittel and Gerhard Friedrich. 10 vols. Grand Rapids, Mich.: Eerdmans. |
| 1972 | "τυφλός κτλ." In *Theological Dictionary of the New Testament,* 8:270-94. Edited by Gerhard Kittel and Gerhard Friedrich. 10 vols. Grand Rapids, Mich.: Eerdmans. |

Schürer, Emil
| 1973-1987 | *The History of the Jewish People in the Age of Jesus Christ (175 B.C—A.D. 135).* 3 vols. Revised and edited by Geze Vermes, Fergus Millar and Matthew Black. Edinburgh: T & T Clark. |

Schweizer, Eduard
| 1974 | "ψυχή κτλ." In *Theological Dictionary of the New Testament,* 9:637-56. Edited by Gerhard Kittel and Gerhard Friedrich. 10 vols. Grand Rapids, Mich.: Eerdmans. |

Seesemann, Heinrich
| 1967 | "ὀρφανός." In *Theological Dictionary of the New Testament,* 5:487-88. Edited by Gerhard Kittel and Gerhard Friedrich. 10 vols. Grand Rapids, Mich.: Eerdmans. |

Segal, Alan F.
| 1977 | *Two Powers in Heaven: Early Rabbinic Reports About Christianity and Gnosticism.* Studies in Judaism in Late Antiquity 25. Leiden, Netherlands: E. J. Brill. |
| 1987 | "Dualism in Judaism, Christianity and Gnosticism: A Definitive Issue." *The Other Judaisms of Late Antiquity,* pp. 1-40. Brown Judaic Studies 127. Atlanta: Scholars Press. |

Sherwin-White, A. N.
| 1963 | *Roman Society and Roman Law in the New Testament.* The Sarum Lectures 1960-1961. Oxford: Oxford University Press. |
| 1965 | "The Trial of Christ." In *Historicity and Chronology in the New Testament,* pp. 97-116. Theological Collections 6. London: SPCK. |

Sloyan, Gerard S.
| 1991 | *What Are They Saying About John?* New York: Paulist. |

Smalley, Stephen S.
1996   "Mary." In *New Bible Dictionary*, pp. 736-38. 3d ed. Edited
               by I. Howard Marshall, A. R. Millard, J. I. Packer and
               D. J. Wiseman. Downers Grove, Ill.: InterVarsity Press.
1998   *John: Evangelist and Interpreter.* 2d ed. Downers Grove,
               Ill.: InterVaristy Press.
Smith, D. Moody
1992   *John Among the Gospels: The Relationship in Twentieth-
               Century Research.* Minneapolis: Fortress.
Smith, Morton
1978   *Jesus the Magician.* New York: Barnes & Noble.
Smith, R. H.
1976   "Holy Sepulchre, Church of the." In *The Interpreter's Dic-
               tionary of the Bible: An Illustrated Encyclopedia, Supple-
               mentary Volume*, pp. 413-15. Edited by Keith Crim.
               Nashville: Abingdon.
Stählin, Gustav
1971   "σκάνδαλον κτλ." In *Theological Dictionary of the New
               Testament*, 7:339-58. Edited by Gerhard Kittel and Gerhard
               Friedrich. 10 vols. Grand Rapids, Mich.: Eerdmans.
1974   "φιλέω κτλ." In *Theological Dictionary of the New Test-
               ament*, 9:113-71. Edited by Gerhard Kittel and Gerhard
               Friedrich. 10 vols. Grand Rapids, Mich.: Eerdmans.
Staton, John E.
1997   "A Vision of Unity—Christian Unity in the Fourth Gospel."
               Evangelical Quarterly 69:291-305.
Stauffer, Ethelbert
1960   *Jesus and His Story.* Translated by Richard and Clara Win-
               ston. New York: Alfred A. Knopf.
Strack, Hermann L.,
and Paul Billerbeck
1924   *Kommentar zum Neuen Testament aus Talmud und
               Midrasch, Zweiter Band: Das Evangelium nach Markus,
               Lukas und Johannes und die Apostelgeschichte.* Munich:
               Beck.
Strathmann, H., and
R. Meyer
1967   "λαός." In *Theological Dictionary of the New Testament*,
               4:29-57. Edited by Gerhard Kittel and Gerhard Friedrich.
               10 vols. Grand Rapids, Mich.: Eerdmans.
Streeter, Burnett Hillman
1926   *The Four Gospels: A Study of Origins Treating of the
               Manuscript Tradition, Sources, Authorship and Date.*
               London: Macmillan.

Talbert, Charles H.
  1992   *Reading John: A Literary and Theological Commentary on
                  the Fourth Gospel and the Johannine Epistles.* New York:
                  Crossroad.

Taylor, Walter F., Jr.
  1992   "Unity/Unity of Humanity." In *Anchor Bible Dictionary,*
                  6:746-53. Edited by David Noel Freedman. 6 vols. New
                  York: Doubleday.

Temple, William
  1945   *Readings in St. John's Gospel.* London: Macmillan.

Thompson, Marianne Meye
  1988   *The Humanity of Jesus in the Fourth Gospel.* Philadelphia:
                  Fortress.
  1996   "The Historical Jesus and the Johannine Christ." In *Explor-
                  ing the Gospel of John: In Honor of D. Moody Smith,* pp.
                  21-42. Edited by R. Alan Culpepper and C. Clifton Black.
                  Louisville, Ky.: Westminster John Knox.

Tolkien, J. R. R.
  1965   "On Fairy-Stories." In *Tree and Leaf.* Boston: Houghton
                  Mifflin.

Tolmie, D. F.
  1995   *Jesus' Farewell to the Disciples: John 13:1—17:26 in
                  Narratological Perspective.* Biblical Interpretation Series 12.
                  Leiden: E. J. Brill.

Torrey, Charles C.
  1931   "The Date of the Crucifixion According to the Fourth
                  Gospel." *Journal of Biblical Literature* 50:227-41.

Turner, M. M. B.
  1992   "Holy Spirit." In *Dictionary of Jesus and the Gospels,* pp.
                  341-51. Edited by Joel B. Green, Scot McKnight and
                  I. Howard Marshall. Downers Grove, Ill.: InterVarsity Press.

Vanderkam, James C.
  1992   "Calendars, Ancient Israelite and Early Jewish." In *Anchor
                  Bible Dictionary,* 1:814-20. Edited by David Noel Freed-
                  man. 6 vols. New York: Doubleday.

von Wahlde, Urban C.
  1981   "The Witnesses to Jesus in John 5:31-40 and Belief in the
                  Fourth Gospel." *Catholic Biblical Quarterly* 43:385-404.
  1989   *The Earliest Version of John's Gospel: Recovering the Gospel
                  of Signs.* Wilmington, Del.: Michael Glazier.

Wallace, Daniel B.
  1996   *Greek Grammar Beyond the Basics: An Exegetical Syntax
                  of the New Testament.* Grand Rapids, Mich.: Zondervan.

Ward, R. Somerset
1994   *To Jerusalem: Devotional Studies in Mystical Religion.*
                Library of Anglican Spirituality. 1931. Reprint, Harrisburg,
                Penn.: Morehouse.
Wenham, David
1995   "How Jesus Understood the Last Supper: A Parable in
                Action." *Themelios* 20:11-16.
1997   *John's Gospel: Good News for Today.* Leicester, U.K.: Relig-
                ious and Theological Students Fellowship Press.
Wenham, John
1992   *Easter Enigma: Are the Resurrection Accounts in Conflict?*
                A Latimer Monograph. 2d ed. Grand Rapids, Mich.: Baker.
Westcott, Brooke Foss
1908   *The Gospel According to St. John: The Greek Text with
                Introduction and Notes.* 2 vols. Edited by A. Westcott. Lon-
                don: Macmillan. Reprint, Grand Rapids, Mich.: Baker, 1980.
Westerholm, S.
1988   "Temple." In *International Standard Bible Encyclopedia,*
                4:759-76. Rev. ed. Edited by Geoffrey W. Bromiley. 4 vols.
                Grand Rapids, Mich.: Eerdmans.
1992   "Clean and Unclean." In *Dictionary of Jesus and the Gos-
                pels,* pp. 125-32. Edited by Joel B. Green, Scot McKnight
                and I. Howard Marshall. Downers Grove, Ill.: InterVarsity
                Press.
Whitacre, Rodney A.
1982   *Johannine Polemic: The Role of Tradition and Theology.*
                SBL Dissertation Series 67. Chico, Calif.: Scholars Press.
Wijngaards, John
1986   *The Gospel of John and His Letters.* Vol. 11 of Message of
                Biblical Spirituality. Wilmington, Del.: Michael Glazier.
Willett, Michael E.
1992   *Wisdom Christology in the Fourth Gospel.* San Francisco:
                Mellen Research University Press.
Williamson, H. G. M.
1992   "Samaritans." In *Dictionary of Jesus and the Gospels,* pp.
                724-28. Edited by Joel B. Green, Scot McKnight and
                I. Howard Marshall. Downers Grove, Ill.: InterVarsity Press.
Wise, Michael O.
1992   "Temple." In *Dictionary of Jesus and the Gospels,* pp. 811-
                17. Edited by Joel B. Green, Scot McKnight and I. Howard
                Marshall. Downers Grove, Ill.: InterVarsity Press.
Witherington, Ben, III
1995   *John's Wisdom: A Commentary on the Fourth Gospel.*
                Louisville, Ky.: Westminster John Knox Press.

Wülfing von Martitz,
Peter, Georg Fohrer,
Eduard Schweizer,
Eduard Lohse,
Wilhelm Schneemelcher
1972   "υἱός κτλ." In *Theological Dictionary of the New Testament*, 8:334-99. Edited by Gerhard Kittel and Gerhard Friedrich. 10 vols. Grand Rapids, Mich.: Eerdmans.

Young, Richard A.
1994   *Intermediate New Testament Greek: A Linguistic and Exegetical Approach*. Nashville, Tenn.: Broadman and Holman.

Zeitlin, Solomon
1932   "The Date of the Crucifixion According to the Fourth Gospel." *Journal of Biblical Literature* 51:263-71.